ESV Expository Commentary

VOL. IV

Ezra–Job

EDITORS

———

Iain M. Duguid
James M. Hamilton Jr.
Jay Sklar

EXPOSITORY
Commentary

VOL. IV

———

Ezra–Job

Ezra–Nehemiah
W. Brian Aucker

Esther
Eric Ortlund

Job
Douglas Sean O'Donnell

WHEATON, ILLINOIS

ESV Expository Commentary, Volume 4: Ezra–Job

Copyright © 2020 by Crossway

Published by Crossway
    1300 Crescent Street
    Wheaton, Illinois 60187

Cover design: Jordan Singer

First printing 2020

Printed in Italy

Unless otherwise indicated, Scripture quotations are from the ESV® Bible (The Holy Bible, English Standard Version®), copyright © 2001 by Crossway, a publishing ministry of Good News Publishers. Used by permission. All rights reserved.

Scripture quotations marked KJV are from the *King James Version* of the Bible.

The Scripture quotation marked MESSAGE is from *THE MESSAGE*. Copyright © 1993, 1994, 1995, 1996, 2000, 2001, 2002 by Eugene H. Peterson. Used by permission of NavPress. All rights reserved. Represented by Tyndale House Publishers, Inc.

Scripture quotations marked NAB are from *The New American Bible*, revised edition. Copyright © 2010, 1991, 1986, 1970 Confraternity of Christian Doctrine, Inc., Washington, DC. All rights reserved.

Scripture quotations marked NASB are from *The New American Standard Bible®*. Copyright © The Lockman Foundation 1960, 1962, 1963, 1968, 1971, 1972, 1973, 1975, 1977, 1995. Used by permission.

Scripture quotations marked NEB are from the *New English Bible*. Copyright © 1961, 1970 by Cambridge University Press and Oxford University Press. All rights reserved.

Scripture quotations marked NET are from *The NET Bible®*. Copyright © 2003 by Biblical Studies Press, L.L.C. www.netbible.com. All rights reserved. Quoted by permission.

Scripture quotations marked NIV are taken from The Holy Bible, New International Version®, NIV®. Copyright © 1973, 1978, 1984, 2011 by Biblica, Inc.™ Used by permission. All rights reserved worldwide.

Scripture quotations marked NJB are taken from *The New Jerusalem Bible*. Copyright © 1985 by Darton, Longman & Todd, Ltd. Used by permission.

Scripture quotations marked NJPS are taken from *Tanakh: The Holy Scriptures: The New JPS Translation according to the Traditional Hebrew Text*. Copyright © 1985 by the Jewish Publication Society. Used by permission.

The Scripture quotation marked NLT is from *The Holy Bible, New Living Translation*. Copyright © 1996, 2004. Used by permission of Tyndale House Publishers, Inc., Wheaton, IL, 60189. All rights reserved.

Scripture quotations marked NRSV are from *The New Revised Standard Version*. Copyright © 1989 by the Division of Christian Education of the National Council of the Churches of Christ in the U.S.A. Published by Thomas Nelson, Inc. Used by permission of the National Council of the Churches of Christ in the U.S.A.

Scripture quotations marked RSV are from *The Revised Standard Version*. Copyright © 1946, 1952, 1971, 1973 by the Division of Christian Education of the National Council of the Churches of Christ in the U.S.A.

Scripture quotations marked AT are the author's translation.

All emphases in Scripture quotations have been added by the authors.

Hardcover ISBN: 978-1-4335-4640-2

Crossway is a publishing ministry of Good News Publishers.

LEGO	31	30	29	28	27	26	25	24	23	22	21	20
15	14	13	12	11	10	9	8	7	6	5	4	3	2	1

CONTENTS

TABLES

PREFACE

TO THE ESV EXPOSITORY COMMENTARY

The Bible pulsates with life, and the Spirit conveys the electrifying power of Scripture to those who lay hold of it by faith, ingest it, and live by it. God has revealed himself in the Bible, which makes the words of Scripture sweeter than honey, more precious than gold, and more valuable than all riches. These are the words of life, and the Lord has entrusted them to his church, for the sake of the world.

He has also provided the church with teachers to explain and make clear what the Word of God means and how it applies to each generation. We pray that all serious students of God's Word, both those who seek to teach others and those who pursue study for their own personal growth in godliness, will be served by the ESV Expository Commentary. Our goal has been to provide a clear, crisp, and Christ-centered explanation of the biblical text. All Scripture speaks of Christ (Luke 24:27), and we have sought to show how each biblical book helps us to see the "light of the knowledge of the glory of God in the face of Jesus Christ" (2 Cor. 4:6).

To that end, each contributor has been asked to provide commentary that is:

- *exegetically sound*—self-consciously submissive to the flow of thought and lines of reasoning discernible in the biblical text;
- *biblically theological*—reading the Bible as diverse yet bearing an overarching unity, narrating a single storyline of redemption culminating in Christ;
- *globally aware*—aimed as much as possible at a global audience, in line with Crossway's mission to provide the Bible and theologically responsible resources to as many people around the world as possible;
- *broadly reformed*—standing in the historical stream of the Reformation, affirming that salvation is by grace alone, through faith alone, in Christ alone, taught in Scripture alone, for God's glory alone; holding high a big God with big grace for big sinners;
- *doctrinally conversant*—fluent in theological discourse; drawing appropriate brief connections to matters of historical or current theological importance;
- *pastorally useful*—transparently and reverently "sitting under the text"; avoiding lengthy grammatical/syntactical discussions;
- *application-minded*—building brief but consistent bridges into contemporary living in both Western and non-Western contexts (being aware of the globally diverse contexts toward which these volumes are aimed);

- *efficient in expression*—economical in its use of words; not a word-by-word analysis but a crisply moving exposition.

In terms of Bible translation, the ESV is the base translation used by the authors in their notes, but the authors were expected to consult the text in the original languages when doing their exposition and were not required to agree with every decision made by the ESV translators.

As civilizations crumble, God's Word stands. And we stand on it. The great truths of Scripture speak across space and time, and we aim to herald them in a way that will be globally applicable.

May God bless the study of his Word, and may he smile on this attempt to expound it.

—The Publisher and Editors

CONTRIBUTORS

Editors

IAIN M. DUGUID

PhD, University of Cambridge

Professor of Old Testament, Westminster Theological Seminary

JAMES M. HAMILTON JR.

PhD, The Southern Baptist Theological Seminary

Professor of Biblical Theology, The Southern Baptist Theological Seminary;
Preaching Pastor, Kenwood Baptist Church, Louisville

JAY SKLAR

PhD, University of Gloucestershire

Professor of Old Testament, Covenant Theological Seminary

Authors

W. BRIAN AUCKER

PhD, University of Edinburgh

Professor of Old Testament and Director of ThM Program,
Covenant Theological Seminary

(Ezra–Nehemiah)

ERIC ORTLUND

PhD, University of Edinburgh

Lecturer in Old Testament and Biblical Hebrew, Oak Hill College

(Esther)

DOUGLAS SEAN O'DONNELL

PhD, University of Aberdeen

Senior Pastor, Westminster Presbyterian Church, Elgin, Illinois

(Job)

ABBREVIATIONS

General

Aram.	Aramaic	i.e.	that is
AT	Author's Translation	lit.	literal, literally
c.	circa, about, approximately	LXX	Septuagint
cf.	confer, compare, see	mg.	marginal reading
ch., chs.	chapter(s)	MT	Masoretic Text
ed(s).	editor(s), edited by, edition	NT	New Testament
e.g.	for example	OT	Old Testament
esp.	especially	repr.	reprinted
et al.	and others	rev.	revised (by)
etc.	and so on	trans.	translator, translated by
ff.	and following	v., vv.	verse(s)
Gk.	Greek	vol(s).	volume(s)
Hb.	Hebrew	vs.	versus
ibid.	*ibidem*, in the same place		

Bibliographic

AB	Anchor Bible
ABCS	Asia Bible Commentary Series
ABRL	Anchor Bible Reference Library
AnBib	Analecta Biblica
ApOTC	Apollos Old Testament Commentary
AS	*Aramaic Studies*
BCOTWP	Baker Commentary on the Old Testament Wisdom and Psalms
CCSL	Corpus Christianorum: Series Latina
COS	*The Context of Scripture*. Edited by William W. Hallo and K. Lawson Younger, Jr. 3 vols. Leiden: Brill, 1997–2002.
DSBS	Daily Study Bible Series
EML	Everyman's Library

EPSC   Evangelical Press Study Commentary

HAR   *Hebrew Annual Review*

JBL   *Journal of Biblical Literature*

NA[28]   Nestle-Aland, *Novum Testamentum Graece*, 28th rev. ed. Edited by Barbara Aland, Kurt Aland, Johannes Karavidopoulos, Carlo M. Martini, and Bruce Metzger in cooperation with the Institute for New Testament Textual Research, Münster/Westphalia; German Bible Society, 2012.

NAC   New American Commentary

NCBC   New Century Bible Commentary

NIBCOT   New International Biblical Commentary on the Old Testament

NICOT   New International Commentary on the Old Testament

NIDOTTE   *New International Dictionary of Old Testament Theology and Exegesis.* Edited by Willem A. VanGemeren. 5 vols. Grand Rapids, MI: Zondervan, 1997.

NIVAC   NIV Application Commentary

NSBT   New Studies in Biblical Theology

OTE   Old Testament for Everyone

OTG   Old Testament Guides

OTL   Old Testament Library

PL   Patrologia Latina. Edited by Jacques-Paul Migne. 217 vols. Paris, 1844–1864.

PNTC   Pillar New Testament Commentary

PTW   Preaching the Word

REC   Reformed Expository Commentary

SBLDS   Society of Biblical Literature Dissertation Series

SBLMS   Society of Biblical Literature Monograph Series

SHBC   Smyth & Helwys Bible Commentary

THOTC   Two Horizons Old Testament Commentary

TOTC   Tyndale Old Testament Commentaries

TTT   Teach the Text Commentary Series

UBSHS   United Bible Societies Handbook Series

WBC   Word Biblical Commentary

WTJ   *Westminster Theological Journal*

WUNT   Wissentschaftliche Untersuchungen zum Neuen Testament

Books of the Bible

Gen.	Genesis		Nah.	Nahum
Ex.	Exodus		Hab.	Habakkuk
Lev.	Leviticus		Zeph.	Zephaniah
Num.	Numbers		Hag.	Haggai
Deut.	Deuteronomy		Zech.	Zechariah
Josh.	Joshua		Mal.	Malachi
Judg.	Judges		Matt.	Matthew
Ruth	Ruth		Mark	Mark
1 Sam.	1 Samuel		Luke	Luke
2 Sam.	2 Samuel		John	John
1 Kings	1 Kings		Acts	Acts
2 Kings	2 Kings		Rom.	Romans
1 Chron.	1 Chronicles		1 Cor.	1 Corinthians
2 Chron.	2 Chronicles		2 Cor.	2 Corinthians
Ezra	Ezra		Gal.	Galatians
Neh.	Nehemiah		Eph.	Ephesians
Est.	Esther		Phil.	Philippians
Job	Job		Col.	Colossians
Ps., Pss.	Psalms		1 Thess.	1 Thessalonians
Prov.	Proverbs		2 Thess.	2 Thessalonians
Eccles.	Ecclesiastes		1 Tim.	1 Timothy
Song	Song of Solomon		2 Tim.	2 Timothy
Isa.	Isaiah		Titus	Titus
Jer.	Jeremiah		Philem.	Philemon
Lam.	Lamentations		Heb.	Hebrews
Ezek.	Ezekiel		James	James
Dan.	Daniel		1 Pet.	1 Peter
Hos.	Hosea		2 Pet.	2 Peter
Joel	Joel		1 John	1 John
Amos	Amos		2 John	2 John
Obad.	Obadiah		3 John	3 John
Jonah	Jonah		Jude	Jude
Mic.	Micah		Rev.	Revelation

Apocrypha and Other Noncanonical Sources Cited

1 Esd.	1 Esdras
1 Macc.	1 Maccabees
Sir.	Sirach

EZRA

W. Brian Aucker

EZRA

Overview

Ezra, along with Nehemiah, recounts a series of homecomings. Although there is long-standing scholarly debate concerning the authorship of Ezra-Nehemiah and the relationship of those books to Chronicles, Ezra-Nehemiah has traditionally been viewed as a unified work, a position taken in this commentary.[1] As such, Ezra-Nehemiah comprises three sections: Ezra 1:1–11; Ezra 2:1–Nehemiah 7:73a; and Nehemiah 7:73b–13:31. The short first section (Ezra 1:1–11) is an introduction narrating the initial authorization granted by Cyrus, king of Persia, for the Jewish exiles to return to the Promised Land. This occurs as the result of the divine decree from the "mouth of Jeremiah" (1:1).

The second section (Ezra 2:1–Neh. 7:73a), the largest, is framed by two nearly identical lists (Ezra 2:1–70; Neh. 7:6–73a).[2] Generally speaking, this second section describes movements to Jerusalem that result in three different building projects, each with its own historical context. The first two of these projects are found in Ezra; the third will take place in Nehemiah (see below). More specifically, the second section begins with a large list of individual names and numbers (Ezra 2), followed by two movements (chs. 3–6; 7–10). The first begins by noting the people are "gathered as one man to Jerusalem" (3:1). Here, as a unified people, they begin altar and temple reconstruction under the leadership of Zerubbabel and Jeshua (ch. 3). Ongoing resistance to the building projects spans a wide chronological range throughout the reigns of several Persian kings. This results in cessation of the work (ch. 4). However, a prophetic call to restart temple reconstruction leads to a supportive decree from Darius and the successful completion of the temple (516 BC) and its resulting dedication (5:1–6:18). The first movement ends with a joyful Passover celebration (6:19–22).

The second movement (chs. 7–10) takes place fifty-seven years later and is described in two parts: (1) authorization and return (chs. 7–8); (2) conflict and resolution (chs. 9–10). After a brief introduction (7:1–10), Ezra the priest

---

1 See Title, Author, and Date of Writing for support of this point.
2 The core ideas for this broad structure are indebted to Tamara Cohn Eskenazi, *In an Age of Prose: A Literary Approach to Ezra-Nehemiah*, SBLMS 36 (Atlanta: Scholars, 1988), 37–126. Eskenazi observes, "This major repetition [i.e., Ezra 2–Nehemiah 7] re-presents the major character, provides continuity for the section as a whole and unifies the events in between" (39).

is granted authority to lead another return to Jerusalem and is given tasks by King Artaxerxes, especially the responsibility of instructing God's people in the "laws of your God" (7:25–26). Preparations for the return are followed by a brief description of the journey itself, concluding with burnt offerings (ch. 8). Homecomings, however, are not always easy, and the joy of return is short-lived. An internal crisis arises with a report of serious "faithlessness" among returnees, as men have married "foreign wives." In response, Ezra mourns and confesses (ch. 9). Proposals from within the community lead to the formation of a commission that investigates and promotes confession, repentance, and atonement (ch. 10). Resolution takes place within one year of the initial departure (7:9; 10:17), with a final list (10:18–44). The book of Nehemiah then recounts wall building—the third construction project (Nehemiah 1–7)—along with a conclusion (Nehemiah 8–13).

Title, Author, and Date of Writing

The titles for the books of Ezra and Nehemiah arise from the names of two main figures within them. When discussing the authorship and date of Ezra, we must keep Nehemiah in view, for multiple lines of evidence show their unified treatment.[3] Division into two separate books was first attested by Origen (AD 185–254) and from there to the Vulgate of Jerome (AD 342–420). The author of Ezra is unknown. Within recent academic discussion, a number of proposals regarding authorship and composition have been made: (1) the persons Ezra and Nehemiah each authored the book bearing his name; (2) Ezra authored both Ezra-Nehemiah and Chronicles; (3) Ezra-Nehemiah was part of the same work as Chronicles but authored or edited by a person or persons other than Ezra (i.e., "the Chronicler"); and (4) Ezra-Nehemiah was the work of one or more authors/editors/compilers distinct from the Chronicler.

While unanimity is lacking, option 4 has displaced position 3 as the recent consensus. How and when the various sources evident in these books were joined to form the whole also continues to be a focus of scholarly discussion. A precise date for final composition of the whole is not possible. Most estimates for completion range from 400 to 300 BC. The first-person account of Ezra, the so-called Ezra Memoir underlying the narrative of Ezra 7–10, indicates the completion of at least some of the material closer to the timing of the reported events (see brief treatment under Genre and Literary Features).

---

3 The view that these were originally one book is the majority position. Among external reasons for this position: (1) the unity of Ezra-Nehemiah is attested in nearly all ancient manuscripts, including the LXX and early rabbinic and patristic traditions; (2) we must count them as one to make sense of Josephus's numbering of the biblical books (*Against Apion* 1.8); (3) the Masoretes, medieval Jewish textual scholars, regarded the two books as one. Note, for example, that the middle verse of the two books is placed at Nehemiah 3:32 in a Masoretic marginal note—clearly not the middle of Nehemiah. Furthermore, the typical Masoretic notation that ends each biblical book in Hebrew is not found at the end of Ezra but is found at the end of Nehemiah. These and other points are enumerated in H. G. M. Williamson, *Ezra, Nehemiah*, WBC 16 (Waco, TX: Word, 1985), xxi–xxii. Features within the books also support this position: evidence of the use of nearly identical lists of returnees (Ezra 2; Nehemiah 7); comparable use of decrees from Persian kings; and the presence of Ezra at the beginning of the final section of Nehemiah (chs. 8–13). For these internal features and others supporting unity, see Paul L. Redditt, *Ezra, Nehemiah*, SHBC 9b (Macon, GA: Smyth & Helwys, 2014), 30.

Date of the Book's Events; Occasion

The multiple temporal notices in Ezra, frequently tied to the reigns of Persian kings, enable reasonably precise dating for the events recounted within the book. The events in Ezra 1–6 took place from 538 to 516 BC. The Babylonian Nebuchadnezzar (605–562) captured Jerusalem in 586 (2 Kings 25). However, in 539, Babylon fell to the Persian king Cyrus the Great (559–530). By this reckoning, the "first year of Cyrus" (Ezra 1:1; 5:13; 6:3) is 538, the year of the first exilic return. It is during the "second year" (520; 4:24) of the reign of Darius (522–486) that temple rebuilding began again in earnest after external and internal factors brought rebuilding to a standstill. A second notice associated with Darius marked completion of the second temple on the "third day of the month of Adar" in Darius's sixth year (516; 6:15). All of the events in Ezra 7–10 took place during a one-year period in 458, the seventh year of Artaxerxes I (464–423).

The occasion for the book's writing may be inferred from key texts (6:14–18; 7:10; 9:8–9). In the aftermath of the chastening due to loss of home, land, temple, and king (i.e., exile), the author wanted readers to know that *the* covenant promise remains: God is still their God, and they are still his people. The book interprets the people's very existence and the beneficence and cooperation of Persian kings during this time as evidence for the dogged, "steadfast" love of God (9:8–9). This people, to whom "belong the adoption" (Rom. 9:4; cf. Ex. 4:22–23), remained sons and daughters. As such, the old stories of the Law and the Prophets were still their stories, and their calling to be a distinctive people remained. Consequently, the book also exhorted its priests, as exemplified by Ezra, to pursue wholehearted study of the Word of God and to seek holiness—not only for themselves but also for their people (Ezra 7:10; 10:10–11; cf. Mal. 2:4–7).

Genre and Literary Features

With its companion, Nehemiah, which is followed by Esther in Protestant tradition, Ezra is part of the postexilic literature that concludes the Historical Books of the OT (Joshua–Esther).[4] Like many of the Historical Books, Ezra is broadly identifiable as biblical historiography. That means that the book of Ezra provides a written account of past events. From numerous lines of inquiry that could have been pursued, the writer selected and ordered a range of sources to provide literary shape to the book for a purpose unashamedly theological in its presentation of events.

Those sources used in Ezra have their own particular generic identifications and perspectives worthy of study in themselves. Nowhere is the personal viewpoint so apparent than in the first-person accounts of events found in Ezra-Nehemiah, conveniently called "memoirs" by most scholars (Ezra 7–10).[5] Beyond

---

4 As in the Protestant tradition, Ezra and Nehemiah follow Chronicles in the Catholic canonical order. Within the Hebrew Bible, Ezra-Nehemiah are traditionally placed after Esther and Daniel and before rather than after Chronicles in the division known as the "Writings."
5 Strictly speaking, the first-person account covers Ezra 7:27–9:15. Ezra 7:1–26 and 10:1–44 are often included in this category since it is assumed a first-person account was the source of the current third-person

the first-person source, the book includes royal decrees (1:2–4; 6:3–5), letters in Aramaic to and edicts from kings (4:8–16; 4:17–22; 5:6–17; 6:6–12; 7:12–26), inventories of temple vessels (1:9–11; 8:25–27), lists and genealogies (2:1–63; 7:1–5; 8:1–14; 10:18–43), and prayer (9:6–15).[6]

Theology of Ezra

A SOVEREIGN GOD WHO GATHERS A CHASTISED PEOPLE

Through the experience of exile, God had chastised an unrepentant people. Yet in mercy he also granted those who remained ("a remnant"; 9:13) the privilege to return to Jerusalem and the land from which they had been expelled seventy years earlier. These events are viewed as the fulfillment of past prophecies, particularly that of Jeremiah (Ezra 1:1). In his sovereign power, God "stirred" kings (1:1–4; 6:14, 22; 7:27), other individuals (1:5–6; 5:1–2; 7:13), and families (2:1–63; 7:7; 8:1–14) to bring about a homecoming of "returned exiles" (2:1; 4:1; 6:16–21; 8:35; 9:4; 10:7, 16). God's power is most evidenced in his "hand" that works through events (7:6, 9, 28; 8:18, 22, 31). Any good that comes to the people, whether protection from external threats (4:5–6; 5:3–5; 8:31) or the reversal of the policies of once-hostile rulers like Artaxerxes (4:7–22; cf. 7:6, 27–28), is viewed as the bounty and steadfast love of the divine King (3:11; 5:12–13; 9:8–9).

A HOLY GOD WHO CREATES A DISTINCT PEOPLE

Israel was separated out from the nations to be a holy and priestly nation (Ex. 19:5–6; Lev. 11:45). As God's "son," (Ex. 4:22–23) they were to serve and worship him in covenantal fidelity (Ezra 5:11). That task persists in Ezra. Like the first exodus community, this "second exodus" community requires an altar and temple in order to fulfill its priestly calling (1:2–4; 3:3–6; 5:15; 6:19–22; 8:35). To lead and instruct them in holiness, God provides "priests and Levites" (esp. 8:15–20), mentioned in nearly every chapter. When the conflict of mixed marriages threatens the "holy race" (i.e., "offspring"; cf. 9:2 ESV mg.) it is Ezra—the priest—who mediates in confession and repentance (ch. 9) in order to purify and preserve the "remnant" by calling them to separate from their foreign wives (10:10–11). Mixing with the "peoples of the land" is ritual impurity with the potential of leading them to return to the idolatry that characterized so much of the preexilic period and led to their demise in the first place (5:12; 9:7, 14). And yet this was no exclusivism based solely on ethnic or racial identity. As in the first exodus, any who separate themselves to worship the Lord may partake in the Passover (6:21; cf. Ex. 12:48).

A FAITHFUL GOD WHO SPEAKS TO A LISTENING PEOPLE

From the start, the question for Israel was "Did God actually say?" (cf. Gen. 3:1). The Israelites' questioning of God's word revealed itself throughout their history

---

narrative in those chapters. Some scholars include Nehemiah 8 as part of the Ezra Memoir; others add Nehemiah 9–10 as well. See Williamson, *Ezra, Nehemiah*, xxviii–xxxii. The Nehemiah Memoirs will be addressed in that book's Introduction.

6 This list draws from sources identified in Williamson, *Ezra, Nehemiah*, xxiii–xxiv.

in their consistent disobedience to the voice of the Lord through his prophets (e.g., 1 Sam. 15:19). However, something has changed. The Israelites now see that there is a chance to get it right. In Ezra there is a renewed understanding that prospering comes by submission to the prophetic voice (5:1–2; 6:14–15). There is interest in performing according to the written "Law of Moses" (3:2; 6:18). There is submission to the leadership of Ezra the priest, steeped in his understanding of the law (7:6, 10; 10:3–4). There is awe and sorrow for sin rarely evident elsewhere in the Historical Books (9:4; 10:1, 9). Clearly, the fight with iniquity remains, "but even now there is hope for Israel in spite of this" (10:2).

Relationship to the Rest of the Bible and to Christ

In the book of Ezra, past history shapes the present portrait. God's covenantal people are reenvisioned as

- Abraham's offspring repeating his ancient journey from Mesopotamia to the Promised Land (Ezra 2:1–3:1; 8:31–32; cf. Gen. 12:1–3);
- chastised and restored to the land according to prophetic promise (Ezra 1:1; cf. Jer. 29:10–14; 30:3; 31:27–28);
- a people led out of Babylonia in a new exodus, with support provided by others (Ezra 1:5–11; 5:14–15; 7:20; 9:8–9; cf. Ex. 12:33–36);
- sacrificing and taught "according to the Law of Moses, with the renewal of the Feast of Booths (Ezra 3:2, 4; 7:10; cf. Josh. 23:6; 1 Kings 2:3; Lev. 23:33–36; Deut. 16:13–15) as well as Passover and the Feast of Unleavened Bread, even for nonmembers of the community (Ezra 6:19–22; cf. Ex. 12:48–49; 13:3–10);
- heeding the call to separate themselves from the "peoples of the lands" (Ezra 9:1–2) upon reentering the land, as in Joshua's day (Deut. 7:1–3);
- rebuilding the temple (Ezra 6:14–18) and restoring its treasures (Ezra 1:7–11; 7:19; 8:30; cf. 1 Kings 6:1–38; 7:51) with worship practices according to Davidic instruction (Ezra 3:10–11; cf. 1 Chron. 16:34, 37–42);
- threatened but saved from enemies seeking their demise (Ezra 4:1–3, 17–22; 8:31; cf. Judg. 2:14–16);
- breaking faith with the Lord, like Achan, and still needing to confess, repent, and atone for fear of God's wrath against community impurity (Ezra 9:10–11; 10:14–15; cf. Josh. 7:1, 19).

No direct citations of Ezra-Nehemiah occur in the NT. However, the relationship to Christ is found in his roles as king, priest, and prophet, themes suggested in Theology of Ezra. When these roles are found in the text of Ezra, they provide bridges to Christ. Beyond this, the book offers a glimpse into fulfillment of the great prophetic promises of a final restoration (Isa. 60:19–21; Jer. 31:33; 32:37–44; Ezek. 36:33). The story of a gathered remnant of an elect nation in a rebuilt temple in Jerusalem, still in need of ongoing purification, looks forward to the final ingathering by Jesus of his universal body, the church, the purified of all nations, worshiping God in the new Jerusalem. At that time the glory of all the kings of the earth shall enter the city of God.[7]

Preaching from Ezra

While the individual Response sections throughout the commentary offer further prompts for the development of sermon outlines and application, several wider principles may be kept in mind. First, if at all possible, one should preach through Ezra-Nehemiah as one unit. As noted already, these books have been traditionally viewed as one book and ideally would be best treated together in a sermon series. The climactic point of the book comes in the covenant renewal and final celebration (Nehemiah 8–12). If left out, Ezra is a story looking for an ending.

Next, one should keep in mind the several historical contexts. Early in a sermon series on Ezra-Nehemiah it may be necessary to address two things: (1) The varied historical settings of Ezra within the Persian period. Many people will never have read Ezra-Nehemiah and thus remain unware that Ezra 1–6 takes place well before Ezra the priest enters the scene in chapter 7. Congregants may also be helped to note the biblical interconnection with the prophets Haggai and Zechariah within the narrative (5:1–2; 6:14–16). (2) It may be helpful at some point to provide an overview of the Historical Books (Joshua–Esther), or at least 2 Kings 24–25, into which Ezra fits as the next part of the concluding chapters.

Finally, the preacher must focus on the congregation of the Lord in the book. While Ezra is an important figure, and the book presents important principles of leadership, Ezra is not first and foremost a book about leadership. It is not Ezra who is the main character; rather, God and his redeemed assembly take center stage. Once we make allowance for the changing historical contexts, the means of grace presented in Ezra—*worship, atoning sacrifice, prayer, Passover, the Word of God, the gathered fellowship*—remain relevant for the "Israel of God" (Gal. 6:16) in every age.

Interpretive Challenges

THE CHRONOLOGICAL ORDER OF EZRA AND NEHEMIAH

According to the biblical presentation, Ezra arrives in Jerusalem in 458 BC, the seventh year of Artaxerxes I (464–423; Ezra 7:7–8). Within the year (7:9; 10:17) Ezra deals with the problem of mixed marriages (chs. 9–10). His ministry and arrival occur thirteen years before Nehemiah, whose initial governorship is dated to Artaxerxes's twentieth year (445; cf. Neh. 1:1). After wall completion, both Nehemiah and Ezra are present at the reading of the Law of Moses and the dedication of the wall that follow (Neh. 8:9; 12:26, 36, 38).

However, a long-standing debate concerns whether Ezra arrived not under Artaxerxes I in 458 but under Artaxerxes II (404–359), whose seventh year was

---

7 See the very helpful theological essays in David J. Shepherd and Christopher J. H. Wright, *Ezra and Nehemiah*, THOTC (Grand Rapids, MI: Eerdmans, 2018), 111–211.

398. If so, this reverses the chronological order, such that Ezra would follow well after Nehemiah. The major arguments for the reversed order are as follows:[8]

First, if the activities of Ezra and Nehemiah overlap, why do they interact so little within the biblical text? Given Ezra's calling to give instruction in the Law (Ezra 7:10), why does he not read the law publicly until some thirteen years after his initial arrival, when Nehemiah is also present (Neh. 8:9)? Otherwise, both men are found together only in the procession at the wall dedication (Neh. 12:31, 36, 38, 40).[9] In response, the lack of interaction is not surprising, given the particular calling and purposes of each individual. In addition, the Torah instruction in Nehemiah 8 occurs as part of a "liturgical celebration by the revived community."[10] While the text of Ezra 9–10 offers no evidence of reading of the Law, Ezra does in fact apply the Law to the specific issue of mixed marriages. Whatever else happened prior to the arrival of Nehemiah is not deemed significant to the wider history being recounted.

With respect to the mixed marriage issue, why are Nehemiah's later, milder attempts at reformation required (Neh. 13:23–27) if Ezra has previously successfully dealt with the crisis by overseeing divorces? In this view, Ezra actually fails in his reforms. Accordingly, some claim that Ezra's harsher, legal actions requiring separation (Ezra 10:11) better fit sometime after Nehemiah's initial milder attempts at reformation. However, Nehemiah's approach to the problem seems to presuppose the prior interpretation and application of the law by Ezra (Ezra 9:12; Neh. 13:25).[11]

Finally, the most complex argument for the reversed order arises from the high-priestly succession. In Ezra 10:6, Ezra stays in the chamber of "Jehohanan [i.e., Johanan] the son of Eliashib." The high priest who is a contemporary of Nehemiah is Eliashib (Neh. 3:1, 20; 13:28). Associated with Eliashib are multiple men with names comparable to Jehohanan: Jonathan (Neh. 12:10–11) and Johanan (Neh. 12:22–23). Following from these texts, some interpreters assume: (1) that Johanan was Eliashib's grandson rather than his son, as explicitly stated in Ezra 10:6 and Nehemiah 12:22–23; (2) that Jonathan (Neh. 12:10–11) is a scribal mistake for Johanan; (3) that Eliashib, the high priest of Nehemiah's day, is identical to Eliashib in Ezra 10:6. Furthermore, a letter among the extrabiblical Elephantine Papyri mentions Johanan as the high priest in 410 BC. It is therefore suggested that the Johanan of Nehemiah 12:22–23 is this same high priest whose chamber Ezra occupies, although he is not called "high priest" at Ezra 10:6. Since each of these points is built upon disputed assumptions, however, they are not strong support from which to argue that Ezra follows Nehemiah.

Overall, each of these and many other arguments in support of the reverse

8 The multiple special studies and alternative proposals exceed the purview of this commentary. An accessible, moderately detailed overview is found in Derek Kidner, *Ezra and Nehemiah: An Introduction and Commentary*, TOTC 12 (Downers Grove, IL: InterVarsity Press, 1979), 161–175. For a concise summary of pros and cons of alternative chronologies see David M. Howard Jr., *An Introduction to the Old Testament Historical Books* (Chicago: Moody Press, 1993), 321–325.

9 Some scholars raise the possibility that Nehemiah's presence at Nehemiah 8:9 and Ezra's presence at Nehemiah 12:36 are editorial additions, not part of the original text. See David J. A. Clines, *Ezra, Nehemiah, Esther*, NCBC (Grand Rapids, MI: Eerdmans, 1984), 232; Williamson, *Ezra, Nehemiah*, 279.

10 Mervin Breneman, *Ezra, Nehemiah, Esther*, NAC 10 (Nashville: B&H, 1993), 44.

11 Williamson, *Ezra, Nehemiah*, xliii.

order have received cogent responses. Although an alternative date for Ezra's arrival remains possible, none of the arguments demand adoption of any of the various proposals. Increasingly, scholars maintain the traditional view that Ezra precedes Nehemiah, a position assumed in this commentary.[12]

THE IDENTITY OF SHESHBAZZAR

The name Sheshbazzar is found only in Ezra. Called "the prince of Judah," he is one of the leaders of the initial return and is given responsibility by Cyrus for returning the original temple vessels (1:8, 11). Later, within the letter to Darius, two new pieces of information are given. We learn that Cyrus made Sheshbazzar "governor" (5:14) and that "this Sheshbazzar" laid the temple foundation (5:16). The problem is that the actual laying of the temple foundation (3:8, 10) that follows immediately from chapter 1 is attributed to Zerubbabel (2:2; 3:2, 8; 5:2; cf. Neh. 7:7; 12:1). Note also that in Haggai, Zerubbabel rather than Sheshbazzar consistently receives the title "governor" (Hag. 1:1, 14; 2:2, 21). What is the best way to explain these observations?

It has been suggested that Sheshbazzar and Zerubbabel are the same person, with Sheshbazzar functioning as his official name and Zerubbabel his personal name. If so, it is odd that the significance of these alternative names is never explained, as might be expected (cf. Dan. 1:6–7). Likewise, it is likely that both names are Babylonian. Having two names is not unusual, but Daniel, for example, has both a Hebrew and Babylonian name. Most importantly, in Tattenai's letter to Darius, the elders (Ezra 5:9–10) and Zerubbabel (5:1–5) describe the work of Sheshbazzar using phrases that make Sheshbazzar active in a prior time and clearly distinct from Zerubbabel (5:14–16).

A more probable position sees the two as separate individuals with different functions and importance at various points in the period of early return (i.e., 538–516 BC). Sheshbazzar is granted an official appointment as governor by Cyrus (cf. 2:63) and tasked with leading the initial returnees and building the temple. Given this official responsibility and in royal correspondence with Darius, he is then highlighted for his role in laying the temple foundation as required by Cyrus. At some point prior to the temple restart in 520 he disappears from the scene. For the returnees, Zerubbabel is the more prominent leader, taking the lead with the altar and temple construction attributed to him in Ezra 3 and Haggai.

Outline

    I. The Lord and Cyrus Issue Decrees and the Community Responds (1:1–11)

      A. The Decrees of the Lord and Cyrus (1:1–4)

        1. Temporal and Prophetic Notice of the Decrees (1:1)

        2. Cyrus's Decree (1:2–4)

---

12 Along with the previously mentioned Kidner and Howard, Clines also holds to the traditional order. He lists thirteen arguments for the reversed order and then briefly counters each argument (Clines, *Ezra, Nehemiah, Esther*, 17–20). Others who hold to the traditional order include Williamson, *Ezra, Nehemiah*, xxxix–xliv; Joseph Blenkinsopp, *Ezra-Nehemiah: A Commentary*, OTL (Philadelphia: Westminster, 1988), 139–144; and more recently Redditt, *Ezra-Nehemiah*, 164.

EZRA 1:1–11

1 In the first year of Cyrus king of Persia, that the word of the Lord by the mouth of Jeremiah might be fulfilled, the Lord stirred up the spirit of Cyrus king of Persia, so that he made a proclamation throughout all his kingdom and also put it in writing:

2 "Thus says Cyrus king of Persia: The Lord, the God of heaven, has given me all the kingdoms of the earth, and he has charged me to build him a house at Jerusalem, which is in Judah. 3 Whoever is among you of all his people, may his God be with him, and let him go up to Jerusalem, which is in Judah, and rebuild the house of the Lord, the God of Israel— he is the God who is in Jerusalem. 4 And let each survivor, in whatever place he sojourns, be assisted by the men of his place with silver and gold, with goods and with beasts, besides freewill offerings for the house of God that is in Jerusalem."

5 Then rose up the heads of the fathers' houses of Judah and Benjamin, and the priests and the Levites, everyone whose spirit God had stirred to go up to rebuild the house of the Lord that is in Jerusalem. 6 And all who were about them aided them with vessels of silver, with gold, with goods, with beasts, and with costly wares, besides all that was freely offered. 7 Cyrus the king also brought out the vessels of the house of the Lord that Nebuchadnezzar had carried away from Jerusalem and placed in the house of his gods. 8 Cyrus king of Persia brought these out in the charge of Mithredath the treasurer, who counted them out to Sheshbazzar the prince of Judah. 9 And this was the number of them: 30 basins of gold, 1,000 basins of silver, 29 censers, 10 30 bowls of gold, 410 bowls of silver, and 1,000 other vessels; 11 all the vessels of gold and of silver were 5,400. All these did Sheshbazzar bring up, when the exiles were brought up from Babylonia to Jerusalem.

Section Overview

In its two scenes Ezra 1 establishes expectations and objectives for the rest of the book by providing readers with its setting, characters, and important themes. The first scene depicts the proclamations of kings (1:1–4); the second, the response of their subjects (vv. 5–11).

In the first scene the text employs royal voices, both human and divine,[13] to recount a weighty historical moment in Israel's ongoing story. On the one hand, the initial events are related through the proclamation issued by a human monarch, Cyrus, to his subjects (vv. 2–4). On the other, this proclamation accomplishes the objectives of a greater monarch, the Lord God, who is described as having

---

13 Eskenazi, *Age of Prose*, 42.

sovereignly foretold these events through the prophet Jeremiah (Ezra 1:1). When the King of kings speaks, his objectives are accomplished.

Ezra's opening verses, which parallel the concluding verses of 2 Chronicles, also introduce the Lord's people, depicting them as subjects of Cyrus and beneficiaries of the decree. Their return to Jerusalem to rebuild the house of the Lord provides the main objective for their wider mission as the Lord's community (v. 3), while others provide the necessary material assistance to support this objective (v. 4).

This leads to the second scene, in which these exiles under Cyrus's rule commence movement toward Jerusalem (vv. 5–11). They go not empty-handed but with various treasures given them by those who are near (vv. 5–6) and by Cyrus himself (vv. 7–8). The chapter concludes with an accounting of former temple treasures that, having been exiled like the people, will now return to Jerusalem (vv. 9–11). The obedience of the human subjects—royals and commoners alike—is attributed to God's sovereign "stirring," an unseen action that rouses the spirit and shapes the chapter (vv. 1, 5).

Section Outline

I. The Lord and Cyrus Issue Decrees and the Community Responds (1:1–11)
   A. The Decrees of the Lord and Cyrus (1:1–4)
      1. Temporal and Prophetic Notice of the Decrees (1:1)
      2. Cyrus's Decree (1:2–4)
   B. The Exiles Respond and Return with Treasures (1:5–11)
      1. Report of Treasures to Returnees from "All Who Were about Them" (1:5–6)
      2. Report of Treasures to Returnees from Cyrus (1:7–8)
      3. Specifics of Treasures Brought Up by Sheshbazzar (1:9–11)

Comment

1:1 The initial verse establishes the historical setting for the subsequent events and provides the political and theological foundation for much of the narrative that follows in Ezra-Nehemiah. At the human level, the animating force of the action is the oral and written proclamation of the Persian king Cyrus II. Although he reigned over the Persian Empire from 559 to 530 BC, he did not defeat the Neo-Babylonian Empire (where Israel lived in exile) until 539. Thus the "first year" is dated from that point (539–538), with the decree generally understood to have been issued in 538 (cf. Introduction: Date of the Book's Events; Occasion).

Fortunately for God's people, this human king's proclamation fulfills the Lord's word given through the prophet Jeremiah in the fourth year of Jehoiakim, Judah's next-to-last king (609–597; cf. Jer. 25:1). At that time, the Lord informed his people that their failure to listen to his word (Jer. 25:7) would result in their subjugation to Babylon for seventy years, after which he would bring them home (Jer. 25:11–14; 29:10–14; 32:42–44; cf. 2 Chron. 36:21). The beginning and end of this seventy-year period is much debated. Suggestions for the range of dates have included: (1) from the replacement of Jehoahaz with Jehoiakim at the hands of Pharaoh Neco II in 609 (2 Kings 23:34) to Cyrus's defeat of the Babylonians in 539; (2) from the fall of Jerusalem in 586 to the completion of the temple in 516; and (3) from the first year of Nebuchadnezzar II's rule (605) to Cyrus's decree in 538 (here taking the seventy years as approximate).

Though the date range is difficult to determine, what is clear is the Lord causes the proclamation of a human king, Cyrus, to fulfill his divine proclamation through Jeremiah. The Lord's sovereignty over the hearts of kings is not uncommon in Scripture (Ex. 14:8; Deut. 2:30; Prov. 21:1), nor will this be the last time we encounter such sovereignty in Ezra (Ezra 6:22; 7:27). The text explicitly states that the Lord "stirred up the spirit of Cyrus king of Persia." In the present context, the word translated "stirred" expresses God's sovereignty in rousing to action either human rulers (1 Chron. 5:26; Jer. 51:11; Hag. 1:14) or nations (2 Chron. 21:16; Isa. 13:17; Jer. 50:9). As foretold by the prophet Isaiah, the Lord stirs up Cyrus with particular force: "'I have stirred him up in righteousness, and I will make all his ways level; he shall build my city and set my exiles free, not for price or reward,' says the LORD of hosts" (Isa. 45:13; cf. 41:2, 25; 44:28).

1:2–4 The importance of this proclamation cannot be overstated. In it, Cyrus refers to the divine actor behind his reign, the principle location at which most of the book's action transpires, and the primary charge set upon him (v. 2). With respect to the divine actor, the decree mentions God five times. In the first mention, the divine being is none other than "the LORD, the God of heaven." "God of heaven" is common in postexilic texts (Ezra 1:2; 5:11, 12; 6:9, 10; 7:12, 21, 23 [2x]; Neh. 1:4, 5; 2:4, 20; Dan. 2:18, 19, 37, 44) and especially in communication between the Jews and Persians.[14] The remaining references identify God by his great covenantal promise as the God who is with his people and whose temple is at Jerusalem. The decree's fourfold repetition of "Jerusalem" confirms the city's prominence within the wider story of Ezra-Nehemiah as the home of God's people and the place toward which all action moves and in which nearly all action takes place. Most importantly, Cyrus is charged with renovating God's house in Jerusalem (Ezra 1:2), the major task in the first movement of Ezra (chs. 3–6).

The expressions in these verses, however, must not be viewed as Cyrus's embrace of the covenant established by the Lord for his people. Instead, they should be read in light of the Cyrus Cylinder inscription (an ancient clay cylinder written to defend the claims of its king), which credits the primary Babylonian god, Marduk, with establishing Cyrus as "king over all the world." It also describes the Persian policy of restoring to temples the images (i.e., statues) of their gods previously taken to Babylon. Cyrus restores the gods of various peoples (not just Israel), thus emphasizing his own benevolence toward those gods and also his desire for those peoples' prayers. In addition, he pronounces his generosity toward

---

14 Williamson, *Ezra, Nehemiah*, 12.

the people who dwell in cities over which he now rules. The proclamation of 1:2–4 is therefore politically expedient; Cyrus does for Judah what he does for other nations.[15] In this case, however, the providence of the living God has moved his heart to act. The Lord raises up and deposes rulers for purposes about which such rulers may be oblivious.

In this case, the Lord's immediate purpose is to bring his homeless people home to rebuild his house (i.e., temple). But a deeper goal exists. In abandoning the covenant, God's people had abandoned their priestly role (Ex. 19:5–6); by restoring them to Jerusalem to rebuild his temple, the Lord revives their priestly function in the world.

The author of Ezra takes up Cyrus's proclamation as one of his sources and expresses it in a manner relevant to his audience. Defining the homeless in more detail, the king's words function as a net to catch any among his subjects ("among you") who identify themselves as the Lord's people ("his people") and to encourage them to carry out the temple rebuilding (Ezra 1:3). On the one hand, hearers will be forced to ask themselves, "Am I among his people?"[16] The answer to this question will make all the difference, since a positive response will result in the recipient's playing an active part in God's restorative work in Jerusalem. On the other hand, returning is not required. Cyrus's decree urges and encourages rather than demands.

The desired action focuses on three related requests. The first expresses hope of God's presence, which stands outside human control. Consistent biblical testimony demonstrates that success in God's plan for his people comes only through his willing presence with them (Ex. 33:15–16; Deut. 31:6; Josh. 1:5; 1 Kings 8:57; Matt. 1:23). Human effort at kingdom advancement bears no genuine fruit without the reality of this central covenantal assurance. The second and third requests are essential to fulfilling Cyrus's primary charge to "build him a house at Jerusalem" (Ezra 1:2). Hearers must be moved both to "go up" to Jerusalem and to commence the work of rebuilding (v. 3).

An interpretive question in verse 4 concerns whether the assistance for the Lord's people comes from Cyrus's Jewish or Gentile subjects. This commentary supports the latter. The Hebrew translated "survivor" (*sha'ar*) generally describes what is *left over* or *remains*. In the context of Ezra 1, it refers to anyone who *survives* and, by extension, to a "remnant." Accordingly, the phrase "each survivor" (v. 4) more precisely describes "his people" (v. 3), the favored community that now benefits from this call for assistance. Several texts with comparable contexts support this approach (Neh. 1:3; Hag. 2:3; cf. Hag. 1:12, 14). Having identified the beneficiaries, we now turn to the question of the source of their assistance. Cyrus initially directs his proclamation "throughout all his kingdom" (Ezra 1:1) before singling out the Lord's people from this wider population (v. 3). He then calls on each local

15 Blenkinsopp, *Ezra-Nehemiah*, 75.
16 Some translations (KJV) and commentators translate the beginning of 1:3 as a question: "Who is there among you of all his people?" See Jacob M. Myers, *Ezra-Nehemiah: Introduction, Translation, and Notes*, AB 14 (Garden City, NY: Doubleday, 1965), 3.

population, i.e., "the men of his place," to support these returning survivors, later called "exiles" (v. 11). These "men of his place" (v. 4) correspond to "all who were about them" (v. 6) in the descriptive response. In other words, gifts to the Lord's people come from those who are not his people, i.e., Gentile neighbors. In further support, many note this is in keeping with the first exodus: God's action brings a release from captivity and gracious support from unexpected sources (cf. comment on 1:5–6).[17]

1:5–6 Response to the proclamation begins with the mention of four groups (Judah, Benjamin, priests, and Levites) who "rose up . . . to go up" (v. 5). This verbal combination, typically used of calls to action in war contexts (Josh. 8:1; Judg. 18:9; Jer. 6:4), is used here to describe the initial movement toward building a worship site (cf. Gen. 35:1, 3).[18] Judah and Benjamin, the tribal remains of the southern kingdom exiled by Nebuchadnezzar, receive particular mention as the new seed to be planted in the land (cf. Jer. 31:27). Benjamin was historically part of the northern kingdom but remained loyal to the southern-based Davidic king when the northern tribes departed, dividing the kingdom (2 Chron. 11:1–4). This mention of part of Israel reveals a concern for all Israel (Ezra 6:17; 8:35) and continues with the reference to priests and Levites, who play an indispensable role in strengthening the people (2 Chron. 11:13–17). Laymen, temple personnel, and all others respond because God "stirs" their spirit to action. Just as he has stirred Cyrus to give his people permission to return (Ezra 1:1), God now stirs them to respond, motivating them to go. Mention of these four groups prepares the reader for the detailed list that follows in chapter 2.

In keeping with the king's decree (1:4), the returnees' Gentile neighbors "made strong their hands" (cf. KJV), a Hebrew idiom that may be accurately rendered "aided" (ESV) or "encouraged" (NASB).[19] The range of materials given—precious metals, beasts, goods, and other gifts (v. 6)—includes what previously has been generically described as "silver" (v. 4) but is now more specifically identified as "vessels of silver." This phrase also occurs in a comparable context in the exodus story, where God moves the Egyptians to show favor to his people (Ex. 3:21–22; 11:1–3; 12:35–36). The giving of gifts in Ezra 1 suggests a new exodus (Isa. 43:14–21; 48:20–21), in which the Lord not only calls his people to action but again provides what is needed to fulfill the calling.

Meanwhile, the words used to describe the aid rendered and items given make it clear this calling involves temple rebuilding. For example, the phrase translated "with gold" is frequently, though not exclusively, found in such contexts (Ex. 31:4; 35:32; 1 Kings 9:11; 2 Chron. 2:7, 14; 9:18). Likewise, the noun form, "freewill offering" (Ezra 1:4), and the verbal form, "freely offered" (v. 6), often refer to gifts

---

17 Philip A. Noss and Kenneth J. Thomas, *A Handbook on Ezra and Nehemiah*, UBSHS (New York: UBS, 2005), 38–39. An alternate view sees the proclamation as calling on Judeans who decide not to return to Jerusalem, rather than Gentile neighbors, to render material support (Williamson, *Ezra, Nehemiah*, 4–5, 14–15). Either way, the call is directed at those not returning, whether Jewish or Gentile.

18 Cf. comment on 3:1–3.

19 Elsewhere, the idiom is found in Ezra-Nehemiah at Ezra 6:22; Nehemiah 2:18.

given for the tabernacle (Ex. 35:29) and the first temple (1 Chron. 29:5, 6, 9 [2x], 14, 17 [2x]). The wider range of Scripture thus underscores that the items mentioned are intended not primarily for general support but to aid this second exodus community in second-temple reconstruction.

1:7–8 A more wooden translation of verse 7 reveals the wordplay used to contrast Cyrus with Nebuchadnezzar II, king of Babylon (605–562 BC). Cyrus "brought out" the vessels of the Lord's house that Nebuchadnezzar had previously "brought out" (ESV "carried away") from Jerusalem during the reign of the Judean king Jehoiachin (2 Kings 24:13).[20] Whenever he defeated a people, Nebuchadnezzar usually took their idols and placed them in the temple of his gods to show their supposed subservience and bondage to the Babylonian gods.[21] But, since the Israelites had no idols in their temple (Ex. 20:4–5), he used the temple vessels as a substitute, placing them in the temple of his gods to suggest that the Lord had been defeated.

In reality, however, it was the Lord himself who had orchestrated Nebuchadnezzar's victory. The writer of Ezra alludes here to Jeremiah 27, using the same phrase "vessels of the house of the LORD" (Ezra 1:7; cf. Jer. 27:16; 28:3, 6) and evoking the Lord's clear statement there that he would raise up Nebuchadnezzar to take the vessels as a punishment against faithless Israel (Jer. 27:6, 16–22). Just as the Lord had sovereignly overseen their removal by one king, he now sovereignly oversees their return by another.

Because in Israel's case Cyrus has no temple idols to return, he instead returns the temple vessels under oversight of "Mithredath the treasurer" and "Sheshbazzar the prince of Judah" (Ezra 1:8). These names further ground the events in a Babylonian-Persian context. Mithredath is a well-known Persian name, and the word for "treasurer" (*gizbar*) is of Persian origin, occurring only here in the OT. On the other hand, Sheshbazzar is likely a Judean who has been given a Babylonian name.[22]

1:9–11 The chapter ends with the designation and numbering of the vessels mentioned in verse 8. The primary interpretive challenges concern: (1) the translation of terms occurring only here in the OT; (2) the quantity of items listed; and (3) the relevance of the list.

The terms for "basins" and "censers" are rare, and a wide range of translations are suggested in the lexicons, English versions, and commentaries; the ESV rendering is reasonable. With respect to the numbers, the total of the items listed (2,499) clearly does not match the concluding sum (5,400).[23] This may be the result of a

---

20 Nebuchadnezzar's first year (605 BC) dovetails with the fourth year of Jehoiakim, king of Judah (609–597; cf. Jer. 25:1). Some temple vessels were removed at this time (Dan. 1:2). After Jehoiakim's death, the majority of temple vessels departed during the short reign of his son Jehoiachin (2 Kings 24:8), in the eighth year of Nebuchadnezzar's reign (598/597).

21 Williamson observes, "Their deposit in the temple of the victor's god was intended to underline to their devotees the inability of their god to save" (*Ezra, Nehemiah*, 16). A parallel event occurs in 1 Samuel 4–6: the Lord permits the ark to be taken captive by the Philistines and brought to the house of Dagon, where he topples the Philistine god.

22 For discussion of the identity of Sheshbazzar, see Introduction: Interpretive Challenges: The Identity of Sheshbazzar.

23 These numbers differ from such English versions as the RSV, whose individual items and sum total 5,469 because it follows the numbers found in the deuterocanonical book *1 Esdras* 2:13–14.

textual corruption, or perhaps the lists in verses 9–10 are partial, while verse 11 offers a total of all items. Either way, verse 11 seeks to show the relevance of the list by connecting the circumstances of the vessels with that of the people. In each case, God's care is underscored by use of the verb "to lead up, bring up." Due to the Lord's sovereign direction of Cyrus, Sheshbazzar's task to "bring up" the vessels parallels the exiles, who are "brought up from Babylonia to Jerusalem" by the Lord's sovereign hand. Nation follows after nation and still, through a sovereign God who is faithful to his covenant, the people of God persist in their calling to build his house and worship.

Response

Ezra-Nehemiah opens with God's people, at times scattered among the powerful kingdoms of Egypt and Assyria, now disoriented and displaced under the rule of the Babylonians and then the Persians. Losing one's place and purpose must rank among the most difficult of human experiences. The Bible calls this loss "exile" (Lam. 1:1–3; cf. Ezra 4:20; Psalm 137). But the Scriptures also assert, especially through the prophets, that though the Lord willed the exile to chastise an unrepentant people (Jer. 7:3–7; 20:4–5; 21:3–7; Ezek. 39:23–24), he also willed to restore them to their home (Jer. 29:10–14; Lam. 4:22; Ezek. 39:25–28).

As of Ezra 1, however, this has not yet happened. In the aftermath of Jerusalem's capture, temple destruction, and apparent loss of kingship, the Lord's people are confronted with unrelenting waves of confusion about his reign. Does he care? Has he gone? Is he sleeping? With no answer seemingly forthcoming, the cry has persisted that God would act to liberate his people. Drawing on imagery from the first exodus, the prophet Isaiah had earlier epitomized the prayers of God's people: "Awake, awake,[24] put on strength, O arm of the LORD; awake, as in days of old, the generations of long ago" (Isa. 51:9). Indeed, this passage affirms the "ransomed of the LORD" will return to Zion (Isa. 51:11). Later, God proclaimed through the prophet Jeremiah that his people would return to Jerusalem (Jer. 30:1–3, 18). Of course God is not asleep (Ps. 121:3). Rather, the God of heaven acts to confirm his lordship even over international affairs. The fulfillment of this promise begins in 538 BC, as the Lord "awakes" in Cyrus a willingness to permit the return of the first exiles.

The gracious act of bringing exiles home, of restoring them to the land, expresses once more the central covenantal promise: God remains their God and they are still his people (Zech. 10:8–10). The Lord's mercy to the community must stimulate each member to identify with his people (Ezra 1:3) and embrace the fruit of repentance (Jer. 31:17–20). Once exiled due to covenantal unfaithfulness (Jer. 11:9–11; Ezra 5:12), the renewed people are returned to rebuild his house. Redeemed people must therefore plea for God to stir and create in them a willingness to meet their joyful obligation.

---

24 The same word translated "stirred" in Ezra 1:1, 5.

Political and historical contexts change. Rulers and nations rise and fall. At times the church is tolerated, at times oppressed. Nevertheless, God is King over nations and grants his people participation in his purposes in every age. The book of Exodus repeatedly states that the goal of freedom from Egypt was the establishment of a worshiping community (Ex. 5:1; 7:16; 8:1; 10:3). The obligation to be a kingdom of priests (Ex. 19:5–6) included the construction of a tabernacle, "that I may dwell in their midst" (Ex. 25:8). The construction of a more permanent temple under Solomon reflected the durability of these covenantal realities (1 Kings 8:1–11; Ezra 5:11). As redeemed servants of God, the main task persists into the present: to build a worshiping community. However, the Lord is the sovereign builder of his house, establishing Jesus Christ, son of David, as the cornerstone and his people as living stones and priests (1 Pet. 2:4–6, 9–10; 1 Cor. 3:10–11, 16–17; Eph. 2:19–22). From bondage to freedom, from Babylonia to Jerusalem to the new Jerusalem, the Lord brings his people home to their original purpose and ultimate destiny. In that new creation, the Lord will dwell with his people forever (Rev. 21:1–4), and they will worship him with their lives (Rev. 21:22–27).

OVERVIEW OF

EZRA 2:1– NEHEMIAH 7:73a

Moving into the second major section of the book (Ezra 2:1–Neh. 7:73a) prompts several initial observations. The placement of the lengthy, nearly identical "census lists" at Ezra 2:1–70 and Nehemiah 7:6–73a bookends the beginning and end of this section.[25] Broadly, the section is composed of three distinct episodes describing the movement of exiles that begins "over there" (i.e., Babylonia) and ends "over here" (i.e., Jerusalem).[26] In that sense, the lists represent a single community not abandoned by God but granted a central role at this major redemptive moment. Most of the action takes place within this second section, as shown by three reconstructive tasks associated with each episode. The words *temple* (Ezra 3–6), *Torah* (Ezra 7–10), and *wall* (Neh. 1:1–7:73a) provide a simple way to consider the accomplished task for each episode in this section.

---

25 On the literary function of these nearly identical chapters, see section on Nehemiah 7:5–73a. For helpful side-by-side comparisons see C. F. Keil, *The Books of Ezra, Nehemiah, and Esther*, trans. Sophia Taylor, Biblical Commentary on the Old Testament by C. F. Keil and F. Delitzsch (1873; repr. Grand Rapids, MI: Eerdmans, 1966), 33–45.

26 These structural observations are indebted to Eskenazi, *Age of Prose*, 37–40.

EZRA 2:1–70

2 Now these were the people of the province who came up out of the captivity of those exiles whom Nebuchadnezzar the king of Babylon had carried captive to Babylonia. They returned to Jerusalem and Judah, each to his own town. [2] They came with Zerubbabel, Jeshua, Nehemiah, Seraiah, Reelaiah, Mordecai, Bilshan, Mispar, Bigvai, Rehum, and Baanah.

The number of the men of the people of Israel: [3] the sons of Parosh, 2,172. [4] The sons of Shephatiah, 372. [5] The sons of Arah, 775. [6] The sons of Pahath-moab, namely the sons of Jeshua and Joab, 2,812. [7] The sons of Elam, 1,254. [8] The sons of Zattu, 945. [9] The sons of Zaccai, 760. [10] The sons of Bani, 642. [11] The sons of Bebai, 623. [12] The sons of Azgad, 1,222. [13] The sons of Adonikam, 666. [14] The sons of Bigvai, 2,056. [15] The sons of Adin, 454. [16] The sons of Ater, namely of Hezekiah, 98. [17] The sons of Bezai, 323. [18] The sons of Jorah, 112. [19] The sons of Hashum, 223. [20] The sons of Gibbar, 95. [21] The sons of Bethlehem, 123. [22] The men of Netophah, 56. [23] The men of Anathoth, 128. [24] The sons of Azmaveth, 42. [25] The sons of Kiriath-arim, Chephirah, and Beeroth, 743. [26] The sons of Ramah and Geba, 621. [27] The men of Michmas, 122. [28] The men of Bethel and Ai, 223. [29] The sons of Nebo, 52. [30] The sons of Magbish, 156. [31] The sons of the other Elam, 1,254. [32] The sons of Harim, 320. [33] The sons of Lod, Hadid, and Ono, 725. [34] The sons of Jericho, 345. [35] The sons of Senaah, 3,630.

[36] The priests: the sons of Jedaiah, of the house of Jeshua, 973. [37] The sons of Immer, 1,052. [38] The sons of Pashhur, 1,247. [39] The sons of Harim, 1,017.

[40] The Levites: the sons of Jeshua and Kadmiel, of the sons of Hodaviah, 74. [41] The singers: the sons of Asaph, 128. [42] The sons of the gatekeepers: the sons of Shallum, the sons of Ater, the sons of Talmon, the sons of Akkub, the sons of Hatita, and the sons of Shobai, in all 139.

[43] The temple servants: the sons of Ziha, the sons of Hasupha, the sons of Tabbaoth, [44] the sons of Keros, the sons of Siaha, the sons of Padon, [45] the sons of Lebanah, the sons of Hagabah, the sons of Akkub, [46] the sons of Hagab, the sons of Shamlai, the sons of Hanan, [47] the sons of Giddel, the sons of Gahar, the sons of Reaiah, [48] the sons of Rezin, the sons of Nekoda, the sons of Gazzam, [49] the sons of Uzza, the sons of Paseah, the sons of Besai, [50] the sons of Asnah, the sons of Meunim, the sons of Nephisim, [51] the sons of Bakbuk, the sons of Hakupha, the sons of Harhur, [52] the sons of Bazluth, the sons of Mehida, the sons of Harsha, [53] the sons of Barkos, the sons of Sisera, the sons of Temah, [54] the sons of Neziah, and the sons of Hatipha.

[55] The sons of Solomon's servants: the sons of Sotai, the sons of Hassophereth, the sons of Peruda, [56] the sons of Jaalah, the sons of Darkon, the sons of Giddel, [57] the sons of Shephatiah, the sons of Hattil, the sons of Pochereth-hazzebaim, and the sons of Ami.

[58] All the temple servants and the sons of Solomon's servants were 392.

59 The following were those who came up from Tel-melah, Tel-harsha, Cherub, Addan, and Immer, though they could not prove their fathers' houses or their descent, whether they belonged to Israel: 60 the sons of Delaiah, the sons of Tobiah, and the sons of Nekoda, 652. 61 Also, of the sons of the priests: the sons of Habaiah, the sons of Hakkoz, and the sons of Barzillai (who had taken a wife from the daughters of Barzillai the Gileadite, and was called by their name). 62 These sought their registration among those enrolled in the genealogies, but they were not found there, and so they were excluded from the priesthood as unclean. 63 The governor told them that they were not to partake of the most holy food, until there should be a priest to consult Urim and Thummim.

64 The whole assembly together was 42,360, 65 besides their male and female servants, of whom there were 7,337, and they had 200 male and female singers. 66 Their horses were 736, their mules were 245, 67 their camels were 435, and their donkeys were 6,720.

68 Some of the heads of families, when they came to the house of the LORD that is in Jerusalem, made freewill offerings for the house of God, to erect it on its site. 69 According to their ability they gave to the treasury of the work 61,000 darics[1] of gold, 5,000 minas[2] of silver, and 100 priests' garments.

70 Now the priests, the Levites, some of the people, the singers, the gatekeepers, and the temple servants lived in their towns, and all the rest of Israel[3] in their towns.

---

[1] A *daric* was a coin weighing about 1/4 ounce or 8.5 grams [2] A *mina* was about 1 1/4 pounds or 0.6 kilogram [3] Hebrew *all Israel*

Section Overview

The census list continues the story from the prior chapter and functions to mark out the returning community. Rather than describing a singular return, the list most likely reflects a series of returns at various times in the early Persian period (538–516 BC).[27]

Individual names in Ezra 2 constitute an idealized community, the "holy seed" ready for implant in the land (Ezra 9:2 AT). The listing of names and numbers may initially appear haphazard. However, the paragraph demarcations in the ESV nicely support the chapter organization. The introductory statement regarding individual leaders and persons who return from captivity (2:1–2a) balances the concluding notices concerning the whole assembly (vv. 64–67), the freewill offerings (vv. 68–69), and the final summation (v. 70), all of which prepare for chapter 3.

The body of chapter 2 then speaks of these initial returnees according to three broad groups: those considered laity (vv. 2b–35), various classes of temple servants (vv. 36–58), and those unable to authenticate their position as legitimate members of Israel (vv. 59–63). A chapter focusing on a wide cross section of the exilic community raises the question of purpose. Why provide a list of mostly unknown persons and priests named and numbered among the community of

---

27 Williamson offers a number of reasons for this assessment. For example, Sheshbazzar, an important figure in the initial return (1:8, 11; 5:14–16) is not listed among the leadership (*Ezra, Nehemiah*, 30–31). Clines holds a similar position and adduces comparable reasons. (*Ezra, Nehemiah, Esther*, 43–44)

God's people who return to Jerusalem? We will return to this question in the Response section below.

Section Outline

II. The Community Rebuilds Temple, Torah, and Wall according to the Decrees (Ezra 2:1–Neh. 7:73a)

    A. The List of Exiles Returning (Ezra 2:1–70)

        1. Introduction to People and Leaders Who Came Up out of the Captivity (2:1–2a)

        2. The Number of the Men of the People of Israel (2:2b–35)

        3. The Temple Personnel (2:36–58)

        4. Those Who Could Not Prove Their Descent (2:59–63)

        5. Summary Statements (2:64–70)

Comment

2:1–2a The initial verses of chapter 2 fit their context as they expand upon the major geographical shift from Babylonia to Jerusalem that concluded the prior chapter. Using verbal repetition, "Now these were the people of the province *who came up*" links back to "when the exiles *were brought up*," which concluded the prior chapter (1:11). This clause also looks forward to the detailed list of persons that follows. The prior chapter interpreted its events as undergirded by God, who "had stirred" the spirit of these people (1:5), motivating their willingness to bear further hardship by returning to Jerusalem. A new day dawns, with future inhabitants given a new place and a new status under new leaders.

A new start in life may require actual geographical movement from one place to another, from one provincial location to another. The term "province" (*medinah*) is an Aramaic loanword referring to smaller administrative divisions, of which there were 127 in the Persian Empire (cf. Est. 1:1). In Ezra-Nehemiah the term "province" applies not only to Babylonia (Ezra 7:16) but to the province of Judah (i.e., Yehud) as well (Ezra 5:8; Neh. 1:3). The latter province lies in a wider region called "Beyond the River."[28] Although not always consistently applied in academic discussion, the technical term *satrapy* was used for the wider region. In light of Ezra 1:11, the immediate literary context of 2:1–2 so emphasizes the movement from Babylonia to Jerusalem that "province" likely refers to the province of Babylonia as the place of origin. Alternatively, Judah as a destination province may be in view. In either case, the movement *from* Babylon back *to* Judah is clear.

Beyond the geographical shift to a new place, the people further assume a new status as those released from the "captivity of [the] exiles." Those Nebuchadnezzar had exiled ("carried captive") were the displaced inhabitants of Jerusalem (2 Kings 24:14; Jer. 29:1) who are now freed "from the captivity" (Ezra 3:8; 8:35; Neh. 1:2, 3; 8:17).[29]

---

28 Ezra 4:10, 11, 16, 17, 20; 5:3, 6; 6:6, 13; 7:21, 25; 8:36; Nehemiah 2:7, 9; 3:7.
29 The ESV at places translates the phrase "survived the exile" (Neh. 1:2, 3).

The astonishing ascent of so many from an old province to a new one and from a place of captivity to one of freedom testifies to God's loving-kindness. Restoration to home and freedom demands a further response of obedience to the task issued in the proclamation of Cyrus. The prior chapter clarified that central task as the rebuilding of the house of God. New leaders, listed by name, provide further evidence of the Lord's loving-kindness in his continual provision for his people to help them accomplish their restored mission. Therefore, past provision of leaders to represent and instruct the Lord's people persists in the postexilic period. Undermining an expected mention of twelve leaders to complement the twelve tribes of Israel (cf. Ezra 6:17; 8:24, 35), the text of Ezra 2:2 lists only eleven names. However, numerical expectations are met by the parallel list in Nehemiah 7:7, which, while diverging at a number of points, most obviously differs with the inclusion of a twelfth name, Nahamani.[30] Among those listed, Zerubbabel and Jeshua hold primacy of place by virtue of their position at the head of this list, their role within the Ezra-Nehemiah narrative, and further mention of them by the postexilic prophets Haggai and Zechariah.

Zerubbabel's name ("seed of Babylon") heads the list. He features in the OT only in the postexilic books, being mentioned twenty times in Ezra, Nehemiah, Haggai, and Zechariah. The biblical texts assert his Davidic lineage as son of Shealtiel (Ezra 3:2, 8; 5:2; Neh. 12:1) and grandson of Jehoiachin (i.e., Jeconiah, 1 Chron. 3:16–19).[31] His descent reveals a royal ancestry and history inextricably tied to both Israel's past and her future (cf. Ezek. 1:2). This makes him first in line for the Davidic throne. Nebuchadnezzar had exiled Jehoiachin in 597 BC at only eighteen years of age (2 Kings 24:12), while Nebuchadnezzar's son Evil-merodach (562–560) released him from prison in 561 (2 Kings 25:27–30). Now, only twenty-three years after his grandfather's release from prison, Zerubbabel leads this early group liberated from captivity.

The whole trajectory of the return to Jerusalem revolves around heeding the decree to rebuild the temple. References to Zerubbabel in Ezra only confirm this purpose, typically focusing on his leadership in the return (Ezra 2:2) and more particularly on his role in renewing the worship of the Lord. He does so by building the altar (3:2, 8), resisting opposition to the rebuilding (4:2–3), and submitting to the prophetic call to renew the work on the temple (5:1–2; 6:14; cf. Hag. 1:12). By using a title given later to Nehemiah (Neh. 5:14), the book of Haggai clarifies Zerubbabel's leadership role by applying to him the designation "governor" (Hb. *pekhah*; Hag. 1:1, 14; 2:2, 21). References to Zerubbabel in Zechariah's fifth vision (Zechariah 4) promise divine assurance in completing the temple even though opposition threatens. Within the NT, the name Zerubbabel

---

30 The divergences in the initial names of leaders range from noteworthy differences to minor variations in spelling.

31 At 1 Chronicles 3:19 we find the only other mention of Zerubbabel in the OT. Chronicles may be considered postexilic, since it was written in the postexilic period; however, its history ends where Ezra's postexilic story begins (2 Chron. 36:22–23). Chronicles informs us that Zerubbabel is the son of Pedaiah, Shealtiel's younger brother. Some speculate that Pedaiah married the widow of Shealtiel, implying levirate marriage (cf. Deut. 25:5–10). See brief discussion in Kidner, *Ezra and Nehemiah*, 41n15.

appears solely in the genealogies of Jesus Christ, the son of David (Matt. 1:12–13; Luke 3:27).

Jeshua, the second figure in the list of leaders, shares a name common to various biblical figures, occasionally making it difficult to distinguish one individual from another. Surpassing the frequency of the name Zerubbabel, which always refers to the same person, the name Jeshua occurs twenty-eight times in Ezra-Nehemiah, always with the spelling "Jeshua." A number of occurrences in Ezra-Nehemiah explicitly or implicitly point to the priest who, along with Zerubbabel, leads an early wave of exiles to Jerusalem (Ezra 2:2; 3:2, 8, 9; 4:3; 5:2; 10:18; Neh. 7:7; 12:1, 7, 10, 26). His ancestry is given as "the son of Jozadak" (Ezra 3:2; 5:2; 10:18; Neh. 12:26) or "Jehozadak" (Hag. 1:1, 12, 14; 2:2, 4; Zech. 6:11). Like Zerubbabel's grandfather Jehoiachin, Jeshua's predecessor Jozadak, also a priest, experienced exile at the hand of Nebuchadnezzar (1 Chron. 6:15). As the postexilic prophets clarified Zerubbabel's function as governor, so Haggai and Zechariah, using the more common spelling "Joshua," frequently call Jeshua "high priest" (Hag. 1:1, 12, 14; 2:2, 4; Zech. 3:1, 8; 6:11). Both Zerubbabel and Jeshua grew up with a deep experience of what exile meant.

The multiple mentions in the Bible of other names in the list warrant brief discussion. The Nehemiah listed in Ezra 2:2 differs from the later Nehemiah, who rebuilds the Jerusalem walls, and the Mordecai listed here differs from the one known from the book of Esther. (As in our day, it was not uncommon for more than one person to have the same name in ancient Israel.) The Seraiah of Ezra 2:2, later mentioned in the list of priests and Levites returning with Zerubbabel and Jeshua (Neh. 12:1), differs from other mentions of the name (Ezra 7:1; Neh. 10:2; 11:11; 12:12).[32] Like Seraiah, Rehum is later listed with the initial return and is identified with the priests and Levites (Neh. 12:3).[33] The names Bigvai and Baanah differ from persons of the same name who later sign the covenant document (Neh. 10:16, 27). Other names in the list receive mention only here or in the parallel text at Nehemiah 7:7 and so remain otherwise unknown.

2:2b–35 The initial comment and identification of leaders (vv. 1–2a) is followed by the first list comprising the returning laity named "the number of the men of the people of Israel" (v. 2b). Many cultures preserve family background and place of origin as important markers of identity and community belonging (cf. Jonah 1:8),[34] and these two markers structure this list. Persons are grouped according to seventeen family names (Ezra 2:3–19) and twenty-two geographical locations (vv. 20–35). Many of the same names appear elsewhere in Ezra-Nehemiah, especially in the list of the people who seal the covenant document (Neh. 10:1–27). The geographical names are consistent with the prior mention of Judah and Benjamin

---

32 Seraiah, the ancestor of Ezra (Ezra 7:1), may be the similarly named priest whom Nebuchadnezzar struck down at Riblah (2 Kings 25:18–21//Jer. 52:24–27). Both 1 Chronicles and Jeremiah contain multiple mentions of the name Seraiah (e.g., 1 Chron. 4:13, 14, 35; Jer. 36:26; 40:8; 51:59, 61).

33 The parallel at Nehemiah 7:7 reads "Nehum" rather than "Rehum," probably due to a scribal error. Elsewhere Rehum functions as "commander" (Ezra 4:8, 9, 17, 23) during Artaxerxes's reign (464–423 BC), a Levite who helps in wall repair (Neh. 3:17), and a name on the sealed covenant document (Neh. 10:25).

34 Joseph Too Shao and Rosa Ching Shao, *Ezra & Nehemiah*, ABCS (Singapore: Asia Theological Association, 2007), 26.

(Ezra 1:5), as nearly all of the places mentioned fall in the province of Judah and a majority specifically within the former territory of Benjamin.[35]

2:36–58 The earlier notice of those stirred up to return mentions Judah and Benjamin, followed by the priests and Levites (1:5). The same order occurs in chapter 2: the "men of the people of Israel" (v. 2b)—revealed as residents of Judah and Benjamin (vv. 20–35)—are followed by priests, Levites, and other temple servants (vv. 36–58). Specifically, the chapter progresses from priests (vv. 36–39) to those who assist their work: Levites (vv. 40–42), temple servants (vv. 43–54), and the sons of Solomon's servants (vv. 55–57). The treatment of temple personnel concludes with a summary statement (v. 58).

2:36–39 Priests and Levites feature prominently in Ezra-Nehemiah.[36] The primary responsibility for temple worship and sacrifice at the altar falls to the priests, a role restricted to descendants of Aaron (Num. 3:10). The names Jedaiah, Harim, and Immer also head three of the twenty-four priestly divisions organized by David according to 1 Chronicles 24:7–18. While the name Pashhur (Ezra 2:38) does not distinguish one of these priestly divisions, the name of Malchijah, his father, does (cf. 1 Chron. 24:9; Neh. 11:12). The priestly role, their foremost mention in the list of temple officials, and the equivalent numbers (4,289) in both Ezra 2:36–38 and Nehemiah 7:39–42 attest to priests' importance in the corporate life of Israel.

2:40–42 The Levites are those members of the tribe of Levi not of Aaronic descent.[37] In the corporate life of God's people, the Levites functioned to guard and care for the physical transport and needs of the tabernacle. Beside this, they assisted the priests (Num. 3:6–9). Further, David had allocated some Levites for particular roles as gatekeepers and musicians in the Lord's house and still others to care for temple vessels and worship preparation (1 Chron. 9:14–34).[38] Even adding the seventy-four Levites to the numbers of gatekeepers and singers, the total number (341) is significantly lower than the number of priests. This shortage of Levites and speculated reasons for their lower numbers will be addressed in the comment on Ezra 8:15–20, where the problem confronts Ezra.

2:43–54 These verses distinguish the temple servants from the sons of Solomon's servants that follow (vv. 55–58). Apart from 1 Chronicles 9:2, the Hebrew term

---

35 John D. Currid and David P. Barrett provide a map labeling all these named locations in the *Crossway ESV Bible Atlas* (Wheaton, IL: 2010), 180. For detailed treatment of specific items in the list see Blenkinsopp, *Ezra-Nehemiah*, 85–87.

36 Priests and Levites are found together in every chapter of Ezra except 4 and 5 (Ezra 1:5; 2:70; 3:8, 10, 12; 6:20; 7:7; 8:15, 29, 30, 33; 9:1; 10:5). In Nehemiah, after the mention at 7:73, they are dominant in the final section (Neh. 8:9, 13; 9:38; 10:28, 34, 38; 11:3, 20; 12:1, 22, 30, 44; 13:5, 13, 30).

37 J. G. McConville, *Ezra, Nehemiah, and Esther*, DSBS (Louisville: Westminster John Knox, 1985), 16.

38 The relationship between the Levites and the singers/gatekeepers is uncertain. In 2:40–42 the latter two seem distinct from Levites; however, elsewhere gatekeepers and singers are considered Levites (1 Chron. 9:26, 33–34; 23:3–6; Ezra 3:10). The term "singers" refers to musicians broadly (cf. 1 Chron. 15:16, 19, 27; 2 Chron. 5:12–13; 23:13) with all occurrences in 1 and 2 Chronicles, Ezra, and Nehemiah. Beyond other occurrences in Ezra 2 (vv. 41, 65 [2x], 70), the singers are found at Ezra 7:7; 10:24; Nehemiah 7:1, 44, 67 (2x), 73; 10:28, 39; 11:22, 23; 12:28; and particularly at the dedication of the wall (Neh. 12:28, 29, 42, 45, 46, 47; 13:5, 10). For "gatekeepers," see Ezra 2:42, 70; 7:7; 10:24; Nehemiah 7:1, 45, 73; 10:28, 39; 11:19; 12:25, 45, 47; 13:5.

translated "temple servants" (*netinim*, "given ones") occurs only in Ezra-Nehemiah to classify a group separate from priests, Levites, singers, or gatekeepers.[39] Their precise role and status remain uncertain. As Levites were given to support the priests in temple work (Num. 3:9; 8:19), so also had the temple servants been given by David and his officials to support the work of the Levites (Ezra 8:20), and they likely performed menial tasks. Perhaps they were descended from the Gibeonites and likewise enlisted as "cutters of wood and drawers of water" (Josh. 9:23, 27).[40] The inclusion of numerous non-Israelite names among the thirty-five families listed makes it possible they are non-Israelites. The mention of Meunim (Ezra 2:50), defeated during the monarchy (1 Chron. 4:41; 2 Chron. 20:1; 26:7), may indicate a history for some as war captives. Certainly, the placement of both the temple servants and the sons of Solomon's servants among the "whole assembly" (Ezra 2:64), and yet separate from the male and female servants listed as property (v. 65), suggests that both of these groups are free rather than enslaved.[41] They enjoy membership in the congregation, as evidenced in participation in the later covenant renewal (Neh. 10:28–29).

2:55–58 Ten family names classify the "sons of Solomon's servants," a group of limited occurrences outside of the lists in Ezra 2 and Nehemiah 7 (cf. Neh. 11:3). Like the temple servants, their beginning and function is uncertain, though some scholars trace their source to Solomon's forced labor of the Canaanite remnant (1 Kings 9:20–21).[42] Perhaps their mention at the end of the temple personnel in Ezra 2 encourages the view that they perform temple duties even more basic than the temple servants'. The single number of 392 for both temple servants and the sons of Solomon's servants (v. 58) shows a connection between them, though the specific nature of that connection remains unclear.

2:59–62 The Bible claims consistently that the earth is the Lord's (Ex. 9:28; Ps. 24:1; 1 Cor. 10:26). As such, God had granted a particular place as a land inheritance, the space where his redeemed people would live out their calling to reflect his glory to the world (Gen. 12:7; Ex. 32:13; Lev. 20:24; Josh. 1:6). For this reason, the legitimacy of membership among returnees arises in the postexilic period in light of claims to property and land (Ezra 2:70; Neh. 11:3). Particularly for the laity, those unable to confirm descent will lose not only land inheritance; they will also forfeit the full rights and privileges of community membership. Three families among the laity (Ezra 2:59–60) and three among the priesthood (vv. 61–63) are unable to prove by genealogical record "whether they belonged to Israel."[43] As for those

---

39 Ezra 2:43, 58, 70; 7:7, 24; 8:17, 20; Nehemiah 3:26, 31; 7:46, 60, 73; 10:28; 11:3, 21.

40 The list of returned exiles in 1 Chronicles 9 intimates a connection between temple servants and Gibeonites. After a similar order of cultic personnel as seen in Ezra 2, the chapter concludes with a Gibeonite genealogy in the exact location where the temple servants are mentioned in Ezra 2, i.e., after singers and gatekeepers (1 Chron. 9:35–44).

41 For the argument that these were freemen see Baruch A. Levine, "The Netînîm," *JBL* 82/2 (1963): 207–212. For discussion of the issues and treatment of particular names in this list see Clines, *Ezra, Nehemiah, Esther*, 56–57.

42 Blenkinsopp, *Ezra-Nehemiah*, 91.

43 Special mention of "sons of Barzillai" (2:61) refers to descendants of a priest whose wife came from the daughters of Barzillai the Gileadite. The family took the name of Barzillai, an aged man who supported David during Absalom's rebellion (1 Kings 2:7; cf. 2 Sam. 17:27–29; 19:31–40).

among the priesthood, the stakes are even higher. The high calling, qualifications, and previous failure of the preexilic priesthood reawakens in the postexilic community the necessity of a consecrated priesthood. The need for renewed priestly service rendered at the altar in a reconstructed temple makes this all the more important. Until further inquiry, these priests are declared ritually unsuitable for priestly duties and privileges.

2:63 The explicit identity of the "governor" (Hb. *tirshata'*; cf. KJV) is uncertain. Three main options are usually given: (1) In a different historical context, the term applies to Nehemiah (Neh. 8:9; 10:1; cf. *1 Esd.* 5:40), so the same could be true here. (2) In the parallel passage noting offerings of the community, the governor provides a gift (Neh. 7:70), suggesting his identity as a Jew.[44] The title may therefore refer to Zerubbabel who, though never called "governor" in Ezra-Nehemiah (cf. Neh. 12:47), is identified elsewhere as "governor" using the more common term *pekhah* (Hag. 1:1, 14; 2:2, 21). (3) If reflective of the earliest period of return, when divine inquiry is limited (see further below), it best points to Sheshbazzar (Ezra 1:11), likewise called "governor" using *pekhah* (5:14).

In any case, the governor establishes a waiting period until a priest can seek divine knowledge in this matter by means of Urim and Thummim, one of three legitimate means of discerning God's will (the other means being prophets and dreams; 1 Sam. 28:6). The Lord had commanded Moses that the Urim and Thummim be carried in the "breastpiece of judgment" worn by the high priest who entered into the Lord's presence (Ex. 28:28–30; Lev. 8:8; Num. 27:21; Deut. 33:8). It appears from 1 Samuel 14:41–42 that their use provided a "yes" or "no" answer to direct inquiry, comparable to lot-casting. Therefore, proper use demanded not merely a priest but a high priest *with* Urim and Thummim *and* a rebuilt temple where God's presence is manifest such that the priest can go before the Lord with the breastpiece.[45] These conditions await fulfillment, because the return of Jeshua the priest and the completion of the temple has not yet occurred.

2:64–70 The chapter summary provides totals for the numbers of persons and animals who return (vv. 64–67) as well as an accounting of provisions for the future work (vv. 68–69). With an initial movement from Babylon to Jerusalem inaugurated, the chapter concludes with the exiles' having arrived "in their towns" (v. 70).

2:64–67 Variations exist between these verses, the parallel list in Nehemiah, and the deuterocanonical *1 Esdras* 5:41. However, all three number 42,360 as the quantity of returning exiles (Ezra 2:64; cf. Neh. 7:66). Obviously, the community of God's people contains numerous individuals. As a multitude of cells combine to form one body, so also the individual persons listed in this chapter form a single entity known as the "whole assembly." The Lord knows each one by name, and, as members of the wider covenant community, each plays a role in God's restorative plan.

---

44 Williamson, *Ezra, Nehemiah*, 37.
45 See the reasoned discussion in Keil, *Ezra, Nehemiah, and Esther*, 43.

2:68–69 This chapter addresses the central task: reestablishing the worship of the Lord in a rebuilt house "on its site." With the temple in ruins, and despite personal economic concerns, the "heads of families" act in faith and determination in a manner consistent with parallel biblical events from the past. Throughout the biblical story the giving of "freewill offerings" reveals individual and corporate spiritual health and makes possible the raising of both the tabernacle (Ex. 35:29) and the first temple (1 Chron. 29:5–6, 9). Contributions toward God's ongoing mission flow not from demand or taxation (2 Chron. 24:6) but freely and with the goal that he might dwell once more among them. Debate persists on how to understand the currency offered; however, the total weight of gold would be approximately 1,133 pounds (514 kg) and of silver 6,250 pounds (2,835 kg).[46]

2:70 The chapter begins by describing the return of a corporate entity, the "people of the province" returning "each to his own town" (v. 1). The final verse functions to frame this movement. Participants in this new redemptive moment include leaders and those associated with temple service (priests, Levites, etc.), as well as "all the rest of Israel in their towns." Abraham's offspring has now returned from Mesopotamia to the Promised Land.

Response

While the purpose of this list is open to debate,[47] and while the names and numbers listed in Ezra 2 provide such a challenge that they are often passed by, several important theological themes are on display here. These may be summarized as follows: *The Lord, for the sake of the world, keeps his promises to a redeemed community in which each member embraces the covenant from the heart.*

First, the list points to a God who keeps his promises to a redeemed community. God had promised through the prophets that the seed of his people, a remnant, would survive and be sown in the land once more (Hos. 2:23; Jer. 31:27). That seed would not only survive but also "be fruitful and multiply" (Jer. 23:3; cf. Jer. 31:8; Ezek. 37:26). While both Ezra and Nehemiah look forward to further resettlements, Ezra 2 recounts the faithful response of Abraham's seed, risking all to return to Jerusalem to rebuild the temple. The offspring of Abraham, ultimately comprising Jews and Gentiles (Ezra 6:21; Gal. 3:28–29), multiplies under the apostolic testimony of a risen Messiah (Acts 6:1, 7; 12:24; 16:5; 19:18–20). And in the new heavens and new earth, the city of God, the new Jerusalem, will descend from heaven to earth, with God himself and the Lamb as the temple, and "the glory and the honor of the nations" will enter that new Jerusalem (Rev. 21:26; cf. Jer. 33:9).

The list also confirms the importance to God of each member and his or her place within his covenant community. Just as the precious temple vessels were

---

46 Clines, *Ezra, Nehemiah, Esther*, 61. The Persian "daric" refers to a gold coin weighing about 0.3 ounces (8.5 g); it was associated with the Persian king Darius I (522–486 BC). Alternatively, this may be a Greek loanword and so translated "drachmas" (NASB, NJB). The term *mina* (Hb. *maneh*) refers not to a coin but to a unit of measure, with one mina equaling approximately 20 ounces (570 g).

47 Commentators provide various answers regarding the purpose of such a list: a generic census list; a list required for tax or land purposes; a list that distinguishes true Israelites from others in the land.

numbered and transported to Jerusalem (Ezra 1:7–11), the precious individual persons, numbered and transported, constitute the covenant community in Ezra 2. This is in keeping with the rest of the biblical story, in which we see the Lord's ongoing determination to set his love upon this particular corporate entity chosen to enter with him into a relationship of mutual obligation and covenantal loyalty (Ex. 24:3–8; Josh. 24:14–28). As will become increasingly apparent, the list of persons represents, in part, the remnant of that ancient collective called to be a holy, treasured possession (Deut. 7:6–11).

At this point in the story, belonging to that people requires, at minimum, the important proof of descent (Ezra 2:59–62). However, in the wider biblical scope, the individual does not belong to the covenant people by virtue of mere external proof or simple physical presence. True faith—embracing God's covenant from the heart—is necessary to belong truly to his people (Ex. 20:5–6; Deut. 6:1–9; 7:9–11). Not surprisingly, in another context that looks forward to return from exile (Deut. 30:1–3), the external expression of genuine faith must arise from an internal circumcision of the heart (Deut. 10:16; 30:6). Later the apostle Paul will insist that this perspective endures into the NT era: the true member of God's covenant people is one marked by circumcision of the heart (Rom. 2:28–29; 9:6–8; cf. Matt. 13:24–30).

Finally, like the church, this restored covenant community exists not for itself. In every age the redeemed community must strive as God's image-bearers to reflect his character to a burdened world. It is no accident that the matching communal lists at Ezra 2 and Nehemiah 7 serve as a frame around the main things to be done: rebuilding the temple and city wall (Ezra 3–Nehemiah 6). It is *these people* (Ezra 2; Nehemiah 7) who must do *these things* (temple and wall rebuilding) at *this time*. And the reason to do these tasks in particular comes down to one word: *worship*. The first exodus community was called out of Egypt in order to worship (Ex. 4:23; 5:1; 7:16; 8:1, 20; 9:1). Comparably, the main thing to be done by this new exodus community (Isa. 48:20–21; 52:8–12; Jer. 23:7–8) is to worship the Lord in a rebuilt temple motivated by grateful obedience to his commands (Torah) in the security of a renewed city (wall). Like the membership roster of a modern congregation, this list contains persons named and known at one time but who will mostly fade from historical view. No matter: God frees his people in every age to take responsibility and act. Investment in the ongoing act of worship requires each to faithfully play his or her role in the forward progress of the kingdom—and to do so boldly, knowing that the Lord will provide.

EZRA 3:1–13

3 When the seventh month came, and the children of Israel were in the towns, the people gathered as one man to Jerusalem. ²Then arose Jeshua the son of Jozadak, with his fellow priests, and Zerubbabel the son of Shealtiel with his kinsmen, and they built the altar of the God of Israel, to offer burnt offerings on it, as it is written in the Law of Moses the man of God. ³They set the altar in its place, for fear was on them because of the peoples of the lands, and they offered burnt offerings on it to the LORD, burnt offerings morning and evening. ⁴And they kept the Feast of Booths, as it is written, and offered the daily burnt offerings by number according to the rule, as each day required, ⁵and after that the regular burnt offerings, the offerings at the new moon and at all the appointed feasts of the LORD, and the offerings of everyone who made a freewill offering to the LORD. ⁶From the first day of the seventh month they began to offer burnt offerings to the LORD. But the foundation of the temple of the LORD was not yet laid. ⁷So they gave money to the masons and the carpenters, and food, drink, and oil to the Sidonians and the Tyrians to bring cedar trees from Lebanon to the sea, to Joppa, according to the grant that they had from Cyrus king of Persia.

⁸Now in the second year after their coming to the house of God at Jerusalem, in the second month, Zerubbabel the son of Shealtiel and Jeshua the son of Jozadak made a beginning, together with the rest of their kinsmen, the priests and the Levites and all who had come to Jerusalem from the captivity. They appointed the Levites, from twenty years old and upward, to supervise the work of the house of the LORD. ⁹And Jeshua with his sons and his brothers, and Kadmiel and his sons, the sons of Judah, together supervised the workmen in the house of God, along with the sons of Henadad and the Levites, their sons and brothers.

¹⁰And when the builders laid the foundation of the temple of the LORD, the priests in their vestments came forward with trumpets, and the Levites, the sons of Asaph, with cymbals, to praise the LORD, according to the directions of David king of Israel. ¹¹And they sang responsively, praising and giving thanks to the LORD,

"For he is good,
    for his steadfast love endures forever toward Israel."

And all the people shouted with a great shout when they praised the LORD, because the foundation of the house of the LORD was laid. ¹²But many of the priests and Levites and heads of fathers' houses, old men who had seen the first house, wept with a loud voice when they saw the foundation of this house being laid, though many shouted aloud for joy, ¹³so that the people could not distinguish the sound of the joyful shout from the sound of the people's weeping, for the people shouted with a great shout, and the sound was heard far away.

Section Overview

The opening chapters of many biblical books function as introductions. Ezra 1 has established the setting and characters essential to this historical account. Royal proclamations, human and divine, trigger the events, with a primary focus upon the faithfulness of the Lord. His promise to restore his people remains firm. And yet, like father Abraham before them, the Lord's people must respond and move from Babylonia to Israel, and, once there, rebuild the house of the Lord (Ezra 1:3).

The second major section of Ezra-Nehemiah (Ezra 2:1–Neh. 7:73a) begins with a list in Ezra 2. This list details the remnant community that responded to the royal and divine proclamations and "came up out of the captivity" (Ezra 2:1). As seed sown by the Lord (Jer. 31:27; Hos. 2:23), this people must look to God, who alone gives growth (1 Cor. 3:7). Following on, Ezra 3 is the first of four pericopes (3:1–13; 4:1–24; 5:1–6:18; 6:19–22) constituting the first episode (Ezra 3–6) of the section (Ezra 2:1–Neh. 7:73a). In this episode the remnant community commences its first and primary mission: reestablishing a beachhead of worship of the Lord in the land by rebuilding the temple.

With temporal markers to clarify structure, the initial scenes relate two crucial building projects. The first scene recounts the rebuilding of the altar in the seventh month, with its attendant sacrifices and celebrations, particularly the Feast of Booths (Ezra 3:1–7). Following on, the second scene describes restoration of the temple foundation in the "second year" (3:8–9). The successful construction of altar and foundation leads naturally to communal praise, with a fusion of joy and melancholy in the final scene (3:10–13).

Section Outline

II.B. First Movement: Altar, Opposition, and Temple (3:1–6:22)
    1. Rebuilding Begins: Altar and Temple Foundation (3:1–13)
        a. Seventh Month: Altar and Offerings, Feast of Booths Celebrated (3:1–7)
        b. Second Year, Second Month: Temple Building Begins (3:8–9)
        c. Praising the Lord for the Foundation Laid (3:10–13)

Comment

3:1–3 Words and phrases function as the cohesive glue that connects the various chapters of Ezra. "Babylonia" and "Jerusalem" (1:11; 2:1) link chapters 1 and 2, while the mention of "towns" (2:70; 3:1) links chapters 2 and 3. Together they reveal the key movement from exile to return. Apart from the collection of freewill offerings (2:68–69) the text says nothing about the specific time or actions that occur between return and resettlement. However, action in chapter 3 begins specifically in the seventh month (v. 1), perhaps still within the first year of Cyrus (1:1), though this is not explicit.

Sacrifice requires an altar. The verbs "arise" (Hb. *qum*) and "build" (*banah*) summarize in part the task of the postexilic community from the start (1:5) and will do so in the future (5:2; Neh. 2:18, 20; 3:1). Jeshua, Zerubbabel, and other leaders get to work (Ezra 3:2). Arising and building in the setting of Ezra-Nehemiah not only repeats previous canonical patterns from the Solomonic temple (1 Chron. 22:19; 2 Chron. 6:10);[48] these verbs likewise fulfill the prior divine promises and commands. Through Cyrus, God himself will see to it that Jerusalem is inhabited and rebuilt (Isa. 44:26–28; 58:12)—but not yet. While the security of walls around Jerusalem will bolster the sense of security required for the flourishing of the people, and a rebuilt temple will provide a place for proper worship, the returnees first rise and erect the altar "in its place" (Ezra 3:3). Setting the altar and temple on their prior foundations establishes continuity with the past, an important feature of this chapter.[49] The reference to altar rebuilding and the notice that "fear was on them because of the peoples of the lands" (v. 3) seems to lack connection.[50] Where previously have we seen this pattern of altar building in the context of enemies?

By rebuilding the altar as one of the first things accomplished upon entry into the land, the returnees repeat the patterns of altar constructions by Abraham (Gen. 12:6–7) and Joshua (Josh. 8:30–35; cf. Deut. 27:1–8) upon first entrance into Canaan. Each of these prior altar-building events occurred in the context of real or potential enemies (Gen. 12:6; Josh. 8:28–29; 9:1–2). Now, in Ezra, upon return to the land, setting up the altar "in its place" in the seventh month has some analogy. Gathering "as one man" typically occurs in contexts of human conflict (Judg. 6:16; 20:1, 8, 11; 1 Sam. 11:7; 2 Sam. 19:14) or the Lord's judgment (Num. 14:15). The two "one man" gatherings found in Ezra-Nehemiah (Ezra 3:1; Neh. 7:73b–8:1) occur in the context of rejoicing and sacrifice during the seventh-month assembly. However, as with Abraham and Joshua, the context of altar construction and sacrifice foreshadows conflicts externally and distresses internally (Ezra 4:1–5, 6, 7–23; 9:1–2; 10:2; Neh. 2:10, 19; 4:1, 7; 6:1–2, 7; 13:3, 23–27). This provides a nuanced but important theological point reverberating throughout Ezra-Nehemiah and all of Scripture: in the present time God's people must carry out their mission to worship the true and living God, but in doing so they must not only expect conflict but trust the Lord in the midst of it.

3:4–6a These events occur in the seventh month, known as Tishri (September/ October)—Israel's most holy month.[51] The month included some of the most sacred festivals of the calendar year: the Feast of Trumpets on the first day of the month (Lev. 23:23–25), the Day of Atonement on the tenth day (Lev. 23:26–32), and the Feast of Booths[52] on the fifteenth (Lev. 23:33–36; 39–43; Deut. 16:13–15). Both the first day of this celebratory month (Trumpets) and the twenty-second day (Lev. 23:36) called for a "holy convocation" (Lev. 23:24; Num. 29:1). The latter

---

48 The verbs may also describe building projects that provoke the Lord (1 Kings 16:32–33; 2 Kings 21:2–3)!
49 Williamson, *Ezra, Nehemiah*, 45; Blenkinsopp, *Ezra-Nehemiah*, 97.
50 For further examination of "the peoples of the lands," cf. comment on 4:4–5.
51 Prior to exile, Tishri was also known by the Phoenician name Ethanim (1 Kings 8:2). For a chart showing the Hebrew calendar, see the *ESV Study Bible*, 34.
52 Some English versions translate "Festival of Tabernacles." Another name is "Feast of Ingathering" (Ex. 23:16).

gathering occurred on the eighth day after the seven-day Feast of Booths,[53] a celebration that receives explicit mention in Ezra and later in Nehemiah as the people gather as "one man" (Ezra 3:1, 4; Neh. 8:14). Previously, this important feast coincided with the placement of the ark in its permanent dwelling place and the dedication of the first temple (1 Kings 8:2, 65). Now Ezra 3 will bind altar reconstruction to the laying of the second temple foundation, even repeating the song of the first dedication (v. 11; cf. 2 Chron. 5:13).

The Feast of Booths, alongside Passover / Unleavened Bread and the Feast of Weeks, is one of the three great feasts celebrated in Israel (Leviticus 23; Deut. 16:16–17; 2 Chron. 8:13). Its name comes from the use of temporary shelters or "booths" constructed and lived in during the Israelites' deliverance from Egypt (Lev. 23:43). The feast celebrates God as Creator and Redeemer. First, the people rejoice in God's creative work as he blesses them yearly with the produce of the autumn harvest, closing one year and beginning another (Deut. 16:13–15). However, the festival also functions to provoke a redemptive memory for current and future generations. In celebrating the festival, all members of the covenantal community are reminded not only of God's provision of food but also of his redemptive actions during the wilderness pilgrimage (Lev. 23:43).

The repetition of "burnt offerings" in nearly every verse of this first scene (Ezra 3:2, 3, 4, 5, 6) not only focuses attention on the renewal of the daily burnt offerings (Ex. 29:38–42; Num. 28:6) but also suggests the increased sacrifices required during the eight days of the Feast of Booths (cf. Num. 29:12–38). What is more, this chapter also mentions the restarting of four other types of sacrifices: daily and monthly sacrifices (Num. 28:11–15), other "appointed feasts," and freewill offerings (Lev. 7:16–18; 22:17–23). Thus, before wall or temple begins, the Israelites must first restore the altar in order to sacrifice burnt offerings.

However, success requires another kind of restoration. God's word, "as it is written in the Law of Moses" and "according to the rule" (Ezra 3:2, 4; 2 Chron. 23:18), provides the motivation. Mosaic instruction (Torah) must have primacy of place in the restored covenant community. As during the exodus and its aftermath, so also for the postexilic generation: God alone provides for their needs, God alone has brought them up out of exile, and God alone, through Torah, reveals how they should live as a "wise and understanding people" among the nations (Deut. 4:5–8).

3:6b–7 The abundance of biblical references cited in the comments on 3:1–6a expose the deep roots of the past as they break through the soil of the postexilic present. Altar reconstruction and reinstitution of sacrifice in the important seventh month provide only the initial steps of rebuilding and renewal. The narration now pauses (v. 6b) to introduce the next construction project, which occupies the rest of the chapter: the necessity of laying the temple foundation (vv. 8–13). Not only in Solomon's day (1 Kings 6:37) but also for the postexilic prophets (Hag. 2:18;

---

[53] The celebration is mentioned at Leviticus 23:34; Deuteronomy 16:13, 16; 31:10; 2 Chronicles 8:13; Ezra 3:4; Zechariah 14:16, 18, 19; John 7:2.

Zech. 8:9–13), laying the foundation becomes a significant signpost for the returning community.

The need for a temple foundation, coupled with the prior mention of "everyone
who made a freewill offering" (Ezra 3:5),[54] provides a natural bridge to the presentation of material offerings for construction (v. 7). The word for "made a freewill
offering" in verse 5 most frequently describes either the offering of oneself for service (Judg. 5:2, 9; Neh. 11:2) or, most often and in the current context, the willingness to offer one's resources freely for temple construction (Ezra 1:6; 2:68). Those
returning do both; they uproot their lives to return to Jerusalem and once more
give materially. The people have a new start, and yet their actions are in keeping
with the past actions of their forefathers, whether those who gave heart-motivated
offerings for the tabernacle in Moses' day (Ex. 35:20–29) or David and others who
offered freely for the first temple (1 Chron. 29:1–9). This latter comparison gains
further support from the presence of "the Sidonians and the Tyrians" who bring
"cedar trees" in preparation for temple building (Ezra 3:7); such a combination
occurs elsewhere only in reference to work David did to prepare for the temple
(1 Chron. 22:4). Certainly the work moves forward by Cyrus's royal "grant," a word
used only here in the OT to express both authorization and empowerment; yet
David's presence is in the background and will soon break through in a more
explicit expression (cf. Ezra 3:10). This forms yet one more point of continuity
with the previous temple.

3:8–9 Like the first paragraph, the second begins with a temporal marker describing events in the "second year" and "second month" (v. 8), the latter the same month
in which Solomon began to build the temple (1 Kings 6:1). Debate persists as to
the historical referent of "second year." Does this refer to the second year of Cyrus
(537 BC) or that of Darius (520)? Some claim the latter since Haggai's initial oracle
to Zerubbabel and Jeshua (i.e., Joshua) was delivered in the second year of Darius
in the sixth month (Hag. 1:1). Haggai also informs us that the temple yet "lies in
ruins" (Hag. 1:4, 9) and concurs with Ezra that completion occurred under the
leadership of Zerubbabel and Jeshua (Ezra 5:1–2; 6:15; Hag. 1:1, 12). On this basis,
Haggai 2:15–18 ostensibly refers to building the temple foundation in Haggai's
day, confirmed by Zechariah 4:9. By this interpretation, the foundation laid in Ezra
3:8, 10 cannot refer to Cyrus's second year but must refer to Darius's second year,
when the foundation was completed.[55]

However, some temple work began before that year, since at some point it
ceased and remained dormant through the reign of Cyrus and into the reign of
Darius (Ezra 4:3–5, 24). Taking the description of Haggai as referring to completely new construction in his day is not demanded. The twofold mention of
the people's coming "to the house" (2:68; 3:8) need only mean they arrived at the

---

54 Lit., "And all who freely offered freewill offerings to the Lord."
55 In light of other considerations, Williamson explains his position that Ezra 3:1–6 refers to an altar built
in the day of Cyrus, while 3:7–4:3 describes the start of the work on the temple in the time of Darius (*Ezra,
Nehemiah*, 44, 47, 64). According to Williamson, no work at all was done on the temple until Darius's reign.

general location of the temple, since it was not yet built. The position taken in this commentary is that 3:8 most naturally resumes 2:68 and refers to the absolute beginning of temple rebuilding, in the second month of the second year after their initial return (c. 537 BC) under Sheshbazzar (1:8; 5:16). Haggai then refers to a restart on the twenty-fourth day of the sixth month in 520, after a lengthy period of delay (Hag. 1:14–15; cf. Ezra 5:1–2) and with now Zerubbabel taking the lead.[56]

Those who have returned are one in purpose with the preexilic community not only because of the comparable task of temple building found in each period; each also gives freely to the work and each receives supplies from the Phoenicians. The mention of building construction begun in the "second month" (Ziv) adds to this presentation since it was also in Ziv that Solomon began to build the temple (1 Kings 6:1) and in Ziv that the temple foundation was established (1 Kings 6:37). This pattern is repeated here.

The burden of restoration resides not only with the leaders Jeshua and Zerubbabel; all the building projects in Ezra-Nehemiah involve all of the people of God, unified in purpose. This requires involvement of other "priests" and "kinsmen" (also translated "brothers," Ezra 3:2, 8, 9) and indeed the whole community in altar construction and temple beginnings. Specifically, by using comparable expressions, the remainder of the paragraph functions to show the united effort of the Levites. They are not only "appointed . . . to supervise the work" (v. 8); specific men heading the Levitical families likewise "stand together . . . to supervise" the workmen (v. 9 AT). The family names mentioned (Jeshua, Kadmiel, Hodaviah [Judah?])[57] occur in several lists of the Levites throughout Ezra-Nehemiah (Ezra 2:40//Neh. 7:43; 9:4–5; 10:9). All of this underscores the postexilic role of the Levites in supervising the work of the temple (1 Chron. 23:2–6; 2 Chron. 34:12–13).

3:10–11a Three nouns—builders, priests, and Levites—now summarize the important aspects of the chapter, preparing for the song of jubilant response that follows. The postexilic community does not follow the previous efforts of Hezekiah or Josiah, as vital as they were to revitalizing national devotion to the Lord. Rather, Chronicles and Ezra-Nehemiah present the renewed worship in the second temple as shaped according to David's earlier instructions, especially his organization of the Levitical musicians (1 Chron. 6:31; 25:6). The pre- and postexilic community thus unify in following the lead of their ideal king in worship.[58] In song, the biblical citation that follows breathes in God's goodness and exhales his steadfast love (Ezra 3:11). Understanding the other prominent contexts where the refrain occurs only deepens its application. This song was used not only when the ark was brought into the first temple (2 Chron. 5:13); it was also sung earlier, when

---

56 For a comparable argument, see Leslie C. Allen and Timothy S. Laniak, *Ezra, Nehemiah, Esther*, NIBCOT 9 (Peabody, MA: Hendrickson, 2003), 31–32.

57 Text critical issues in Ezra 3:9 lead commentators to view Judah as a corruption of the similar Hodaviah based on Ezra 2:40.

58 On this important perspective see Dean R. Ulrich, "David in Ezra-Nehemiah," *WTJ* 78/1 (2016): 49–64. David is named in Ezra 3:10; 8:2, 20; Nehemiah 3:15, 16; 12:24, 36, 37 (2x), 45, 46.

David brought the ark into Jerusalem with the climactic request to "gather and deliver us from among the nations" (1 Chron. 16:34–35). The returning remnant now sings the same song, rejoicing in the privilege to see this prayer answered. Perhaps most relevant, Jeremiah cites this very song as the one that will be sung when Jerusalem's fortunes are restored and thank offerings are found once more in God's house (Jer. 33:10–11).[59]

3:11b–13 The completed foundation results in a description of the communal song of praise as "shouting a great shout" (vv. 11b, 13 AT). Elsewhere, only with the ark's presence in war contexts do we find this exact expression (Josh. 6:4–5, 20; 1 Sam. 4:5). Worship often brings varied responses, reflecting the range of human emotion. For some, the shout signals great joy at the arrival of this moment long desired. For others, haunted by past memory, the song brings out the unresolved sorrow of a temple now ruined, with no hope of attaining its former glory (cf. Hag. 2:3). So the chapter ends as it began: with the people of God gathered together, perhaps ready for conflict but also yearning for the renewed presence of the Lord in the Land of Promise.

Response

The physical return of the rejoicing exiles necessitates a spiritual return as well. The command to arise and build and the attendant restoration of sacrifices show that God desires our repentance under submission to his Word: all peoples must "repent and believe in the gospel" (Mark 1:15). The purpose of the distresses he brings upon his people are so that they will return to him (Amos 4:6–11) in order to dwell with him. Entering his presence requires purification, and this comes through the sacrifices established initially through Moses. For this reason, the first act of the returnees is restoration of the altar for sacrifice. With the coming of Christ, God himself finally and fully provides for both the purification of his people and their entrance into his throne room through their embrace of the once-for-all sacrifice of the unblemished Messiah (Heb. 9:11–14; 10:10). The sound of our great shout must also be heard far away (Ezra 3:13), both rejoicing in Christ's victory on the cross and sorrowing for our past rebellion that led him there.

This postexilic community is a part of an ongoing story with a glorious ending. Their exile surely brought times of desperate discouragement that caused them to question God's goodness (Psalms 79; 137). Through it all, God sovereignly guided their paths, although in the midst of this ongoing trial his precise leading often remained unclear (Ps. 77:19–20). Now, with their gathering from the nations, God has begun to restore their fortunes, as he had promised (Deut. 30:3; Jer. 30:3; 33:10–11). As the whole community makes a new start on the rebuilding of the temple (Ezra 3:8), they experience a mixture of joy and sorrow: joy at their current restoration but sorrow at what has been lost (vv. 11–12). Their response is concentrated in first bringing contributions for construction (v. 7) and then a song

---

59 Portions of this song are also a refrain in Psalms 118 and 136.

of worship when the foundation is completed (v. 11). With that song they sing to one another of the Lord's unchanging goodness and steadfast love.

In every age, the people of God will face times of both exhilaration and dejection. Like the returnees, no matter our circumstance we must respond in worship as we remind one another that God's faithfulness endures into eternity as our sure hope. Fear of the "peoples of the lands" may be real and persistent (v. 3; 4:4). Times of confusion, darkness, and tribulation may arise individually or corporately. However, those wholeheartedly devoted to Christ and his cause must never view such experiences as the end. David not only acquired cedars from Lebanon to be used in temple construction (1 Chron. 22:4; cf. Ezra 3:7); he also sang that the faithful have access to the very throne room of the Lord, the true King (Psalm 24). We endure under God's protection, knowing that through David's greater Son— the Lamb who is also our Shepherd—tribulation will give way to our tribute's entrance into the throne room of God. One day, the wealth of the nations will be offered to the Lord in ongoing joyful praise (Isa. 60:10–13; Rev. 21:24–27).

EZRA 4:1–24

4 Now when the adversaries of Judah and Benjamin heard that the returned exiles were building a temple to the LORD, the God of Israel, ²they approached Zerubbabel and the heads of fathers' houses and said to them, "Let us build with you, for we worship your God as you do, and we have been sacrificing to him ever since the days of Esarhaddon king of Assyria who brought us here." ³But Zerubbabel, Jeshua, and the rest of the heads of fathers' houses in Israel said to them, "You have nothing to do with us in building a house to our God; but we alone will build to the LORD, the God of Israel, as King Cyrus the king of Persia has commanded us."

⁴Then the people of the land discouraged the people of Judah and made them afraid to build ⁵and bribed counselors against them to frustrate their purpose, all the days of Cyrus king of Persia, even until the reign of Darius king of Persia.

⁶And in the reign of Ahasuerus, in the beginning of his reign, they wrote an accusation against the inhabitants of Judah and Jerusalem.

⁷In the days of Artaxerxes, Bishlam and Mithredath and Tabeel and the rest of their associates wrote to Artaxerxes king of Persia. The letter was written in Aramaic and translated.¹ ⁸Rehum the commander and Shimshai the scribe wrote a letter against Jerusalem to Artaxerxes the king as follows: ⁹Rehum the commander, Shimshai the scribe, and the rest of their associates, the judges, the governors, the officials, the Persians, the men of Erech, the Babylonians, the men of Susa, that is, the Elamites, ¹⁰and the rest of the nations whom the great and noble Osnappar deported and settled in the cities of Samaria and in the rest of the

province Beyond the River. [11](This is a copy of the letter that they sent.) "To Artaxerxes the king: Your servants, the men of the province Beyond the River, send greeting. And now [12]be it known to the king that the Jews who came up from you to us have gone to Jerusalem. They are rebuilding that rebellious and wicked city. They are finishing the walls and repairing the foundations. [13]Now be it known to the king that if this city is rebuilt and the walls finished, they will not pay tribute, custom, or toll, and the royal revenue will be impaired. [14]Now because we eat the salt of the palace[2] and it is not fitting for us to witness the king's dishonor, therefore we send and inform the king, [15]in order that search may be made in the book of the records of your fathers. You will find in the book of the records and learn that this city is a rebellious city, hurtful to kings and provinces, and that sedition was stirred up in it from of old. That was why this city was laid waste. [16]We make known to the king that if this city is rebuilt and its walls finished, you will then have no possession in the province Beyond the River."

[17]The king sent an answer: "To Rehum the commander and Shimshai the scribe and the rest of their associates who live in Samaria and in the rest of the province Beyond the River, greeting. And now [18]the letter that you sent to us has been plainly read before me. [19]And I made a decree, and search has been made, and it has been found that this city from of old has risen against kings, and that rebellion and sedition have been made in it. [20]And mighty kings have been over Jerusalem, who ruled over the whole province Beyond the River, to whom tribute, custom, and toll were paid. [21]Therefore make a decree that these men be made to cease, and that this city be not rebuilt, until a decree is made by me. [22]And take care not to be slack in this matter. Why should damage grow to the hurt of the king?"

[23]Then, when the copy of King Artaxerxes' letter was read before Rehum and Shimshai the scribe and their associates, they went in haste to the Jews at Jerusalem and by force and power made them cease. [24]Then the work on the house of God that is in Jerusalem stopped, and it ceased until the second year of the reign of Darius king of Persia.

[1]Hebrew *written in Aramaic and translated in Aramaic,* indicating that 4:8–6:18 is in Aramaic; another interpretation is *The letter was written in the Aramaic script and set forth in the Aramaic language* [2]Aramaic *because the salt of the palace is our salt*

Section Overview

This chapter, the second of four pericopes constituting the first movement in Ezra-Nehemiah (Ezra 3–6), follows the conflicted emotion accompanying foundation completion (3:13). It introduces the major theme of *opposition*. The earlier reference to fear ("because of the peoples of the lands"; 3:3) foreshadows the extended exposition of this theme in chapter 4. Indeed, unending hostility to the efforts of God's people as well as their attendant trust in him are themes central to both the book and the whole biblical story.

Beyond this, questions arise concerning the narrative location and historical content of the chapter. Why does the narrative, grounded in the age of Cyrus (559–530 BC) and Darius (522–486) (4:4–5), suddenly flash forward several decades to include a snapshot of Ahasuerus's reign (486–465) (v. 6) and the extended example of events under Artaxerxes (465–423) (vv. 7–23), only to return to Darius's reign at the end (v. 24; cf. v. 5)? Likewise, the topic of temple construction shifts to a focus on wall and city rebuilding (v. 12), projects suited to Nehemiah's day. While these features may present interpretive challenges, the position and content of the chapter make sense once we accept that its burden is not to present a strict historical sequence but rather to set forth the message that repeated confrontations face the returned exiles throughout the postexilic period.[60]

The message is vital, as is the medium through which it is delivered. The extended example of opposition during Artaxerxes's reign comes not through stories but through a series of letters. Adversaries entreat Artaxerxes for action against the builders (vv. 7–16) and then receive his decree in return (vv. 17–22). The chapter concludes by reporting the force of his pronouncement (v. 23) before returning us to the storyline (v. 24). These letters not only recall the importance of royal edicts in Ezra-Nehemiah (cf. Ezra 1:1; Neh. 2:7–8); they also launch a stretch of text that concludes the first movement (Ezra 4:8–6:18)—text written not in Hebrew but in Aramaic, a language suitable for addressing the head of the empire.

Section Outline

II.B.2. Opposition Tries to End the Reconstruction Projects (4:1–24)
   a. Leaders Reject the Offer of Adversaries to Help Rebuild Temple (4:1–3)
   b. Opposition during the Reigns of Cyrus and Darius (4:4–5)
   c. Opposition during the Reign of Ahasuerus (4:6)
   d. Opposition during the Reign of Artaxerxes: An Example (4:7–23)
   e. Temple Building Ceases until the Second Year of Darius (4:24)

Comment

4:1–3 The initial scene of the chapter typifies the conflicts to follow. The "returned exiles" (v. 1; lit., "the sons of the exile")[61] are opposed by those whom we assume are not a part of the exilic community. The exiles are further specified as the tribes of "Judah and Benjamin" (cf. 1:5), two tribes who long ago had remained faithful to the Davidic king at the time of kingdom division (1 Kings 12:20–21; 2 Chron. 11:12) and who now willingly bear the responsibility of rebuilding the temple.

In what follows, Zerubbabel and Jeshua represent Israel in dialogue with the "adversaries." The author gives no explicit reason as to why this group deserves such a title. Why should the kind offer "Let us build with you, for we worship your God as you do" be met with such an exclusivist reply: "We alone will build" (Ezra 4:2–3)?[62]

---

60 Kidner, *Ezra and Nehemiah*, 53: "From this point onwards right to the end of Nehemiah there is conflict. Nothing that is attempted for God will now go unchallenged, and scarcely a tactic be unexplored by the opposition."

61 The exact phrase is found elsewhere at Ezra 6:19, 20; 8:35; 10:7, 16 and translated "returned exiles" in the ESV. See related phrases at Ezra 2:1//Nehemiah 7:6 ("people of the province"); Ezra 6:21 ("the people of Israel who had returned from exile").

62 Other statements comparable to "You have nothing to do with us" (4:3) are found in similar contexts of exclusive devotion to the Lord (Josh. 22:24; 2 Kings 3:13) (Clines, *Ezra, Nehemiah, Esther*, 75).

No doubt, a strict interpretation of Cyrus's decree necessarily excludes non-Israelites from the building process (cf. 1:3).[63] However, a more reasoned theological response relevant to the original audience requires further explanation.

"Adversaries," sometimes translated "enemies" (Hb. *tsar*), are found throughout the Bible.[64] The term first occurs in Melchizedek's blessing of Abraham (Gen. 14:20) and refers broadly to anyone who oppresses Israel (Num. 10:9; 24:8).[65] In this chapter the adversaries are equated with the "people of the land" (Ezra 4:4). Elsewhere in Nehemiah, the term for "adversaries" refers to those willing to kill the wall rebuilders (Neh. 4:11), and Nehemiah 9:27 reminds Israel that they were given into the hands of "their enemies" in the period of the judges due to their rejection of God's word.[66] In short, although the historical specificity of the enemies varies over time, there is a parallel established between being subject to "adversaries" (i.e., "enemies") in the day of the judges and being subject now to the "people of the land" (cf. comment on Ezra 4:4–5).

The "adversaries" further specify themselves as descendants of those relocated by the Assyrian king Esarhaddon (681–669 BC), sacrificing to the Lord ever since (v. 2). The Assyrian practice of repopulating defeated regions with non-natives seemingly continued over a long period after Samaria's fall (722), when an unnamed "king of Assyria," likely Sargon II (721–705), transferred non-natives and brought them to the cities of Samaria.[67] Afterward, he sent a priest who could teach them about "the law of the god of the land" (2 Kings 17:24–28). Unfortunately, this resulted in syncretistic practices that combined worship of the Lord with worship of the gods of the nations from which these adversaries came. It is in this light that we must understand the leadership's decision to reject the offer of help. Cooperating with descendants of those who, in their evaluation, manifested a toxic religious stew would lead to sure compromise and perhaps grant inroads into control of the temple itself.[68]

4:4–5 These verses clearly contrast the "people of the land" with the "people of Judah." The phrase "people of the land/earth"[69] appears in the Bible with varied contexts and referents. In some contexts God desires for "all the peoples of the earth" to know him and his relationship with Israel (Josh. 4:24; 1 Kings 8:43, 60). At other times, God's protective care and special relationship to his distinct people dispel their own fear of the people of the land (Num. 14:9; Deut. 28:10).

---

63 Williamson, *Ezra, Nehemiah*, 50.
64 This term is found most frequently in the Psalms. The other term for "enemy" in Ezra-Nehemiah is *'oyeb* (Ezra 8:22, 31; Neh. 4:15; 5:9; 6:1, 16; 9:28). Williamson, *Ezra, Nehemiah*, 49, calls the adversaries in Ezra 4:1–3 "ill-defined."
65 Remarkably, the first use of the synonym "enemy" (*'oyeb*) in the Bible is located at the similarly significant Genesis 22:17.
66 Significantly, the parallel statement in Nehemiah 9:30 again equates the adversaries with the "peoples of the lands" (cf. Ezra 4:1, 4).
67 The practice of resettlement continues into the reign of Osnappar (likely Assurbanipal, 669–627 BC), who followed his father to the throne after a period of civil war (Ezra 4:10).
68 On the latter point see Blenkinsopp, *Ezra-Nehemiah*, 108. These persons should not be identified as the Samaritans of the later Samaritan-Jewish conflict. Such a position is anachronistic (Clines, *Ezra, Nehemiah, Esther*, 73; Williamson, *Ezra, Nehemiah*, 49; Blenkinsopp, *Ezra-Nehemiah*, 107).
69 Occasionally we find slight variations in form and translation, such as "common people" (Lev. 4:27), "peoples of the lands" (Ezra 3:3), or "peoples of the earth" (1 Kings 8:43).

Occasionally in 2 Kings the phrase appears to refer not to the nations (outsiders) but to those who are faithful to the Davidic king (e.g., 2 Kings 11:14, 18–20).

But what of the twelve appearances of the phrase in Ezra-Nehemiah (Ezra 3:3; 4:4; 9:1, 2, 11; 10:2, 11; Neh. 9:24, 30; 10:28, 30, 31)? A quick perusal shows that Israel's identification with (or, conversely, not separating from) the people of the land is much more than a rejection of a kind offer to help, an act of prideful exclusion, or a case of crass nationalism (cf. Ezra 6:21). For returnees to cooperate with the peoples of the land in this new start would indicate ongoing unfaithfulness and a failure to remain faithful to their calling to be God's distinct people (Ex. 19:5–6; 1 Kings 8:53), the type of compromise that had led them to this very point in the first place.

Further, in Ezra 4 the "people of the land" seek to frustrate the temple rebuilding (cf. vv. 1, 4) These opponents do not attack and then withdraw. Instead they press unrelentingly, as expressed by three similar verbal forms: weakening hands (cf. Jer. 38:4), making builders afraid, and bribing counselors—perhaps government officials—to subvert the very plans of the people (lit., "hiring counselors against them to frustrate their counsel"). The expression "all the days of Cyrus … even until the reign of Darius" reveals a nearly twenty-year period of opposition (from around 538 to 520 BC).

4:6 In verses 6–23 opposition is expressed in the form of four letters of accusation. Verse 6 moves forward chronologically, briefly noting a written accusation from the reign of Ahasuerus (486–465 BC), also known as Xerxes, the king prominent in the book of Esther. The particular allegations and historical issues are unmentioned.

4:7 Two further letters of accusation (vv. 7, 8–16) are from the reign of Artaxerxes (464–423 BC), followed by his reply to the second letter (vv. 17–22). Artaxerxes is portrayed in the narrative as reigning from Ezra 7 through Nehemiah 13 (cf. Ezra 7:1; Neh. 2:1; 13:6).[70] The first letter (Ezra 4:7) receives only the briefest notice, and, apart from specifying the senders and the receiver, the text provides no further explanation. We know little about the persons mentioned here.[71] The observation that this letter was "written in Aramaic" (v. 7b), the imperial language of the Persian Empire, is clear enough. However, the meaning of the concluding comment, "and translated," is uncertain. The Hebrew attests a second occurrence of the word "Aramaic" at the end of verse 7. Some take the two references to Aramaic together to refer to both the Aramaic script and the Aramaic language (NIV; cf. second NIV mg.). Alternatively, the initial reference to Aramaic may mean that it was written in Aramaic and translated (i.e., "read") in either Aramaic (NEB) or Persian for the king.[72] In this view, the second instance of "Aramaic" at the end of

---

70 See Introduction: Interpretive Challenges: The Chronological Order of Ezra and Nehemiah on Artaxerxes and the chronological challenges of Ezra-Nehemiah.

71 The Mithredath mentioned in Cyrus's day (Ezra 1:8) is not the same person as that of Ezra 4:7 (Mithredath was a common Persian name). Bishlam and Tabeel are found only here in Ezra-Nehemiah.

72 Kidner, *Ezra and Nehemiah*, 57n47. He highlights the NEB: "written in Aramaic and read aloud in Aramaic." Clines (*Ezra, Nehemiah, Esther*, 77) and Blenkinsopp (*Ezra-Nehemiah*, 112) opt for Persian. Williamson suggests

verse 7 is a scribal notice informing the reader that what follows in Ezra 4:8–6:18 is in Aramaic (cf. ESV mg.; see NET, NJPS).[73]

4:8–11a The second, more extensive letter contains several components: narrative framework (vv. 8, 11a) and preamble (vv. 9–10); greeting (v. 11b); and information and request (vv. 12–16). Apart from the descriptors "commander" and "scribe," we have no further information on Rehum[74] or Shimshai (v. 8). Verses 9–10 repeat their names and add other "associates" (cf. v. 17), identified using seven terms for officials (e.g., "judges") as well as specific ethnic groups tied to places (e.g., "the Elamites").[75] The letter writers desire Artaxerxes to believe that their expressed loyalty includes everyone but the Jews of Jerusalem. In short, all the nations have once more fully aligned against Jerusalem (cf. Ps. 2:2; Jer. 34:1). Even descendants of those earlier exiled by the Assyrian king Assurbanipal (also known as Osnappar; Ezra 4:10) join the opposition.

4:11b The greeting comes explicitly to Artaxerxes from those who further qualify as "your servants" and name their province as "Beyond the River," following on the first mention of the name in verse 10. The term refers to the satrapy (that is, a province ruled by a governor; cf. 5:3) that included Judea and Samaria along with Syria.[76]

4:12–16 The letter itself displays an effective rhetoric. Remarkably, the writers never directly ask the king to stop the building project. Instead, they initially suggest that the ongoing rebuilding of Jerusalem will have an unfavorable economic impact. Clearly, the rebuilding effort mentioned here must refer to some period before the later restart by Nehemiah approved by Artaxerxes (c. 445 BC; cf. Neh. 1:3; 2:1). While not always evident in translation, some form of the verb "to know" (e.g., "be it known") occurs in every one of these verses, often functioning as a not-so-subtle accusation. Jerusalem's asserted rebellion against prior kings (2 Kings 18:19–20; 24:20) expresses only a partial truth (2 Kings 16:7–9). The rhetoric here seeks to ignite Artaxerxes to action for reasons of economy and pride. The repetitive language (Ezra 4:13, 16) encircling the central request (vv. 14–15) moves beyond *what* is happening to *why* it matters by highlighting the imagined negative impact of tax evasion[77] upon the king's treasury. Playing on royal fears of rebellion, the implication is that Artaxerxes must demand cessation of work or risk not only loss of income but potentially his grip on the whole province itself (v. 16).

---

that "and translated" indicates that the letter in front of the author had previously been translated from Aramaic into Hebrew (*Ezra, Nehemiah*, 61).

73 Aramaic is found also in 7:12–26.

74 Since Rehum is an adversary, this cannot be the same Rehum who returned with Zerubbabel (Ezra 2:2; Neh. 12:3), nor the signer of the covenant (Neh. 10:25). The translation "commander" can have a military connotation, but that is not necessary here; the word refers simply to a high official like a chancellor or assistant to the governor.

75 Uncertainty persists with respect to the exact referent for some of these. This is reflected in varied English translations of the terms. For example, the ESV differs from KJV in that the latter treats all seven names in 4:9 as if referring to ethnic groups (so-called gentilics): e.g., Dinaites, Apharsathchites, Tarpelites, and so on.

76 "Beyond the River" (Ezra 4:10, 11, 16, 17, 20; 5:3, 6; 6:6, 8, 13; 7:21, 25; 8:36; Neh. 2:7, 9; 3:7) is occasionally translated "Trans-Euphrates" (cf. NIV). The term "province" in ESV is supplied as a further descriptor.

77 The phrase is from Kidner, *Ezra and Nehemiah*, 59.

To this end, the adversaries must soften the king to hear the inference of their letter. The elements that precede the "therefore" of verse 14b do so by establishing their ostensible motivations. First, the phrase "because we eat the salt of the palace" is a figure of speech in which a part ("the salt") stands for the whole: regular dining at the king's table. Basically, they argue that their habitual dining at the palace drives the loyalty expressed by the very writing of the letter itself.[78] Second, they appeal to concern for royal pride, stating their fear that any inaction on their part may end in seeing the king disgraced. Such are the stated motivations that lead to the primary request that he search the available archives, past and present (v. 15). In so doing, they claim the king will "find" and "learn" the numerous reasons the city was destroyed in the first place. Like a virus constantly reproducing itself in order to destroy its host, they suggest that Jerusalem's past history of fomenting sedition can be resolved only by destruction. Therefore, the king must act promptly to shut down city and wall reconstruction.

4:17–22 The earlier request (v. 15) generated the hoped-for results, as the records confirm the city's habitual insurrection (v. 19). Some debate exists as to whether the Aramaic verb translated "plainly" (*meparash*; v. 18) should be understood to mean that the letter was read with "clarity," with "accuracy," "in translation," or "word for word" (as opposed to a summative report).[79] In any case, Artaxerxes communicates that he has heard the message and now acts upon it by decree. Some take the reported rule of "mighty kings . . . over Jerusalem" (v. 20) to signify the domination and income of David and Solomon (1 Kings 4:21; Ps. 72:10) or perhaps later kings. While this is conceivable, the earlier mention of "tribute, custom, and toll" referred to potential lost revenue for Artaxerxes himself (Ezra 4:13 AT). The phrase "tribute, custom, and toll" now repeated in verse 20 (cf. 7:24) more likely denotes levies obtained by the previous mighty kings of Assyria and Babylonia, of whom Artaxerxes is now the successor. In either case, the letter of the adversaries is effective, as Artaxerxes now grants authority to demand the cessation of work (4:21). Nevertheless, by retaining "until a decree is made by me" (v. 21b), Artaxerxes leaves himself room for a possible later reversal, a permission in fact eventually granted to Nehemiah (Neh. 2:7–8).

4:23 This illustrative account of opposition in Artaxerxes's reign concludes with a final set of observations. Finally granted royal authority, the adversaries implement the king's wishes not only by making the building cease (cf. v. 21)—and doing so immediately (cf. v. 22)—but also "by force and power," which is likely a reference to an armed threat.[80] There is some speculation that the opponents go beyond the king's orders and actually destroy the work already done on the

---

78 This is the reason why some translations, rather than "salt-eating" at 4:14, use the language of "loyalty," "service," or "obligation" (NIV, NASB). Consistent dining at the king's table and its related obligations may also be related to the permanence expressed in the phrase "covenant of salt" (Num. 18:19; 2 Chron. 13:5).
79 Note the ESV translation of the cognate Hebrew verb (*meparash*) as "clearly" in Nehemiah 8:8 and a similar range of English alternatives (cf. ESV mg.).
80 Clines cites 1 *Esdras* 2:30 NEB: "with cavalry and a large body of other troops and stopped the builders" (*Ezra, Nehemiah, Esther*, 82).

walls (cf. v. 12), perhaps providing correlation with the destruction mentioned in Nehemiah 1:3.[81] In any event, the original audience better understands that the delays in rebuilding the temple, wall, and city were due in part to the unending external resistance faced by the exiles.

4:24 After the chronological advance through the reigns of Cyrus, Darius, Ahasuerus, and Artaxerxes, the word "then" heading this verse does not refer to something that happens directly after verse 23, during Artaxerxes's reign. Instead we are returned to the earlier narrative time indicated at verse 5 and the restart of temple reconstruction under Darius, an event recounted fully in the next chapter. The verb translated "stop," "made cease" with regard to the walls (vv. 21, 23) now occurs twice ("stopped," "ceased") with regard to the temple. In returning to Darius's reign, the narrative theme is again underscored: every attempt at forward progress encounters resistance.

Response

Missionaries serving in difficult places will especially appreciate the external threats and resistance presented in this chapter, as will congregations who may face opposition in their local contexts. In both cases, wisdom demands a balanced approach when assessing opposition to the church's witness and practice. On the one hand is the real danger of seeing everyone and everything as a personal theological adversary. In doing so we run the risk of rejecting the world and being in constant conflict with it. Like Elijah, we view ourselves and our tribe as the exclusive keepers of orthodoxy, arrayed against the forces of evil (1 Kings 19:10, 14). On the other hand, it is folly to deny, ignore, or underestimate the very real teeth-baring and flesh-tearing enemies of God's rule and God's people. The Scriptures unequivocally point to the Devil as the chief adversary in our fight for faith and the animating power behind the suffering of the church (Matt. 4:1–10; 1 Pet. 5:8–9; Rev. 2:10–11).

While the fundamental enemies of the church are primarily spiritual (Eph. 6:12), they are physical as well. The smaller skirmishes in any one moment of the biblical-theological story are physical manifestations of the great primal conflict established between the offspring of the woman and the offspring of the Serpent (Gen. 3:15; Heb. 2:14; Rev. 12:9). Resistance arises especially as God's people persist in fulfilling their calling for the sake of the world. This is seen repeatedly in the OT (Gen. 14:17–24; Ex. 1:12; Josh. 10:10) and also in the NT: the words and experiences of both the Lord Jesus (John 15:18–25; Matt. 26:3–4; Acts 2:23) and the apostolic testimony (Acts 9:1, 23; Phil. 1:28; 1 Tim. 1:13) bear witness to resistance from flesh-and-blood adversaries (and teach us to expect the same today). This same resistance is exactly what we see in the initial chapters of Ezra, as the people of God must rebuild their broken world in order to fulfill their calling amid the enemies of God, who use all means available to thwart that forward progress. This

---

81 Clines, *Ezra, Nehemiah, Esther*, 82; Blenkinsopp, *Ezra-Nehemiah*, 115.

is especially clear in Ezra 4, in which we see that true antagonists employ several means, with increasing intensity, to stop God's work.[82]

First, the enemies attempt to *infiltrate* by stressing their desire to help. With their language they assert their indistinguishable purpose, dedication to God, and sacrificial service (v. 2). In this case the leaders wisely reject the offer, sensing that it is not sincere. This does not mean that rejection is always the route to take—after all, the support and assistance of outside kings was essential to enabling temple rebuilding in the first place (6:22). But there are many times in which we must maintain an appropriate separation from the world (10:11; Rom. 12:2; 2 Cor. 6:14–7:1).[83] In all of this, the call of the Lord to wise innocence remains as crucial today as it was to his first followers (Matt. 10:16).

The second tactic of the adversaries is *discouragement*. While the Israelites in this chapter may have breathed a sigh of relief at the success of their first parry against their opponents (Ezra 4:3), they are not now able to rest. As noted above (cf. comment on 4:4–5), their defensive move only exposes the enemy's real motivation as they press the advantage in order to discourage. This is a primary weapon that the Enemy of our souls uses to this day. Many of us can remember some instance in which we worked with all of our might, only to see our efforts spoiled, destroyed, or otherwise thwarted by elements out of our control. In such moments, frustration piles up and we lose the courage to go on. Yet, while human hands may weaken and fail, God's hand does not (e.g., Ezra 7:6, 9, 28). The Lord hears our faltering cries: "They all wanted to frighten us, thinking, 'Their hands will drop from the work, and it will not be done.' But now, O God, strengthen my hands" (Neh. 6:9).

The final tactic of the adversaries is *intimidation*. While likely stopping short of actual physical harm, Rehum and company succeed in strong-arming with both written accusation and the threat of military force (Ezra 4:13, 23). Their half-truths concerning Jerusalem's history of revolt and the ostensible loss of revenue result in the king's decree in their favor—and against that of the Israelites. No longer interested in showing how similar they are to the people of God, the adversaries include themselves among those of the world loyal to the king (vv. 9–10), as opposed to the singularly problematic Jerusalem presented as the sole enemy of the empire.[84] The antidote must await events in the next chapter. For now, it is enough to remind ourselves that the solution to all external opposition rests with the Lord's anointed: "The adversaries of the LORD shall be broken to pieces; against them he will thunder in heaven. The LORD will judge the ends of the earth; he will give strength to his king and exalt the horn of his anointed" (1 Sam. 2:10; cf. Ps. 72:8–11). This is the hope the church clings to today, knowing that such victory is found in God's ultimate Anointed One, Jesus Christ, before whom every knee will one day bow to acknowledge him as Lord of all (Phil. 2:10–11).

---

82 This concept is indebted to McConville, *Ezra, Nehemiah, and Esther*, 26ff.
83 Note particularly in 2 Corinthians 6:16–18 the collection of OT passages on separation that Paul applies to the Corinthian church.
84 McConville, *Ezra, Nehemiah, and Esther*, 27–28.

EZRA 5:1–17

5 Now the prophets, Haggai and Zechariah the son of Iddo, prophesied to the Jews who were in Judah and Jerusalem, in the name of the God of Israel who was over them. [2] Then Zerubbabel the son of Shealtiel and Jeshua the son of Jozadak arose and began to rebuild the house of God that is in Jerusalem, and the prophets of God were with them, supporting them. [3] At the same time Tattenai the governor of the province Beyond the River and Shethar-bozenai and their associates came to them and spoke to them thus: "Who gave you a decree to build this house and to finish this structure?" [4] They also asked them this:[1] "What are the names of the men who are building this building?" [5] But the eye of their God was on the elders of the Jews, and they did not stop them until the report should reach Darius and then an answer be returned by letter concerning it.

[6] This is a copy of the letter that Tattenai the governor of the province Beyond the River and Shethar-bozenai and his associates, the governors who were in the province Beyond the River, sent to Darius the king. [7] They sent him a report, in which was written as follows: "To Darius the king, all peace. [8] Be it known to the king that we went to the province of Judah, to the house of the great God. It is being built with huge stones, and timber is laid in the walls. This work goes on diligently and prospers in their hands. [9] Then we asked those elders and spoke to them thus: 'Who gave you a decree to build this house and to finish this structure?' [10] We also asked them their names, for your information, that we might write down the names of their leaders.[2] [11] And this was their reply to us: 'We are the servants of the God of heaven and earth, and we are rebuilding the house that was built many years ago, which a great king of Israel built and finished. [12] But because our fathers had angered the God of heaven, he gave them into the hand of Nebuchadnezzar king of Babylon, the Chaldean, who destroyed this house and carried away the people to Babylonia. [13] However, in the first year of Cyrus king of Babylon, Cyrus the king made a decree that this house of God should be rebuilt. [14] And the gold and silver vessels of the house of God, which Nebuchadnezzar had taken out of the temple that was in Jerusalem and brought into the temple of Babylon, these Cyrus the king took out of the temple of Babylon, and they were delivered to one whose name was Sheshbazzar, whom he had made governor; [15] and he said to him, "Take these vessels, go and put them in the temple that is in Jerusalem, and let the house of God be rebuilt on its site." [16] Then this Sheshbazzar came and laid the foundations of the house of God that is in Jerusalem, and from that time until now it has been in building, and it is not yet finished.' [17] Therefore, if it seems good to the king, let search be made in the royal archives there in Babylon, to see whether a decree was issued by Cyrus the king for the rebuilding of this house of God in Jerusalem. And let the king send us his pleasure in this matter."

[1] Septuagint, Syriac; Aramaic *Then we said to them,* [2] Aramaic *of the men at their heads*

Section Overview

Ezra 5:1–6:18 is the climactic moment within the first movement of Ezra (chs. 3–6). In response to steady opposition (ch. 4), the Lord grants hope from two directions. First, he sends prophets to prompt his discouraged people to restart temple building. Although this leads certain officials to challenge the activity, a letter to Darius results not only in confirmation of Cyrus's decree but also to further declaration from Darius permitting and supporting reconstruction.

This entire section is set up as a chiasm, in which the first half (5:1–17) mirrors the second (6:6–18), with a pivot in the middle (6:1–5). This structure encourages us to read 5:1–6:18 as one pericope with seven "scenes" (see Section Outline below).[85]

In the matching first (a) and last (a') scenes (5:1–2; 6:14–18) there is explicit mention of prophetic activity. Coming at the beginning and end of this section, the prophets' work serves in a manner akin to the temple's foundation stones and roof and underscores that true flourishing occurs only through obedience to the revealed prophetic word. We also see an emphasis on God's sovereign working through human actions, as completion of the required task comes by both divine and human edicts (6:14).

In response to the prophetic reignition of the building process, Persian authorities in the second scene (b) investigate the exiles to determine authority (why they build) and identity (5:3–5). Their inquiry ends as orders are carried out explicitly by the very authors of the investigation (b') (6:13).

The core of the pericope consists of three royal communications. A letter from Tattenai to King Darius (c) reports the questions of the investigation and details the answers of the Israelite elders (5:6–17). In the matching scene (c'), Darius replies to Tattenai with his own decree supporting the rebuilding of the temple (6:6–12). In between, the central scene (d) details the seeking and finding of Cyrus's decree (6:1–5). This vindicates the returnees as obedient to the prophetic word and compliant with Persian authority (cf. 4:15).

In the comments that follow, the focus will be on the first three scenes (Ezra 5); the remaining four scenes will be the focus of the next chapter (Ezra 6:1–18).

Section Outline

II.B.3. Prophetic Restart to Reconstruction Yields Epistolary Support
      with Temple Completion (5:1–6:18)
     a. Prophets Support Zerubbabel and Jeshua in Rebuilding (5:1–2)
        b. Tattenai and Associates Question Leaders' Authority to Rebuild
           (5:3–5)
           c. Letter from Tattenai Requests Confirmation of Cyrus's
              Decree (5:6–17)
              d. Archive Search Finds Cyrus's Decree (6:1–5)

---

85 I am grateful to my student Cary Smith for pointing out this structure.

        c'. Letter to Tattenai Supports Rebuild by Darius's Decree
           (6:6–12)

      b'. Tattenai and Associates Heed Darius's Order (6:13)

   a'. Prophetic Support Leads to Temple Completion and Dedication
      (6:14–18)

Comment

5:1–2 The OT prophets, God's appointed spokesmen who are endowed with God's authority, arise at specific moments in redemptive history. Here the postexilic prophets Haggai and Zechariah are with the leaders and people, "supporting them" (v. 2). As such they inject life into the people, revitalizing the work begun initially in 538 BC but dormant until 520, the second year of Darius's reign (4:24; Hag. 1:15). Like an endurance athlete lacking oxygen and out of nutrition, the returnees are exhausted, weakened, and floundering. Troubled by opponents, they lay fatigued and failing, their will and purpose adrift. Before them a temple corpse leads them to believe that God had abandoned his rule over them (Isa. 63:17–19).

Enter these prophets, administering the nourishment of God's word, their very presence reminding the disheartened that the God of Israel yet remains "over them" (Ezra 5:1). They are still his people, called by his name as his very possession (Ex. 19:5). He still blesses them, guards them, and gives them his peace (Num. 6:24–27). Indeed, Haggai blends rebuke for the self-interest that has contributed to their current sorry state (Hag. 1:3–6) with the comfort that the Lord is still present as their God. As earlier with Cyrus and the community (Ezra 1:1, 5), so now by the prompting of the prophetic word God once more "stirs" the spirit of Zerubbabel, Jeshua, and the whole remnant (Hag. 1:12–15; Zech. 4:8–9) to arise and build. With the altar in its place (Ezra 3:3) and the temple foundation established (3:10), the beginning is made on God's house proper (5:2).

5:3–5 The events here occur "at the same time" (v. 3), promoting the view that the words of prophetic succor barely reach Zerubbabel and Jeshua before, as in chapter 4, immediate challenges arise to the building project. Those challenges come in the form of enquiries from Tattenai "the governor" and Shethar-bozenai, the latter individual otherwise unknown and his role unstated (although he was likely an assistant or secretary; cf. 4:9). A collective group known as "their associates" round out the authorities.[86] This triad (Tattenai, Jeshua, and associates) stands toe to toe with the aforementioned triad of Zerubbabel, Jeshua, and their prophetic reinforcements (5:2).

---

86 The term "associate" or "colleague" at 5:3 (4:7, 9, 17, 23; 5:3, 6; 6:6, 13) occurs frequently in Aramaic bureaucratic correspondence of the period. At 5:6 and 6:6 these same "associates" are further specified by the word that follows, *'afarsekaye'* (KJV "Apharsachites"), translated "the governors" (ESV). These are investigators with authority to troubleshoot problems for the empire and enact punishment (Clines, *Ezra, Nehemiah, Esther*, 85–86). The term differs from the comparable word, *'afarsatkaye'* (Ezra 4:9), translated variously: "the governors" (ESV); "the lesser governors" (NASB); "the rulers" (NET); "officials" (NJPS, NIV); "envoys" (NRSV). Other terms translated "governor" include *tirshata'* (2:63) and *pekhah*, a title applied to Tattenai as "governor" in the current context (5:3).

The title "governor" (Aram. *pekhah*) was pliable, as attested by its bestowal upon numerous persons with varying levels of responsibility.[87] Elsewhere, others called "governor" include Sheshbazzar (v. 14) and, in Darius's later response, an unnamed "governor of the Jews" (6:7). In this historical context, the referent must be Zerubbabel, according to Haggai (Hag. 1:1, 14; 2:2, 21). Later under Artaxerxes, Nehemiah will also be called "governor" (Neh. 5:14; 12:26).[88] In the context of Ezra 5:3, the title grants to Tattenai the requisite authority to investigate the building project, especially since his oversight as governor of the province "Beyond the River" (5:3, 6; 6:6, 13) includes the province of Judah (5:8).[89]

Investigative authority in hand, the group headed by Governor Tattenai "came to" the group headed by Zerubbabel. Unlike Rehum in the prior chapter, Tattenai asks questions and reports the reply without asserting sedition. Nonetheless, given that his questions come at precisely "the same time" as the prophetic support to rebuild the temple is given, it seems we are once again witnessing a face-off between the power of God and of men. Moreover, while the combination of verb and prepositional phrase translated "came to" (v. 3) occurs nowhere else in the Aramaic portions of the Bible, a parallel Hebrew phrase frequently expresses aggression, as attested elsewhere by the ESV translation "came against" or "came upon" (e.g., Gen. 34:25, 27; 1 Sam. 12:12; 30:23; 2 Kings 7:6; 2 Chron. 20:2, 12, 22; 28:20; Zech. 12:9; 14:16).[90] Most importantly, the narrator tells us that only the watchful, caring eye of God prevents the cessation of the building project, even if temporarily (Ezra 5:5; cf. Deut. 11:12; Ps. 33:18). Why provide this potent theological interpretation of events unless Tattenai is in fact making some attempt to halt construction?

Fortunately, he offers no show of force (cf. Ezra 4:23) but simply asks two questions: Who granted you permission to build? And who are you? (cf. 5:9–10). With the first question he seeks to discover who exactly has given the Jewish leaders permission both "to build" and "to finish" the structure (v. 3). The word "structure" (Aram. *usharna'*) testifies to the advanced nature of the work; it likely refers to the wood used within the walls themselves in accordance with a construction method common in the ancient Near East (5:8; 6:4; cf. 1 Kings 6:36; 7:12). Other possibilities for this "structure" include the wood lining interior walls, parallel to those in Solomon's temple (1 Kings 6:14–18), or even to the temple furnishings themselves (Ezra 6:5). The mention of the report and the official reply from Darius (5:5) prepare us for the crucial content of Ezra 5:6–6:18 that follows.

5:6–10 As in the previous letter to Artaxerxes (4:11) and other notable royal documents (4:23; 7:11), we learn that what follows is a copy of a document from

---

87 Williamson, *Ezra, Nehemiah*, 77.
88 In Ezra-Nehemiah the term translated "governor" (*pekhah*) is in the singular or plural at Ezra 8:36; Nehemiah 2:7, 9; 3:7; 5:14 (2x), 15, 18; 12:26. A Persian equivalent, always with the definite article ("the governor," *hattirshata'*), is found at Ezra 2:63 and Nehemiah 7:65, 70, and applied to Nehemiah at Nehemiah 8:9; 10:1.
89 There is an extrabiblical cuneiform document that names Tattenai, corroborating his title as governor and noting that he was deputy to an individual named Ushtani, who was appointed by Darius I in 520 BC.
90 Joshua Berman, "The Narratological Purpose of Aramaic Prose in Ezra 4.8–6.18," *AS* 5/2 (2007): 165–191.

Tattenai and others to the king. Although new to Darius, most of the information in the narrative introduction to the letter (5:6–7a), and even the questions in the letter itself, repeat prior information (vv. 9–10; cf. vv. 3–4).

The new information given in verse 8 reveals Tattenai's real concern using verbal forms (participles) describing the status of a building project moving quickly toward completion. Within wider biblical use, the mention of a work that "prospers" typically points to the success of God's people in carrying out the mission he has given them (Gen. 24:40; 39:2, 3; Josh. 1:8; 2 Chron. 7:11). Likewise, in Ezra-Nehemiah prospering or success comes through submission to the prophetic word (Ezra 6:14) or as an answer to prayer (Neh. 1:11; 2:20). The mention of timber "laid in the walls" is consistent with the "structure" noted above in Ezra 5:3, while the phrase translated "huge stones" (cf. 6:4) may refer to size or to the technique by which they were shaped to fit in place.[91] Finally, the diplomatic phrase "the great God" reflects respect rather than the elevation of Israel's God above all others.

5:11–17 Nested within the quoted letter, these verses report the response of "those elders" to the questions initially posed (vv. 9–10; cf. vv. 3–4). The elders, found only in 5:1–6:18, are titled more fully "the elders of the Jews" (5:5; 6:7, 8, 14), likely referring to their role as representatives of the people. Their response begins by answering the second question (Who are you?), albeit obliquely. Rather than submitting the individual names requested, the collective identify themselves as "servants of the God of heaven and earth" (5:11).

What follows in verses 11–12 begins the answer to the first question (Who granted you permission to build?). These verses are a remarkable synopsis of biblical history, moving from God's work as creator of heaven and earth (Genesis 1–2) to the climactic moment of temple construction under Solomon (1 Kings 6–8) to the low point of Israel's history in Nebuchadnezzar's temple destruction and population deportation (2 Kings 25:8–11).[92] The reference to Solomon as the great king serving the great God makes perfect sense in this context, considering that the elders' description of Solomon's work on the first temple includes both its "building" (Aram. *benah*) and its "finishing" (*kelal*), actions that parallel the binding together of "building" and "finishing" projects found throughout the current and prior pericopes (Ezra 4:12, 13, 16; 5:3, 9, 11; 6:14).

The adversative "but because" heading verse 12 provides the theological rationale for the sack of Jerusalem by Nebuchadnezzar's human army (cf. Judg. 6:1; 13:1; 2 Kings 17:20; 1 Chron. 6:15; Jer. 21:7; Neh. 9:30). This balances Rehum's

---

91 The phrase "huge stones" (5:8) does not use the typical adjective to describe the size of the stone found elsewhere (e.g., Gen. 29:2; Deut. 27:2; Josh. 10:11). The actual language of Ezra 5:8 might be woodenly rendered, "rolling stones," with the assumption that since they need to be rolled they must be large. Williamson opts for "dressed stone," with emphasis on technique of preparation rather than size (*Ezra, Nehemiah*, 70). This is the basis of some translations that render "hewn" or "cut" stone (NJPS, NAB). Blenkinsopp, *Ezra-Nehemiah*, 118, has "worked stones."

92 For the argument that temple completion under Solomon is the climactic moment in OT history, see Graeme Goldsworthy, *Christ-Centered Biblical Theology: Hermeneutical Foundations and Principles* (Downers Grove, IL: IVP Academic, 2012), 24–27.

half-truth alleging that Jerusalem fell primarily because of its rebellion against kings (Ezra 4:15; cf. 2 Kings 18:7; 24:1, 19–20). In summary, how do the elders answer the question of identity? "We are servants of God," they reply in effect, "with a celebrated royal history and a temple, now leveled in crumbled layers of ash, wood, and stone because of our unfaithfulness."

God leaves neither temple nor people in a state of disrepair (Ezra 5:13–16). Like the apostle Paul's "therefore" in Romans 8:1, the adversative "however" (Ezra 5:13) throws a grace punch to the gut of the "but because" in verse 12. Although the shattered temple and exile reveal God's anger at sin, yet, through Cyrus's decree, the Lord ordains his people to rebuild and repopulate. That decree—its timing and contents—along with the fact that the temple vessels pilfered previously by Nebuchadnezzar and placed in the temple of Babylon are returned to Sheshbazzar, repeat information that opens Ezra, the only other place where Sheshbazzar is named (vv. 13–14; cf. 1:8, 11). That information, now repeated some eighteen years later, answers the question of the expressed authority under which they rebuild. Further fresh details about Sheshbazzar, previously unstated but perhaps assumed, fill out his portrait. First, we learn that Cyrus granted him the title and authority of "governor" (*pekhah*).[93] With this authority, the imperatives "take … go and put" highlight his task with respect to restoring the valuable temple vessels in a house yet to be built.

The grammatical prominence of "this Sheshbazzar" and the description of the temple status that follows in 5:16 raise two questions. First, why does the text highlight Sheshbazzar's role in laying the temple foundation when he is unmentioned in chapter 3, where that work is instead attributed to Zerubbabel and Jeshua? Second, the earlier narrative indicated that work on the house of God had ceased from some time during Cyrus's reign until Darius's second year (4:4–5, 24; Hag. 1:1–2). This appears to contradict the temporal markers "and from that time until now" and the concluding verbal forms that seem to indicate ongoing building activity throughout the entire period.

The answer to the first question hinges on the identification of Sheshbazzar and his connection to Zerubbabel (cf. Introduction: Interpretive Challenges: The Identity of Sheshbazzar). The position adopted here is that Sheshbazzar and Zerubbabel are separate individuals, each acting within his own sphere of influence. Crediting Sheshbazzar rather than Zerubbabel with laying temple foundations makes sense within an official administrative document that stresses Sheshbazzar's role as governor.[94] Concerning the second issue, the simplest explanation assumes good-faith communication. A construction project can be started, face a lengthy work stoppage before completion, and still be accurately described as being "in building" during the period of delay. Understandably, the elders seek to present themselves as compliant with Cyrus's call to rebuild. It is therefore reasonable to

---

93 Earlier Sheshbazzar was called "prince of Judah" (1:8), and the text mentions an unnamed governor (*tirshata'*; 2:63) that may refer to him. See also comment on 5:3–5 and note 86 on the variety of terms translated "governor" by the ESV.
94 Clines, *Ezra, Nehemiah, Esther*, 89.

take the evaluation "until now it has been in building" as true of the wider task without denying specific moments of stasis within the project (cf. Ezra 4:4–5).

Universally, English versions treat 5:16 as the end of the nested quotation that began in verse 11. The final appeal from Tattenai and friends to Darius in verse 17 entreats him to search the royal archives[95] and respond with his will for the matter. The deferential tenor of the request counters the more accusatory tone from Rehum during Artaxerxes's reign (4:15). Tattenai reasonably assumes that if the decree of Cyrus exists, it will be found in Babylon, given the city's status as the prior dwelling place of those now building in Jerusalem.

Response

The repetitive nature of the information in this chapter is clear. The initial questions of Tattenai (5:3–4) are duplicated within the letter (vv. 9–10), and some of the details reported by the elders repeat material from the opening chapter of Ezra. These repeated elements work to focus our attention on those elements that are new. And when the context of the book as a whole is taken into account, these facts are not highlighted in order to identify things unknown to Tattenai or Darius. Instead, the author is seeking to reinvigorate action and to inculcate identity for the original postexilic audience. In doing so he provides important lessons that extend to God's people in all ages.

Faced with fear-producing opposition, the returnees cease working on the various building projects. Their lack of missional motivation, however, is undone in the present chapter by exactly the right antidote. The returnees have been living like a wilting plant unaware of its need for water and are desperately in need of God's refreshing streams. He does not disappoint. The surprising "now the prophets" in verse 1 signals that God sent Haggai and Zechariah to resuscitate the mission by reminding them of his presence and inciting them to action despite the constant opposition. He is with them; they need not fear (Hag. 1:12–15).

Today, examples of opposition to God's people abound. The global church meets pressure from local governments to cease various modes of gospel proclamation. Individual Christians may avoid articulating core biblical truths in order to maintain relationships or security. Pastors are sidelined from ministry by life issues beyond their control. But God is still with us. We must never take for granted God's provision of the prophetic and apostolic decree, delivered once for all to the saints, to motivate us to action (Eph. 4:11–12; 2 Pet. 3:1–3). In the face of opposition, our resolve is strengthened by the apostolic witness, which urges us to obey God rather than men and to do so with fierce gentleness and persuasion in answer to the question, "By what power or by what name did you do this?" (Acts 4:7; cf. Acts 4:19–21; 2 Cor. 5:11; 1 Pet. 3:14–16).

Fulfilling the mission will bring interrogation and confrontation. As noted above, when this happens the returnees must justify both their actions and their

---

95 The ESV translation "royal archives" renders the more wooden "the house of the treasures of the king," sometimes translated "royal treasure house" (NAB) or "royal treasuries" (NJB).

authority to act. More fundamentally, they must also answer the question of identity: Who are you? (Ezra 5:4, 10). By placing their answer within the official letter from a governor to a king, the author seeks to encourage later generations of believers to remember their core identity. The argument is one from greater to lesser: if frail exiles can courageously assert their identity before powerful local and imperial rulers, so too may we be resolute rather than fearful. So who are we? What truths does this text seek to instill?

Before all else, we are "servants of the God of heaven and earth" (v. 11), called to love the Lord rather than to fear man. The elders encourage us to bind ourselves in reverent worship to the God who has made all things. Faced with the choice of leaning into the world with a stance either of love toward God or of fear toward man, we must choose the former, in keeping with the great commandment (Deut. 6:5; 11:1). Indeed, even the elders' use of the title "servant" is significant. While this title is used in the Bible to refer to great leaders—from Abraham, Moses, Joshua, David, and Paul to the messianic figure prophesied by Isaiah (e.g., Isa. 52:13–53:12) and the prophetic line generally (e.g., Jer. 7:25)—it also applies to Israel as a whole. The exhortations in the Major Prophets that command servant Jacob (i.e., Israel) to "fear not" and to trust God's saving power instead would apply easily to the returning exiles (Isa. 44:1–5; Ezek. 28:25–26; Jer. 30:10). And this same command applies equally to God's people today as we submit to the apostolic call to live as free servants (1 Pet. 2:13–16).

But servants often have a past that is shameful. David's preparations and the resulting temple "built and finished" by Solomon his son (Ezra 5:11) were glorious, but they collapsed under God's anger for Israel's sin. The glorious gifts of land, kingship, and temple are all taken away because of the covenantal rebellion enacted by the very kings who were called to covenantal faithfulness (Deut. 17:18–20; 1 Kings 11:9–10; 2 Kings 17:19–23). Similarly, we too have rebelled against a holy God, a rebellion the Bible names as worthy of death (Deut. 24:16; Rom. 3:23; 5:12; 6:23).

But just as the Israelites' sin was not the end of the story, neither has our story ended! We are servants of God deserving of his wrath but met instead by his loving kindness. In Ezra 5, grace is pronounced in verses 12–13, where the "but because" of God's anger meets the "however" of Cyrus's decree—a decree that had come because of God's initiation (1:1). This is his mercy, and as a result a future exists for his returnees as the temple will be rebuilt and the land repopulated. God's mercy means that the failures of their past need not put an end to fruitful service. The same is equally true today: for those who repent and believe the good news of Jesus Christ, the failures of the past are swallowed by the mercies of God in Christ, the one who enables us to serve him faithfully and fruitfully.

Solomon, Zerubbabel, Jeshua, and Sheshbazzar each plays, within his context, a role in temple building. Sheshbazzar established the temple foundations, and "from that time until now it has been in building, and it is not yet finished" (5:16). This shining statement remains true for us in the continuous story of redemption. We are servants of the Lord Jesus, our great King, heir of David, High Priest, and foundation builder. Christ is the cornerstone who has also laid the foundations of his church—but it is not yet finished. Throughout the world he continues building it into a spiritual house (Eph. 2:19–22; 1 Cor. 3:16; 2 Cor. 6:16; 1 Pet. 2:4–6), calling us to labor faithfully at his side until this house fills the whole earth.

EZRA 6:1–18

6 Then Darius the king made a decree, and search was made in Babylonia, in the house of the archives where the documents were stored. [2] And in Ecbatana, the citadel that is in the province of Media, a scroll was found on which this was written: "A record. [3] In the first year of Cyrus the king, Cyrus the king issued a decree: Concerning the house of God at Jerusalem, let the house be rebuilt, the place where sacrifices were offered, and let its foundations be retained. Its height shall be sixty cubits[1] and its breadth sixty cubits, [4] with three layers of great stones and one layer of timber. Let the cost be paid from the royal treasury. [5] And also let the gold and silver vessels of the house of God, which Nebuchadnezzar took out of the temple that is in Jerusalem and brought to Babylon, be restored and brought back to the temple that is in Jerusalem, each to its place. You shall put them in the house of God."

[6] "Now therefore, Tattenai, governor of the province Beyond the River, Shethar-bozenai, and your[2] associates the governors who are in the province Beyond the River, keep away. [7] Let the work on this house of God alone. Let the governor of the Jews and the elders of the Jews rebuild this house of God on its site. [8] Moreover, I make a decree regarding what you shall do for these elders of the Jews for the rebuilding of this house of God. The cost is to be paid to these men in full and without delay from the royal revenue, the tribute of the province from Beyond the River. [9] And whatever is needed—bulls, rams, or sheep for burnt offerings to the God of heaven, wheat, salt, wine, or oil, as the priests at Jerusalem require—let that be given to them day by day without fail, [10] that they may offer pleasing sacrifices to the God of heaven and pray for the life of the king and his sons. [11] Also I make a decree that if anyone alters this edict, a beam shall be pulled out of his house, and he shall be impaled on it, and his house shall be made a dunghill. [12] May the God who has caused his name to dwell there overthrow any king or people who shall put out a hand to alter this, or to destroy this house of God that is in Jerusalem. I Darius make a decree; let it be done with all diligence."

[13] Then, according to the word sent by Darius the king, Tattenai, the governor of the province Beyond the River, Shethar-bozenai, and their associates did with all diligence what Darius the king had ordered. [14] And the elders of the Jews built and prospered through the prophesying of Haggai the prophet and Zechariah the son of Iddo. They finished their building by decree of the God of Israel and by decree of Cyrus and Darius and Artaxerxes king of Persia; [15] and this house was finished on the third day of the month of Adar, in the sixth year of the reign of Darius the king.

¹⁶And the people of Israel, the priests and the Levites, and the rest of the returned exiles, celebrated the dedication of this house of God with joy. ¹⁷They offered at the dedication of this house of God 100 bulls, 200 rams, 400 lambs, and as a sin offering for all Israel 12 male goats, according to the number of the tribes of Israel. ¹⁸And they set the priests in their divisions and the Levites in their divisions, for the service of God at Jerusalem, as it is written in the Book of Moses.

¹A *cubit* was about 18 inches or 45 centimeters ²Aramaic *their*

Section Overview

The third pericope (Ezra 5:1–6:18) of the first episode (chs. 3–6) consists of a concentric structure of seven scenes or segments (cf. Section Outline) and culminates with temple completion. The previous chapter concluded with two requests of the king: first, that Darius order a search of the archives to confirm the elders' assertion that temple rebuilding was proceeding under the aegis of Cyrus's decree (5:13), and second, that he deliver his decision. These issues shape expectations for the current chapter. Will Darius locate the decree of Cyrus so central to these early chapters of Ezra? Will Darius, like Artaxerxes later (4:21), permit or instead shutdown this rebuilding project? Those questions are answered directly (6:1–18).

The initial inquiry is answered by the search for and discovery of Cyrus's decree (d) (6:1–5). Given the event's importance, it comes appropriately in the very center of the structure identified in the Section Outline below. It also sets off a series of events that mirror the events of chapter 5. The prior letter to Darius (c) (5:6–17) is balanced by the letter from Darius (c') describing his own decree (6:6–12). In response, the named authorities permit the very building activity (b') (6:13) they once questioned (b) (5:3–5). The pericope concludes by highlighting by means of narration the completion of the temple with the prophetic support (a') (6:14–18) previously expressed (a) (5:1–2).

Section Outline

II.B.3. Prophetic Restart to Reconstruction Yields Epistolary Support
       with Temple Completion (5:1–6:18)
    a. Prophets Support Zerubbabel and Jeshua in Rebuilding (5:1–2)
       b. Tattenai and Associates Question Leaders' Authority to Rebuild
           (5:3–5)
          c. Letter from Tattenai Requests Confirmation of Cyrus's
              Decree (5:6–17)
             d. Archive Search Finds Cyrus's Decree (6:1–5)
          c'. Letter to Tattenai Supports Rebuild by Darius's Decree
              (6:6–12)
       b'. Tattenai and Associates Heed Darius's Order (6:13)
    a'. Prophetic Support Leads to Temple Completion and Dedication
       (6:14–18)

Comment

6:1–5 Darius does the next thing expected and orders the search for Cyrus's decree in Babylonia, that is, the wider region (i.e., satrapy) of which Babylon was the capital (v. 1; cf. 5:17).[96] The search ends in Ecbatana, approximately 280 miles (450 km) northeast of Babylon.[97] The decree's eventual location in Ecbatana makes sense: previously (550 BC) Cyrus had captured this fortified capital ("citadel") of Media, whereupon it became the summer residence of the Persian kings and thus a natural place to keep official documents.

The decree begins by identifying its date: "the first year of Cyrus" (6:3), his initial regnal year after taking Babylon (538–537) and assuming the title "king of Babylon" (5:13). Compared with the decree described previously (1:2–4), the archived decree (6:3–5) reveals several unique features. Temple rebuilding becomes the primary topic, as attested by the dual repetition of "the house" (v. 3). Specifications describe temple size, project funding from royal resources, a stone-to-timber construction ratio consistent with Solomon's temple (1 Kings 6:36), and an explicit command to return vessels to the temple. The clause "let its foundations be retained" encourages maintenance of the original temple footprint and is in keeping with other notices that the temple was built "on its site" (Ezra 2:68; 5:15–16; 6:7). The mention of these details, and particularly the notice concerning temple boundaries, may function to limit the amount of financial support needed by limiting the final size of the building.

Two problems surround the temple's dimensions. First, its dimensions are open-ended. Its height and breadth are fixed at 60 cubits each (v. 3; c. 90 ft. x 90 ft. [27 m x 27 m]), but its length is not stated. Second, the first temple was 30 cubits high, 20 cubits wide, and 60 cubits long (c. 45 ft. x 30 ft. x 90 ft. [13.5 m x 9 m x 27 m]; 1 Kings 6:2). This makes the new temple six times the size of Solomon's original, a size not only at odds with prior instructions to retain the former foundations but also in conflict with the assumption that the rebuilt temple was much smaller in scope (Ezra 3:12; Hag. 2:3).

An irrefutable solution to this problem is not possible. Some commentators resolve the issue by asserting scribal error and adopting the dimensions of the first temple (1 Kings 6:2). This solution does not have strong support from ancient versions.[98] Others reasonably assume that the listed height and breadth are the size for the facade only, allowing for a smaller inner structure. A third solution considers the impact of the dimensions on a postexilic audience. It accepts that Cyrus's decree granted permission for a larger structure than was actually built. Assuming that the unstated length was also 60 cubits (the length of the first temple), then the resulting structure would have been a perfect cube analogous to the smaller cubic structure of the Most Holy Place (1 Kings 6:20). This would also align with

---

96 The same Aramaic term (*babel*) is used for both Babel and Babylonia (cf. 2:1), making it sometimes unclear which is in mind. Either translation is possible here.

97 Noss and Thomas, *Ezra and Nehemiah*, 129.

98 Blenkinsopp notes that "this necessitates rather drastic textual surgery" (*Ezra-Nehemiah*, 125).

the ideal dimensions of Ezekiel's vision of temple (Ezek. 42:15–20), land (Ezek. 47:13–48:29), and city (Ezek. 48:30–35).

In short, while the building's actual footprint would have followed that of the original, the idealized dimensions given here would have signified to the original audience not only the holiness of the space but also the fact that the times of renewal promised by Ezekiel were at hand. Further, in the wider sweep of Ezra-Nehemiah, reconstruction of a wood-and-stone temple represents only the first stage in an expanding "house of God." The fully completed holy space would move beyond the rebuilt temple to include the reconstitution of a "holy people" under Torah (Ezra 7–10; esp. 8:28) and the rebuilding of Jerusalem itself (Nehemiah 1–7). Only then would this "perfected" space be ready for the restored community to commence in the "holy city" the covenant renewal celebration that ends the book of Nehemiah (Neh. 11:1).[99]

6:6–12 Darius responds and balances the prior inquiry (5:6–17). Cyrus's decree is found, but its contents are reported to Tattenai only indirectly. Instead, Darius offers his decision (6:6–7), including a decree for the payment of costs (vv. 8–10), the mention of severe warnings against disobedience (vv. 11–12a), and a call to action (v. 12b).

"Now therefore" marks the beginning of Darius's instructions to the authorities. In unequivocal language he answers the question of what to do about temple rebuilding. His response functions like a restraining order: they must "keep away" and "let . . . alone" the work of rebuilding. This suffocates any temptation of the authorities to prevent the work. Positively, the "elders of the Jews" (cf. 5:9) and the unnamed "governor of the Jews" (here Zerubbabel; cf. comment on 5:3–5) are regranted permission to rebuild. This positive outcome provides real world evidence that the protecting "eye of their God" is on them (5:5).

To return to Darius's decree, it is clear that he saves the best for last (6:8–10). In a remarkable series of commands, he subverts expectations, going beyond merely staving off harassment from outsiders. Remarkably, Darius commands that Tattenai and his associates work on behalf of those they once disturbed. But how? In restating prior commands (v. 4b), Darius reiterates that the empire will finance the project. The irony must not be missed. In a later letter, Artaxerxes will be warned that rebuilding of the Jerusalem walls will impact royal revenue (4:13).[100] In short, royal tribute will now be used to pay costs "in full," likely distributed by Tattenai himself!

Moreover, this rebuilding is to happen speedily. The phrase translated "and without delay" (6:8) may indicate concern for the payment not to be delayed, but a more probable interpretation understands the concern to be for the rebuilding

---

99 The solution proposed here was inspired by the idea of an idealized structure in the work of Eskenazi, who suggests that Cyrus's open-ended decree leaves room for further expansion of the "house of God," an expansion that takes place under Ezra and Nehemiah during the reign of Artaxerxes. See Eskenazi, *Age of Prose,* 56–57.
100 Recall that the letter addressed to Artaxerxes in Ezra 4:8ff., although earlier in the book, recounts a period of opposition under Artaxerxes that is chronologically in the future.

not to be interrupted. This interpretation is supported by the specific verb used here (Aram. *betel*), which always refers to the cessation of a building project in Ezra (4:21, 23, 24 [2x]; 5:5; 6:8).[101] The beginning and ending of verse 9 ("And whatever is needed . . . let that be given . . . without fail") expand the lavish generosity of a king who provides not only the place of worship but the animals and other elements required for sacrifice. Nonetheless, while Darius may be known as the "friend of all the gods,"[102] he remains a king with political motivations, requesting prayers for a long life for himself and his progeny (v. 10). Like Cyrus before him, Darius embraces a hope that his pious actions will prompt the gods to look favorably upon his reign.[103]

The letter shifts topics in verses 11–12. Both Scripture and other ancient texts contain threats of punishment for disobedience or attempts to amend royal edicts or covenants (e.g., Deut. 28:15–68). Specifically, those rebelling against Darius face the threat of public humiliation and death by bodily suspension on a beam (Ezra 6:11). There is evidence of this gruesome practice in Scripture (e.g., Deut. 21:22–23; Josh. 8:29; 10:26–27) and throughout the ancient Near East into the Classical era, including Roman crucifixion. The Persian practice of bodily suspension described in Ezra 6:11 is consistent with Darius's actions described elsewhere.[104] Likewise, Darius calls upon God (i.e., "the God of Heaven"; vv. 9–10), "who has caused his name to dwell" in the Jerusalem temple, to "overthrow any king or people" (v. 12a) who dare "alter" his decree. Describing the temple as the place where God's name dwells is more typical of the Jews themselves (Deut. 12:5, 11; 1 Kings 14:21), and it is unlikely that Darius understands the ramifications since it implies that God, not Darius, possesses Jerusalem. In summary, the logic of Ezra 6:11–12 is that anyone who alters or violates the royal decree also threatens God's *house* and thereby will meet grave consequences as well as the defilement of his own *house* (cf. 2 Kings 10:27).

6:13 In verse 12 Darius concluded his edict and its threats for disobedience by stating: "Let it be done with all diligence." He thus dictates expectation of thorough compliance consistent with other royal edicts (7:21, 26). In 6:13 his servants clearly obey, doing "with all diligence" just as he had said.

6:14–18 The repetition of several themes found in Ezra 1–6 shows that 6:14–15 are key verses. The temple was completed "by decree of the God of Israel," the

---

101 In context, the verb *btl* may be broadly rendered *to stop, bring to an end, make cease*. The NET maintains the original word order in its translation of 6:8: "From the royal treasury, from the taxes of Trans-Euphrates the complete costs are to be given to these men, so that there may be no interruption of the work."

102 This title was given him by the Egyptians, who also received his beneficence. See John H. Walton, Victor H. Matthews, and Mark W. Chavalas, *The IVP Bible Background Commentary: Old Testament* (Downers Grove, IL: IVP Academic, 2000), 466.

103 The Cyrus Cylinder reads: "May all the gods whom I settled in their sacred centers ask daily of Bel and Nabu that my days be long and may they intercede for my welfare." See "Cyrus Cylinder," trans. Mordechai Cogan (*COS* 2.124:315–316).

104 The Behistun Inscription, located in western Iran, recounts Darius's ascension to power and his treatment of four rebels by impaling. In the nineteenth century this inscription was central to the deciphering of cuneiform script. For the practice of bodily suspension generally see David W. Chapman and Eckhard J. Schnabel, *The Trial and Crucifixion of Jesus*, WUNT 344 (Tübingen: Mohr Siebeck, 2015), 322–324; for Persia and Media specifically see 376–390. See also Esther 2:23; 5:14; 6:4; 7:9–10; 8:7; 9:13–14, 25.

divine King. This divine decree was mediated by the prophetic word: the return from exile was from the start a fulfillment of the word of Jeremiah (1:1). Now, near the end of this first narrative movement (chs. 3–6), the narrative return of the prophets Haggai and Zechariah, who reinvigorated the rebuilding effort (5:1–2), offers a fitting conclusion. As is the case throughout Scripture, true success for the people of God comes only *through* submission to the prophetic word.[105] So the temple is restarted, and its completion takes place as foretold by the prophetic word, a fact that further confirms that these prophets are from the Lord (cf. Zech. 4:9).

However, Ezra-Nehemiah also acknowledges the importance of human action. Human kings do not act apart from the will of the divine King, and their decrees contribute to the rebuilding of the temple as well as the remaining building projects in the book. This is the case particularly for Artaxerxes, who has nothing to do with construction of the temple but whose later decrees play a vital part in permitting the "reconstruction" projects of Ezra (Ezra 7–10, people under Torah) and Nehemiah (Nehemiah 1–6, the city of Jerusalem)—projects also ordained by God.[106] For now, the first building project (the temple) concludes in the final month of the calendar (Adar) in Darius's sixth year. This may approximate the promised seventy years of Jeremiah (Ezra 1:1; Jer. 25:11–12; 29:10–14).[107]

Temple completion leads to "dedication" (Hb. *khanukkah*) with joy (Ezra 6:16–18).[108] This is neither the first nor the last time the returnees will experience the unrestrained radiance of joy against the backdrop of former sorrows (3:12, 13; 6:16, 22; Neh. 8:10, 12, 17; 12:27, 43 [2x], 44). In restoration of worship they find their deepest identity, calling, and fulfillment. Certainly, the sacrificial numbers pale in comparison to the first temple dedication, yet they may be patterned after the offerings there (1 Kings 8:62–63) or after those offered at the tabernacle's completion (Numbers 7). The offering of twelve male goats, one for each tribe "for all Israel," is significant for several reasons. First, it evidences a unified view of Israel beyond the focus on only "Judah and Benjamin" (Ezra 1:5; 4:1; 10:9). This unified "people of Israel" includes priests, Levites, and all returning exiles (6:16). Second, and of central importance, the "sin" or "purification" (NJPS) offering is graciously given to a people whose treasonous covenant rebellion had led to exile (Jer. 11:6–11). As such, the blood of the sin offering purifies a people whose defilement and dishonor touch every aspect of their lives.[109]

It is not clear whether the offering includes purification of the temple itself (Lev. 4:3–12), but this would not be surprising given past history and current context.

---

105 Some English translations seem to lessen the connection between the prophetic ministry and the final positive outcome (cf. NET, NJPS, NIV).

106 Note the fitting comment of Allen and Laniak with respect to the author's mention of Artaxerxes: "He jumped to the final phase of the saga, Nehemiah's building work to restore the holy city as the corollary of the new temple" (*Ezra, Nehemiah, Esther*, 50).

107 Adar occurs February/March. Depending on the reckoning of regnal years, Darius's sixth year is identified as either 515 or 516 BC. The building began in Darius's second year (4:24), calculated as September 21, 520 (Hag. 1:15).

108 The Aramaic term *khanukkah* will later become synonymous with the December holiday—known today as Hanukkah—celebrating temple purification and repair after desecration by Antiochus IV Epiphanes (*1 Macc.* 4:36–61).

109 The primary texts for the purification offering are found at Leviticus 4:1–5:13. An excellent discussion is found in Jay Sklar, *Leviticus*, TOTC 3 (Downers Grove, IL: IVP Academic, 2014), 107–118 (esp. 108).

The explicit mention of "male goats" rather than a bull, female goat, or lamb may point to the sin offering for leaders as representatives of the people (Lev. 4:22–26). At its core, the purification offering would remove defilement of the rebuilt temple (Lev. 15:31; Hag. 2:14).[110]

The final verse (Ezra 6:18) mentions Moses and alludes to David, both in terms of their connection to the first temple. While Moses is present in Ezra-Nehemiah primarily as the deliverer of the law, here "Book of Moses" (6:18; Neh. 13:1) likely refers to his establishment of the general duties of priests and Levites, which would have been followed in the first temple (Exodus 29; Leviticus 8; Numbers 18). As for David, his role in shaping worship is alluded to in the mention of the divisions and sections he assigned to priests, Levites, and others in the first temple (Ezra 3:10; 1 Chronicles 23–26; cf. 1 Chron. 22:13). In both cases, the connection to the first temple helps establish that this second temple is a legitimate house of worship.

Response

The exilic community has experienced incomprehensible loss and heartache, but now the sun is rising. Those suffering, whether from displacement or from loss of identity, business, occupation, home, material possessions, or loved ones, will resonate with that imperceptible moment when the light begins to shine and hope returns. To be human is to taste sorrow in its multiple dimensions, and yet this is not the final destiny of God's flock. The returning community shows the church in every age, no matter its hardships, that we may celebrate with joy the many facets of God's grace.

God's grace topples the temptation to lose hope. Circumstances, of our own creation or others' (Ezra 5:12), may result in a grim pessimism that believes nothing will ever change. But thankfully, even relentless affliction can, through God's grace, issue in joy (2 Cor. 8:1–2). In the case of the returnees, God works even in the actions of Persian kings. The finding of the decree of Cyrus, a result never guaranteed, emboldens them to complete the temple. However, more work remains to be done by Ezra the priest, Nehemiah the governor, and all the people to extend the building project beyond the temple in order to include great joy for all Jerusalem (Neh. 12:27–43). And so it is for us. Our global disciple-making mission (Matt. 28:19–20) concludes in an ideal Jerusalem for the redeemed community (Rev. 21:15–16).

However, God does more than we can ask or think (Eph. 3:20), with grace that overflows our expectations. In the case of the returnees, gaining vindication and support from Cyrus's decree to continue building would be sufficient, but God prompts Darius to go further in commanding that the temple be resurrected with imperial finances (Ezra 6:8). Because of God's sovereign work, Tattenai and

---

110 Clines states that the sin offering "would have been made in order to decontaminate the temple or altar from any impurity brought upon it during its building (cf. Ezek. 43:18–27)" (*Ezra, Nehemiah, Esther*, 96).

associates, representatives of the empire, are commanded to support the work of temple construction. There may be times when even those who question the missional work of God's people and their authority to act suddenly find themselves supplying the very materials required for the work (cf. 4:13, 21–22; Neh. 2:7–8). Indeed, Darius even offers "whatever" sacrifices are required for worship (Ezra 6:9); receiving them from the hand of men, the people of God offer them back to God (v. 17). These are God's gifts through God's agent to God's people; his grace does indeed overflow our expectations.

Finally, in the face of opposition God's grace prospers his people through his Word. In 520 BC that word came through the prophets Haggai and Zechariah, who exhorted a discouraged people to persevere in their task. That task—temple completion ("building and prospering")—was a result of submission to the prophetic word (v. 14; cf. 5:1–2). This truth echoes throughout the Scriptures: the people of God prosper and succeed in their mission to be his people and bring his glory throughout all the earth only as they obey God's will and Word (Josh. 1:8; 1 Chron. 22:11–13; Neh. 1:11; 2:20; Ps. 1:3).

That final prophetic Word has appeared in the coming of Jesus Christ, who is not only our Prophet (John 6:14; cf. Deut. 18:15–19) but also our Priest and King. Jesus issues the divine decree to "repent and believe in the gospel" (Mark 1:15). If rejection of the royal decree and opposition to God's purposes for his people result in warnings of severe judgment in Darius's day (Ezra 6:11), what will become of those who rebel against the final Word of the divine King (2 Thess. 1:4–10)? Yet Christ has appeared and willingly bore the shame and punishment due to us (Rom. 6:23; Heb. 12:2; 1 John 4:10). We prosper in submission to his Word and by embracing his sacrifice. Jesus, the great Prophet, Priest, and King, builds his repentant and believing people into a great temple, granting them success to "proclaim [his] excellencies" (1 Pet. 2:4–9) in all the world.

EZRA 6:19–22

[19] On the fourteenth day of the first month, the returned exiles kept the Passover. [20] For the priests and the Levites had purified themselves together; all of them were clean. So they slaughtered the Passover lamb for all the returned exiles, for their fellow priests, and for themselves. [21] It was eaten by the people of Israel who had returned from exile, and also by every one who had joined them and separated himself from the uncleanness of the peoples of the land to worship the LORD, the God of Israel. [22] And they kept the Feast of Unleavened Bread seven days with joy, for the LORD had made them joyful and had turned the heart of the king of Assyria to them, so that he aided them in the work of the house of God, the God of Israel.

Section Overview

This passage is the fourth and final pericope of Ezra 3–6, four chapters that form the first of three movements from Babylon to Jerusalem. The remainder of Ezra describes the second movement (chs. 7–10), while in Nehemiah we find the third (Neh. 1:1–7:4).

More particularly, Ezra 6:19–22 comes about one month after the climactic temple completion and celebration (vv. 13–18). The text describes how the Israelites celebrate two important feasts: Passover (vv. 19–21) and the Feast of Unleavened Bread (v. 22). What is more, it emphasizes their joy in doing so, for the Lord has given them joy and encouraged them by accomplishing his will through multiple human kings.

Section Outline

II.B.4. Temple Completed with Festal Celebrations (6:19–22)[111]
    a. Feast of the Passover Celebrated (6:19–21)
    b. Feast of the Unleavened Bread Celebrated (6:22)

Comment

6:19–21 With these verses the narrative returns to the Hebrew language after the large sweep of Aramaic text detailing the correspondence to and from Persian kings (4:8–6:18). The return to Hebrew not only marks this as a conclusion to the Aramaic portion; it further functions as a capstone to Ezra 1–6. The temporal notice also helps to distinguish this paragraph as its own pericope. The letter from Artaxerxes to Ezra in the next chapter will offer the final example of Aramaic text in Ezra-Nehemiah (Ezra 7:12–26).

It is the "returned exiles" who keep the Passover.[112] To this point in Ezra, the restored community is also identified as the "people of the province" (2:1), the "people of Israel" (2:2)—synonymous with "sons of Israel" (6:16)[113]—"the whole assembly" (2:64), or simply "the people" (3:1, 11). This corporate language highlights the role of the entire community as an important "character" not only in this concluding pericope but throughout Ezra-Nehemiah.

We have already seen the Israelites celebrate the Feast of Booths (Ezra 3:4), which took place in the fall, in the seventh month (Tishri). Now, years later, having completed the temple, Israel celebrates Passover / Unleavened Bread, another of its great feasts. It took place in the first month, a little over one month after the completion of the temple, which occurred in the final month of the previous year (i.e., Adar; 6:15). This first month was known as Abib prior to the exile (Ex. 13:4; 23:15; 34:18; Deut. 16:1) and as Nisan after the Babylonian captivity (Neh. 2:1; Est. 3:7).[114]

---

111 The literary structure of 5:1–6:18 and the temporal notice in 6:19 encourage separating out 6:19–22.
112 The Hebrew is "sons of exile" (*bene haggolah*) or simply "the exile(s)" (*haggolah*) and is found within Ezra-Nehemiah almost exclusively in Ezra (Ezra 1:11; 2:1; 4:1; 6:19, 20, 21; 8:35; 9:4; 10:6, 7, 8, 16; Neh. 7:6).
113 English translations often translate "sons of Israel" with the more inclusive "people of Israel."
114 Not January of the Gregorian calendar but March/April. Clines believes the date in this case to be on or about April 21, 515 BC (*Ezra, Nehemiah, Esther*, 96). Others believe the year to be 516. See, e.g., F. Charles Fensham, *The Books of Ezra and Nehemiah*, NICOT (Grand Rapids, MI: Eerdmans, 1982), 95.

In terms of procedure, the Passover lamb was to be sacrificed by the elders at twilight on the fourteenth day of the first month (Ex. 12:6, 21) and its blood placed on the doorposts (Ex. 12:22). From that day and for the following seven days until the twenty-first day Israel was to eat unleavened bread (Ex. 12:18).

The Passover's symbolism was rich, memorializing the protection of Israel's firstborn from judgment even as the death of the firstborn befell Egypt in the final plague (Ex. 12:12–13, 26–27). Along with Unleavened Bread, Passover reminded Israel of God's great redemptive act in the exodus from Egypt, their freedom from slavery (Ex. 12:17), and the haste with which they departed Egypt (Deut. 16:3) to worship in the wilderness (Ex. 5:1).[115] In the context of Ezra, the relevance for the returning community is clear: as they consider their newfound though partial freedom in a new exodus (cf. 1:6), they rejoice that they have returned to the Land of Promise to worship their covenantal Lord in a completed and dedicated temple. In other words, just as Passover was celebrated in connection with the first exodus, so is it celebrated again with a second exodus.

In Ezra 6, Passover celebration occurs only as the priests and Levites, responsible for leading in worship, "purify themselves." Similar ritual purification rites are repeated later during wall dedication (Neh. 12:30) and the general reforms instituted by Nehemiah (13:22). Concern for ritual uncleanness and the need for purification to celebrate the Passover in particular (Num. 9:6ff.) will persist into the NT era (John 11:55). Though the purification rites for the priests and Levites are not specified in Ezra 6, they likely follow those previously established for each group (priests: Lev. 22:1–9; Levites: Num. 8:5–22). Some ambiguity exists in Ezra 6:20 as to whether both priests and Levites or Levites alone sacrifice the Passover. The ESV translation implies that some priests *and* Levites are involved in the sacrifice on behalf of the wider community and of other priests (and themselves). In support, it could be noted that reconsecrated priests and Levites played an important role in Passover celebration during Hezekiah's restoration (2 Chron. 30:13–22). Even then, however, the Levites were singled out as those who sacrificed the Passover lambs on behalf of some who were not consecrated (2 Chron. 30:17), and during Josiah's reforms the Levites took sole responsibility for Passover sacrifice (2 Chron. 35:3–6). The possibility for exclusive Levitical work persists here as well.

Overall, renewed public worship in a rebuilt and dedicated temple as well as the prior mention of "sin offering" (Ezra 6:17) echo an analogous moment in Leviticus at which tabernacle completion is followed by priestly and assembly consecration. Immediately after the tabernacle's consecration in Leviticus 8, the priests make sin offerings on behalf of themselves and the people to prepare the whole community to meet with the Lord (Lev. 9:1–7).[116] After these offerings in Leviticus, the Lord appears in glory (Lev. 9:22–24; cf. Ex. 40:34–38). This takes place again after the completion of the first temple (1 Kings 8:10–11), and Ezekiel, having seen a

---

115 Other notable Passover celebrations in the OT are associated with entrance into the land as commanded by Moses (Ex. 12:27; Josh. 5:10–11), the cleansing of the temple under King Hezekiah (2 Chronicles 29–30), and the reforms directed by King Josiah (2 Kings 23:12–23).
116 Sklar, *Leviticus*, 149. On the topic of the ritual states of holiness, purity, and impurity, see pp. 44–50.

vision of the Lord's glory departing the temple (Ezek. 11:22–25) speaks of a day on which it will again return (43:1–10). Sadly, there is no evidence in Ezra that such a return takes place.

As Ezra 6 continues, verse 21 describes not one but two main groups of participants who eat the Passover meal. As expected, Passover is eaten by the people of Israel who are *returning* from the exile (cf. Ex. 12:47). However, another group— seemingly "not Israel"—is mentioned and includes all who are *separating themselves* from the "uncleanness" of the "peoples of the land"[117] in order to worship Israel's God, the Lord. It is likely that "uncleanness" here refers to Gentile idolatry and its associated practices (Ezra 9:1–2), while the word for "separating themselves" (Hb. *nibdal*) may refer not simply to physical separation but also to a distinction between that which is clean and that which is unclean, between holy and profane (Lev. 10:10; 11:47).[118]

The use of the word does several things. In this context, the action would mean demonstrating that they are the Lord's holy people by adhering to his laws covering both ritual and moral purity, in this way distinguishing themselves from the nations (Lev. 20:24–26; 1 Kings 8:53). Naturally, they would need to be circumcised as well in order to participate in the Passover (Ex. 12:48–49; Num. 9:14), marking themselves as members of the covenant community. The fact that non-Israelites can do so, however, shows that faith, not ancestry, is the true entry point into the covenant community, and the mention of non-Israelites seeking to join Israel and worship the Lord counters the seeming exclusivity of Ezra 4:1–3.[119]

6:22 As with Passover, the returned exiles keep the Feast of Unleavened Bread instituted by God to remind them of his great redemptive act in freeing them from Egypt (Ex. 12:14–20; 13:3–10; Deut. 7:8). For the moment, all of the trauma and displacement, the opposition and inertia of seventy-plus years transforms into a new state of mind and heart. Exile is over. The people have returned home. Temple and feasts marking them as God's people are restored. They freely worship and celebrate this feast with a newfound joy not simply arising from within but given by the God who makes them glad (2 Chron. 30:21; Ps. 92:4).

However, they rejoice in another sovereign work of God, one that points to an additional theme central to Ezra-Nehemiah. The positive actions of pagan kings toward Israel, here "the king of Assyria," find no explanation save in the sovereign choice of the God who moves the human heart for good (Ezra 6:22; Prov. 21:1; cf. 1 Kings 18:37) or ill (Ex. 4:21; 7:3–4; Isa. 10:5–11).[120] The Lord had sent prophetic support to assist in the temple restart (Ezra 5:1–2), and this verse

---

117 It is certainly possible that this group includes Jews who had not gone into exile (Clines, *Ezra, Nehemiah, Esther*, 97).

118 The use of this word also readies us for an important conflict in chapters 9–10; see further comments there.

119 Kidner, *Ezra and Nehemiah*, 68.

120 The reference to Assyria, while odd, need not necessarily reflect scribal error or anachronism. Rather, Persian kings *are* now ruling over the former territories of the Assyrians and Babylonians and may be viewed as inheritors of those former regimes. By way of analogy, there is evidence of the incorporation of Persian kings into Babylonian king lists; see Fensham, *Ezra and Nehemiah*, 96.

makes clear his overarching sovereignty throughout this episode: the God who first stirred the king's heart to prompt a return now changes the heart of a king toward Israel so that, in turn, the king strengthens them to build the house of God.[121] As the next chapter makes clear, this will not be the last time that kings will strengthen the hands of God's servants to build his house.

Response

The verses of the current pericope express once more the call to rejoice—but for a different reason. Joy arose in the prior pericope as a response to the many facets of God's grace in light of temple completion (6:16). And yet Jeremiah, prior to exile, had warned in his great "temple sermon" (Jer. 11:1–17) that temple presence is of little value in the face of a chronic and resolute lack of repentance. Being the people of God means much more than the presence of a nice building and the restoration of requisite services. Having a place for corporate worship is indeed a cause for gladness, but being genuine members of God's people and worshiping him with sincere faith is what leads to far deeper joy.

Today the Lord's Supper provides a regular opportunity to do so; in it, the Lord gives us the chance to worship him as we remember and celebrate our redemption from slavery to sin. In Israel's day, Passover and Unleavened Bread called the people to remember the exodus, the great redemptive event of the OT. In Ezra 6:21, participants in the Passover are those joined to Israel who have separated from the "uncleanness of the peoples of the land." This call is relevant to Israel (Isa. 52:11–12) and the church as well (1 Cor. 6:14–18). Our Lord, in celebrating the Passover, instituted the meal for his disciples in light of his coming death and resurrection, the great redemptive event of world history (Matt. 26:19–30). This "Lord's supper" (1 Cor. 11:20–29) in part marks out members of his body as distinct from the world (1 Cor. 10:16–21). God confirms his promises to us, and we grasp those promises by faith as we see the sacrifice of "Christ, our Passover lamb" (1 Cor. 5:7) presented to us in visible words. As the true Israel, we celebrate redemption from our bondage and renew our covenant with him.

---

121 The clause translated "he aided them" (ESV), "to encourage them" (NASB), "to give them support" (NJPS) may be woodenly rendered "to strengthen their hands."

EZRA 7:1–28

7 Now after this, in the reign of Artaxerxes king of Persia, Ezra the son of Seraiah, son of Azariah, son of Hilkiah, [2] son of Shallum, son of Zadok, son of Ahitub, [3] son of Amariah, son of Azariah, son of Meraioth, [4] son of Zerahiah, son of Uzzi, son of Bukki, [5] son of Abishua, son of Phinehas, son of Eleazar, son of Aaron the chief priest— [6] this Ezra went up from Babylonia. He was a scribe skilled in the Law of Moses that the LORD, the God of Israel, had given, and the king granted him all that he asked, for the hand of the LORD his God was on him.

[7] And there went up also to Jerusalem, in the seventh year of Artaxerxes the king, some of the people of Israel, and some of the priests and Levites, the singers and gatekeepers, and the temple servants. [8] And Ezra[1] came to Jerusalem in the fifth month, which was in the seventh year of the king. [9] For on the first day of the first month he began to go up from Babylonia, and on the first day of the fifth month he came to Jerusalem, for the good hand of his God was on him. [10] For Ezra had set his heart to study the Law of the LORD, and to do it and to teach his statutes and rules in Israel.

[11] This is a copy of the letter that King Artaxerxes gave to Ezra the priest, the scribe, a man learned in matters of the commandments of the LORD and his statutes for Israel: [12] "Artaxerxes, king of kings, to Ezra the priest, the scribe of the Law of the God of heaven. Peace.[2] And now [13] I make a decree that anyone of the people of Israel or their priests or Levites in my kingdom, who freely offers to go to Jerusalem, may go with you. [14] For you are sent by the king and his seven counselors to make inquiries about Judah and Jerusalem according to the Law of your God, which is in your hand, [15] and also to carry the silver and gold that the king and his counselors have freely offered to the God of Israel, whose dwelling is in Jerusalem, [16] with all the silver and gold that you shall find in the whole province of Babylonia, and with the freewill offerings of the people and the priests, vowed willingly for the house of their God that is in Jerusalem. [17] With this money, then, you shall with all diligence buy bulls, rams, and lambs, with their grain offerings and their drink offerings, and you shall offer them on the altar of the house of your God that is in Jerusalem. [18] Whatever seems good to you and your brothers to do with the rest of the silver and gold, you may do, according to the will of your God. [19] The vessels that have been given you for the service of the house of your God, you shall deliver before the God of Jerusalem. [20] And whatever else is required for the house of your God, which it falls to you to provide, you may provide it out of the king's treasury.

[21] "And I, Artaxerxes the king, make a decree to all the treasurers in the province Beyond the River: Whatever Ezra the priest, the scribe of the Law of the God of heaven, requires of you, let it be done with all diligence, [22] up to 100 talents[3] of silver, 100 cors[4] of wheat, 100 baths[5] of wine, 100 baths of oil, and salt without prescribing how much.

23 Whatever is decreed by the God of heaven, let it be done in full for the house of the God of heaven, lest his wrath be against the realm of the king and his sons. **24** We also notify you that it shall not be lawful to impose tribute, custom, or toll on anyone of the priests, the Levites, the singers, the doorkeepers, the temple servants, or other servants of this house of God.

25 "And you, Ezra, according to the wisdom of your God that is in your hand, appoint magistrates and judges who may judge all the people in the province Beyond the River, all such as know the laws of your God. And those who do not know them, you shall teach. **26** Whoever will not obey the law of your God and the law of the king, let judgment be strictly executed on him, whether for death or for banishment or for confiscation of his goods or for imprisonment."

27 Blessed be the Lᴏʀᴅ, the God of our fathers, who put such a thing as this into the heart of the king, to beautify the house of the Lᴏʀᴅ that is in Jerusalem, **28** and who extended to me his steadfast love before the king and his counselors, and before all the king's mighty officers. I took courage, for the hand of the Lᴏʀᴅ my God was on me, and I gathered leading men from Israel to go up with me.

[1] Aramaic *he* [2] Aramaic *Perfect* (probably a greeting) [3] A *talent* was about 75 pounds or 34 kilograms [4] A *cor* was about 6 bushels or 220 liters [5] A *bath* was about 6 gallons or 22 liters

Section Overview

Structurally, we remain in the second section of the book (Ezra 2:1–Neh. 7:73a). Altar and temple reconstruction have been the major building projects of the first episode (Ezra 3–6). Episode two (chs. 7–10) presents its own "building project," the reconstitution of God's people under Torah. Three pericopes, roughly defined as setting, conflict, and resolution, form this episode. The first pericope (chs. 7–8) of this episode sets the stage, as Ezra is introduced to lead a second return by a decree of Artaxerxes. The major conflict to be addressed is then introduced in the second pericope (ch. 9), with a report to Ezra that the "holy seed" of Israel has mixed with the "peoples of the lands" through intermarriage (9:2 AT). Resolution comes in the final pericope (ch. 10), through communal confession and repentance. Through it all, Ezra shows himself to be a dedicated priest and model of pastoral care who prays for and suffers with his flock.

Two large "scenes" (chs. 7; 8) make up the first pericope, which, like the prior return under Cyrus, begins in Babylon and ends in Jerusalem. Scene one brings Ezra center stage, grounding his vocation in priestly genealogy (7:1–6). A brief summary follows, describing those who returned from Babylonia with Ezra (7:7–9) and concluding with a key verse (7:10). Little action occurs in this opening scene because the letter from Artaxerxes commissioning Ezra's task dominates the textual space (7:11–26). First-person narration signals the conclusion, as Ezra praises God for his sovereignty and steadfast love (7:27–28). Following our treatment of chapter 7, the next section of the commentary will analyze scene two (ch. 8), describing events surrounding the actual journey to Jerusalem.

Section Outline

II.C. Second Movement: Ezra Reconstitutes the People under Torah
(7:1–10:44)

1. Ezra Receives a Decree and Leads Another Return to Jerusalem
(7:1–8:36)

a. Ezra Receives a Decree from Artaxerxes (7:1–28)

(1) Introduction of Ezra: His Genealogy and Vocation (7:1–6)

(2) Summary Statement about the Return to Jerusalem
(7:7–10)

(3) Authorization via Artaxerxes's Letter (7:11–26)

(4) Ezra Blesses God's Sovereignty and Steadfast Love (7:27–28)

Comment

7:1–6 Opened by "Now after this" (v. 1), these verses begin a new episode, with a new character and setting. After temple completion (6:14–18) and Passover celebration (6:19–22) in the sixth year of Darius (516 BC; 6:15), fifty-seven years pass until the story enters a new historical moment in 458, the seventh year of Artaxerxes (7:7).[122] New episodes may require new participants, as is the case here. The priestly genealogy (vv. 1–5) listed after Ezra's name postpones the topic, which is finally arrived at in verse 6: "Ezra went up from Babylonia." The suspicion that "going up" envisions Jerusalem as the destination (cf. 1:3) will soon be confirmed (7:7; 8:32).

The genealogy of Ezra begins by naming him "the son of Seraiah, son of Azariah" (7:1) which could mean that Seraiah is his actual father or simply that Seraiah is one of his ancestors if "Seraiah" refers to the preexilic priest of the same name executed by the Babylonians (2 Kings 25:18–21). The name Ezra is itself a form of the Hebrew "Azariah," meaning "Yahweh has helped," underscoring an important theme illustrated throughout the book so far. Moving further back in time, the genealogy traces the high-priestly line back to "Aaron the chief priest" (Ezra 7:5). Although Ezra is not a high priest, joining him to this esteemed line of sixteen priests prepares us for his key role of reconstituting the people under the instruction of the law.[123]

At the end of this one long genealogical sentence, the narrator establishes not just any Ezra but *this* Ezra with *these* credentials as the character around whom the episode orbits. A verb finally appears, informing us that this Ezra "*went up from Babylonia.*" Use of this repeated verb (vv. 6, 7, 9, 28) looks back to Cyrus's decree (1:3) and anticipates the main action to follow. The mention of Ezra's skill

---

122 There is debate on the chronological order of the persons Ezra and Nehemiah (cf. Introduction: Interpretive Challenges: The Chronological Order of Ezra and Nehemiah). If the Artaxerxes mentioned here is Artaxerxes I (464–423 BC), then Ezra arrives in his seventh year (458) and before Nehemiah in his twentieth (445; Neh. 2:1). That position is assumed in this commentary. If this is Artaxerxes II (404–359), then Ezra returns in 398, many years after Nehemiah. Some scholars hold to a third option, in which the "seventh" year of Artaxerxes I should be read as the "thirty-seventh year," which again places Ezra's arrival after Nehemiah's (cf. Neh. 1:1).

123 Shepherd and Wright, *Ezra and Nehemiah*, 30. In keeping with what sometimes occurs in biblical genealogies, the list in Ezra passes over a number of generations; a more extensive list of priests can be found at 1 Chronicles 6:1–15.

as a "scribe" further informs our interpretation, since this word indicates he is more than a quick copyist. The term applies to a Persian administrative official who functioned clerically or as a diplomat/lawyer to aid the king in document interpretation (cf. 4:8).[124] And while Ezra may have served the Persian king with respect to Jewish affairs (cf. Neh. 11:24), the scribal skill expressed focuses overtly on his expert understanding in the Law (Torah) of Moses, probably referring to the Pentateuch according to most assessments.[125]

Ezra's teaching of the law may support Artaxerxes's goal of kingdom stabilization[126] even while he serves as diplomat of the divine King, interpreting his law as given to Moses. In translation it is easy to miss the clear parallelism in the dual uses of the verb "to give" (Hb. *natan*) in Ezra 7:6. It describes the source of divine law ("the LORD, the God of Israel, *had given*") and the human law ("the king *granted* [i.e., gave] him all that he asked"), instilling a sense of dependence of the latter upon the former. The phrase "hand . . . on" occurs six times in Ezra 7–8 (7:6, 9, 28; 8:18, 22, 31) and twice in Nehemiah (Neh. 2:8, 18). The granting of human favor is explicable only by God's gracious hand. Whatever Ezra's precise purpose for leaving Babylon, these features of his life, skill, and royal favor must be kept in mind.

7:7–10 The major categories of persons listed as those who also "went up" to Jerusalem with Ezra in 458 BC (v. 7; cf. 8:1–14) reveal an order identical to the prior inventory (2:2, 36, 40–42, 43).[127] While "Ezra" (7:8) is not found in the original (cf. ESV mg.), its addition properly clarifies him as the singular subject of the verb. A departure and arrival on the first day of the first and fifth months, respectively (v. 9), means a spring trip beginning in Nisan (March/April) and ending in Ab (July/ August).[128] This is in keeping with the typical northwest route along the Euphrates, which required a journey of four months and approximately 900 miles (1,450 km). God's bountiful favor is noted once more with the idiom "the hand of God" (vv. 6, 9) to explain his safe arrival.

The final verse (v. 10) is key for all of Ezra 7–10. The conjunction "for" may be taken to explain why the grace of 7:9b holds true, that is, *because* of Ezra's devotion, God expressed his favor.[129] However, verse 10 is better considered as a summary explaining Ezra's heart motivation and its attendant actions as the very basis of his willingness to go to Jerusalem and fulfill his calling as an ideal priest. What does it mean for Ezra to "set his heart"? Negatively, to not set one's heart means

---

124 Walton, Matthews, and Chavalas, *IVP Bible Background Commentary: Old Testament*, 468. The scribe or secretary played a role in Israel as well (e.g., 2 Sam. 8:17; 20:25). Beyond text production, scribes could negotiate (2 Kings 18:18–27), function as messengers (2 Kings 19:2–7) and oversee temple treasure (2 Kings 12:10–11). See Blenkinsopp, *Ezra-Nehemiah*, 136.

125 Clines, *Ezra, Nehemiah, Esther*, 103. Within Jewish tradition Ezra has a high standing as a "second Moses" and more than any other "stamped Israel with its lasting character as the people of the book" (Kidner, *Ezra and Nehemiah*, 70). For the development of these ideas in Second Temple Judaism, see especially *2 Esdras* 14. Into the NT period, scribes were identified as students and teachers of Scripture (Matt. 2:4; Luke 5:17; 1 Tim. 1:7).

126 A 460-BC revolt in Egypt was quelled between 456 and 454. Ezra's journey comes at its height, and Artaxerxes would do all that he could to limit further rebellions to the north. See Walton, Matthews, and Chavalas, *IVP Bible Background Commentary: Old Testament*, 469, at 7:23.

127 See comments on 2:1–70 for discussion of particular categories, i.e., priests, Levites, etc.

128 If 458 BC was the year, then the dates of departure and arrival were April 8 and August 4, respectively.

129 Fensham, *Ezra and Nehemiah*, 101.

rebellion, stubbornness, vacillation, and doing evil—the equivalent of unbelief (Ps. 78:8; 2 Chron. 12:1, 14; 20:33). Alternatively, to set one's heart means loving obedience, a teachable spirit, commitment to the Lord, and the pursuit of righteousness growing as the fruit of a life yearning for the law of the Lord (Psalms 112; 119; Acts 2:42). The "Law of the Lord" parallels the later "statutes and rules" (cf. Neh. 1:7; 9:13; 10:29) and summarizes all of God's law.[130] The three objects of his heart direction (to study, do, and teach) show him to be a model priest.

7:11–26 In this second correspondence of Artaxerxes (cf. 4:11, 17, 23) Ezra receives an expansive mandate by royal decree. After a narrative introduction (7:11) the majority of the chapter (vv. 12–26) produces the letter to Ezra in Aramaic, the language of official communication.[131] The letter is clearly structured, with instructions to Ezra authorizing a return to Jerusalem and expectations on the use of funds (vv. 12–20). Next Artaxerxes directs his treasurers (vv. 21–24) and concludes with final specifics for Ezra's task (vv. 25–26).

7:11–20 Ezra's activity becomes clear in the abundant second-person-singular addresses ("you," "your").[132] After the introduction (vv. 11–12), Ezra's authorization to lead a return (v. 13) and the trip's purpose and provisions for the temple are explicated (vv. 14–16). Instructions for use of the offerings conclude the paragraph (vv. 17–19), with permission to draw further from the treasury if needed (v. 20).

Aspects of Ezra's calling as priest *and* scribe are indissolubly linked together in this "copy" of a king's letter (v. 11; cf. 4:11, 23; 5:6), again relating these to his learning in the "commandments of the Lord."[133] Artaxerxes's description of Ezra (7:12) therefore parallels the narrator's (v. 11) and matches not only Ezra's prior introduction (vv. 1–10) but also the rest of Ezra and Nehemiah (Ezra 7:21; Neh. 8:9; 12:26). The repetition must drive home a concern essential for the returning exiles: Ezra's administrative and temple service, along with his instruction of the community, does not arise from personal aggrandizement but is granted by divine and human kings.

The earlier notice that Ezra was granted "all that he asked" (Ezra 7:6) leaves his specific requests unreported; this letter fills the gap. As later with Nehemiah (Neh. 2:5, 8), it is easy to imagine Ezra requesting from Artaxerxes permission to return to Jerusalem. The king affirms and grants royal permission to Ezra to lead any "who *freely offers* to go" up (Ezra 7:13). Elsewhere in the chapter and book this verb indicates freewill offerings (vv. 15, 16; 1:6; 2:68; 3:5). In 7:13 the verb refers to laymen or clerics who now offer themselves as "living sacrifices" to repopulate Jerusalem (cf. Neh. 11:2; Ezra 1:3).

---

130 Beyond Exodus 20–23 this would include Leviticus (Lev. 26:46) and Deuteronomy, with its extensive use of the phrase "statutes and rules" (cf. Deut. 4:1, 5, 8, 14, 45; 5:1, 31; 6:1, 20; 7:11; 11:32; 12:1; 26:16, 17).
131 The authenticity of the letter, even though it is shaped by its implicit Jewish concerns, is accepted by nearly all scholars (Williamson, *Ezra, Nehemiah*, 98–99). For a brief summary of arguments for and against see Fensham, *Ezra and Nehemiah*, 103–104.
132 There are thirteen instances of "you" and "your" that refer particularly to Ezra in 7:13–20.
133 See also 7:6, 10. Blenkinsopp suggests that the two titles (i.e., priest and scribe) summarize the two tasks of Ezra's mission: evaluation of the cult (priest) and further establishment of the judicial system (scribe) (*Ezra-Nehemiah*, 148).

Ezra's reasons for seeking to return may be reverse engineered in light of the two explicit verbal complements in the letter. First, he wants to "make inquiries about Judah and Jerusalem according to the Law of [his] God, which is in [his] hand" (7:14).[134] The sense is that Ezra desires to perform a spiritual checkup on the community of "Judah and Jerusalem," including an evaluation of temple practices, in light of the law of Moses. This spiritual evaluation will actually uncover serious illness requiring drastic medicine (chs. 9–10), so Ezra must further request of the king what he needs to accomplish his tasks. This includes the presence of the letter itself,[135] as well as the second verbal complement. Ezra is sent to "carry" a bevy of freewill offerings to meet the needs of temple worship. These come from the king and his counselors, Ezra's own community, and even the wider province (7:15–16; cf. 1:4–6)![136]

Having received the requested offerings, Ezra receives further instructions on their use, perhaps upon initial arrival (7:17–19).[137] The purchase and offering of all manner of sacrifices, the human-determined but God-constrained boundaries for spending whatever funds remain, the command to deliver additional vessels given for ritual service, and the option to draw from the king's finances as required all reveal the king's unspoken trust in Ezra's character—a trust not misplaced, as chapter 8 will show (8:25ff.).

7:21–24 Artaxerxes addresses his treasurers with a second decree (v. 21; cf. v. 13). Although he places upper limits on the amount of silver, wheat, etc., his provisions are still generous.[138] It remains an open question as to whether some of these goods can be used for travel, but temple essentials drive the primary concern in verse 23. This verse provides the rationale for why a Persian king would agree to any of this in the first place: his actions reflect the Persian practice of restoring the temples and proper worship among subjugated peoples. He joins Cyrus in commanding the return of temple "vessels" (v. 19; cf. 1:7–8; 5:14–15; 6:5) and Darius in giving sacrificial provisions (7:17; cf. 6:9–10). These actions are meant to appease the local community and placate the potential wrath of the gods toward his empire and progeny. The tax relief for the temple personnel (7:7, 24) likewise mirrors the precedent of former kings.

7:25–26 If verses 15–20 express and detail Ezra's task to "carry," verses 25–26 further explicate what it means to "make inquiries" (v. 14). Again addressing Ezra

---

134 Not "in his hand" in the sense of carrying actual scrolls; rather, this is a figure of speech meaning "mastery" or "readily available." Also at 7:25.
135 Nehemiah similarly asks Artaxerxes to give him letters approving passage and provisions for his mission (Neh. 2:7–8). While it is admittedly speculative, it seems that input from Ezra or another Jewish official in the composition of such an important letter is not out of the question.
136 As in Ezra 1, gifts from the province perhaps come from non-Jews. The mention of "his counselors" (7:15) and "seven counselors" (7:14) refers to input from dependable advisers (cf. Est. 1:14). No external Persian inscriptions mention these counselors, but other ancient texts note the Persian practice of a private counsel.
137 Williamson, *Ezra, Nehemiah*, 102.
138 Commentators and translations will vary on estimates, revealing the danger of attempting modern equivalencies for ancient biblical measurements. Blenkinsopp estimates these measurements at three and three-quarter tons of silver, 650 bushels of wheat, and 600 gallons each of wine and oil (*Ezra-Nehemiah*, 149–150). Clines lowers approximations for the nonsilver goods and considers them a reasonable annual donation. Both scholars single out the amount of silver as extraordinary (*Ezra, Nehemiah, Esther*, 104).

directly, Artaxerxes grants to him expanded jurisdiction due to his expertise in the law of God, here called "the wisdom of your God that is in your hand." This wisdom, grounded in precedent from Deuteronomy (Deut. 1:16–17; 16:18; 17:8–13), shapes the appointment of "magistrates and judges" to ensure ongoing instruction and compliance with God's law.[139] And yet, Ezra's service belongs even more to the "God of heaven" (Ezra 7:12, 21, 23). In evaluating the community, Ezra teaches more than external compliance to legal dictates.[140] As the exile has shown, these are of little value unless bound to inward motivations of faith and love for the Lord (Deut. 6:4–9; 2 Chron. 29:31; Ps. 51:16–17; Matt. 23:23). So important is his task that Ezra and his appointed officials have authority to enforce a continuum of Persian penalties upon any who are disobedient to the law of God or king (Ezra 7:26; 10:8).

7:27–28 The final paragraph returns to Hebrew and commences the first-person address of the so-called Ezra Memoir (7:28–9:15). In his own voice Ezra erupts in praise to God, interpreting theologically the content of this chapter by defining the "God of our fathers" in two ways. First, the Lord acts in the king's heart. The blossoming of Artaxerxes's private concerns and motivations into a desire to "beautify" God's house has no explanation apart from the God who plants the seed of his own purposes within the king (cf. Isa. 60:7, 13).[141] Second, Ezra rejoices that God uses him. Throughout this process the Lord makes Ezra a recipient of "steadfast love" (Hb. *hesed*). The expressed favor of king and court to this servant of the Word makes sense to him only as a visible manifestation of God's gracious hand upon his shoulder.

Response

The highs and lows of God's restored community are tempered by a fifty-seven-year stasis (cf. comment on 7:1–6). We are tempted to believe that during these stretches of silence God no longer takes interest in his people. This must be resisted. Fortunes may change quickly. With Ezra we praise God that he reveals his sovereignty in all things and especially his continual concern to build his church.

We praise God for building his church by providing leaders. In his timing, he did so by providing Ezra, a name whose longer form (Azariah) means "the LORD has helped." Indeed, he has. The Lord brought Ezra not simply as a leader but as a priest and scribe "skilled in the Law of Moses" (v. 6). As such, Ezra "had set his heart to study the Law of the LORD, and to do it and to teach his statutes and rules in Israel" (v. 10). This resolve made Ezra akin to an immovable fence post, cemented deeply below the freeze line, resistant to the hurricane force winds of ministry. The pastorate is fraught with distractions, many of them important and worthy of

---

139 Shepherd and Wright, *Ezra and Nehemiah*, 34.
140 The importance of Ezra's teaching ministry is expressed by the verb "to know," occurring three times in 7:25 (the last of which translated as "teach," that is, "cause to know").
141 It is unclear what "beautify" means in 7:27, but the context points to Artaxerxes's provision of sacrificial offerings. The Isaiah passages refer to both sacrificial offerings (Isa. 60:7) and wood from Lebanon (Isa. 60:13) as elements to "beautify" the temple.

attention. And yet Ezra shows us the one thing that matters. Only a deep love for God combined with an unrelenting, persistent, and unyielding determination to study his Word can shape the faithful application (i.e., "doing") of ministry. Only then can we teach with humility. And it is the teaching ministry that was a core component of priestly duty (Deut. 17:9–11; Ezek. 44:23; Mal. 2:7–9) and best parallels the work of biblical exposition. The need for informed and sound pastoral instruction in churches cannot be refuted if the current state of biblical and theological knowledge among professed Christians is as dire as recent polls indicate. Nor is this service to God's Word merely an OT concern (Acts 6:4; 2 Tim. 2:15).

We also praise God for building his church by moving in the hearts of kings. Artaxerxes's decree to stop the wall (Ezra 4:21–22; cf. Neh. 2:1) likely occurs at least several years before Nehemiah's arrival in 445 BC. Artaxerxes's concern for his own economic loss expressed in that setting (Ezra 4:13, 21–22) stands in sharp contrast with the favors he showers in Ezra 7: his own explicit offerings (vv. 15, 21); permission to gather offerings from other sources (v. 16); a desire to see treasure spent on the temple (v. 17); and overall trust in Ezra's integrity (vv. 18, 20). All of this is summarized as a royal willingness to "beautify the house of the LORD" (v. 27). While the benevolence of politicians may have precedent in local custom or practice, ultimately God directs even the decisions of the politically powerful (Prov. 21:1). Any largesse toward the church from the hand of men has its ultimate source in the Lord. The occasional dramatic story of goodwill offered to Christian churches, pastors, or missionaries serving in environments hostile to the gospel bears this out.

Finally, we praise God for building his church through his evident steadfast love and gracious hand upon us. Ezra interprets the public and favorable disposition of the king, his counselors (cf. Ezra 7:14–15), and "all the king's mighty officers" (v. 28) as real expressions of God's "steadfast love," the hand of divine bounty resting upon him (v. 28). All of this evident goodness results in Ezra's taking courage, enabling him to gather the "leading men" for the return to Jerusalem. Therefore, God's goodness increases valor and prepares Ezra for the next stage of kingdom advancement narrated in chapter 8. The Lord has ultimately shown steadfast love and goodness to his people in the very public life, death, and resurrection of Jesus Christ from the dead (1 Pet. 1:3–5). This definitive expression of God's steadfast love and good hand increases our courage to work in our various callings to advance his kingdom.

EZRA 8:1–36

8 These are the heads of their fathers' houses, and this is the genealogy of those who went up with me from Babylonia, in the reign of
Artaxerxes the king: ²Of the sons of Phinehas, Gershom. Of the sons of
Ithamar, Daniel. Of the sons of David, Hattush. ³Of the sons of Shecaniah, who was of the sons of Parosh, Zechariah, with whom were registered 150 men. ⁴Of the sons of Pahath-moab, Eliehoenai the son of
Zerahiah, and with him 200 men. ⁵Of the sons of Zattu,¹ Shecaniah the
son of Jahaziel, and with him 300 men. ⁶Of the sons of Adin, Ebed the
son of Jonathan, and with him 50 men. ⁷Of the sons of Elam, Jeshaiah
the son of Athaliah, and with him 70 men. ⁸Of the sons of Shephatiah,
Zebadiah the son of Michael, and with him 80 men. ⁹Of the sons of Joab,
Obadiah the son of Jehiel, and with him 218 men. ¹⁰Of the sons of Bani,²
Shelomith the son of Josiphiah, and with him 160 men. ¹¹Of the sons of
Bebai, Zechariah, the son of Bebai, and with him 28 men. ¹²Of the sons
of Azgad, Johanan the son of Hakkatan, and with him 110 men. ¹³Of
the sons of Adonikam, those who came later, their names being Eliphe-
let, Jeuel, and Shemaiah, and with them 60 men. ¹⁴Of the sons of Bigvai,
Uthai and Zaccur, and with them 70 men.

¹⁵I gathered them to the river that runs to Ahava, and there we camped
three days. As I reviewed the people and the priests, I found there none
of the sons of Levi. ¹⁶Then I sent for Eliezer, Ariel, Shemaiah, Elnathan,
Jarib, Elnathan, Nathan, Zechariah, and Meshullam, leading men, and for
Joiarib and Elnathan, who were men of insight, ¹⁷and sent them to Iddo,
the leading man at the place Casiphia, telling them what to say to Iddo
and his brothers and³ the temple servants at the place Casiphia, namely,
to send us ministers for the house of our God. ¹⁸And by the good hand of
our God on us, they brought us a man of discretion, of the sons of Mahli
the son of Levi, son of Israel, namely Sherebiah with his sons and kinsmen, 18; ¹⁹also Hashabiah, and with him Jeshaiah of the sons of Merari,
with his kinsmen and their sons, 20; ²⁰besides 220 of the temple servants,
whom David and his officials had set apart to attend the Levites. These
were all mentioned by name.

²¹Then I proclaimed a fast there, at the river Ahava, that we might humble ourselves before our God, to seek from him a safe journey for ourselves,
our children, and all our goods. ²²For I was ashamed to ask the king for a
band of soldiers and horsemen to protect us against the enemy on our way,
since we had told the king, "The hand of our God is for good on all who
seek him, and the power of his wrath is against all who forsake him." ²³So
we fasted and implored our God for this, and he listened to our entreaty.

²⁴Then I set apart twelve of the leading priests: Sherebiah, Hashabiah,
and ten of their kinsmen with them. ²⁵And I weighed out to them the
silver and the gold and the vessels, the offering for the house of our God
that the king and his counselors and his lords and all Israel there present

had offered. 26 I weighed out into their hand 650 talents[4] of silver, and silver vessels worth 200 talents,[5] and 100 talents of gold, 27 20 bowls of gold worth 1,000 darics,[6] and two vessels of fine bright bronze as precious as gold. 28 And I said to them, "You are holy to the LORD, and the vessels are holy, and the silver and the gold are a freewill offering to the LORD, the God of your fathers. 29 Guard them and keep them until you weigh them before the chief priests and the Levites and the heads of fathers' houses in Israel at Jerusalem, within the chambers of the house of the LORD." 30 So the priests and the Levites took over the weight of the silver and the gold and the vessels, to bring them to Jerusalem, to the house of our God.

31 Then we departed from the river Ahava on the twelfth day of the first month, to go to Jerusalem. The hand of our God was on us, and he delivered us from the hand of the enemy and from ambushes by the way. 32 We came to Jerusalem, and there we remained three days. 33 On the fourth day, within the house of our God, the silver and the gold and the vessels were weighed into the hands of Meremoth the priest, son of Uriah, and with him was Eleazar the son of Phinehas, and with them were the Levites, Jozabad the son of Jeshua and Noadiah the son of Binnui. 34 The whole was counted and weighed, and the weight of everything was recorded.

35 At that time those who had come from captivity, the returned exiles, offered burnt offerings to the God of Israel, twelve bulls for all Israel, ninety-six rams, seventy-seven lambs, and as a sin offering twelve male goats. All this was a burnt offering to the LORD. 36 They also delivered the king's commissions to the king's satraps[7] and to the governors of the province Beyond the River, and they aided the people and the house of God.

[1] Septuagint; Hebrew lacks *of Zattu* [2] Septuagint; Hebrew lacks *Bani* [3] Hebrew lacks *and* [4] A *talent* was about 75 pounds or 34 kilograms [5] Revocalization; the number is missing in the Masoretic Text [6] A *daric* was a coin weighing about 1/4 ounce or 8.5 grams [7] A *satrap* was a Persian official

Section Overview

The previous chapter introduced the current episode (Ezra 7–10), which consists of three pericopes covering setting (chs. 7–8), conflict (ch. 9), and resolution (ch. 10). Chapter 7 functioned as Act 1, introducing Ezra (7:1–10) and presenting Artaxerxes's letter (7:11–26). Through it all, God's bountiful and providential hand upon Ezra led to praise of the Lord and to the increase of Ezra's courage (7:27–28). In chapter 8, Act 2 of the setting, Ezra himself recounts the congregation's preparations and eventual arrival in Jerusalem.

Four nouns summarize the current chapter: *congregation, proclamation, separation,* and *culmination*. Before Ezra departs from Babylonia he gathers his *congregation* (8:1–20) by seeking out the "leading men from Israel to go up" with him (7:28b). The resulting effort is then presented as a genealogy (8:1–14). Unfortunately, the lack of Levites delays the congregation's departure when Ezra must take steps to correct the deficiency (vv. 15–20). In light of the dangers inherent in their journey, Ezra issues a *proclamation* of a fast to seek God's care (vv. 21–23). With the third noun, *separation*, Ezra marks out holy priests to guard holy vessels (vv. 24–30). As will be seen, this advances themes relevant not only to the final chapters of Ezra and the beginning of Nehemiah but also to God's people in all ages. Finally, the *culmination* of Ezra 7–8 describing the journey and arrival occurs in the final two paragraphs (8:31–36), in which the Lord's protection and the delivery of temple treasures are recounted (vv. 31–34) and temple offerings and the delivery of Artaxerxes's commissions are summarized (vv. 35–36).

Section Outline

II.C.1.b. Ezra and Exiles Journey from Babylonia to Jerusalem (8:1–36)
    (1) Congregation: Ezra Gathers the Returnees (8:1–20)
    (2) Proclamation: Ezra Calls for Fasting and Prayer (8:21–23)
    (3) Separation: Holy Priests to Guard Holy Vessels (8:24–30)
    (4) Culmination: Departure and Delivery (8:31–36)

Comment

8:1–14 Ezra first gathers the congregation that will travel with him, here made up of leaders (vv. 1–14) and Levites (vv. 15–20).[142] The former are called "heads" (v. 1), referring to the "leading men" just mentioned in 7:28b[143] and consisting of important rulers, whether priests or laymen. The list here recalls chapters 1–2, where Cyrus's initial edict (1:2–4) was followed in chapter 2 by a list of twelve leaders (2:2)[144] and seventeen family names (2:3–19). Now, eighty years later (458 BC), Artaxerxes's decree is followed by a slightly smaller list based on the genealogy of those who returned to Jerusalem with Ezra (8:1–14).

The formulaic pattern begins "of the sons of X," with "X" identifying a noteworthy kinship group. Of these fifteen names, the first three—Phinehas, Ithamar, and David—identify priestly and royal luminaries from Israel's past. Those of Aaron's priestly line include his grandson Phinehas, son of Eleazar (cf. 7:5; Num. 4:16; Deut. 10:6; Num. 25:7–8; Josh. 24:33), and Aaron's son Ithamar (Ezra 8:2; Ex. 6:23). Eleazar and Ithamar and their descendants represent major divisions in David's priestly organization (1 Chron. 24:1–6).[145] Perhaps this makes sense of the mention of David that follows, since David's role in directing and shaping Israel's worship is the primary thrust of the mentions of David in Ezra-Nehemiah (Ezra 3:10; 8:20; Neh. 12:24, 36, 45, 46).[146] Somewhat easy to miss is the fact that the remaining names, from Parosh (Ezra 8:3) through Bigvai (v. 14), refer to twelve family leaders already named in 2:3–15. In other words, among those who now return with Ezra are some with priestly and royal connections and others from families whose prior generations had returned with Zerubbabel and Jeshua.

The pattern "of the sons of X" is then followed by a specifically named patriarch and his father's name. These identify the actual "heads of their fathers' houses" (8:1)

---

142 The "gathering" of the people for assembly occurs often in these books once the persons Ezra and Nehemiah enter the history (Ezra 7:28b; 8:15; 10:1, 7, 9; Neh.1:9; 5:16; 7:5; 13:11). This shows the importance of the people as a corporate entity.
143 The Hebrew word is the same in both verses.
144 Strictly speaking there are eleven leaders mentioned in Ezra 2:2, but twelve if we restore Nahamani found in the parallel Nehemiah text (Neh. 7:7).
145 These two sons remained to Aaron after the deaths of his other sons, Nadab and Abihu (Lev. 10:1–15).
146 Beside the genealogical notice at Ezra 8:2, the remaining references to David are in the context of the "city" or "house of David" (Neh. 3:15; 12:37) or the "tombs of David" (Neh. 3:16).

who return with Ezra to Jerusalem, whether Gershom or Daniel (not the prophet), Ebed or Jeshaiah, etc. The relationship between these persons and other similarly named individuals in Ezra-Nehemiah is not always clear (e.g., Daniel at Ezra 8:2; Neh. 10:6). Other names, like Zechariah, are not only common in the OT but much more frequent in Ezra-Nehemiah, such that connections remain even more elusive.

The formulaic pattern concludes by providing the number of males who return with the family leader. The representative males (1,496), including extended families, provide an estimated total of 5,000 or more, still much lower than the 42,360 listed in the first return (Ezra 2:64).[147]

This genealogy reminds the postexilic community that although these families experience historically disparate stages of return, they are bound together as one people of God. The twelve familial "heads" in chapter 8 repeat family names of those who returned under Zerubbabel in chapter 2. This "all Israel" perspective becomes even more apparent by the close of the chapter (8:35). If Ezra, the priest and expert in the law of Moses, compiled this list (cf. v. 34), then the fronting of Phinehas, Ithamar, and David makes sense—it brings to the surface Ezra's mission and its concern for priestly leadership, proper worship, and obedience to the law of Moses for all Israel, matters that persist throughout the chapter and the rest of the book of Ezra.

8:15–20 During Ezra's three-day assessment at the "river" (or "canal"; NET, NIV) to Ahava, he finds no "sons of Levi" or any other temple assistants (cf. 7:7). The absence of Levites would make the routine work of the priests less efficient, since Levites assisted them in their duties. With respect to the present concern, Ezra needs Levites to accomplish his mission of bearing royal gifts to Jerusalem (7:15; 8:24–30). Finally, Levites are needed for the instruction of the people (Neh. 8:7–8) and to ensure that the workers at God's house are not neglected (Neh. 10:38–39). The abandonment of the house of God was a key cause of exile in the first place (2 Chron. 24:18–19).

Earlier, the number of priests registered (4,289) dwarfed the Levites, singers, and gatekeepers (341; cf. Ezra 2:36–39, 40–42). The reason for the smaller numbers of Levites is unknown. Conjectures include the possibility that fewer Levites actually went into exile, being numbered among the poor remaining in the land (Jer. 39:9–10), or that the exiled Levites were hesitant or unwilling to return to their former temple work since, with no temple in Babylonia, they were forced to find new means of supporting their families in the meantime.

To solve the need for Levites, Ezra establishes a commission of nine "leading men" (Ezra 8:16; cf. 7:28; 8:1), accompanied by two others. None of the commission are identified explicitly as Levites, though the latter two, called "men of insight," are able to instruct.[148] They are sent to present their need of "ministers for the

---

147 Williamson, *Ezra, Nehemiah*, 110. The number 1,496 totals only those men who accompany heads of families. It does not include the later reference to additions (8:18–20).

148 These "men of insight" likely have a special function as "teachers" (NASB, NET) or "instructors" (NJPS), although they are not Levites. In Chronicles the term (Hb. *mebîn*) refers to the teaching function of the Levites (1 Chron. 25:8; 2 Chron. 35:3; Neh. 8:7–8). See Blenkinsopp, *Ezra-Nehemiah*, 165.

house of our God" to Iddo, an otherwise unknown "leading man" at Casiphia.[149] While the term "ministers" may broadly apply to servants or assistants in a non-worship setting (Ex. 24:13; Josh. 1:1; 1 Kings 19:21), the current context makes Ezra's concern for God's house clear: he needs Levites to join him (1 Chron. 16:4; 2 Chron. 13:10; 23:6).

Because of the "hand of our God on us," thirty-eight Levites willingly overturn their lives to serve. Similarly, 220 "temple servants" is a significant quantity when compared to the 392 present at the first return (Ezra 2:58).[150] And yet quality is just as important as quantity. Sherebiah arrives (8:24; Neh. 8:7; 9:4–5), with a reputation for wisdom and competent service (Ezra 8:24; Neh. 8:7; cf. 2 Chron. 30:22), along with Hashabiah and Jeshaiah. Each man has deep Levitical roots traceable back to Merari (a son of Levi)—a fact whose relevance will be apparent in due course (Ezra 8:24–30).

8:21–23 A form of the verb "seek" (Hb. *baqash*) occurs once in each verse as a key word in the paragraph ("implored" in v. 23). Ezra continues preparations by proclaiming a fast to attune his people to seek God humbly for their needs (Isa. 58:2–14). Very real dangers exist in transporting families, property, and treasure (Ezra 7:15; 8:25) over vast distances. Consequently, in requesting "a safe journey" (lit., "a straight way"; cf. Isa. 40:3–4; Jer. 31:9) they seek and receive the Lord's protection (Ezra 8:23, 31b).

In verse 22, Ezra shows how he grows the faith of his people. Artaxerxes had been informed that Israel's God was both gracious and just, doing good to "all who seek him" as well as expressing wrath to "all who forsake him" (cf. Ex. 34:6–7; 20:5–6; 1 Chron. 28:9; 2 Chron. 15:2). By forgoing military accompaniment on this occasion, Ezra defines his community as seekers of God who trust him wholly and receive his beneficence. Neither reliance upon "soldiers and horsemen" nor the taking of precautions is a sinful act in itself (cf. Ezra 8:29, 34; Neh. 2:9). However, the notice that the Lord "listened to our entreaty" vindicated their public trust in God before the Persian king (Ezra 8:23; cf. Ps. 20:7) and further strengthens their faith.

8:24–30 For Israel to embrace her mission shows obedience and trust. The act of "setting apart" (v. 24) is an action laden with theological and missional importance. From the beginning of creation God separated one thing from another (Gen. 1:4, 6, 7, 14, 18). He further separated Israel from all the other peoples he had made and gave them dietary laws as an outward expression of their holy status (Lev. 20:24–26; 1 Kings 8:53). One tribe, the Levites, was separated from other tribes to transport the tabernacle (Num. 3:1–4:49; 8:5–19). Later David, in light of temple construction, organized the Levites to assist the priests in worship (1 Chron. 23:24–32). Further, among the Levites, Aaron and his sons were separated as priests (Ex. 29:1) and commanded not only to perform ritual separation (i.e., "to

---

149 Like Ahava (8:15), the precise location of Casiphia is unknown, though it is likely near Ahava.
150 The number includes the "sons of Solomon's servants" (Ezra 2:58). Only at 8:20 do we find the establishment of the temple servants (Hb. *netinim*) by David. For discussion of this group, cf. comment on 2:43–54.

distinguish") between the holy things and the common things but also to teach these things to the Lord's people (Lev. 10:8–11; 1 Chron. 23:13).

In view of this backstory, Ezra's separating out twelve "leading priests" alongside twelve Levites (Ezra 8:24)[151] indicates they have been set aside for a very important task. Having assigned the responsibility to inventory and transport the wide-ranging contributions "for the house of our God" (v. 25; cf. 7:15–16), Ezra now delegates that task to these men and specifically names Sherebiah and Hashabiah, descendants of Merari and recent additions to the numbers of Levites (8:24; cf. vv. 18–19). The amounts Ezra weighs into "their hand" (i.e., entrusts to them; v. 26) indicate a physically demanding task. For these Levites to bear this heavy load is relevant, since historically the Merarites were the Levites responsible for the weightiest items in tabernacle transportation (Num. 7:6–9; cf. 3:36–37).

Ezra then provides the rationale for the selection of these men (Ezra 8:28–29): only holy servants (Ex. 39:30; Lev. 21:6; 1 Kings 8:4) may bear these consecrated vessels and offerings (2 Chron. 5:1, 5) set aside from common use for the holy house of a holy God. Israel's history shows the consequences of behavior to the contrary (Lev. 10:1–3; Josh. 7:1; 2 Sam. 6:6–8). Success in this endeavor requires not only physical labor but also diligent guardianship until these items arrive safely at their destination in the storerooms of the second temple.

8:31–34 In these final paragraphs Ezra completes his mission by leading his people to Jerusalem (vv. 31–32; cf. 7:13). The departure from Ahava on the "twelfth day" of the first month (8:31–32) differs from the departure date identified in 7:9 as the "first day of the first month." Practically, this discrepancy accounts for the initial three-day camp at Ahava (8:15), the gathering of Levites (vv. 15–20), the call for a fast (vv. 21–23), and the setting apart of priests and Levites (vv. 24–30). Further, these dates have theological significance. Departure in the first month (Nisan) reflects that of the exodus from Egypt (Ex. 12:2; Num. 33:3). Ezra's actual departure date on the twelfth day would be two days before the Passover celebration on the fourteenth day of that month. This means that, like the first exodus, the travelers will be celebrating Passover early in their journey. This also means that this narrative in Ezra picks up at a point in the liturgical calendar where the last episode left off (Ezra 6:19–22). Like Moses, Ezra's "exodus" will be followed by application of the law and a covenant with the people (7:14, 25–26; 10:5).[152]

Ezra likewise delivers the offerings to the temple chiefs as instructed (8:33; cf. 7:15–16, 19). His careful accounting of the offerings he carries was earlier expressed by means of the verb "weighing out" (Hb. *shaqal*) or its cognate noun, "weight" (8:25, 26, 29, 30). Those who first received this holy treasure now deliver it directly "into the hands" (v. 33) of two priests, Meremoth and Eleazar, and two

---

151 Sherebiah and Hashabiah are unquestionably Levites (8:18–20; Neh. 10:11–12) even though they are named alongside the twelve priests in Ezra 8:24. It is better therefore to read the text to refer to twelve priests "*together with*" (NET) twelve Levites (i.e., Sherebiah, Hashabiah, and ten of their fellow Levites). The end of the paragraph confirms this reading as both "priests and Levites" take on responsibility of transport to Jerusalem (8:30). See Kidner, *Ezra and Nehemiah*, 75; Williamson, *Ezra, Nehemiah*, 114.

152 See Blenkinsopp for these and other suggestions on the significance of the dates (*Ezra-Nehemiah*, 138–139).

Levites, Jozabad and Noadiah (cf. Neh. 13:13). Accuracy is emphasized by three more occurrences of "weighed" or "weight" in Ezra 8:33–34 and the note that everything is counted and the totals recorded (v. 34).

8:35–36 Finally, in compliance with Artaxerxes's prior commands (7:17), the offerings to God are made (8:35). It may be noted that even eighty years after the first return, the remnant is still considered to be "from captivity" (v. 35; cf. 2:1; 3:8) and "returned exiles" (8:35; cf. 4:1; 6:16). Beyond this, the unity of Israel hinted at in the chapter's opening genealogy and Ezra's setting apart twelve priests and twelve Levites (8:24)—naturally symbolic of Israel's twelve tribes—now moves to center stage as twelve bulls are offered "for all Israel" as a burnt offering.[153] Given the prior prayer and fasting (vv. 21–23) and assumed gratitude for a safe journey, these burnt offerings would be to offer praise to God for his faithfulness.[154] The twelve goats for the sin offering effect purification for the whole congregation (cf. comment on 6:14–18). Together they reveal a reconstituted people, "all Israel," wholly dedicated to the Lord.

The delivery of the "king's commissions" (8:36) refers to Artaxerxes's letter (7:12–26) and particularly the directions to the "treasurers" (7:21–24), along with the broad legal authorization granted to Ezra in the province (7:25–26). With the final delivery of these to both regional and provincial administrators (i.e., satraps and governors), assistance reaches the people and God's house (8:36; cf. 7:23), and the pericope reaches its fitting conclusion.

Response

The chapter shows the Lord gathering his people, providing them shepherds, protecting them in their long journey, and bringing them safely home to Jerusalem. In terms of the first of these, the Lord's servant Ezra gathers the congregation to make the long journey to Jerusalem (8:15). In this way the Lord begins to fulfill many biblical prophecies—using the phrase "I will gather"—to fulfill the promised restoration of his beleaguered, exiled remnant. This promise ripples from the Major Prophets (Isa. 43:5–7; 54:7; 56:8; Jer. 32:37; Ezek. 11:17) to the Minor Prophets (Mic. 2:12; 4:6; Zeph. 3:19; Zech. 10:8–10). This ingathering finds its completion in Christ Jesus, who gathers his scattered people, both Jews and Gentiles, in this age (John 11:51–52; cf. John 10:16; Acts 15:15–18) and finally in the age to come (Matt. 3:12; 13:30, 47–50; 25:31–32; 2 Thess. 2:1).

With regard to shepherding, Ezra recognizes the need for Levites to shepherd this gathered people. The absence of Levites is a genuine threat to both proper worship and instruction of the people and, by extension, a threat to their mission as God's people (Ezra 8:15). It is the Lord himself who provides the needed shepherds, "ministers for the house of our God" (vv. 17–18). Notice, however, that the actor is

---

153 Burnt offerings are offered elsewhere in Ezra after altar reconstruction (3:2–6). Darius also provides burnt offerings as part of his decree (6:9), and perhaps these are assumed to be part of the dedication (6:16–17).
154 If the reading of "seventy-two lambs" found in *1 Esdras* 8:66 is accepted, then all of the burnt offerings are divisible by twelve.

not "my God" but "our God," a phrase repeated throughout the chapter (vv. 17, 18, 21, 22, 23, 25, 30, 31, 33). This not only reveals the necessary connection between God, the true Shepherd, and his whole flock; it also shows the Lord's concern to provide ministers for his "house," the temple. Those who are "separated" or "set apart" (v. 24) for this work must, with utmost solemnity, live consistently with their holy status. Only then can they faithfully "guard . . . and keep" (v. 29) the holy vessels, treasures for which they are responsible. In our redemptive moment, the connection between the holiness of shepherds and the holy vessels of the church that he leads, i.e., God's people, is never clearer than in Paul's instructions to Timothy (2 Tim. 2:15–21).[155] Greater still, we have a Great High Priest, Jesus Christ, who sanctifies us as his holy vessels, guarding and keeping us for his presence (Rom. 15:16; 1 Cor. 1:2; 1 Thess. 5:23; 1 Pet. 1:15–16; 5:1–3).

Finally, under God's protection, Ezra must lead his congregation from Babylon to arrive safely home in Jerusalem. As noted above, the eventual return of holy vessels by holy priests and Levites to the house of the Lord (Ezra 8:28; cf. Isa. 52:11–12) evokes the return of this holy people to their home in Jerusalem (Ezra 1:11–2:1). In the face of the dangers inherent in such a long journey, preparations to return include the humble pursuit of the good hand of God through prayer and fasting (cf. 8:21–23). The Lord willingly answers these prayers for protection by providing a "straight way" (i.e., "safe journey," v. 21; cf. Isa. 40:3–4; Ps. 5:7–8; Prov. 3:5–6). Throughout, God's gracious hand displays his favorable oversight of the Jerusalem trip, whether in initial permission from Artaxerxes or in the people's eventual safe arrival in Jerusalem (Ezra 7:6, 9, 28; 8:22, 31). We too ground our safe homecoming into God's presence in the new Jerusalem not in our genealogy (vv. 1–14), our willingness to serve (vv. 18–20), our prayer (v. 21), or even our holy status (v. 28), but in the mercy of our Father (Luke 15:17–24) and the priestly work of his Son (Heb. 10:10–14). As John Newton so beautifully states, "'Tis grace has brought me safe thus far, and grace will lead me home."

EZRA 9:1–15

9 After these things had been done, the officials approached me and said, "The people of Israel and the priests and the Levites have not separated themselves from the peoples of the lands with their abominations, from the Canaanites, the Hittites, the Perizzites, the Jebusites, the Ammonites, the Moabites, the Egyptians, and the Amorites. [2] For they have taken some of their daughters to be wives for themselves and for their sons, so that the holy race[1] has mixed itself with the peoples of the lands. And in this faithlessness the hand of the officials and chief men has

---

155 Robert W. Yarbrough, *The Letters to Timothy and Titus*, PNTC (Grand Rapids, MI: Eerdmans, 2018), 392–394.

been foremost." [3] As soon as I heard this, I tore my garment and my cloak and pulled hair from my head and beard and sat appalled. [4] Then all who trembled at the words of the God of Israel, because of the faithlessness of the returned exiles, gathered around me while I sat appalled until the evening sacrifice. [5] And at the evening sacrifice I rose from my fasting, with my garment and my cloak torn, and fell upon my knees and spread out my hands to the LORD my God, [6] saying:

"O my God, I am ashamed and blush to lift my face to you, my God, for our iniquities have risen higher than our heads, and our guilt has mounted up to the heavens. [7] From the days of our fathers to this day we have been in great guilt. And for our iniquities we, our kings, and our priests have been given into the hand of the kings of the lands, to the sword, to captivity, to plundering, and to utter shame, as it is today. [8] But now for a brief moment favor has been shown by the LORD our God, to leave us a remnant and to give us a secure hold[2] within his holy place, that our God may brighten our eyes and grant us a little reviving in our slavery. [9] For we are slaves. Yet our God has not forsaken us in our slavery, but has extended to us his steadfast love before the kings of Persia, to grant us some reviving to set up the house of our God, to repair its ruins, and to give us protection[3] in Judea and Jerusalem.

[10] "And now, O our God, what shall we say after this? For we have forsaken your commandments, [11] which you commanded by your servants the prophets, saying, 'The land that you are entering, to take possession of it, is a land impure with the impurity of the peoples of the lands, with their abominations that have filled it from end to end with their uncleanness. [12] Therefore do not give your daughters to their sons, neither take their daughters for your sons, and never seek their peace or prosperity, that you may be strong and eat the good of the land and leave it for an inheritance to your children forever.' [13] And after all that has come upon us for our evil deeds and for our great guilt, seeing that you, our God, have punished us less than our iniquities deserved and have given us such a remnant as this, [14] shall we break your commandments again and intermarry with the peoples who practice these abominations? Would you not be angry with us until you consumed us, so that there should be no remnant, nor any to escape? [15] O LORD, the God of Israel, you are just, for we are left a remnant that has escaped, as it is today. Behold, we are before you in our guilt, for none can stand before you because of this."

[1] Hebrew *offspring* [2] Hebrew *nail*, or *tent-pin* [3] Hebrew *a wall*

Section Overview

The second return from Babylonia to Jerusalem is recounted in two acts (Ezra 7; 8). By the good hand of God, referenced in all stages of the journey (7:6, 9, 28; 8:18, 22, 31), the community surmounts many challenges. Appropriately, the prior chapter concluded with offerings of praise to God for safe arrival. With the setting established, the returned exiles have readied themselves for a new life in the land.

However, conflict arises. Playing out in another two acts, chapters 9 and 10 recount the crisis of intermarriage and provide a case study for Ezra's ministry. In his calling from the Lord, his specialty is the law of God, and he has devoted himself to its study and practice and to teaching it to others (7:10). Likewise, the human king Artaxerxes has authorized him to "make inquiries about Judah and Jerusalem according to the Law of your God" (7:14). The crisis of intermarriage (ch. 9) provides an immediate situation for him to put this knowledge and skill to work.

The chapter consists of three parts. Officials inform Ezra that intermarriage has led to the mixing of the returned exiles with the "peoples of the lands" (9:1–2). Desolated by the news, Ezra mourns (vv. 3–4). His prayer of confession covers the remainder of the chapter (vv. 5–15), further subdivided into four parts (vv. 5–7, 8–9, 10–11, 12–15). Ezra concludes, "None can stand before you because of this," preparing us for the resolution in the next and final chapter.

Section Outline

II.C.2. Mixed Marriages: Crises and Resolution (9:1–10:44)

    a. Crisis: Report Leads to Mourning and Confession (9:1–15)

        (1) Report to Ezra about Lack of Separation of the "Holy Seed" (9:1–2)

        (2) Response of Ezra: Acts of Mourning (9:3–4)

        (3) Prayer of Ezra: Confession at Evening Sacrifice (9:5–15)

Comment

9:1–2 "After these things" marks a new pericope subsequent to events depicted in Ezra 8:35–36. Four months have passed since Ezra's arrival (cf. 7:8 with 10:9),[156] and Ezra recounts the story in first-person narrative.

Some leaders, "the officials" (Hb. *hassarim*), approach Ezra in crisis. These persons may be synonymous with those already established as "the heads of fathers' houses" (8:29) or with "rulers" of administrative districts (Neh. 3:9). While the problem clearly envelopes the whole community, the accusation singles out "officials" and others labeled "chief men" (Ezra 9:2).[157] This latter group refers to lower-level leaders. In short, persons who have previously returned from exile, and particularly leaders, are censured for not "separat[ing] themselves from the peoples of the lands" (v. 1).[158]

This intermixing is forbidden since it puts the returnees in contact with the abominations of the "peoples of the lands," abominations associated with enemies from Israel's past.[159] For the returnees this list of enemies would evoke

---

156 Many interpreters consider Ezra's teaching ministry and reading of the law (Nehemiah 8) to have had its original literary setting between his arrival in Jerusalem in the fifth month (Ezra 7:8) and the mixed marriage crisis in the ninth month (10:9). In this view, Ezra's reading of the law took place during this temporal gap in the seventh month (Neh. 8:1–2) and prompted the intermarriage confession. For arguments, see Williamson, *Ezra, Nehemiah*, 127–128, 283–286.

157 This plural noun, translated "officials" (Hb. *sarim*; 9:1, 2; cf. 8:20; 10:8, 14), has a wide range of meaning. Other occurrences in Ezra are translated "officers" (7:28), "leading" (priests) (8:24; 10:5), "lords" (8:25), "chiefs" (of priests) and "heads" (of fathers) (8:29). The plural noun rendered "chief men" (*seganim*; 9:2) is found only here in Ezra but frequently in Nehemiah (Neh. 2:16 [2x]; 4:14, 19; 5:7, 17; 7:5; 12:40; 13:11), where it is almost always translated "officials" in the ESV. See also the comment on "nobles and officials" at Nehemiah 2:11–16.

158 For the theological significance of being "separate," see comment on 8:24–30. If those coming to Ezra include themselves in the wrongdoing, then this is a confession, not simply an accusation.

159 See comments on 4:1–5; 6:19–21 for discussion of "peoples of the land" as adversaries and non-Israelites who are distinct from returning exiles. One interpretive challenge is that not all of the nations listed in 9:1

God's original promise to bring Israel to the land and fight for them (Ex. 3:8, 17; 23:23; Josh. 3:10). Israel was commanded to drive out these nations and inherit the land as a gift (Deut. 31:3–6; Josh. 1:1–6; 21:43–45). It was in part due to these nations' abominations that intermarriage with them was originally prohibited (Ex. 34:11–16; Deut. 7:1–5; Judg. 3:5–6). In this context "abominations" likely refer to false worship and related practices that the Lord deems reprehensible (Deut. 12:31; 20:18; 2 Kings 21:1–7). Sadly, for Israelites to intermarry and express fidelity and devotion to their foreign human spouses means adultery and breaking faith with the Lord as their Husband (Hos. 2:16–20).

The key word "faithlessness" (Ezra 9:2, 4; 10:6) and its comparable verb (10:2, 10; translated "to break faith" or "to act treacherously") have various uses. They may refer to treating what is holy as common inadvertently (Lev. 5:15), disobeying commands outright (Josh. 7:1; 22:16–20), or pursuing the "gods of the peoples of the land" (1 Chron. 5:25) and can be found in parallel to stiff-necked unbelief (2 Chron. 30:7–8). King Solomon, by his marriage to foreign women (Neh. 13:23–27; 1 Kings 11:1–13), was the supreme model of acting "treacherously." The actual concern is not ethnicity or race. Instead, the major dynamic is wholehearted engagement to be the Lord's (Deut. 6:4–9). Indeed, outsiders who separated themselves "from the uncleanness of the peoples of the land" were permitted to join *with* Israel and participate in the benefits of the community (Ezra 6:21–22; cf. Ex. 2:21; 12:38; Josh. 6:25; Ruth 1:4; 4:13–22; 2 Kings 5:1–19).[160]

Another concern over the intermarrying is ritual impurity. By intermarrying, the "holy race" (lit., "holy seed," "offspring") becomes unholy—not for genetic reasons but because by mixing with the ritually impure they themselves become impure (cf. Deut. 23:2; Ps. 106:34–39). In turn, becoming unholy threatens their elect status as Abraham's offspring (Gen. 17:7–9; Deut. 7:6–8), mixing together what the Lord has kept apart. Not only so, but "holy seed" identifies the promised remnant preserved and replanted after the judgment of exile (Isa. 6:13; Jer. 31:27–28; Neh. 9:2) and *the* offspring, Jesus Christ, who was promised to rule over that holy seed (Gen. 3:15; 22:17–18; Jer. 33:25–26; Gal. 3:16). Israel was to be careful always to guard this holy seed.

9:3–4 Ezra immediately responds with a series of public actions in front of the temple (cf. 10:1). In grief he tears his garments (9:3, 5) and removes his hair, signifying humiliation, death, and mourning (Job 1:20; Isa. 15:2; Joel 2:12–13).[161] There may be a wordplay here, as the *ma'al* ("faithlessness"; Ezra 9:2) of the people

existed in Ezra's day. One solution is to suggest that the list is stereotypical, intentionally describing the different nations in terms that resonate with Israel's history. Another is to follow versions that translate 9:1 along the lines of the NIV: "have not kept themselves separate from the neighboring peoples with their detestable practices, like those of the Canaanites, Hittites . . ." (so also NET). In this case, the actual nations of Ezra's day are being compared to Israel's past enemies.

160 This is exemplified best in the marriage of Ruth, a Moabite woman, to Boaz, great-grandfather of King David.

161 Tearing garments is imagery for nakedness and thus death and humiliation, while the pulling out of hair was a modification to shaving the head in mourning, an act forbidden to Israel (Deut. 14:1–2) so as not to mourn like surrounding nations (Clines, *Ezra, Nehemiah, Esther*, 121). Here Ezra mourns the death of the community (Williamson, *Ezra, Nehemiah*, 133).

leads to the tearing of Ezra's *me'il* ("cloak"; v. 3). When one is overcome by excessive sorrow, a proper response may be stunned silence (Job 2:13). So too Ezra sits "appalled," mourning this corporate death for a breach of faith (cf. Josh. 7:1, 6).

In contrast to the excitement of the prior gathering (Ezra 7:28; 8:15), persons now gather continuously about Ezra in solidarity with his mourning (9:4b).[162] They assemble because they are "trembling" with fear and awe at God's word (cf. Isa. 66:2, 5), perhaps considering the impact of the words found in Ezra 9:2 (cf. Deut. 7:3). They also mourn the "faithlessness" of returned exiles. Having suffered the physical and mental effects of exilic trauma that came because of faithlessness (2 Chron. 36:14–20), who could blame them for fear and trembling in the face of a new outbreak of faithlessness?

9:5–15 After an introductory statement (v. 5) Ezra's public confession flows in four parts. He initially confesses the past iniquities of his people (vv. 6–7). The remaining segments all begin with the Hebrew conjunction *we'attah* ("But now," v. 8; "And now," v. 10; "Therefore," v. 12). Key words throughout include "give/grant" (vv. 7, 8 [2x], 9 [2x], 12, 13), "guilt" (vv. 6, 7, 13, 15), and "remnant" (vv. 8, 13, 14, 15).

9:5–7 Ezra confesses past iniquities and present results. The temporal notice ("at the evening sacrifice")[163] and new actions ("I rose . . .") make verse 5 the introduction to the prayer. By arising from his fasting, Ezra leaves behind his prior acts of self-affliction to embrace agonizing confession. Ripping garments and hair leads him to bended knees and hands "spread out . . . to the LORD" (cf. 1 Kings 8:54). It is personal for Ezra. The verbs "I am ashamed and blush,"[164] frequently found together (Isa. 45:16, 17; 50:7), express the reality of Ezra's first-person emotional pain at this corporate failure. Had the community responded in Jeremiah's day in like manner, perhaps exile could have been delayed or averted (Jer. 6:13–15; 8:8–12; Ezek. 36:25).

Ezra's shame and dishonor before God arise from "our iniquities" (Ezra 9:6, 7, 13), which resulted in "our guilt" (vv. 6, 7, 13, 15; 10:10, 19). Using metaphors, Ezra characterizes their iniquity (i.e., violations of God's standards) as having "risen higher than our heads," while the resulting guilt (i.e., liability to punishment) extends to heaven itself. His historical abstract in 9:7 focuses on prior judgments. Their "great guilt" stretches from ancestral past to the present. The "cumulative iniquities"[165] that gave rise to that guilt resulted in conquest ("given into the hand"), further detailed as death, servitude (exile), and financial loss.[166] These summarize the extensive consequences for covenantal breach found in the Pentateuch (Lev. 26:14–39; Deut. 28:15–68). The personal shame ends in corporate "utter shame, as it is today." Although the heat of judgment has passed, effects

---

162 By means of the verbal form, the text gives the impression of an ever-expanding gathering of co-mourners.
163 This was the ninth hour (3 p.m.; cf. Ps. 141:2; Dan. 9:21; Acts 3:1).
164 The Hebrew verb *kalam*, translated "blush," is elsewhere rendered "put to . . . dishonor" (Ps. 35:4), "confounded" (Isa. 45:16, 17; "humiliated," NASB), or "disgraced" (Isa. 50:7).
165 Fensham, *Ezra and Nehemiah*, 128.
166 Perhaps Ezra has the broad period in mind from the period of the judges through the Assyrian and Babylonian domination and into his present Persian period.

remain. By including himself with "we, "our," or "us" in nearly every verse of the entire confession, Ezra shows himself to be a faithful priest, fully identifying with the iniquity, guilt, and punishment of his people.

9:8–9 "But now" (Hb. *we'attah*) marks the eye of the storm, described as a "brief moment" of God's favor. This refers to the short eighty years from Cyrus to Artaxerxes. These verses, saturated with the goodness of God, function rhetorically to interpret God's character and Israel's recent history. The words "favor" (v. 8) and "steadfast love" (*hesed*; v. 9) form two hubs from which four spokes extend.

In verse 8 the Lord shows favor: *to leave* a remnant, *to give* a secure hold, *to brighten* the eyes, and *to give* reviving. This "favor" is often found in parallel with "prayer," in which cases it is translated "plea," as in a plea for mercy (1 Kings 8:28, 30, 45, 49). With the "LORD our God" as its source, "favor" explains Israel's continued existence as a people. Several nouns throughout Ezra's prayer may be translated "remnant" (*peletah*, Ezra 9:8, 13, 14, 15; *she'erit*, v. 14). This English term may refer to anyone who escapes or survives a disaster. Here it is a technical term for the postexilic community that experienced deliverance (Neh. 1:2; Hag. 1:12; Zech. 8:6). With the second verbal complement, "*to give* us a secure hold," Ezra uses the term for "peg" ("secure hold"; cf. ESV mg.) to communicate a rebuilt temple ("his holy place"; cf. Ps. 24:3; Lev. 10:17; 14:13) that has provided them a sense of stability. From these, the final two verbal complements result. Where there was once mourning and death (cf. Pss. 13:2–3; 38:9–10; Ezek. 37:1–14), there is now restored vigor ("brighten our eyes"; cf. 1 Sam. 14:29) in an enlivened community ("grant us . . . reviving").

Repeating key themes from Ezra 9:8 (e.g., reviving, temple presence), the first half of verse 9 provides an important truth: when God's people are most oppressed, his steadfast love (*hesed*) is most evident. As earlier (cf. 7:27–28; Hos. 2:19–20), the favorable acts of Persian kings are confirmation of God's covenantal commitment: *to give* reviving, *to set up* the house, *to repair* its ruins, *to give* a wall. Of all the elements of exilic judgment (Ezra 9:7), subjection to Persian kings persists, and yet God has not forsaken them. If "protection" (*gader*, "wall"; cf. NASB) is interpreted as Nehemiah's rebuilt wall, then Ezra must have arrived after the wall was built by Nehemiah (445 BC). However, its use as a figure of speech elsewhere (e.g., "wall of protection"; cf. Hos. 2:6; Ezek. 13:5; 22:30) promotes a figurative use here.[167] While the protection envisioned includes that of Persian kings, the context of the Lord's faithfulness remains the source of all restorative work among his people (Isa. 31:5; Zech. 8:1–5).

9:10–11 "And now" (Hb. *we'attah*) sets off the third subdivision of the confession. With "after this," Ezra strains to find a way forward. How could God's people

---

[167] Of course, other reasons for a figurative interpretation may be adduced. Judah obviously had no wall around it, which encourages us to take "wall" as figurative. Second, the earlier use of "peg" ("secure hold") shows metaphorical use. Finally, the Hebrew word *gader* ("wall") refers to a wall or fence enclosing a vineyard. The only possible referent to a "city wall" for this term is in Micah 7:11, and even that interpretation is not certain (Williamson, *Ezra, Nehemiah*, 136).

continually "forsake" his commandments when God had so evidently not forsaken them? These "commandments" do not come from a specific place in Scripture. Instead, Ezra presents a collage of scriptural phrases summarizing the incessant prophetic call to covenantal fidelity from Moses onward (Deut. 18:15; 2 Kings 17:13, 23; 21:10–12; 24:2; Jer. 7:25–26).[168]

The statement in Ezra 9:11 provides the rationale for the introduction of the specific commandment that follows (v. 12). The word "impure" most frequently refers to the ritual impurity of menstruation (Lev. 15:19–24), which was considered highly defiling due to the loss of human blood.[169] Normal bodily functions were not a moral issue. However, in the joining of "land" and "impurity," ritual uncleanness becomes a metaphor for moral uncleanness (Ezek. 36:17–18; cf. Isa. 64:6; Lam. 1:17).[170] The worship of false gods and associated "abominable practices" (Deut. 18:9; cf. 2 Kings 16:3; 21:2; Ezek. 16:47) made the land and persons in it unclean and led to the removal not only of its original inhabitants (Lev. 18:24–30) but eventually of both Israel and Judah.

9:12–15 Although the marker "therefore" (Hb. *we'attah*; v. 12) clearly continues Ezra's prayer and the patchwork of scriptural passages begun in verse 11, it also transitions to the specific prohibition against intermarriage (vv. 12, 14; cf. Deut. 7:3; Neh. 10:30) and Ezra's implicit call to repent in his conclusion. Associated with the commandment not to intermarry is the command to "never seek their peace or prosperity" (Ezra 9:12). This nearly verbatim citation was originally given in the context of illicit relationships and applied to the Moabites and Ammonites (Deut. 23:2–6)—both the offspring of illicit relationship (Gen. 19:30–38). Through obedience to this command, Israel would fulfill her calling to inherit and pass on the land to her children (i.e., "be strong") and likewise experience the blessings of its produce (Deut. 6:11; 11:8–12; Josh. 1:6–9; 5:12; 14:9; 1 Chron. 28:8).

These commandments were given because of God's love for his people and their missional call to be holy; obedience to them was a way for them to express their love for him (Deut. 7:1–8; Josh. 23:11–13; John 14:15). The mitigation of punishment in the middle of Ezra 9:13 ("seeing that you . . . have given us such a remnant as this") explains the whole rationale of verses 13–14—judgment is not the end. Even in judgment, God's abundant mercy has been evident by virtue of their ongoing existence as a people—it might have been worse. In light of such mercy, how could they now persist in intermarrying and risk the destruction of the surviving remnant? Ezra's concluding statement in verse 15 confesses unequivocally that the Lord is "just" (NASB "righteous") and that his past judgments that left them as only a remnant were true and right (Deut. 32:4–6; 2 Chron. 12:6; Ps. 119:137). Ezra also confesses their guilt without qualification, implying that the righteous God would be justified in utterly destroying them. In light of their

---

168 A key phrase found in Ezra 9:11 and throughout the OT is "my [or his] servants the prophets" (2 Kings 17:13, 23; Jer. 25:4; 29:19; 35:15; Amos 3:7).
169 Sklar, *Leviticus*, 202–203.
170 Ezra 9:11 and Ezekiel 36:17 are the only places at which the word translated here as "impurity" is brought together with words translated "land" or "earth."

continued existence, hope yet remains. How will they respond to Ezra's public prayer of confession and its implicit call to repent?

Response

Sin brings mourning. By his outward acts of mourning, Ezra separates himself and sits "appalled" (9:4) as prior rejoicing turns to lamentation (8:35–36; Amos 8:10). He admits that intermarriages run the risk of dissolving the remnant into the surrounding culture. And he is devastated, tearing his clothes and pulling out his hair as one might do to mourn death. It is true that, unlike in the ancient Near East, many cultures today no longer tear garments or hair in response to the emotional distress of death. But understanding the depth of our sin as a kind of death that demands such a response will help us to mourn sin's presence more appropriately.

The intermarriage prohibition and the command to "never seek their peace or prosperity" (Ezra 9:12) become easy targets for uniform dismissal of the OT. Yet the call to be holy and separate from the world remains an important principle for the church in all ages. This is true of Jesus' teaching (Matt. 5:14; John 17:14–17) and apostolic discipleship (2 Cor. 6:14–7:1; Eph. 1:4; 5:27; 1 Pet. 1:15–16; 2 John 10). It must also be noted that these commands provide no justification today for prohibiting marriage between persons of different tribes, races, or nations. Rather, the issue concerns ultimate heart commitments (2 Cor. 2:15–16). Moreover, these commands do not mean complete separation from those who do not follow Christ (1 Cor. 5:9–10). Gaining the proper balance between cultural engagement and separation requires God's wisdom both individually and corporately, even as we seek another city "whose designer and builder is God" (Heb. 11:8–10; cf. Phil. 3:20).

Amid the sin of this chapter, it is the steadfast love of God that motivates obedience and is the only source of new life (Ezra 9:8–9). While we live, hope remains. God does not treat us as our sins deserve but preserves a people for their good and his glory. Ezra twice focuses on the escaped remnant as evidence of God's faithful love to his people. Instead of demanding repentance, Ezra urges them to ponder the question of how they shall then live in response to God's mercy (vv. 8, 13–14). The historical circumstances of the apostle Paul's day differed, but the principle yet remains: separation from the world and presentation of ourselves as "living sacrifices" does not earn God's favor but is a response to the merciful love he shows us in Christ, a love that motivates holiness (Rom. 12:1–2).

We may note, finally, how Ezra models the role of mediator on behalf of his people. Like a faithful pastor, Ezra knows when to identify with the congregation in its sin and suffering. At times, as with the prophet Elijah, the pronouns "I" and "they" may produce distance in addressing the people's unfaithfulness (1 Kings 19:10). Conversely, Ezra intercedes for the community and numbers himself with the transgressors using "our," "we," or "us" throughout his confession (even though he himself has not intermarried). Their iniquity and guilt are his, and he longs for their holiness. The definitive expression of such a mediator comes in the "one mediator" Christ Jesus (1 Tim. 2:5–6), the faithful High Priest who was numbered with the transgressors and identified fully with their sins (Isa. 53:12). In "faithlessness" (Ezra 9:2; cf. Rom. 4:16) no one can stand before God. However, in union with Jesus Christ, our sins are removed, his righteousness is ours, and we stand with the righteous remnant in the city of the living God (2 Cor. 5:21; Heb. 12:22–24). In light of this, let us be quick to confess sin, turn from it, and look to God for the mercy he makes so freely available to us in Jesus.

EZRA 10:1–44

10 While Ezra prayed and made confession, weeping and casting himself down before the house of God, a very great assembly of men, women, and children, gathered to him out of Israel, for the people wept bitterly. ²And Shecaniah the son of Jehiel, of the sons of Elam, addressed Ezra: "We have broken faith with our God and have married foreign women from the peoples of the land, but even now there is hope for Israel in spite of this. ³Therefore let us make a covenant with our God to put away all these wives and their children, according to the counsel of my lord¹ and of those who tremble at the commandment of our God, and let it be done according to the Law. ⁴Arise, for it is your task, and we are with you; be strong and do it." ⁵Then Ezra arose and made the leading priests and Levites and all Israel take an oath that they would do as had been said. So they took the oath.

⁶Then Ezra withdrew from before the house of God and went to the chamber of Jehohanan the son of Eliashib, where he spent the night,² neither eating bread nor drinking water, for he was mourning over the faithlessness of the exiles. ⁷And a proclamation was made throughout Judah and Jerusalem to all the returned exiles that they should assemble at Jerusalem, ⁸and that if anyone did not come within three days, by order of the officials and the elders all his property should be forfeited, and he himself banned from the congregation of the exiles.

⁹Then all the men of Judah and Benjamin assembled at Jerusalem within the three days. It was the ninth month, on the twentieth day of the month. And all the people sat in the open square before the house of God, trembling because of this matter and because of the heavy rain. ¹⁰And Ezra the priest stood up and said to them, "You have broken faith and married foreign women, and so increased the guilt of Israel. ¹¹Now then make confession to the LORD, the God of your fathers and do his will. Separate yourselves from the peoples of the land and from the foreign wives." ¹²Then all the assembly answered with a loud voice, "It is so; we must do as you have said. ¹³But the people are many, and it is a time of heavy rain; we cannot stand in the open. Nor is this a task for one day or for two, for we have greatly transgressed in this matter. ¹⁴Let our officials stand for the whole assembly. Let all in our cities who have taken foreign wives come at appointed times, and with them the elders and judges of

every city, until the fierce wrath of our God over this matter is turned away from us." [15] Only Jonathan the son of Asahel and Jahzeiah the son of Tikvah opposed this, and Meshullam and Shabbethai the Levite supported them.

[16] Then the returned exiles did so. Ezra the priest selected men,[3] heads of fathers' houses, according to their fathers' houses, each of them designated by name. On the first day of the tenth month they sat down to examine the matter; [17] and by the first day of the first month they had come to the end of all the men who had married foreign women.

[18] Now there were found some of the sons of the priests who had married foreign women: Maaseiah, Eliezer, Jarib, and Gedaliah, some of the sons of Jeshua the son of Jozadak and his brothers. [19] They pledged themselves to put away their wives, and their guilt offering was a ram of the flock for their guilt.[4] [20] Of the sons of Immer: Hanani and Zebadiah. [21] Of the sons of Harim: Maaseiah, Elijah, Shemaiah, Jehiel, and Uzziah. [22] Of the sons of Pashhur: Elioenai, Maaseiah, Ishmael, Nethanel, Jozabad, and Elasah.

[23] Of the Levites: Jozabad, Shimei, Kelaiah (that is, Kelita), Pethahiah, Judah, and Eliezer. [24] Of the singers: Eliashib. Of the gatekeepers: Shallum, Telem, and Uri.

[25] And of Israel: of the sons of Parosh: Ramiah, Izziah, Malchijah, Mijamin, Eleazar, Hashabiah,[5] and Benaiah. [26] Of the sons of Elam: Mattaniah, Zechariah, Jehiel, Abdi, Jeremoth, and Elijah. [27] Of the sons of Zattu: Elioenai, Eliashib, Mattaniah, Jeremoth, Zabad, and Aziza. [28] Of the sons of Bebai were Jehohanan, Hananiah, Zabbai, and Athlai. [29] Of the sons of Bani were Meshullam, Malluch, Adaiah, Jashub, Sheal, and Jeremoth. [30] Of the sons of Pahath-moab: Adna, Chelal, Benaiah, Maaseiah, Mattaniah, Bezalel, Binnui, and Manasseh. [31] Of the sons of Harim: Eliezer, Isshijah, Malchijah, Shemaiah, Shimeon, [32] Benjamin, Malluch, and Shemariah. [33] Of the sons of Hashum: Mattenai, Mattattah, Zabad, Eliphelet, Jeremai, Manasseh, and Shimei. [34] Of the sons of Bani: Maadai, Amram, Uel, [35] Benaiah, Bedeiah, Cheluhi, [36] Vaniah, Meremoth, Eliashib, [37] Mattaniah, Mattenai, Jaasu. [38] Of the sons of Binnui:[6] Shimei, [39] Shelemiah, Nathan, Adaiah, [40] Machnadebai, Shashai, Sharai, [41] Azarel, Shelemiah, Shemariah, [42] Shallum, Amariah, and Joseph. [43] Of the sons of Nebo: Jeiel, Mattithiah, Zabad, Zebina, Jaddai, Joel, and Benaiah. [44] All these had married foreign women, and some of the women had even borne children.[7]

[1] Or *of the Lord* [2] Probable reading; Hebrew *where he went* [3] Syriac; Hebrew *And there were selected Ezra . . .* [4] Or *as their reparation* [5] Septuagint; Hebrew *Malchijah* [6] Septuagint; Hebrew *Bani, Binnui* [7] Or *and they put them away with their children*

Section Overview

A surviving remnant arrives in Jerusalem in the fifth month (Ezra 7:9). Some four months later (cf. 10:9) officials confront Ezra with a crisis: the returned exiles are intermarrying with the peoples of the land (9:1–2). In response, Ezra mourns (9:3–4) and confesses publicly the sin of the escaped remnant (9:5–15). Rather than demanding repentance, he identifies with the iniquities of the people and offers gentle pastoral care, presenting God's mercy to stir up the conscience of his people (9:8–9, 13–14). The current chapter offers resolution in a second "act" and draws the second movement of Ezra-Nehemiah (Ezra 7–10) to a close.

This chapter has a concentric structure.[171] Beginning with a community proposal to make a covenant before the Lord to send away foreign wives and the encouraging of Ezra to make this happen (10:1–4), the chapter concludes (vv. 18–44) with a list of those who "pledged themselves to put away their wives" (v. 19). Within this outer frame, Ezra withdraws, fasts, and mourns after first placing the community under oath to do as they have covenanted (vv. 5–6). The investigation then occurs in summary form in verses 16–17. Moving more centrally, we see verses 7–8 report the proclamation from "the officials and the elders" to "come" to Jerusalem within three days. In comparable language, a counterproposal arises for the guilty to "come at appointed times" (vv. 12–15). Central to the chapter, Ezra brings a full-orbed indictment and a call to confession and repentance (vv. 9–11).

Section Outline

II.C.2.b. Resolution: Confession and Repentance of the People (10:1–44)
      (1) Shecaniah Confesses and Proposes a Covenant (10:1–4)
        (2) Ezra Places Community under Oath and Withdraws (10:5–6)
          (3) Proclamation Calls for an Assembly at Jerusalem (10:7–8)
            (4) Ezra Calls for Public Confession and Separation
                (10:9–11)
          (3') Assembly Confesses and Calls for the Guilty to Come
              (10:12–15)
        (2') Authorities Resolve the Intermarriage Crisis (10:16–17)
      (1') A Register of Those Married to Foreign Wives (10:18–44)

Comment

10:1–4 The terms *confession, covenant,* and *repentance* provide an abstract for the chapter. Ezra's prior activities were told chiefly in his own voice (7:27–9:15); the text now returns to third-person narrative. Ezra's actions, however, are not new. The grammar stresses the incessant praying, confessing, and weeping of Ezra found in the prior chapter. His "casting himself down" parallels prior actions (9:4–5), now making clear that all this took place "before the house of God" (10:1). Ezra's core action remains confession for "iniquities" (9:6, 7, 13; cf. Neh. 9:2) and "faithlessness" (Ezra 9:2, 4).[172] It was the community's persistent transgressions and breaking of the covenant that brought on the flood of judgments that culminated in exile (Lev. 26:14–39). Yet even in exile the Lord has provided the way forward: confession for iniquity and faithlessness, along with offering atoning sacrifice, will restore the relationship (Lev. 26:40–45; 16:21).[173]

---

171 A *concentric* structure has a single center (A-B-C-B'-A'), while the dual-centered structure is best identified as *chiastic* (A-B-C-C'-B'-A'). Jerome T. Walsh, *Style and Structure in Biblical Hebrew Narrative* (Collegeville, MN: Liturgical Press, 2001).
172 Recall from the discussion at 9:1–2 that this word may also be translated to "break faith" or to commit "treachery."
173 Leviticus 26:40 is the only place in the OT that brings together the terms "confess," "iniquity," and both the noun and verb referring to "treachery" ("in their *treachery* whereby *they acted treacherously* against me"; AT).

In response to Ezra's very public expressions of sorrow, an ever-expanding crowd of equally mournful confessors gather (Ezra 10:1; cf. 9:4), defined here as a "very great assembly."[174] Shecaniah, among the seventy "sons of Elam" who have returned with Ezra (8:7), represents the community in offering a way forward. His confession is a model. First, he admits the heart issue: "We have broken faith" (10:2). He next specifies the fundamental expression of their faithlessness, namely, marrying foreign women.[175] The pain and risk for Shecaniah are great, given the involvement of six men from his own clan, reaching perhaps even to his own father (v. 26).[176] Third, Ezra's prayer had concluded by observing their very real danger before God "because of this" (9:15). Shecaniah picks up this exact phrase, noting "hope for Israel *in spite of this*." Such hope comes by way of a suggested resolution in the form of a covenant.

Underneath all of this is the need for everything to be done "according to the Law" (10:3). Divorce was known and regulated in Israel (Deut. 24:1–4), yet no particular law existed for this marital situation.[177] Shecaniah must propose that the community commit to apply the ancient covenantal obligations in this new setting, calling on God to witness their solemn promise to "separate" (Ezra 10:11; cf. Ex. 23:32–33; 34:15–16; Deut. 7:1–3). The suggestion to adopt this drastic measure arises not because of Ezra's demand but because of his confession and sorrow (i.e., "the counsel of my lord"; Ezra 10:3). It is also likely that this proposal is the fruit of Ezra's instruction over the preceding four months.

Acceptance arises from those with utmost regard for God's Word and its call to holiness (i.e., "those who tremble at the commandment"; v. 3; cf. 9:4; Isa. 66:2). It is impossible to specify what it means to "put away" foreign wives and children. Minimally, this must entail the dissolution of the marital relationship and removal from full participation in the community. The closing imperatives—"arise," "be strong," and "do it"—implore Ezra to proceed with all haste. By so doing, he will help Israel fulfill her mission to inherit the land and follow Torah (Josh. 1:6, 7, 9; 23:6). In this Ezra receives the full support of the community.

10:5–6 Ezra responds to Shecaniah's call to "arise" (v. 4), as both verses 5 and 6 begin with that same Hebrew verb (translated "withdrew" in v. 6). Ezra's actions fulfill part of his priestly task under the divine King, as he is taking action to lead them in the ways of God. However, these actions are also consistent with a primary task assigned to Ezra by Artaxerxes, since applying God's law was the very thing he was commanded to do (7:14, 25–26). One of his first steps is to use his royal authority to lead various constituencies to "take an oath" (10:5) and promise obedience, an

---

174 The noun translated "assembly" (Hb. *qahal*; 10:1, 12, 14) will be translated "congregation" in 10:8. The gathering here is not for worship (e.g., 2 Chron. 30:25), but the term is used of a gathering for religious purposes (Deut. 9:10; 10:4).

175 The use of the verb to describe marrying foreign women is unusual and found only here (10:2, 10, 14, 17, 18) and in Nehemiah (13:23, 27). This atypical use may point to the illegitimacy of these unions (Williamson, *Ezra, Nehemiah*, 150).

176 It is difficult to say with certainty whether Jehiel, Shecaniah's father (10:2), is to be identified with the Jehiel in 10:26.

177 If Deuteronomy 24:1–4 is in view in these separations, then perhaps their wives' foreign background is considered "indecency" by men and divorce thereby justified (Williamson, *Ezra, Nehemiah*, 151).

important beginning step in the making of the covenant Shecaniah has proposed (v. 3; cf. Ex. 19:8; 24:3, 7).

Given the caprice of human nature and the sober choices that come before people when sin is prominent, outcomes are rarely assured. Knowing this, Ezra continues to fast and pray, but this time more privately (10:1; cf. 9:3–4) in a room associated with the temple. Such rooms were used both as storerooms (8:29; Neh. 10:38) and to provide Levites a room after being on duty (1 Chron. 9:27, 33; 23:28). Whether Ezra spends the entire night[178] in prayer or some shorter time, it is easy to imagine him alone, sitting, fasting, reflecting, beseeching God for strength and wisdom for all involved in this crisis.

10:7–8 The time elapsed between verses 1–6 and the issuance of the proclamation is unknown. Nevertheless, the three-day requirement for gathering reveals a desire for quick resolution. The proclamation identifies the judgments incurred by any who ignore it. First, the threat that property "be forfeited" applies a form of *haram*, a Hebrew verb often used to refer to persons or property permanently consecrated to the Lord for either destruction or service (e.g., Ex. 22:20; Lev. 27:29; Josh. 2:10; 6:17–18, 21; 7:1). In this context, forfeiture of property likely means its dedication to temple use rather than destruction (Lev. 27:21, 28; Num. 18:14). Anyone refusing to join the assembly to discuss the issue of separation will himself be separated (i.e., "banned") from the congregation.

10:9–11 These verses represent the climactic moment of the chapter. In gathering at the "open square," the people return to the location of Ezra's public prayer (v. 1). The tribes of Judah and Benjamin, tribes prominent among the returned exiles (1:5; 4:1), heed the call to gather within the time allotted.[179] The ninth month (Chislev, November/December) coincides with the rainy season. Heavy rain and falling temperatures saturate and make to shiver an assembly that is already trembling with apprehension over the upcoming confrontation.

Returning to prior themes, Ezra now indicts and exhorts.[180] As he urges his people to holiness, he is called "Ezra the priest" for the first time since chapter 7 (10:10; cf. 7:21). His previous use of the pronouns "we," "us," and "our," showing priestly identification with their iniquity (cf. comment on 9:5–7), gives way to accusation with an explicit use of the pronoun "you." His surgical diagnosis of their heart disease leads to a clear identification of their resulting symptoms (i.e., "*you* have broken faith and *you* have married"; 10:10 AT). Like a good surgeon,

---

178 The ESV has adopted a simple and contextually appropriate emendation here (cf. ESV mg.). Note also that the names Jehohanan, Johanan, Jonathan, and Eliashib occur many times in Ezra-Nehemiah. This makes it difficult to discern the connection with the two men named in Ezra 10:6. On the identities of Jehohanan and Eliashib and their role in the debate on the chronological order of Ezra and Nehemiah, see Williamson, *Ezra, Nehemiah*, 151–154.

179 It is also possible that these tribal references are better interpreted as geographical areas. Given the reduced size of Judea in the Persian period, those within this minor province would be within 20 miles (32 km) of Jerusalem, easily covered within the time allotted (so Clines, *Ezra, Nehemiah, Esther*, 128–129).

180 Note throughout these verses the presence of words and themes such as "separate," "intermarriage," "guilt," "faithlessness," "peoples of the land," "foreign wives," all of which are found explicitly or inferred in some form in 9:1–2, 6–7, 13; 10:2–3.

he also warns of the dangers of their current condition: if the "guilt" of Israel has already led to God's wrath (9:13–14), how much more if they keep adding to Israel's guilt (10:10)?

With "now then," Ezra commands repentance using three interwoven commands (v. 11). The central command, "do his will," shows that no mere external act will suffice. For Ezra's hearers, trembling under the weight of cold and conviction, this is much needed motivation to submit their whole selves to do what pleases God (cf. Pss. 40:8; 50:14), especially the practical call for separation (Lev. 20:22–26).[181] By obeying the command to "*make* confession," the assembly recognizes that the God of their past ("your fathers") and present is a just God (cf. Ezra 9:15). Finally, obeying the final command realizes the first two: "*separate yourselves.*" Although clearly referring to separation from foreign wives, the use of this language elsewhere in Ezra shows that intermarriage remains symptomatic of wider assimilation with "peoples of the lands" (6:21; 9:1). If so, the ritual purity of the whole community is at stake.

10:12–15 By responding concisely in content ("It is so") and tone ("with a loud voice"), the assembly agrees with Ezra's exhortation, offering no further excuses. However, the people do propose a delay due to mitigating factors. They build their case by adding consideration upon consideration: the numbers of people *and* the weather *and* the lack of strength *and* the potential length of the task.[182] Like the frequent "I have sinned" (e.g., Josh. 7:20; 1 Sam. 15:24; 2 Sam. 12:13; Luke 15:18), "we have greatly transgressed" clarifies their multiplied wrongdoing (cf. Ezra 9:6–7).[183] Comparable language elsewhere expresses acts of rebellion, especially in the political sphere (1 Kings 12:19; 2 Kings 1:1; 8:22). With respect to the Lord, "multiplied transgression" or "greatly transgressed" shows utter contempt for his authority (Isa. 59:12–13) leading, if unrepented, to inevitable judgment (Jer. 5:6).

The proposal includes a commission (Ezra 10:14). Participants include "officials" (cf. 9:1; 10:8) who will "stand," i.e., represent the whole congregation, who "cannot stand" (cf. v. 13). Joining these will be "elders and judges of every city," perhaps to provide evidence or ensure justice for the accused. Most importantly, anyone guilty of intermarriage must come at the time called. The fear of eradication of the remnant (9:14–15) motivates this proposal in an effort to turn away threatened wrath. Comparable vocabulary is used when grave sin threatens through judgment the very existence of the whole people (Ex. 32:12, 14; Num. 25:4; Josh. 7:1, 26; 2 Kings 23:26; 2 Chron. 29:10; 30:6–9; Jonah 3:9).

Support is substantial but not unanimous. The ESV captures well the ambiguity of the final verse of the scene. Attention is sharpened by the word "only," which strongly suggests a contrast between four men and the community decision. There are two men (Jonathan, Jahzeiah) who "opposed this" and two others

---

181 Blenkinsopp, *Ezra-Nehemiah*, 193.
182 For the sake of a more elegant and readable translation the conjunction "and" is either not translated or rendered more contextually with "nor" (ESV), "furthermore" (NET), "besides" (NIV), etc.
183 Ezra earlier used metaphorical language to speak of mounting iniquity and guilt (9:6–7).

(Meshullam, Shabbethai) who "supported them." Much hinges, therefore, on the referent of "this." Perhaps "this" refers to the proposed separation itself, and so all four men stand opposed to that community decision, preferring a more lenient approach. Alternatively, "this" might refer not to the call for divorce but to its plan for implementation (Ezra 10:14). In this view, they prefer a more rigorous approach, desiring either increased swiftness of implementation or severity, or both. Most likely, these men prefer the more rigorous option. This conclusion is based primarily upon Shabbethai's identity as a Levite and Meshullam's position of leadership and presence with Ezra in his return (8:16).[184]

10:16–17 The initial oath (vv. 5–6) now reaches its summative conclusion. The notice that the returned exiles "did so" intimates that they effect the proposal (v. 14). With the details of the commission's inquiries left to the imagination, it is impossible to know how divorce laws or Deuteronomy 24:1–4 applies, if at all. At a minimum, it appears that the investigation progresses carefully.

"Ezra the priest" continues his task of purifying a "holy race" (Ezra 9:2). With the final use of the verb "to separate" (Hb. *badal*), he "selected" officials to serve on the commission (10:16).[185] The representative "officials" (v. 14), now identified as "heads of fathers' houses" (cf. 1:5; 2:68; 4:2, 3; 8:1, 29), are carefully selected by clan and designated specifically by name. The scene concludes by noting that the commission starts its work almost immediately, on the "first day of the tenth month" (cf. 10:9), and finishes in approximately three months, justifying the initial concerns for how long the process might take (v. 13).[186]

10:18–44 The book's final list (cf. 2:1–70; 8:1–14) presents over one hundred men guilty of marrying non-Israelite women.[187] These paltry numbers, relative to the numbers of people associated with the first return (2:64), may indicate a practice of intermarriage more limited than first perceived.[188] As in 8:1–14, the priests (10:18–22) and Levites (vv. 23–24) precede the laity ("Israel") (vv. 25–43). The chapter concludes with a single summary statement (v. 44).

10:18–22 Those first mentioned are related to Jeshua, the high priest, a noted leader in the first return (e.g., 2:2, 36; 3:2; 5:2). Citation of the "sons of" Immer, Harim, and Pashhur (10:20–22; cf. 2:36–39) suggests guilt among all the priestly families. The general dereliction of priestly duty in the period matches

---

184 For a lengthy analysis and support for this conclusion, see Williamson, *Ezra, Nehemiah*, 156–157. None of the men is mentioned in the list of those who took foreign wives (10:18–44), so they would have no reason, in principle, to oppose separation. An individual named "Meshullam" is mentioned in the list that follows (10:29) but is unlikely to be the same person. It is improbable that the Meshullam who recently returned with Ezra would have married within the four months since his arrival. For a lengthy analysis, see Williamson, *Ezra, Nehemiah*, 156–157.

185 The ESV accepts a minor textual emendation by which Ezra makes the selections himself; the MT is silent on how the commission is chosen (cf. ESV mg.).

186 Kidner, *Ezra and Nehemiah*, 81.

187 The ESV text lists 27 priests and Levites and 84 laymen. Blenkinsopp provides an excellent discussion (*Ezra-Nehemiah*, 195–201).

188 While the list may evidence some editorial arrangement, there is no reason to accept the suggestion that it was originally longer and has been abbreviated here. For rigorous arguments supporting this view, see Williamson, *Ezra, Nehemiah*, 157–158. Clines also holds that the list is complete (*Ezra, Nehemiah, Esther*, 131).

Malachi 1:6; 2:1–4; the onerous sin of leaders, who have special obligations for marriage (cf. Lev. 21:7, 13–14), is not ignored. Repentance encompasses two actions for all those on the list (Ezra 10:19). First is a pledge (lit., "they gave their hand") promising determination to keep the covenantal promises and dismiss the foreign wives (cf. 1 Chron. 29:24). Second is acknowledgment of guilt by means of the guilt offering (cf. Lev. 5:14–19). Taking foreign wives is an act of faithlessness (cf. Lev. 5:15) and a serious covenantal breach, demanding a guilt offering to make atonement.[189]

10:23–24 The lower number of Levites may be due to relative reduction of numbers as evidenced in other lists (2:36–42; 8:15). Unlike in 2:43–58 and 8:20, neither the "sons of Solomon's servants" nor "temple servants" (2:55–58) receive mention, either because no intermarriage is found among them or because the list focuses on higher-level cult personnel.

10:25–43 Many of the names of the laity here reappear in lists in Nehemiah, but connection between these occurrences is uncertain. Eleven family heads are named (ESV), or perhaps twelve if the inexplicable Hebrew name "Machnadebai" (v. 40) is read as either "of the sons of Azzur" or more likely "of the sons of Zaccai" (cf. 2:9, e.g., NAB).[190] Of those named, only Binnui and Machnadebai are not found in chapter 2; lesser overlap occurs with those named in chapter 8.

10:44 The abrupt concluding verse provides little insight into what happens to these families. The first half of the verse states the obvious, while the second half notes only that both women and their children are impacted ("and some of the women had even borne children").[191] Women and children taking steps to separate themselves and "worship the LORD, the God of Israel" (6:21) remains a possibility. The importance of kinship connections in the ancient Near East may prompt others to return to former communities. The lack of closure certainly readies us to revisit the problem in Nehemiah.

Response

The Lord desires his people to be wholly committed to him. Occasionally, those responsible for shepherding others (e.g., pastors, elders and deacons, teachers, parents, etc.) must confront persons or congregations under their care concerning actions or relationships that threaten faithful discipleship. In this chapter, such confrontation comes in Ezra's call for confession, doing the will of God, and repentance. It requires the community to consider the ways in which they "have broken faith" (10:10) and lived in a manner contrary to their professed walk before God. A faithful response means submission to God's will as revealed in his Word

---

189 Keil, *Ezra, Nehemiah, and Esther*, 133. On the guilt or reparation offering as required for serious betrayals of covenantal loyalty, see Sklar, *Leviticus*, 118–123.

190 The textual issues in 10:25–43 are addressed by Williamson, *Ezra, Nehemiah*, 144. One example is the twice named "Bani" (10:29, 34); some suggest reading "Bigvai" (cf. 2:14) for the latter.

191 The second half provides numerous translation challenges. The alternative translation based on *1 Esdras* 9:36 reads, "And they put them [i.e., wives] away with their children" (RSV).

and a willingness to evaluate the insidious ways our hearts may have acclimatized to sinful cultural norms.

Rarely in the OT do we read of such a visceral community response to God's command as described here—particularly weeping over sin (v. 1) and the vigorous confession and unambiguous agreement to "separate . . . from the peoples of the land and from the foreign wives" (vv. 11–12). This principle is analogous to Paul's instruction to the Corinthian church to guard against hazardous relationships with unbelievers (2 Cor. 6:14–7:1; cf. Matt. 18:7–9). Confession may result in being numbered among the transgressors (Ezra 10:18–44). However, we must remember that the servant of the Lord was also numbered among the transgressors for our sake (Isa. 53:12).

With this demand to separate, the Lord exhibits both truth and grace, judgment and mercy. Loving God requires that we reflect his character by embracing with love the people and cultures of the world while, at the same time, rejecting the world's sensibilities. Consequently, the call to pursue and preserve holiness is required of believers in every age (Lev. 11:44–45; 1 Pet. 1:15–16). The follower of Jesus Christ lives in a tension between exclusivity and separation from the world on the one hand and missional responsibility to and engagement with the world on the other. Jesus' own claims to be the exclusive Savior of the world are ruthlessly rigorist (Matt. 10:5–6; 15:22–28; John 10:7–8; 14:6; cf. Acts 4:12). If these claims of the Lord Jesus result in the charge of intolerance by some contemporary people, there is little hope that Ezra will escape a similar indictment.

It is understandable why some would view Ezra's lack of inclusivity as detestable, or at least his interpretation of the law that results in these divorces. And yet Ezra, with the authority of empire behind him (Ezra 7:14, 26), is otherwise deferential in approach, fervent in prayer, heartbroken by sin, and faithful as an ideal priest, willing to allow a commission to have the final say in the matter. Ezra's concern for the purity of the community groans under the weight of women and children expelled from the congregation because they are "foreign." Given his character, he must view the decision to separate as the less bad of two bad choices.

This leads to a final point: the Lord preserves his people in holiness for the sake of the world. The separation from and exclusion of foreign wives that concludes Ezra likewise concludes Nehemiah (Neh. 13:23–27). Widening the canonical scope, this challenging ethical issue has some analogies with events that open the Historical Books. In Joshua, those entering the land are commanded to separate from the "peoples of the lands" lest they "be a snare and a trap to you" (Josh. 23:12–13; cf. Ex. 23:23–33; Lev. 20:23–24, 26; Deut. 20:16–18). This highlights the fact that the preservation of a priesthood and people, a "holy race" (Ezra 9:2) that is "holy to the LORD," is the very reason for Israel's existence (Ex. 28:36; Deut. 7:6; 14:2; 26:16–19). Israel exists to be a kingdom of priests (Ex. 19:6), teaching the world how to know and worship the Lord and interceding on the world's behalf. Separation from sin is actually for the sake of the inclusion of the nations

(Josh. 6:25; 1 Kings 17:8–9; 2 Kings 5:15; Isa. 56:1–8). This is why preserving this returned community in holiness is so important.

As in Ezra's community, the calling to be a kingdom of priests and our position as "sojourners and exiles" persists for the Lord's people today (1 Pet. 2:9–12). The follower of Christ is commanded: "Do not love the world or the things in the world. If anyone loves the world, the love of the Father is not in him" (1 John 2:15). However, there is a goal in mind: "Keep your conduct among the Gentiles honorable, so that when they speak against you as evildoers, they may see your good deeds and glorify God on the day of visitation" (1 Pet. 2:12; cf. Matt. 5:16). The call to separation from sin combined with mission on the world's behalf has the purpose of drawing the nations into relationship with the Lord. Ultimately, rejection of the "peoples of the land" in the OT is meant to preserve a remnant, and from this "holy offspring" (Ezra 9:2 ESV mg.) comes Jesus Christ, the *Holy Offspring* (Gal. 3:16, 19). His life, death, resurrection, and reign mean finally the inclusion of—rather than separation from—the Gentiles (Isa. 49:6; Luke 4:25–27; Acts 1:8; 13:46–48; Rom. 11:17–24; Gal. 3:16, 19; Col. 3:11).

NEHEMIAH

W. Brian Aucker

NEHEMIAH

Overview

Nehemiah completes the story of the homecoming and restoration of God's people begun in Ezra. The book opens with the news that the exiles in Jerusalem are in "great trouble and shame" and the city walls in disrepair (1:1–3). Nehemiah laments this problem before both divine (1:4–11) and human kings (2:1–8) and is granted permission to journey to Jerusalem to rebuild the wall. The accomplishment of the wall rebuilding is recounted in Nehemiah 3–6. However, as in Ezra (e.g., Ezra 4; 9), trouble is encountered from adversaries without (Neh. 2:10, 19–20; 4:1–23; 6:1–19) and disobedience from the community within (ch. 5). The remarkable speed of wall completion is evidence of the "help of our God" (6:16), but the need to repopulate the city also becomes apparent at this time (7:1–4) as Nehemiah considers the genealogy of the people (7:5–73a).

The climax of Nehemiah and of Ezra-Nehemiah as a whole is recounted in 7:73b–13:31. The theological highpoint is reached with a covenant-renewal ceremony (7:73b–10:39), concluding with the vital pledge, "We will not neglect the house of our God" (10:39). After Jerusalem is repopulated (11:1–12:26), the culmination of Ezra-Nehemiah is reached at 12:27–13:3 as a purified community dwells within a purified city (12:30). The conclusion then narrates a series of reforms associated with the temple, Sabbath, and separation (13:4–31). These reforms remind the people to be ever vigilant in their calling to be a people holy to the Lord.

Title, Author, and Date of Writing

The book opens by informing the reader that these are the "words of Nehemiah," a major figure in the book (1:1). He is "cupbearer to the king" (1:11b) and appointed "governor in the land of Judah" (5:14). Discussion of authorship and of date of final composition are inextricably tied to compositional questions, including the sources used to compile Ezra-Nehemiah and the relationship of 1–2 Chronicles to Ezra-Nehemiah. As with the first-person accounts of Ezra (i.e., the "Ezra Memoir"), the conventionally titled "Nehemiah Memoir" (Neh. 1:1–7:5a; 12:27–43; 13:4–31) may be dated close to the time of the events it recounts (cf. Genre and Literary Features). Nehemiah 13:6 provides an earliest possible date of 433 BC for the memoirs' consolidation. If, as seems likely, the list of priests and Levites in 12:1–26 is a later addition, the reference to the high priest Johanan (12:23) in office at the very end of the fifth century points to a latest possible date for the work of an editor. We may then infer that at least some of the sources were combined by around 400.[1] In this commentary, Ezra-Nehemiah are considered two parts of a literary unity. For this and proposals on authorship see Introduction to Ezra: Title, Author, and Date of Writing.

Date of the Book's Events; Occasion

Two notices link Nehemiah's actions to the reign of the Persian king Artaxerxes I (464–423 BC). The first refers to the twentieth year of Artaxerxes's reign (445), when Nehemiah requested permission to return to Jerusalem to rebuild the wall (2:1). The second mentions the thirty-second year of Artaxerxes (433), when Nehemiah visited him (although purpose and length of stay are not specified; 13:6). This chronological range also fits with what is known of Sanballat from extrabiblical texts. Sanballat led those opposed to Nehemiah's mission (Neh. 2:10, 19; 4:1; 6:1–2, 5, 12, 14; 13:28). His name is found in a letter of the Elephantine papyri. This collection of Aramaic correspondence was discovered at Elephantine, a Jewish colony located near the southern border of Egypt. The letter, dated 407, is addressed to "Bagavahya governor of Judah." He was governor of Judah soon after Nehemiah. The addendum of the letter mentions a prior letter sent to "Delaiah and Shelemiah sons of Sanballat governor of Samaria."[2] It appears that by the last decade of the fifth century Sanballat was elderly and his sons had taken over the administrative responsibilities of the governorship. Similarly, the letter mentions the high priest Jehohanan, most certainly to be identified with "Johanan the son of Eliashib" (Neh. 12:22–23). This also accords with the chronology of Nehemiah's earlier service under Artaxerxes I when Eliashib was high priest (3:1).[3]

The occasion for the book of Ezra-Nehemiah must be inferred from its contents. The book provides an account of how Nehemiah gained permission from Artaxerxes to rebuild the wall of Jerusalem (Nehemiah 1–2), its successful completion in the face of external opposition and internal injustice (Nehemiah 3–6), and the impact of this achievement upon the community (Nehemiah 7–13). It may therefore be viewed as an apology to counter the charge that wall reconstruction was an act of sedition, with the wall being rebuilt for cultural, political, or economic reasons (Ezra 4:11–16; Neh. 2:19; 6:5–9).[4]

By themselves, purely secular reasons for the book are unsatisfactory. God's Word, especially his Law, exists to shape a people. The book of Nehemiah teaches the "remnant . . . who . . . survived the exile" (1:3) that God is still their God and

---

1 H. G. M. Williamson contends that the Ezra and Nehemiah memoirs were brought together by around 400 BC and Ezra 1–6 was added as a final stage of composition around 300; *Ezra, Nehemiah*, WBC 16 (Waco, TX: Word, 1985), xxxvi. This latter position is challenged by Joseph Blenkinsopp in *Ezra-Nehemiah: A Commentary*, OTL (Philadelphia: Westminster, 1988), 43–44. He also argues for the common authorship of 1–2 Chronicles and Ezra-Nehemiah (47–54). David J. A. Clines also holds the Chronicler to be responsible for Ezra-Nehemiah and posits a date of about 400; *Ezra, Nehemiah, Esther*, NCBC (Grand Rapids, MI: Eerdmans, 1984), 12–14.
2 "Request for Letter of Recommendation (First Draft)," trans. Bezalel Porten (*COS* 3.51:130).
3 Williamson, *Ezra, Nehemiah*, 151, 168.
4 Manfred Oeming, "The Theological Ideas behind Nehemiah's Wall," in *New Perspectives on Ezra-Nehemiah: History and Historiography, Text, Literature, and Interpretation*, ed. Isaac Kalimi (Winona Lake, IN: Eisenbrauns, 2012), 131–149.

he longs for them to dwell with him. The exemplary prayers of both Nehemiah and the community illustrate for later generations how God has remained faithful to his covenant and attentive to their pleas for help (1:5–6; 9:32). Their ongoing trouble, shame, and distress still matter to the Lord (1:3, 7; 9:33–34, 37). The faithful would also learn that God prospers the work of his people (2:20; 6:16). Therefore, in response to his mercies, they must confess their sin (1:6–7; 9:2, 29, 37) and hear and obey God's Word (8:1–3, 8, 14, 18; 9:3; 10:29). Their pledge to covenantal faithfulness (9:38–10:39) entails their support of temple function and faithful worship (10:32–39; 12:44–47; 13:10–14) and their practicing of that which sets them apart as a holy people. This includes Sabbath keeping (10:31; 13:15–18) and a proper separation from the nations (10:30; 13:1–3, 23–28). Such matters transition to the theological features discussed below.

Genre and Literary Features

Nehemiah shares with Ezra the broad genre classification of historiography, that is, an account of past events shaped literarily for theological purposes.[5] Similar to the "Ezra Memoir," a prominent feature of the book is Nehemiah's first-person narration, conveniently called the "Nehemiah Memoir" (Neh. 1:1–7:5a; 12:27–43; 13:4–31).[6] Most of this autobiographical material narrates events within the first year of Nehemiah's return and only briefly his several illustrative attempts at reform more than a decade later.

Also like Ezra, Nehemiah contains multiple subgenres presented as part of this single literary work. These include historical narrative (1:1–3; 2:1–20; 4:1–3, 6–23; 5:1–18; 6:10–13, 15–19; 7:1–5; 7:73b–8:18; 9:1–5a; 11:1–2; 12:27–47; 13:1–13, 15–22a, 23–28, 30–31a); a report of correspondence (6:1–9a); prayers both long (1:4–11a; 9:5b–37) and short (4:4–5, 5:19; 6:9b, 14; 13:14, 22b, 29, 31b); and a first-person account of the covenant adopted by the people (9:38; 10:28–39). Along with these, the book includes multiple lists: persons who worked on the wall (3:1–32); a genealogy of returned exiles (7:6–7:73a); those who signed the covenant (10:1–27); persons who repopulated Jerusalem (11:3–24); villages settled outside of Jerusalem (11:25–36); and priests and Levites (12:1–26). The combination of archival material and the interweaving of first- and third-person narrative are unique features to biblical literature.[7]

Theology of Nehemiah; Relationship to the Rest of the Bible and to Christ

Nehemiah demonstrates multiple connections with nearly every portion of the OT canon but particularly with the Pentateuch, Historical Books, and Prophets. There are no direct quotations of Nehemiah in the NT (cf. 9:6; Acts 4:24).

---

5 For the canonical location of Nehemiah, cf. Introduction to Ezra: Genre and Literary Features.
6 While often included in the memoir, there is debate on who is responsible for the origins and inclusion of 3:1–32 and 7:6–72a in Nehemiah's first-person account.
7 Michael W. Duggan, *The Covenant Renewal in Ezra-Nehemiah (Neh. 7:72b–10:40): An Exegetical, Literary, and Theological Study*, SBLDS 164 (Atlanta: SBL, 2001), 37; Tamara Cohn Eskenazi, *In an Age of Prose: A Literary Approach to Ezra-Nehemiah*, SBLMS 36 (Atlanta: Scholars, 1988), 180.

GOD SECURES HIS EXILED PEOPLE IN A WALLED CITY

The rebuilding of the altar and temple (Ezra 3–6) is followed by the reconstitution and repentance of the people under God's Law (Ezra 7–10). Then, through
the efforts of Nehemiah and the people, God rebuilds a second physical structure,
the wall, by once more working his purposes in history through the decision of a
Persian king (Neh. 2:1–8; 6:16; cf. Ezra 1:1; 6:14). The house of God, once burned,
has been rebuilt. A people once exiled have been brought home (2 Kings 25:9–11;
Neh. 7:4; 11:1–2). The wall of Jerusalem, once battered by the Babylonians (2 Kings
25:10) and halted later by Artaxerxes's command (cf. Ezra 4:21–24), is rebuilt by
the command of that same king. All of this is undergirded by prayer (Neh. 2:4–5;
6:15–16),[8] the answers to which show that God is attentive to the ongoing "trouble
and shame" of his people (1:3).

Of course, when Nehemiah is mentioned it is the wall of Jerusalem that comes
to mind. But the significance of the wall is that it enables God's people to live in
Jerusalem, his holy habitation. This is the location of his temple and the place where
he chooses to have his name dwell (1:9; Deut. 12:5, 11, 14, 18, 26; 1 Kings 8:27–30;
Isa. 60:14). Stated differently, what the wall accomplishes is the ability of the people
to live once more with God in their midst, fulfilling biblical themes and promises
running from the Pentateuch to the Prophets. In the Pentateuch, God promised that
he would dwell with and walk among his people (Lev. 26:11–12). Even the curse of
exile was not the end but would be met with gracious restoration (Deut. 30:1–5).

Likewise, from the beginning of Ezra-Nehemiah prophetic words undergird
both the certainty of exile (Jer. 25:8–11) and the command to return and rebuild
(Ezra 1:1; 6:14; cf. Isa. 41:2; 44:26–45:1; 58:12; 61:4; Jer. 25:12–14; 29:10–14). The
Lord had promised that he would "gather" his long-suffering remnant (Neh. 1:9),[9]
a promise found in both the Major (Isa. 54:7; 56:8; Jer. 32:37; Ezek. 11:16–17) and
the Minor Prophets (Mic. 2:12; 4:6; Zeph. 3:18–20; Zech. 10:8–10). This promise of
restoration, together with the promise of God's dwelling in the midst of his regath-
ered people, form the foundation of Nehemiah's opening prayer (Neh. 1:8–9).

GOD MAINTAINS A COVENANT WITH HIS REPENTANT PEOPLE

However, the concerns of Ezra-Nehemiah go beyond the physical structures of
temple and wall. Indeed, while Ezra and Nehemiah are important leaders, the
emphasis falls upon the role of the restored community, evident in the lists of
people in the second half of Nehemiah (7:6–73a; 10:1–27; 12:1–26).[10] The wall
had been destroyed as part of Israel's chastisement for past iniquities. Its rebuilding would signal God's covenantal faithfulness and restoration of his people.
Therefore, it is no accident that immediately following completion of a physical
wall the people determine to renew the covenant, beginning with the reading of
the Law (ch. 8) and concluding with renewed covenantal promises. The covenant

---

8 Oeming, "Theological Ideas," 141.
9 Cf. Introduction to Ezra: Theology of Ezra; and the Response section on Ezra 8.
10 Eskenazi draws special attention to the role of the people in *Age of Prose*. See especially the treatment of
the renewed covenant (chs. 8–10) on 96–111.

functions like a wall itself, erecting important markers of corporate identity: obedience to God's Law (10:29), a recommitment to separation and Sabbath practices (10:30–31), and the promise not to "neglect the house of our God" (10:39). Such remarkable corporate repentance and determination to walk in God's statutes are alluded to in earlier prophetic promises (Jer. 32:39–40; Ezek. 11:19; 36:26–28).

The literary and theological center of the covenant and spiritual peak of Ezra-Nehemiah is the great redemptive-historical prayer of the Levites (Neh. 9:5–37) that follows the initial readings of the Law (8:1–8, 18). The impact of that reading is dramatic, resulting in evidences of repentance, further reading of the Law, and worship (9:1–5a). Stirrings of spiritual renewal lead to the prayer itself, whose themes carry forward the penitential prayers of both Ezra (Ezra 9:6–15) and Nehemiah (Neh. 1:5–11). Covering creation to their present moment, the prayer offers a summary and theological interpretation of Israel's entire story with nearly limitless connections to the rest of the OT. Rhetorically, the prayer marks out the community's cry for salvation in the face of slavery and oppression (9:36–37) and an implicit recommitment to the Lord and his Word. Although the people's fathers showed signs of ongoing unbelief (9:16–17, 26, 29–30), God is still the God who "keeps covenant and steadfast love" (9:32), as Nehemiah had prayed previously (1:5). His mercies, so apparent in their history (9:17, 19, 27–28, 31), still remain possible for those who keep his covenant.

GOD GIVES JOY TO HIS PURIFIED PEOPLE

The dedication of the wall is the celebration of a completed building project. However, it is also much more. The sacrifices and especially the rejoicing that dominate the grand finale (12:43) are offered up by a people thankful that their faithful God has kept his promises to them. They celebrate their restoration as a purified people, the true Israel, inhabiting Jerusalem, God's holy city (12:27–30; 11:1, 18). And yet, as the final chapter of Nehemiah shows, they must be vigilant to persevere in repentance and faithfulness (13:4–31) and not forsake the house of God (13:11; cf. 10:39).

This portrait of the hope of a purified community dwelling with God in his holy city finds its completion in Christ Jesus. In Christ, God has shown himself faithful to the everlasting covenant made first with Abram (Gen. 12:1–3; 17:7, 13, 19; Gal. 3:16). He has secured both home and inheritance for his exiled people (Matt. 5:5; John 14:2–3; 1 Pet. 1:1, 17; 2:11). Through his atoning death Christ has cleansed both Jew and Gentile by faith (Eph. 5:26; Titus 2:14; 1 John 1:7–9). He gathers his scattered people in this age (John 10:16; 11:51–52; Acts 15:15–17) and finally in the age to come (Matt. 3:12; 13:30, 47–50; 25:31–32; 2 Thess. 2:1). The destiny of the "ransomed of the LORD" is Zion (Isa. 35:10), the "holy city, the new Jerusalem" (Rev. 21:2–4), where they will dwell with God. Until that day the redeemed continue God's mission and testify to his goodness and expand his kingdom. All this is done with the "help of our God" so that the nations might hear, fear, and turn to him (Neh. 6:16; 12:43).

Preaching from Nehemiah

With its thirteen chapters composed primarily of narrative, Nehemiah could be preached in a moderately short sermon series. However, as noted in the Introduction to Ezra, the congregation would benefit from working through both books in canonical order, because the climactic point of Ezra-Nehemiah is the covenant renewal and final celebration in Nehemiah 7:73b–13:3. A series on both books could be done within half a year or shorter if several chapters are addressed per sermon (e.g., Ezra 1–2; Neh. 11:1–12:26).

An old nursery rhyme begins, "Here's the church and here's the steeple, open the door and see all the people." It is easy to focus on the physical structures, church and steeple, and neglect the population within. That danger also exists in preaching through Nehemiah. Leadership and the congregational support of building programs are important features of the book and could quickly become the main thing of a sermon series. Although this would not be inappropriate if carefully done, it is not the primary emphasis of the book.[11] As in all good preaching, the attention of any sermon series on Ezra-Nehemiah must remain on the person and work of the Lord. Through his sovereign power a penitent remnant rebuilds both temple and wall. In his great mercy and covenantal faithfulness God spares this remnant, and they respond by renewing their covenant. At its core this represents the great covenantal promise, "You shall be my people, and I will be your God" (Ezek. 36:28). It is this core covenantal theme of the ingathering of a purified people that culminates in the person and work of Christ and points to its final conclusion with a holy people dwelling and rejoicing with God in his holy city (Neh. 11:1; 12:30, 43; Rev. 21:1–4).

Like any book of Christian Scripture, Nehemiah presents its own difficulties and rewards in preaching. Particular challenges will arise from varied lists within the book (cf. Genre and Literary Features). Passages like this should not be neglected. In the Response sections in this commentary, every effort has been made to think sermonically in order to provoke further reflection for users of this commentary. More positively, the prayers (Neh. 1:4–11; 9:5b–37) demonstrate a rich connection to the rest of the Bible. These reveal to congregations how a positive view of the Law shaped the repentance and worship of God's ancient people (9:1–5a) and should continue to guide the redeemed community.

Interpretive Challenges

WERE EZRA AND NEHEMIAH CONTEMPORARIES?

At the covenant renewal in Nehemiah 7:73b–10:39, Ezra and Nehemiah are found together for the first time (8:9).[12] This implies a gap of at least thirteen years

---

11 See "Leadership and Ezra-Nehemiah," the concluding essay in David J. Shepherd and Christopher J. H. Wright, *Ezra and Nehemiah*, THOTC (Grand Rapids, MI: Eerdmans, 2018), 188–211.
12 Elsewhere, only the event of wall dedication brings them together (12:31, 33, 36). They are also mentioned together at the end of the lists of priests and Levites at 12:26. The Azariah mentioned in the list of covenant signees at 10:2 may be Ezra, though this is debated. If this is Ezra, it provides another instance in which both men are found in a list, since Nehemiah is mentioned at 10:1. Clines notes that the suggestion that Ezra's name is an editorial insertion at 12:36 is held by most scholars and "very plausible" (*Ezra, Nehemiah, Esther,*

between Ezra's arrival in Jerusalem (458 BC; cf. Ezra 7:8) and his reading of the Law at the Water Gate (Neh. 8:2–3)—at the earliest 445 (cf. Neh. 2:1). This lack of interaction and thirteen-year gap are part of the larger debate of the chronological order of Ezra and Nehemiah (cf. Introduction to Ezra). The crux of the problem for many commentators is how Ezra could possibly have waited so many years to heed the explicit and initial charge of Artaxerxes (Ezra 7:12) to implement "the Law of your God" (Ezra 7:14, 25–26). In other words, we have no evidence that he actually followed through with the charge placed upon him by Artaxerxes. Writing on Nehemiah 12:27–43, one commentator states it clearly: "The question of whether Ezra and Nehemiah were ever together in Jerusalem has been one of the major topics of debate in regard to these books."[13]

This lack of cooperation leads many to believe that Ezra's reading of the Law at Nehemiah 7:73b–8:18 (and some include Neh. 9:1–37) was part of Ezra's earlier reform and originally located not in Nehemiah but placed between Ezra 8 and 9.[14] In other words, the events of Nehemiah 8 are believed to have occurred in the year of Ezra's arrival in Jerusalem. Not only would this mean that Ezra actually taught the Law as required by Artaxerxes; placing this event in Ezra would also fit chronologically. For example, Ezra arrived in Jerusalem in the fifth month (Ezra 7:8) and commenced his marriage reforms in the ninth month (10:9), and it would make good sense that these reforms took place in response to his reading of the Law in the seventh month, which happens to be the very month (though of a different year) mentioned in Nehemiah 8:2, 14.[15]

Proponents of this approach therefore hold that Ezra's reading of the Law was editorially placed in Nehemiah either by accident or for thematic or theological purposes—to show that covenant renewal was the climax of Ezra-Nehemiah.[16] As a result, Nehemiah's name at 8:9 must have been added by an editor or scribe who placed the text in its current location and also changed Ezra's first-person narrative into a third-person narrative.[17] In addition, if Nehemiah 8 was originally part of Ezra 7–10, the historical settings of Nehemiah 9–10 must also be addressed, given their connections with what precedes in Nehemiah 8 (cf. Neh. 9:1).[18] Blenkinsopp's comment on 9:1–5 seems fitting to the whole of 7:73b–10:39 when he states that there are as many opinions as there are commentators.[19]

It is not possible to address the multiple interlocking arguments fully here.[20] However there are several points to consider. First, while it is true that Ezra does not read the Law in Ezra 7–10, this does not mean that he did not apply it. This is

---

232). However, he also notes that "it cannot be proved that Ezra's participation is unhistorical." Editorial insertion of Ezra's name is asserted by Blenkinsopp, *Ezra-Nehemiah*, 346.

13 Williamson, *Ezra, Nehemiah*, 372.

14 Ibid., 283–286, calls this view a "widespread and wholly correct scholarly consensus" (283). Both Clines (*Ezra, Nehemiah, Esther*, 180–182) and Blenkinsopp (*Ezra-Nehemiah*, 45) concur.

15 An alternative suggestion is that Nehemiah 8 follows Ezra 10, since in 1 *Esdras*, Neh. 7:73–8:13 follows immediately after Ezra 10:44 as a more optimistic conclusion to the marriage reforms.

16 Williamson, *Ezra, Nehemiah*, 286.

17 Ibid., 147

18 Duggan, *Covenant Renewal*, 8–9.

19 Blenkinsopp, *Ezra-Nehemiah*, 294.

20 For arguments supporting the biblical presentation that Ezra and Nehemiah were contemporaries see Derek Kidner, *Ezra and Nehemiah: An Introduction and Commentary*, TOTC 12 (Downers Grove, IL: InterVarsity

clear in his prayer (Ezra 9:10–12). Second, the Law reading on the first day of the seventh month (Neh. 8:2) also fits well chronologically in Nehemiah since it follows the prior temporal notice that wall completion occurred in Elul, the sixth month (Neh. 6:15). Third, there is a tendency to question the contemporaneous ministries of Ezra and Nehemiah while ignoring the possibility that they may indeed have been contemporaries.[21] If the ministries of Ezra and Nehemiah did not overlap, how did the actual course of events (i.e., that they were not contemporaries) lead to the current canonical shape in which they are placed together? It is plausible but difficult to accept that the final editor brought Ezra and Nehemiah together as contemporaries merely for theological purposes. Finally, as Clines notes, if one is not willing to accept the reconstruction and to view Nehemiah's name at 8:9 as the work of the editor, the alternatives are to (1) emend the dates of Ezra's arrival (Ezra 7:7–8) or (2) suppose that Ezra did not read the Law until Nehemiah's arrival.[22] The latter position is reasonable. The fact that cooperation between Ezra and Nehemiah is discussed only in a limited way in Ezra-Nehemiah does not mean there was not more cooperation; it only means that detailing the cooperation was not important to the story that is preserved.

Outline

I. The Lord and Cyrus Issue Decrees and the Community Responds (Ezra 1:1–11)

II. The Community Rebuilds Temple, Torah, and Wall according to the Decrees (Ezra 2:1–Neh. 7:73a)

    A. The List of Exiles Returning (Ezra 2:1–70)[23]

    B. First Movement: Altar, Opposition, and Temple (Ezra 3:1–6:22)

    C. Second Movement: Ezra Reconstitutes the People under Torah (Ezra 7:1–10:44)

    D. Third Movement: Nehemiah's Ministry Commences (Neh. 1:1–7:4)

        1. Nehemiah Offers a Prayerful Request (1:1–11)

        2. Nehemiah Receives Permission and Arrives in Jerusalem (2:1–20)

        3. Wall-Gate Restoration (3:1–3:32)

        4. Builders Make Progress with Some Trepidation (4:1–24)

        5. Governor Nehemiah Shows "Interest" for All (5:1–19)

        6. Enemy Attempts to Frighten Nehemiah Cannot Stop the Wall (6:1–7:4)

Press, 1979), 161–175. Kidner addresses the question of "infrequent co-operation" as the first of four "apparent anomalies" that led to the view that Ezra followed Nehemiah chronologically (cf. Introduction to Ezra).
21 For examples, see Williamson, *Ezra, Nehemiah*, 282, and Clines, *Ezra, Nehemiah, Esther*, 232.
22 Clines, *Ezra, Nehemiah, Esther*, 185.
23 In this commentary Ezra and Nehemiah are treated as one book. In order to show how the whole coheres, the large blocks of text from Ezra are included before the start of Nehemiah at point II.D. The core ideas for this broad structure are indebted to Eskenazi, *Age of Prose*, 37–126. She observes, "This major repetition [i.e., Ezra 2–Nehemiah 7] re-presents the major character, provides continuity for the section as a whole and unifies the events in between" (39). Others argue for treating Nehemiah as a literary work independent of Ezra; see Mark J. Boda, "Prayer as Rhetoric in the Book of Nehemiah," in *New Perspectives on Ezra-Nehemiah: History and Historiography, Text, Literature, and Interpretation*, ed., Isaac Kalimi (Winona Lake, IN: Eisenbrauns, 2012), 267–284 (esp. 276, 284).

NEHEMIAH 1:1–11

1 The words of Nehemiah the son of Hacaliah.

Now it happened in the month of Chislev, in the twentieth year, as I was in Susa the citadel, **2** that Hanani, one of my brothers, came with certain men from Judah. And I asked them concerning the Jews who escaped, who had survived the exile, and concerning Jerusalem. **3** And they said to me, "The remnant there in the province who had survived the exile is in great trouble and shame. The wall of Jerusalem is broken down, and its gates are destroyed by fire."

⁴ As soon as I heard these words I sat down and wept and mourned for days, and I continued fasting and praying before the God of heaven. ⁵ And I said, "O LORD God of heaven, the great and awesome God who keeps covenant and steadfast love with those who love him and keep his commandments, ⁶ let your ear be attentive and your eyes open, to hear the prayer of your servant that I now pray before you day and night for the people of Israel your servants, confessing the sins of the people of Israel, which we have sinned against you. Even I and my father's house have sinned. ⁷ We have acted very corruptly against you and have not kept the commandments, the statutes, and the rules that you commanded your servant Moses. ⁸ Remember the word that you commanded your servant Moses, saying, 'If you are unfaithful, I will scatter you among the peoples, ⁹ but if you return to me and keep my commandments and do them, though your outcasts are in the uttermost parts of heaven, from there I will gather them and bring them to the place that I have chosen, to make my name dwell there.' ¹⁰ They are your servants and your people, whom you have redeemed by your great power and by your strong hand. ¹¹ O Lord, let your ear be attentive to the prayer of your servant, and to the prayer of your servants who delight to fear your name, and give success to your servant today, and grant him mercy in the sight of this man."

Now I was cupbearer to the king.

Section Overview

In current editions of the Hebrew Bible, this first chapter of Nehemiah follows immediately from the end of Ezra with no break, since Ezra and Nehemiah were treated historically as one book. The introductory section of Ezra-Nehemiah (Ezra 1) began by narrating the initial return of Israelites under Zerubbabel and Jeshua by authority of the Persian king Cyrus (538 BC).

The second section (Ezra 2:1–Neh. 7:73a) began with the list of returnees who rebuilt the temple, completed in 516. More than half a century later, Ezra then led a second return to Jerusalem under the authority of Artaxerxes in the latter's seventh year (458; Ezra 7–8). This was followed by the crisis of mixed marriages and the final list of those who pledged to put away their foreign wives (Ezra 9–10). This second section of Ezra-Nehemiah (Ezra 2:1–Neh. 7:73a) concludes in the book of Nehemiah. The major conflict facing a new figure named Nehemiah focuses on the reestablishment of Jerusalem's wall (Neh. 1:1–7:4). The episode begins with Jerusalem's wall and gates in disrepair and concludes with the city secured (1:3; 7:1–4). It may also be noted that Nehemiah, like Zerubbabel and Ezra, receives authority to act from a Persian king, although now in the "twentieth year" of that king's reign (1:1; 2:1) and so thirteen years after Ezra's return (445).

The title for the book (Neh. 1:1a) is followed by the commencement of narration. A report is brought to Nehemiah on the sorry state of Jerusalem's defenses and the shame brought on the returnees as a result (vv. 1b–3). He responds immediately with the second major prayer in Ezra-Nehemiah (vv. 4–11; cf. Ezra 9:6–15), a prayer dense with allusions to Deuteronomy. The unit closes with a surprising notice of Nehemiah's status (Neh. 1:11b).

Section Outline

   II. The Community Rebuilds Temple, Torah, and Wall according to the Decree (Ezra 2:1–Neh. 7:73a) . . .

      D. Third Movement: Nehemiah's Ministry Commences (Neh. 1:1–7:4)

         1. Nehemiah Offers a Prayerful Request (1:1–11)

           a. Title: Nehemiah's Words (1:1a)

           b. Nehemiah Receives Word That Jerusalem Is in Disrepair (1:1b–3)

           c. Nehemiah Fasts and Offers a Prayer (1:4–11a)

           d. Notice: Nehemiah's Vocation (1:11b)

Comment

1:1a The opening parallels several prophetic introductions (Jer. 1:1; Amos 1:1) and wisdom texts attributed to specific persons (Prov. 30:1; 31:1; Eccles. 1:1). Nehemiah's name means "Yahweh has comforted," but apart from being called Hacaliah's son (Neh. 1:1; 10:1) and having a brother named Hanani (1:2), nothing else is known of Nehemiah's upbringing or family background. He uses first-person narrative much more than Ezra (Neh. 1:1–7:5; 12:31–43; 13:4–31),[24] leading to the book's very personal feel.

1:1b–3 Nehemiah begins by stating the time and his location when approached by "certain men from Judah," including his brother Hanani (7:2). This is likely his actual brother, or a near relative (as opposed to "brother" referring simply to a fellow Jew). Whether Hanani arrived in Susa with the group or simply introduced them to Nehemiah is uncertain. Susa, nearly always identified with "the citadel," was an elevated region upon which sat the king's palace (e.g., Est. 1:2, 5; 2:3). It was also the name of the city (Est. 3:15). Both city and citadel were located about 225 miles (362 km) east of Babylon; the citadel functioned as the winter residence of the Achaemenid (i.e., Persian) kings.[25] Its winter use therefore makes sense of the group's arrival in the month of Chislev (November/December), the ninth month (cf. Ezra 10:9).[26] The notice of these events "in the twentieth year" likely refers to the twentieth year (445 BC) of Artaxerxes I (464–423; cf. Neh. 2:1), thirteen years since Ezra's arrival.[27] The text states neither Nehemiah's particular purpose in Susa nor the purpose of this group of persons who travel from Judah to see him.

---

24 These portions are known in the secondary literature as the "Nehemiah Memoirs."

25 The term "Achaemenid dynasty" to refer to the reigns of Persian kings arises from the earliest founder of the dynasty, Achaemenes. The dynasty stretches back just under a century before Cyrus (559–530 BC). The summer residence of the Persian kings, Ecbatana, is mentioned in Ezra 6:2.

26 Ran Zadok, "Some Issues in Ezra-Nehemiah," in *New Perspectives on Ezra-Nehemiah: History and Historiography, Text, Literature, and Interpretation,* ed. Isaac Kalimi (Winona Lake, IN: Eisenbrauns, 2012), 161.

27 Nisan (March/April; Neh. 2:1) started the calendrical year for Persian and Jewish calendars. Therefore, the meeting in the ninth month, Chislev (1:1b–4), could not happen in the same year as that mentioned in 2:1 but must be in Artaxerxes's nineteenth year. If Nehemiah is following a regnal rather than calendar year, however, both months would fall within Artaxerxes's twentieth year. The best alternative suggestion is that the new year began in the autumn, in which case Chislev and Nisan would occur in the same year; F. Charles Fensham, *The Books of Ezra and Nehemiah,* NICOT (Grand Rapids, MI: Eerdmans, 1982), 150. However, there is no evidence as early as Nehemiah's day for this later Jewish liturgical practice. Williamson provides a solid discussion of the various proposals (*Ezra, Nehemiah,* 169–170).

Nehemiah expresses several concerns to the group. First, he wonders about persons living in Judea ("the province"), but the language "who escaped, who had survived the exile" is somewhat ambiguous. It may refer to those who remained in the land and never went into exile or to those who returned to Jerusalem from Babylon, or perhaps both. The noun translated "escaped" is rendered "remnant" at Ezra 9:8, 13, 15 and is found elsewhere with the verb rendered "survived" only at Ezra 9:8, 15. There "remnant" is a technical term for the community that has returned from Babylon. Here Nehemiah likely broadens the reference to any Jewish survivor now in Judah.[28] The nature of his concern for the city of Jerusalem is not further specified.

The inquiry about people and place receives a reply that drives Nehemiah's response and the whole story that follows. "The remnant . . . who had survived the exile" is described as enduring "great trouble and shame" (Neh. 1:3)—but why? First, they cannot escape the ongoing vision of their destroyed city, provoking a constant reminder of past guilt, defeat, and death (cf. Ezra 9:7). Beyond this, their defenseless state due to failed walls and gates threads its way through the story and must be remedied (Neh. 1:3; 2:8, 13, 15, 17; 3:13, 15; 6:1; 7:1; 12:30, 31, 37). Finally, opponents would point out the impotence or unwillingness of their God to deliver them (cf. 2 Kings 18:28–35). While "shame" may arise for numerous reasons, in this context it refers to the taunts and insults suffered at the hands of their enemies due to their weakened state (Jer. 24:9). The following chapter confirms this, making it clear that "trouble" and "derision" (= "shame") arise from the sorry condition of Jerusalem's gates and wall (Neh. 2:17).

1:4 Nehemiah's inclination to act finds initial expression in his anguished response. Like Ezra's (Ezra 9:3–5), Nehemiah's response is immediate, emotive, and God directed: "I sat down and wept and mourned." The past tense translation should not be viewed as if they started and stopped at once.[29] Rather, the two verbal forms that follow ("fasting and praying") include all of these actions to summarize that Nehemiah's ongoing activity lasts "for days." In this way, the prayer that follows summarizes what Nehemiah prays over several months.

It may be noted that Jerusalem's degraded defenses resulting from Nebuchadnezzar's onslaught is not new news to Nehemiah. That trauma is long past and the results seared into the mind of the postexilic community (cf. Lamentations). Besides, the very presence of the group "from Judah" (Neh. 1:2) as well as the letters in Ezra (Ezra 5:6–17; 6:1–12; 7:7–26; cf. Jer. 29:1) evidence the effective communication between Jerusalem and Persia. So why does he respond so strongly? The text does not say. Perhaps Nehemiah mourns the lack of tangible progress in all reconstruction in the intervening period. Alternatively, perhaps the initial start is obstructed or reversed by the forceful opposition of Rehum (Ezra 4:11–16, 23). In this view, the event is indeed recent, which may explain Nehemiah's passionate response.

---

28 Clines, *Ezra, Nehemiah, Esther*, 137; Williamson, *Ezra, Nehemiah*, 171.
29 Cf. NET: "When I heard these things I sat down abruptly, crying and mourning for several days."

1:5 Ezra's prayer focused primarily on the specific problem of mixed marriages (Ezra 9:6–15). Overall, Nehemiah's prayer is more generic, overflowing with biblical references, especially from Deuteronomy, centering upon Israel's covenantal relationship with the "Lord God of heaven."[30] The prayer begins and ends by asking God to "be attentive" (Neh. 1:6, 11a). The central supplication to "remember" (vv. 8–10) provides a key synopsis of the covenantal blessings and curses.

As is fitting, Nehemiah first recalls God's character (v. 5). With the title "great and awesome God" he invokes the Lord's power and justice, especially his works in dealing with Israel's enemies (Neh. 4:14; 9:32; Deut. 7:21; 10:17; Ps. 66:3; Dan. 9:4). Opponents may continually threaten Israel's security due to Jerusalem's lack of wall and gates, but Israel must not let past trauma deter their current comfort in the God who has done great and awesome things for them (2 Sam. 7:23). These past deliverances do not simply reveal God's overwhelming power; they also provide the core of his self-identification as the God of utter fidelity and devotion to his people. And yet, as in a committed marriage, each partner must express reciprocal love in mutual obligation and responsibility. Nehemiah thus underscores that the favor of the covenant-keeping God of steadfast love rests upon those who "love him and keep his commandments" (Neh. 1:5; cf. Deut. 7:9; Josh. 22:5; 1 Kings 8:23; Dan. 9:4). A God faithful to his people seeks a people devoted to their God (Ex. 6:7; Jer. 7:23; 11:4; 24:7; 31:33).

1:6–7 Using human physical characteristics, Nehemiah first requests that God's ears and eyes be especially attentive to hear his words and see his agony (1 Kings 8:28–29; 2 Chron. 6:40; 7:15; Ps. 130:2; Isa. 37:17). His prayer, offered "before you day and night," exemplifies the kind of petitions he makes over four months (cf. Neh. 1:1; 2:1). Knowing his own covenantal failures and those of the postexilic community, his prayer rightly starts with confession (Ezra 10:1; Dan. 9:4, 20). Acknowledgment of sin is welcomed by the Lord and does not disqualify further identification of his people as "your servants" (Neh. 1:6, 10, 11). Like Ezra, by his use of "we" Nehemiah identifies with the sin of his community and further admits to the sin in his own family. Although not mentioning specific sins, the combination of "the commandments, the statutes, and the rules" references the comprehensive teaching of Moses as the expression of God's will for his people. Obedience to Mosaic instruction reflects love for God and distinguishes the true Israel (Lev. 26:15; Deut. 5:31; 6:1; 7:11; 8:11; 11:1; 26:17; 30:16; 1 Kings 8:58; 2 Kings 17:34, 37; Neh. 9:13; 10:29). Unfortunately, God's people have failed miserably in this regard, and Nehemiah's language emphatically expresses that in their not heeding Moses' instructions they have "acted very corruptly." With these generic admissions it is easy to forget the danger that sin poses. In the presence of a holy God, failure to keep these commandments is synonymous with hating God, and judgment remains the outcome barring repentance and atonement (Ex. 20:5–6; Deut. 7:10; 9:18–19; Isa. 6:5).

---

30 Cf. comment on Ezra 1:2–4 for the phrase "God of heaven."

1:8–10 These verses express the core of the prayer and the grace of the passage and may be summarized with *Remember your word* (vv. 8–9) and *Remember your people* (v. 10).

Broadly, verses 8–9 summarize the concluding portions of any covenant document, in which we find the curses for those who refuse obedience and the blessings for those who embrace and keep the covenant (e.g., Leviticus 26; Deuteronomy 27–28). More specifically, these verses use the language of Deuteronomy 30:1–5[31] to point to its particular promise: the Lord will restore his people from exile when they repent.

The verses begin by recalling the Lord's warnings. Verse 8b emphasizes the pronoun—"if *you* are unfaithful"—and uses the strong verb "to be unfaithful" (Hb. *ma'al*) to describe the people's sin. This verb (Ezra 10:2, 10; Neh. 1:8; 13:27) and its related noun ("faithlessness"; Ezra 9:2, 4; 10:6) most recently characterized the sorrowful events at the end of Ezra.[32] They describe any treacherous act against the Lord, a condition which, if met, brings about the judgment, also described with another emphatic pronoun: "*I* will scatter you among the peoples" (cf. Lev. 26:33; Deut. 4:27–28; 28:64; Jer. 9:13–16; Ezek. 12:15; 20:18–26; 22:15). The Lord had fulfilled these threats in their recent experience.

However, judgment is never the end of the story for the remnant, and Nehemiah 1:9 turns quickly to hope. By God's merciful correction, faithless treachery may be turned to confession and repentance: "If you return" (cf. Lev. 26:40–45; Deut. 4:29–31). It is then that the God who scatters shows himself also to be the God who gathers. Indeed, he will go to the "uttermost parts of heaven" to retrieve the repentant. This promise not only summarizes Deuteronomy 30:1–5 but is an overture of hope woven throughout the prophets (Isa. 43:5; Jer. 23:3; 29:14; 31:8, 10; 32:37; Ezek. 11:16–20; 34:11–16; 36:24; 37:21; Mic. 4:6–7; Zeph. 3:18–20; Zech. 10:8–10). In further links to Deuteronomy, the Lord has promised to bring them "to the place that I have chosen, to make my name dwell there," namely, his temple home in Jerusalem (Neh. 1:9; cf. Deut. 12:5–6, 11; 14:23; 1 Kings 12:27). And herein resides the problem: Jerusalem's current condition brings "great trouble and shame" (Neh. 1:3).

In sum: positively, the people of Israel are no longer characterized as "verse 8 people," chastised, scattered, and languishing under covenant curses. Instead, they are "verse 9 people," experiencing covenant blessings, now returning to God through confession, reaffirming their determination to keep the commandments, and, in this moment of favor (Ezra 9:8), gathered and restored by God. Negatively, they await the completed restoration and repopulation of Jerusalem.

Nehemiah then further defines those who experience God's redeeming favor: they are both "your servants" and "your people" (Neh. 1:10). In other words, they are not simply servants but also Israel, offspring of the patriarchs and heirs to the covenant promises, a fact to which Moses returns on more than one occasion to

---

31 "Scatter" (Deut. 30:3), "gather" (Deut. 30:3), "outcasts" which are "in the uttermost parts of heaven" (Deut. 30:4), and "return" and obey commandments (Deut. 30:2); Shepherd and Wright, *Ezra and Nehemiah*, 51.
32 For more detailed discussion of the term, cf. comment on Ezra 9:1–2.

plead for the Lord to turn away wrath and not destroy them in the face of their unfaithfulness (Ex. 32:13–14; Deut. 9:29). More specifically, Nehemiah echoes a prayer previously uttered by Solomon, who asks the attentive God to "hear in heaven" the confession of his servants, "if they turn again," and to grant forgiveness and restoration after exile (1 Kings 8:27–36). In fact, it is "*your* servants" and "*your* people" who are those redeemed by "*your* great power" and "*your* strong hand." The prevailing use of this language recalls the numerous events of salvation surrounding the exodus from Egypt.[33] So Nehemiah pleads for God to exhibit once more the power that redeemed them.

1:11a Nehemiah summarizes his prayer by once again asking God to "be attentive" (v. 11; cf. v. 6). He makes his final appeal for answered prayer not only for himself as "servant" but also in solidarity with all of those who are "servants." Notice, however, the impact of repentance. They are characterized no longer as those who have "sinned against you" (v. 6) but as those "who delight to fear your name" (cf. Ezra 9:4; 10:3), that is, those who delight to acknowledge the Lord as the one who is to be worshiped reverently and whose commandments are to be obeyed faithfully (cf. Deut. 6:13; 10:20; 28:58). Nehemiah's request for success "today" prepares the reader for his upcoming audience with the king (Neh. 2:1–8). He knows that only God's mercy could succeed in changing the mind of "this man," soon revealed as Artaxerxes. Nehemiah's difficult situation is clarified when we remember that it was Artaxerxes's prior decree that had stopped wall reconstruction (Ezra 4:21).

1:11b In a surprising ending, "this man" (v. 11a) seems connected with the king for whom Nehemiah is cupbearer. In the ancient Near East, this influential post was held by one who was trusted to taste the king's wine and granted royal access as a confidant.[34] In the first part of this verse, Nehemiah pleads with God to "give success" and "grant . . . mercy" before Artaxerxes (cf. 2:8; Ezra 1:1; 5:5; 6:14; 7:27). Presently, we are uncertain what this entails but can make an educated guess. Artaxerxes had once stopped the wall construction (Ezra 4:21–23). Accepting the call to rebuild those very walls to alleviate "trouble and shame" (Neh. 1:3) will mean Nehemiah must request permission from Artaxerxes to do so, a dangerous request that may be viewed as sedition and threat (Ezra 4:16, 22; Neh. 6:6–7). This prepares us for what follows in the next chapter.

Response

Nehemiah responds to the "great trouble and shame" of the remnant (1:3) with prayer that is persistent (v. 4), penitent (vv. 6–7), and purposeful (vv. 8–11). His confidence in approaching the Lord is grounded in God's covenant faithfulness

---

33 For "great power" and "strong hand" with respect to the exodus, cf. Exodus 6:1; 13:3, 9, 14, 16; 14:31; 32:11; Deuteronomy 4:37; 7:8; 9:26, 29; 2 Kings 17:36; Jeremiah 32:21. These are sometimes associated with the Lord's "outstretched arm": Exodus 6:6; Deuteronomy 4:34; 5:15; 7:19; 9:29; 11:2; 26:8; 2 Kings 17:36; Psalm 136:10–15; Jeremiah 32:21.
34 The probability of Nehemiah being a eunuch in the royal court receives little support beyond several LXX manuscripts that have misread "cupbearer" as "eunuch," two words that in Greek have some formal similarity.

and steadfast love (v. 5). Although our particular life experiences of "trouble and shame" will vary, we also may approach the throne of grace for our own needs and on behalf of those who need to know the steadfast love of God (Heb. 4:16).

First, we see Nehemiah's persistence in prayer. His weeping and mourning are not one-time events but last continually, "for days" (Neh. 1:4). Nehemiah knows that for the sake of the remnant he must act to rebuild the wall, but he realizes that his ongoing sorrow and need require ongoing supplication. Therefore he pleads continually, confronting the past and committing to God his future course before Artaxerxes. He asks the Lord to "be attentive" (v. 6) to his prayer not because he fears God's inattention. Rather, he knows that he must not presume upon the grace of the "great and awesome God" (v. 5; cf. 9:32). Nehemiah also knows that in the past God's "great power" and "strong hand" manifested itself in redemption from Egypt (1:10). We know that in these last days this redemptive power was revealed in the ministry, death, resurrection, and current reign of our Lord Jesus Christ (Luke 4:36; Acts 10:38; 1 Cor. 1:18, 24; 6:14; Eph. 1:19–21; Phil. 3:10; Heb. 1:3). We endure in prayer knowing that as God revealed his power to save in the past, he may once more reveal his strength in our present situation (Neh. 1:11).

However, there are occasions in which our distress is due to past unfaithfulness. On behalf of the remnant, Nehemiah confronts the past, confessing their corrupt acts in the broadest terms as a failure to keep "the commandments, the statutes, and the rules" of the covenant (v. 7; Ex. 34:1; Jer. 31:32). He does not simply confess the sins of others but implicates his own particular family in the collective transgressions that led to exile (Neh. 1:6). Key to Nehemiah's logic is his belief that the confession of verses 6–7 is equivalent to returning to God and therefore may move the Lord to complete the good work once begun.[35]

As Nehemiah prays, he does so purposefully, praying Scripture and especially asking God to "remember the word" (v. 8). In that covenantal word, the Lord promised to gather his repentant outcasts in a restored Jerusalem (v. 9; cf. Deut. 30:1–5). Because Nehemiah knows that God is powerful, he believes the Lord can act, and because he knows that God is faithful to his word, Nehemiah believes that he will act (Neh. 1:10–11).

In sum, the repentant people of God respond to the steadfast love of God, on the one hand, by loving him and obeying his commandments (vv. 5, 9). On the other hand, we also confess our sin, admitting we have not kept those commandments, which seemingly disqualifies us from the very homecoming for which we long. But rather than disqualifying us, genuine repentance actually provides evidence of his grace and mercy in our lives, fueling our desire to respond faithfully to his love (v. 9; cf. Deut. 30:6; 1 John 1:9).[36] And that evidence means we are numbered among his gathered outcasts and welcomed into the home where he dwells.

---

35 John Goldingay provides an excellent reflection upon the role of Nehemiah's prayer; *Old Testament Theology*, vol. 1, *Israel's Gospel* (Downers Grove, IL: InterVarsity, 2003), 766–768.
36 Lacking but implied in Nehemiah's reference to Deuteronomy 30:1–5 is the need for the exilic community to experience God's enabling grace, the "circumcision of the heart," which results in wholehearted devotion and life (Deut. 30:6).

NEHEMIAH 2:1–20

2 In the month of Nisan, in the twentieth year of King Artaxerxes, when wine was before him, I took up the wine and gave it to the king. Now I had not been sad in his presence. ²And the king said to me, "Why is your face sad, seeing you are not sick? This is nothing but sadness of the heart." Then I was very much afraid. ³I said to the king, "Let the king live forever! Why should not my face be sad, when the city, the place of my fathers' graves, lies in ruins, and its gates have been destroyed by fire?" ⁴Then the king said to me, "What are you requesting?" So I prayed to the God of heaven. ⁵And I said to the king, "If it pleases the king, and if your servant has found favor in your sight, that you send me to Judah, to the city of my fathers' graves, that I may rebuild it." ⁶And the king said to me (the queen sitting beside him), "How long will you be gone, and when will you return?" So it pleased the king to send me when I had given him a time. ⁷And I said to the king, "If it pleases the king, let letters be given me to the governors of the province Beyond the River, that they may let me pass through until I come to Judah, ⁸and a letter to Asaph, the keeper of the king's forest, that he may give me timber to make beams for the gates of the fortress of the temple, and for the wall of the city, and for the house that I shall occupy." And the king granted me what I asked, for the good hand of my God was upon me.

⁹Then I came to the governors of the province Beyond the River and gave them the king's letters. Now the king had sent with me officers of the army and horsemen. ¹⁰But when Sanballat the Horonite and Tobiah the Ammonite servant heard this, it displeased them greatly that someone had come to seek the welfare of the people of Israel.

¹¹So I went to Jerusalem and was there three days. ¹²Then I arose in the night, I and a few men with me. And I told no one what my God had put into my heart to do for Jerusalem. There was no animal with me but the one on which I rode. ¹³I went out by night by the Valley Gate to the Dragon Spring and to the Dung Gate, and I inspected the walls of Jerusalem that were broken down and its gates that had been destroyed by fire. ¹⁴Then I went on to the Fountain Gate and to the King's Pool, but there was no room for the animal that was under me to pass. ¹⁵Then I went up in the night by the valley and inspected the wall, and I turned back and entered by the Valley Gate, and so returned. ¹⁶And the officials did not know where I had gone or what I was doing, and I had not yet told the Jews, the priests, the nobles, the officials, and the rest who were to do the work.

¹⁷Then I said to them, "You see the trouble we are in, how Jerusalem lies in ruins with its gates burned. Come, let us build the wall of Jerusalem, that we may no longer suffer derision." ¹⁸And I told them of the hand of my God that had been upon me for good, and also of the words that the king had spoken to me. And they said, "Let us rise up and build."

So they strengthened their hands for the good work. [19] But when Sanballat the Horonite and Tobiah the Ammonite servant and Geshem the
Arab heard of it, they jeered at us and despised us and said, "What is this
thing that you are doing? Are you rebelling against the king?" [20] Then I
replied to them, "The God of heaven will make us prosper, and we his
servants will arise and build, but you have no portion or right or claim[1]
in Jerusalem."

[1] Or *memorial*

Section Overview

The events of the prior chapter lead naturally to the events that follow. Nehemiah,
aware of the "great trouble and shame" confronting the remnant (Neh. 1:1–3),
has confessed sin and implored God's favor based on his covenantal faithfulness
to a repentant people (1:6–10). More specifically, Nehemiah asked for success
before "this man," one we assume to be the king before whom he functions as
cupbearer (1:11).

Temporally, the narrative advances several months and is told in two larger
scenes. First, Nehemiah gains permission from Artaxerxes to return to Judah
(2:1–8). Next, Nehemiah pursues action in Jerusalem in the days following his
arrival (vv. 9–20). Each scene ends by ascribing all glory to God for any success
(vv. 8b, 20).

These scenes may be considered more closely. After an initial introduction to
the chapter (v. 1), the opening scene begins as a series of three royal inquiries (vv. 2,
4, 6), followed immediately by Nehemiah's replies (vv. 3, 5, 7–8a). The concluding
verses advance beyond simple answers as Nehemiah requests authorizing letters
and supplies to enable his work.

The second scene (vv. 9–20) takes place in the province "Beyond the River" (v. 9)
and may also be further subdivided. Nehemiah's arrival, though supported by
the king, is met with opposition from specific persons (vv. 9–10). We then read of
Nehemiah's nighttime expedition through Jerusalem as he inspects the walls and
gates of the city (vv. 11–16). The chapter concludes with Nehemiah openly discussing his plans with leaders and issuing a call to "rise up and build" (vv. 17–18). The
scene ends as it had begun, with reference to the specific individuals who opposed
the rebuilding effort (vv. 19–20; cf. v. 10).

Section Outline

II.D.2. Nehemiah Receives Permission and Arrives in Jerusalem (2:1–20)
- a. Nehemiah Requests and Receives Permission to Go to Judah
     (2:1–8)
- b. Nehemiah Arrives, Inspects the Walls, and Proposes to Rebuild
     (2:9–20)
     - (1) Nehemiah Arrives in Jerusalem; Adversaries Hear (2:9–10)
     - (2) Nehemiah Inspects the Walls at Night (2:11–16)

(3) Nehemiah Exhorts the Community to Rise and Rebuild
    (2:17–18)
(4) Adversaries Hear and Accuse Nehemiah of Rebellion (2:19–20)

Comment

2:1 This verse's temporal notice, providing historical context, leaps ahead approximately four months, from the ninth month, Chislev (November/December; 1:1), to the first month, Nisan (March/April; 2:1). However, both months occur in the "twentieth year" (1:1; 2:1). Thus both months (Chislev, Nisan) likely occur within the twentieth regnal year, rather than calendar year, of Artaxerxes (c. 445 BC).[37] The text further defines the setting as "when wine was before him," meaning a time when wine was served. Whether a private dinner or a banquet is in view is left unstated, though the language makes the latter more likely given the importance of the "wine banquet" as an institution for the Persians. During the preceding four months Nehemiah constantly prays (cf. comment on 1:4), seeking just the right time to bring his needs to the king.[38]

We also learn that the ensuing dialogue takes place at the precise moment in the dinner when Nehemiah actually presents the wine to the king.[39] As the end of the prior chapter marked background information with "Now" (1:11b), so here the narrative pauses briefly to provide relevant detail also marked with "Now." Nehemiah "had not been sad in his presence"—we may assume that to this moment he has silently borne the heavy emotional toll and pastoral concern for his people and for their city.

2:2–3 Three concise questions from the king (vv. 2, 4, 6) are followed by Nehemiah's responses (vv. 3, 5, 7–8a). In the interlude, just before each of his own replies, Nehemiah provides further information for his readers.

Nehemiah's facial cues give rise to the king's first question concerning the source of his "sadness of the heart," since it clearly does not arise from illness (v. 2). The three words translated "sad," "sadness," and in the next verse "be sad" are all built on the same Hebrew root (*ra'*; "evil, sad, misfortune") and underline Nehemiah's heightened state of sorrow. Significantly, his internal distress matches the external "trouble" (*ra'ah*) of Jerusalem's current state (1:3; 2:17). These are countered below with words built on an opposite root (*tob*; "good") and translated as "pleases" (vv. 5, 7), "find favor" (v. 5), "it pleased" (v. 6), and the "good" hand of God (v. 8). The relevance of this will be seen in verse 10.[40]

---

37 Cf. note 27.
38 During the first night of the new year (Zarathustra's birthday) the Persians celebrated with a banquet at which it was customary for the king to grant favors. It is possible that Nehemiah chose this opportune time to present his request. See Joseph Fleishman, "Nehemiah's Request on Behalf of Jerusalem," in *New Perspectives on Ezra-Nehemiah: History and Historiography, Text, Literature, and Interpretation*, ed. Isaac Kalimi (Winona Lake, IN: Eisenbrauns, 2012), 249.
39 Herbert Edward Ryle, *The Books of Ezra and Nehemiah with Introduction, Notes and Maps*, Cambridge Bible for Schools and Colleges (Cambridge: Cambridge University Press, 1897), 159, cited in Williamson, *Ezra, Nehemiah*, 177.
40 This interpretation is supported by J. G. McConville, who states, "The contrast between good (*tob*) and evil (*ra'*) pervades the chapter in a way that is not immediately obvious from the English translation"; *Ezra, Nehemiah, and Esther*, DSBS (Louisville: Westminster John Knox, 1985), 82.

Before Nehemiah's reply, readers learn that he is "very much afraid," although he does not tell us why. Generally speaking, he may simply fear the king's negative response. More specifically, however, his facial sadness is a serious breach of court etiquette, placing him at risk for rebuke or demotion (cf. Est. 4:11). For a Zoroastrian king like Artaxerxes, cheerfulness is viewed as gratitude toward the god Ahura Mazda. On the other hand, he would consider sadness a "sign of ingratitude and evil intentions" attributed to the god of evil. As a "weapon of evil," sadness would strike at a core religious value for Zoroastrians.[41] Equally damaging, Nehemiah's goal of rebuilding Jerusalem may be viewed as seditious, as will soon be confirmed (Neh. 2:19; 6:6). Artaxerxes has previously demanded the cessation of wall construction in Jerusalem for exactly this reason (Ezra 4:12–13, 21–22).

Wishing the king a long life, though customary (Neh. 2:3; Dan. 2:4; 3:9; 5:10; 6:6, 21), is all the more pertinent since, above all else, the cupbearer must evidence unimpeachable loyalty. This may also provide insight into Nehemiah's prayer for "mercy" in the king's sight (Neh. 1:11). He tells the king what readers already know: his sorrowful countenance is due to the unhappy state of the city. He only describes the city as the place where his ancestors are buried (cf. 2:5). "Jerusalem," the focus of denunciation as "that rebellious and wicked city" (Ezra 4:12), is wisely unmentioned. With a personal appeal to his obligations to the dead ("my fathers' graves"), Nehemiah hopes to provoke a sympathetic response from the king and distance himself further from political motivations.

2:4–5 The king's second question probes exactly what Nehemiah wants, transitioning into the second bit of information in the pause. Recognizing the tipping point of the conversation, Nehemiah prays, likely offering up little more than "give success and grant mercy" (cf. 1:11).[42] Such concise prayers are characteristic of Nehemiah (4:4–5, 9; 5:19; 6:9) and especially those asking God to "remember" (5:19; 6:14; 13:14, 22, 29, 31). As in his first reply, Nehemiah remains highly deferential, submitting himself to the king's wishes and identifying himself clearly as a servant before the king. With Nehemiah's response, Artaxerxes learns that he desires to be sent to an unnamed city, that this city is in Judah, and that he seeks to rebuild it.

2:6–8a With the queen present, the king finally questions the length of Nehemiah's stay and the time of his return.[43] In narrating his reply, Nehemiah moves away from dialogue, only recording the king's favorable response and that Nehemiah "had given him a time." This functions as the third interlude before Nehemiah's

---

41 Fleishman, "Nehemiah's Request," 250–251; for Artaxerxes as a Zoroastrian, see 247.

42 Shepherd and Wright, *Ezra and Nehemiah*, 53.

43 Nehemiah's purpose for recollecting the queen's presence is uncertain. Whether women were present at Persian royal wine banquets remains debated (Fleishman, "Nehemiah's Request," 252–253). The Hebrew noun translated "queen" (*shegal*) is not the usual word for queen and is found elsewhere only at Psalm 45:9 (cf. Dan. 5:2–3, 23: Aram. *shegal*, ESV "wives"). Her presence might in some way benefit Nehemiah, since according to Herodotus Persian queens in this period were powerful; John H. Walton, Victor H. Matthews, and Mark W. Chavalas, *The IVP Bible Background Commentary: Old Testament* (Downers Grove, IL: IVP Academic, 2000), 473. Alternatively, her presence may be intended to indicate that the conversation takes place not at a banquet but in a private setting.

final bold requests (vv. 7–8a); the phrase "So it pleased the king" is an amazing reversal of the prior decree (Ezra 4:21) and a strong statement of support for Nehemiah's request.

Seizing the opportunity, Nehemiah presses further by asking Artaxerxes for two specific letters. The first, "to the governors," will provide safe passage and perhaps necessary supplies along the journey. The word translated "governors" is a somewhat malleable term applying equally to rulers of a larger province or to those of smaller districts within a province (Neh. 3:7; cf. Ezra 8:36).[44] These officials, akin to the earlier Rehum and Shimshai (Ezra 4:8), are the sort of high-ranking administrators that might challenge Nehemiah's authority. Nehemiah knows that he must prepare for opposition.

The second letter, to a Jewish official named Asaph, requests timber from Artaxerxes's forest for three construction projects.[45] First, wood is needed for the gates of "the fortress of the temple." This defensive structure may be associated with the Tower of the Hundred or the Tower of Hananel (Neh. 3:1; cf. 7:2) found on the less defensible northern side of the temple complex and a likely precursor to the Antonia Fortress of Herod's temple.[46] In addition, wood is needed to beam the various other gates within the city wall and for wall reconstruction itself (cf. 3:3, 6; Ezra 5:8). Finally, Nehemiah needs wood for his own residence, likely to repair one previously constructed.

2:8b The heightened concern expressed at the end of Nehemiah's lengthy prayer (1:11), the succinct prayer of verse 4, the daring of Nehemiah's request, and Artaxerxes's prior aversion to wall construction make the favorable reply of the king all the more remarkable. As predominantly in Ezra (7:6, 9, 28; 8:18, 22, 31), so here in Nehemiah: human benevolence is attributed to divine sovereignty expressed in bountiful blessing, a fact that Nehemiah will relate later for a final time (Neh. 2:18).

2:9–10 After the completion of Nehemiah's audience with Artaxerxes (v. 8b), a geographical notice signals a new paragraph. This short subscene establishes Nehemiah's authority derived from both Artaxerxes's letter (v. 7) and his military escort. This show of strength may indicate that Nehemiah already holds the position of governor (5:14).

Evidence for authority is necessary, given the introduction of Sanballat the Horonite (2:10, 19; 4:1, 7; 6:1, 2, 5, 12, 14; 13:28). A nonbiblical letter from the area of Elephantine testifies to his position as governor of Samaria at a much later date (407 BC), although he may already hold the position in Nehemiah's day.[47] His daughter marries into the family of the high priest Eliashib (13:28).

44 Cf. comment on Ezra 5:3–5.
45 Asaph is otherwise unknown. The location of this forest is also uncertain, though some commentators suggest Lebanon due to its source of cedar earlier in the Persian period (Ezra 3:7).
46 Blenkinsopp, *Ezra-Nehemiah*, 215.
47 By the time of the letter from Elephantine, Sanballat is aged and his sons are functioning in his place. His name is Babylonian (= "Sin [the moon God] gave life"), though it is not clear if he himself is (note that Zerubbabel is also a Babylonian name though the one bearing it is Jewish). His sons are Delaiah and Shelemiah,

Joining Sanballat in opposition to Nehemiah is Tobiah (2:10, 19; 4:3 [cf. 4:1], 7; 6:1, 12, 14), "the Ammonite servant" (2:10) well connected to the nobles of Judah (6:17–18) and related to another priest named Eliashib (13:4, 7).[48] Tobiah may be a fellow Jew and Sanballat's equivalent, with a Persian appointment as governor to Transjordan Ammon. Alternatively, he may be an Ammonite (Neh. 13:1; cf. Judges 11; 2 Sam. 10:1–14) with Persian rank, though ultimately subordinate to Sanballat.[49] Whatever the case, these men do enjoy some measure of power and authority.

The way their response is described is significant. Earlier, words built on the root for "evil" to describe Nehemiah's own emotional state gave way to words built on the root for "good" to describe the ways in which the Lord was answering Nehemiah's prayer and showing him favor (cf. comment on Neh. 2:2–3). Clearly, bringing about such good is the Lord's desire. Now there is a reversal: as Nehemiah seeks the city's "welfare" (also built on the root for "good"), this results in Sanballat and Tobiah's great displeasure (v. 10)[50] and clearly puts them in opposition not only to Nehemiah but also to the Lord. This is especially ironic in light of the meaning of Tobiah's name ("Yahweh is good"). And why such a strong response? Likely because Nehemiah's authority now threatens the political, economic, or even religious status of Sanballat and Tobiah.[51]

2:11–16 A new paragraph begins with another geographical and temporal notice (v. 11; cf. Ezra 8:32). In what follows, Nehemiah narrates his out-and-back inspection of the wall and gates, the evaluation stage of his mission. The description of this inspection—from the triple reminder that all these events occur at "night" (vv. 12, 13, 15) to the "few men" with him to the solitary beast Nehemiah rides—all build a picture of covert activity. The plans God has placed within him ("into my heart"; v. 12) remain unspoken, perhaps even to the men with him and certainly from all others, and the theme of secrecy also closes the paragraph (v. 16). It seems that Nehemiah fears the potential damage done by opponents or resistance from within the Jerusalem community if his plans are exposed prematurely.

Nehemiah exits through the Valley Gate, likely located on southwest side of Jerusalem's wall and providing access to the Central (or Tyropoeon) Valley.[52] He journeys southward to the Dung or "Rubbish" Gate at the southernmost tip of

---

Hebrew names with "Yah," a shortened form of Yahweh likely indicating that Sanballat is a worshiper of the Lord. His identification as "the Horonite" likely means that he comes from one of several places containing the name "Horon," perhaps Upper and Lower Beth-horon (Josh. 16:3, 5), northwest of Jerusalem.

48 Commentators generally agree that the Eliashib of 13:4, 7 is not to be identified with the high priest of the same name (3:1; 13:28). When Tobiah and Sanballat are mentioned together, Sanballat is always named first until Nehemiah 6:12, 14, where the order is reversed. Afterward, Tobiah is referenced by himself (6:17, 19; 13:5, 8) or in relation to Eliashib (13:4, 7). The Tobiah at Ezra 2:60//Nehemiah 7:62 may be an ancestor of Nehemiah's opponent (Blenkinsopp, *Ezra-Nehemiah*, 92).

49 See Kidner, *Ezra and Nehemiah*, 89, 110, and Blenkinsopp, *Ezra-Nehemiah*, 219, for the former position and Williamson, *Ezra, Nehemiah*, 183, for the latter. Tobiah's relationship to the prominent "Tobiads" who ruled Ammon in the third century BC is not certain.

50 Lit., "and it displeased them a great displeasure" (cf. Jonah 4:1).

51 Clines, *Ezra, Nehemiah, Esther*, 145.

52 For a representation of the locations in this paragraph, cf. map, *ESV Study Bible*, 827.

the City of David. The verbal forms communicate ongoing inspections all along the 500-yard (c. 450-meter) stretch between these two gates (cf. 3:13). The Dragon Spring location is uncertain, but given the word order it was probably located somewhere between the two gates.[53] The locations for the Fountain (or Spring) Gate and the King's Pool remain debated, though it is conjectured that the former was located near the southeast corner, where it led to the water source called En-rogel located 650 feet (200 m) south of the city. Given the increased destruction debris, Nehemiah then proceeds on foot (2:14).

The verbal forms "ascending" and "inspecting" suggest that although he has abandoned the line of the wall due to increased rubble, he continues his examination as he travels northward along the floor of the Kidron Valley located east of the city.[54] Given the sudden loss of topological details, it seems likely that "and I turned back" (v. 15) means he does not continue north to circumnavigate the city but retraces his steps. The scene ends, again stressing Nehemiah's success in hiding his activities from everyday citizens ("Jews"), priests, the "nobles" and "officials,"[55] and any others ("the rest").

2:17–18 The timing of the next event is unstated. However, the sudden quotation ("Then I said to them") and repetition of terms that had first prompted Nehemiah to action ("trouble," "gates burned," "derision" = "shame"; cf. 1:3), along with his use of "us" and "we," suggest a rhetorical strategy designed to elicit immediate reaction from the community. Furthermore, as a concluding flourish, Nehemiah testifies that due to the Lord's good hand Artaxerxes had altered the king's policy regarding the wall (cf. 2:8b). The community must hear unequivocally that Nehemiah comes with both divine and royal approval.

The prompt and unified response, "Let us rise up and build," reveals unequivocal success. These verbs not only summarize the postexilic task of building that binds the people of Ezra and Nehemiah's era with those who returned under Zerubbabel and Jeshua (Ezra 1:5; 3:2; 5:2). They also echo David's original charge to Solomon (1 Chron. 22:19), fulfill prophecy (Isa. 44:26; 58:12), and anticipate the future messianic servant's ministry (Isa. 61:4; Amos 9:11). The people will indeed arise and build (Neh. 2:18; 3:1).

Finally, it may be noted that in other contexts the idiom "weaken the hands" describes discouragement leading to work stoppages due to hostility (Ezra 4:4; Neh. 6:9). The very opposite occurs now: God's work surging through Nehemiah steels community resolve so that they "strengthened their hands for the good."[56] As the community adopts a courageous resolve to do the Lord's work, they also wait

---

53 Otherwise translated "Dragon's Well" (NASB), "Jackals' Spring" (NJPS), or "Jackal Well" (NIV). Other popular identifications for this spring include the Pool of Siloam and En-rogel.

54 Williamson, *Ezra, Nehemiah*, 190; Blenkinsopp, *Ezra-Nehemiah*, 222.

55 The plural (Hb. *seganim*; 2:16) is always translated "officials" by ESV. This fluid term may describe Persian administrators, provincial governors, or simply community leaders (2:16 [2x]; 4:14, 19; 5:7, 17; 7:5; 12:40; 13:11). Their exact function is never clarified. Often the officials are teamed with "nobles" (*khorim*; 2:16; 4:14, 19; 5:7; 7:5), whose own leadership function is sometimes difficult to distinguish from the officials' (although they have been called "hereditary Judean nobility" in Blenkinsopp, *Ezra-Nehemiah*, 252).

56 The Hebrew reads "for the good thing," that is, the good work; the ESV adds "work" to make this clear.

patiently to receive "the good" from him. As 2:20 will show, any prospering of their work in the face of resistance comes only through God's benevolence (2 Sam. 10:12).

2:19–20 Sanballat and Tobiah move from displeasure (v. 10) to mocking taunts upon hearing of the actual determination to rebuild Jerusalem. They are joined by a powerful though less engaged opponent, "Geshem the Arab" (v. 19; 6:1, 2, 6). Several extrabiblical inscriptions attest to his fame and influence in northwest Arabia and beyond; one names him "king of Kedar" (cf. Isa. 21:13–17).[57] Jerusalem is therefore surrounded by enemies to the north (Samarians), east (Ammonites), southeast (Arabs), and west (city of Ashdod; cf. 4:7).[58] In 2:19 they accuse the entire community (the "you" is plural) of rebellion, a view earlier espoused (Ezra 4:12–13, 21–23; cf. Neh. 6:5–6).

Rather than defending himself by referring to the "king's letters" (2:9), Nehemiah demarcates a firm line between "us" and "you" (v. 20). His words remind God's "servants," who have recently determined to "arise and build," that they must trust in the "God of heaven" (cf. 1:5; 2:4) to prosper their work. At the same time, Nehemiah excludes his opponents and declares independence by using legal terminology. First, they have "no portion," meaning that they have no political association within the nation (cf. 2 Sam. 20:1; 1 Kings 12:16). Their lack of "right" refers to their loss of legal authority. The meaning of "claim" (or "memorial"; cf. ESV mg.) is unclear, though in this context it probably refers to a denial of participation in worship (cf. Ezra 4:3). In summary, Nehemiah lets his opponents know that they have "no civic, legal, or religious rights" in the city.[59]

Response

Nehemiah's prayers bear fruit. The King of kings has redeemed his servants before, and Nehemiah trusts that he will do so again (1:10–11; cf. 2:20). It is God's goodness that prompts Nehemiah's courage to speak to Artaxerxes, to evaluate his situation realistically in order to challenge his people, and to remain steadfast when threatened by opposition.

Nehemiah speaks not without significant fear, however. But God-empowered courage bridges the gap between fear and the voicing of his concerns (vv. 2–3). Artaxerxes's unexpected support for Nehemiah's mission, freeing him from his cupbearing duty, provides evidence of the good hand of the Lord, who does more than Nehemiah can ask or imagine (vv. 8, 20). This assures us that God hears our short, passionate pleas (v. 4). Through God's providence we trust that this world's powers will support the kingdom advancement they may have once so adamantly resisted (Ezra 4:8–22).

---

57 Geshem's name is inscribed on a fifth-century-BC silver vessel donated by his son (Kainu) and found in Egypt at Tell el-Maskhuta. Geshem's influence extended to Edom, the Negev, and northern Egypt (Clines, *Ezra, Nehemiah, Esther*, 148).

58 A view supported by Blenkinsopp, who adds the city of Ashdod to the west (*Ezra-Nehemiah*, 226).

59 Philip A. Noss and Kenneth J. Thomas, *A Handbook on Ezra and Nehemiah*, UBSHS (New York: UBS, 2005), 294. Williamson (*Ezra, Nehemiah*, 192) and Blenkinsopp (*Ezra-Nehemiah*, 226–227) are in agreement on the sense of the biblical terminology described here.

God opens these remarkable doors and Nehemiah steps through, embracing his assigned mission to restore God's glory by alleviating Jerusalem's shame (Neh. 2:17; Isa. 62:6–7). In this it is not personal aggrandizement but his people's "welfare" that motivates him (Neh. 2:10). More importantly, he states that he has acted upon what "God had put into my heart to do for Jerusalem" (v. 12). Effective service for God means knowing what needs to be done and doing it. This includes assessing whether we are actually seeking the best for those under our care and whether the actions we envision are in keeping with the Lord's will. This demands a candid analysis of the situation and planning for our task.

The Holy Spirit's leading and godly motivation are consistent with prudence and evaluation, as is evident in Nehemiah's inconspicuous nighttime evaluation (vv. 11–16). While it is unlikely that Nehemiah circumnavigates the whole city (cf. comment on 2:11–16), he sees enough of the city's demise to know "the trouble we are in" (v. 17). Whether the church thrives or struggles in our time, only a realistic evaluation of its situation and challenges will enable its members to "rise up and build" (vv. 17–18), a primary task to which God's people are called.

In Ezra 4, opponents adopted a progressive strategy advancing from infiltration to discouragement to full-blown intimidation. In Nehemiah 2 there is no pretense; the enemies of God, sensing the slightest aroma of kingdom advancement, move immediately to displeasure and accusation (vv. 10, 19). There are times when friendship with the Lord means hostility with the world, and seeking the welfare of God's people may end in ridicule (v. 19; cf. James 4:4). When confronted with opposition, Nehemiah remains steadfast in his hope that God's good hand will prosper his servants in their calling and exclude enemies from the holy city (Neh. 2:8, 18, 20; cf. Josh. 1:8). When facing opposition in our service to the Lord, we can be assured of no less.

NEHEMIAH 3:1–32

3 Then Eliashib the high priest rose up with his brothers the priests, and they built the Sheep Gate. They consecrated it and set its doors. They consecrated it as far as the Tower of the Hundred, as far as the Tower of Hananel. [2] And next to him the men of Jericho built. And next to them[1] Zaccur the son of Imri built.

[3] The sons of Hassenaah built the Fish Gate. They laid its beams and set its doors, its bolts, and its bars. [4] And next to them Meremoth the son of Uriah, son of Hakkoz repaired. And next to them Meshullam the son of Berechiah, son of Meshezabel repaired. And next to them Zadok the son of Baana repaired. [5] And next to them the Tekoites repaired, but their nobles would not stoop to serve their Lord.[2]

⁶ Joiada the son of Paseah and Meshullam the son of Besodeiah repaired the Gate of Yeshanah.³ They laid its beams and set its doors, its bolts, and its bars. ⁷ And next to them repaired Melatiah the Gibeonite and Jadon the Meronothite, the men of Gibeon and of Mizpah, the seat of the governor of the province Beyond the River. ⁸ Next to them Uzziel the son of Harhaiah, goldsmiths, repaired. Next to him Hananiah, one of the perfumers, repaired, and they restored Jerusalem as far as the Broad Wall. ⁹ Next to them Rephaiah the son of Hur, ruler of half the district of⁴ Jerusalem, repaired. ¹⁰ Next to them Jedaiah the son of Harumaph repaired opposite his house. And next to him Hattush the son of Hashabneiah repaired. ¹¹ Malchijah the son of Harim and Hasshub the son of Pahath-moab repaired another section and the Tower of the Ovens. ¹² Next to him Shallum the son of Hallohesh, ruler of half the district of Jerusalem, repaired, he and his daughters.

¹³ Hanun and the inhabitants of Zanoah repaired the Valley Gate. They rebuilt it and set its doors, its bolts, and its bars, and repaired a thousand cubits⁵ of the wall, as far as the Dung Gate.

¹⁴ Malchijah the son of Rechab, ruler of the district of Beth-haccherem, repaired the Dung Gate. He rebuilt it and set its doors, its bolts, and its bars.

¹⁵ And Shallum the son of Col-hozeh, ruler of the district of Mizpah, repaired the Fountain Gate. He rebuilt it and covered it and set its doors, its bolts, and its bars. And he built the wall of the Pool of Shelah of the king's garden, as far as the stairs that go down from the city of David. ¹⁶ After him Nehemiah the son of Azbuk, ruler of half the district of Beth-zur, repaired to a point opposite the tombs of David, as far as the artificial pool, and as far as the house of the mighty men. ¹⁷ After him the Levites repaired: Rehum the son of Bani. Next to him Hashabiah, ruler of half the district of Keilah, repaired for his district. ¹⁸ After him their brothers repaired: Bavvai the son of Henadad, ruler of half the district of Keilah. ¹⁹ Next to him Ezer the son of Jeshua, ruler of Mizpah, repaired another section opposite the ascent to the armory at the buttress.⁶ ²⁰ After him Baruch the son of Zabbai repaired⁷ another section from the buttress to the door of the house of Eliashib the high priest. ²¹ After him Meremoth the son of Uriah, son of Hakkoz repaired another section from the door of the house of Eliashib to the end of the house of Eliashib. ²² After him the priests, the men of the surrounding area, repaired. ²³ After them Benjamin and Hasshub repaired opposite their house. After them Azariah the son of Maaseiah, son of Ananiah repaired beside his own house. ²⁴ After him Binnui the son of Henadad repaired another section, from the house of Azariah to the buttress and to the corner. ²⁵ Palal the son of Uzai repaired opposite the buttress and the tower projecting from the upper house of the king at the court of the guard. After him Pedaiah the son of Parosh ²⁶ and the temple servants living on Ophel repaired to a point opposite the Water Gate on the east and the projecting tower. ²⁷ After him the Tekoites repaired another section opposite the great projecting tower as far as the wall of Ophel.

²⁸ Above the Horse Gate the priests repaired, each one opposite his own house. ²⁹ After them Zadok the son of Immer repaired opposite his own house. After him Shemaiah the son of Shecaniah, the keeper of the East Gate, repaired. ³⁰ After him Hananiah the son of Shelemiah and Hanun the sixth son of Zalaph repaired another section. After him Meshullam the son of Berechiah repaired opposite his chamber. ³¹ After him Malchijah, one of the goldsmiths, repaired as far as the house of the temple

servants and of the merchants, opposite the Muster Gate,[8] and to the upper chamber of the corner. [32] And between the upper chamber of the corner and the Sheep Gate the goldsmiths and the merchants repaired.

[1] Hebrew *him* [2] Or *lords* [3] Or *of the old city* [4] Or *foreman of half the portion assigned to*; also verses 12, 14, 15, 16, 17, 18 [5] A *cubit* was about 18 inches or 45 centimeters [6] Or *corner*; also verses 20, 24, 25 [7] Some manuscripts *vigorously repaired* [8] Or *Hammiphkad Gate*

Section Overview

This chapter recounts the faithful corporate response to the call to "rise up and build" the wall and gates of Jerusalem (Neh. 2:17–18). The narrative is told as if construction is already completed; however, we will learn that opposition actually occurs during its construction (4:1, 7–8) and that the doors put in place in this chapter (cf. 3:1, 3, 6, 13, 14, 15) are not actually set until later (6:1). Although ten gates, four towers, and other structures are found throughout the chapter, the precise location of most of these remain unknown.[60] Nevertheless, without this chapter we would lack vital information for postulating Jerusalem's topography in Nehemiah's day (cf. 2:13–15).

Earlier, under Hezekiah (c. 715–686 BC), Jerusalem's walls were expanded westward across the Central Valley to surround the Western Hill. The commentary below follows the current consensus that Nehemiah's walls surrounded a much smaller city comprising only the Temple Mount to the north and the City of David to the south, with both located on the Eastern Hill, east of the Central Valley.[61] Among the many details in this chapter we will meet over fifty named individuals, families, towns, and groups of varied vocations who work on the construction. Details are specific enough to include repairs done near the homes of particular individuals (e.g., 3:10, 23), even noting the work from the door to the end of the home of the high priest (vv. 20–21)!

The Section Outline below follows the ESV decision to rely upon the presence of the noun "gate" as a paragraph marker (3:1, 3, 6, 13 [2x], 14, 15, 28), since it is gate repair that dominates the chapter.[62] Metaphorically, these seven paragraphs function like literary building blocks as section by section the work progresses. Beginning at the Sheep Gate, located along the northern wall (vv. 1–2), work progresses counterclockwise to the western side of the city, including the Fish Gate (vv. 3–5) and Gate of Yeshanah (vv. 6–12), then moves southward to the Valley Gate (v. 13) and Dung Gate (v. 14). From this southernmost point work then follows the eastern side, from the Fountain Gate to the Water Gate (vv. 15–27). The final paragraph, beginning with repair of the Horse Gate, completes the 1.5-mile (2.4-km) circuit by arriving at the Sheep Gate, where the chapter had begun (vv. 28–32; cf. v. 1).

---

60 For possible locations, cf. map, *ESV Study Bible*, 827.

61 For an argument for a more robust wall rebuild that also includes the Southwest Hill of the preexilic period, see David Ussishkin, "On Nehemiah's City Wall and the Size of Jerusalem during the Persian Period: An Archaeologist's View," in *New Perspectives on Ezra-Nehemiah: History and Historiography, Text, Literature, and Interpretation*, ed., Isaac Kalimi (Winona Lake, IN: Eisenbrauns, 2012), 101–130.

62 The noun "gate" occurs also at 3:26 and 3:29, 31, 32. However, in these final cases the referents mark the location or limit the work rather than describing the explicit repair of the gate itself.

Section Outline

II.D.3. Wall-Gate Restoration (3:1–3:32)

    a. Of the Sheep Gate (3:1–2)

    b. Of the Fish Gate (3:3–5)

    c. Of the Gate of Yeshanah to the Tower of the Ovens (3:6–12)

    d. Of the Valley Gate to the Dung Gate (3:13)

    e. Of the Dung Gate (3:14)

    f. Of the Fountain Gate to the Projecting Tower (3:15–27)

    g. Of the Horse Gate to the Sheep Gate (3:28–32)

Comment

3:1–2 It is vital to consider *who* begins the work, *where* the work begins, and *how* the work proceeds. The narrative impresses upon readers that work commences without delay. It is relevant that the work begins with Eliashib, the high priest, and his fellow priests ("his brothers"). Eliashib repeats the actions of his grandfather Jeshua (or Joshua), the former high priest (12:10; Hag. 1:12), who also "rose up" and "built" both altar and temple (cf. Ezra 3:2; 5:2). Although Eliashib's family later nurtures questionable relationships that require Nehemiah's attention (Neh. 13:28–29), at this point the high priest makes clear his commitment to Jerusalem's renewal.

It is no coincidence that priestly rebuilding begins at the Sheep Gate, located along the northern portion of wall, and moves westward toward the named towers.[63] The Sheep Gate was so named due to its function as the entrance through which sheep were brought for sacrifice (cf. John 5:2). The priority of the priestly work here, and its proximity to the temple, would remind the people of their call to be a worshiping and sacrificing people. This also suggests the high priest's role in helping the remnant live out its calling to be a holy nation and kingdom of priests (Ex. 19:5–6). For this to happen fully, Jerusalem must be secured. Along with this, the northern side of the city, being most open to attack, probably experienced significant Babylonian destruction.[64] By beginning here, the narrative highlights a pastoral point: the work of restoration must begin at the point of greatest need.

For this reason, the work begins with "consecration" of both gate and tower. By consecrating their part of the work, the priests set the tone for a project that will restore the "holy city" (Neh. 11:1, 18). The narration moves counterclockwise as a connected work. For the first time we read both "next to him" and "next to them" (3:2), a phrase that occurs in some form in nearly every verse from verse 2 to verse 15 (cf. vv. 17, 19), followed by the comparable "after him," which heads nearly every verse from verse 16 to verse 31.[65] Section by section the wall is connected and those who do the building work side by side.

---

63 The "Tower of the Hundred" probably headquartered one hundred men, while the "Tower of Hananel" (3:1; 12:39; Jer. 31:38; Zech. 14:10) was likely identical to the "fortress of the temple" (Neh. 2:8) and the "castle" (7:2). In the Roman period, the site was occupied by the Antonia Fortress (Clines, *Ezra, Nehemiah, Esther*, 151).
64 Some commentators note a subtle shift in verb frequency from the use of "build" in 3:1–3 (cf. 3:13–15), emphasizing greater destruction along this stretch, to the verb "repair" used elsewhere.
65 Cf. comment on 3:15–27 for possible explanation of this division.

3:3–5 The rebuilding of the "Fish Gate" by the "sons of Hassenaah" (cf. Ezra 2:35) follows. The uncertain gate location, perhaps at the northwest corner, may have provided access to the fish market (cf. Neh. 13:16). With respect to gate structures, for the first time we encounter the refrain that workers "laid its beams [3:3, 6; cf. 2:8] and set its doors, its bolts, and its bars" (3:3, 6, 13, 14, 15). These actions actually conclude the construction process (6:1; 7:1). The key verb translated "repaired" occurs thirty-five times in the chapter, in nearly every verse.[66] To some interpreters this suggests something less than the complete rebuild required at the more compromised northern wall.[67]

Regarding the builders, Meremoth "son of Uriah" (3:4) is earlier identified as the priest who accepts gifts from Ezra (Ezra 8:33); he will also repair a second section of wall, near the high priest's house (Neh. 3:21). Meshullam "son of Berechiah" has a daughter who marries Tobiah's son (6:18), suggesting his elevated social status. Like the prior reference to "men of Jericho" (3:2; cf. Ezra 2:34), the mention of "Tekoites" (Neh. 3:5) underscores work crews originating from specific towns (cf. vv. 7, 13). The observation that some of their prominent members "would not stoop to serve their Lord" could imply prideful rebellion against God's purposes.[68] Alternatively, their refusal to work may indicate rejection of some aspect of the building effort under human leaders, including Nehemiah (cf. "lords"; 3:5 ESV mg.; NASB "masters"). Given the use of the word translated "Lord" elsewhere in Nehemiah, the former option seems more probable (1:11; 4:14; 8:10; 10:29). While the text remains vague on what motivates the work embargo, the unity of purpose otherwise expressed in the chapter is remarkable. Perhaps prompted by negligence of their nobles, the Tekoites seek to repair another section along the eastern wall (3:27).

3:6–12 This paragraph describes work along the western wall, moving southward. Several structures are noted. The "Gate of Yeshanah" (cf. 12:39) may have provided access to a little-known town near Bethel called Yeshanah. For grammatical and other reasons some translations render this "Old Gate" (RSV, NASB) or, with a minor textual emendation, "Mishneh Gate" (NAB). "Mishneh" refers to a newer portion of the city sometimes rendered as "Second Quarter" (2 Kings 22:14; Zeph. 1:10) or "New Quarter" (NJB). This portion was likely uninhabited in the Persian period.[69] The "Broad Wall," the next structure mentioned (Neh. 3:8), fortified the preexilic Mishneh.[70] The description "and they restored Jerusalem" (v. 8) is alternatively rendered "and they forsook Jerusalem" and may mean that at this point the earlier preexilic wall line was abandoned.[71] The location of the final place

---

66 The verb is absent only in 3:1, 2, 3, 25, 26.
67 Blenkinsopp, *Ezra-Nehemiah*, 234.
68 The idiom, "Their nobles did not bring their neck into the service of their Lord" (AT), uses imagery of oxen refusing subjection to the yoke (Jer. 27:11–12). If this is synonymous with being "stiff-necked" (so Williamson, *Ezra, Nehemiah*, 196), then their refusal moves beyond pride to unbelief.
69 The Mishneh Gate was the portal to the "New" or "Second" Quarter of Jerusalem, which had expanded in the days of Hezekiah and Manasseh (Williamson, *Ezra, Nehemiah*, 205).
70 Philip J. King and Lawrence E. Stager, *Life in Biblical Israel* (Louisville: Westminster John Knox, 2001), 219.
71 The presence of the Hebrew verb *'azab*, here translated "and they restored," is the subject of ongoing debate, as is its presence in Sanballat's question at 4:2. Typically the verb is glossed "to abandon" or "to forsake"; however, in this context, most translations and interpreters opt for a translation "to restore" by accepting an alternative Ugaritic root (cf. Ex. 23:5).

mentioned, the "Tower of the Ovens," is uncertain, though it was somewhere between the Broad Wall and the Valley Gate (cf. 12:38). Typically, interpreters associate the ovens with bakers, assuming their presence near both palace and temple (cf. "the bakers' street"; Jer. 37:21,).

Several named individuals and groups are worthy of mention. Like Meremoth (Neh. 3:4), "Malchijah the son of Harim" (v. 11) marks another strong connection with the book of Ezra. He was one who agreed to divorce his foreign wife (Ezra 10:31). Also like Meremoth and several other builders, Malchijah repairs a second section of wall. Unlike with them, however (cf. Neh. 3:4, 21; 3:5, 27; perhaps 3:18, 24), the text at verse 11 does not indicate the first section of wall Malchijah repaired. This will be so of several others who repair "another section" without mention of the first (cf. vv. 19, 20, 30). Beside association by family or geography, some workers are identified with professions, such as "goldsmiths" (vv. 8, 31, 32), "perfumers" (v. 8), and later "merchants" (vv. 31, 32), perhaps working at locations adjacent to where they formerly plied their trades or sold their goods. The mention of Shallum and the specific work of his daughters (v. 12), while perhaps indicating his lack of sons, fits the chapter's overall portrait of widespread community collaboration in the rebuilding effort.

Several items in the chapter provide detail on governmental administration in the period. In keeping with the Babylonians' establishing Gedaliah as governor at Mizpah (2 Kings 25:23; Jer. 40:7ff.), that town is further specified as a governmental center and residence of the Persian governor during official visits to the province (Neh. 3:7).[72] Also, for the first time mention is made of one of the "rulers" of a "district"; five such rulers are in fact mentioned, with several of the districts further divided into smaller administrative "half-districts" (vv. 9, 12, 14, 15, 16, 17, 18). Careful attention to these verses shows that assistance came not only from within Jerusalem but also from a number of places outside of it. For example, the men of Gibeon and Mizpah (v. 7) as well as the rulers from these various subdistricts offered their assistance. These include Malchijah of Beth-haccherem (v. 14), Shallum of Mizpah (v. 15), Nehemiah of Beth-zur (v. 16), and Hashabiah and Bavvai of Keilah (vv. 17–18). We may also include Ezer, "ruler of Mizpah" (v. 19), who manages the town itself rather than the wider district of the same name (cf. v. 15).

3:13 It was from the "Valley Gate" that Nehemiah initially commenced his nocturnal inspection (2:13). It had been fortified in the eighth century BC by King Uzziah (2 Chron. 26:9). Reconstructions that assume a more limited scope of repair to include the City of David and Temple Mount of the Eastern Hill, but not the Western Hill, assume that the gate overlooked the Central Valley.[73] The text mentions no further gate repair until the Dung Gate, some 500 yards (c. 450 m) to the south.

---

72 Blenkinsopp, *Ezra-Nehemiah*, 235.

73 Williamson, *Ezra, Nehemiah*, 188; Blenkinsopp, *Ezra-Nehemiah*, 221–222. For those who include the Western Hill in reconstruction, the gate would be located in the Hinnom Valley (Ussishkin, "Nehemiah's City Wall," 124). Persian-period remains located along the western slope of the Southeast Hill were excavated by Crowfoot in the early twentieth century. These have been tentatively identified as the remains of the Valley Gate, though this identification has been challenged by Ussishkin ("Nehemiah's City Wall," 109–114).

3:14 The report of repair to the "Dung Gate," which provided access to the city dump in the Hinnom Valley, brings the construction to its southernmost point. The gate is often identified with the "Potsherd Gate" (Jer. 19:2).

3:15–27 The second half of the chapter describes work along the eastern side of the city. The "Fountain Gate" (v. 15) marks the final gate whose repair is explicitly mentioned. In this latter half of the chapter the dominant phrase "after him/them," rather than "next to him/them," heads nearly every verse of the final two paragraphs (vv. 15–27, 28–32). Attention shifts from identifying features along the wall itself (vv. 1–15) to locating work based on markers beyond the wall (e.g., "tombs of David"; v. 16). Often, construction takes place "opposite" city landmarks well known to the earliest audience (vv. 16, 19, 25, 26, 27) or with reference to gates (vv. 28, 29, 31) or the locations of specific houses (vv. 16, 20, 21, 23, 24, 25). This varied shift in description, occurring at just this point, corresponds to the place where the preexilic wall line, along with its gates, was abandoned in favor of a new wall line farther up the slope of the eastern ridge (cf. 2:14).[74]

3:15–16 The "Fountain Gate" (v. 15) is likely named for its access to water at En-rogel.[75] Whether the "Pool of Shelah of the king's garden" or the separate "artificial pool" (v. 16) should be identified with the previously mentioned "King's Pool" (2:14) is far from certain. The former seems more probable.[76] Only here in the chapter is it stated that a gate is "covered." This is also the only time the verb occurs in the OT. It may indicate that a roof or timbers are placed over it (cf. NET: "he . . . put on its roof") and so may be parallel to "they laid its beams" (3:3, 6). Davidic kings were buried in the "tombs of David" (v. 16) within the City of David located in the southern part of the eastern ridge (1 Kings 2:10; 11:43; 14:31; 15:8; etc.); however, the precise location remains unknown.

3:17–21 Though not all persons described here are Levites, these verses provide a general description of their work along several wall sections. Some Levites hold administrative positions as rulers of half-districts. Hashabiah (v. 17) is probably the Levite of 10:11 and perhaps the returnee of Ezra 8:19. The reference to Levitical support is appropriate given construction near the home of Eliashib, the high priest (Neh. 3:20–21). Meremoth, also a priest (v. 21; cf. Ezra 8:33), now works on a second segment of wall (cf. v. 4) along the whole length of Eliashib's home, while Eliashib and other priests rebuild along the northern wall (cf. v. 1).

3:22–26 Several priests repair near their own residences (v. 23; cf. v. 28). There is uncertainty about the topographical features of the "buttress" (vv. 19, 24, 25)[77] and the "corner" (vv. 24, 31, 32). Others, like the "tower" and the "court of the guard," are noted in reference to the king's palace located somewhere on the Ophel (v. 25;

---

74 Williamson, *Ezra, Nehemiah*, 200; Blenkinsopp, *Ezra-Nehemiah*, 231.
75 Cf. comment on 2:11–16 for locations of the Fountain Gate and En-rogel.
76 Blenkinsopp, *Ezra-Nehemiah*, 222. Williamson provides a lengthy discussion (*Ezra, Nehemiah*, 189–190, 207).
77 Or "corner" (cf. 3:19 ESV mg.; NJPS "the angle"). The term may indicate some directional turn in the wall. It differs from the word translated "corner" (Hb. *pinnah*) in 3:24, 31, 32.

cf. Jer. 32:2). Pedaiah, possibly a Levite (Neh. 13:13; cf. Ezra 2:3; 8:3; 10:25; Neh. 10:14), joins with the temple servants (cf. comment on Ezra 2:43–54) in repairs that finish at a point opposite the "Water Gate" (Neh. 3:26). That gate provided access to the Gihon Spring, the ancient water supply for the city. If it stood "on the east" side of the wall, then it was part of the old wall and outside of the new line of Nehemiah's wall, while the "projecting tower" was inside.[78]

3:27 The mention of the Ophel (v. 26) carries over to the work of the Tekoites (cf. v. 5), who repaired as far as its wall. "Ophel" typically refers to the hill rising north of the City of David toward the Temple Mount. At one time its wall may have represented the northernmost fortification of the City of David, prior to northward expansion of the city with Solomon's building of the temple.[79]

3:28–32 This final wall segment is located in the city's northeast corner. Here priests repair near their own homes, which neighbor the temple precinct. The "Horse Gate" (v. 28) may have been part of the preexilic wall and located lower on the slope (cf. Jer. 31:40). If so, "above the Horse Gate," refers to repairs done higher up the slope. Alternatively, some postulate its location within the royal-temple complex itself (cf. 2 Kings 11:16).

On the other hand, the "East Gate" (Neh. 3:29) was within the wall of the temple complex, making it likely that Shemaiah, its keeper, was a Levite (cf. 2 Chron. 31:15). The language that follows describing Meshullam's second section of work "opposite his chamber" (Neh. 3:30; cf. v. 4) suggests a priest's dwelling within the temple area (Ezra 10:6; Neh. 12:44; 13:7; cf. Jer. 35:2, 4) and may anticipate the later "chamber" conflict with Tobiah (Neh. 13:4–9), who was related to Meshullam by marriage (6:18).

Although conceivably a gate of the temple court, if the "Muster Gate" (3:31) was instead a city gate it was the northernmost gate along the eastern side.[80] Likewise, the twice-mentioned "upper chamber of the corner," perhaps a watchtower, provides the final northeastern landmark at the city corner, where it joins the northern line of the wall. The goldsmiths (cf. v. 8) repair alongside merchants who live in this area of the city (vv. 31–32), perhaps proximate to a market north of the temple. As these tradesmen repair toward the west they close the circuit, uniting with priests who began the chapter at the Sheep Gate (v. 1).

Response

Grinding verse by verse through the topographical features of this chapter builds its own analogy to the hard work of stone-by-stone wall reconstruction. An impor-

---

78 Clines, *Ezra, Nehemiah, Esther*, 156; Williamson, *Ezra, Nehemiah*, 287.

79 If the wall of Ophel ran east to west, then Nehemiah's wall crossed at right angles with it. Alternatively, the wall of Ophel may have been incorporated within the south-north progression of Nehemiah's wall north of the Water Gate. The precise relationship of this wall of Ophel with the one mentioned in the building project of the kings Jotham (2 Chron. 27:3) and later Manasseh (2 Chron. 33:14) is uncertain (Blenkinsopp, *Ezra-Nehemiah*, 238).

80 Williamson, *Ezra, Nehemiah*, 211. Note also that the significance of the name is unknown. For example, in the ESV footnote *Hammiphkad* is a transliteration of the Hebrew (cf. KJV: *Miphkad*).

tant question is why this chapter resides here at all. Why recount the completion of the entire rebuilding project whole and at once, rather than serially and progressively? The chapter's presence clearly impedes narrative progress, evidenced by the that fact that Nehemiah promptly returns to an earlier temporal moment when the wall was incomplete and opposition to it vigorous (4:1–9; 6:1–14). Why remove the tension by actually telling readers at the start that the remnant community succeeded in its determination to "rise up and build" (2:18)? Several reasons may be noted.

Obviously, we learn that the wall gets rebuilt. By reading the finished story before the progressive account of wall construction—including opposition—God's people will learn that his purposes cannot be thwarted; the Lord will repair Jerusalem (2:20). He is not only the creator of Israel but also the redeemer of Israel, "who says of Jerusalem, 'She shall be inhabited,' and of the cites of Judah, 'They shall be built, and I will raise up their ruins'" (Isa. 44:26)—a prophecy that includes Cyrus's appointment as ruler in order to rebuild both Jerusalem and its temple (Isa. 44:28). Likewise, we know the end of the biblical story even in the midst of kingdom advancement and opposition. The new Jerusalem will be built and God will dwell with his people (Rev. 21:1–4).

Second, the work's completion confirms that the Lord will rebuild Jerusalem through the work of his chosen servant. Nehemiah's earlier assertion that God had "put into my heart" (Neh. 2:12; cf. 2:18) to rebuild Jerusalem would be difficult for people to confirm or deny. However, by showing the successful completion up front, the Lord validates to the reader that Nehemiah is a trustworthy servant of the divine King himself. To cite Isaiah once more: the Lord "confirms the word of his servant" (Isa. 44:26). The same may be seen with God's ultimate servant, Jesus. As God confirms Nehemiah through a rebuilt Jerusalem, so Jesus, *the* servant, is confirmed in his resurrection and ascension. The conquering church is built through the apostolic witness to these events, a mission that is ongoing for the church (Acts 2:29–33; Matt. 16:18).

Finally, this text describes the enlisting of the entire remnant community, both unified and diverse, in the work of renewal. Remarkable cooperation exists among the range of workers: men and women, priests and laymen, Levites and tradesmen, locals and nonresidents, administrators and citizens. In comments on the final verse (Neh. 3:32), when the tradesmen link up with priests back at the Sheep Gate, one interpreter observes how this "symbolizes the whole enterprise."[81] The leadership and organization required to gain such sustained support and effort from varied persons with diverse interests and abilities is itself a gift of God, for which he is to be praised (Eph. 4:11–16). Here we might underscore Nehemiah's wise pastoral strategy to place persons at the very locations wherein they have the highest personal stake, i.e., near their own homes.[82] Called to serve the Lord in every historical moment, the one body of Christ is granted diverse gifts, talents,

---

81 Kidner, *Ezra and Nehemiah*, 98.
82 Williamson, *Ezra, Nehemiah*, 212.

and functions among its multiform members (Rom. 12:3–8; 1 Corinthians 12). Assured victory in the Lord Jesus Christ, members working side by side in kingdom advancement are encouraged to faithfully repair their assigned segment of the wall.

NEHEMIAH 4:1–23

4^1 Now when Sanballat heard that we were building the wall, he was angry and greatly enraged, and he jeered at the Jews. ² And he said in the presence of his brothers and of the army of Samaria, "What are these feeble Jews doing? Will they restore it for themselves?² Will they sacrifice? Will they finish up in a day? Will they revive the stones out of the heaps of rubbish, and burned ones at that?" ³ Tobiah the Ammonite was beside him, and he said, "Yes, what they are building—if a fox goes up on it he will break down their stone wall!" ⁴ Hear, O our God, for we are despised. Turn back their taunt on their own heads and give them up to be plundered in a land where they are captives. ⁵ Do not cover their guilt, and let not their sin be blotted out from your sight, for they have provoked you to anger in the presence of the builders.

⁶ So we built the wall. And all the wall was joined together to half its height, for the people had a mind to work.

⁷³ But when Sanballat and Tobiah and the Arabs and the Ammonites and the Ashdodites heard that the repairing of the walls of Jerusalem was going forward and that the breaches were beginning to be closed, they were very angry. ⁸ And they all plotted together to come and fight against Jerusalem and to cause confusion in it. ⁹ And we prayed to our God and set a guard as a protection against them day and night.

¹⁰ In Judah it was said,⁴ "The strength of those who bear the burdens is failing. There is too much rubble. By ourselves we will not be able to rebuild the wall." ¹¹ And our enemies said, "They will not know or see till we come among them and kill them and stop the work." ¹² At that time the Jews who lived near them came from all directions and said to us ten times, "You must return to us."⁵ ¹³ So in the lowest parts of the space behind the wall, in open places, I stationed the people by their clans, with their swords, their spears, and their bows. ¹⁴ And I looked and arose and said to the nobles and to the officials and to the rest of the people, "Do not be afraid of them. Remember the Lord, who is great and awesome, and fight for your brothers, your sons, your daughters, your wives, and your homes."

¹⁵ When our enemies heard that it was known to us and that God had frustrated their plan, we all returned to the wall, each to his work. ¹⁶ From that day on, half of my servants worked on construction, and half held the spears, shields, bows, and coats of mail. And the leaders stood behind the whole house of Judah, ¹⁷ who were building on the wall. Those who carried burdens were loaded in such a way that each labored on the work

with one hand and held his weapon with the other. [18] And each of the builders had his sword strapped at his side while he built. The man who sounded the trumpet was beside me. [19] And I said to the nobles and to the officials and to the rest of the people, "The work is great and widely spread, and we are separated on the wall, far from one another. [20] In the place where you hear the sound of the trumpet, rally to us there. Our God will fight for us."

[21] So we labored at the work, and half of them held the spears from the break of dawn until the stars came out. [22] I also said to the people at that time, "Let every man and his servant pass the night within Jerusalem, that they may be a guard for us by night and may labor by day." [23] So neither I nor my brothers nor my servants nor the men of the guard who followed me, none of us took off our clothes; each kept his weapon at his right hand.[6]

[1] Ch 3:33 in Hebrew [2] Or *Will they commit themselves to God?* [3] Ch 4:1 in Hebrew [4] Hebrew *Judah said* [5] The meaning of the Hebrew is uncertain [6] Or *his weapon when drinking*

Section Overview

The thematic flow of Nehemiah 4–6 mirrors, at a smaller level, the flow of all of Ezra 2–Nehemiah 7. Just as the whole book narrates opposition to building projects (Ezra 3–6; Nehemiah 2–6), with internal challenges of the community in between (Ezra 7–10), so these three chapters in Nehemiah narrate wall building in two chapters (Nehemiah 4; 6) surrounding the economic problems internal to the community (Nehemiah 5).

Nehemiah 3 paused the flow of the storyline to tell readers that the wall gets built.[83] What the Lord had placed in Nehemiah's heart to do for the city and its people (2:8, 12, 18) was presented as accomplished, with doors, bolts, and bars already set (3:3, 6, etc.; cf. 6:1). The people did indeed successfully "rise up and build" because God had promised that it would be so (Isa. 44:26–28), a truth about which his people sing (Psalm 147).[84] Now, with this conclusion already narrated, Nehemiah 4:1–23 backtracks to recount the progress of wall building as well as the adversarial reaction of their enemies. This ebb and flow of rebuilding progress followed by the opposition shapes the chapter. Indeed, this important theme is found in Nehemiah 2; 4; and 6 (cf. table 2.1). Table 2.1 clarifies the principle that, as the kingdom advances, the opposition's tactics will adapt (esp. 4:6–14). In all cases the opposition responds to what they "heard" (vv. 1, 7; 6:1). Enemy tactics shift from verbal taunts (4:1–6), to serious physical threat to the community (vv. 7–14), to the later attempt at intimidating leadership (6:1–14). In the current chapter this results in the establishment of a defensive posture by the community and the recognition that God has thwarted enemy actions (4:15–23).

---

83 As Clines notes, the narrative resumes here from Nehemiah 2:20 (*Ezra, Nehemiah, Esther*, 158).
84 God will advance and sustain his people in every age to accomplish his redemptive purposes. This bolsters the faithful to endure in their varied callings.

TABLE 2.1: Nehemiah's Pattern of Progress and the Adversaries' Responses[85]

Action	Adversaries	Adversaries "Hear" and React	Counter-Response
Nehemiah arrives (2:9)	Sanballat, Tobiah (2:10)	Are greatly displeased (2:10)	Action: Nehemiah goes to Jerusalem (2:11)
People determined to build (2:17–18)	Sanballat, Tobiah, Geshem (2:19)	Jeer, despise, accuse (2:19)	Verbal response: "God . . . will make us prosper" (2:20)
Building the wall (4:1)	Sanballat, Tobiah (4:1, 3)	Are enraged, taunt (4:1–3)	Nehemiah prays for God to act against foes (4:4–5)
Wall *joined* together (Hb. *qashar*) to half its height (4:6)	Sanballat, Tobiah, Arabs, Ammonites, Ashdodites (4:7)	Are very angry, *plot* together (Hb. *qashar*) to fight against Jerusalem (4:7–8)	Community prays and sets a guard (4:9)
		Death threats to the community (4:11)	Nehemiah reminds people: "Remember the Lord" (4:14)
God frustrates plans of enemies (4:15)	Enemies (4:15)	Hear that God has frustrated their plan (4:15)	Work resumes with increased defensive posture (4:15–23)
Wall completed but doors not yet set (6:1)	Sanballat, Tobiah, Geshem (6:1)	Plot to do Nehemiah harm (6:1–9)	Nehemiah prays for strength (6:9)
	Shemaiah hired by Sanballat, Tobiah (6:10, 12)	Plot to give Nehemiah a bad name (6:10–13)	Nehemiah prays for God's intervention (6:14)
Wall completed with doors set (6:15; 7:1)	All enemies, Tobiah (6:16–17)	"Fell greatly in their own esteem" (6:16)	Work accomplished with the help of God (6:16)

Section Outline[86]

II.D.4. Builders Make Progress with Some Trepidation (4:1–23)

    a. Adversaries Hear and Jeer; Prayer and Progress (4:1–6)

    b. Adversaries Hear and Plot; Prayer and Protection (4:7–14)

    c. Adversaries Hear; Weapons and Workers (4:15–23)

Comment

4:1–6 After the narration of wall construction as a whole (3:1–32), the chapter begins with wall building in progress. In the ESV, the scene is treated in two paragraphs (4:1–5, 6); the first of these may be further subdivided between the rage and verbal taunts of Sanballat and Tobiah (vv. 1–3) and Nehemiah's brief prayer for deliverance (vv. 4–5). The final verse (v. 6), a separate paragraph, then provides a summary on the building project.

---

85 The idea for table 2.1 was prompted by the exposition of these themes in Blenkinsopp, *Ezra-Nehemiah*, 225.
86 The scenic structure gains independent support from both Kidner (*Ezra and Nehemiah*, 98–102) and Blenkinsopp (*Ezra-Nehemiah*, 242–253). In Hebrew the versification is 3:33–4:17.

4:1–3 The presence of Sanballat, joined by Tobiah for the third time (cf. 2:10, 19), forebodes trouble for the postexilic community.[87] Initially displeased greatly by Nehemiah's presence and his resolve to do good to Jerusalem (2:10) and later raising the specter of rebellion (2:19), Sanballat, hearing of actual progress, becomes not only angry but also "greatly enraged" (4:1). This results in a litany of verbal assaults in the form of peppered rhetorical questions all categorized as "jeering," whose major goal appears to be the destruction of the morale of the builders.[88] These questions are likely the abstract of a longer speech delivered before "his brothers" (v. 2), not necessarily kin but rather allies who share his disdain at the prospects of a renewed Jerusalem. Overall, Sanballat's anger leads to ridicule of God's people, which is equivalent to provocation of the Lord (v. 5).[89]

First, Sanballat makes fun of the community with a personal attack by defining them as the "feeble Jews." At one time this may have been an accurate assessment, since the related verbal form (Hb. *'amal*, "to grow feeble, to languish") elsewhere describes the languishing state of Jerusalem's walls and gates in the aftermath of Babylonian destruction (Lam. 2:8–9). Regardless of whether the presence of the "army of Samaria" implies Sanballat's authority to command an organized fighting force or is simply a local show of power to counter Nehemiah's "army and horsemen" (Neh. 2:9), its mention intimates that his underlying goal may go beyond mocking to enlist his hearers in physical threats against Jerusalem (cf. 4:8, 11).

Moving beyond personal attack, the question of whether they will "restore it for themselves" questions their competence—can forty-one work details apparently composed of clerics, laymen, and tradesmen rather than professional contractors actually build a functioning defensive structure?[90] The third question ("Will they sacrifice?") indirectly asks whether they will ever finish since sacrifices would, in the end, be offered to the Lord in a concluding celebration (12:27, 38, 43) just as at two prior climactic moments (Ezra 6:16–17; 8:35). This leads naturally to the next question, "Will they finish up in a day?" which implies a lack of realism on the builders' part regarding the arduous nature of the work. Finally, the question of whether the builders will "resuscitate" charred limestone rubble challenges the sanity of a people who would rebuild their wall from weakened stones. The assumed fragility of the final product is summarized by Tobiah's added statement of ridicule that an animal as small as a fox could knock it down (Neh. 4:3).

4:4–5 In turning to God the faithful admit their need and submit their defense to him. This is the first time, though not the last, that Nehemiah pleads for God's help for the community in light of rising opposition (cf. 6:14; 13:28–29). As the

---

87 For further introduction to these persons, cf. comment on 2:9–10.

88 J. I. Packer calls this "psychological warfare" in *A Passion for Faithfulness: Wisdom from the Book of Nehemiah* (Wheaton, IL: Crossway, 1995), 99.

89 Different forms of the Hebrew verb *ka'as* are used to describe both Sanballat's anger (4:1) and the Lord's provocation (4:5).

90 See also comment on 3:6–12 (at 3:8) and note 71 for a comparable use of the verb *'azab*, translated in both places by the ESV as "restore." Other translation options based on the predominant gloss of the verb "to abandon" or "to forsake" include: (1) "Are they going to give up [i.e., "abandon"]?" (Neh. 3:34 NJB) or, with a slight emendation of the prepositional phrase, (2) "Will they commit [i.e., "abandon"] themselves to God?" Cf. ESV footnote and discussion in Williamson, *Ezra, Nehemiah*, 213, and Blenkinsopp, *Ezra-Nehemiah*, 242.

enemies "heard" (4:1), so now Nehemiah implores God to "hear" (v. 4) their taunts and vindicate his "feeble" (v. 2) people. To bring reproach upon the Lord's people is to bring reproach upon the Lord himself (1 Sam. 17:26, 45). It was this very reproach (= "shame") that moved Nehemiah to action in the first place (Neh. 1:3). He yearns for poetic justice such that the vicious words that have made the community "despised" (Hb. *buzah*) will someday turn back upon Sanballat and Tobiah so that they become as "plunder" (*bizzah*) and captives—as the exiles themselves have only recently experienced. Like David (Ps. 109:6–20) and particularly Jeremiah (Jer. 18:18–23), Nehemiah asks God to find his opponents guilty with no hope of forgiveness for iniquity or removal of their sin for this offense, the very opposite of what God does for his repentant people (Ps. 85:1–3). But this is not personal vengeance. They have provoked God himself[91] by mocking his people, and Nehemiah leaves vindication of God's flock in God's hands.

4:6 While Sanballat may have succeeded in rousing his own supporters, his first attempt at harming morale fails miserably. In answer to Nehemiah's short prayer, the Lord renews the heart of the people to work. In fact, "So we built the wall" provides a somewhat abrupt summation to the prior material, emphasizing that the work progresses to "half its height" in a seeming act of willful, God-trusting defiance.

4:7–14 This second scene, just like the first, moves from a report that the adversaries "heard" (vv. 7–8; cf. v. 1) to a community response of prayer (v. 9; cf. vv. 4–5). The final paragraph (vv. 10–14) then provides further evaluations from each group and an advancement in the builders' defensive strategy. It concludes with the reminder to "remember the Lord."

4:7–9 Like the binding of a broken bone, the progress of closing the wall fractures is described metaphorically with imagery of healing. The rare noun *arukah*, here translated "repairing" (v. 7; 2 Chron. 24:13; Isa. 58:8; Jer. 8:22; 30:17; 33:6), in Jeremiah describes the promise of restored health after exile, remarkably also preceded by a verse promising that foes will go into captivity and the plunderers will become plunder (Jer. 30:16–17)—just as Nehemiah has recently prayed (Neh. 4:4)!

The relationship between events in verses 6–8 is cemented by descriptions of the wall ("joined together"; v. 6) and the enemies ("plotted together"; v. 8) that both use a form of the verb *qashar* ("to join," "to league together," "to conspire"). Hearing of the building progress, the collective is now "very angry" (v. 7), mirroring the prior individual emotion of Sanballat (v. 1). Enemies from Samaria in the north are now joined by allies from the south (Arabs), east (Ammonites), and west

---

91 The objective pronoun "you" in the clause "they have provoked you" (4:5) is not present in the Hebrew, but its addition (cf. ESV, KJV) helpfully clarifies the object of the verb. The verb is predominantly used of the provocation of the Lord, and occasionally the object must be made explicit (e.g., 1 Kings 21:22 ["me"]; 2 Kings 21:6 ["him"]; 2 Kings 23:19 ["the LORD"]). The prepositional phrase "in the presence of" rules out "the builders" as the direct object of the verb. See Williamson, *Ezra, Nehemiah*, 214.

(Ashdodites). Perhaps Tobiah and Geshem work their respective Ammonite and Arab connections to gain support (2:19). Ashdod, a former Philistine city, is at this time the name of a province under Persian rule (cf. 13:23). When these enemies band together, the Israelite remnant community is now threatened on all sides by forces outnumbering their own (cf. Josh. 11:1–5). What does the community do? As Nehemiah has previously prayed and acted (Neh. 2:4–5), the people respond with prayer combined with prudent action for around-the-clock self-defense (4:9).

4:10–14 "In Judah it was said" suggests this is a regularly repeated song or saying. In spite of progress, the interminable demands of the work bring on a "dispiriting weariness" and frank admission of the inability of the remnant community to complete the job.[92] The complaint about "too much rubble" may reflect the increased destruction of homes along the eastern slope overlooking the Kidron Valley. These dwellings, especially near the wall, were dismantled to augment city defenses in the face of the Babylonian siege (cf. Jer. 33:4). As for the surrounding foes, whether Sanballat and his allies would have actually attacked, given Nehemiah's authorization from Artaxerxes, is beside the point. The difficulty of the labor, combined with the threat of possible assault and desire to kill, generates the intended impact on morale.

The text is silent as to how the Judeans actually become aware of these increased threats. While Nehemiah 4:12 presents interpretive challenges (cf. ESV mg.), it suggests that Jews sympathetic to Jerusalem's plight because they live near its enemies and are aware of their plotting become increasingly distressed and converge often ("from all directions . . . ten times") to communicate their concerns. Aware of the increased saber-rattling, they fear for the safety of loved ones building in Jerusalem. Their message, "You must return to us," represents a call to those from surrounding towns and villages (cf. 3:2, 5, 7) to abandon the Jerusalem mission and return home to relative safety.[93]

This interpretation makes sense of Nehemiah's actions that follow. Given information about real death threats in order to "stop the work" (4:11) and the possibility of desertion of the work by those living outside of Jerusalem (v. 12; cf. v. 22), Nehemiah adopts alternative tactics (v. 13), including a strategic cessation of work (vv. 13–14; cf. v. 15). Although the text is difficult, the sense may be that at some point along the wall that is least elevated ("in the lowest parts") and most visible to outside observation ("in open places") he arms and stations the people "by their clans" (v. 13). This would give the impression of a unified force poised for conflict and show the enemies that any advantage of a surprise attack has been lost. A gathering at one place, rather than distribution of men at various vulnerable points along the wall, also makes better sense of the three verbs that

---

92 McConville, *Ezra, Nehemiah, and Esther*, 91. McConville and others suggest 4:10 is a kind of song intended to keep the work progressing. Clines nicely sets forth its rhythmical nature, often found in laments (*Ezra, Nehemiah, Esther*, 162).

93 Williamson, *Ezra, Nehemiah*, 226; Blenkinsopp, *Ezra-Nehemiah*, 249. This seems more likely than the idea that the Jerusalem wall builders are being urged to return to their particular towns or villages in order to defend the villages themselves. It is the rebuilding of Jerusalem that attracts the ire of the foes.

immediately head verse 14, describing Nehemiah's address to boost morale for the whole community.[94]

At no point should the wisdom of establishing communal defense imply a lack of trust in God. In "remembering" that the Lord is "great and awesome," they also remember that he is faithful to his covenant (1:5; 9:32; Dan. 9:4) and will defend his people in the present as he has in the past. The Lord's implied presence not only dispels the fear of man, as earlier in their history (cf. Ex. 14:13; Num. 14:9; Deut. 3:22; 7:21; 20:3–4; Josh. 10:25); it further braces the community to fight for their families, those who are most precious to them (Neh. 4:14; cf. 2 Sam. 10:12).

4:15–23 Like the first two scenes (vv. 1–6, 7–14), the final one begins by observing that "our enemies heard" (cf. vv. 1, 7). What follows may be viewed in two paragraphs. The first (vv. 16–21) is bounded by an identical Hebrew phrase translated variously in the ESV by "worked on construction" (v. 16) and "labored at the work" (v. 21).[95] Here both workers and weapons feature prominently as Nehemiah readies the community for possible conflict (vv. 19–20). The final paragraph recounts Nehemiah's ongoing concern for security (vv. 22–23).

4:15 This verse provides an introduction to what follows. Previously when the enemies heard of an advance in the wall-building project, they responded with anger and further action (vv. 1–3, 7–8). Now they respond with silence. As the walls go up, the former threats come tumbling down. Enemies once able to "frustrate [the] purpose" of God's people in rebuilding (Ezra 4:5) can do so no longer. God blesses Nehemiah's strategy (cf. comment on Neh. 4:10–14) and "frustrate[s] their plan [= "purpose"]" (cf. Ps. 33:10–11), for a time silencing the derision of Sanballat and Tobiah, as Nehemiah had prayed (Neh. 4:4). The work stoppage implied in verses 13–14 is now also reversed, and the work restarts.

4:16–18 The temporal notice "from that day on" (v. 16) now indicates a fourth shift in tactics, as Nehemiah organizes how the work will proceed until project completion (cf. 6:15).[96] He takes several steps to balance work and defense as well as to maintain morale. Wisely, half of Nehemiah's servants "worked on construction" while he withdraws the other half to provide a visible guard detail in case of attack. The referent of "my servants" (4:16, 23; 5:10, 16; 13:19) is not certain, though it may represent those who function as his private militia in his role as governor (cf. 2:9).[97] The weapons of the latter, including shields and coats of mail, which limit their ability to work, indicate a more formally armed troop (cf. 4:13). Beyond his servants, Nehemiah takes steps with three other groups, each with an assigned task. First, the "leaders" (v. 16) stand apart to supervise progress along

---

94 Williamson (*Ezra, Nehemiah*, 226–227) and Blenkinsopp (*Ezra-Nehemiah*, 249–250) take a comparable approach.
95 Another option is that of the ESV, which places 4:21 as the head of a final paragraph (4:21–23).
96 The three earlier tactics included prayer and work to counter the initial verbal taunts of Sanballat (4:1–6), prayer and setting a guard in light of the general threat of gathering forces (4:7–9), and Nehemiah's own arming of a visible force along with a verbal boost of their morale in the face of specific intelligence (4:10–14). These perceptive observations are found in Kidner, *Ezra and Nehemiah*, 101.
97 A suggestion made in Clines, *Ezra, Nehemiah, Esther*, 163.

specific segments of the wall and to keep watch for potential danger.[98] Next, "those who carried burdens" (v. 17), that is, who bring supplies or clear rubble, do so while maintaining their need to make use of an easily wielded weapon. Likewise, the builders are armed at the hip, needing two available hands to continue the work (v. 18).

4:19–20 Although the threat diminishes, Nehemiah stresses the need for all to remain vigilant given their dispersal around the wall perimeter. As he had earlier exhorted the nobles, officials,[99] and the rest of the people to "remember the Lord" and fight (v. 14), so now he implores this same triad to gather to him for battle should they hear the trumpeter's blast (vv. 18, 20; cf. Judg. 3:27; 6:34). All the while Nehemiah encourages the embrace of Israel's well-worn adage, "Our God will fight for us" (cf. Ex. 14:14; Deut. 1:30; Josh. 10:14, 42; 2 Chron. 32:5–8).

4:21 This verse is taken as a conclusion to the current paragraph, since it summarizes prior content. It recounts in nearly identical language that "We [i.e., Nehemiah and his servants] labored at the work" (cf. v. 16, "My servants worked on construction"); like verse 16, it reiterates that half of the servants stand guard, implying that the other half work.[100] The notice that Nehemiah's servants work and watch from sunrise to beyond sunset (v. 21) transitions to the final paragraph of the chapter.

4:22–23 With "I also said" Nehemiah once more addresses the people (cf. vv. 19–20) and implements a final strategy, calling for workers to remain within the city. Concern over desertions may be valid (cf. v. 12), and keeping builders within Jerusalem will improve efficiency to ensure their "labor by day" (v. 22). However, the primary reason to limit travel remains the city's security. This appeal would also increase the safety of those living outside the city who might endanger themselves by commuting daily back and forth to their nearby villages.

The concluding verse highlights the exemplary leadership of Nehemiah and his support staff, whether kinsmen, servants, or guard, in order to stress their endurance and preparedness. The final clause of verse 23, "each kept his weapon," is clear enough and fits the context well, though how to take the final Hebrew word, translated "at his right hand," remains elusive.[101] As translated in the ESV

---

98 These "leaders" (Hb. *sarim*), typically considered tribal representatives, are translated consistently as "rulers" in the wall building of 3:9, 12, 14, 15, 16, 17, 18, 19. Other translations include "officers," "governor," and "princes" (2:9; 4:16; 7:2; 9:32, 34, 38; 11:1; 12:31, 32). See also comment on Ezra 9:1–2.

99 For "nobles" and "officials" (4:14, 19), cf. note 55. Blenkinsopp (*Ezra-Nehemiah*, 252) provides a good evaluation, particularly for the "officials" (Hb. *seganim*).

100 This assessment is reached independently from C. F. Keil, *The Books of Ezra, Nehemiah, and Esther*, trans. Sophia Taylor, Biblical Commentary on the Old Testament by C. F. Keil and F. Delitzsch (1873; repr. Grand Rapids, MI: Eerdmans, 1966), 206.

101 The concluding phrase reads "each his weapon the water" (cf. ESV mg.). For this reason, while most English translations maintain some rendering of "each his weapon," differences arise in the treatment of the final word, "the water." Some versions maintain the word with the sense that each person carries his weapon "even to/at the water" (NASB, NJPS) or more explicitly "even when he went for water," i.e., for drinking (NIV, NET). Others conclude that the reference to the water implies washing. This reproduces some form of the Latin Vulgate (KJV, CSB). Finally, some translations accept a proposed emendation to a verbal form "each kept . . . at/in his right hand" (ESV, NRSV, NJB). The rationale for this is further explained in Williamson (*Ezra, Nehemiah*, 221) and Blenkinsopp (*Ezra-Nehemiah*, 250), who both adopt this final approach.

it suggests that even at rest they remain fully dressed, with weapons located at their right hand, at the ready.

Response

Like a seed, the driving message of the chapter—"Our God will fight for us" (4:20)—must be planted in our hearts so that it can grow and be recalled often as we press into the world. Indeed, the fact that the Lord will fight for us makes clear that we will face opposition in this world. This is exactly what takes place in this chapter with Nehemiah.

From the start, Nehemiah's concern for the good of Jerusalem is met by Sanballat's great displeasure, jeering, and accusation of rebellion (2:10, 19). This soon evolves into great rage, ending for a time in mockery (4:1–3). If this stratagem was also employed against the Lord Jesus himself (Matt. 27:29, 41; Mark 10:34), his individual disciples and the church must expect no less (Matt. 10:24–25; 2 Pet. 3:1–3; Jude 17–18). And this opposition does not always stop after the first try. As table 2.1 in the Section Overview above reveals, scoffers, intent upon evil, are adaptive and unrelenting. We should not be surprised if our adversaries, faced with initial failure, develop alternative strategies. The joining together of the wall (Neh. 4:6) leads to the joining together (= conspiring) of an array of forces now "very angry" and advancing with real death threats (vv. 7, 11). The church in many parts of the world understands such threats all too well.

Knowing that the Lord is their defender, Nehemiah and the people pray (vv. 4–5, 9). This may appear an obvious observation, but we must be reminded to pray, since prayer is often not our intrinsic reaction to ridicule. Instead, doubting that God will actually fight for us, we may insist upon defending ourselves. As this chapter ably shows, there may come a time for self-defense. However, self-defense must never be placed before turning to God. We admit the need of our "feeble" abilities (v. 2) in the face of overwhelming odds. By calling upon God to judge his enemies in the face of threatened harm, Nehemiah adopts a posture frequent in the psalms (e.g., Pss. 5:10; 35:4–8; 58:6–9; 59:11–17; 109:6–20) and especially in Jeremiah 18:18–23. He entrusts his situation to God not for personal vengeance but so that the Lord would thwart the schemes of Abraham's cursors (Gen. 12:3) and vindicate his own holy name (Neh. 4:5; cf. Ex. 34:6–7). We entrust to God the rage of the nations (Ps. 2:1–3), knowing that he has installed his king, the Lord Jesus, as ruler over all (Ps. 2:6–8) and as the one through whom final justice will be brought to bear (Ps. 2:9). In the meantime, we plead that he would use his weak and feeble people to bring flourishing to the world (1 Cor. 1:26–29; 2 Cor. 10:10).[102]

Knowing that God fights for his people, they are emboldened to take action. Several times in the chapter prayer combines with building and guarding (Neh. 4:4–6, 9). Occasionally the broken world and overwhelming opposition combine with our own frailty to bring real demoralization. In these moments, the tasks the

---

102 For a nuanced and concise treatment of curses in Psalms, see C. John Collins, "Introduction to the Psalms," in *ESV Study Bible*, 938.

Lord places upon us may seem more than we can bear. For Nehemiah's people, the massive rubble pile and unending project dominate their vision (vv. 10–11, 19). In response, he reminds them to lift their eyes and "remember the Lord, who is great and awesome" (v. 14). This language recalls God's covenantal promise to be with this people, a presence that necessarily puts to flight the fear of man (Deut. 7:21). Further, at Nehemiah's behest they unite in a force of mutual support and defense (Neh. 4:13), remembering that the fight for those they love is also a fight of faith (1 Tim. 6:12; 2 Tim. 4:7). Only as we "remember the Lord" (Neh. 4:14) who "will fight for us" (v. 20) are we free to play our role (vv. 16–18) and return "each to his work" (v. 15).

NEHEMIAH 5:1–19

5 Now there arose a great outcry of the people and of their wives against their Jewish brothers. ²For there were those who said, "With our sons and our daughters, we are many. So let us get grain, that we may eat and keep alive." ³There were also those who said, "We are mortgaging our fields, our vineyards, and our houses to get grain because of the famine." ⁴And there were those who said, "We have borrowed money for the king's tax on our fields and our vineyards. ⁵Now our flesh is as the flesh of our brothers, our children are as their children. Yet we are forcing our sons and our daughters to be slaves, and some of our daughters have already been enslaved, but it is not in our power to help it, for other men have our fields and our vineyards."

⁶I was very angry when I heard their outcry and these words. ⁷I took counsel with myself, and I brought charges against the nobles and the officials. I said to them, "You are exacting interest, each from his brother." And I held a great assembly against them ⁸and said to them, "We, as far as we are able, have bought back our Jewish brothers who have been sold to the nations, but you even sell your brothers that they may be sold to us!" They were silent and could not find a word to say. ⁹So I said, "The thing that you are doing is not good. Ought you not to walk in the fear of our God to prevent the taunts of the nations our enemies? ¹⁰Moreover, I and my brothers and my servants are lending them money and grain. Let us abandon this exacting of interest. ¹¹Return to them this very day their fields, their vineyards, their olive orchards, and their houses, and the percentage of money, grain, wine, and oil that you have been exacting from them." ¹²Then they said, "We will restore these and require nothing from them. We will do as you say." And I called the priests and made them swear to do as they had promised. ¹³I also shook out the fold¹ of my garment and said, "So may God shake out every man from his house and from his labor who does not keep this promise. So may he be shaken out and emptied." And all the assembly said "Amen" and praised the LORD. And the people did as they had promised.

¹⁴ Moreover, from the time that I was appointed to be their governor in the land of Judah, from the twentieth year to the thirty-second year of Artaxerxes the king, twelve years, neither I nor my brothers ate the food allowance of the governor. ¹⁵ The former governors who were before me laid heavy burdens on the people and took from them for their daily ration[2] forty shekels[3] of silver. Even their servants lorded it over the people. But I did not do so, because of the fear of God. ¹⁶ I also persevered in the work on this wall, and we acquired no land, and all my servants were gathered there for the work. ¹⁷ Moreover, there were at my table 150 men, Jews and officials, besides those who came to us from the nations that were around us. ¹⁸ Now what was prepared at my expense[4] for each day was one ox and six choice sheep and birds, and every ten days all kinds of wine in abundance. Yet for all this I did not demand the food allowance of the governor, because the service was too heavy on this people. ¹⁹ Remember for my good, O my God, all that I have done for this people.

[1] Hebrew *bosom* [2] Compare Vulgate; Hebrew *took from them for food and wine after* [3] A *shekel* was about 2/5 ounce or 11 grams [4] Or *prepared for me*

Section Overview

The paint hardly dries on the canvas of the prior chapter's portrait of unity in the face of external opposition before the sketch for the next painting begins. The unity revealed in the two previous chapters quickly transitions to complaints from some members of the body that others within the community are exploiting current events for economic advantage.

The structure of this chapter is straightforward. The initial scene begins with a "great outcry" arising from three specific groups (Neh. 5:1–5). Some are struggling for enough food, others find it difficult to maintain their land and homes due to famine, and a final group cannot pay the royal taxes. Nehemiah's response marks out the start of the next scene (vv. 6–13). The seriousness of the situation is expressed in the charges raised against the "nobles and officials" concerning the injustice of their economic practices. Nehemiah's rebuke and exhortation challenge them to a better way and lead to genuine repentance. The favorable outcome encourages Nehemiah to clarify further his own practices during his whole period as governor (vv. 14–18). He testifies unequivocally that his concern for his people and fear of God have motivated his own financial sacrifice. The chapter ends with Nehemiah's first prayer asking God to remember his work (v. 19).

Section Outline

II.D.5. Governor Nehemiah Shows "Interest" for All (5:1–19)
    a. Economic Hardship Expressed with a Great Outcry (5:1–5)
    b. Nehemiah Rebukes Leadership for Their Unjust Practices (5:6–13)
    c. Nehemiah Rejects Governor's Food Allowance (5:14–18)
    d. Nehemiah's First Prayer Asking God to Remember His Deeds (5:19)

Comment

5:1 The "great outcry" is the occasioning incident that begins the chapter. The expression indicates a significant level of emotional distress, often in the context of war or injustice (Gen. 27:34; Ex. 3:9; 11:6; 12:30; 1 Sam. 4:13–14; 2 Kings 8:5; Jer. 48:3–5; 49:21; Zeph. 1:10). Rather than from a sudden attack of outsiders upon Jerusalem (Neh. 4:11), this verbal protest arises from men ("the people"), explicitly joined by "their wives," and directed internally "against their Jewish brothers." Several factors may have brought these submerged complaints to the surface. First, although the wall-construction process was too short to have caused this disruption (cf. 6:15), Nehemiah's demand that builders remain in Jerusalem (4:22) would increase the pressure upon those with understaffed local farms. Wives, absent their husbands, would become burdened with the August/September harvest of grapes, dates, and late figs. This would also be the ideal time for creditors to exact payment.[103] Further, we may surmise that hostile neighbors, unsympathetic to Jerusalem's plight, may have restricted commercial transactions with the local population. These prior factors only exacerbate the underlying problem, namely, a famine increasing the need to procure food.

5:2–4 Each of these verses begins with identical words in the Hebrew, with each providing increasing detail of the complaint. The basic problems are food and money. In the first group (v. 2) we find those most desperate within the community. They are landless, and their sole concern is acquisition of grain in order to "keep alive" their children. Similar to the first group, the second complainants share the basic need to "get grain" (v. 3). However, unlike the first group, they yet possess fields and vineyards, but since these are their only source of income, they are "mortgaging" (from the Hb. verb ʿarab) them, along with their houses, because of the "famine" (from the noun raʿab). The reason for the famine is never stated (cf. Hag. 1:6, 10–11; 2:17). The subtle shift in focus of the final group is their need to borrow money, putting up property as collateral. It seems that they have enough food but are in arrears on the king's tax and now must borrow to pay their fixed annual taxes.[104] Those who cannot pay are in serious danger of losing their fields and vineyards to creditors.

5:5 The statement "Now our flesh is as the flesh of our brothers, our children are as their children" summarizes the impact upon all three prior groups. This expression employs the strongest kind of statement of identity, claiming in no uncertain terms that they are family (cf. 1 Kings 22:4; 2 Kings 3:7). It is hoped that their economically advantaged "Jewish brothers" will feel the full desperation of

---

103 Some commentators argue that 5:1–13 is historically displaced and comes from a time much later in Nehemiah's governorship. One main argument is that the wall-building period is much too short for such a crisis to arise. Certainly, the time is short. However, the wall is completed on the twenty-fifth day of Elul (approx. mid-September), which meant construction began in mid-July. The complaints would have arisen in August or September, at the crucial point of harvest. Williamson (*Ezra, Nehemiah*, 235–236) provides a lengthy discussion supporting the text's current historical setting. Similar arguments are found in Blenkinsopp, *Ezra-Nehemiah*, 256.
104 In Ezra 4:13, 20, the noun is translated "tribute."

those forced to pledge their older children to debt-slavery to serve creditors until the family debt is paid. True, this is a better option than loss of property, which would forever prevent them from redeeming their children. It is also true that this kind of debt payment was permitted and regulated within Mosaic legislation, but there is also particular concern for the treatment of the Israelite as "brother" (Ex. 21:2–11; Lev. 25:39–46 [cf. 2 Kings 4:1–2]; Deut. 15:12–18). It is this kinship connection that is appealed to now.[105]

Unfortunately, some daughters have "already been enslaved," doubtless an incredibly heavy and painful burden to their parents. Because some creditors have already received the land's produce and perhaps even the land itself as payment on defaulted loans, the idiom "there is no power for our hand" (i.e., "it is not in our power to help") reveals that those enslaving their children have no other option for payment (cf. Deut. 28:32). In short, the tragic reality is that some of their own Jewish brothers have taken up the role of foreign oppressors. The mention of "brothers" (Neh. 5:1, 5, 7, 8) as well as the loss of people and property nicely transitions to the next scene.

5:6–13 In light of the "great outcry" (vv. 1–5), Nehemiah first contends with the leaders in the community (vv. 6–11). After their positive response (v. 12) the scene concludes with Nehemiah's enacted warning (v. 13).

5:6–11 To this point in the book Nehemiah has never described himself as "angry" in spite of the rage rising from adversaries (4:1, 7). Now, when the disadvantaged within the community are oppressed by "their Jewish brothers" (5:1), he expresses anger due to "their outcry." In the response that follows, Nehemiah not only exhorts but also provides a model for handling community strife.

In the face of a potentially volatile situation, he pauses to reflect (v. 7), even though the ethical landscape is clear to him (v. 9) and his role as governor (v. 14) provides the necessary authority to confront the "nobles and officials" (2:16; 4:14, 19; 7:5).[106] The charges brought are less a formal lawsuit and closer to a concise reprimand, although this is debated.[107] Debate also surrounds the specific charges (5:10–11). He may be rebuking the making of loans at interest (i.e., "exacting of interest," ESV; cf. NIV), a practice counter to the Lord's explicit instructions (Ex. 22:25–27; Lev. 25:35–37; Deut. 23:19–20).[108] Alternatively, it is proposed that although the loans were made in a legal way, persons are "seizing the collateral" (NET).[109] Although not ideal (Prov. 22:26–27), giving and receiving a pledge to

---

105 On OT slavery see J. G. McConville, *Deuteronomy*, ApOTC 5 (Downers Grove, IL: IVP Academic, 2002), 261–263; Jay Sklar, *Leviticus*, TOTC 3 (Downers Grove, IL: IVP Academic, 2014), 307–310.
106 On these groups, see brief discussion in note 55.
107 Fensham, for example, takes Nehemiah's charges as a "lawsuit" that cannot take place in an ordinary court since some of the judges are among the accused (*Ezra and Nehemiah*, 193). Others take this as more informal (Clines, *Ezra, Nehemiah, Esther*, 168).
108 The Pentateuchal texts use the more typical Hebrew noun for "interest" (*neshek*) or its cognate verb "to lend on interest" (*nashak*). Nehemiah 5 instead uses the noun (*masha'*; 5:7) and the cognate verb (*nashah*; 5:10, 11), translated "exacting interest" (5:7) "lending" (5:10), and "exacting" (5:11).
109 This position is espoused in Clines, *Ezra, Nehemiah, Esther*, 168–169; Williamson, *Ezra, Nehemiah*, 233; and Blenkinsopp, *Ezra-Nehemiah*, 259.

guarantee a loan was permissible within certain guidelines (cf. Ex. 22:25–27; Deut. 24:6, 10–13, 17). Now those lines have been crossed and the creditors are seizing pledges of people and property. This impacts the ongoing ability of the poor to sustain the lives of their families (cf. Neh. 5:11). A third option holds that they are "pressing claims on loans" (NJPS), perhaps demanding immediate payment.

In any event, the "great outcry" (v. 1) results in a "great assembly" (v. 7). The aggrieved and the offenders, as "Jewish brothers" (vv. 1, 8), gather in a family meeting. The family language amplifies the anguish of relational dysfunction. Nehemiah first addresses the problem of those persons now in servitude (vv. 8–9; cf. v. 5). In strong contrast to the nobles and officials, Nehemiah includes himself among those buying back (i.e., redeeming) "Jewish brothers" sold to pay debt. They are destitute and unable to redeem themselves (Lev. 25:47–49). The repetition of the verb "to sell" (Neh. 5:8) reveals the incongruity of situation. As if being enslaved to Gentiles were not distressing enough, brothers with economic advantage are actually doing the selling, a forbidden act (Ex. 21:8; Lev. 25:42; Deut. 24:7)! Following the guilty silence of the accused, Nehemiah's evaluation that such actions are "not good" reveals that the offenders know their guilt warrants the rebuke. They are harming their brothers. These actions also show that they do not "walk in the fear of our God" (Neh. 5:9). This colossal failure to reflect the Lord's compassion in the world strikes at the very core of Israel's missional purpose for following God's gracious law (Deut. 8:6; 10:12; 13:4; 2 Chron. 6:31; Jer. 44:7). Rather than wondering at Israel as a "wise and understanding people" and marveling at the God who would shape this people by his instruction (Deut. 4:5–8), the nations offer only "taunts" (cf. Neh. 1:3, 2:17; 4:4).

With "moreover" (5:10), Nehemiah turns to the loss of property (vv. 3–5, 11). On its own, his loan of "money and grain" is not contrary to Mosaic legislation. Rather, the problem is that some are profiting from the unhappy plight of others (cf. Lev. 25:35–38; Ezek. 22:12). "Let us abandon" (Neh. 5:10) may suggest Nehemiah's inclusion among those profiting; on the other hand, he immediately excludes himself with the rebuke, "*you* [not we] have been exacting" (v. 11). At its heart, his call to "restore" (v. 12) is a call for all to repent and offer a truly compassionate response to bless those now in economic peril. Nehemiah first calls for the immediate restoration of all land and property seized either as collateral or because of the inability of debtors to pay. Less certain is his second proposal calling for the return of "the percentage" (lit., "the hundredth of"). This may refer to a monthly interest of 1 percent based on a yearly 12 percent, or it may refer to an unspecified amount of interest. In any event, rather than "tell" its principles by quoting specific Pentateuchal texts (cf. Ex. 22:25–27; Deut. 15:10–11), the chapter "shows" them through the narrative action.

5:12a No debate, no counterproposal, no verbal pushback arises from the creditors—only the unambiguous "We will restore . . . we will do as you say." This suggests true repentance. It is open to debate whether Nehemiah is requiring the cancellation of all debts. The statement that they will "require nothing" of their debtors may imply that creditors are willing to cancel fully the original loan also. While that is possible, they may be still expecting payment of principal but be willing to release what they had seized as security for repayment.[110]

5:12b–13 Nehemiah concludes by first requiring an oath sworn before priests (cf. Ezra 10:5).[111] Next, their offense expressed by a triple repetition of the verb "to sell" (Neh. 5:8) is met with threefold use of the verb "to shake out" (*na'ar*; v. 13). Moving from his own symbolic action "I also shook out"—like emptying one's pockets—then to God as the subject of the verb "may [he] shake out," he concludes with the threat to the oath takers, "may he be shaken out," implying the loss of all they own. Notably, when God is the subject of this verb, it always refers to judgment (Job 38:13), including when the Lord "shook off" (i.e., "overthrew") Pharaoh's army in the exodus (Ex. 14:27; Ps. 136:15).[112] In short, if they do not "do as they had promised" (Neh. 5:12), they risk a judgment similar to that experienced by one of Israel's archetypal enemies. The community, both the aggrieved and the repentant, issue an affirmative "Amen," and the praise that follows is joined with the narrative evaluation that they did "as they had promised."

5:14–18 This previously narrated event gives Nehemiah pause to reflect at a later time on his own generosity as governor. Repeated terms in the introduction (vv. 14–15) and conclusion (v. 18) make clear that his focus is on his generosity to his fellow Jews in contrast to the lack of generosity among his predecessors.

The opening verses (vv. 14–15) envision the whole twelve-year stretch (445–443 BC) encompassing Nehemiah's first tenure as "their governor."[113] This provides the first verification of his early service as governor (2:1, 7, 9). (As 13:6 makes clear, at a later point he will serve a second term of unknown length.) Moreover, the reference to "former governors" (5:15) accords with the prevalent references to governors throughout Ezra-Nehemiah. Without further specification it is uncertain if these prior governors include only those associated with the province of Judah (Ezra 5:8; cf. Ezra 2:1//Neh. 7:6; 1:3; 11:3), such as Sheshbazzar (Ezra 5:14) and Zerubbabel (Hag. 1:1), or whether the reference is broader and could include Tattenai (Ezra 5:6; 6:6) or some other unnamed "governors" (Ezra 4:9; 8:36; Neh. 2:7, 9; 3:7).

More importantly, the paragraph focuses especially on Nehemiah's conduct in contrast to that of his predecessors. In particular, Nehemiah determined that he and his family (i.e., "my brothers") would abstain from the "food allowance of the governor" (5:14), a phrase repeated in verse 18 to underscore his relinquishing

---

110 Williamson states that "if property that had been seized in lieu of repayment was to be returned, it is clearly implied that this also involves cancellation of the original loan" (*Ezra, Nehemiah*, 241). Some commentators qualify "require nothing" with "by way of pledge," claiming Nehemiah could not possibly have required the cancellation of all debts as a gift. With this interpretation, the sense is that creditors expect repayment on the original loan but give up what they had seized as guarantee of repayment. See Clines, *Ezra, Nehemiah, Esther*, 169; Leslie C. Allen and Timothy S. Laniak, *Ezra, Nehemiah, Esther*, NIBCOT 9 (Peabody, MA: Hendrickson, 2003), 111, 114.
111 Clearly "them" of 5:12b refers not to the priests but to the "nobles and officials" who took the oath.
112 For "shook off" as a translation, see the ESV footnotes at Exodus 14:27; Psalm 136:15.
113 On the noun *pekhah* and other terms translated "governor," cf. comment on Ezra 5:3–5.

of the allowance typically rendered to the office holder. This was not what his predecessors had done. By means of a repeated verb (*kabad*, "to be/make heavy"), he notes that prior governors had made "heavy" the service of the people (vv. 15, 18; cf. 1 Kings 12:10, 14). In the Persian context, this heavy burden refers not to the relatively short-lived wall building but to the assessment of imperial taxes. Not only was the king's tax to be paid (Neh. 5:4; cf. Ezra 4:13, 20), governors were allowed to take additional taxes for provincial administration, projects, and support for their household. With respect to the latter, prior governors had acted accordingly by taking their daily "forty shekels."[114] Perhaps predictably, the subordinate tax collectors were even more oppressive (cf. Neh. 9:37; Luke 22:25). In all this Nehemiah has acted differently, being motivated by the two great commandments: his reverence for God expressed in love for his brothers (Neh. 5:15, cf. vv. 8–9). Throughout his tenure he refused to exacerbate the situation by imposing more taxes than necessary.

In addition to his compassionate care, two further points illustrate the nature of Nehemiah's governorship. First, it was king-like in nature, keeping with what was expected of a governor in the Persian period. Hosting 150 men daily at his table is a clear example of this. Those present included "Jews and officials," perhaps corresponding to the "nobles and officials" mentioned elsewhere (2:16; 4:14, 19; 5:7; 7:5). Also included were Persians and perhaps Judeans who had been granted land for past service to the king, satrap, or governor.[115] The amount of food noted, modest by ancient Near Eastern royal standards, is significant, and leftovers would be redistributed to others.[116] With respect to the "nations" (5:17), their mention further highlights Nehemiah's responsibility as governor to entertain Persian diplomats or perhaps Jews visiting Jerusalem from outside of the province. That this was done "at my expense" (v. 18) likely indicates that meals were resourced from farmlands available to him in his gubernatorial role. Overall, he reiterates points made in verses 14–15 concerning his refusal to take the food allowance.

Second, Nehemiah's governorship was characterized by his dedication to building the wall. This is noted in verse 16, which sits at the center of the paragraph, portraying the dedication of Nehemiah and supporting attendants ("my servants," cf. 4:16) to their work upon the wall. The mention of not acquiring land underscores his rejection of material acquisition in general, coheres with prior suggestions that Nehemiah acquired no land from those in need of loans (5:3, 5, 11), and is perhaps one more way in which he contrasts with his predecessors.

5:19 Nehemiah's own heavy burden of public ministry includes the potential that his efforts and sacrifice would fail. Now, as elsewhere (cf. 13:14, 22, 31), we

---

114 A challenging textual issue surrounds the phrase "for their daily ration" (5:15; cf. ESV mg.). The current translation is based on the Latin Vulgate and the presence of a comparable phrase, "for each day," found at 5:18. This daily income came to approximately 1 pound (450 g) of silver per day (Clines, *Ezra, Nehemiah, Esther*, 171).
115 See Lisbeth S. Fried, "150 Men at Nehemiah's Table? The Role of the Governor's Meals in the Achaemenid Provincial Economy," *JBL* 137/4 (2018): 821–831.
116 Fried, who makes this point, notes that the amount of meat would be approximately 800 pounds (360 kg) per day ("150 Men," 827).

overhear his plea that God would make fruitful his overall conduct, in accordance with God's will, not only for his life but also in the lives of those whom he has faithfully represented and served.

Response

In his role as governor Nehemiah was attentive to the cry of the distressed (5:1–5), exhorted the guilty to repent (vv. 6–13), and forswore his privilege for the sake of others (vv. 14–18). Each of these three realities is easily seen in the ministry of the Lord Jesus and now, by extension, must be characteristic of the church as we bear his image as the body of Christ.

First, God's people are to hear the cry of the oppressed. God did not ignore Israel's cries in the past (Ex. 3:7; Neh. 9:9), and the Scriptures, especially the Psalms, abound with the promise that he hears us in our current distress (Pss. 18:6; 25:14–18; 31:7; 81:7; 106:44; 107:1–43). God's people are to imitate God's actions in this regard. The "great outcry" (Neh. 5:1) that heads the chapter overflows with deep anguish and loss. Rather than blaming those in economic distress for their current financial problems, Nehemiah "heard their outcry" (v. 6) and responded with anger appropriate to the injustice they faced. Certainly, it is vital for local congregations to attend to needs beyond itself; however, our first responsibility is to hear the cry of anguish among God's own people. By showing that we "love one another," we bear Christ's image to the world (John 13:34–35; 1 John 3:17).

Second, God's people must be concerned about repentance. Through Nehemiah's courageous and compassionate response the Lord confronts, brings repentance, and ultimately restores bounty to the community. Note Nehemiah's approach. In the face of his anger, Nehemiah pauses to consider a measured response—private reprimand followed by public discussion and rebuke. In all this he does not fail to admit his own complicity. It may also be noted that in the practical exhortation "Return!" (Neh. 5:11) we find the only imperative to the community in the whole chapter. The biblical basis for this is never made explicit, but a wealth of Pentateuchal texts undergird the ethics of the entire narrative (cf. comment on 5:6–11). The exhortation to repent is met initially with silence rather than self-justifying excuses and is followed by a genuine statement of repentance: "We will restore" (v. 12). It was injustices against neighbor that, in part, brought prophetic indictment in the past (Amos 4:1; 8:4–6; Isa. 5:8–10; 10:1–4; Jer. 22:11–17; Ezekiel 18). Now, with repentance, there is hope of fruitfulness and new life.

Finally, God's people must be willing to give up their own privileges for the sake of others. In view of the heavy burdens upon his people, Nehemiah refused to take the food allowance privileged him as governor. His reason was simply but powerfully stated as "the fear of God" (Neh. 5:15). Even in fulfilling his divine call to rebuild Jerusalem (v. 16), Nehemiah did not take advantage of others in ways his leadership may have permitted. His life was one of sacrifice for others. Similarly, when the church sacrifices its financial security or social standing for the sake of wider ministry goals, it bears Christ to the world (Phil. 2:3–8). The two great commandments, love of God and neighbor (Matt. 22:36–40), pulsate throughout this chapter, with God's redeeming love as the motivation to love and sacrifice for others. As in the first exodus, the Lord had once more restored to the remnant a measure of freedom in the land—how dare they now use that freedom to enslave their fellows? Their covenant-keeping God had chosen them to be his people. This meant they must walk in the "fear of God" (Neh. 5:9, 15), keeping and obeying his commandments, holding fast their love for him as well as their brothers. These remain persistent expressions of biblical discipleship (1 Pet. 2:16–17) and are a central way we fulfill our calling to "be a specimen of love,"[117] modeling a new humanity to the world.

NEHEMIAH 6:1–7:4

6 Now when Sanballat and Tobiah and Geshem the Arab and the rest of our enemies heard that I had built the wall and that there was no breach left in it (although up to that time I had not set up the doors in the gates), [2] Sanballat and Geshem sent to me, saying, "Come and let us meet together at Hakkephirim in the plain of Ono." But they intended to do me harm. [3] And I sent messengers to them, saying, "I am doing a great work and I cannot come down. Why should the work stop while I leave it and come down to you?" [4] And they sent to me four times in this way, and I answered them in the same manner. [5] In the same way Sanballat for the fifth time sent his servant to me with an open letter in his hand. [6] In it was written, "It is reported among the nations, and Geshem[1] also says it, that you and the Jews intend to rebel; that is why you are building the wall. And according to these reports you wish to become their king. [7] And you have also set up prophets to proclaim concerning you in Jerusalem, 'There is a king in Judah.' And now the king will hear of these reports. So now come and let us take counsel together." [8] Then I sent to him, saying, "No such things as you say have been done, for you are inventing them out of your own mind." [9] For they all wanted to frighten us, thinking, "Their hands will drop from the work, and it will not be done." But now, O God,[2] strengthen my hands.

[10] Now when I went into the house of Shemaiah the son of Delaiah, son of Mehetabel, who was confined to his home, he said, "Let us meet together in the house of God, within the temple. Let us close the doors of the temple, for they are coming to kill you. They are coming to kill you by night." [11] But I said, "Should such a man as I run away? And what man such as I could go into the temple and live?[3] I will not go in." [12] And I understood and saw that God had not sent him, but he had pronounced the prophecy against me because Tobiah and Sanballat had hired him. [13] For this purpose he was hired, that I should be afraid and act in this

---

117 McConville, *Ezra, Nehemiah, and Esther*, 100.

way and sin, and so they could give me a bad name in order to taunt me. [14] Remember Tobiah and Sanballat, O my God, according to these things that they did, and also the prophetess Noadiah and the rest of the prophets who wanted to make me afraid.

[15] So the wall was finished on the twenty-fifth day of the month Elul, in fifty-two days. [16] And when all our enemies heard of it, all the nations around us were afraid and fell greatly in their own esteem, for they perceived that this work had been accomplished with the help of our God. [17] Moreover, in those days the nobles of Judah sent many letters to Tobiah, and Tobiah's letters came to them. [18] For many in Judah were bound by oath to him, because he was the son-in-law of Shecaniah the son of Arah: and his son Jehohanan had taken the daughter of Meshullam the son of Berechiah as his wife. [19] Also they spoke of his good deeds in my presence and reported my words to him. And Tobiah sent letters to make me afraid.

7 Now when the wall had been built and I had set up the doors, and the gatekeepers, the singers, and the Levites had been appointed, [2] I gave my brother Hanani and Hananiah the governor of the castle charge over Jerusalem, for he was a more faithful and God-fearing man than many. [3] And I said to them, "Let not the gates of Jerusalem be opened until the sun is hot. And while they are still standing guard, let them shut and bar the doors. Appoint guards from among the inhabitants of Jerusalem, some at their guard posts and some in front of their own homes." [4] The city was wide and large, but the people within it were few, and no houses had been rebuilt.

[1] Hebrew *Gashmu* [2] Hebrew lacks *O God* [3] Or *would go into the temple to save his life*

Section Overview

This textual unit concludes the wall reconstruction, the "third movement" in Ezra-Nehemiah (Neh. 1:1–7:4).[118] As in the book of Ezra (Ezra 4:1–24; 5:3–5), external adversaries threaten the community throughout the entire project. This is especially apparent whenever they "heard" about progress on the wall.[119] The main leaders in this opposition are Sanballat, Tobiah, and Geshem (Neh. 2:19). Now these individuals (6:1) press their final attack against Nehemiah in an attempt to keep him from completing his work. "Fear" is the key verb that structures 6:1–19, occurring in the final verse of each of the first three paragraphs to describe the fear of man (6:1–9, 10–14, 15–19). In the final paragraph the verb is turned on its head when it identifies Hananiah as a "God-fearing man" (7:2). It is the second type of fear that helps one avoid the first.

Hearing that the wall is almost done, enemies make several attempts to meet with Nehemiah through a series of letters. They attempt to frighten him into stopping the work. He rebuffs each of their advances because he perceives their

---

118 The first movement described the building of the altar and temple under Zerubbabel (Ezra 3–6), while the second movement described the reconstitution of the people under the instruction of the law by Ezra (Ezra 7–10).
119 See the Section Overview of 4:1–23 for how throughout chapters 2, 4, and 6 enemies hear of building progress and react negatively.

intention to harm him (6:1–4). Nehemiah denies the rumors of Sanballat's final letter, clarifies Sanballat's motivation, and prays to the Lord for strength (6:5–9).

Next, Shemaiah is hired to pronounce a prophecy to entice Nehemiah to meet him in the temple because "they are coming to kill you" (6:10). Nehemiah again refuses to meet because he recognizes the dishonorable motives and knows that Tobiah and Sanballat are behind the hiring (6:11–13). As in the first paragraph, the second concludes with prayer (6:14; cf. 6:9).

In the third paragraph it is the enemies who now fear because they "heard" (6:16) that the wall has been completed with God's help (6:15–16). However, even this good news leads to further letters between nobles and Tobiah and subsequent communication with Nehemiah. For the final time Nehemiah concludes that letters have been sent "to make me afraid" (6:17–19).

The final paragraph connects with the first by mentioning that the doors are set up (7:1; cf. 6:1). Nehemiah then appoints officials and establishes security practices for the city. The unit concludes by observing that Jerusalem is still in need of repopulation and sufficient housing (7:4).

Section Outline

II.D.6. Enemy Attempts to Frighten Nehemiah Cannot Stop the Wall
   (6:1–7:4)
   a. Enemies Write Letters in Order to Frighten (6:1–9)
   b. Prophets Deceive in Order to Frighten (6:10–14)
   c. Wall Completion; Tobiah Writes Letters in Order to Frighten
      (6:15–19)
   d. Nehemiah Acts for the Security of Jerusalem (7:1–4)

Comment

6:1–4 With only the doors left to hang at the gates, the opponents change tactics by pressing Nehemiah directly. Sanballat and Geshem the Arab, likely representing Tobiah and all the opposition, request a meeting with Nehemiah (v. 2).[120] Sanballat is probably governor of Samaria at this time (cf. comment on 2:9–10). Neither the purpose of the meeting nor the precise location of "Hakkephirim" is known.[121] Its setting in the "plain of Ono" (cf. Ezra 2:33//Neh. 7:37; 11:35) would place it outside the province of Judah near its northwest border, surrounded by the hostile provinces of Samaria and Ashdod.[122] To get there, Nehemiah would have to leave the work that remains and "come down" (6:3), likely referring to a geographical descent from the higher elevation of Jerusalem. Nehemiah's states unequivocally that the opponents are up to no good (v. 2). His evaluation would not be difficult

---

120 For Sanballat and Tobiah, cf. comment on 2:9–10; for "Geshem the Arab" (6:1, 6), cf. comment on 2:19–20.
121 It has been suggested that this is the village Kafr Ana, southeast of the port city of Joppa.
122 Whether it was inside or outside of the province is debated. References to exiles who settled there (Ezra 2:33; Neh. 11:35) may imply that Ono was within the province of Judah. It was about 7 miles (11 km) southeast of Joppa, approximately 27 miles (43 km) northwest of Jerusalem, and around 25 miles (40 km) southwest of Samaria.

given the past behaviors of these men and the distance of the suggested meeting location. Why not meet in Jerusalem?

Nehemiah's diplomatic but terse response does not reject the offer directly (v. 3). Instead, he emphasizes the work that would stop in his absence. He refuses to allow a meeting with these men to deter his course of action, despite their ongoing attempts (v. 4). Completing the wall is the very reason he was authorized to return (2:8; 5:16). Nehemiah considers his calling a "great work," referring to its size (cf. 4:19), and elsewhere a "good work," since it advances only due to God's goodness (2:18).

6:5–8 The phrase "in the same way" (v. 5)[123] leads us to expect a similar attempt. Instead, an alternative approach is adopted. The stated goal of this fifth letter, "Let us take counsel together," shows that Sanballat still seeks an audience with Nehemiah (v. 7b; cf. v. 2). However, to compel that meeting, he writes an "open" (i.e., unsecured) letter. Typically, official documents, written on leather or papyrus, were tied up and impressed with a clay seal to protect their contents and indicate authenticity. Because an unsecured letter would encourage rumors, it would naturally prompt Nehemiah to wonder how far its contents were publicly known. Sanballat feigns concern to coerce Nehemiah to meet him by raising the specter that Artaxerxes will hear about the contents of the letter (v. 7b). These contents include allegations of Nehemiah's sedition rumored "among the nations" and confirmed by the important figure Geshem[124] (v. 6). "Nations" refers here to the provincial adversaries surrounding Judah (4:7; 5:9).

Three times Sanballat uses the pronoun "you" (6:6) to identify Nehemiah as the very one who, according to reports, is inciting rebellion and seeking kingship for himself. It is these items, Sanballat suggests, that provide the reason for "why *you* are building the wall" (cf. 2:19). Nehemiah understands the underlying threat: Artaxerxes may hear these interpretations of his wall building and assume they are true. Sanballat is likely aware of the alleged Jewish rebellion made known to Artaxerxes in an earlier letter. Those prior accusations had ended wall construction (Ezra 4:13, 16, 21–22). Sanballat now hopes for the same.

These "reports" also claim that Nehemiah has "set up" (i.e., appointed or designated) prophets to proclaim his royal status (Neh. 6:7). Though unstated, perhaps this rumor plays on prophetic promises of messianic kingship (Hag. 2:20–23; Zech. 6:12–13). In his unambiguous denial, Nehemiah accuses Sanballat of complete fabrication of these charges, "inventing them out of your own mind" (Neh. 6:8; cf. 1 Kings 12:33). Clearly Nehemiah is loyal to Artaxerxes and, with no known Davidic heritage, has neither claim to nor desire for the throne.

6:9 The key word "fear" makes its first appearance (vv. 9, 13, 14, 19; 7:2). Nehemiah quickly perceives that this fear's ultimate purpose is to make "their hands . . . drop." This figurative language means "to discourage" or "to demoralize" (cf. Ezra 4:4).

---

123 This identical phrase appears two times in 6:4, translated "in this way" and "in the same manner."
124 The ESV footnote, "Gashmu," indicates the Hebrew name here that most interpreters take as an equivalent of Geshem (cf. 6:1).

The enemies hope the hands of the wall builders will weaken and the work cease. It is clear from earlier attempts that Sanballat and company will stop at nothing to see this happen (Neh. 4:7–9, 11). Throughout, Nehemiah and his community trust the Lord for his protection (2:4; 4:4–5, 9; 6:14). All this encourages us to see Nehemiah's final request, "strengthen my hands," as a prayer to God, countering discouragement and showing his implicit trust in the Lord.[125]

6:10–13 Tobiah and Sanballat shift strategy by hiring Shemaiah to pronounce a prophecy against Nehemiah (v. 13). Several uncertainties arise in the introduction (v. 10). Apart from his lineage, nothing is known of Shemaiah. Whether he is a priest or an otherwise unknown prophet is uncertain. His name is relatively common, even within Ezra-Nehemiah.[126] The prophetic connection seems more likely, given the prophetic focus that follows (vv. 12, 14). Likewise, no explanation is given for why Nehemiah enters Shemaiah's house nor why Shemaiah is "confined to his home" or by whom (cf. Jer. 36:5). However one interprets this restriction,[127] Shemaiah suggests that they "meet together in the house of God" (cf. Neh. 6:2).

What follows is more apparent. For impact, Shemaiah twice repeats that Nehemiah's life is under threat of assassination, although by whom he does not specify. The assumed suspects must include Sanballat, Geshem, and Tobiah. Refuge can be found at the horns of the altar (1 Kings 1:50–53; 2:28), but this is located in the open courtyard, not within the temple itself. Likewise, Nehemiah is not in a situation in which sanctuary law would apply (cf. Ex. 21:12–14). Rather, Shemaiah is suggesting that Nehemiah hide out "within the temple" itself, that is, in the very sanctuary.

Nehemiah responds by means of two rhetorical questions (Neh. 6:11). First, to "run away" to the temple for refuge would be contrary to his character and calling as governor. It would fly in the face of the authority granted him by Artaxerxes (5:14) and the clear evidence of God's gracious approval (2:8, 20). Nehemiah has capable armed defenders if he is actually under threat (2:9; 4:23). With the second rhetorical question, Nehemiah addresses the danger of entering the temple. Entering as a layman would profane the sanctuary and place him under a legal threat of death (cf. Num. 18:1–7). Additionally, contact with a holy God could lead to death (Ex. 33:20; Deut. 5:24–25).[128] Nehemiah views the whole act—both fleeing and defiling the sanctuary—as "sin" (Neh. 6:13), a lack of trust in God.

---

125 As the ESV footnote observes, "O God" is not present in the Hebrew. The Greek translation (LXX) may be rendered, "But now I strengthened my hands." The lack of the words "O God" leads some English translations to render this as Nehemiah's determination rather than a prayer (e.g., NAB: "But instead, I now redoubled my efforts").

126 Shemaiah is the name of one of the leading men who returned with Ezra (Ezra 8:13, 16; cf. Ezra 2:60), a priest who took a foreign wife (Ezra 10:21), and a priest who sealed the covenant (Neh. 10:8). It is possible that these last two are the same priest. Elsewhere, the name is attested in both prophetic (1 Kings 12:22; Jer. 26:20; 29:24–32) and Levitical circles (1 Chron. 9:14; 15:11; 24:6; Neh. 11:15).

127 The clause reads, "and he was *confined*," to which the ESV adds "to his home." Williamson provides a list of six suggestions from varied studies for how to interpret this verb translated "confined" (*Ezra, Nehemiah*, 249). He concludes, albeit hesitantly, that the suggestion to take it as "harassed, worried" fits the context best, rendering it "who was *looking extremely worried*" (245).

128 An alternative translation takes "and live" not as contrasted with dying but as a purpose clause meaning "in order to live." See the ESV footnote to 6:11 (cf. NASB, NET). By this alternative, Nehemiah builds upon the point made in the first rhetorical question.

Like the earlier attempts to deceive (vv. 8–9), Nehemiah immediately perceives that "God had not sent him" (v. 12; cf. Jer. 14:14–15; 28:15). According to Sanballat, prophets had proclaimed "concerning you" (Neh. 6:7). From this prior event, Nehemiah infers that Shemaiah too has been hired to make prophetic pronouncement "against me" (v. 12).[129] He further explicates the complex logic. Fear is the goal of the false prophets (vv. 13–14); however, it is not an end in itself. It is hoped that fear would initiate flight, and flight would end in Nehemiah's cowering in the sanctuary and violating standards of holiness. This "sin," if committed, would provide a final glorious opportunity for enemies to deride Nehemiah's good name (cf. 2:17, 19; 4:1–5; 5:9). Public shame would then weaken community support and further delay or stall wall completion.

6:14 Refusing retaliation, Nehemiah prays his second "remember" prayer (cf. 5:19; 13:14, 22, 29, 31). In spite of their deceptive web, Nehemiah trusts God by placing Tobiah and Sanballat in the Lord's hand, entreating his vengeance (cf. 4:4; Jer. 11:18–20).[130] Under this prayer he also incorporates their allies: numerous false prophets, including a prophetess named Noadiah (cf. Ezek. 13:17–19), although why she is singled out is unknown. The key word closes the paragraph: all of these persons "wanted to make me afraid" (Neh. 6:14; cf. v. 9).

6:15–16 "The wall was finished" in only 52 days—in Elul, the sixth month (August/September). Now for the final time "our enemies heard" (v. 16).[131] These enemies were once the purveyors of contempt and fear. Finally the tables are turned. They now experience the fear and the discouragement they had once hoped to instill in Israel.[132] The fear of these adversaries increases all the more since all this has happened "with the help of our God"; through prayer, enemy taunts have fallen back upon their own heads (4:4–5). God's expressed "good" (Hb. *tobah*; cf. comment on 6:17–19) toward Jerusalem and the resulting fear among the nations again fulfills his word through the prophet Jeremiah (Jer. 33:9; cf. Ezra 1:1).

6:17–19 The phrase "in those days" suggests these verses pertain to the state of affairs throughout the period. The building project clearly had the support of some nobles (4:14, 19).[133] The important official "Meshullam the son of Berechiah" (6:18) had also shown enthusiasm for the project (3:4, 30). Others leaders may have shifted allegiance under the threatened rumors (6:6–7). Some "nobles of Judah"

---

129 For a fuller argument tracing these inferences within the text, see Shepherd and Wright, *Ezra and Nehemiah*, 75–76, and the supporting literature noted there. Alternatively, it is possible that God has provided this insight to Nehemiah.

130 For the first time, in 6:12, 14 Tobiah is mentioned before Sanballat. This may indicate that Tobiah, given his connections to the community (cf. 6:17–19), takes the lead in this final attempt to stop Nehemiah. The mention of the temple (6:10) may also hint at his further role in the final chapter (13:4–9). Sanballat, on the other hand, disappears from the narrative, mentioned only once more in the book, by way of family connection (13:28).

131 On the prevalence of this concept, cf. table 2.1 in the Section Overview of 4:1–23.

132 The idiom "fell greatly in their eyes" occurs only here in the OT. It has the sense of being humbled and is translated variously as "fell greatly in their own esteem" (ESV), "lost their self-confidence" (NIV), or "were greatly disheartened" (NET).

133 On "nobles," cf. note 55.

are singled out for their ongoing correspondence with Tobiah (v. 17; cf. 13:17), although the content of these letters is unspecified. Evidently Tobiah, along with his son, is socially well-connected with important families in Jerusalem.[134] Exactly how the explicit marital links to Shecaniah (cf. 3:29; 7:10) and Meshullam caused those in Judah to be "bound by oath" to Tobiah is uncertain. This "oath" may indicate agreements made with him by those who desire a more open trade policy or may point to other kinds of business associations that would favor Tobiah's economic interests.[135]

It is possible to view the nobles' actions positively or negatively. Positively, the exchange of letters between the nobles and Tobiah may indicate their attempts to mediate reconciliation with Nehemiah.[136] The nobles therefore attempt to sway Nehemiah's opinion of Tobiah by speaking of "his good deeds" (Hb. *tobotayw*).[137] Negatively, the letters may actually function to keep Nehemiah's adversaries aware of his strategies, plans, and actions. Indeed, if Tobiah is so interested in the "good" (*tobah*) of Jerusalem, why was he initially so displeased at Nehemiah's presence (2:10)? Whatever the motive of the nobles, Tobiah's goal has always remained the intimidation of Nehemiah (6:19), a purpose consistent with the rest of the chapter (cf. vv. 9, 16).

7:1–4 The final paragraph expresses Nehemiah's concern for the security and repopulation of the city. The paragraph is treated here with 6:1–19 rather than 7:5–73a for several reasons. First, it repeats that the wall was built, adding new information about the reset doors (cf. 6:1, 15). Second, the key verb "fear" is used for the final time (7:2). Third, what follows in 7:5–73a is separated by being labeled a "genealogy," a repeated list of persons that encloses the entire second section (Ezra 2:1–Neh. 7:73a). In particular, verses 1–3 hold together with the theme of "appointment."

First, gatekeepers, singers, and Levites (Neh. 7:1; cf. Ezra 2:70//Neh. 7:73a; Ezra 7:7; Neh. 10:28; 12:47; 13:5) are appointed, although by whom and for what purpose is unstated.[138] Typically the mention of gatekeepers, along with musicians and Levites, suggests those gatekeepers who secure the temple. However, the context here suggests their role in guarding the gates of the city. Their work is augmented by the presence of singers and Levites who join in securing the city (13:22). The mention of the latter hints at the ongoing need for temple worship within a secured "holy city" (11:1).

Nehemiah also gives two men charge "over Jerusalem" (7:2). Hanani, Nehemiah's brother, was among those who first brought him news of the broken-down wall (1:2). It is therefore fitting that he is found again at its completion. A second man,

---

134 Recall that Tobiah is either a fellow Jew or of Ammonite ancestry. If the latter, then this provides another example of Jewish intermarriage with foreigners. Cf. comment on 2:9–10.
135 Kidner, *Ezra and Nehemiah*, 111; Clines, *Ezra, Nehemiah, Esther*, 177. The latter point is made by Blenkinsopp, *Ezra-Nehemiah*, 274.
136 Fensham calls this "diplomatic negotiations" (*Ezra and Nehemiah*, 208). A similar position is espoused by Williamson, *Ezra, Nehemiah*, 261.
137 The verbal construction indicates that their positive reports about Tobiah were ongoing.
138 For a discussion of these groups, cf. comment on Ezra 2:40–42.

Hananiah, is identified as "governor of the castle." The term "governor" here refers not to a political appointment, since Nehemiah is governor of Judah at this time (5:14).[139] Instead this refers to Hananiah's role as a commander of the fortress (i.e., "castle") probably associated with the temple (cf. 2:8; 3:1). His selection is based on both his superior reverence for God and his evident trustworthiness (cf. Ex. 18:21).

The second half of Nehemiah 7:3 refers to a final appointment of city residents who would guard at particular posts along the wall and at locations near their own homes (cf. 3:23, 28, 29). That much is clear. The interpretation of the first half of the verse is less certain, although the verbs "opened" and "shut" clearly concern some kind of atypical practice. It appears that Nehemiah commands Hanani and Hananiah not to open Jerusalem's gates at dawn, as would be typical, but to delay for several hours later until the sun grew hotter (cf. 1 Sam. 11:9, 11). Then, at day's end, he calls for complete securing of doors combined with a call for guards to remain on duty.[140]

The final verse succinctly covers three topics: city size, population, and housing. Evaluating the walled city as one that is "wide and large," i.e., spacious (Judg. 18:10; 1 Chron. 4:40), must be relative to the reduced population "within it." Recent analysis suggests that settlement during the Persian period included only the enclosed City of David, with a population estimated at between 400 and 500. At this time the Western Hill was unoccupied.[141] Clearly, some already inhabited the city in their own homes (Neh. 7:3; cf. 3:23, 28, 29), so that the final clause ("no houses") must indicate that additional housing is still needed. Perhaps the few inhabitants provide the rationale for institution of unique security measures.[142] In any event, the genealogy that follows intimates that Jerusalem's rebuilding will include repopulation (cf. ch. 11).

Response

God's people are called to be a worshiping community, advancing God's kingdom and testifying to his glory in all the earth (1 Chron. 28:8; Ps. 8:1–2; Rev. 5:13). That mission is sure to raise the ire of those who despise this goal or question how it is being accomplished. Achievement of that mission is possible only by prayer, persistence, and trust in the Lord's protection.

The completion of the wall leads to opponents' turning their subtle attacks directly upon Nehemiah himself, intending to engender fear and distraction

---

139 The noun translated "governor" (Hb. *sar*) generally refers to an official, leader, prince, or other position of authority. Multiple times it is translated "ruler" in chapter 3. Particularly relevant are 3:9, 12, which mention two men identified as "ruler of half the district of Jerusalem." Perhaps Hanani and Hananiah now assume these roles.

140 Alternatively, rather than leaving the gates closed *until* the "sun is hot," the gates were not to be opened *during* the hottest part of the day, i.e., when people and guards were resting and the city was most vulnerable to attack. Therefore, the guards are called to secure the gates at this time of heightened vulnerability. Arguments for this interpretation are found in Williamson, *Ezra, Nehemiah*, 266–267, and Blenkinsopp, *Ezra-Nehemiah*, 274–275. The latter translates: "The gates of Jerusalem are not to be left open *during* the hottest part of the day, but *while* they are still on guard duty they are to shut and bar the gates" (274, emphasis added).

141 Ussishkin, "Nehemiah's City Wall," 116–117. One's view of the city's size will depend upon the extent of wall reconstruction, a debated topic. See Section Overview of Nehemiah 3:1–32 and note 61.

142 Clines, *Ezra, Nehemiah, Esther*, 178.

(Neh. 6:9, 14, 19). Such distractions can potentially derail even the most dedicated pastors, congregations, and institutions. The adversarial strategies—the calls to "meet together" with intent to harm (6:2, 7, 10), the false allegations (6:6–8), the fictional death threats of false prophets (6:10)—seek to strike the leader and thereby weaken community resolve and make "their hands . . . drop from the work" (6:9). Prior attacks had actually achieved that result (Ezra 4:4)[143] and intimidation had successfully shut down wall reconstruction (Ezra 4:12, 21).

Prayer is our proper response in the face of such opposition. As before (Neh. 1:4–11; 2:4; 4:4–5, 9), Nehemiah again prays to the Lord as the only one able to strengthen weak hands (6:9). Even so, Nehemiah has no assurance that Tobiah and Sanballat will ever relent. With no desire to seek his own vengeance, Nehemiah also prays for the Lord to remember the deeds of Tobiah and Sanballat and bring them to justice (6:14). We must pray for strength in weakness even as we plead for the Lord to bring an end to those opposing gospel advancement.

Nehemiah not only prays but also persists in the Lord's work, knowing that there is more work to do (7:1–4). As a leader, he understands the importance of his calling and subordinates all else to its accomplishment. In this case, even though the wall is completed, the work of repopulation (ch. 11) and covenant renewal (chs. 8–10) yet remain. Building projects are not an end in themselves. With altar, temple, and wall in place, the "voice of gladness" must be restored to the city (Jer. 33:10–11; cf. Neh. 12:43) and Jerusalem must be repopulated with a worshiping community (7:4). Those committed to testifying to the gospel of the grace of God in Christ (Acts 20:24) must likewise be singularly persistent. There are very few priorities that should cause this "great work" to be stopped (Neh. 6:3–4).

In order to aid in the city's restoration, Nehemiah prays and establishes its security (7:1–3; cf. 4:9). However, he does so with the full assurance that all of this is accomplished "with the help of our God" (6:16). Only the Lord's ongoing protection could possibly explain the speed and completion of a work so burdened by adversaries and the "taunts of the nations" (5:9). The God of great reversals will make afraid those who seek to frighten his flock. We pray about and persist in his work. However, any success in ministry is ultimately due only to his protection: "Our help is in the name of the LORD" (Ps. 124:8).

---

143 In Ezra-Nehemiah the idiom "slacken the hands" (i.e., "make drop the hands" or "discourage") occurs only at Ezra 4:4; Nehemiah 6:9.

NEHEMIAH 7:5–73a

⁵Then my God put it into my heart to assemble the nobles and the officials and the people to be enrolled by genealogy. And I found the book of the genealogy of those who came up at the first, and I found written in it:

⁶These were the people of the province who came up out of the captivity of those exiles whom Nebuchadnezzar the king of Babylon had carried into exile. They returned to Jerusalem and Judah, each to his town. ⁷They came with Zerubbabel, Jeshua, Nehemiah, Azariah, Raamiah, Nahamani, Mordecai, Bilshan, Mispereth, Bigvai, Nehum, Baanah.

The number of the men of the people of Israel: ⁸the sons of Parosh, 2,172. ⁹The sons of Shephatiah, 372. ¹⁰The sons of Arah, 652. ¹¹The sons of Pahath-moab, namely the sons of Jeshua and Joab, 2,818. ¹²The sons of Elam, 1,254. ¹³The sons of Zattu, 845. ¹⁴The sons of Zaccai, 760. ¹⁵The sons of Binnui, 648. ¹⁶The sons of Bebai, 628. ¹⁷The sons of Azgad, 2,322. ¹⁸The sons of Adonikam, 667. ¹⁹The sons of Bigvai, 2,067. ²⁰The sons of Adin, 655. ²¹The sons of Ater, namely of Hezekiah, 98. ²²The sons of Hashum, 328. ²³The sons of Bezai, 324. ²⁴The sons of Hariph, 112. ²⁵The sons of Gibeon, 95. ²⁶The men of Bethlehem and Netophah, 188. ²⁷The men of Anathoth, 128. ²⁸The men of Beth-azmaveth, 42. ²⁹The men of Kiriath-jearim, Chephirah, and Beeroth, 743. ³⁰The men of Ramah and Geba, 621. ³¹The men of Michmas, 122. ³²The men of Bethel and Ai, 123. ³³The men of the other Nebo, 52. ³⁴The sons of the other Elam, 1,254. ³⁵The sons of Harim, 320. ³⁶The sons of Jericho, 345. ³⁷The sons of Lod, Hadid, and Ono, 721. ³⁸The sons of Senaah, 3,930.

³⁹The priests: the sons of Jedaiah, namely the house of Jeshua, 973. ⁴⁰The sons of Immer, 1,052. ⁴¹The sons of Pashhur, 1,247. ⁴²The sons of Harim, 1,017.

⁴³The Levites: the sons of Jeshua, namely of Kadmiel of the sons of Hodevah, 74. ⁴⁴The singers: the sons of Asaph, 148. ⁴⁵The gatekeepers: the sons of Shallum, the sons of Ater, the sons of Talmon, the sons of Akkub, the sons of Hatita, the sons of Shobai, 138.

⁴⁶The temple servants: the sons of Ziha, the sons of Hasupha, the sons of Tabbaoth, ⁴⁷the sons of Keros, the sons of Sia, the sons of Padon, ⁴⁸the sons of Lebana, the sons of Hagaba, the sons of Shalmai, ⁴⁹the sons of Hanan, the sons of Giddel, the sons of Gahar, ⁵⁰the sons of Reaiah, the sons of Rezin, the sons of Nekoda, ⁵¹the sons of Gazzam, the sons of Uzza, the sons of Paseah, ⁵²the sons of Besai, the sons of Meunim, the sons of Nephushesim, ⁵³the sons of Bakbuk, the sons of Hakupha, the sons of Harhur, ⁵⁴the sons of Bazlith, the sons of Mehida, the sons of Harsha, ⁵⁵the sons of Barkos, the sons of Sisera, the sons of Temah, ⁵⁶the sons of Neziah, the sons of Hatipha.

⁵⁷The sons of Solomon's servants: the sons of Sotai, the sons of Sophereth, the sons of Perida, ⁵⁸the sons of Jaala, the sons of Darkon,

the sons of Giddel, [59] the sons of Shephatiah, the sons of Hattil, the sons of Pochereth-hazzebaim, the sons of Amon.

[60] All the temple servants and the sons of Solomon's servants were 392.

[61] The following were those who came up from Tel-melah, Tel-harsha, Cherub, Addon, and Immer, but they could not prove their fathers' houses nor their descent, whether they belonged to Israel: [62] the sons of Delaiah, the sons of Tobiah, the sons of Nekoda, 642. [63] Also, of the priests: the sons of Hobaiah, the sons of Hakkoz, the sons of Barzillai (who had taken a wife of the daughters of Barzillai the Gileadite and was called by their name). [64] These sought their registration among those enrolled in the genealogies, but it was not found there, so they were excluded from the priesthood as unclean. [65] The governor told them that they were not to partake of the most holy food until a priest with Urim and Thummim should arise.

[66] The whole assembly together was 42,360, [67] besides their male and female servants, of whom there were 7,337. And they had 245 singers, male and female. [68] Their horses were 736, their mules 245,[1] [69] their camels 435, and their donkeys 6,720.

[70] Now some of the heads of fathers' houses gave to the work. The governor gave to the treasury 1,000 darics[2] of gold, 50 basins, 30 priests' garments and 500 minas[3] of silver.[4] [71] And some of the heads of fathers' houses gave into the treasury of the work 20,000 darics of gold and 2,200 minas of silver. [72] And what the rest of the people gave was 20,000 darics of gold, 2,000 minas of silver, and 67 priests' garments.

[73] So the priests, the Levites, the gatekeepers, the singers, some of the people, the temple servants, and all Israel, lived in their towns.

[1] Compare Ezra 2:66 and the margins of some Hebrew manuscripts; Hebrew lacks *Their horses . . . 245*
[2] A *daric* was a coin weighing about 1/4 ounce or 8.5 grams [3] A *mina* was about 1 1/4 pounds or 0.6 kilogram [4] Probable reading; Hebrew lacks *minas of silver*

Section Overview

This chapter provides an example of one way that repetition works in biblical narrative. The list encountered initially in Ezra 2 (Ezra 2:1–70) is now repeated in Nehemiah 7:5–73a, where it closes the second major section of Ezra-Nehemiah (Ezra 2:1–Neh. 7:73a).[144] That large section recounts three major movements of people and the three vital tasks associated with each movement: temple (Ezra 3:1–6:22), Torah (Ezra 7:1–10:44), and wall (Neh. 1:1–7:73a).[145] The list in Nehemiah not only inventories names and numbers of leaders, lay persons, and temple personnel but identifies them as those who returned "at the first" (Neh. 7:5). Likely this does not refer to a solitary initial return in 538 BC but represents a composite of the entire chronological period narrated in Ezra 1–6. When treating the two lists, commentators reasonably refer readers to prior comments on Ezra 2:1–70. While that practice continues here for particulars, numerous general questions remain. Beyond marking the start and finish of a major section, how should we view these lists in their particular literary and historical contexts? What type of text is this? What

---

144 Cf. Introduction to Ezra for discussion of the sources found in Ezra-Nehemiah.
145 See further detailed discussion at Ezra 2. The structural observations are indebted to Eskenazi, *Age of Prose*, 37–40.

may be said about its origin? What are some other differences between the lists? At this point in Ezra-Nehemiah, how does the list function as the story advances?

The location and presentation of a work of art shapes its interpretation. So it is with the individual contexts of Ezra 2 and Nehemiah 7. While these chapters unify Ezra-Nehemiah structurally, the varied literary and historical contexts in which each resides stimulate further considerations. The first appearance of the list in Ezra 2, which opens the second major section of Ezra-Nehemiah, sits historically in the transitional period that looks back to exile and forward to temple completion (538–516 BC). This occurred approximately fifty-seven years prior to the ministries of Ezra and Nehemiah. The community described in the first appearance of the list, propelled by divine and royal proclamations, represents a second exodus community: it is the Lord's remnant as a new beginning, the newly planted seed fulfilling his promises of renewal likened to the restoration of Eden (Jer. 24:5–7; 31:27–28; Ezek. 36:35). Those represented in this list gather as "one man" (Ezra 3:1), heeding the prophetic imperative and rebuilding the temple (Ezra 6:14–15).

The list in Nehemiah 7, though an identical "painting," hangs in a different literary and historical gallery. On the one hand, it represents the conclusion to the second major section of Ezra-Nehemiah. The initial list in Ezra represented the community that had first returned to build the altar and temple under Zerubbabel. Nearly one hundred years later, the wall is completed under governor Nehemiah (Neh. 6:15; 7:1), after which the list is repeated. However, in Nehemiah the list does more than conclude. It represents the solidarity of purpose and the unity of the people in Nehemiah's day with those from the past. Along with this, it keeps the focus on the people who are needed to repopulate Jerusalem now that the city has been secured by a wall (7:4, 73; 11:1–2).[146] Finally, it provides a transition to a new beginning, preparing for what follows. Earlier in Ezra, the "one man" represented a community gathered to build the altar. Now in Nehemiah, they again gather as "one man" (8:1), this time not to build a physical structure but to commence a full-orbed covenant renewal (7:73b–10:39).

Section Outline

II.E. List of Exiles Repeated (7:5–73a)
1. Nehemiah Moved to Enroll by Genealogy (7:5)
2. The People of the Province Who Came Up out of the Captivity (7:6–7a)
3. The Number of the Men of the People of Israel (7:7b–38)
4. The Temple Personnel (7:39–60)
5. Those Who Could Not Prove Their Descent (7:61–65)
6. Summary Statements (7:66–73a)

---

146 As one scholar notes, "The double quotation of the same census list provides continuity between two different eras since, in both cases, the list serves to identify the members of the true Israel of the postexilic era, whether as reentering the land and beginning to build the temple (Ezra 2:1–3:1) or as preparing to repopulate Jerusalem (Neh. 7:6–72; 11:1)" (Duggan, *Covenant Renewal*, 33). There is general agreement that 11:1–2 is a narrative continuation of chapter 7 (esp. 7:4–5, 73), with its concern for the need to repopulate Jerusalem (Clines, *Ezra, Nehemiah, Esther*, 211; Williamson, *Ezra, Nehemiah*, 344–345; Blenkinsopp, *Ezra-Nehemiah*, 322–323).

Comment

7:5 The verse contains the only instance of the noun translated "genealogy" (Hb. *yakhas*) in the OT. More common is the verb (*yakhas*), found only in Chronicles, Ezra, and Nehemiah, which either describes the recording of someone in a genealogical list or translates more simply as "genealogy" (cf. Ezra 8:1).[147] Therefore Nehemiah identifies the text as "the book of the genealogy" (*sefer hayyakhas*) rather than as a "census" (cf. Ex. 30:12; Num. 1:2, 49). He does not inform us where he found this genealogy, but he uses it for his own narrative purposes.

The first-person statement (i.e., "my heart," "I found") gives the reason for the list in Nehemiah. As the initial decree of Cyrus was stirred by the Lord (Ezra 1:1), and the later decree of Artaxerxes was likewise incited by God's work "into the heart of the king" (Ezra 7:21, 27), so Nehemiah recognizes that the motivations of his own heart and the actions that follow are due to God's prompting.[148] As previously (Neh. 2:12), God once again acts upon this leader's heart such that Nehemiah resolves to gather the community to enroll them by genealogy. It is this stated purpose and Nehemiah's reported find of the genealogy that provides a significant difference between the lists in Ezra 2 and Nehemiah 7.

7:6–73a Cf. comments on Ezra 2:1–70.

Excursus on Ezra 2//Nehemiah 7 Genealogy

Manifold studies in the history of interpretation reach no consensus regarding whether Ezra 2 or Nehemiah 7 represents the original list or location.[149] Attention to detailed variations between the lists goes beyond the purposes of this commentary, but the differences may be generally grouped along a spectrum from minor to more significant.

On the one end, minor differences between the lists include the presence or absence of linguistic elements such as prepositions, conjunctions, and definite articles. Infrequently, verbal forms vary slightly between the two (Ezra 2:2; Neh. 7:7).

To move along our spectrum: the names listed express relative consistency with limited disparity. Many times names match exactly in spelling and order of location. At other times the spelling of names differs slightly or the order differs by a shift in position (cf. Ezra 2:16–20 and Neh. 7:21–25). More substantive deviation occurs when: (1) a name is present in one list (e.g., Magbish in Ezra 2:30; Nahamani in Neh. 7:7) but absent in the opposing list's parallel verse; or (2) a name in one list differs dramatically in another (e.g., "Jorah" at Ezra 2:18 reads "Hariph" at Neh. 7:24).

---

147 1 Chronicles 4:33; 5:1, 7, 17; 7:5, 7, 9, 40; 9:1, 22; 2 Chronicles 12:15; 31:16, 17, 18, 19; Ezra 2:62; 8:1, 3; Nehemiah 7:5, 64.

148 In this context Kidner makes the remarkable statement that of "all biblical characters, Nehemiah is perhaps the most explicit on 'the practice of the presence of God'" (*Ezra and Nehemiah*, 112).

149 Some hold that an original list placed first in Nehemiah 7 later found a home in Ezra 2 (Clines, *Ezra, Nehemiah, Esther*, 44–45; Williamson, *Ezra, Nehemiah*, 28–32, 267–269). Others give prominence to an insertion first in Ezra 2 and then a weaving into Nehemiah 7 (Blenkinsopp, *Ezra-Nehemiah*, 83, 43–44). Of course, the possibility exists that a list or even two different lists were grafted into each context by a common author or editor (i.e., the Chronicler or some other author[s]). This last position is held by Paul L. Redditt, *Ezra-Nehemiah*, SHBC 9b (Macon, GA: Smyth & Helwys, 2014), 74–79.

This leads to the more apparent similarities and differences in the numbers within the two lists. For example, the numbers given in Ezra 2:2b–35 and Nehemiah 7:7b–38 that describe the "men of the people" match at fifteen places. Some numbers differ by a single figure (i.e., plus or minus 1) whether in the ones-, tens-, hundreds-, or thousands-digit place.[150] Scribal misreading is the most likely explanation.[151] On the other hand, the names and numbers for the priests are identical in each list (cf. Ezra 2:36–39; Neh. 7:39–42), as are the combined numbers of temple servants and sons of Solomon's servants (cf. Ezra 2:58; Neh. 7:60). Significantly, the final summary number of the full assembly is 42,360 in each (Ezra 2:64; Neh. 7:66).[152]

Finally, the chapter conclusions at both Ezra 2:68–69 and Nehemiah 7:70–72 evidence the most notable variations. This makes sense, as each list was adapted to fit its distinctive context. While both Ezra 2:68 and Nehemiah 7:70, 71 begin "some of the heads of the fathers" (AT), they immediately diverge. In Ezra, where the focus is on the return and the temple, the new historical and literary moment is marked by the addition, "when they came to the house of the LORD that is in Jerusalem" (2:68). The mention of voluntary offerings for the house of God follows. On the other hand, rather than this explicit focus on return and temple, the contextual emphasis in Nehemiah is more generic, stating only that the leaders gave "to the work" (7:70) and "into the treasury of the work" (7:71). Likewise, Nehemiah's list also details the contribution of the governor "to the treasury" (7:70), a notice unparalleled in Ezra (2:69).

Response

The response following Ezra 2 centered on God's faithfulness in keeping his promises to the redeemed community, on the role of the individual in the context of the community, and on the community as a worshiping people in a rebuilt temple. Although these points apply also to the repeated list in Nehemiah 7, the varied context and other themes in the latter promote new considerations. So, how does the list in Nehemiah 7 advance the story in its context?

At this point, the people might be tempted to believe that the work is done and to celebrate the completion of the wall, believing that the conclusion of that structure is the highpoint, the top of the mountain. We rightly celebrate such climactic moments, but we must not mistake success for the finish and as an opportunity to rest indefinitely. Mountain climbers and cyclists know all too well the "false summit." What appears from below as the peak, when reached, reveals

---

150 For example, each of the following differs by one number in its respective digit(s): Adonikam differs by one at the ones digit (666 [Ezra 2:13]); 667 [Neh. 7:18]); Bigvai at the tens and ones digits (2,056 [Ezra 2:14]; 2,067 [Neh. 7:19]; Zattu at the hundreds digit (945 [Ezra 2:8]; 845 [Neh. 7:13]); and Azgad at the thousands and hundreds digits (1,222 [Ezra 2:12]; 2,322 [Neh. 7:17]).

151 Kidner, *Ezra and Nehemiah*, 42, 48; Clines, *Ezra, Nehemiah, Esther*, 45; Blenkinsopp, *Ezra-Nehemiah*, 85–86.

152 The total holds for 1 *Esdras* 5:41 as well. Note that, if added separately, each list total does not equal 42,360. The numbers in Ezra 2:3–60 add up to 29,818 while those in Nehemiah 7:8–62 equal 31,089. The total in 1 *Esdras* is 30,143 (Kidner, *Ezra and Nehemiah*, 48). The text is silent on the reason for the differences and no consensus has been reached on the discrepancy. Some have suggested that the total includes women (Williamson, *Ezra, Nehemiah*, 37–38). According to 1 *Esdras* 5:41, the total included Israelites from twelve years old.

itself only to be another stage in a long climb. So it is for the people in Nehemiah's day. Much good work has been accomplished, and yet so much more remains to be done—otherwise the dedication of 12:27–13:3 would take place at this point. Fortunately, they recognize that, along with the repopulation of Jerusalem (ch. 11), they still need a deeper restoration under the Law of Moses, full repentance, and covenant renewal (chs. 8–10). While God's people rightly rejoice in a job well done, lethargy lurks if they believe their mission to be completed.

Instead, whatever God accomplishes in us or through us must, in due time, propel further kingdom service. This means that while the people of God have returned to the land, those written in the genealogy must willingly sacrifice to repopulate the city of God with true worshipers (11:1–2). So it is that this moment in Ezra-Nehemiah functions as an archetype. This genealogy represents the true Israel, those authentic members of the family of Abraham (Neh. 7:61). As members of the body of Christ, we are included in that people, children of Abraham (Rom. 4:11–12) and those who have been circumcised of heart (Rom. 2:28–29). As such we ask ourselves how we must resist the danger of lethargy, working and praying in our historical moment to populate the city of God further with true worshipers of him.

Ultimately, those of every nation graced with salvation in Christ look forward to inhabiting that city whose builder is God (Heb. 11:10, 16; 12:22). But it is even more remarkable than this. As the first list leads to temple and the second list to repopulation of Jerusalem, so the "one who conquers" is both pillar in the temple of God and inhabitant in the new Jerusalem (Rev. 3:12). With this in mind, we must not see God's work in and through us as an end in itself. We do not exist or work to "please ourselves" but "with one voice glorify the God and Father of our Lord Jesus Christ" through our mutual love (Rom. 15:1, 6) and through serving the Lord in our various callings until he returns (1 Cor. 15:58; 2 Cor. 9:8; Eph. 4:28; Col. 3:23; 1 Thess. 4:11).

NEHEMIAH 7:73b–8:18

And when the seventh month had come, the people of Israel were in their towns.

8 And all the people gathered as one man into the square before the Water Gate. And they told Ezra the scribe to bring the Book of the Law of Moses that the LORD had commanded Israel. ² So Ezra the priest brought the Law before the assembly, both men and women and all who could understand what they heard, on the first day of the seventh month. ³ And he read from it facing the square before the Water Gate from early morning until midday, in the presence of the men and the women and those who could understand. And the ears of all the people were attentive to the Book of the Law. [4] And Ezra the scribe stood on a wooden platform that they had made for the purpose. And beside him stood Mattithiah, Shema, Anaiah, Uriah, Hilkiah, and Maaseiah on his right hand, and Pedaiah, Mishael, Malchijah, Hashum, Hashbaddanah, Zechariah, and Meshullam on his left hand. [5] And Ezra opened the book in the sight of all the people, for he was above all the people, and as he opened it all the people stood. [6] And Ezra blessed the LORD, the great God, and all the people answered, "Amen, Amen," lifting up their hands. And they bowed their heads and worshiped the LORD with their faces to the ground. [7] Also Jeshua, Bani, Sherebiah, Jamin, Akkub, Shabbethai, Hodiah, Maaseiah, Kelita, Azariah, Jozabad, Hanan, Pelaiah, the Levites,[1] helped the people to understand the Law, while the people remained in their places. [8] They read from the book, from the Law of God, clearly,[2] and they gave the sense, so that the people understood the reading.

[9] And Nehemiah, who was the governor, and Ezra the priest and scribe, and the Levites who taught the people said to all the people, "This day is holy to the LORD your God; do not mourn or weep." For all the people wept as they heard the words of the Law. [10] Then he said to them, "Go your way. Eat the fat and drink sweet wine and send portions to anyone who has nothing ready, for this day is holy to our Lord. And do not be grieved, for the joy of the LORD is your strength." [11] So the Levites calmed all the people, saying, "Be quiet, for this day is holy; do not be grieved." [12] And all the people went their way to eat and drink and to send portions and to make great rejoicing, because they had understood the words that were declared to them.

[13] On the second day the heads of fathers' houses of all the people, with the priests and the Levites, came together to Ezra the scribe in order to study the words of the Law. [14] And they found it written in the Law that the LORD had commanded by Moses that the people of Israel should dwell in booths[3] during the feast of the seventh month, [15] and that they should proclaim it and publish it in all their towns and in Jerusalem, "Go out to the hills and bring branches of olive, wild olive, myrtle, palm, and other leafy trees to make booths, as it is written." [16] So the people went out and brought them and made booths for themselves, each on his roof, and in their courts and in the courts of the house of God, and in the square at the Water Gate and in the square at the Gate of Ephraim. [17] And all the assembly of those who had returned from the captivity made booths and lived in the booths, for from the days of Jeshua the son of Nun to that day the people of Israel had not done so. And there was very great rejoicing. [18] And day by day, from the first day to the last day, he read from the Book of the Law of God. They kept the feast seven days, and on the eighth day there was a solemn assembly, according to the rule.

[1] Vulgate; Hebrew *and the Levites* [2] Or *with interpretation*, or *paragraph by paragraph* [3] Or *temporary shelters*

Section Overview

The people have completed their building tasks according to commands of the Lord and the edicts of Persian kings. The concluding section (Neh. 7:73b–13:31) provides the finale of the whole of Ezra-Nehemiah. The entire section consolidates prior themes, including conviction of sin and covenant renewal under God's Word, proper worship under priests and Levites, the repopulation of Jerusalem, wall dedication, and the need for ongoing reform. These are retold under four broad headings: covenant renewal (7:73b–10:39), habitation of Jerusalem with a list of priests and Levites (11:1–12:26; cf. 7:4–5), wall dedication (12:27–43), and Nehemiah's reforms (12:44–13:31).

The section begins with the reconstituted community focusing on God's Word and undertaking covenant renewal. In the current chapter Ezra returns to the story as Nehemiah's first-person account (Nehemiah Memoir) gives way temporarily.[153] The reading of the Law and the celebration of the Feast of Booths (7:73b–8:18) is followed by a redemptive-historical covenant confession (9:1–37) and then concludes with the sealing and obligations of the covenant (9:38–10:39).

The major theme of chapter 8 is the renewal of the people under the ministry of biblical instruction on the first and second day of the seventh month (8:2, 13). First, the people gather to hear the Law read and explained (7:73b–8:12). Then Ezra helps the people study the Law. They recognize and remedy their failure to keep the Feast of Booths as prescribed (8:13–18). The events of both days conclude with "great rejoicing" (8:12, 17). Key words include "people," "Law" (i.e., Torah), and "understand" (8:2, 3, 7, 8, 9, 12).

Section Outline

   III. The Community Rejoices: Covenant Renewal and Community
       Reconstitution (Neh. 7:73b–13:31)

      A. Covenant Renewal (7:73b–10:39)

         1. The Law Is Read and the Feast of Booths Celebrated
           (Neh. 7:73b–8:18)

           a. The Law Is Read: The People Understand and Rejoice
              (7:73b–8:12)

              (1) Gathering of the People; the Law Is Read and
                  Understood (7:73b–8:8)

              (2) The People Celebrate with "Great Rejoicing" (8:9–12)

           b. The Law Is Studied; the Feast of Booths Is Celebrated
              (8:13–18)

              (1) Gathering of the People; the Law Is Studied (8:13–15)

              (2) The Feast of Booths Is Celebrated with "Great
                  Rejoicing" (8:16–18)

Comment

7:73b–8:3 As a general introduction, these verses describe the setting (both the time and place of the reading of the Law) as well as the persons who deliver and hear the message. It is best to keep 7:73b as the heading of what follows rather

---

153 The convenient title "Nehemiah Memoir" applies to the first-person accounts in Nehemiah 1:1–7:73a; 12:27–43; 13:4–31. See Introduction to Nehemiah: Genre and Literary Features.

than the conclusion of the prior chapter.[154] As with the pattern found in Ezra (cf. Ezra 2:1–70; 3:1), the gathering of the people as "one man" follows the lengthy list of names in Nehemiah (cf. 7:6–73a with 7:73b–8:1), both occurring in the seventh month. The unified community, "all the people," participates in this climactic moment (8:1, 3, 5 [3x], 6, 7 [2x], 9 [2x], 11, 12, 13, 16).[155] They meet at the Water Gate, located on the eastern side of the city and providing ready access to water via the Gihon Spring, the city's water supply (cf. 3:26; 8:1, 3, 16; 12:37). For this reason it is a center of communal life.[156]

The excitement of wall completion in Elul (August/September), the sixth month (6:15), leads naturally to these events, specified as days one and two of the seventh month (8:2, 13; Tishri = September/October), the holiest month in Israel's calendar.[157] Although the year is not specified, this would have occurred in 445 BC.

The first day of the seventh month was historically a holy convocation and a day of rest begun with a trumpet blast to remind the people to prepare for this most holy month (Lev. 23:24–25). The people show themselves vital to the action because it is the "assembly" (Neh. 8:2) rather than the leaders who initiate the action of the chapter by asking Ezra to bring the Law (8:1). As previously, Ezra acts to instruct in the Law only after being approached by others (cf. Ezra 9:1). At his initial return to Jerusalem, Ezra had been authorized by Artaxerxes to bring the Law with him from Babylon to Jerusalem in order to instruct the people in the "laws of your God" (Ezra 7:12, 25–26). Now returning to the narrative, Ezra once more carries out his assigned duties as scribe and priest, both a reader and a teacher of the Law (Neh. 8:1, 2, 4, 5, 6, 8, 13). More importantly he fulfills his calling from the Lord (Ezra 7:6, 10, 12; cf. Deut. 33:10).[158]

While the people make their request known and Ezra responds to that request, it is the living message of God's Word (i.e., Law or Torah) that takes center stage from beginning to end (cf. Neh. 8:1, 18). Emphasis falls on the people's hunger for its message and their "understanding" of its meaning (8:2, 3, 7, 8, 9, 12). They are identified as those who "heard" and whose "ears . . . were attentive" (8:2–3). The reading of the Law goes on for several hours (8:3). It is first identified as "the Book of the Law of Moses that the LORD had commanded Israel" (8:1), the longest title granted it in the chapter.[159]

---

154 Clines, *Ezra, Nehemiah, Esther*, 181; Williamson, *Ezra, Nehemiah*, 277; Blenkinsopp, *Ezra-Nehemiah*, 282.
155 Most of the verses cited here read "all the people." The prominence of "people" as a key word is supported by Eskenazi, *Age of Prose*, 97.
156 Kidner, *Ezra and Nehemiah*, 114–115.
157 On the important festivals associated with the seventh month, cf. comment on Ezra 3:4–6a.
158 Ezra was authorized to return to Jerusalem in 458 BC to "teach" the "laws of your God" (Ezra 7:25). Why would he delay some thirteen years before doing so at this moment? This perplexing delay persuades many commentators that the text of Nehemiah 8 (and perhaps chs. 9–10) was historically and literarily connected with the Ezra Memoir and was moved to this point in Nehemiah at some point in its editorial history. Williamson calls this viewpoint a "widespread and wholly correct scholarly consensus" (*Ezra, Nehemiah*, 285). See ibid., 282–287, and Blenkinsopp, *Ezra-Nehemiah*, 45, 284, 286, for fuller argumentation. Space does not permit an assessment of the complex arguments and varied opinions (cf. Introduction to Nehemiah: Interpretive Challenges). For an alternative position see the references in note 163.
159 Elsewhere in the chapter it is called "the Law" (8:2, 7, 9, 13), "the Book of the Law" (8:3), "the Law of God" (8:8), "the Law that the LORD had commanded by Moses" (8:14), and "the Book of the Law of God" (8:18). The title "Law of Moses" is found also at Joshua 8:31, 32; 23:6; 2 Kings 14:6; 23:25; Malachi 4:4.

8:4–8 Further details of the reading are now provided. The occasion is dignified and solemn, with the Word of God as the focus. It is literally raised above the people (vv. 4–5a). An elevated platform (lit., "tower of wood") is constructed, wide enough to include Ezra and the thirteen leading men, likely laity, who stand and face the crowd. These men perhaps assist Ezra in reading.[160] The people rise immediately at the opening of the scroll (i.e., "book")—they know they are about to hear the very words of the divine king (v. 5b; Ex. 33:10). Further, as prayer and blessing are often accompanied by the raising of hands (Pss. 28:2; 63:4; 134:2) so also here. Ezra blesses and exalts "the great God" (Neh. 8:6; cf. Deut. 10:17; Ezra 5:8; Neh. 1:5; 9:32; Ps. 95:3; Jer. 32:18; Dan. 2:45; 9:4; Titus 2:13), and the people respond physically. They move upward in praise with hands lifted and then downward in submissive worship with heads and bodies prostrate toward the ground itself (Gen. 24:48; Ex. 4:31; 12:27; 34:8; 2 Chron. 20:18). The intensity of their affirmation of Ezra's blessing of the Lord is evidenced by their response: "Amen, Amen" (Neh. 8:6; 1 Chron. 16:36; Pss. 41:13; 72:19; 89:52).

The reading of the Book of the Law is necessary, but that Word must also be understood. The twofold presence of the verb translated "understand" opening the paragraph (Neh. 8:2–3) is balanced by its double repetition at the conclusion (vv. 7–8). The thirteen helpers on the platform parallel the mention of thirteen Levites.[161] How is their work accomplished? In order to meet their obligation to teach (Deut. 33:10), the Levites apparently move among the people, who "remained in their places" (Neh. 8:7). The final verse (v. 8) summarizes the whole. An interpretive question in this verse surrounds the verbal form (Hb. *meporash*) translated "clearly" in the first half of the verse. One basic sense of the word is "to make distinct, clear, or plain" (cf. Lev. 24:12; Num. 15:34). By this interpretation, the reading (i.e., "they read") is done by those on the platform in an articulate, careful manner so that it is comprehensible to the hearers. Alternatively, another sense of the verb is "to separate" or "divide into parts." The idea is that the reading is done in a systematic, paragraph-by-paragraph manner. There is likely some value in both of these ideas.[162] What is clear is that those on the platform perform the reading and the Levites explain the meaning of what is heard (i.e., "they gave the sense"), with the result that the people understand.

8:9–12 Nehemiah's presence with those who are instructing is now noted.[163] Ezra and the Levites are again mentioned, and the teaching ministry of the Levites is

---

160 Kidner, *Ezra and Nehemiah*, 115. If these persons were priests or Levites they probably would have been designated as such by the text (Williamson, *Ezra, Nehemiah*, 289).

161 The Hebrew text at 8:7 reads "and the Levites" (cf. ESV mg.). Most modern translations and commentators delete the conjunction ("and") so that "the Levites" is a title that applies to all those in the list. For support of this position, see Clines, *Ezra, Nehemiah, Esther*, 184. He observes that most of the names found here are also identified in other lists of Levites within the book (9:4–5; 10:9–13; 11:16).

162 See ESV footnote for these options. Blenkinsopp (*Ezra-Nehemiah*, 288) opts for "distinctly" (i.e., "clearly") and Williamson (*Ezra, Nehemiah*, 291) for "paragraph by paragraph." It may be that both senses are appropriate (so Kidner, *Ezra and Nehemiah*, 116). "Translate" is another option not as widely held. In this view the reading in Hebrew is translated into Aramaic by the Levites (cf. NASB; Fensham, *Ezra and Nehemiah*, 217). Similar interpretive options hold for the cognate Aramaic verb at Ezra 4:18 (cf. comment on Ezra 4:17–22).

163 Nehemiah 8:9 and 12:26, 36 provide the only places where Ezra and Nehemiah are mentioned together and appear to function as contemporaries. From this and the singular verbs in 8:9, 10 ("he said") some scholars

reiterated (v. 9). Likewise, the people are once more prominent. What is new and remarkable is the intense response to hearing the words of the Law proclaimed. The depth of emotion is evident in their mourning, the repetition of "weep" and "grieve," and the fact that the leaders must offer comfort and compassion to a sorrowing community. The reason for this communal bereavement will soon become apparent: all are convicted of sin for breaking faith with their covenant-keeping Lord (9:1–2, 32–33; cf. Ezra 10:11; Neh. 1:6–7).

A time for broken hearts and confession of sin will come. For now, a response of joy and rest is fostered—and for a surprising reason. Three times the people are reminded that this first day of the seventh month is set apart as holy (Lev. 23:23–25; Num. 29:1–6). Such a holy convocation should lead to joy rather than gloom or despondency (Num. 10:10). Grief must also be banished because, in spite of their iniquities, God has continued to help his people (Neh. 6:16). The Holy One of Israel is ever gracious and faithful; he remains their place of refuge (i.e., "strength"; Isaiah 12). In this context, joy in the Lord, their stronghold, means worshipful celebration with delicious food ("fat") and drink, a foretaste of God's future abundant blessing (Isa. 25:4–6; 55:1–2). And this is not only for themselves. They must also "send portions" to others. This probably refers to meeting the needs of the poor and sojourners who are otherwise unable to share in the collective joy (cf. Est. 9:19, 22; Jer. 31:13).

All of this leads to the response of an obedient community. The prior four imperatives, "go . . . eat . . . drink . . . send" (Neh. 8:10), are explicitly obeyed in the concluding verse (v. 12). As the verb "understand" was found beginning and ending the prior paragraph (vv. 2–3, 7–8), so it opens and closes this one (vv. 9, 12). The teaching of God's Word has found its mark in their hearts—they understand what God is communicating to them in "the words" of his Law. The chapter concludes as it began, with emphasis on "all the people." Now however, they are dispersed with "great rejoicing" (v. 12).

8:13–15 With the people dispersed (v. 12) the heads of extended families gather on the second day. These household leaders represent the entire community (v. 13; Ezra 1:5; 3:12; 4:2, 3; 8:1). They come to Ezra "the scribe," a biblical scholar (cf. Ezra 7:10), not simply to hear the Law read but to "study" (ESV) or "gain insight" (NASB) into its words (Neh. 8:13; cf. Jer. 8:7). The language parallels the earlier work of the Levites in Nehemiah 8:8, who "gave the sense" (ESV) or were "imparting insight" (NET). Much more must be gleaned from God's Law, and the larger gathering is an inefficient way to do so. Practically, the smaller group of leaders could be instructed and then carry back important teaching to their familial units (Deut. 4:10; 6:7; Ps. 78:4–8).

By studying what the "LORD had commanded by Moses" they recognize widespread communal neglect to keep the "Feast of Booths." That festival was to be held

---

conclude that the verse, and the wider text, is an insertion and therefore not original. For a spirited defense of the biblical text and the fact that Ezra and Nehemiah play "an inextricable part in the other's life work," see Eskenazi, *Age of Prose*, 98–99. Likewise, in an appendix Kidner treats the textual and grammatical challenges raised to the "infrequent co-operation" of Ezra and Nehemiah (*Ezra and Nehemiah*, 163–165).

in only thirteen days! Four Mosaic texts describe the Feast of Booths. The prime candidate for what was found "written" (Neh. 8:15) and studied on this occasion is Leviticus 23:33–36, 39–43. These verses connect most directly with Nehemiah 8:13–18 since both mention: (1) the gathering of "palm" and other "leafy trees" (v. 15; Lev. 23:40); (2) the command to "dwell in booths" (Neh. 8:14; Lev. 23:42–43); (3) the call to "rejoice" (Neh. 8:17; Lev. 23:40); and (4) the eighth day as a "solemn assembly" (Neh. 8:18; Lev. 23:36). Perhaps a second text, Deuteronomy 31:9–13, is also read. There Moses commands the reading of "this law before all Israel" during the Feast of Booths at every seventh year. A third Pentateuchal text to mention the Feast of Booths, Deuteronomy 16:13–17, is more of a summary in nature, though it does share the call to "rejoice in your feast" (Deut. 16:14; cf. Ex. 23:16; 34:22). The final text, Numbers 29:12–38, does not use the words "Feast of Booths" but is clearly describing it, giving details for the sacrifices required on days one through eight.[164] Whichever of these four texts is read, it is clear that emphasis is placed on making the contents of God's Word known to all ("proclaim it and publish it in all their towns and in Jerusalem"; Neh. 8:15; cf. Deut. 31:12–13). In this case, the centrality of biblical instruction leads to the reinstitution of an important festival for the whole community.

8:16–18 The familial heads take these instructions to their households. The community has carefully heeded the four previous commands (cf. vv. 10, 12). Now the call to "go out . . . bring . . . make" is also directly obeyed (vv. 15, 16). Celebration of the Feast of Booths garners widespread support. Almost a century after the initial return, the assembly still identifies itself as those "who had returned from the captivity" (v. 17; Ezra 2:1; 3:8; 8:35; Neh. 1:2, 3). In terms of location, booths are built at the home ("roof" and "court"), publicly in the "courts of the house of God," and finally in the wider public squares before gates.[165] These domestic and civil locations suggest that the leadership obeys the call to "proclaim" and "publish" the need to keep the festival (8:15; cf. "proclaim" at Lev. 23:2, 4, 24, 37).

The statement in Nehemiah 8:17 that they had not lived in booths in the period "from the days of Jeshua" (i.e., "Joshua") is not meant to be taken literalistically. The feast was observed under Solomon (1 Kings 8:2, 65–66; 2 Chron. 7:8–10; 8:13) and more recently (Ezra 3:1, 4). Instead, the statement is designed to draw a parallel between Joshua's community and the postexilic returnees, with each community moving from exile to settlement (cf. Josh. 8:34–35; Hos. 12:9). As in Joshua's day, God has again preserved and settled his pilgrim people as a new exodus community who gather in worship before him. The promised offspring of Abraham are restored to the land (Neh. 9:8; Gen. 12:7; 13:15–16; 17:7–8; Jer. 3:14; 29:14).

---

164 In fact, Numbers 29 provides details for the sacrifices required during the various feasts of the seventh month. On the significance of the Feast of Booths, cf. comment on Ezra 3:4–6a.

165 Likely, those coming into Jerusalem from rural areas built in these public areas (Williamson, *Ezra, Nehemiah*, 296). See comment on 7:37b–8:3 for the location of the "Water Gate" (8:1). The "Ephraim Gate" (2 Kings 14:13//2 Chron. 25:23) is not mentioned in the wall building of Nehemiah 3. Its precise location is unknown. However, its placement between the Broad Wall and the Gate of Yeshanah in 12:38–39 suggests a location in the northwest segment of the wall. The homes of the period had flat roofs and were often built around a central courtyard.

The chapter concludes with two related observations. From the first day of the feast to the last, Ezra continues to read the Law to the people, underscoring its centrality to their corporate life. In keeping with this, the text also notes their obedience to the Law, keeping the feast throughout its seven days and ending it on the eighth with the "solemn assembly, according to the rule" laid down in the Law (Neh. 8:18, cf. Lev. 23:36; Num. 29:35). God's Word, and obedience to it, are the foundation for his people.

Response

The census of 7:5–73a had prepared for the repopulation of Jerusalem. However, it also leads to this remarkable moment when "all the people," so prominent throughout the chapter (8:1, 3, 5, 6, 9, 11, 12, 13), gather again as "one man" (v. 1). In the past they had gathered as "one man" to rebuild the altar and celebrate the "Feast of Booths" (Ezra 3:1–4). What is unique in the current setting is that they gather not to rebuild a physical structure but to look to God for a spiritual renewal under instruction in the "Book of the Law," also prominent in the chapter. The chapter is structured in two parts (Neh. 7:73b–8:12, 13–18), with each part emphasizing the gathering of the people, instruction in God's Word, and their response to its proclamation.

Time and again the Lord had characterized his people as those who "did not listen" to his instruction (Judg. 2:17; Ps. 81:8–16; Prov. 5:13; Isa. 65:12; 66:4; Jer. 7:22–28; 17:23; 34:14; 44:5). They were obstinate and unbelieving. In consequence God gave them over to their stubborn hearts (Ps. 81:12; Rom. 1:24–25) and sent them into captivity (2 Kings 21:8–15; Jer. 36:29–31). And yet judgment is never the end of the story. Now something new has occurred (cf. 2 Chron. 34:14–21). As the community gathers to hear the Word read, they are convicted of sin and weep (Neh. 8:9–10). These expressions of tenderness and conviction may be an early fulfillment of the new covenant promise that "they shall all know me" (Jer. 31:34).[166] They are not only attentive to the Word; they also obey its neglected instructions (Neh. 8:2–3, 14–16). These responses are inexplicable apart from the work of the Spirit of God.

The acts of the people in this chapter (gathering, instruction, response) must characterize all who embrace Christ as Savior and Lord in every cultural and historical setting (Heb. 10:24–25). Ultimately, our gathering and instruction in God's Word are not ends in themselves but a vital part of our calling to be a worshiping people (Neh. 8:6). All of this results in "great rejoicing" (vv. 12, 17) and obedience (vv. 13ff.) to the Word proclaimed.

In worship, those who name the name of Jesus rejoice that they are members of his body, a people identified and preserved by God as the offspring of Abraham (Rom. 4:9–18; 9:6–8; 11:17–20; Gal. 3:29). We also rejoice that God provides

---

166 "To have *understood* what God was saying was what made the occasion. It was a step from blind religiousness towards some degree of divine-human fellowship. Its full flowering would be in the new covenant with its assurance, 'they shall all know me'; but the old covenant already held much promise of its successor." Kidner, *Ezra and Nehemiah*, 118.

instruction in his gracious Word and has so worked in us by his Spirit that we desire to gather and hear the message of the cross that is foolishness to the world (1 Cor. 2:12–16; Mark 4:10–20). We likewise praise God that he has called some persons to "study" that Word and teach it to others (Neh. 8:13; Eph. 4:11–14; 2 Tim. 2:2). Ezra—a scribe and priest—does not make himself the most important thing. Rather, he knows that he is a servant of the Word, a minister called to open and expound the Scriptures for others (Acts 6:4).

Finally, while mourning and weeping for sin are at times an appropriate response in worship as we are convicted by God's Word (Neh. 8:9–11), we also must remember grace in our grief. For Israel, the "holy" day is a call to celebration, with feasting and "sending portions." Likewise, the "solemn assembly" concluding the Feast of Booths celebration is combined with "great rejoicing" (v. 17; 2 Chron. 7:8–10). For Christian congregations this should be especially so in our weekly Sabbath celebration. We gather and rejoice in worship under instruction of the Scriptures. In doing so we remember that grief and exile is not the end: "The joy of the LORD is your strength" (Neh. 8:10; Isa. 35:10).

NEHEMIAH 9:1–37

9 Now on the twenty-fourth day of this month the people of Israel were assembled with fasting and in sackcloth, and with earth on their heads. ² And the Israelites¹ separated themselves from all foreigners and stood and confessed their sins and the iniquities of their fathers. ³ And they stood up in their place and read from the Book of the Law of the LORD their God for a quarter of the day; for another quarter of it they made confession and worshiped the LORD their God. ⁴ On the stairs of the Levites stood Jeshua, Bani, Kadmiel, Shebaniah, Bunni, Sherebiah, Bani, and Chenani; and they cried with a loud voice to the LORD their God. ⁵ Then the Levites, Jeshua, Kadmiel, Bani, Hashabneiah, Sherebiah, Hodiah, Shebaniah, and Pethahiah, said, "Stand up and bless the LORD your God from everlasting to everlasting. Blessed be your glorious name, which is exalted above all blessing and praise.

⁶² "You are the LORD, you alone. You have made heaven, the heaven of heavens, with all their host, the earth and all that is on it, the seas and all that is in them; and you preserve all of them; and the host of heaven worships you. ⁷ You are the LORD, the God who chose Abram and brought him out of Ur of the Chaldeans and gave him the name Abraham. ⁸ You found his heart faithful before you, and made with him the covenant to give to his offspring the land of the Canaanite, the Hittite, the Amorite, the Perizzite, the Jebusite, and the Girgashite. And you have kept your promise, for you are righteous.

⁹ "And you saw the affliction of our fathers in Egypt and heard their cry at the Red Sea, ¹⁰ and performed signs and wonders against Pharaoh and

all his servants and all the people of his land, for you knew that they acted arrogantly against our fathers. And you made a name for yourself, as it is to this day. ¹¹ And you divided the sea before them, so that they went through the midst of the sea on dry land, and you cast their pursuers into the depths, as a stone into mighty waters. ¹² By a pillar of cloud you led them in the day, and by a pillar of fire in the night to light for them the way in which they should go. ¹³ You came down on Mount Sinai and spoke with them from heaven and gave them right rules and true laws, good statutes and commandments, ¹⁴ and you made known to them your holy Sabbath and commanded them commandments and statutes and a law by Moses your servant. ¹⁵ You gave them bread from heaven for their hunger and brought water for them out of the rock for their thirst, and you told them to go in to possess the land that you had sworn to give them.

¹⁶ "But they and our fathers acted presumptuously and stiffened their neck and did not obey your commandments. ¹⁷ They refused to obey and were not mindful of the wonders that you performed among them, but they stiffened their neck and appointed a leader to return to their slavery in Egypt.[3] But you are a God ready to forgive, gracious and merciful, slow to anger and abounding in steadfast love, and did not forsake them. ¹⁸ Even when they had made for themselves a golden[4] calf and said, 'This is your God who brought you up out of Egypt,' and had committed great blasphemies, ¹⁹ you in your great mercies did not forsake them in the wilderness. The pillar of cloud to lead them in the way did not depart from them by day, nor the pillar of fire by night to light for them the way by which they should go. ²⁰ You gave your good Spirit to instruct them and did not withhold your manna from their mouth and gave them water for their thirst. ²¹ Forty years you sustained them in the wilderness, and they lacked nothing. Their clothes did not wear out and their feet did not swell.

²² "And you gave them kingdoms and peoples and allotted to them every corner. So they took possession of the land of Sihon king of Heshbon and the land of Og king of Bashan. ²³ You multiplied their children as the stars of heaven, and you brought them into the land that you had told their fathers to enter and possess. ²⁴ So the descendants went in and possessed the land, and you subdued before them the inhabitants of the land, the Canaanites, and gave them into their hand, with their kings and the peoples of the land, that they might do with them as they would. ²⁵ And they captured fortified cities and a rich land, and took possession of houses full of all good things, cisterns already hewn, vineyards, olive orchards and fruit trees in abundance. So they ate and were filled and became fat and delighted themselves in your great goodness.

²⁶ "Nevertheless, they were disobedient and rebelled against you and cast your law behind their back and killed your prophets, who had warned them in order to turn them back to you, and they committed great blasphemies. ²⁷ Therefore you gave them into the hand of their enemies, who made them suffer. And in the time of their suffering they cried out to you and you heard them from heaven, and according to your great mercies you gave them saviors who saved them from the hand of their enemies. ²⁸ But after they had rest they did evil again before you, and you abandoned them to the hand of their enemies, so that they had dominion over them. Yet when they turned and cried to you, you heard from heaven, and many times you delivered them according to your mercies. ²⁹ And you warned them in order to turn them back to your law. Yet they acted presumptu-

ously and did not obey your commandments, but sinned against your rules, which if a person does them, he shall live by them, and they turned a stubborn shoulder and stiffened their neck and would not obey. [30] Many years you bore with them and warned them by your Spirit through your prophets. Yet they would not give ear. Therefore you gave them into the hand of the peoples of the lands. [31] Nevertheless, in your great mercies you did not make an end of them or forsake them, for you are a gracious and merciful God.

[32] "Now, therefore, our God, the great, the mighty, and the awesome God, who keeps covenant and steadfast love, let not all the hardship seem little to you that has come upon us, upon our kings, our princes, our priests, our prophets, our fathers, and all your people, since the time of the kings of Assyria until this day. [33] Yet you have been righteous in all that has come upon us, for you have dealt faithfully and we have acted wickedly. [34] Our kings, our princes, our priests, and our fathers have not kept your law or paid attention to your commandments and your warnings that you gave them. [35] Even in their own kingdom, and amid your great goodness that you gave them, and in the large and rich land that you set before them, they did not serve you or turn from their wicked works. [36] Behold, we are slaves this day; in the land that you gave to our fathers to enjoy its fruit and its good gifts, behold, we are slaves. [37] And its rich yield goes to the kings whom you have set over us because of our sins. They rule over our bodies and over our livestock as they please, and we are in great distress.

[1] Hebrew *the offspring of Israel* [2] Septuagint adds *And Ezra said* [3] Some Hebrew manuscripts; many Hebrew manuscripts *and in their rebellion appointed a leader to return to their slavery* [4] Hebrew *metal*

Section Overview

The covenant renewal of Nehemiah 7:73b–10:39 is the first of four major units in the final section of Nehemiah (7:73b–13:31). As this unit begins, the Law is twice read and explained on the first two days of the seventh month. The community responds with weeping, rejoicing, and celebration of the neglected Feast of Booths (8:18).

The current chapter (9:1–37) follows this renewed attention to the Law with worship and confession as the core of covenant renewal. For a third time the people assemble under Levitical instruction to hear the Law read (v. 1; cf. 8:1, 13). This results in a call to prayer (9:1–5). The prayer includes praise, repentance, and a lengthy confession reciting God's unrelenting faithfulness, especially in giving the land, and the people's consistent failure to love him (vv. 6–31). The confession is structured as a redemptive-historical summary, the most complete review of the biblical story in the entire OT.[167] Its epochs are nicely indicated in the ESV by five paragraphs: creation to the call of Abraham (vv. 6–8); exodus to Sinai (vv. 9–15); rebellion and the wilderness (vv. 16–21); possession of the land (vv. 22–25 [Joshua]);

---

167 Nehemiah 9 is comparable to a historical psalm like Psalm 106, which covers exodus to exile (cf. Ps. 106:7, 47). Other OT summaries include Deuteronomy 1–3; Joshua 24:2–13; 1 Samuel 12:6–13; Psalms 78; 105; 136. The question of genre, whether it is prose or poetry, and other questions of classification are treated at length in Williamson, *Ezra, Nehemiah*, 305–307.

cycles of disobedience, mercy, and prophetic warning (vv. 26–31 [Judges to Kings]). The final paragraph, with a shift marked by "Now," brings the history up to the current moment. It functions as both a concluding confession and lament and an implicit petition for God's deliverance (vv. 32–37).

Section Outline

III.A.2. Redemptive-Historical Covenant Confession (9:1–37)
  a. Assembly with Reading, Confession, and a Call to Prayer (9:1–5)
  b. Creation to Abrahamic Covenant (9:6–8)
  c. Exodus and the Red Sea Crossing to Mount Sinai (9:9–15)
  d. Rebellion and the Forty-Year Wilderness Period (9:16–21)
  e. The Land as an Expression of the Lord's Goodness (9:22–25)
  f. Cycles of Sin, Subjugation, Supplication, and Salvation (9:26–31)
  g. Petition and Lament in Light of the Lord's "Great Goodness" (9:32–37)

Comment

9:1–5 As in the prior chapter, here the description of setting and persons involved (vv. 1–3) is followed by the actions of the Levites in leading worship (vv. 4–5). The text does not state where this assembly takes place. Mentions of "this month" refer to the seventh month (8:2, 13). Action on the twenty-fourth day means it follows soon after the prior "solemn assembly" of the twenty-second day (8:18). That day was the eighth following the seven days of the Feast of Booths (Lev. 23:33–36).

  In spite of the shift from rejoicing to penitence, the current actions are consistent with the previous chapter. The response of weeping and mourning has revealed the prior impact of the reading of the Law (Neh. 8:9–12). This is now expressed through fasting (cf. Ezra 8:21–23; 10:6), sackcloth, and earth upon the people's heads (Est. 4:1; Jonah 3:5–6; Dan. 9:3). These are outward forms of mourning and repentance, death and burial. The people (lit., "seed of Israel"; cf. Neh. 9:2 ESV mg.) remain the major focus throughout. Their "separation" from foreigners is not marital (cf. Ezra 9:1–2; 10:1–2); it is a separation in order to come before their God and applies to the entire confessing community (Neh. 10:28; cf. Ezra 6:21). They again *stand* and *read* (Neh. 9:3–5; 8:4–5), followed now by *confession* and *worship*. This occurs over a significant part of one day (9:3; cf. 8:3). Certainly, it is surprising that Ezra is not named (though cf. 9:6 ESV mg.). However, the Levites again play their part (v. 4), as they did in the previous chapter (8:7), again confirming the compatibility of chapters 8 and 9.[168]

  The "stairs [lit., "the ascent"] of the Levites" (9:4) may refer to the steps of an otherwise unknown structure used to elevate the Levites before the people

---

168 Some interpreters offer reasons why it is inappropriate to read chapter 9 in light of chapter 8. These include the sudden shift from joy to penitence, Ezra's absence, and language like "seed" and "separation" (Neh. 9:2) more typical of Ezra (cf. Ezra 9:1–2; 10:8, 11, 16). The conclusion is that Nehemiah 9 has been relocated from Ezra 8–10. Some of these concerns have been addressed above and in the Introduction to Nehemiah: Interpretive Difficulties. For a full discussion, see Williamson, *Ezra, Nehemiah*, 308–310.

on such occasions.[169] Two sets of eight Levites are mentioned, with five names shared in common. It appears that one set begins by crying out publicly for deliverance ("cried with a loud voice"; v. 4b; cf. 1 Sam. 28:12; 2 Sam. 19:4; Est. 4:1; Ezek. 11:13). The second group then issues the invitation to praise ("stand up and bless the LORD"; Neh. 9:5b) and puts the general cry of distress into words with the prayer of confession that follows (cf. v. 37).[170] The doxology heading the prayer begins like a hymn of praise, exalting the "glorious name" of their covenant-keeping Lord (v. 5b).[171] The whole confession that follows is intended to bless God's name.

9:6 The doxology (v. 5b) leads to a simple but profound proclamation: "You are the LORD." There is only one incomparable God worthy of that name (2 Kings 19:15). Like Genesis 1 the prayer moves from heaven to earth, naming the Lord as the sole Creator and Preserver of *all* (four times) creation. The whole prayer is dominated by the works of God ("you made," "you chose," etc.). The worshiping "host of heaven" may refer to angelic servants (1 Kings 22:19; Ps. 8:5) or to all of the heavenly bodies (cf. Gen. 2:1). Ironically, the Israelites had exchanged worship of the creator for worship of the "host of heaven" he had made. Such worship was a prominent expression of covenantal disobedience and had led to exile (Deut. 4:19–20; 2 Kings 17:16; 21:3–5; 23:4; Jer. 8:2; 19:13).

9:7–8 The phrase "You are the LORD" ties verses 6–7 together. The God who created all things (v. 6) also chose Abram in particular (v. 7). The God who created Adam and placed him in the garden (Gen. 2:7–9, 15) also chose Abram and brought him from Mesopotamia to the land of promise (Gen. 11:28, 31; Deut. 10:15). Through Abram's offspring God purposed to redeem and recreate all things. The rebellions of Genesis 3–11 would be healed.

By renaming Abram as Abraham ("father of a multitude") the Lord summarized the promises of the everlasting covenant made with Abraham (Gen. 17:1–5; 22:17–18). That covenant included the giving of the "land of the Canaanite," of descendants to inhabit that fruitful land, and of blessing—especially the promise to be Abraham's God and the God of his children (Gen. 12:1–3; 15:18–21; 17:6–8; 26:3; Ex. 6:7; Jer. 7:23). The verb "to give" (Hb. *natan*) is a key word throughout the confession, where God is the primary subject.[172]

---

169 Kidner suggests an analogy with the later Herodian temple, where fifteen steps led from the court of the women to the court of Israel (*Ezra and Nehemiah*, 121). According to the Mishnah, the Levites used to sing on these steps. The translation "platform" (NASB, NJPS) may suggest the wooden platform of 8:4. However, the word translated "platform" is a different noun than that translated "stairs" in 9:4, and the sense of the latter is of a more permanent structure (Williamson, *Ezra, Nehemiah*, 311).

170 Jeshua, Bani (i.e., Binnui), and Kadmiel were Levitical leaders (cf. 10:9; 12:8). It seems unlikely that these same names, along with Shebaniah and Sherebiah, refer to different individuals in the separate lists. Rather, all five play a role in both the cry of distress of the first group and then the confession of the second. Another option is that originally both lists were identical and differences between the two arose in textual transmission (Blenkinsopp, *Ezra-Nehemiah*, 295).

171 Cf. 1 Chronicles 16:29; Psalms 66:1–4; 72:18–19; 96:7–9.

172 The Lord is the subject of the verb "give" 17 of 19 times: 9:8 (2x), 10 ("performed"), 13, 15 (2x), 20 (2x), 22, 24, 27 (2x), 30, 35 (2x, "set"), 36, 37 ("set"). God gives a covenant, land, signs and wonders, commandments, bread and water, his good Spirit, kingdoms and peoples, victory over and defeat at the hands of enemies, saviors, and his great goodness. Where Israel is the subject of the verb it refers to "giving" rebellion: 9:17 ("appointed"), 29 ("turned").

God not only covenants with Abraham; he also evaluates his heart. Abraham demonstrated an ongoing intention to walk after God by faith (Gen. 15:6). Sometimes this is called a "circumcised heart" (Deut. 10:16; 30:6; Rom. 2:28–29; 4:9–12). All of this is relevant to a postexilic people who, like Abraham, have also journeyed from Mesopotamia. They are bolstered by the faith expressed by Abraham their father. More importantly, they are comforted that God remains true to his word and keeps his promises (Neh. 9:8). They still exist as Abraham's offspring, and the Lord is still their God. Most importantly, in context, the Lord has remained faithful to return them to the land.

9:9–11 The language of these verses clearly evokes Exodus 1–15. Seeing their miserable state (Ex. 2:23–25; 3:7), God performed "signs and wonders." These mighty acts were accomplished to deliver his people from slavery (Ex. 7:3–4; Deut. 6:22; 26:8; 34:11). Hearing "their cry at the Red Sea" (Neh. 9:9; Ex. 14:10–15), God divided the waters. His people passed through, but their enemies were cast like "a stone into mighty waters" (Neh. 9:11; Ex. 15:5, 10; Isa. 43:15–17). These themes of slavery and freedom, judgment and deliverance are relevant to the postexilic praying audience. God will also hear their cry for help in their slavery (Neh. 9:4, 36).

The purpose of this deliverance was that the Lord's glory as savior might spread abroad as it was "to this day" (v. 10b; cf. v. 5b). In mistreating their forebears, the Egyptians "acted arrogantly,"[173] behavior already known by Jethro, Moses' father-in-law (Ex. 18:11). But when Jethro learned of the mighty ways in which the Lord had rescued his people, he came to the same conclusion as the postexilic community: "Now I know that the LORD is greater than all gods" (Ex. 18:10–11; cf. Neh. 9:32 and also Ex. 14:17–18).

9:12–15 These verses abridge the travel to Sinai and the giving of the Law there (Exodus 13–31). The pillar of cloud and fire and the fact that "you came down" signal God's presence, deliverance, guidance, and protection (Ex. 13:21–22; 14:19; cf. Ex. 3:8). However, the Lord also met their physical needs with "bread from heaven" and water in the wilderness, clear references to events in Exodus 16–17 (esp. 16:4; 17:6).

More importantly, the Lord again kept his covenant promises. He had promised Abraham that the families of the earth would be blessed in him (Gen. 12:3). But how? One important way was through the Lord's descending to speak to Moses his instructions for his newly delivered people (Neh. 9:13–14; Ex. 19:20). Especially singled out is the "holy Sabbath" (Neh. 9:14; Ex. 20:8–11; 31:13–17; Neh. 13:15–22). Along with receiving God's law, taking possession of the land, sworn as a gracious gift, is once more stressed (9:8, 15; Ex. 6:8). Here God would plant them as a kingdom of priests and a holy nation (Ex. 19:5–6). In short, by obeying these commandments in that place, the Lord would shape a new humanity, a people of grace and justice and blessing to all the nations (Neh. 9:8, 15; cf. Ex. 19:5–6; Deut. 4:1–8).

---

173 The sense of the verb is a pride that defies a greater authority, here the Lord (Ex. 18:11; Jer. 50:29). In its later application to Israel the ESV translates this "acted presumptuously" (Neh. 9:16, 29). Like Egypt, Israel's pride leads to complete disregard of the Lord in the face of clear commandments (e.g., Deut. 1:43).

9:16–31 After the attention given to God's beneficence the final three paragraphs alternate between human disobedience and the Lord's merciful response ("they" vs. "you"). This is apparent in the A-B-C-B'-A' pattern of the whole, with the land promise located centrally (table 2.2).

TABLE 2.2: Chiasm of Disobedience and Grace

Human Disobedience	Divine Response
(A) "acted presumptuously" (v. 16)	"gracious and merciful" (v. 17)
(B) "committed great blasphemies" (v. 18)	"great mercies" (v. 19)
(C) the land as the Lord's gift (vv. 22–25)	
(B') "committed great blasphemies" (v. 26)	"great mercies" (v. 27)
(A') "acted presumptuously" (v. 29)	"great mercies"; "gracious and merciful" (v. 31)

9:16–17a, 18 The bleak evaluation piles up. Like the Egyptians, they had "acted presumptuously" (vv. 16, 29; cf. note 173). They had "stiffened their neck" (cf. v. 29), which parallels hardening one's heart (2 Chron. 36:13). Comparable language characterizes them after the golden calf incident (Ex. 32:9; 33:3, 5; 34:9). The idiom is nearly synonymous with unbelief (Deut. 10:16; 2 Kings 17:14ff.; 2 Chron. 30:8–9; Prov. 29:1) and is likened to a refusal to listen to God's Word (Jer. 7:26; 17:23; 19:15).[174] Here the latter sense is prominent. They refused to "obey" (lit., "hear"; Neh. 9:16, 17) the good teaching received (vv. 13–14). They forgot ("were not mindful") of the signs and wonders of their deliverance (vv. 9–11). Perhaps most dramatically, by their idolatry they "committed great blasphemies" (v. 18), showing contempt for the things of God.[175]

Two significant examples are referenced. First, the desire for other leadership following the report of the spies (Numbers 13–14; esp. 14:4). This revealed their ingratitude and rejection of Moses' authority in order to "return to their slavery in Egypt" (Neh. 9:17).[176] More importantly, it showed a refusal to embrace God's gift of the land. Second, the golden calf incident (v. 18; Exodus 32–34; esp. 32:4, 8) provided *the* paradigm of idolatry (Ex. 20:3–4).

9:17b, 19–21 "But you" (v. 17b) and "Even when" (v. 18a) reveal the Lord's response. Every mention of their "great blasphemies" (vv. 18, 26) is answered with his "great mercies" (vv. 19, 27). Indeed, the entire rebellious recitation is framed by the "gracious and merciful" Lord (vv. 17, 31). These terms head the list of God's

---

174 The idiom may refer to a beast refusing its master's will. It is sometimes translated "stubborn" or "obstinate" (Deut. 9:6, 13; 31:27; Isa. 48:4). Stephen equates it with being uncircumcised in heart and ears, which he interprets as a resistance to the Holy Spirit (Acts 7:51).

175 The noun translated "blasphemies" here occurs infrequently (9:18, 26; 2 Kings 19:3//Isa. 37:3; Ezek. 35:12). Other English translations translate it as "impieties," "provocations," "insults," and "contempt." Its sense can be discerned from the cognate verb in comparable contexts of rejection of the Lord (Num. 14:22–23; 16:30; Isa. 1:4) and especially of breaking the covenant (Deut. 31:20). This is parallel with unbelief (Num. 14:11). The noun then describes the results of these treacherous actions.

176 The Hebrew reads "in their rebellion" (cf. KJV, NIV, NJPS). With support of some ancient manuscripts, a change of one letter makes this "in Egypt," an emendation accepted by most English translations. The comparable language in Numbers 14:4 also supports this.

benevolent characteristics, including forgiveness, patience, and an unrelenting faithfulness (v. 17b), wedged between the two examples of rebellion (vv. 16–17a, 18). Beginning with the golden calf incident, this description of the Lord forms a consistent thread of testimony throughout the OT (Ex. 34:6; Pss. 86:15; 103:8; 145:8; Joel 2:13; Jonah 4:2).

Practically, this meant that, in spite of their rejection of him, the Lord "did not forsake them" (Neh. 9:17, 19, 31). This is evidenced in the fact that even after the description of these rebellions (vv. 16–18), God's mercies persisted through his presence in the guiding pillars (v. 19; cf. v. 12), his instruction (v. 20a; cf. vv. 13–14),[177] physical sustenance (vv. 20b–21; cf. v. 15a) and his giving of the land (vv. 22–25, 15b).[178] In all this time "they lacked nothing" (v. 21; Deut. 2:7; 8:9). This is truly amazing grace!

9:22–25 The land promise now receives full attention. The key words "possession," "land," and "gave" from verse 15b are carried forward.[179] Attention to the land reveals its importance to the postexilic community (vv. 36–37). No mention is made of failure, sin, or rebellion. Instead, obedience is stressed in the repetition of "took possession" as the grateful response of faith to God's actions:

- You (= "Lord") gave, allotted//they took possession (v. 22; Num. 21:21–31, 33–35; Deut. 2:24–3:11);
- You multiplied their children (cf. Neh. 9:8), brought them (i.e., led), told them to enter and to possess (v. 23; cf. Deut. 7:1–2)//they entered and took possession (Neh. 9:24);
- You subdued and gave over the Canaanites (v. 24)//they captured and took possession (v. 25; Joshua 1–12).

The climactic verse, Nehemiah 9:25, summarizes the overflowing grace of God. These underserved items, repeating Deuteronomy 6:10–11, indicate security (fortified cities), fertility (rich = "fat" land), shelter (houses), water (cisterns already hewn), and food (vineyards, etc.). The final verbs lead to the summary: "[they] delighted themselves in your great goodness." God had placed his people in a new Eden.

9:26–31 The period from Judges–2 Kings is painted with the broadest of strokes. The cycle of sin, subjugation, supplication, and salvation, characteristic of Judges (Judg. 2:11–23), typifies the entire history.[180] This cycle is repeated twice in Nehemiah 9:26–28. In verses 29–31 the cycle begins for a third time by mentioning sin

---

177 The law (9:13–14) is here parallel to "your good Spirit to instruct them" (9:20a). In this context, the verb translated "instruct" (Hb. *sakal*) is associated with the success arising from the study and observance of the law (Josh. 1:7–8; Williamson, *Ezra, Nehemiah*, 314). The work of God's "good Spirit" is elsewhere linked with the Lord's teaching his will (Ps. 143:10; cf. Ps. 51:11–13).

178 The observation that these varied expressions of God's faithfulness are repeated and paralleled both before (9:12–15) and after (9:19–21) the rebellion of 9:16–18 is found in Williamson, *Ezra, Nehemiah*, 314–325.

179 Williamson, *Ezra, Nehemiah*, 316.

180 Other suggested links to Judges include "rest" (Judg. 3:11, 30; 5:31; 8:28) and "did evil again" (Judg. 3:12; 4:1; 10:6; 13:1).

and subjugation, but the associated supplication and salvation are saved for the final paragraph (vv. 32–37).

9:26 "Nevertheless" marks the contrast between God's "great goodness" (v. 25) and their disobedience (Deut. 6:10–12; 8:7–20). Rejection or embrace of the Lord's law (Hb. *torah*) meant rejection or embrace of Lord himself (Neh. 9:26, 29). This was evident particularly in the sometimes violent rejection of the prophetic warnings (1 Kings 18–19; 2 Kings 6:31; 17:13–20; 2 Chron. 24:20–22; Jer. 26:20–23; Matt. 23:30, 37). The people's refusal to repent and obey (cf. Neh. 9:16–17) is again described as "great blasphemies" (cf. v. 18), which suggests ongoing idolatry (cf. 1 Kings 12:28; 2 Kings 17:16; Hos. 13:2). But once more their sin was met with God's "great mercies" (Neh. 9:26–27; cf. 18–19).

9:27–28 The cycle described above is repeated in each verse. The Lord now chastises his people for their incessant sin (vv. 26, 28) by empowering enemies over them (vv. 27, 28).[181] As in Egypt (v. 9), the people again "cried out" (Neh. 9:27, 28; cf. Judg. 2:18) and "you heard" (vv. 27, 28). The Lord countered oppressors who oppress with "saviors who saved" (cf. Judg. 2:16; 3:9, 15). The repetitions of the cycle are indicated in the final clause, "many times you delivered them" (Neh. 9:28; cf. v. 30).

9:29–31 Only sin and subjugation are present in the third presentation of the cycle (though see further at v. 31). Again prophets warn in order to motivate repentance (v. 29; 2 Kings 17:13, 15; Amos 4:6–13; Zech. 1:1–4). This was a matter of life and death (cf. Lev. 18:5; Deut. 30:15–20). Obedience as an embrace of life was always set before Israel, not as a means of earning God's favor but as way of loving the one who had already redeemed them. Covenantal faithfulness maintained fellowship with God and kept them under the canopy of his favor (Deut. 4:1; 5:33; 8:1; Amos 5:14; John 14:21).

They again rejected the prophetic message. As in the wilderness period they "acted presumptuously"[182] and "did not obey" (Neh. 9:29; cf. vv. 16–17). Rather than embrace God's good instruction (v. 13), they "sinned against your rules" (v. 29). Whereas God *gave* them many good gifts, they *gave* him only rejection. This is once again expressed in the metaphor of a stiffened neck (vv. 16–17) and stubborn shoulder—an animal refusing its yoke.[183] The Spirit who had instructed them (v. 20) was also the Spirit who warned them through the prophets (Zech. 7:11–14; cf. 2 Chron. 24:19; Jer. 6:10; 11:7; 2 Pet. 1:21). The long-suffering of the Lord lasted over "many years," likely a reference to the entire era of kingship.[184] The result was that they "would not give ear" (i.e., did not pay attention or heed instruction). Jeremiah equated this to having "uncircumcised" ears (Jer. 6:10; Acts 28:25–27).

---

181 For the first time in the chapter, "gave them" has a negative connotation. This is emphasized in 9:27, which may be translated: "And you [the Lord] gave them into the hand of their *oppressors* and they *oppressed them*, and in the time of *their oppression* . . ."

182 Cf. note 173.

183 In the clause "turned a stubborn shoulder," the verb "turned" translates the Hebrew word *natan* ("to give"). As noted in the comment on 9:7–8, this is a key word.

184 The verb "bore" (i.e., prolong, extend, continue) has "steadfast love" as its object at Psalms 36:10; 109:12; Jeremiah 31:3.

As in the days of the judges (Neh. 9:27), they became subject to the "peoples of the lands," here a reference to Assyrian and Babylonian exile.[185] However, judgment is never the end for the Lord's people. Ultimately, the existence of Ezra-Nehemiah as a book and this very prayer of the restored community confirms God's preservation of a remnant. So while supplication and salvation are not explicitly mentioned here, the mention of the Lord's "great mercies" and his identification as a "gracious and merciful" God (vv. 17, 31) form the basis of the supplication about to come.

9:32–37 These verses now finish the prior cycle begun in verses 19–31 by providing the missing supplication. The current generation indirectly pleads that God would once again provide salvation from their oppressors.

9:32–35 In other narrative summaries, "and now" marks a shift from a review of the past to a challenge for the people in the present (Deut. 4:1; Josh. 24:14; 1 Sam. 12:13, 16). In the current confession it marks the main petition from the present generation, asking God not to minimize the accumulated "hardship . . . upon us."[186]

Their supplication is grounded in God's omnipotent but compassionate character. He is "our God," who is far above all things (Deut. 10:17). Yet he is also the Lord who comes close to his people in covenant faithfulness (Neh. 9:17, 32; cf. 1:4–5; Jer. 32:18). Joined to the entire preexilic community, they agree that God's chastisements were deserved. Assyria and Babylonia had oppressed them from the eighth to fifth centuries, culminating in their current status under the Persians. Even in this God has been righteous and faithful in all his dealings with Israel (Neh. 9:33; cf. v. 8b).

Verses 34–35 summarize their primary transgressions. They have rejected God's Word and worshiped idols. The latter is inferred by the language "serve" and "wicked works" often associated with the worship (i.e. service) of foreign gods (Judg. 2:19; Ps. 106:28–29; Jer. 2:26–27; 11:9–17). This is even more reprehensible given the Lord's "great goodness" and especially the bounteous land ("rich land"; cf. Neh. 9:25).

9:36–37 The concluding lament of "great distress" (v. 37) repeats the key word-group from verse 27 (*oppress, oppressors*, etc.). Not only their fathers' sins but "our sins" have brought about this state of affairs. The twofold "Behold, we are slaves" (v. 36; cf. Jer. 2:14) surrounds the central reminder of the land's abounding gifts. The blessings of Nehemiah 9:22–25 are now inverted. Rather than exerting their will over the "peoples of the lands," they are now subjugated to the kings God has set (i.e., "given") over them.[187] They no longer control the land's produce or even their own bodies — the latter likely referring to forced labor or military service (Lev. 26:17; Deut. 28:30b–31, 39–40, 48). They leave to God's mercy their unspoken need

---

185 For "peoples of the lands," cf. comment on Ezra 4:4–5.

186 The noun "hardship" elsewhere describes the experience under the Egyptians, in the journey in the wilderness, and in the Babylonian exile (Ex. 18:8; Num. 20:14; Lam. 3:5).

187 The translations "as they would" (9:24b) and "as they please" (9:37) render the same Hebrew phrase. Israel was once able to exert its will over others, but now others are exerting their will over Israel.

for salvation. Having confessed their past and present covenantal unfaithfulness, they are ready to renew the covenant (Nehemiah 10).[188]

Response

This prayer is the confession and cry of an entire community. It takes the form of a redemptive-historical summary that moves chronologically from creation to the postexilic present. The story retells the front end of Israel's gospel, the good news of a covenantal relationship established by the Lord. We must also remember that it is the front end of our story, as the early church did by weaving it into the preaching of the gospel fulfilled ultimately in Jesus Christ (Acts 7:2–53; 13:17–41).[189] Since the people already know their story, what is the point of retelling it in a confession? Stated differently, what good does it do to pray their past?

Praying their story helps to shape their identity and spiritually reform the postexilic community. It defines and situates them as the people of God. Renewed interest in the goodness of God's law (Neh. 9:3, 13) had been further revived by the prior instruction from Ezra and the Levites (8:2–3, 13). In its light, they remember the indissoluble link with their forefathers as they lament both prior chastisements and their current situation as "slaves this day" (9:33, 36). All this is justified "because of our sins" (v. 37). Their entire history illustrates a refusal to heed God's Word, a refusal to return to him in spite of repeated prophetic warnings, and a refusal to live faithfully in gratitude for his gifts, especially the land (vv. 8, 15, 22–25, 35–37). In light of the story, their need to repent becomes crystal clear.

In praying their story, they also bear witness to the God who keeps his promise. These promises that end in Jesus Christ (2 Cor. 1:20) begin with the Lord, the creator and sustainer of all things (Neh. 9:6, 32) who had also chosen and covenanted with Abraham and his descendants (vv. 7–8), promising he would bring blessing to the nations through them (Gen. 12:3). Thus while confession of sin is important, it is not Israel's primary vocation. Rather, they are first called to testify to the glory of God, to praise his "glorious name" and "great goodness" (Neh. 9:5, 25, 35), and thereby bless the nations by making God known to them (cf. Acts 26:16–18). The core of this testimony is their ongoing recitation of his mighty acts in delivering them from their bondage in Egypt (Neh. 9:9–11; Ps. 96:2–3). Moreover, by obeying his good commandments, they would form a new humanity placed in the midst of the nations (Neh. 9:13–14, 22–25). In their current "great distress" they therefore remember that God is righteous and faithful and has kept his promises in the past (vv. 8, 33); surely he will do so again in the future.

This in turn gives them hope in the God of "great mercies" (vv. 19, 27, 31). In praying their story, the postexilic community remembers that because of the Lord's mercies they still have a chance to play the part he has called them to play in his story. Indeed, the grave sins of the wilderness period were met with God's

---

188 Nehemiah 9:38 in English is 10:1 in Hebrew and will be treated with the following chapter.
189 On the function of story summaries, see Michael D. Williams, "Story Summaries: Key Points for Understanding the Bible's Big Story and Our Place within It," *Presbyterion* 45/1 (Spring 2019): 41–58.

self-identification as "gracious and merciful" (vv. 17, 31). Repeatedly he had shown himself to be a God of inexhaustible patience, ever ready to forgive their ongoing disobedience and save them when they cried out (v. 27). So now they are crying out to God again (v. 4). In contrast to their past contempt for God's instruction, they have returned to God, ready to embrace his law once more. They prepare to "make a firm covenant" (v. 38), seeking once more to be agents of divine blessing in their own day.

Today, Jew and Gentile in Christ continue as members of this people God has created, elected, ransomed, blessed, forgiven, and restored. Indeed, he did not "make an end of them" (v. 31). This is the front end of the gospel story, culminating in the coming of Jesus the Messiah (Acts 7:52–53; 13:16–33)—a story that molds our identity. Likewise, with the postexilic community we may cry out in our own individual and corporate distress (Neh. 9:37) with confidence that the same Lord is our God, still gracious, merciful, and ready to forgive (v. 17b). In recounting these great deeds of the Lord and embracing his good law (v. 13) we testify to the goodness of his care for his people. Finally, in remembering his mercies and the sins of our fathers we are prompted to repent where necessary and to play our part in the mission to declare his glory among the nations.

NEHEMIAH 9:38–10:39

38 1 "Because of all this we make a firm covenant in writing; on the sealed document are the names of[2] our princes, our Levites, and our priests.
10 [3]"On the seals are the names of[4] Nehemiah the governor, the son of Hacaliah, Zedekiah, 2 Seraiah, Azariah, Jeremiah, 3 Pashhur, Amariah, Malchijah, 4 Hattush, Shebaniah, Malluch, 5 Harim, Meremoth, Obadiah, 6 Daniel, Ginnethon, Baruch, 7 Meshullam, Abijah, Mijamin, 8 Maaziah, Bilgai, Shemaiah; these are the priests. 9 And the Levites: Jeshua the son of Azaniah, Binnui of the sons of Henadad, Kadmiel; 10 and their brothers, Shebaniah, Hodiah, Kelita, Pelaiah, Hanan, 11 Mica, Rehob, Hashabiah, 12 Zaccur, Sherebiah, Shebaniah, 13 Hodiah, Bani, Beninu. 14 The chiefs of the people: Parosh, Pahath-moab, Elam, Zattu, Bani, 15 Bunni, Azgad, Bebai, 16 Adonijah, Bigvai, Adin, 17 Ater, Hezekiah, Azzur, 18 Hodiah, Hashum, Bezai, 19 Hariph, Anathoth, Nebai, 20 Magpiash, Meshullam, Hezir, 21 Meshezabel, Zadok, Jaddua, 22 Pelatiah, Hanan, Anaiah, 23 Hoshea, Hananiah, Hasshub, 24 Hallohesh, Pilha, Shobek, 25 Rehum, Hashabnah, Maaseiah, 26 Ahiah, Hanan, Anan, 27 Malluch, Harim, Baanah.
28 "The rest of the people, the priests, the Levites, the gatekeepers, the singers, the temple servants, and all who have separated themselves from the peoples of the lands to the Law of God, their wives, their sons, their daughters, all who have knowledge and understanding, 29 join with their

brothers, their nobles, and enter into a curse and an oath to walk in God's Law that was given by Moses the servant of God, and to observe and do all the commandments of the LORD our Lord and his rules and his statutes. [30] We will not give our daughters to the peoples of the land or take their daughters for our sons. [31] And if the peoples of the land bring in goods or any grain on the Sabbath day to sell, we will not buy from them on the Sabbath or on a holy day. And we will forego the crops of the seventh year and the exaction of every debt.

[32] "We also take on ourselves the obligation to give yearly a third part of a shekel[5] for the service of the house of our God: [33] for the showbread, the regular grain offering, the regular burnt offering, the Sabbaths, the new moons, the appointed feasts, the holy things, and the sin offerings to make atonement for Israel, and for all the work of the house of our God. [34] We, the priests, the Levites, and the people, have likewise cast lots for the wood offering, to bring it into the house of our God, according to our fathers' houses, at times appointed, year by year, to burn on the altar of the LORD our God, as it is written in the Law. [35] We obligate ourselves to bring the firstfruits of our ground and the firstfruits of all fruit of every tree, year by year, to the house of the LORD; [36] also to bring to the house of our God, to the priests who minister in the house of our God, the firstborn of our sons and of our cattle, as it is written in the Law, and the firstborn of our herds and of our flocks; [37] and to bring the first of our dough, and our contributions, the fruit of every tree, the wine and the oil, to the priests, to the chambers of the house of our God; and to bring to the Levites the tithes from our ground, for it is the Levites who collect the tithes in all our towns where we labor. [38] And the priest, the son of Aaron, shall be with the Levites when the Levites receive the tithes. And the Levites shall bring up the tithe of the tithes to the house of our God, to the chambers of the storehouse. [39] For the people of Israel and the sons of Levi shall bring the contribution of grain, wine, and oil to the chambers, where the vessels of the sanctuary are, as well as the priests who minister, and the gatekeepers and the singers. We will not neglect the house of our God."

[1] Ch 10:1 in Hebrew [2] Hebrew lacks *the names of* [3] Ch 10:2 in Hebrew [4] Hebrew lacks *the names of* [5] A *shekel* was about 2/5 ounce or 11 grams

Section Overview

Nehemiah 8–10 may be broadly conceived as a covenant renewal, a climactic moment of reform prompted by several readings of the Law. A third reading of the "Book of the Law" on the twenty-fourth day (9:1) results in fasting, confession, and worship. Israel's entire history of rebellion and God's steadfast love is recounted in a prayer shaped as a redemptive-historical covenant confession. The steadfast love of the Lord has not forsaken them (9:17, 19, 31), although how the Lord will answer their current "great distress" (9:37) is left to his merciful character.

Having considered the past, they reflect on their obligations and so determine to renew their covenant as the Lord's people. The first half of the chapter begins with a resolution to write a covenant document (9:38) and continues with the names of those whose names are affixed (10:1–27). The second half of the chapter reveals the covenant's content. It commences with a general commitment to the Lord's commandments (10:28–29) and concludes with detailed promises from the unified people (10:30–39a). The promise to reject mixed marriages (10:30) and reform Sabbath practices (10:31) is followed by the pledge that they will fulfill certain obligations associated with the temple (10:32–39a). The final verse summarizes the recommitment: "We will not neglect the house of our God" (10:39b).

Section Outline

III.A.3. The Sealing and Promises of the Renewed Covenant (9:38–10:39)

    a. Determination to Make and Seal a Covenant (9:38–10:27)

        (1) The Covenant Made in Writing (9:38)

        (2) The Covenant Sealed with Names (10:1–27)

    b. The Covenant Promises of the Whole Community (10:28–39)

        (1) The Whole Community Enters into a Curse and Oath (10:28–29)

        (2) The Promises Made (10:30–39)

            (a) To Reject Mixed Marriages (10:30)

            (b) To Maintain Sabbath Observances (10:31)

            (c) To Give One Third of a Shekel for God's House (10:32–33)

            (d) To Bring Offerings to the House of the Lord (10:34–39a)

            (e) Summary: "We Will Not Neglect the House of Our God" (10:39b)

Comment

9:38[190] "Because of all this" transitions from the reading of the Law on the first day of the seventh month (8:2), the celebration of the Feast of Tabernacles ending on the twenty-second day of the month (8:18), and the prayer of confession on the twenty-fourth day of the month (9:1). The covenant renewal that follows in the current chapter functions as the conclusion of chapters 8–9 as the people recommit to the Law.[191] In the forefront is their current "great distress" (9:37), leading to the decision to renew the covenant. The explicit pronoun ("we") implicates the entire community in the resolve to enter this "firm covenant."

The standard word for "covenant" (Hb. *berit*) is not used here. That this chapter represents a covenant-renewal ceremony is supported by the presence of the verb "cutting" (*karat*), typical of covenant making.[192] It is followed by a word that has the sense "faith(fulness), support" (*'amana*)[193] Taken together, the phrase refers to

---

190 Nehemiah 9:38 in English is equivalent to 10:1 in Hebrew.

191 Numerous scholars argue that the covenant renewal of chapter 10 fits best chronologically after chapter 13 (Clines, *Ezra, Nehemiah, Esther*, 199–200; Williamson, *Ezra, Nehemiah*, 330–331; Blenkinsopp, *Ezra-Nehemiah*, 311; Allen and Laniak, *Ezra, Nehemiah, Esther*, 138–139). In contrast, Eskenazi (*Age of Prose*, 124–125) and Duggan (*Covenant Renewal*, 257, 289) argue that the regulations adopted by the community in chapter 10 actually provide the rationale for the related reforms undertaken later by Nehemiah in 13:4–31.

192 The idiom "cutting a covenant" is prevalent in the OT. Cf. Genesis 15:18; Exodus 24:8; Joshua 24:25; 2 Samuel 5:3; Nehemiah 9:8.

193 The sense of the word as "agreement" is found only in 9:38. A related sense is found at 11:23, where it is translated "fixed provision" (ESV) or "firm regulation" (NASB).

"making a faithful [i.e., firm] (thing)" (thus ESV's "firm covenant"), made in writing as a unilateral and "voluntary act of the people."[194] The categories of signatories (princes, Levites, priests)[195] are reflected in the detailed list that follows. The "sealed document" may indicate personal imprints into wax or clay, or perhaps actual signatures.[196] Those who seal the document now pledge in solemn agreement their determination to abide in the Lord's instruction.

10:1 The initiative of a united people is demonstrated by a document bearing eighty-four names in four groups. Nehemiah and Zedekiah head the list, perhaps highlighting their role as civil authorities. This is not the first time that the term "governor" has been used or applied specifically to Nehemiah (cf. 8:9).[197] Zedekiah is otherwise unknown. He may be a chief official under Nehemiah or a secretary to Nehemiah identical with "Zadok the scribe" (13:13; cf. Ezra 4:8).

10:2–8 A second group of signatories follows, with twenty-one priestly names. Within this list, only six individuals are not found in the lists either of initial priestly houses associated with Zerubbabel and Jeshua (12:1–7) or of those of Joiakim, Jeshua's successor (12:12–21). In other words, fifteen of the priestly names that seal the covenant represent family names or "chiefs of the priests" (12:7) rather than individuals.[198] Ezra may not be listed because of his inclusion under a separate priestly division, such as Seraiah or Azariah (Ezra 7:1; cf. 1 Chron. 6:14). Alternatively, Azariah, a lengthened form of Ezra, may refer to him. Pashhur and Amariah (i.e., Immer; Neh. 10:3), along with Harim (v. 5), are named among the four priestly families (Ezra 2:36–39). Other names listed are found elsewhere in Ezra-Nehemiah (e.g., Daniel; Ezra 8:2), though correlation between individuals remains uncertain.

10:9–13 Seventeen Levitical names follow. The first three names, Jeshua, Binnui, and Kadmiel, are set apart from fellow Levites, "their brothers" (v. 10). These three joined with Zerubbabel in the first return (Ezra 2:40; Neh. 12:1, 8). Jeshua and Kadmiel, "along with the sons of Henadad," had organized initial work on the temple (Ezra 3:9). They function here as ancestral names of Levitical family groups.

However, there are also what appear to be personal names in this list. At least ten of the names are found among the Levites who either instruct in the Law (Neh. 8:7) or lead in worship and confession (9:4–5).[199] Interestingly, listed among these Levites are Hashabiah (10:11) and Sherebiah (v. 12). These may be the very men

---

194 Eskenazi, *Age of Prose*, 104.
195 For the noun translated "princes" at 9:32, 38, cf. comment on Ezra 9:1–2 (where the noun is translated "officials"). For the priests and Levites, cf. comments on Ezra 2:36–42.
196 The phrase "the names of" is absent in the Hebrew of 9:38 and 10:1 but is added by implication (cf. ESV mg.).
197 This is the final instance of the Persian term "the governor" (*hattirshata'* = "the Tirshatha" [KJV]). For varied terms that are translated as "governor," cf. comments on Ezra 2:63; 5:3–5.
198 The six not shared with either list are Pashhur, Malchijah, Obadiah, Daniel, Baruch, and Meshullam. As noted in the commentary, Pashhur was also the name of a priestly family according to Ezra 2:38. See Kidner, *Ezra and Nehemiah*, 134, which provides a helpful comparative table listing all the names in Nehemiah 10:2–8, 12:1–7, 12–21.
199 Noss and Thomas, *Ezra and Nehemiah*, 463.

who willingly joined the depleted ranks of Levites (Ezra 8:18–19). Hashabiah is also a builder of the wall (Neh. 3:17). Both names are placed among the "chiefs of the Levites" (12:24). It is difficult to know whether the overlapping names in these varied contexts refer to the same individuals.[200]

10:14–27 The majority of the signers are lay representatives, forty-four "chiefs [= heads] of the people" (v. 14; cf. 8:13)—perhaps synonymous with "our princes" (9:38). The names of some of these lay leaders appear to be ancestral names found elsewhere in the book. For example: (1) the first twenty-one names from Parosh to Magpiash (excepting Bunni, Azzur, and Hodiah) are found in the major lists of the community at Ezra 2//Nehemiah 7 in nearly the same order; (2) thirteen of the names are shared with the list of wall builders in Nehemiah 3 and in a nearly identical order; and (3) four names are also listed among Ezra's lay leaders in Nehemiah 8:4 (Hashum [10:18], Meshullam [v. 20], Anaiah [v. 22], and Maaseiah [v. 25]).[201] This way of unifying the community binds them chronologically, tying the past returnees with the reconstituted people of the present. This is analogous to the way that past and present are joined in the confessional prayer of chapter 9.

10:28–39 All of the assembly joins with the representatives (9:38) to enter into "a curse and an oath" (10:28–29). The final portion of the chapter affirms the specific obligations comprising four categories (vv. 30–39a). It concludes with a summary statement (v. 39b).

10:28–29 The traditional divisions of people, priests, Levites, and so on (Ezra 7:7; Neh. 7:73) are now given to make clear that all are involved (even if not mentioned explicitly in the lists of 10:1–27). The list ends with the inclusion of children, whose presence at the first reading of the Law was merely implied as "all who could understand" (8:2). The central clause reflects the repentance of the assembly: all those loyal to the Lord have "separated themselves *from*" the seductions promoted by the "peoples of the lands" (cf. 9:24, 30) in order to move *toward* the Law (Torah) of God (cf. Ezra 6:21; 9:1–2; Isa. 56:1–8).

Along with the people, the Law of God plays an important role in all of Nehemiah 8–10.[202] The people had rebelled against these right, true, and good commandments (9:13, 16, 26). Now, arm in arm with the signatories ("their brothers, their nobles"), they characterize their repentance by three actions: to walk in, to observe, and to do the Mosaic instructions. Together these actions express the profound embrace of God's law as a way of life for an entire community. Restoring the centrality of the Law to their public and private lives is key to the purposes for which God has distinguished them from the world yet for the world (Lev. 18:4;

---

200 Kidner, *Ezra and Nehemiah*, 125.
201 Blenkinsopp, *Ezra-Nehemiah*, 313. For details on variations in names and their orders compared to Ezra 2 and Nehemiah 7, see Clines, *Ezra, Nehemiah, Esther*, 203–204. Clines believes the names from 10:14 to 10:27 are probably family rather than personal names. In this view, the names from Meshullam (10:20) to the end are newer kinship names developed in the century since the first return. A table comparing names in chapters 3 and 10 is found in Williamson, *Ezra, Nehemiah*, 329.
202 Cf. note 159.

26:3; Deut. 6:4–10; 11:22–24; Josh. 22:5). The physical and spiritual restoration was foretold in the prophets (Ezek. 11:16–20; 36:24–28).

This momentous commitment is bound by "a curse and an oath" An oath (Hb. *shebu'ah*) is a sworn promise to keep the stated stipulations that follow (Neh. 10:30ff.; 2 Chron. 15:12–14). The curse (*'alah*) appeals to God to bring penalties upon them if they break the oath. Those penalties are unstated. The earlier confession had underscored God's righteousness in bringing "all that has come upon us" (Neh. 9:32–33; Dan. 9:11).[203] Those judgments, resulting from covenantal disobedience, are likely the kinds of penalties in mind now (Lev. 26:14–45; Deut. 27:15–26; 29:10–21).

10:30–39 Four categories of obligations relevant to the community are embraced. The people promise to reject mixed marriages (v. 30), to maintain Sabbath and related observances (v. 31), and to provide for God's house (vv. 32–39a). The last may be further subdivided into imposition of a temple tax (vv. 32–33) and offerings brought to the house of the Lord (vv. 34–39a). The chapter closes with a concluding statement (v. 39b). As will be seen below, at times the community takes known instructions from the Pentateuch and applies them to their current covenant renewal.[204]

10:30 General statements concerning separation (v. 28; 9:2) result in the specific rejection of mixed marriages. Placing this obligation first shows their renewed resolve to be holy. The Lord had highlighted the dangers associated with such marriages in the aftermath of the golden calf incident (Ex. 34:10–17). Intermarriage among the initial inhabitants of the land was also proscribed by Moses (Deut. 7:1–6). More recently, Ezra had shepherded the community through intermarriage violations (Ezra 9–10), as would Nehemiah later (Neh. 13:23–29). The people promise explicitly to obey these prior Mosaic prohibitions. The expressed concerns are not national or racial but religious; intermarriage had indeed promoted false worship and idolatry, as Israel's history attested.[205]

10:31 As with the first promise, Sabbath keeping was a strong marker of identity for God's people as a sign of the Mosaic covenant (Ex. 20:8–11; 31:12–17; Deut. 5:12–15). The people understand its importance, having recently mentioned the "holy Sabbath" in their confession (Neh. 9:14). Profaning it was a serious covenant breach that had resulted in repeated prophetic warnings (Jer. 17:19–27; Ezek. 20:12–13, 16, 20, 21, 24). Sabbath instructions regarding work cessation did not address commerce or the purchase of food. However, the desire to get on with trade had fostered Sabbath resentment and even injustice (Amos 8:4–7;

---

203 These two nouns are together in the OT only at Numbers 5:21; Nehemiah 10:29; Daniel 9:11.

204 McConville provides an admirable discussion of the ways that known laws are reapplied by the postexilic community (*Ezra, Nehemiah, Esther*, 133–134). As Duggan observes, "None of the stipulations actually quotes verbatim a text in the Pentateuch. Each of them represents rather an interpretive reading of the legislation (*Covenant Renewal*, 288).

205 We will not reiterate the theological importance of the theme. Cf. comments on Ezra 6:19–21; 9:1–2 and the Response section to Ezra 9:1–15.

cf. Isa. 58:13–14). Certainly the prohibition of trade within the community was already assumed. However, for a repentant people the validity of purchasing goods from the "peoples of the land" would be an important question of present application. Rather than flirting with compromise, they determine to prohibit all Sabbath transactions with outsiders and expand this to include other holy days (cf. Neh. 13:15–22).

Maintaining the Sabbath principle to be a distinct people extends to the cessation of land cultivation and full harvest as well as the "exaction of every debt" in the sabbatical year. The latter implies total forgiveness of debts.[206] These seventh-year observances were already part of Mosaic instruction (Lev. 25:1–7; Deut. 15:1–18). Whether the people are seeking to synchronize these to the same calendar year is unclear. The debt-release purpose of having "no poor among you" (Deut. 15:4) would be relevant to a community recently embroiled in its own debt crisis (Neh. 5:1–13) and their more recent concern for those in need (8:10).[207]

10:32–33 The remainder of the obligations in the chapter relate to temple support, commencing with a temple tax. Every verse in verses 32–39 contains the phrase "the house of our God/the LORD."

The language "take on ourselves the obligation" (v. 32; lit., "commands") shows the whole community bearing responsibility for the support of the temple. The verbal complement that follows—"to give yearly" (a temple tax)—expresses the main action. Persian kings had previously financed temple function (Ezra 6:7–10; 7:11–24; 8:25–30). With the increasing use of coinage in this period and perhaps waning royal support, the people now pledge themselves to give a third part of a shekel to maintain worship—the very core of their calling. There is no explicit Pentateuchal law requiring such a tax. In the past, freewill offerings had been welcomed for tabernacle service (Ex. 25:1–2; 36:3–5). At Exodus 30:11–16 a half-shekel tax is levied upon each adult during the census for the "service of the tent of meeting" (Ex. 30:16; cf. Ex. 38:25; 2 Chron. 24:4–14). The assembly may be applying the spirit of this Exodus passage and expanding it to include an annual charge.

These funds will support the seven elements listed (Neh. 10:33). The "show-bread" or "bread of the Presence" describes the twelve rows of bread placed on the table in the Holy Place as a permanent thank offering (Ex. 25:23–30). The others mentioned broadly follow Numbers 28–29. These include daily ("regular"), weekly ("Sabbath"), monthly (new moon), and festival offerings. The "holy things" are associated with other public offerings (2 Chron. 29:33; 35:13). The "sin offerings to make atonement" refers to purification or penitence at special public occasions (2 Chron. 29:20–21; Ezra 6:16–17; 8:35).[208] Finally, "work" (Hb. *mela'kah*) in the

---

206 Clines, *Ezra, Nehemiah, Esther*, 206. The idiom may be translated "And we will forgo . . . the debt of every hand," that is, the deed of debt held in the hand of the one to whom the debt was due (Noss and Thomas, *Ezra and Nehemiah*, 470).

207 Shepherd and Wright, *Ezra and Nehemiah*, 92–93.

208 It is less likely that these "sin offerings to make atonement" refer to sacrifices on the Day of Atonement since the latter would be included among the "appointed feasts" (Clines, *Ezra, Nehemiah, Esther*, 208; Blenkinsopp, *Ezra-Nehemiah*, 317). The half-shekel temple tax persists into the NT (Matt. 17:24–27).

concluding phrase (Neh. 10:33b) likely refers to maintenance of temple buildings (2 Kings 12:15).[209]

10:34–39 The fivefold presence of the verb "bring" (vv. 34, 35, 36, 37, 39) unifies these verses. It signifies the offerings and contributions brought to the house of the Lord.[210] These offerings are further differentiated as the wood offering (v. 34); firstfruits, firstborn, and other contributions brought "to the priests" (vv. 35–37a); and tithes for the work of the Levites (vv. 37b–39a). A summary statement concludes the chapter (v. 39b).

10:34 The fire of the altar was to burn perpetually—the referent to "as it is written in the Law" (v. 34; Lev. 6:8–13). However, no known Pentateuchal law mandates how the wood was to be supplied. The community meets this obligation by lot-casting in order to divide the labor between families through a yearly work rotation (cf. Josh. 9:27). Again, the implications of the law are applied to a contemporary need.

10:35–37a The focus shifts to offerings brought "to the priests" (vv. 36, 37a) for their support. It begins with the firstfruits of the land. Israel was commanded to bring the "best of the firstfruits of your ground," whether barley in early spring or wheat in late spring (Ex. 23:19; 34:22, 26; Lev. 23:9–22; Deut. 26:1–11). The latter festival was called the Feast of Harvest/Weeks (Ex. 23:16; 34:22; Lev. 23:15–22). By offering the firstfruits of their grain they thank the Lord as their provider and as the only one worthy of their best.[211] The scope of the promise in Nehemiah 10:35 expands to include "all fruit."

The firstborn is analogous to the firstfruits (v. 36). After the initial Passover, the Lord commanded Israel to set apart (i.e., consecrate) all the firstborn as holy. This reminded them of God's deliverance of their firstborn in Egypt (Ex. 13:1–2, 11–16). Because they belong to the Lord, the firstborn of clean animals must be sacrificed and unclean animals and firstborn children redeemed with a price (Ex. 34:19–20; Num. 18:15–17). This shows the postexilic community to be in solidarity with those redeemed at the time of the exodus.

The list concludes with several other of their best (i.e., first or prime) agricultural products to be brought "to the priests, to the chambers" (Neh. 10:37a; cf. Num. 18:12; Deut. 18:4).[212] The dough offering, by analogy to firstfruits, likewise recalls God's provision upon entering the land (Num. 15:20–21; cf. Lev. 7:14). In sum, all of these contributions support the priests as they minister in the temple, as noted in Numbers 18:12–20.

10:37b–39a The presence of "to bring" at verse 37a extends to the tithes (or tenth part) of the land's production brought to the Levites (v. 37b).[213] Ancient instructions

---

209 Williamson, *Ezra, Nehemiah*, 336.
210 The presence of "shall bring up" in 10:38 translates a different verb.
211 See discussion in Sklar, *Leviticus*, 282–284.
212 The word "chambers" (Hb. *lishkot*) at Nehemiah 10:37b, 38, 39 specifies rooms used for storage (cf. Neh. 13:4–5).
213 The Hebrew of 10:37 has only one occurrence of the verb "to bring," but in the ESV there are two. The translation has added the second to clarify that "and to bring" applies to the contributions brought to the Levites.

for priestly contributions (Num. 18:12–20) were followed by similar instructions concerning tithes for the Levites (Num. 18:21–24). These tithes functioned as the reward for their service at the tabernacle. Evidently the postexilic community gives Levites responsibility for the collection of the tithe outside of Jerusalem. This collection is overseen by priests, perhaps insuring accountability for all parties.[214] Based on Numbers 18:26, the Levites themselves are responsible for bringing a tenth of the tithe they receive into the storehouse within the temple precinct (Neh. 10:38; Num. 18:26). "For" (Neh. 10:39a) connects this with the prior obligations, and the phrase "to the chambers" receives its final mention (vv. 37, 38, 39a). In this way the verse summarizes all of the items offered by both laity and Levites.

10:39b "We will not neglect [= "forsake"] the house of our God" summarizes verses 32–39a as a renewed commitment to maintain temple worship and support of temple personnel. The failure to do so is a recurring theme of the postexilic prophets. Haggai and Zechariah urge the reconstruction of God's house and note the danger of its neglect (Ezra 6:14; Hag. 1:2–6; 2:17–19; Zech. 1:16–17; 4:8–9; 8:9–13). Through Malachi the Lord decries the failure to bring the tithe "into the storehouse" (Mal. 3:8–10). Later Nehemiah will be provoked to ask, with respect to the neglect of tithes for Levites, "Why is the house of God forsaken?" (Neh. 13:10–14).

Response

The prophetic word provokes a chain of events in Ezra-Nehemiah (Ezra 1:1). Altar and temple reconstruction (Ezra 1–6), reconstitution under the law (Ezra 7–10), and rebuilding of the wall (Nehemiah 1–7) are all milestones leading to this moment of covenant renewal, the highpoint within Nehemiah 8–10. A renewed passion for God's instruction transforms a spiritually lethargic community. Ultimately it leads to a confession and prayer reminding them of God's steadfast love (Neh. 9:17, 32; cf. 1:5). God has not forsaken them (9:31). How should they respond to such faithfulness and evident care? They must respond to the Lord's grace by committing themselves to him in at least three ways.

First, they must commit to God's Word, for returning to the law is equivalent to returning to the Lord himself (cf. 9:26, 29). The use of OT discipleship language (walk, observe, do) affirms their revived desire to obey (10:29; cf. 9:13). In this way a wholly united community takes its stand by signing this "firm covenant" (9:38; 10:28–29). Such public acts of piety should not be dismissed. Having just recounted the deeds of their forefathers, they know where their own sin has led (9:30, 37). Christian denominations, churches, and individuals find precedent here for recommitting themselves to God and his Word in such public ways. In so doing we confess our constant need for the Lord to shape us by his Word and keep us by his Spirit; otherwise, we will fall away.

Committing oneself to the Lord also means embracing his mission. The com-

---

214 It is possible that the phrase "the priest, the son of Aaron" refers to the high priest (Clines, *Ezra, Nehemiah, Esther*, 210) though Williamson observes, "There were many more than one Aaronic priest" (*Ezra, Nehemiah*, 325).

munity recommits to its long-standing mission to be a distinct people who, at the same time, witness to the nations (Ex. 19:5–6; Deut. 7:1–10). Negatively, they separate themselves from "the peoples of the lands" (Neh. 10:28; cf. 9:2). In his prior prayer of confession, Ezra called upon the people not to intermarry with the nations due to the threat posed to the holy seed (Ezra 9:12). Now it is this entire community that makes explicit their determination to do so (Neh. 10:30). They further express their commitment to keeping the Sabbath day holy by not purchasing goods from foreigners (10:31). This call to distinguish oneself from the world while remaining in it as salt and light persists for the church today (Matt. 5:13–16; John 17:14–21; 1 John 2:15). We mark ourselves out by naming Jesus Christ as our Lord (Rom. 10:8–13), by honoring the day of worship, by uniting with him in our baptism, by participating in the Lord's Supper, and above all by our obedience to him. In everything we state publicly that we are God's people.

Separating *from* the nations, the people move *to* the Law of God (Neh. 10:28–29). This movement leads naturally to an ongoing commitment to worship him. Of course the praise of the Lord was a key aspect of their identity and the goal of their return (Ezra 1:3; 3:10–11; Neh. 8:6; 9:3, 6). Its importance is clear from the quantity of text dedicated to the subject and the evident repetition of the phrase "the house of our God" (10:32–39). The obligations espoused include the "temple tax," given willingly to fund regular and special times of worship (10:32–33), the practical division of labor that provides wood for offerings (10:34), and the multiform promises "to bring" ongoing support for those who minister in the temple (10:35–39). Throughout, the spirit of the law is taken up and further applied in their covenant renewal. We are exhorted in the church today to share that commitment to give, labor, and support the worship of God at his house, especially by supporting the physical needs of those who lead the church (1 Cor. 9:13–14; Gal. 6:6). In doing so we join our voices to the Israelites of Nehemiah 10 in affirming, "We will not neglect the house of our God" (v. 39).

NEHEMIAH 11:1–12:26

11 Now the leaders of the people lived in Jerusalem. And the rest of the people cast lots to bring one out of ten to live in Jerusalem the holy city, while nine out of ten[1] remained in the other towns. [2] And the people blessed all the men who willingly offered to live in Jerusalem.

[3] These are the chiefs of the province who lived in Jerusalem; but in the towns of Judah everyone lived on his property in their towns: Israel, the priests, the Levites, the temple servants, and the descendants of Solomon's servants. [4] And in Jerusalem lived certain of the sons of Judah and of the sons of Benjamin. Of the sons of Judah: Athaiah the son of Uzziah, son

of Zechariah, son of Amariah, son of Shephatiah, son of Mahalalel, of the sons of Perez; [5] and Maaseiah the son of Baruch, son of Col-hozeh, son of Hazaiah, son of Adaiah, son of Joiarib, son of Zechariah, son of the Shilonite. [6] All the sons of Perez who lived in Jerusalem were 468 valiant men.

[7] And these are the sons of Benjamin: Sallu the son of Meshullam, son of Joed, son of Pedaiah, son of Kolaiah, son of Maaseiah, son of Ithiel, son of Jeshaiah, [8] and his brothers, men of valor, 928.[2] [9] Joel the son of Zichri was their overseer; and Judah the son of Hassenuah was second over the city.

[10] Of the priests: Jedaiah the son of Joiarib, Jachin, [11] Seraiah the son of Hilkiah, son of Meshullam, son of Zadok, son of Meraioth, son of Ahitub, ruler of the house of God, [12] and their brothers who did the work of the house, 822; and Adaiah the son of Jeroham, son of Pelaliah, son of Amzi, son of Zechariah, son of Pashhur, son of Malchijah, [13] and his brothers, heads of fathers' houses, 242; and Amashsai, the son of Azarel, son of Ahzai, son of Meshillemoth, son of Immer, [14] and their brothers, mighty men of valor, 128; their overseer was Zabdiel the son of Haggedolim.

[15] And of the Levites: Shemaiah the son of Hasshub, son of Azrikam, son of Hashabiah, son of Bunni; [16] and Shabbethai and Jozabad, of the chiefs of the Levites, who were over the outside work of the house of God; [17] and Mattaniah the son of Mica, son of Zabdi, son of Asaph, who was the leader of the praise,[3] who gave thanks, and Bakbukiah, the second among his brothers; and Abda the son of Shammua, son of Galal, son of Jeduthun. [18] All the Levites in the holy city were 284.

[19] The gatekeepers, Akkub, Talmon and their brothers, who kept watch at the gates, were 172. [20] And the rest of Israel, and of the priests and the Levites, were in all the towns of Judah, every one in his inheritance. [21] But the temple servants lived on Ophel; and Ziha and Gishpa were over the temple servants.

[22] The overseer of the Levites in Jerusalem was Uzzi the son of Bani, son of Hashabiah, son of Mattaniah, son of Mica, of the sons of Asaph, the singers, over the work of the house of God. [23] For there was a command from the king concerning them, and a fixed provision for the singers, as every day required. [24] And Pethahiah the son of Meshezabel, of the sons of Zerah the son of Judah, was at the king's side[4] in all matters concerning the people.

[25] And as for the villages, with their fields, some of the people of Judah lived in Kiriath-arba and its villages, and in Dibon and its villages, and in Jekabzeel and its villages, [26] and in Jeshua and in Moladah and Beth-pelet, [27] in Hazar-shual, in Beersheba and its villages, [28] in Ziklag, in Meconah and its villages, [29] in En-rimmon, in Zorah, in Jarmuth, [30] Zanoah, Adullam, and their villages, Lachish and its fields, and Azekah and its villages. So they encamped from Beersheba to the Valley of Hinnom. [31] The people of Benjamin also lived from Geba onward, at Michmash, Aija, Bethel and its villages, [32] Anathoth, Nob, Ananiah, [33] Hazor, Ramah, Gittaim, [34] Hadid, Zeboim, Neballat, [35] Lod, and Ono, the valley of craftsmen. [36] And certain divisions of the Levites in Judah were assigned to Benjamin.

12 These are the priests and the Levites who came up with Zerubbabel the son of Shealtiel, and Jeshua: Seraiah, Jeremiah, Ezra, [2] Amariah, Malluch, Hattush, [3] Shecaniah, Rehum, Meremoth, [4] Iddo, Ginnethoi, Abijah, [5] Mijamin, Maadiah, Bilgah, [6] Shemaiah, Joiarib, Jedaiah, [7] Sallu, Amok, Hilkiah, Jedaiah. These were the chiefs of the priests and of their brothers in the days of Jeshua.

8 And the Levites: Jeshua, Binnui, Kadmiel, Sherebiah, Judah, and Mattaniah, who with his brothers was in charge of the songs of thanksgiving. 9 And Bakbukiah and Unni and their brothers stood opposite them in the service. 10 And Jeshua was the father of Joiakim, Joiakim the father of Eliashib, Eliashib the father of Joiada, 11 Joiada the father of Jonathan, and Jonathan the father of Jaddua.

12 And in the days of Joiakim were priests, heads of fathers' houses: of Seraiah, Meraiah; of Jeremiah, Hananiah; 13 of Ezra, Meshullam; of Amariah, Jehohanan; 14 of Malluchi, Jonathan; of Shebaniah, Joseph; 15 of Harim, Adna; of Meraioth, Helkai; 16 of Iddo, Zechariah; of Ginnethon, Meshullam; 17 of Abijah, Zichri; of Miniamin, of Moadiah, Piltai; 18 of Bilgah, Shammua; of Shemaiah, Jehonathan; 19 of Joiarib, Mattenai; of Jedaiah, Uzzi; 20 of Sallai, Kallai; of Amok, Eber; 21 of Hilkiah, Hashabiah; of Jedaiah, Nethanel.

22 In the days of Eliashib, Joiada, Johanan, and Jaddua, the Levites were recorded as heads of fathers' houses; so too were the priests in the reign of Darius the Persian. 23 As for the sons of Levi, their heads of fathers' houses were written in the Book of the Chronicles until the days of Johanan the son of Eliashib. 24 And the chiefs of the Levites: Hashabiah, Sherebiah, and Jeshua the son of Kadmiel, with their brothers who stood opposite them, to praise and to give thanks, according to the commandment of David the man of God, watch by watch. 25 Mattaniah, Bakbukiah, Obadiah, Meshullam, Talmon, and Akkub were gatekeepers standing guard at the storehouses of the gates. 26 These were in the days of Joiakim the son of Jeshua son of Jozadak, and in the days of Nehemiah the governor and of Ezra, the priest and scribe.

1 Hebrew *nine hands* 2 Compare Septuagint; Hebrew *Jeshaiah, and after him Gabbai, Sallai, 928* 3 Compare Septuagint, Vulgate; Hebrew *beginning* 4 Hebrew *hand*

Section Overview

The theme of repopulation opened and closed the chapter that followed the completion of the wall (Neh. 7:4–5, 73a). However, that storyline paused to consider the essential task of community restoration under God's law (7:73b–10:39). Multiple readings of the Law had concluded with the writing of a "firm covenant" (9:38). This repentant people had recommitted to walk, observe, and do God's Law (10:29), and to not neglect God's house (10:39b).

The narrative now returns to Jerusalem's repopulation and care for God's house (11:1–12:26). It links several lists and consists of two parts. The first part directly addresses the repopulation theme (11:1–36). Those who gave of themselves to relocate to Jerusalem (11:1–2) include laypersons (11:4–9), priests (11:10–14) and Levites (11:15–18), along with gatekeepers and temple servants (11:19–21). This is followed by comments concerning Levitical overseers, singers, and the command of the king (11:22–24). The first part ends with a second list of villages and settlements of Judah and Benjamin located outside Jerusalem (11:25–36). This expansion beyond Jerusalem signals the importance of the land promise so prevalent in chapter 9.

The second part of this section deals with the care for God's house, evidenced by an aggregated list of priests and Levites (12:1–26). These verses include four lists of priests and Levites (12:1–9, 10–11, 12–21, 24–25), a note on sources (12:22–23), and a conclusion (12:26). Read contextually, this list of priests and Levites, the final of the major lists in Ezra-Nehemiah, supplements the records of 11:1–36 and transitions to the priestly and Levitical service evidenced at the climactic wall dedication of 12:27–47.

Section Outline

III.B. Habitation of Jerusalem and Its Villages; a List of Priests and
        Levites (11:1–12:26)
    1. Jerusalem and Its Villages Populated (11:1–36)
        a. The People Chosen and Willing (11:1–2)
        b. Those Who Lived in Jerusalem (11:3–24)
        c. Those Who Lived in Villages outside Jerusalem (11:25–36)
    2. A List of Priests and Levites (12:1–26)
        a. Priests and Levites Who Came Up with Zerubbabel and Jeshua
            (12:1–9)
        b. The Genealogy of the High Priests (12:10–11)
        c. Priests in the Days of Joiakim (12:12–21)
        d. A Brief Note on Sources (12:22–23)
        e. Levites in the Days of Joiakim (12:24–26)

Comment

11:1–36 The lists of repopulated settlers in Jerusalem (vv. 1–24) and its villages (vv. 25–36) may appear awkward in this literary context. However, the logic of covenant renewal (ch. 10) followed by settlement in Jerusalem may be loosely analogous to the movement from covenant renewal in Deuteronomy to the settlement period of Canaan in Joshua–Judges.[215]

11:1–2 Some "leaders" ("princes" in 9:32, 34) determine to live in Jerusalem, but other inhabitants are needed. Their ancestors once cast lots to apportion the land (Num. 26:55–56; Josh. 14:2) and recently cast lots to determine the work schedule for the wood offering.[216] Now lots are cast to determine whom God will "bring" into Jerusalem to repopulate the city. This key verb ("to bring") recently referred to the offering of firstfruits and contributions brought to the house of the Lord (Neh. 10:34–39). Some of these were called the "tithes from our ground" (10:37–38). Now, one in ten families, or a tithe, become living sacrifices. They are brought not into the holy temple but into Jerusalem, "the holy city" (11:1, 18; Isa. 48:2; Joel 3:17; Dan. 9:24) while nine out of ten remain in other cities.

The sacrificial imagery persists with the Hebrew verb *nadab* ("willingly offered");

---

215 Shepherd and Wright, *Ezra and Nehemiah*, 95.
216 Ibid.

Neh. 11:2), used of making freewill offerings for temple construction (1 Chron. 29:5–6, 9; Ezra 1:6; 2:68). More pointed are the military connotations of voluntary service (Judg. 5:2, 9; cf. Ps. 110:3). These chosen and volunteering families rightly receive a blessing that God would prosper their commitment. For returnees, even a limited loss of agricultural income, along with the abandonment of ancestral lands (cf. Neh. 11:3), would add to the disruption already associated with relocation.

11:3–6 The two groups inside and outside of Jerusalem are reintroduced (v. 3). This prepares for the two major units that follow (vv. 4–24, 25–36). Each group comprises the traditional strata of the community attested in Ezra 2 and Nehemiah 7 (i.e., laymen ["Israel"], priests, Levites, etc.).[217] Rather than identification by family names (Parosh, Shephatiah, etc.), tribal and clan names are used, evoking the exodus/settlement imagery.[218] The "chiefs of the province" (11:3) are the various family heads listed throughout verses 4–24. They are contrasted with those outside of Jerusalem, who each remain "on his [own] property," i.e., his ancestral possession (vv. 3, 20; Lev. 25:10; 1 Chron. 9:2).

The lay tribes, Judah and Benjamin (Neh. 11:4), were loyal to the southern kingdom (1 Kings 12:21–23) and representative tribes of the return (Ezra 1:5). The parallel list at 1 Chronicles 9:2–21 includes the northern tribes Ephraim and Manasseh (1 Chron. 9:3), perhaps to represent all Israel.[219] Two sons of Judah, Athaiah and Maaseiah, are identified by their clans, Perez and Shelah, respectively.[220] The description of the sons of Perez as "valiant men" has a military connotation elsewhere in these books (Ezra 8:22; Neh. 2:9; 11:14). The defense of Jerusalem is an important aspect of its repopulation (7:2–3; cf. 4:13, where defense is established by clans).[221]

11:7–9 Sallu is the only named descendant of Benjamin (cf. 1 Chron. 9:7–9). Benjamin's men of valor nearly double the Judahite totals (Neh. 11:8).[222] Joel as "overseer" (cf. vv. 14, 22) and Judah as "second over the city" may have succeeded Hanani and Hananiah (7:2) as military leaders. A less likely option is that Judah is in charge of the city's second or "New Quarter" (cf. NIV).

11:10–14 The list that follows the lay leaders presents the priestly houses whose members repopulated Jerusalem.[223] One approach to the list counts five of these

---

217 Discussion of the laymen and various temple personnel may be found in the comments on Ezra 2:1–70.
218 Shepherd and Wright, *Ezra and Nehemiah*, 96.
219 The list in 1 Chronicles 9:2–21 shares approximately half of its names with Nehemiah 11:4–19.
220 Perez was a son of Judah by Tamar (Gen. 38:12–29). Shelah was a son of Judah by his Canaanite wife, Shua (Gen. 38:1–6, 26). A slight change in vocalization reads "Shelanite" (cf. Num. 26:20) rather than "Shilonite" (Neh. 11:5).
221 Williamson, *Ezra, Nehemiah*, 348. Alternatively, it may refer to men of exceptional character, capability, or wealth.
222 Two text-critical issues are found in 11:7–8, where the Hebrew may be rendered "Jeshaiah, and after him Gabbai, Sallai, 928" (cf. ESV mg.). The reading "and his brothers" rather than "and after him" (NASB) makes better sense in the context of both verse and passage (11:12, 13, 14, 19). Further, the names "Gabbai, Sallai" may be taken as a corruption of the phrase "men of valor," comparable to the phrase at 11:6. Some English versions translate the Hebrew text (KJV, NASB, NIV, NJPS). Others accept the first but reject the second emendation: "And his brothers, Gabbai, Sallai" (NEB, NAB, NRSV).
223 There are multiple interpretive challenges presented in this list. Fensham provides a succinct discussion of the various difficulties (*Ezra and Nehemiah*, 245–246).

priestly houses (Jedaiah, Jachin, Seraiah, Adaiah, and Amashsai).[224] The latter two names are associated with the important priestly houses of Pashhur and Immer, who returned with Zerubbabel, while the preexilic "Jedaiah" is linked with the house of Jeshua (Neh. 7:39–42//Ezra 2:36–39). Several of these names are also found in the earlier priestly divisions established by David (1 Chron. 24:7, 17). With this first approach, "ruler of the house of God" refers to Seraiah and the names that follow trace his genealogy as the last preexilic high priest (2 Kings 25:18; Jer. 52:24; cf. Ezra 7:1–2). Alternatively, if Jachin is a scribal error for "son of," then the initial list may provide the genealogy of Jedaiah, who is further identified as high priest. The problem is that we know of no postexilic high priest by this name. It is therefore proposed that Jedaiah is known elsewhere by the alternative spellings Joiada or Jehoiada, the successor to Eliashib (Neh. 12:10) and contemporary of Nehemiah (13:28).[225]

In either case, 822 persons who willingly inhabit Jerusalem include those associated with the liturgical service within the temple itself, i.e., "the work of the house." The others that follow may hold less ceremonial duties, such as teaching or defense. The phrase "mighty men of valor" provides an even stronger sense of military function for some of these families than that expressed in 11:6.[226]

11:15–18 Six Levites are mentioned. Shemaiah (cf. 1 Chron. 9:14) is the first of three Levitical chiefs, followed by Shabbethai and Jozabad, who have recently instructed the people in the Law (Neh. 8:7) and were present early in Ezra's ministry (Ezra 10:15, 23). The latter two oversee the "outside work of the house of God" (Neh. 11:16). This probably indicates physical maintenance of the building and collection of tithes and offerings as supplies (10:38).

The singers are here included among the Levites (cf. 7:44; 12:8–9). Mattaniah, a name long associated with the sons of Asaph (cf. 1 Chron. 9:15; 2 Chron. 29:13), receives special mention as praise leader.[227] Bakbukiah as "second among his brothers," likely refers to his role as leader of the antiphonal choir (Neh. 12:9, 25; cf. Ezra 3:11).[228] Abda is attached by descent to Jeduthun. The latter had joined Asaph and Heman as the three families appointed by David to lead worship (1 Chron. 25:1).

11:19–21 Akkub and Talmon are representative familial names of gatekeepers (Ezra 2:42//Neh. 7:45; 12:25). The gatekeepers primarily protect the silver and sanctity of the temple, although their tasks are extensive (1 Chron. 9:17–34). At times gatekeepers are identified as Levites (1 Chron. 9:26; 2 Chron. 23:4; 34:12–13).

---

224 This number may be six rather than five if Joiarib (i.e., Jehoiarib) is not the father of Jedaiah but considered as a separate priestly house, as the parallel at 1 Chronicles 9:10–13 attests (so Blenkinsopp, *Ezra-Nehemiah*, 321).

225 Blenkinsopp represents the first interpretation (*Ezra-Nehemiah*, 325–326), while Clines represents the latter (*Ezra, Nehemiah, Esther*, 215–216). The latter view also requires emending "their brothers" to "his brothers." There is no textual warrant for either of the emendations associated with this latter interpretation. In spite of the textual challenges, Noss and Thomas encourage translators to adopt the text as it currently stands (*Ezra and Nehemiah*, 485).

226 The latter two points are made by Kidner, *Ezra and Nehemiah*, 130.

227 With a very minor change of one consonant to the Hebrew, the ESV reads "praise" instead of "beginning" (cf. ESV mg.). However, "the leader in beginning" (NASB) may preserve a technical term for choir leadership.

228 Noss and Thomas, *Ezra and Nehemiah*, 488. On the singers and gatekeepers and their relationship to Levites, cf. comment on Ezra 2:40–42.

The "rest of Israel" (Neh. 11:20) signals the remainder of laymen, along with priests and Levites, who live outside of the city "on his property" (v. 3), here called "his inheritance." The verse therefore concludes the list of those who inhabit Jerusalem. The expected treatment of the "temple servants" usually found immediately after the gatekeepers (cf. v. 3; Ezra 2:43–53; 7:7, 24; Neh. 7:46–56, 73a) instead follows 11:20 as the first of three supplemental notes (11:21–24). The "temple servants" are not included in the former list because they are already living in Jerusalem "on Ophel," the hill southeast of the Jerusalem temple complex (cf. 3:26–27).[229]

11:22–24 A second note identifies Uzzi, the great-grandson of Mattaniah (cf. v. 17), as overseer of the Levitical singers (cf. vv. 9, 14b, 17). His choral supervision is defined as the "work of the house of God" (v. 22). The "command" (v. 23) refers either to David's initial organization of musicians (12:24; 1 Chronicles 25) or to provisions for worship from the Persian king, including prayers and sacrifices for him (Ezra 6:10; 7:20, 23). The "fixed provision" likely specifies this regular support for the singers as at Nehemiah 12:47, or perhaps the organization of their regular duties (NIV).

The concluding note clearly refers to the Persian king. Pethahiah is otherwise unknown. His commission to be at the king's side (i.e., "hand"; 11:24 ESV mg.) means that he represents local affairs to the Persian authorities.[230] He is descended from Zerah, the third and final major clan of Judah, absent from verses 4–5 (1 Chron. 9:6).

11:25–36 As expected, the "towns of Judah" follow (vv. 3, 20). These are inhabited by the people of Judah (vv. 25–30) and Benjamin (vv. 31–36). "Villages" refers to both smaller settlements and their attached communities (cf. v. 25).

11:25–30 The villages from Dibon through En-rimmon are south, located in the Negeb, while the remainder (Zorah through Azekah) are westward, in the Shephelah.[231] Kiriath-arba (v. 25; i.e., Hebron) and Beersheba, providing the southernmost limit, belonged to preexilic Judah but are now under Edomite-Arab control within the province of Idumea (cf. 2:19).[232] Providing the northernmost limit, the Hinnom Valley sets the southern and western geographical borders of Jerusalem (cf. Josh. 15:8).

The list marks out the ideal provincial boundaries of Judah. A majority of the seventeen places named are also found in approximately the same order at Joshua 15:13–39, where the allotments for Judah are described.[233] This, combined with the

---

229 Breneman, *Ezra, Nehemiah, Esther*, 259. See comment on Ezra 2:43–54 for a discussion of temple servants and comment on Nehemiah 3:27 for Ophel.
230 It is conjectured that he may be the governor two generations after Nehemiah (Clines, *Ezra, Nehemiah, Esther*, 219).
231 Clines believe that most of locations in 11:25–36 are fortified (*Ezra, Nehemiah, Esther*, 220–221). The Shephelah is the transitional region between the coastal plain and the central hill country.
232 Blenkinsopp, *Ezra-Nehemiah*, 329.
233 Of course, many place names in Joshua 15; Ezra 2//Nehemiah 7; Nehemiah 3 are not found in 11:25–36. There are also some names in 11:25–30 found nowhere else in Ezra-Nehemiah. Several of the places would be

description of the people as "encamped" (Neh. 11:30)—an unusual way to describe their settlement—may be an attempt to evoke the ancient land settlement. The people are presented as encamped around the centrally located Jerusalem ("holy city"; vv. 1, 18), even as allotments were once granted a people around the centrally placed tent of meeting (Joshua 15–19, esp. 18:1). "Our list, then, fits very well with the exodus-settlement pattern which we have observed at several points in our reading of Ezra-Nehemiah.... The idea of the land as an encampment around the sanctuary, a reproduction of the arrangement during the wilderness journeying, is based on ancient tradition."[234]

11:31–36 Most of the fifteen places of Benjaminite habitation are located in the hill country and coastal plain (cf. Ezra 2:26–33). Geba through Bethel move generally northward from Jerusalem into the central hill country, Benjamin's original allotment. Anathoth through Ananiah are slightly northeast of the city, tracing a north-to-south trajectory. Ramah and Hazor (not the Hazor of Josh. 11:1) are located just west of Geba. Gittaim through Ono are in the coastal plain, with some located outside of the northwest border of the province.[235] With some Levitical family groups ("divisions") formerly of Judah now dwelling among Benjamin, the picture of a worshiping community around the holy city is complete (Neh. 11:36).[236]

12:1–26 Four lists of priests and Levites (vv. 1–9, 10–11, 12–21, 24–26) are appended to the list of inhabitants of Jerusalem and its environs. The current lists emphasize the continuity of priestly and Levitical temple service from the initial return under Zerubbabel and Jeshua (v. 1) to the more recent wall completion and covenant renewal under Nehemiah and Ezra (v. 26).

12:1–9 Four priestly family or clan names were identified as those who returned with Zerubbabel and Jeshua in 538 BC (Ezra 2:36–39//Neh. 7:39–42). Now 12:1–7 offers a more extensive list of twenty-two family names. These are presented as personal names but also represent the restoration of the priestly divisions known in Zerubbabel's day (Ezra 6:18). Aside from the name Hattush (Neh. 12:2) and variations in spellings there is significant overlap with the names in Joiakim's day (vv. 12–21). Apparently these names persist as the names of priestly divisions.[237] On "Ezra" (vv. 1, 13), cf. comment on 10:2–8. There is significant correspondence with the signers of the covenant at 10:2–8, although neither Iddo (12:4, 16) nor the final six names, Joiarib through Jedaiah, appear there.[238]

---

outside the Persian province of Judah. Williamson provides a brief discussion of challenges associated with the whole (11:25–36) and a succinct list of options concerning how the list may have arisen (*Ezra, Nehemiah*, 349–350).
234 Blenkinsopp, *Ezra-Nehemiah*, 330. Williamson also supports this interpretation, stating, "The people are portrayed in terms of the prototypical cultic community of the wilderness days" (*Ezra, Nehemiah*, 353). See Blenkinsopp (330–332) for a detailed discussion of village locations.
235 On the location of Ono, cf. comment on Nehemiah 6:1–4.
236 Shepherd and Wright, *Ezra and Nehemiah*, 97.
237 For a chart comparing 12:1–7, 12–21 and 10:2–8, see Kidner, *Ezra and Nehemiah*, 134. In his chart Blenkinsopp adds 1 Chronicles 24 (*Ezra-Nehemiah*, 337). See the technical commentaries for varied proposals on the compositional history and relationship between these lists.
238 The presence of the conjunction "and" (Hb. *waw*) before Joiarib, untranslated at both 12:6 and 12:19, may mark these final six names as later editorial additions (Williamson, *Ezra, Nehemiah*, 362; Blenkinsopp, *Ezra-Nehemiah*, 335).

Eight Levitical family names follow (vv. 8–9). Jeshua, Binnui, and Kadmiel are three family heads (cf. 10:9). Judah (= Hodaviah) may also be included as a family name (Ezra 2:40//Neh. 7:43). The remaining four names, here listed among the first returnees, identify individuals also lately encountered. Sherebiah returned with Ezra and served in the recent covenant renewal (Ezra 8:24; Neh. 8:7; 9:4–5; 10:12). These join Mattaniah as liturgical musicians in charge of songs of thanksgiving. Bakbukiah and Unni round out the antiphonal choir (cf. 11:17).

12:10–11 Jehozadak, father of Jeshua, was the high priest of the exile (1 Chron. 6:4–15). The current list is a selective rather than comprehensive continuation of that high priestly line. It spans from the known service of Jeshua at the first return (538 BC) to the less certain time of Jaddua (c. 400 and beyond). Eliashib was known to be high priest in Nehemiah's day, nearly a hundred years after Jeshua (Neh. 3:1; 445). Joiakim falls between Jeshua and Eliashib in the early fifth century, likely in office at Ezra's arrival.[239] Historical questions persist regarding the identities of Jonathan and Johanan (12:11, 23), as well as Jaddua (v. 11).[240]

12:12–21 The priestly divisions ("heads of [the] fathers' houses"; v. 12) in the days of Joiakim (cf. comment on 12:10–11) are identified by twenty-one names. Above we noted twenty-two parallel names in Jeshua's day (vv. 1–7), with only Hattush (v. 2) absent from the current list in verses 12–21 (perhaps accidently lost in transmission). The paired names (e.g., Seraiah/Meraiah; Jeremiah/Hananiah; etc.) make clear that the initial name identifies the priestly division (or family name) while the second provides the personal name of the priest who headed the family in Joiakim's day. As also noted above, Joiarib to Jedaiah (cf. vv. 6–7) are not found among the signers of the covenant (10:2–8). Nearly all of these personal names are unknown to us. However, Zechariah may refer to the prophet whose ministry also overlapped with the high priest Jeshua (Ezra 5:1; 6:14). Iddo, Zechariah's grandfather (Zech. 1:1, 7), is here the name of a priestly division (cf. Neh. 12:4). The head of the family for the Miniamin division has been lost in transmission (v. 17).

12:22–23 Several notes on sources follow. In the previous section (vv. 12–21), priests during the high priesthood of Joiakim were listed "as heads of [the] fathers' houses" (vv. 12–21). The current note further informs the reader that, as with the priests, Levites were also registered by family name rather than as individuals.[241] Such recording spanned the period from Eliashib to his son Johanan (v. 23). The

---

239 Williamson, *Ezra, Nehemiah*, 364; Blenkinsopp, *Ezra-Nehemiah*, 338.
240 On Jonathan and Johanan and their role in the debated chronology of Ezra and Nehemiah, cf. the Introduction to Ezra. Various proposals exist concerning the identity of Jaddua. Josephus (*Antiquities* 11.302, 325–332) places him at the end of the Persian period during the reign of Darius III Codomannus (336–331 BC) as the high priest greeted by Alexander the Great (c. 333). If the high-priestly list is complete, this would make a possible but improbable length of service as high priest. Williamson (*Ezra, Nehemiah*, 363) and Blenkinsopp (*Ezra-Nehemiah*, 336–338) thus contend that Josephus's date is correct but that the list in 12:10–11 is incomplete (that is, it skips a generation or more). Alternatively, it may be that Josephus got his dating wrong or perhaps there was more than one high priest named Jaddua. Kidner (*Ezra and Nehemiah*, 135, 160) takes this approach, arguing that the list does not go farther than the reign of Darius II Nothus (423–404 BC) which was during or just after Nehemiah's lifetime. By this interpretation there were two persons named Jaddua.
241 Williamson, *Ezra, Nehemiah*, 361.

latter was mentioned briefly above in the comment on 12:10–11; as with Jaddua, his name raises questions concerning his identity. According to a letter from the Elephantine papyri (407 BC), Johanan served as high priest in 410 and is referred to as "Jehohanan."[242] These verses further claim that the Levitical family names were recorded in the "Book of the Chronicles," which is not the biblical book but perhaps refers to a temple archive. The referent of "Darius the Persian" is uncertain. If referring to Darius I (522–486), this historical marker fits the literary context of lists already encountered (vv. 1–7, 12–21) and indicates that priestly registration recommenced as early as his reign (cf. Ezra 6:1, 18).[243]

12:24–26 Four or possibly five Levitical family heads are provided ("chiefs" = "heads," as at vv. 12, 22, 23).[244] Jeshua and Kadmiel are ancestral names (Ezra 2:40; 3:9) and the personal names of those who joined with Hashabiah (= Hashabneiah) and Sherebiah in leading worship (Neh. 9:4–5) and signing the covenant (10:9–12; cf. Ezra 8:18–19). "Stood opposite them" (cf. Neh. 12:9) again refers to antiphonal singing. David had organized the Levites as singers and gatekeepers (Ezra 3:10; 1 Chronicles 25–26; 2 Chron. 8:14). Establishment of the former was in keeping with prophetic instruction (2 Chron. 29:25). The phrase "watch by watch" applies elsewhere to the rotating duties of the gatekeepers (cf. 1 Chron. 26:16). Here it is linked to the thanksgiving offering of the choir (1 Chron. 23:30), which prepares for Nehemiah 12:31.

It is best to take the first three Levitical names in verse 25 as equivalent to those in 11:17 (Obadiah = Abda). Likewise, Talmon and Akkub, identified as gatekeeper family names at 11:19, are joined by Meshullam (= Shallum; Ezra 2:42//Neh. 7:45; 1 Chron. 9:17).

The priestly houses of Joiakim's day were known (Neh. 12:12–21). The summarizing historical note (v. 26) stresses that the Levitical families treated in verses 22–25 also served from the time of Joiakim. All are now joined with the subsequent ministries of Nehemiah and Ezra to illustrate the unified and ongoing renewal of temple worship throughout the period.

Response

With renewed vigor the people have recommitted to God's Word, mission, and worship (Nehemiah 10). In response to his grace and their current state of "great distress" (9:37), this commitment culminates in the statement "We will not neglect the house of our God" (10:39). The lists in 11:1–12:26—the final lists in Ezra-Nehemiah— show that very promise being kept. Stated positively, the people care for the house of their God by repopulating his city, refilling his land, and remembering his gifts.

---

242 He is not to be confused with the Jehohanan of Ezra 10:6 according to Williamson (*Ezra, Nehemiah*, 151–154).

243 Other options include Darius II Nothus (423–404 BC), which comports with the time of Johanan's work as high priest, and Darius III Codomannus (336–331), which fits the historical period of Jaddua according to Josephus. Williamson argues for Darius I (*Ezra, Nehemiah*, 364–365).

244 The number is five if, as seems reasonable, the phrase "son of" in 12:24 is a scribal error that should read "Binnui" (cf. 12:8). No other text identifies Jeshua as son of Kadmiel (Ezra 2:40; 3:9; Neh. 7:43; 9:4, 5), and both names are found with Binnui at Nehemiah 10:9; 12:8.

The promise to care for God's house means nothing in the absence of practical and sometimes costly acts of faith. The repeopling of the city was already a concern for Nehemiah (7:4, 73a). However, the people are not called to practical action by Nehemiah, Ezra, or any other leader. Indeed, the leaders of the people are already dwelling in Jerusalem (11:1). Instead, the people, overwhelmingly present by means of the lists of names, take center stage with this act of consecration. The Lord moves in their hearts in order to repopulate Jerusalem, and a variety of people respond. As the tithes were brought into the house of God (10:38), so the people now became the living tithe brought into the "holy city" (11:1, 18). Even though it may be costly, God's people must wholeheartedly offer themselves in order to see his world healthy and thriving (Rom. 12:1).

The people also care for God's house by refilling his land. Israel had long ago received the command to "be fruitful and multiply and fill the earth" (Gen. 1:28). That expansion was initially witnessed in their obedience to enter Canaan under the ministry of Joshua (cf. Neh. 8:17). The settlement allusions persist in this passage. They include the movement from covenant making to habitation of the city and villages (as the movement from Deuteronomy to Joshua), the use of tribal and clan names (as in Joshua), the numerous cities in Nehemiah 11:25–36 present also in Joshua 15, the people encamped around the holy city as they had once encamped around the tent of meeting (Joshua 15–19; 18:1), and Levites scattered within the midst of the people (Neh. 11:36; cf. Josh. 21:41). In sum, by expanding throughout the province they again embraced the hope of a Promised Land whose rich yield goes not to foreign kings.[245] From an NT perspective, this now takes place as the faithful long to see the whole earth filled with God's glory as people from every nation seek Christ as Lord and offer their best to him.

Finally, the restored community fulfills its commitment to care for the house of God by remembering the different gifts he has given to his people. Specifically, the repeated priestly and Levitical names (Neh. 12:1–26) would remind early readers of the multitude of servants God raised up to provide pastoral care even from the earliest return under Zerubbabel. God has consistently provided his people with leaders to offer sacrifice, instruct in his Word, and lead in worship. This reflects the nature of the church: the Lord grants gifts to his people to enable both church and world to flourish. Indeed, the Lord assures us that he will build his church through the gifts he gives (Eph. 4:11–12), a promise we must never take for granted. Most of all, the gift of the priestly line mentioned here (Neh. 12:10–11) is completed finally in Jesus, the Son of God, our Great High Priest (Heb. 4:14).

---

245 Allen and Laniak, *Ezra, Nehemiah, Esther*, 145.

NEHEMIAH 12:27–13:3

27 And at the dedication of the wall of Jerusalem they sought the Levites in all their places, to bring them to Jerusalem to celebrate the dedication with gladness, with thanksgivings and with singing, with cymbals, harps, and lyres. 28 And the sons of the singers gathered together from the district surrounding Jerusalem and from the villages of the Netophathites; 29 also from Beth-gilgal and from the region of Geba and Azmaveth, for the singers had built for themselves villages around Jerusalem. 30 And the priests and the Levites purified themselves, and they purified the people and the gates and the wall.

31 Then I brought the leaders of Judah up onto the wall and appointed two great choirs that gave thanks. One went to the south on the wall to the Dung Gate. 32 And after them went Hoshaiah and half of the leaders of Judah, 33 and Azariah, Ezra, Meshullam, 34 Judah, Benjamin, Shemaiah, and Jeremiah, 35 and certain of the priests' sons with trumpets: Zechariah the son of Jonathan, son of Shemaiah, son of Mattaniah, son of Micaiah, son of Zaccur, son of Asaph; 36 and his relatives, Shemaiah, Azarel, Milalai, Gilalai, Maai, Nethanel, Judah, and Hanani, with the musical instruments of David the man of God. And Ezra the scribe went before them. 37 At the Fountain Gate they went up straight before them by the stairs of the city of David, at the ascent of the wall, above the house of David, to the Water Gate on the east.

38 The other choir of those who gave thanks went to the north, and I followed them with half of the people, on the wall, above the Tower of the Ovens, to the Broad Wall, 39 and above the Gate of Ephraim, and by the Gate of Yeshanah,[1] and by the Fish Gate and the Tower of Hananel and the Tower of the Hundred, to the Sheep Gate; and they came to a halt at the Gate of the Guard. 40 So both choirs of those who gave thanks stood in the house of God, and I and half of the officials with me; 41 and the priests Eliakim, Maaseiah, Miniamin, Micaiah, Elioenai, Zechariah, and Hananiah, with trumpets; 42 and Maaseiah, Shemaiah, Eleazar, Uzzi, Jehohanan, Malchijah, Elam, and Ezer. And the singers sang with Jezrahiah as their leader. 43 And they offered great sacrifices that day and rejoiced, for God had made them rejoice with great joy; the women and children also rejoiced. And the joy of Jerusalem was heard far away.

44 On that day men were appointed over the storerooms, the contributions, the firstfruits, and the tithes, to gather into them the portions required by the Law for the priests and for the Levites according to the fields of the towns, for Judah rejoiced over the priests and the Levites who ministered. 45 And they performed the service of their God and the service of purification, as did the singers and the gatekeepers, according to the command of David and his son Solomon. 46 For long ago in the days of David and Asaph there were directors of the singers, and there

were songs[2] of praise and thanksgiving to God. [47] And all Israel in the days of Zerubbabel and in the days of Nehemiah gave the daily portions for the singers and the gatekeepers; and they set apart that which was for the Levites; and the Levites set apart that which was for the sons of Aaron.

13 On that day they read from the Book of Moses in the hearing of the people. And in it was found written that no Ammonite or Moabite should ever enter the assembly of God, [2] for they did not meet the people of Israel with bread and water, but hired Balaam against them to curse them—yet our God turned the curse into a blessing. [3] As soon as the people heard the law, they separated from Israel all those of foreign descent.

[1] Or *of the old city* [2] Or *leaders*

Section Overview

Much has transpired in the nearly one hundred years since the initial return to the land in 538 BC. The altar and temple have been rebuilt under Zerubbabel and Jeshua, Ezra the priest and scribe has returned with the Law and led the people in repentance, and Nehemiah the governor has overseen the completion of the wall in the face of great opposition. In the final section of Ezra-Nehemiah (Neh. 7:73b–13:31), the people sense that a new time has arrived.

Prompted by the ministry of the Word, this new day begins in earnest with the renewal of the covenant (7:73b–10:39), resulting in the habitation of Jerusalem and its environs (11:1–12:26). Some of the laymen, priests, Levites, and temple personnel who promised not to "neglect the house of our God" (10:39) offer themselves as the living tithe brought into the "holy city" (11:1, 18). Now, in the third episode (12:27–13:3), we encounter the climactic moment not only of this section but of all Ezra-Nehemiah. Each of those men again play their part. However, emphasis falls on the communal celebration led by the priests and Levites (11:1–12:26) as the people gather to give thanks.

The overall structure of the episode is reasonably straightforward. The whole is composed of two parts: wall dedication (12:27–43) and events "on that day" (12:44–13:3). The first scene of the wall dedication focuses on the gathering of priests and Levites and concludes with a purified community (12:27–30). The procession of two great choirs follows in the second scene (12:31–43). Ezra leads a group going south (12:31–37) while Nehemiah follows after the one traveling north (12:38–39). Both choirs join together in the house of God for sacrifices offered "on that day," with abundant rejoicing (12:40–43).

The second part may also be treated as two scenes. In the first (12:44–47), arrangements are made for the care of tithes, contributions, and portions promised earlier (cf. 10:32–39). It concludes with the note that these are "set apart" (i.e., consecrated) for the Levites and the priests. This theme of separation flows into the final scene, where again reading of the Mosaic law "on that day" moves Israel to take seriously its call to be a distinct people (13:1–3).

Section Outline

III.C. Wall Dedication and Events "On That Day" (12:27–13:3)
1. Wall Dedication (12:27–43)
    a. Assembly Gathers for the Dedication (12:27–30)
    b. The Procession of Two Great Choirs (12:31–43)
2. Two Further Events "On That Day": Provisions and Purification (12:44–13:3)
    a. Provision: Contributions for Temple Personnel (12:44–47)
    b. Purification: Reading and Applying the Book of Moses (13:1–3)

Comment

12:27–30 These introductory verses describe the preparations for what follows. We learn that there is a wall dedication "with gladness," that the Levites gather to lead with music, and purification is made for the entire community, gates, and wall. The completion of the temple had been followed by a dedication with rejoicing (Ezra 6:16–18). Many scholars wonder why the similar celebration narrated here does not follow immediately after wall completion in the sixth month, Elul (Neh. 6:15). Perhaps the simplest answer is that dedication is delayed by the need to repopulate and secure Jerusalem (7:3–5, 73; 11:1–24), an action that is itself postponed by the powerful events of Nehemiah 8–10, shaped by the reading of the Law in the seventh month (8:2; 9:1).

While 284 Levites live in Jerusalem (11:18), many others live in towns surrounding the city (11:3, 20). More Levites are needed in Jerusalem due to the magnitude of the celebration (cf. Ezra 8:17). The Levitical role of leading in thanksgiving with music and singing was previously anticipated (Ezra 3:10–13; Neh. 11:17, 22–23; 12:24) and long ago commanded by David (1 Chron. 15:16; 2 Chron. 29:25). The phrase "sons of the singers" (Neh. 12:28) points not to descent but to function as members of a guild or company of musicians. The narrator first describes the locations from which they gather in general terms, "in all their places" (v. 27). This is clarified as *from* the "district" and "villages" (v. 28), and *from* Beth-gilgal and the "region" (lit., "fields"; v. 29). The locations mentioned are a short distance from Jerusalem, either south (Netophah near Bethlehem), east (Beth-gilgal), or north (Geba, Azmaveth).[246] Understandably, the Levites closest to the temple could most easily answer the call to serve at the celebration.

The dedication begins with purification (v. 30). This is expected due to the prior confession of sin (ch. 9) and the holy calling of the community, with their concern to "separate themselves" (9:2; 10:28; 13:3) within the "holy city" (11:1, 18). The need for the priests and Levites to purify themselves (12:30; 13:22) is comparable to Ezra 6:20, the last time we encountered this act (Ezra 6:19–21). The prior listing of priests and Levites suggests the Lord's provision of those able to minister by carrying out both the purification and dedication that follows (Neh. 12:1–26;

---

246 Beth-gilgal, if associated with the Gilgal near Jericho, would be farthest away (c. 18 mi. or 30 km).

cf. v. 44b). The exact rites of purification are not provided. They may include fasting, abstinence from sexual activity, sprinkling with water and washing of one's clothes and body, or a sin offering (Ex. 19:10, 14–15; Num. 8:7–8). Likewise, the process of purification for the wall and gates is unknown.

12:31–43 The second scene (vv. 31–43) begins with a return to Nehemiah's first-person account, the first time we have heard his voice since 7:5. His appointment of two great choirs "that gave thanks" highlights a key word. The single word rendered "thanksgivings" at 12:27 occurs in the initial verse of each part that follows (vv. 31, 38, 40). In each instance it refers to the very purpose of the choirs as those "who gave thanks." They are brought "onto the wall," indicating traversal along its top. Excavation of portions of Nehemiah's wall suggest that it was wide enough for such a procession.

12:31–37 The first choir likely exits at the Valley Gate and moves south toward the Dung Gate, as Nehemiah once did (2:13).[247] The choir is followed by a lay leader, Hoshaiah, and half of the other lay leaders and then seven priests with trumpets led by Ezra (12:33–35a, 36b).[248] Zechariah (v. 35b) is a "son of Asaph," signaling his role as music director. He is followed by eight of "his brothers" (v. 36a AT; ESV "his relatives"). This indicates that they are fellow Levites, not family members (cf. 12:8, 24). Just as trumpets were the prerogative of priests (Num. 10:8; 1 Chron. 16:6; Ezra 3:10), so Levites have the "musical instruments of David" (cf. 2 Chron. 29:26). The order of singers first and musicians last is reflected in the procession of Psalm 68:25. Processional movements at the Fountain Gate (Neh. 12:37) are unclear. The "ascent of the wall" may indicate that the steepness of the wall causes them to abandon it so that they make their way into the City of David via the stairs in order to rejoin the wall at some point to the north, eventually making their way to the Water Gate.

12:38–39 The second thanksgiving choir moves in the opposite direction, north along the wall. Its composition mirrors that of the southern procession. After the choir a lay leader, Nehemiah, and "half of the people" follow (v. 38; cf. v. 32). Although not narrated in the same order, the second procession also has seven priests with trumpets, a Levitical musical director (Jezrahiah), and eight Levites ("the singers") with him (vv. 41–42). All of the place names encountered here are also found in the wall-building episode in chapter 3 except for the Ephraim Gate

---

247 For a discussion of the topography throughout this chapter, cf. comments on Nehemiah 3:1–32.
248 The conjunction "and" in the phrase "*and* certain of the priests' sons with trumpets" (12:35) is best taken as explanatory of what precedes and thus translated "*that is*, certain of the priests' sons with trumpets." By this interpretation the phrase does not point to the names that follow as the trumpeters. Rather, it further identifies the seven priests previously mentioned. This is further supported by the fact that: (1) Zechariah, named as a descendant of "Asaph," was a Levite, not a priest; and (2) trumpeting was a priestly duty (Num. 10:8; 1 Chron. 15:24; 2 Chron. 29:26; Ezra 3:10). This explanation is supported by Williamson, *Ezra, Nehemiah*, 367, and Blenkinsopp, *Ezra-Nehemiah*, 343. For example, the NAB translates: "followed by Hoshaiah . . . along with Azariah, Ezra, Meshullam . . . Shemaiah, and Jeremiah, priests with the trumpets, and also Zechariah, son of Jonathan . . ." The phrase "sons of the priests" or "priests' sons" means they are members of the priestly class (e.g., Neh. 12:28: "sons of the singers"). The narrator may be identifying "Ezra," the second priest in the list (Neh. 12:33), with "the scribe" who was "before them" (i.e., before the priests; 12:36). This would keep the number of priests at seven for both processions (cf. 12:41 for the second procession).

(but see note 165), and the Gate of the Guard. The identity of the latter is unknown though is perhaps best identified with the Muster Gate (cf. 3:31).[249]

12:40–43 The two "great choirs" (v. 31) and the Levites with their instruments (vv. 36, 42) offer responsive thanksgiving (cf. v. 24). The priests are present with their trumpets (vv. 35, 41) along with Nehemiah and the "officials," representing all the people standing "in the house of God."[250] This is no routine ritual but a dedication marked from the start by "gladness" (v. 27). This key word is abundant in the grand finale of verse 43, with the noun (two times) and verb (three times) both present. The verse also resonates with the other building projects as if to envelop the whole of Ezra-Nehemiah. For example, the sacrifices at the altar and temple completion (Ezra 3; 6) are paralleled here by "great sacrifices." Moreover, the emphasis upon thanksgiving (Hb. *todah*) throughout the episode suggests they are peace (fellowship) offerings for thanksgiving (Lev. 7:11–15), offered because of the "great joy" with which God has "made them rejoice," as at the Passover after the temple was rebuilt (Ezra 6:22). Finally, the inclusion of women and children further expresses communal joy, so that the indistinguishable sound once heard at the altar completion among the people (Ezra 3:12–13) is now the exuberant "joy of Jerusalem . . . heard far away."

12:44–47 The temporal marker "on that day" and the key word "rejoice," both of which are found in verses 43 and 44, link this scene with the prior one.[251] At the covenant renewal the people had pledged to bring to the house of God their first-fruits, contributions, and tithes "required by the Law" (v. 44; cf. 10:35–39). Men are now appointed to gather, manage, and distribute these provisions (cf. 13:13). These offerings are given to all "who ministered," including priests and Levites as well as singers and gatekeepers (12:47). This includes their combined service at the recent dedication and their performance of other duties ("service of their God"), along with the Levitical "service of purification" (v. 45; cf. v. 30; 1 Chron. 23:27–32). These contributions are offered not only from a sense of obligation but also from a sense of joy and gratitude to God for those who serve faithfully.[252]

David's command had organized the singers and gatekeepers, and Solomon followed his father's commands (1 Chron. 6:31–32; 25:1–26:32; 2 Chron. 8:14; cf. Neh. 12:24–25). The choral directorships of Jezrahiah (v. 42) and Zechariah,

---

249 Association of the Gate of the Guard with the "court of the guard" as the place of assembly is reasonable but less likely, since the latter was further south and associated with the palace, not the temple (Jer. 32:2); Blenkinsopp, *Ezra-Nehemiah*, 347.

250 Some scholars propose that the laymen must have separated from the clergy and stood in the temple courts (cf. 8:16). Eskenazi (*Age of Prose*, 120) argues that the city itself is now viewed as the "house of God." The people are able to enter because they are purified (12:30), as are the wall and gates that surround the "holy city" (11:1, 18; cf. 3:1).

251 I note this because the celebration at 12:43 is clearly a finale, and there is a need to justify treating 12:44–13:3 with what comes before (i.e., 12:27–43) rather than with what comes after (13:4–31) because of the variations in how commentators handle these final textual units. See also comment on 13:1–3. Those treating 12:44–13:31 as a textual unit note lexical and thematic links between 12:44–13:3 and what follows. These include the use and abuse of temple chambers, provision for the Levites, Sabbath activity, and improper marriage with foreigners.

252 In the Response section on 11:1–12:26 it was noted that gratitude to God for providing pastoral care for his people would be an appropriate response of early readers to the list of priests and Levites in 12:1–26.

a son of Asaph (v. 35), were no postexilic innovation. Rather, they perpetuate a tradition of musical direction and "songs of praise and thanksgiving" traced back to the venerable Asaph, chief of those David had appointed to praise God in song (1 Chron. 15:16–18; 16:4–6). The commitment of Asaph's descendants to the service of God and the remnant community is already apparent from earlier texts (Neh. 7:44; 11:17, 22).

The final verse expands upon 12:44 with a reminder that the daily portions are due and provided for all who serve at the temple. The royal command for the singers' provision "as every day required" (11:23) now includes the gatekeepers.[253] The mention of "the days of" Zerubbabel and Nehemiah indicates that these measures characterize the historical periods when each serves as governor. Finally, the gifts are "set apart" or consecrated for the Levites, and from the Levites the "tithe of the tithe" is "set apart" for the priests ("sons of Aaron"). This is just as the people pledged and the Law requires, a sacred obligation for "all Israel" (cf. 10:38; Num. 18:26–28).

13:1–3 The theme of community purification (cf. 12:30) and the lexical links with "on that day" (cf. 12:43, 44), along with the twice repeated "set apart" (i.e., "consecrated"; Heb. *maqdishim*) in 12:47, helps to connect this final scene to the prior two.[254] It is not surprising that public reading from the Book of the Law again plays an important role in community action, given its impact from the start of the book's final section (cf. 8:3, 8, 18; 9:3). Recent reaffirmation of covenantal obligations began with the specific promise not to intermarry with the "peoples of the land" (10:30). Disobedience in this area, once addressed by Ezra (Ezra 9–10), will need to be addressed again by Nehemiah (Neh. 13:23–27).

However, the specific Mosaic exhortation goes beyond marital relationships to include separation from "all those of foreign descent" (v. 3). The specific text cited is a nearly verbatim summary of Deuteronomy 23:3–5,[255] where it is commanded that the Ammonites and the Moabites be excluded from the "assembly of God," meaning the covenant community gathered for worship, reading of the law, or festivals (cf. Neh. 8:2, 17).[256] However, this is no absolute exclusion of people groups, as witnessed by the welcome received by all who join themselves to Israel, Ruth the Moabitess being a chief example (Ruth 1:16–17; Ezra 6:21; Neh. 10:28; cf. Deut. 23:7–8).

God promised Abraham that his descendants would be a blessing to the nations (Gen. 12:1–3). However, that same promise held out curses for those who dishonored Abraham. Here the latter situation is in view. The reason given is that Ammon and Moab had failed to show Israel hospitality (Num. 21:21–26) and

---

253 The precise phrase "a matter of a day in its day" is found at both 11:23 and 12:47.

254 Shepherd and Wright, *Ezra and Nehemiah*, 101.

255 Cf. comment on Ezra 9:12–15, where Deuteronomy 23:6 is cited by Ezra in the context of separation.

256 Christopher J. H. Wright, *Deuteronomy*, NIBC 4 (Peabody, MA: Hendrickson, 1996), 247. Strictly speaking, Moab had hired Balaam and the Amorites (not Ammonites) had refused passage. Ammon may be included with Moab under the tradition that Balaam was an Ammonite or resident of Ammon (Clines, *Ezra, Nehemiah, Esther*, 237).

explicitly sought to them do them harm by hiring the prophet Balaam to curse them (Numbers 22–24). Likewise, Nehemiah's opponents, led by Tobiah "the Ammonite," had hired a prophet to harm him (Neh. 6:12). This prepares us for his expulsion in 13:4–9.[257]

The command to separate from the "peoples of the land" and the conflicts with those who opposed them has threaded its way through Ezra-Nehemiah (Ezra 3:3; 4:1–24; 5:3–4; 6:21; 9:1–2; 10:2–3, 10–11; Neh. 2:1–20; 4:1–23; 6:1–19; 9:2; 10:28). Compliance is important because Israel has so often failed to embrace God's covenant wholly, thereby neglecting her missional calling to be the Lord's distinct and holy people (Ex. 19:5; Deut. 4:1–8; 6:20–25; 7:1–11).

Response

The postexilic prophet Zechariah repeated the promise that the Lord would regather his people, dwell with them, and "bring good to Jerusalem and to the house of Judah" (Zech. 8:1–8, 14–15; cf. Jer. 23:3–4; 29:10–14).[258] That day has arrived. The people renew the covenant, resulting in a commitment that the house of God would not be neglected (Neh. 10:39). That holy space is expanded to include the "holy city" itself (11:1, 18). The people celebrate the dawn of this new era as the "seed of man" (the holy seed) is resown in the holy city with a people embracing a renewed commitment to the Word of God (Jer. 31:27, 38). All that God had done through and for this restored remnant motivates them to be a joyful, thankful, and consecrated people.

There is always the danger that, apart from God, constructed edifices become objects of trust and pride (Jer. 7:1–7). Wall dedication is no celebration of human accomplishment, nor is wall completion an end in itself. Before the wall could be celebrated, the renewal and recommitment of the people (Nehemiah 8–10) and the repopulation of Jerusalem (11:1–12:26) had to take place. Only then, with God restored to the center of their lives, could their accomplishment be set in its proper context. The two processions surround the entire city and dedicate the work of their hands to the Lord. Their rejoicing is evident in the unrestrained presence of that word in 12:43. True joy cannot be controlled, manufactured, or manipulated. Its source is found in God, who "made them rejoice." When Paul calls the Philippians to rejoice (Phil. 4:4), he does so not in contrast to OT faith but because he understands that joy is always the proper response to the goodness of the Lord.[259]

Naturally, songs of thanksgiving flow from joy at what God has done and motivate the practical step of bringing our offerings to him (Neh. 12:44, 47; Ps. 107:22; Isa. 51:3; 1 Thess. 3:9). The very titles of the choirs as "those who gave thanks" (Neh. 12:31, 38, 40) is translated simply "thanksgivings" in 12:27. When we sing our songs of praise in gratitude to God for his work in our lives, we join that ancient

---

257 Blenkinsopp, Ezra-Nehemiah, 351.
258 For a listing of other prophetic texts with this theme, see the Response section on Ezra 8:1–36.
259 McConville, Ezra, Nehemiah, Esther, 142.

tradition (12:46). In addition, the varied gifts given to the priests and Levites for the "house of our God" are obligations embraced by the whole people at the covenant renewal (10:32–39). And yet they are also offered in gratitude because they "rejoice" over the ministry of the priests and Levites in their midst (12:44). Today as well the NT church has the privilege of joining an esteemed tradition by giving in order to supply the daily needs of those who serve as pastors and leaders in the church. Likewise, the wider ministries of the church, its worship and discipleship, require material support from those who spiritually benefit (1 Cor. 9:11–14). The joy of worship must be met with the joy of giving to support that worship.[260]

The people who set apart offerings are themselves set apart as purified by the priests and Levites (Neh. 12:30; cf. Ex. 19:10). They are ready to meet God in worship, an act that must have its impact beyond the walls of the sanctuary. That impact is seen through their further consecration in obedience to the Book of Moses (Neh. 13:1–3). God's command to be a treasured possession and holy people is never rescinded (Deut. 7:1–11; 14:2; 1 Pet. 2:9). Now they obey God's will by not permitting into the holy assembly those of foreign descent. In this way the episode closes with a deeply theological dynamic for those who love the Lord Jesus Christ. The people of God, purified by Christ their high priest, are set apart for God, submissive to his Word, and destined to dwell with him in his house. Regrettably, those who hate God, curse his people, and refuse to hear his Word will in the end be "separated from all Israel" (Neh. 13:3; cf. Ex. 20:5; Matt. 25:41–46; 2 Thess. 1:8). In light of this, we give ourselves to our Lord more and more, singing with the psalmist:

"Walk about Zion, go around her,
    number her towers,
consider well her ramparts,
    go through her citadels,
that you may tell the next generation
    that this is God,
our God forever and ever.
    He will guide us forever." (Ps. 48:12–14)

---

260 Allen and Laniak, *Ezra, Nehemiah, Esther*, 161.

NEHEMIAH 13:4–31

⁴Now before this, Eliashib the priest, who was appointed over the chambers of the house of our God, and who was related to Tobiah, ⁵prepared for Tobiah a large chamber where they had previously put the grain offering, the frankincense, the vessels, and the tithes of grain, wine, and oil, which were given by commandment to the Levites, singers, and gatekeepers, and the contributions for the priests. ⁶While this was taking place, I was not in Jerusalem, for in the thirty-second year of Artaxerxes king of Babylon I went to the king. And after some time I asked leave of the king ⁷and came to Jerusalem, and I then discovered the evil that Eliashib had done for Tobiah, preparing for him a chamber in the courts of the house of God. ⁸And I was very angry, and I threw all the household furniture of Tobiah out of the chamber. ⁹Then I gave orders, and they cleansed the chambers, and I brought back there the vessels of the house of God, with the grain offering and the frankincense.

¹⁰I also found out that the portions of the Levites had not been given to them, so that the Levites and the singers, who did the work, had fled each to his field. ¹¹So I confronted the officials and said, "Why is the house of God forsaken?" And I gathered them together and set them in their stations. ¹²Then all Judah brought the tithe of the grain, wine, and oil into the storehouses. ¹³And I appointed as treasurers over the storehouses Shelemiah the priest, Zadok the scribe, and Pedaiah of the Levites, and as their assistant Hanan the son of Zaccur, son of Mattaniah, for they were considered reliable, and their duty was to distribute to their brothers. ¹⁴Remember me, O my God, concerning this, and do not wipe out my good deeds that I have done for the house of my God and for his service.

¹⁵In those days I saw in Judah people treading winepresses on the Sabbath, and bringing in heaps of grain and loading them on donkeys, and also wine, grapes, figs, and all kinds of loads, which they brought into Jerusalem on the Sabbath day. And I warned them on the day when they sold food. ¹⁶Tyrians also, who lived in the city, brought in fish and all kinds of goods and sold them on the Sabbath to the people of Judah, in Jerusalem itself! ¹⁷Then I confronted the nobles of Judah and said to them, "What is this evil thing that you are doing, profaning the Sabbath day? ¹⁸Did not your fathers act in this way, and did not our God bring all this disaster¹ on us and on this city? Now you are bringing more wrath on Israel by profaning the Sabbath."

¹⁹As soon as it began to grow dark at the gates of Jerusalem before the Sabbath, I commanded that the doors should be shut and gave orders that they should not be opened until after the Sabbath. And I stationed some of my servants at the gates, that no load might be brought in on the Sabbath day. ²⁰Then the merchants and sellers of all kinds of wares lodged outside Jerusalem once or twice. ²¹But I warned them and said to them, "Why do you lodge outside the wall? If you do so again, I will lay hands

on you." From that time on they did not come on the Sabbath. ²² Then I commanded the Levites that they should purify themselves and come and guard the gates, to keep the Sabbath day holy. Remember this also in my favor, O my God, and spare me according to the greatness of your steadfast love.

²³ In those days also I saw the Jews who had married women of Ashdod, Ammon, and Moab. ²⁴ And half of their children spoke the language of Ashdod, and they could not speak the language of Judah, but only the language of each people. ²⁵ And I confronted them and cursed them and beat some of them and pulled out their hair. And I made them take an oath in the name of God, saying, "You shall not give your daughters to their sons, or take their daughters for your sons or for yourselves. ²⁶ Did not Solomon king of Israel sin on account of such women? Among the many nations there was no king like him, and he was beloved by his God, and God made him king over all Israel. Nevertheless, foreign women made even him to sin. ²⁷ Shall we then listen to you and do all this great evil and act treacherously against our God by marrying foreign women?"

²⁸ And one of the sons of Jehoiada, the son of Eliashib the high priest, was the son-in-law of Sanballat the Horonite. Therefore I chased him from me. ²⁹ Remember them, O my God, because they have desecrated the priesthood and the covenant of the priesthood and the Levites.

³⁰ Thus I cleansed them from everything foreign, and I established the duties of the priests and Levites, each in his work; ³¹ and I provided for the wood offering at appointed times, and for the firstfruits.

Remember me, O my God, for good.

¹ The Hebrew word can mean *evil*, *harm*, or *disaster*, depending on the context

Section Overview

The wall dedication is clearly the climax of Ezra-Nehemiah, with all of the members of a purified, holy community gathered in the holy city (Neh. 12:30) with rejoicing caused by God (12:27–43). The celebration of "that day" (12:43) is followed by two events, also described as occurring "on that day." These are summarized under the two broad themes of provisions (12:44–47) and purification (13:1–3). These themes were likewise present in the prior covenantal obligations, which focused on the provision of tithes for temple service (10:32–39) and purification from the peoples of the land, the latter including proper keeping of the Sabbath (10:30–31). These texts and themes provide a literary bridge to 13:4–31, which presents reforms in both of these areas. Nehemiah first describes those reforms undertaken for the purification and provision for the temple (13:4–14) and then moves on to describe those reforms carried out in the areas of Sabbath and separation (vv. 15–29).

Nehemiah's "I" of first-person address is heard in almost every verse. The passage comprises four pericopes (vv. 4–14, 15–22, 23–29, 30–31), with each ending in a "remember" prayer of Nehemiah (vv. 14, 22, 29, 31).[261] The first three also share

---

261 This structural observation is the basis for treating 13:4–14 together, all being accomplished "for the house of my God" (13:14).

the basic form of a problem Nehemiah faces, a confrontation he engages (vv. 11, 17, 25), and a resolution he enacts. In each case foreign influence is involved. The first pericope concerns the temple, both its misuse (vv. 4–9) and the failure of the people in providing for the temple work of the Levites (vv. 10–13). In the second, Nehemiah confronts the profanation of the Sabbath (vv. 15–22a). In the third vignette the problem of intermarriage is again found among the laity (vv. 23–27) and the priesthood (vv. 28–29). The concluding summary once more underscores the themes of purification and provision, followed by Nehemiah's closing prayer (vv. 30–31).

Section Outline

III.D. Nehemiah's Reforms: Temple, Sabbath, Separation (13:4–31)

    1. Reforms concerning the Temple (13:4–14)

        a. Cleansing of the Temple Chamber (13:4–9)

        b. Neglect of the Temple through Lack of Support for the Levites (13:10–13)

        c. Prayer: "Remember Me" (13:14)

    2. Reforms concerning the Sabbath (13:15–22)

        a. Problem: Goods and Trading on the Sabbath (13:15–16)

        b. Confrontation of Nobles of Judah (13:17–18)

        c. Resolution: Nehemiah's Practices Guard Sabbath Sanctity (13:19–22a)

        d. Prayer: "Remember This" (vv. 22b)

    3. Reforms concerning Separation from Foreign Wives (13:23–29)

        a. Linguistic and Marital Intermixing (13:23–24)

        b. Confrontation (13:25a)

        c. Resolution (13:25b–28)

        d. Prayer: "Remember Them" (13:29)

    4. Summary of Reforms: Purification and Provisions (13:30–31)

Comment

13:4–5 The temporal marker "Now before this" interrupts the expected chronological sequence and, if read as a flashback, suggests that the events in verses 4–14[262] (or perhaps vv. 4–31 as a whole) occurred previously, with "this" referring to the prior wall dedication and other events in 12:27–13:3 linked together by the repeated phrase "on that day" (12:43, 44; 13:1). So far, this presented sequence of events is no problem.[263] The tension arises at verse 6, where Nehemiah states that

---

262 Note that 13:10–14 is placed with 13:4–9, since the former has no separate chronological introduction but begins with a verbal form indicating the next thing in the narrative. English versions express this either with "I also" (ESV, NASB, NIV) or "I then" (NJPS).

263 Eskenazi describes the whole of 13:4–31 as a "coda," continuing, "This coda in Ezra-Nehemiah trails like an afterthought, looping back to a time before the climax of the celebration" (*Age of Prose*, 123). Although Williamson argues that 13:4 is from the final editor, he states that 13:4–31 is presented as a "pluperfect" of the climax of 12:26–13:3 (*Ezra, Nehemiah*, 383–384). Noss and Thomas state, "The situation described here [i.e., 13:4] took place before the dedication of the wall and the events reported in 12:27–13:3" (*Ezra and Nehemiah*, 534).

the events of verses 4–14 (or vv. 4–31) took place during his visit to Artaxerxes in the king's "thirty-second year" (433 BC; cf. 5:14). If so, then the wall dedication in 12:27–43 took place after Nehemiah's return in 433, even though the wall itself was completed in 445 (and one might expect the wall dedication to have taken place shortly thereafter). It may be that after the promises of the covenant renewal (9:38–10:39) and the resettlement of Jerusalem (11:1–12:26), Nehemiah traveled to Babylon (13:6) in 433. Upon his return to Jerusalem he was appalled at the multiple community lapses. For the sake of the people's spiritual health he carried out a series of reforms based on the very obligations the people themselves had previously embraced as part of the covenant renewal. Only after these reforms, narrated in verses 4–14 (or vv. 4–31), did the wall dedication of 12:27–43 take place.[264]

Upon his return to Jerusalem, Nehemiah faced the ritual defilement of the temple precincts. A "large chamber" holding temple supplies and provisions for priests and Levites had been cleared of its contents. This was possible because a priest, Eliashib, had been given authority over the "chambers."[265] The prevalence of this word throughout recalls the other passage in which "chambers" are prominent (10:37–39). There the people had agreed to fill the rooms of the "house of our God" with tithes and all kinds of contributions, which they later offered at the dedication (12:44). Outrageously, temple supplies had now been removed in order for Tobiah to move in.[266]

13:6–7 Beyond Eliashib's unspecified relational connection with Tobiah, nothing more can be said of his motivation. As an aside, Nehemiah explains that these events occurred during his extended visit to Artaxerxes in 433 BC. He discovers this upon his return and calls it "evil"[267] for several reasons. First, use of this sacred space was only for priests and Levites (cf. 6:11). Second, Tobiah held some Ammonite connection (2:10, 19; 4:3), and so Mosaic exclusion from the assembly was relevant (13:1). His presence would defile the temple vicinity itself. Finally, Tobiah consistently opposed the well-being of the community throughout the period. He even took the lead in hiring a prophet to harm Nehemiah (6:12; cf. 13:2).

13:8–9 Tobiah, once "displeased" (Hb. *wayyera'*) that Nehemiah sought the welfare of the people of Israel (2:10), now experiences Nehemiah's "anger" (*wayyera'*). Nehemiah acts unilaterally and immediately by personally casting out the "vessels of the house of Tobiah" (*kele bet-tobiyyah*; AT). This phrase is mirrored precisely in the return of the "vessels of the house of God" (*kele bet ha'elohim*) and other previously removed contents. This restoration and the proper use of the chamber occurs only after it is ritually cleansed by Nehemiah's orders (cf. 2 Chron. 29:15–19). It is not clear if he functions officially as governor or based on his prior authority.

---

264 The hypothesized order of events outlined here is suggested by Shepherd and Wright, *Ezra and Nehemiah*, 103.
265 Commentators generally agree that this Eliashib is not to be identified with the high priest of the same name.
266 For further discussion of Tobiah, cf. comment on Nehemiah 2:9–10.
267 Noss and Thomas note the prevalence of the noun translated "evil" throughout the passage (13:7, 17, 18, 27) and the verb built on the same root in 13:8, "I was . . . angry" (*Ezra and Nehemiah*, 536).

13:10 Nehemiah also learns that the Levites and singers are not receiving their due tithes. This discovery may be provoked by the return of goods to the cleansed chamber (v. 9).[268] This suggests a problem of both supply and distribution (cf. vv. 12–13). Under the current system the Levites are responsible for accepting the community's tithes and transporting them to Jerusalem (10:37b–38). However, the people have not brought them as promised (10:35–39; cf. 12:44). As a result, those "who did the work" of the temple (cf. 12:45) are abandoning their posts to work the fields in their towns (cf. 7:73; 11:20; 12:28–29).[269]

13:11 The loss of the Levites would be detrimental to the spiritual health of the community, given their central role in leading worship (cf. 12:27, 40–42). In response, Nehemiah confronts the lay leaders ("officials") he deems responsible.[270] This is the first occurrence of the verb translated "confronted" in the current passage (13:11, 17, 25). This is not a formal legal complaint but an argument and rebuke for insufficient tithes (cf. Mal. 3:8–10). The rhetorical question "Why is the house of God forsaken?" is an accusation referring to the literal flight of the Levites from their duties (Neh. 13:10). Also implicated is the community for failing to keep the summative promise of their renewed covenant—"We will not forsake the house of our God" (10:39).[271] Nehemiah's swift action solves the immediate problem, the lack of Levites, by gathering and restoring them to their places of service in the temple.

13:12–13 Short term, the supply is renewed with an influx of tithes into the temple storehouses (v. 12). For the long-term problem of distribution, Nehemiah appoints a team of four men of unquestioned integrity. These appointments are later confirmed at the dedication (cf. 12:44).[272] The representatives (priest, scribe, Levite, singer) provide a cross section of constituencies with interest in the gathering, organization, and just distribution of the "portions" due their fellow temple workers (13:10).[273]

13:14 The "remember" prayers uttered by Nehemiah provide structural markers at the end of each pericope (vv. 14, 22, 29, 31). Positively, Nehemiah pleads that God would be ever mindful of his faithful actions (cf. 1:8; 5:19). These "good deeds"[274] are those just narrated, as evidenced by the phrases "house of my God" and "for his service."[275] Negatively, he asks that these not be blotted out—as if kept in a heavenly register (Mal. 3:16). This prayer is neither self-serving nor hubristic but asks that God would bless his work to bear long-term fruit (cf. Heb. 6:10). As

---

268 Clines carefully observes that the Levitical tithes of "grain, wine, and oil" (13:5, 12) are conspicuously absent from the list of items restored after Tobiah's rejection (13:9) (*Ezra, Nehemiah, Esther*, 240).

269 There is no indication that these are connected with the Levitical cities.

270 On the "nobles and officials," cf. note 55. Nehemiah will confront the "nobles" at 13:17. He had previously confronted, i.e., "brought charges" against, both groups at 5:7. He will confront the "Jews" at 13:25 (cf. 13:23).

271 The verb translated "neglect" by the ESV at 10:39 is translated "forsaken" at 13:11. In the latter case the passive form indicates the lack of attention by the officials and the people.

272 Shepherd and Wright, *Ezra and Nehemiah*, 104.

273 Blenkinsopp, *Ezra-Nehemiah*, 356.

274 The translation of *hesed* as "good deeds" reflects a less frequent use of the word with reference to love for God, i.e., acts of devotion motivated by covenantal faithfulness (cf. 2 Chron. 32:32; 35:26).

275 The final phrase is ambiguous and may be translated "his service" (ESV), "its services" (NASB), or "its attendants" (NJPS). The final two refer to temple services or those who lead them.

Kidner states, "To hear God's 'Well done' is the most innocent and most cleansing of ambitions."[276]

13:15–16 The events of the second problem faced by Nehemiah take place "in those days." This provides loose temporal connection with the prior narrative. Nehemiah witnesses a bustle of activity, including preparing, loading, and transporting all kinds of merchandise into Jerusalem. Unfortunately, this occurs on the Sabbath. Foreign influence is again noted with the mention of Phoenicians (Tyrians and Sidonians), well-known traders (Isa. 23:2–3, 8, Ezek. 27:1–3). They have established a trading station for fish and other goods in Jerusalem, likely at the Fish Gate (Neh. 3:3).[277]

13:17–18 This trade leads to the second confrontation, presented as accusatory questions and directed at the "nobles of Judah" (cf. comment on 13:11). Nehemiah calls their profanation of the day "evil" because the people are not observing the Sabbath, a holy covenant sign the Lord has commanded (v. 22; Ex. 20:8–11; 31:12–17). Likewise, they are disregarding their newly adopted obligation to reject Sabbath trade with foreigners (cf. Neh. 10:31). However, this is no recent problem, as both Amos (Amos 8:5) and Jeremiah (Jer. 17:21–22) attest. The latter notes that maintaining Sabbath holiness is a matter of life and death for his hearers. Its persistent denigration would lead to Jerusalem's destruction (Jer. 17:27). Nehemiah warns that a fresh visitation of God's wrath is possible (cf. Ezra 9:14; 10:14). By the very "evil" (Hb. *ra'*) they are now perpetuating, their fathers had brought on them this "disaster" (*ra'ah*), i.e., exile and Jerusalem's destruction.

13:19–22a The threat of God's judgment leads Nehemiah to act. First he denies access to Jerusalem by closing the doors of the gates throughout the Sabbath. He adds short-term security by stationing some of his own guards to ensure no possible entry by persons bearing a burden.[278] Next he disperses the traders by threatening to "lay hands on" them, by either force or arrest. Clearly this is effective. Finally, as part of long-term arrangements (cf. v. 19), the Levitical gatekeepers are commanded to purify themselves and guard the gates as part of their ongoing responsibility to maintain the sanctity of the temple—now expanded to include the holy city (11:1, 18; 12:30; Isa. 52:1; Joel 3:17).[279]

13:22b The former "remember" prayer focused on Nehemiah's "deeds" (Hb. *hesed*) done to care for the temple (v. 14). In this prayer Nehemiah asks God to "spare me" or have compassion based on his "steadfast love" (*hesed*). The need for the manifestation of God's covenant love would be palpable in this situation, as Nehemiah must correct Sabbath neglect among the people, a practice that had, in part, brought about the events of the exile (cf. comment on 13:17–18).

---

276 Kidner, *Ezra and Nehemiah*, 143.
277 Blenkinsopp, *Ezra-Nehemiah*, 360.
278 See Williamson's argument at 4:10 (16) that Nehemiah's "servants" are men who are trained and armed and owe Nehemiah personal allegiance (*Ezra, Nehemiah*, 227–228).
279 Williamson, *Ezra, Nehemiah*, 396.

13:23–24 With "In those days also I saw," the report of the third reform commences like the second had (cf. v. 15). Jewish men are again marrying foreign women. This reverses the earlier pledge that they would not marry the "peoples of the land" (10:30–31).[280] The Ammonites and Moabites were not mentioned among the Pentateuchal lists because those lists prohibited marriage to inhabitants within the land (Ex. 34:11–16; Deut. 7:1–5). However, they are included in Ezra's list (Ezra 9:1–2), likely expanded under the influence of Deuteronomy 23:3–4, 6.

Ashdod is the name of the Persian province west of Judah (cf. comment on Neh. 4:7–9). The Ashdodite marriages are singled out for their impact upon the language acquisition of some of the children of these unions. This may be so because the Ashdodite tongue had less affinity to Hebrew than did the Moabite and Ammonite dialects.[281] Of significance to Nehemiah, the loss of Hebrew, "the language of Judah," would have a harmful impact on social and religious identity. Primarily this would result in the inability to understand the Scriptures or engage meaningfully in worship. Within a generation the loss of the knowledge of the Lord could be precipitous (cf. Judg. 2:10).

13:25 Nehemiah's third "confrontation" is with the actual Judeans who have married foreign wives. Ezra's response to the news of foreign marriages had been internally focused, with mourning and confession on behalf of the community (Ezra 9:3–15). The process ended in repentance and separation of a select group from their foreign wives by community decision (Ezra 10:2–5, 9–15). Nehemiah's reaction is autocratic and externally focused. He administers physical punishment and pulls out hair, probably from the beard. This latter practice expresses public humiliation rather than judicial action. Instead of the forced divorces of Ezra's reforms, Nehemiah seems intent on punishing current and preventing future offenders. The divine sanctions of the oath Nehemiah utters are based on Deuteronomy 7:3 and apply this Scripture to his current context (Neh. 13:25b). Others have already taken a similar oath (10:30; cf. Ezra 9:12).

13:26–27 Some interpret Nehemiah's response to be excessive and even xenophobic. However, Solomon provides the lens through which to interpret the logic of Nehemiah's actions. Nehemiah has a balanced view of both human behavior and God's grace. Solomon was loved by the Lord, who blessed him and his reign (2 Sam. 12:24–25; 1 Kings 3:12–13; 4:20–34). Unfortunately, while Solomon loved the Lord (1 Kings 3:3), he also loved "many foreign women," including Moabites and Ammonites (1 Kings 11:1–2), and he began to love their gods (11:4–8). His spiritual adultery became the parade illustration of covenantal unfaithfulness (i.e., "act treacherously"; Neh. 13:27).[282] The resulting judgment of kingdom

---

280 This particular use of the verb translated "married" is found only in reference to foreign marriages (Ezra 10:2, 10, 14, 17, 18; Neh. 13:23, 27), suggesting the illegitimacy of the unions.
281 What is meant by "language of Ashdod" is unclear. Some argue that it is a non-Semitic language with some historical link to the language once spoken by the Philistines (Williamson, *Ezra, Nehemiah*, 398). For the "language of Judah," see 2 Kings 18:26, 28.
282 For further discussion of "act treacherously," cf. comment on Ezra 9:1–2. In brief, the verb depicts a comprehensive rejection of the Lord and his commands.

division (1 Kings 11:9–12) was cataclysmic for both Israel and Judah and would lead ultimately to their current distress. In this sad trajectory, the people followed their king's lead and "mixed [themselves] with the peoples," becoming indistinguishable from the nations (Hos. 7:8).[283] In so doing they lost their missional purpose. This leads naturally to the greater-to-lesser argument with which Nehemiah closes the paragraph. If even the resplendent Solomon could commit this "great evil and act treacherously," how foolish is it for us to continue to sin likewise and expose ourselves to the just judgment of the Lord as had our ancestors, including our former kings (Neh. 9:33–35).

13:28 The theme of prohibited marriage persists in a specific case. Eliashib was high priest in Nehemiah's time (3:1), and his son Jehoiada (= Joiada) was his successor (12:10–11). Whether Jehoiada is already high priest at this time is uncertain, since "high priest" in the verse could refer to either man. Either way, the reported marriage should horrify the reader. The high priest is held to more stringent standards in marriage. In particular, he is to marry "of his own people" (i.e., tribe; Lev. 21:14). This assures an offspring with a genealogy fully tied to the tribe of Levi (Ex. 29:29–30; Neh. 7:64). It also guarantees that the high priest would "not profane his offspring" (Lev. 21:13–15).[284]

To exacerbate the problem, the unnamed bride is the daughter of Sanballat the Horonite. If he is governor of Samaria at the time, as seems possible, then Sanballat's daughter would be considered a foreign wife.[285] In this manner, the whole passage is framed with reference to Tobiah and Sanballat, the two archenemies of Nehemiah's ministry who brokered influence through their intermarital relationships (cf. Neh. 6:18). The reform ends with neither accusatory question or dialogue but rather Nehemiah's violent expulsion of Jehoiada's son from the community.

13:29 This "remember" prayer differs from the earlier ones (vv. 14, 22). It bears some affinity with earlier imprecations directed against opponents (cf. comments on 4:4–5; 6:14). The reference to "them" indicates the persons mentioned in 13:28, perhaps extended to any priest whose faithless action or questionable genealogy defiles the priesthood itself (7:64). The phrase "covenant of the priesthood and the Levites" is not found in the Pentateuch, but a "covenant with Levi" is mentioned at Malachi 2:4–9. That covenant included the need for the descendant of Levi to fear the Lord, revere his name, and live righteously before God in life and speech. This manner of life was required of all those who instructed God's people. Nehemiah now turns over to the Lord a priest who, by marrying a Gentile, has disqualified himself from instructing the people of God.[286]

---

283 Kidner, *Ezra and Nehemiah*, 144.
284 Sklar, *Leviticus*, 266.
285 Cf. comment on Nehemiah 2:9–10. Sanballat's ancestry is uncertain, but he may have been a descendant of those earlier settled in the north by the Assyrians (2 Kings 17:24; Ezra 4:1–3). The names of his sons, Delaiah and Shelemaiah, are known from extrabiblical texts. These names with an "-iah" ending may indicate that Sanballat identified himself as a worshiper of the Lord (Clines, *Ezra, Nehemiah, Esther*, 144).
286 Clines (*Ezra, Nehemiah, Esther*, 249) and Williamson (*Ezra, Nehemiah*, 401) as well as other commentators suggest the connections with Malachi.

13:30–31a The terms *purification* and *provisions* nicely summarize the final section of Nehemiah. These terms not only apply to verses 4–31 but reach back to the purification of verses 1–3 and 10:30–31 as well as the provisions of 12:44–47 and 10:32–39. Nehemiah had purified the community ("them") of "everything foreign."[287] Tobiah the Ammonite was expelled from the temple and the chambers were "cleansed" (13:4–9), the Sabbath was consecrated, foreign merchants were disbanded, the Levites purified themselves (vv. 15–22), laymen were rebuked for their foreign marriages (vv. 23–27), and the high priest's descendant was banished (v. 28). All that remained was the need for provisions. And so Nehemiah "established" the particular duties of priests and Levites, ensuring proper worship (v. 30; cf. 12:45; 13:11). Finally, he "provided"[288] for the wood offering "at appointed times" (cf. 10:34) as well as firstfruits (cf. 10:35). Both of these were prominent obligations in the covenant renewal but whose collections had lapsed during Nehemiah's absence (cf. 13:5, 9; 12:45).

13:31b In Nehemiah's concluding plea, the shortest "remember" prayer in the book (cf. vv. 14, 22), he turns all over to the Lord, asking him to remember all of his faithful actions (as at 5:19). These actions may include all that God has accomplished through him or the specific events of purification and provision lately recounted. If these events occurred before the dedication (13:4), then the community decisions of 12:44–47 and 13:1–3 may be the answer to his prayer. Certainly, preservation of the book bearing his name shows that God has answered the prayer of Nehemiah.

Response

The calling of the people of God to be a holy people is nonnegotiable (Eph. 1:4–6; 1 Pet. 1:15–16; 2:9–10). This is just as relevant for those in the days of Ezra-Nehemiah as it is for any other era. At a particular moment in the Persian period, God delivers and restores his people to their proper functioning as a purified worshiping community within the holy walls of the holy city (Neh. 12:30; 11:1). That is something to be celebrated.

And yet, until the Lord returns, there is no final celebration. The text of 13:4–31 is placed after the celebration (12:27–47), even though the events occur "before this" (13:4). This sequencing exhorts the faithful in every generation to prevent celebration from leading to carelessness. The church must always be reading and hearing from the Lord's Word (13:1), always repenting and always reforming. The safety and security of our salvation won by Christ must never lead to complacency and negligence as we are to "conduct yourselves with fear throughout the time of your exile" (1 Pet. 1:17).

In various ways the neglect of consecration crept into the community in Nehemiah's absence. Tobiah, an influential enemy with Ammonite connections

---

287 While "them" may refer to recently mentioned priests and Levites (13:29), as a summary statement it may justifiably apply to the whole community.
288 The verb "provided" is not in the Hebrew text: "And I established the duties of . . . and for the wood offering . . ."

(Neh. 13:4; 2:10; 6:17–19), used his relationships to worm his way into the temple. Indeed, the house of the Lord was forsaken not only in this way but with respect to the required tithes for the Levites as well. Promises once made were quickly forgotten (10:35–39) and the service of God impacted (13:10–11). This included the misuse of the Sabbath. By it God affords rest and the opportunity for his people to consider his past goodness, to grow in trust for his provision, and to express their identity as his people distinct from the nations.[289] The failure to keep the Sabbath is perhaps entwined with the disobedience of mixed marriages. So dire is this issue for the holy calling of the people that both Ezra and Nehemiah are forced to address it. Even the high priest's family is implicated.

If the distinctive character, calling, and testimony of God's people is central to all of this, then Nehemiah's vehement response to each is understandable. Consider what it means that God's furniture had been removed from the temple chambers now indwelled by Tobiah. It demands Nehemiah's expulsion of the furniture and the cleansing of the temple (vv. 8–9). At the other end of the passage, Nehemiah chases the high priest's son from the community for his desecration of the priesthood (v. 28). This certainly evokes the comparable actions of the Lord Jesus in cleansing the temple (John 2:13–17). Our great and holy High Priest entered the world to defeat Satan and wash us clean (Heb. 10:19–22; 1 John 1:7–9). He made us members of his holy temple (1 Cor. 3:16–17; Eph. 2:19–22) and gained for us a "Sabbath rest" we could not gain for ourselves (Heb. 4:9–11). As a response to his mercy we must "not neglect the house of our God" (Neh. 10:39) but persist in the "confession of our hope" (Heb. 10:23). Each member of Christ's body is called to be a living tithe, consecrated to him and distinct from the world (Rom. 12:1–2), giving ourselves to good works and walking in the means of grace as his distinct people. With Nehemiah we pray, "Remember us, our God, for good."

---

289 McConville, *Ezra, Nehemiah, Esther*, 147.

ESTHER

Eric Ortlund

ESTHER

Overview

The book of Esther narrates the deliverance of God's people from the schemes of Haman, who plots the death of every Jew in the Persian Empire over a personal insult (Est. 3:6). The book depicts this common biblical theme of deliverance as God's people live in exile, under the authority of a Gentile king, without priests to consult or an army to fight for them. It also shows the kindness of the Lord to a portion of Abraham's seed that seems to have forgotten about him. As argued below, the book's famous silence about God is best interpreted not as a sign that God is uninvolved but as a sign that the Jews living in Persia are Jewish only in regard to their customs and ethnic identity, with no special allegiance to the God of Abraham. One consequence of their spiritual insensitivity is that the real victory God gives his people is muted and obscured. This prompts modern-day believers, who are also living in exile (cf. 1 Pet. 1:1), to consider how they can look for God's deliverance amid hostility, as well as how they can speak about God to spread his fame among the nonbelievers all around them.

Author

The author of Esther reveals nothing about himself in his text. A number of details of Persian life imply he lived there, and his concern for Purim in chapters 8–9 suggests he was Jewish. Otherwise, he obscures his own personality to focus on God's deliverance of his people.

Date and Occasion

The Persian king Ahasuerus is better known as Xerxes I, who ruled from 486 to 465 BC. ("Xerxes" and "Ahasuerus" are Greek and Hebrew renderings of his Persian name.) The book does not record the death of the king or of other major characters, but seems to have been written after Purim had been celebrated for some time (9:19). A date late in Ahasuerus's reign is perhaps the most likely time of composition.

The book's purpose is to explain the original circumstances leading to the creation of the Feast of Purim so that its meaning will never be forgotten. The author wishes his people never to lose the memory of the great deliverance that prompted the first Purim as they continue its celebration.

Genre and Literary Features

Although they are perhaps not very well known, the two most helpful genre classifications for the book of Esther are historical novella and diaspora story. To speak of Esther as a historical novella is in no way to disparage its historical veracity; three references to royal chronicles (2:23; 6:1; 10:2) imply the main events of the narrative can be verified. Rather, this term helps distinguish Esther from more straightforward accounts, such as Ezra or Nehemiah. The book's humor, vivid characterizations, and abundance of coincidences and reversals all imply the author is giving us reliable history in the form of a story. Thus we will have to attend to the book as a story, with characters and unfolding plot, to learn what the narrator would teach us.

But what kind of story is it? Elsewhere in the OT we find the dangers and possibilities of Jewish life in exile brought into sharp focus. The book of Daniel, especially chapters 1–6, is perhaps the best biblical text to compare with the book of Esther. Both books show Jews struggling in foreign settings potentially hostile to them, without the benefits of living in the Promised Land, such as a standing army, priests receiving messages from God, and so on. (The story of Joseph from Genesis may be an early precursor to this, and the noncanonical book of Tobit is another good example of a diaspora story.) Although Esther and Daniel portray God's intervention in the world in very different ways, they both focus on living wisely in exile in a way Ezra and Nehemiah (e.g.) do not, even though both Ezra and Nehemiah held high positions in foreign courts. This leads us to watch for how Esther, through its story, portrays living successfully in exile.

One important feature of this story is its tight structure. The descent of the plot to the point of most danger for the Jews is mirrored perfectly in their deliverance, with the king's sleepless night as the turning point:

(A) The greatness of Ahasuerus (1:1–2)
   (B) Two banquets (for men and women) (1:3–9)
      (C) The elevation of Haman (3:1)
         (D) The edict against the Jews (3:7–15)
            (E) Mordecai informs Esther of the plot against the Jews
               (4:1–9)
               (F) Esther's first banquet with the king and Haman (5:1–8)
                  (G) Turning point: The king's sleepless night (6:1)
               (F') Esther's second banquet with the king and Haman (7:1)
            (E') Esther informs Ahasuerus of the plot against the Jews
               (7:3–6)
         (D') The edict in favor of the Jews (7:7–8:14)
      (C') The elevation of Mordecai (8:15–17)

(B') Two banquets on the two days of Purim (9:1–32)

(A') The greatness of Mordecai (10:1–3)[1]

This chiastic structure is built around a series of feasts located at significant junctures in the story. When Vashti refuses to parade herself during the book's first two feasts, she loses her position as queen, allowing Esther to be crowned in her place, with another banquet (2:18). Haman is exposed during Esther's second banquet, while Mordecai's promotion is accompanied with feasting (8:17). Finally, as noted above, the book's happy ending is celebrated with the Feast of Purim. The book's tight structure serves to clarify its major theme: the perfectly symmetrical reversal of the Jews' fortunes (9:1, 22). The story's feasts do the same, each showing some reversal in power.

The terse and unadorned style of earlier biblical narrative is not reproduced in Esther. The narrator expresses himself in a more convoluted way, perhaps in imitation (or parody?) of the way language was used in the court.

Finally, it should be noted the book is one of the most humorous in the Bible. At several points in the story it is difficult not to laugh at King Ahasuerus and his bumbling, ineffective pomposity or at Haman's being hung on the very gallows he built for Mordecai. The juxtaposition of these comic elements and Haman's terrifying hatred for the Jews is, of course, unexpected. But this may be part of the narrator's strategy: although there is nothing funny about Haman and his hatred of the Jews, the comic interludes in the book give a kind of release. The book prompts us to laugh even amid the most frightening of situations, as deliverance is worked out.

Theology of Esther

The central theological theme of the book of Esther is the deliverance of God's people—and not just their deliverance, but the complete and total reversal of their plight. The book begins with the Jews of Persia powerless before the murderous designs of Haman, who holds authority second only to the king. The exact reversals detailed in the book show the author's worldview: deliverance will come for the Jews (4:14).

Connected to the theme of deliverance is that of providence. Too many coincidences and reversals happen at exactly the right time to attribute the Jews' deliverance to anything other than God's control of all things, no matter how small: the Jewish Esther being chosen out of (probably) hundreds of young women to become queen; the king's sleepless night, during which he is reminded of Mordecai's unrewarded service; Haman being hung on the gallows he built for Mordecai; the king's entrance just as Haman is imploring Esther, as well as his mistaken assumption that Haman is assaulting her. God is, of course, never directly mentioned as acting on his people's behalf. Esther is well known for being the only book in the Bible

---

1 Adapted from Michael V. Fox, *Character and Ideology in the Book of Esther*, 2nd ed. (Grand Rapids, MI: Eerdmans: 2001), 157.

that never directly mentions God. The reason for this is discussed below, under Interpretive Challenges; at this point, it need only be said that it is impossible to avoid the conclusion God is at work to save his people through the power politics of the Persian court.

The book's ending gives much attention to celebrating the deliverance of the Jews at the Feast of Purim. The Jews do not just talk about the actions of Mordecai and Esther, but reenact and embody their deliverance with joyful celebration and gifts to the poor (9:22). Although the feasts and festivals of the old covenant are not binding on new covenant believers, the new covenant does have two rituals (baptism and the Lord's Supper) that symbolically and joyfully reenact God's deliverance of us in Christ.

Another theme of the book is Mordecai and Esther's conduct in the Persian court. Although this commentary will argue that Mordecai and Esther fail to capitalize on a significant blessing in their deliverance from Haman's plot, this does not negate how both show courage and skill throughout the story. This is easiest to see when Mordecai exposes a plot to kill the king—probably at some personal danger to himself—and continues uncomplaining in his work when this action goes unrewarded. For her part, Esther plays her hypersensitive, deeply unwise husband perfectly, avoiding a number of pitfalls as she exposes the plot of the king's favorite adviser—a plot the king had approved. Without whitewashing the imperfections of either character, the narrator seems to be showing us the skill and tact that living in exile will sometimes require, especially when God's people fall under hostile attack.

It is impossible to miss God's love and care for Abraham's seed even when they no longer remember him. The Lord's ancient promises to bless those who bless his people and curse those who curse them still hold true—even if the Persian Jews fail to embody fully the blessing to the nations that the ancient promise to Abraham suggests (Gen. 12:2–3). The string of coincidences in the story shows that the deliverance of the Persian Jews is not simply a result of the strategizing of Mordecai and Esther. God is at work to deliver his people, even though he remains unrecognized by the book's characters.

Finally, it should be noted that the narrator focuses on the relationship between the sexes at a number of points in his story. Like the rest of the ancient world, Persia was a highly patriarchal society. We see a law made that all wives must obey their husbands (Est. 1:20), and Esther is certainly not consulted when taken into the king's harem for the rest of her life (note the passive verbs in 2:8, 16). In fact, part of the book's portrayal involves a none-too-subtle mocking of Persian patriarchy; as the commentary will show, King Ahasuerus, although obsessed with his own honor, never acts or even seems to think for himself, but is always acted upon by those around him—most significantly by Esther, who knows how to flatter her husband to save her people (7:3–6; 8:4–6). It is difficult not to laugh at how threatened the king and his advisers feel by Vashti's refusal to obey (ch. 1), or how they advertise their powerlessness through their decree meant to assert male authority. Although it would be incorrect to set the book of Esther against the apostles' statements on male headship (Eph. 5:22–23; 1 Pet. 3:1–6) or their limitation of some roles in ministry to men (1 Tim. 2:12), Esther does contribute to the Bible's portrayal of male-female relationships by showing Esther (together with Mordecai) working to save her people in a context in which women had virtually no power. The narrator does not want us to miss the thoughtless buffoonery and pomposity of the Persian royal male elite—a carelessness that is potentially lethal. The shifting relationship between Mordecai and Esther, in which Esther will come to take the lead, will be noted throughout the commentary.

Relationship to the Rest of the Bible and to Christ

The salvation of God's people from their enemies is a constant theme in the OT: in the exodus from Egypt, the spiritually empowered warlords of the book of Judges, and Saul's and David's wars with the Philistines (to name only a few examples), the Bible repeatedly shows God saving his people from those who would destroy them. The book of Esther offers a variation on this theme, showing God's deliverance when his people are outside the Promised Land, living in a society hostile to them: it is a deliverance worked out entirely "behind the scenes," in the normal course of the tumult of the Persian court. Even if life for the Jews in Persia was vastly different from that of their ancestors, the same promise of God's deliverance held true.

Although God's people in the new covenant are not constituted as a political body nor engage in physical warfare, the same promise speaks to us as we endure this present evil age (Phil. 1:28; 2 Thess. 1:5–10; Rev. 19:11–21). This is probably the main connection of the book of Esther with the NT: although new covenant believers are not promised complete deliverance from every earthly trial (Rom. 8:35–36), the Lord Jesus does deliver his people from spiritual death within "this present darkness" (Eph. 6:12), even as we live in it. In the greatest reversal of fortunes imaginable, we who deserve death and judgment receive the opposite from God, who is working to deliver us even in our darkest hour. The joy of Purim is a hint of a greater celebration at a greater feast after a greater act of deliverance from a greater enemy (Rev. 19:1–8).

Beyond this, not many specific typological connections between characters and events in Esther and the NT can be found. It is difficult to see Esther prefiguring Christ as she wins a beauty contest and sleeps with a man before she is officially married to him. Mordecai is an admirable man in many ways, but with the possible exception of his being honored publicly (6:10–11), at no point does he adumbrate that greater coming Savior. The contrasts between them and Christ are more significant than the similarities.

Preaching from Esther

The book of Esther can be preached profitably in at least three ways. First and most important, pastors can point to the overarching biblical theme of God's deliverance and how it is worked out through a string of coincidences none of the characters recognize, through the work of God's people living and working in a pagan society. It may even help to awaken modern congregations to our difficult position as the NT describes it, as exiles (1 Pet. 1:1) vulnerable to slander and mistreatment (1 Pet. 3:9–17).

A second way the book of Esther is helpful for God's new covenant people is in its examination of what it looks like to live wisely in exile. Although postexilic books like Esther, Ezra, Nehemiah, and Daniel in no way condemn living and working in pagan society, Esther especially portrays that society as potentially dangerous. Mordecai's exposure of a plot on the king's life is significant in this regard (2:21–23): Mordecai shows loyalty to a king undeserving of it, and does not complain when passed over for a promotion. When Mordecai finally is honored for exposing the plot, no reaction on his part is recorded; he simply goes back to work (6:12). For her part, Esther skillfully manipulates the king, exposing Haman without bruising Ahasuerus's hypersensitive ego. In Mordecai and Esther, we see the kind of courage and resourcefulness living wisely in exile may sometimes require.

Finally, the way Mordecai is repeatedly identified as Jewish when under attack from Haman (3:4, 6, 10, 13; 5:13; 6:10, 13) warns us against any trace of anti-Semitism in our churches. Although national and ethnic identity does not determine our standing before God (Matt. 21:33–46), his promises to his ethnic people remain unbroken, so that all Israel will be saved (Rom. 11:26)—however one might interpret Paul's words. Haman's designs against the Jews of his day returned on his own head—a clear warning to anyone who would scheme against God's people!

Interpretive Challenges

Clearly the greatest interpretive challenge of the book of Esther is the absence of any explicit mention of God. Nor, in fact, is there any mention of Torah, the Promised Land, the temple, or other heroes from the OT. Although a fast is called in chapter 4, no mention is made of prayer during the fast or of worship of God after it. There is no indication that Mordecai and Esther keep dietary laws or observe the Sabbath; indeed, it is not clear if the other Persians even knew they were Jewish. Surely, if they had been keeping these laws, they would have distinguished themselves from the Persians much earlier in the story. The books of Ezra, Nehemiah, and Daniel, written at a similar stage in redemptive history, form stark contrasts to Esther in this regard. How is this silence on all matters theological to be interpreted?

Certainly God does sometimes work in quiet and unobtrusive ways: in Judges 14:4, for example, we are explicitly told that none of the characters in the story realize events are playing out as they are because God is secretly ordering them. Doubtless the narrator of Esther is, at least in part, making a similar implication about the quietness and subtlety of God's work by never mentioning him directly. Furthermore, if we are meant to assume God's activity even when he is unmentioned (as I believe the narrator means us to), perhaps we are meant to assume the same about the religious behavior of the characters. This is what ancient translations did. The Aramaic Targums (later translations and embellishments of the biblical text for Jews who did not speak Hebrew) and the Greek Septuagint of Esther add much religious behavior and speech we would expect from these characters; for instance, the Septuagint records a long prayer by Mordecai after Esther tells him to call a fast (4:16), which is followed by a prayer by Esther where she says she hates sleeping with the king and keeps the dietary restrictions of the law. Similarly, the first Targum to Esther adds that God kept sleep from the king in chapter 6 because of the prayers of Jewish women. But even if these translators simply added text to bring Esther in line with their expectations, it may be that the narrator assumed we would understand (for instance) that Esther and Mordecai were praying fervently when it looked as if Haman might get his wish. Another example of this kind of assumption is found in Mordecai's theologically fraught statement in 4:14. As will be discussed in the commentary, Mordecai uses a theologically loaded word to express his certainty that the Jews will be delivered. Perhaps we are meant to read this in a way similar to Paul's expecting that the Philippians' prayers "will turn out for [his] deliverance" (Phil. 1:19)—clearly, though not explicitly, referring to God's action on his behalf.

The problem with this reading is the sheer number of places God's name is not mentioned where we would expect it to be. By the book's end, the silence has become deafening. If the narrator is asking us to assume that Mordecai and Esther act as devoutly as we would expect, he is asking too much. For instance, Esther apparently does not keep any of the laws that would distinguish her as a Jew in the king's harem (in fact, she never self-identifies as Jewish), even sleeping with a man to see if she pleases him (Est. 2:16–17). No mention of prayer is recorded during the fast (4:16), nor is any mention of praise made after the Jews' fortunes are reversed (9:1). A new festival is added to the Jewish ritual calendar without divine authorization (9:20–23). The book ends by speaking only of Mordecai's greatness—not God's (10:2–3). Even the conversion of some of the Persians in 8:17 is ambiguous; as will be discussed in the commentary on that passage, this probably means only that some Persians adopted Jewish customs. It is possible, in fact, to read this book as a story of Jews who are only culturally Jewish—who have kept some of their ancestral traditions but have lost any knowledge of the God of Abraham. (This would not, in itself, make the book secular, only the characters.) It appears that Purim could be celebrated without any specifically religious activity (similar to how Christmas is celebrated in some homes). The book ends not with praise of God from his people and surrounding Gentiles, but with the Jews safe and secure—a happy ending, to be sure, but one that could have been better (cf. Isa. 45:22–23).

This suggests the narrator is guiding us to the uncomfortable conclusion that the deliverance he records was a real victory, but only a partial one. In the larger context of Scripture, it is impossible not to see God at work "behind the scenes" to deliver his people through Mordecai and Esther. But what if the military and cultural victory for the Jews of Persia had been a spiritual one as well? What if the book ended with many Persians explicitly aligning themselves with the God of Mordecai and Esther, with Mordecai working for the good, not just of his own people but of the Gentiles as well? This, in turn, raises the issue of how God's people can most fully glorify God when he works on their behalf. A number of OT texts emphasize the speech of God's people in praise of the God who intervenes for them (Pss. 96:7–10; 145:6–7; Isa. 43:10–11; 45:20–25; 66:20). Without denigrating the happy deliverance God worked through his courageous servants Esther and Mordecai, it is worth asking how we can most fully exploit God's deliverance of his people so that the interests of his kingdom are best served. We will wrestle with this ambiguity at numerous points in the commentary.

A second difficulty in reading Esther is the moral ambiguity of its heroes and the violence in the story. Mordecai acts sensibly and selflessly, both as a Persian bureaucrat and on behalf of his people, with one exception: his refusal to bow to Haman in chapter 3. Mordecai is probably refusing to do so as a matter of principle: as discussed in the commentary, Mordecai's reasons for not bowing, although not explicit in the text, probably have to do with Haman's being an Agagite, a descendant of the Amalekite king Agag, whom Saul spared in 1 Samuel 15. (That Mordecai is a descendant of Kish, Saul's father, strengthens this connection.) Mordecai's sense of loyalty to his people probably made it difficult for him to genuflect before this Amalekite, with their ancient hostility to Israel. But even if Mordecai's refusal is understandable and in some sense justified, it is still worth asking whether it was wise. His action endangers every Jew in Persia. As a government official, Mordecai probably had to genuflect before many superiors, irrespective of their moral quality. This issue will be discussed further in the commentary.

Esther, for her part, does act with courage and great skill on behalf of her people in chapters 5–7. Before that, however, we are told nothing of her feelings about being taken into the king's harem and sleeping with the king: although she might have loathed her time there, it is possible she enjoyed being part of the beauty contest. But perhaps more troubling is Esther's request of the king for a second day of fighting in 9:13. Although Esther's other requests find moral justification and are harder to criticize, there seems to be no reason for this second day of fighting beyond revenge, for the Jews' enemies had been given only one day to attack the Jews. Esther seems cruel and acts in a way not dissimilar to the enemies of the Jews. The book bearing her name shows God working his deliverance through entirely imperfect people, prompting the reader to reflect on how God's acts of deliverance for his people living in exile might be better stewarded, not in vengeance upon our persecutors but in speaking about the God who works such deliverance.

Outline

I. Setup and Background: Queen Vashti's Deposal (1:1–22)
   A. Ahasuerus's Feast for His Officials and People (1:1–9)
   B. Vashti's Refusal of the King (1:10–12)
   C. The Edict against Vashti (1:13–22)

ESTHER 1:1–22

1 Now in the days of Ahasuerus, the Ahasuerus who reigned from India to Ethiopia over 127 provinces, ²in those days when King Ahasuerus sat on his royal throne in Susa, the citadel, ³in the third year of his reign he gave a feast for all his officials and servants. The army of Persia and Media and the nobles and governors of the provinces were before him, ⁴while he showed the riches of his royal glory and the splendor and pomp of his greatness for many days, 180 days. ⁵And when these days were completed, the king gave for all the people present in Susa the citadel, both great and small, a feast lasting for seven days in the court of the garden of the king's palace. ⁶There were white cotton curtains and violet hangings fastened with cords of fine linen and purple to silver rods[1] and marble pillars, and also couches of gold and silver on a mosaic pavement of porphyry, marble, mother-of-pearl, and precious stones. ⁷Drinks were served in golden vessels, vessels of different kinds, and the royal wine was lavished according to the bounty of the king. ⁸And drinking was according to this edict: "There is no compulsion." For the king had given orders to all the staff of his palace to do as each man desired. ⁹Queen Vashti also gave a feast for the women in the palace that belonged to King Ahasuerus.

¹⁰On the seventh day, when the heart of the king was merry with wine, he commanded Mehuman, Biztha, Harbona, Bigtha and Abagtha, Zethar and Carkas, the seven eunuchs who served in the presence of King Ahasuerus, ¹¹to bring Queen Vashti before the king with her royal crown,[2] in order to show the peoples and the princes her beauty, for she was lovely to look at. ¹²But Queen Vashti refused to come at the king's command delivered by the eunuchs. At this the king became enraged, and his anger burned within him.

¹³Then the king said to the wise men who knew the times (for this was the king's procedure toward all who were versed in law and judgment, ¹⁴the men next to him being Carshena, Shethar, Admatha, Tarshish, Meres, Marsena, and Memucan, the seven princes of Persia and Media, who saw the king's face, and sat first in the kingdom): ¹⁵"According to the law, what is to be done to Queen Vashti, because she has not performed the command of King Ahasuerus delivered by the eunuchs?" ¹⁶Then Memucan said in the presence of the king and the officials, "Not only against the king has Queen Vashti done wrong, but also against all the officials and all the peoples who are in all the provinces of King Ahasuerus. ¹⁷For the queen's behavior will be made known to all women, causing them to look at their husbands with contempt,[3] since they will say, 'King Ahasuerus commanded Queen Vashti to be brought before him, and she did not come.' ¹⁸This very day the noble women of Persia and Media who have heard of the queen's behavior will say the same to all the king's officials, and there will be contempt and wrath in plenty. ¹⁹If it please the king, let a royal order go out from him, and let it be written among the laws of the Persians and the Medes

so that it may not be repealed, that Vashti is never again to come before King Ahasuerus. And let the king give her royal position to another who is better than she. ²⁰ So when the decree made by the king is proclaimed throughout all his kingdom, for it is vast, all women will give honor to their husbands, high and low alike." ²¹ This advice pleased the king and the princes, and the king did as Memucan proposed. ²² He sent letters to all the royal provinces, to every province in its own script and to every people in its own language, that every man be master in his own household and speak according to the language of his people.

¹ Or *rings* ² Or *headdress* ³ Hebrew *to disdain their husbands in their eyes*

Section Overview

The narrator shows how the way was opened for Esther to become queen after Vashti offended her husband. The narrator's portrayal of the pompous self-importance of the Persian court is, at this stage in the story, merely funny; but we already see the potential for danger in the way women are treated and in the foolishness of Persia's rulers.

Section Outline

I. Setup and Background: Queen Vashti's Deposal (1:1–22)
    A. Ahasuerus's Feast for His Officials and People (1:1–9)
    B. Vashti's Refusal of the King (1:10–12)
    C. The Edict against Vashti (1:13–22)

Comment

1:1–4 The book's first sentence is one of its most convoluted. Instead of simply telling us of the king's feast, the narrator sets its context by showing the vast extent of Ahasuerus's kingdom: India and Cush ("Ethiopia") formed the eastern and southern boundaries of the OT's world. Furthermore, with all the complex bureaucracy 127 provinces would require, this kingdom is the opposite of some rural backwater. The second verse focuses on the king of this enormous empire. We are to imagine the secure and glorious rule of this king in the largest and most important part of his kingdom.

King Ahasuerus holds a feast for the officials in his court and army (v. 3). The many classes of royal servants and soldiers hint at the massive undertaking this party must have been. But this feast is not an act of goodwill on Ahasuerus's part: he is showing off; verse 4 might be woodenly translated, "[Ahasuerus] showed the wealth of the glory of his kingdom and the pomp of the splendor of his greatness many days, 180 days." Again, this protracted phrasing implies the wealth, luxury, and hedonistic excess of the Persian court. The purpose of this huge party, involving hundreds of people, is nothing more than pompous royal self-display. And it goes on for 180 days—half a year, in which the government of one of the largest kingdoms imaginable is doing nothing but partying.

1:5–8 Having completed his party for the upper echelon of Persian society, Ahasuerus throws another party for everyone in the capital. If the first party involved hundreds, this would have involved thousands. The narrator scans the scene like a cinematographer: the palace's inner garden is surrounded by curtains of the richest material, hung on silver and marble frames (vv. 5–6a). The furniture is such as only a king could afford (v. 6b), and the cups are made of gold (v. 7). Not only that, but the king gives everyone an open bar; at royal expense, for a full week, everyone drinks as much as he wants (v. 8). These details show the purpose of this party is the same as the first: pompous self-display at a level of excess difficult to imagine. Already the narrator is guiding us to form a certain impression of the context in which Mordecai and Esther live: although one might be impressed by the wealth of the empire, one does not admire it. Verse 8 also gives the first hint of Ahasuerus's passivity; although this example is relatively trivial, it is the first of many in which he lets others do as they please.

1:9 Vashti also holds a feast, this one for the women attending her, in a different part of the palace. Although she will soon distinguish herself from everyone else in the court, at the beginning of the story she is part of it.

1:10–11 With the scene set, we are told of the conflict setting the entire story in motion. The king has been at his wine for a full week (v. 10) and thus is hardly sober when he orders his wife to show herself to everyone. The added detail in verse 10 that this command is communicated by the king's closest eunuchs, all of whom are listed by name, prolongs the note of hollow grandeur and labored ostentation sounded throughout this chapter. The narrator suggests Vashti is being invited to the party not as an equal but as an object: the verb "to show" in verse 11 is the same as in verse 4, implying she will be shown off like the king's wealth. That she is to appear wearing her crown confirms this, as is the stated purpose of her appearance: to display her physical attractiveness. Just as Ahasuerus wanted to show off the wealth of his kingdom, so he wants to show off his wife. He apparently thinks of the two as being in the same basic category: his property.

1:12 But Vashti refuses. Her reasons are not stated. While one can occasionally find statements in commentaries that she disobeys out of arrogance, it is easy to sympathize with her decision not to strut in front of a large group of drunken men who want only to ogle her. What kind of husband would ask this of his wife? We instantly learn, however, the consequences of crossing Ahasuerus: Vashti's preservation of her dignity wins for her only the fiercest anger. The terms used for this anger often portray the most solemn acts of judgment by God (Ps. 89:46; Isa. 64:9; Jer. 4:4; Lam. 5:22; but cf. also Pharaoh's anger in Gen. 40:2). The use of these terms thus gives the king's wrath an ironic twist: God has good reasons for his anger, but Ahasuerus does not.

1:13–15 The king speaks to his advisers about his "problem." We will repeatedly see Ahasuerus unable to act for himself, always relying on others to do his thinking for him. We should note as well another long, complex sentence describing the king's counselors, their role and status, and the king's habit of turning to them, all before hearing what the king says in verse 15. It is, by now, difficult to miss the grandiose complexity of the royal palace. That these men see the face of the king (v. 14) means they can approach the throne uninvited, a privilege extended to no one else (4:11). They also understand the times and are "versed in law and judgment," being legal experts with their finger on the pulse of the nation. This sounds impressive until we hear their advice for resolving this "crisis."

1:16–20 The king states his pseudoproblem in terms of official royal policy: instead of seeking relationship advice, he asks what should be done with this rebel according to legal principle (v. 15). Memucan's interpretation of the incident and recommendation for resolving it reveal a good deal about the Persian court and the men who run it. Instead of finding a way to smooth over this ill-advised move on the king's part, Memucan's first statement could be translated as saying Vashti has "sinned" against the king (ESV "done wrong"; this very common root is used, e.g., by David for his sin in Ps. 51:2, 5, 9). According to Memucan, any refusal of any command from husband to wife is tantamount to a moral fault. Not only that, Memucan says, but Vashti has wronged everyone in the entire empire (Est. 1:16)! This "sin" is so great because, after everyone hears what Vashti has done, no woman will ever be respectful to her husband again, only treating him contemptuously (v. 17). This very day, Memucan warns, a vast rebellion against the established social order is beginning in which propriety and harmony in home and state will descend into nothing but bitter contempt (v. 18). This is, of course, a panicky and frantic overinterpretation of the incident. Vashti is not dishonoring her husband by refusing to come; *he* has dishonored *her* with his request. It is also difficult to believe his fear is realistic—but if it is, what does this say about the level of respect among Persian wives for their husbands? These men are obsessed with honor, defined in terms of absolute obedience from their wives, so that any failure dishonors the husband. The narrator is none-too-subtly showing how fragile and insecure Persian male dominance is, easily threatened by even a reasonable refusal from a woman.

What is to be done to stave off this impending disaster? The king must assert his authority by banishing and deposing his wife (v. 19). Since she refused to come when summoned, she must never be allowed into the king's presence again and her position must be given to another. Only then (according to Memucan) can this crisis be averted and order be restored so that wives honor their husbands (v. 20). The king's edict must be published in every last corner of the kingdom and can never be repealed—an idiosyncrasy of Persian law (cf. Dan. 6:8, 12, 15) that will present problems later in the story.

The narrator's exposure of royal Persian patriarchy verges on satire as we read Memucan's proposed edict. Most humorous of all is that Memucan's advice, instead of quelling this supposed vast rebellion, ensures that every last citizen of

Persia knows that the man in control of 127 provinces has been thwarted by his wife. Seeking to suppress the implications of this rumor, his advice will instead broadcast it. Furthermore, do these men really think something as beautiful and complex as a respectful marriage can be created by fiat? And how do they expect it to be enforced? One also notices that the only qualification for a queen to surpass Vashti is total obedience to the king's every whim. The "honor" (Est. 1:20) they seek from women is hollow, and the way they go about securing it empties it of any meaning.

1:21–22 Ahasuerus, of course, sees none of this; he acts, literally, "according to the word of Memucan" (v. 21), again showing his passivity. Messengers are sent to proclaim the new edict everywhere. We learn that a number of ethnic groups with their own languages live in Persia, a point to which we will return. A final humorous touch is added when the decree is summarized according to men ruling their homes and speaking their own language. Although some marriages may have led to two languages being spoken at home, this was hardly a burning issue of state.

Response

Thus far in the story, the path has been cleared for Esther to rise to royalty and work on behalf of her people in their most desperate time of need. But with the exception of the king, we have not been introduced to any of the story's main characters. Furthermore, the events of this chapter could have been summarized much more briefly. Why are we given this extended tour of the soap opera of the Persian court?

The narrator apparently wants us to see in detail the kind of difficulties our characters will have to face. The king is pompous, superficial, frivolous, unwise, easily angered, and pleased with ridiculous advice. Although he is the supreme authority, he is passive and open to all kinds of outside influence, and will legislate unchangeable laws without much thought. One also sees how it is not justice that drives Persian laws but the needs of its insecure ruler. We are further shown how the Persian court is not an easy place for women—and everything in this story will depend on Esther and her ability to manipulate a man obsessed with receiving honor and submission from women. In many ways, this world is also silly—but those familiar with the story already know how easy it will be for horrifying violence to break out.

The narrator is also setting up a contrast between the strategies of Vashti and Esther. The reader is shown how badly Ahasuerus and those around him react to an independent-minded woman. Esther will have to be much more cunning if she is to save the lives of her people.

Into this unstable world of excess, a world sometimes ridiculous, sometimes frightening, Mordecai and Esther must make their way as they try to achieve something obviously good, but with which no one will help. Our situation as new covenant believers, living and working in the world within this present age, is no different. Mordecai and Esther are in no way condemned in the book for being involved in the Persian court, but the narrator wants us to be fully aware of the real nature of their environment, however much it might pass itself off as a great and glorious kingdom.

ESTHER 2:1–23

2 After these things, when the anger of King Ahasuerus had abated, he remembered Vashti and what she had done and what had been decreed against her. ²Then the king's young men who attended him said, "Let beautiful young virgins be sought out for the king. ³And let the king appoint officers in all the provinces of his kingdom to gather all the beautiful young virgins to the harem in Susa the citadel, under custody of Hegai, the king's eunuch, who is in charge of the women. Let their cosmetics be given them. ⁴And let the young woman who pleases the king¹ be queen instead of Vashti." This pleased the king, and he did so.

⁵Now there was a Jew in Susa the citadel whose name was Mordecai, the son of Jair, son of Shimei, son of Kish, a Benjaminite, ⁶who had been carried away from Jerusalem among the captives carried away with Jeconiah king of Judah, whom Nebuchadnezzar king of Babylon had carried away. ⁷He was bringing up Hadassah, that is Esther, the daughter of his uncle, for she had neither father nor mother. The young woman had a beautiful figure and was lovely to look at, and when her father and her mother died, Mordecai took her as his own daughter. ⁸So when the king's order and his edict were proclaimed, and when many young women were gathered in Susa the citadel in custody of Hegai, Esther also was taken into the king's palace and put in custody of Hegai, who had charge of the women. ⁹And the young woman pleased him and won his favor. And he quickly provided her with her cosmetics and her portion of food, and with seven chosen young women from the king's palace, and advanced her and her young women to the best place in the harem. ¹⁰Esther had not made known her people or kindred, for Mordecai had commanded her not to make it known. ¹¹And every day Mordecai walked in front of the court of the harem to learn how Esther was and what was happening to her.

¹²Now when the turn came for each young woman to go in to King Ahasuerus, after being twelve months under the regulations for the women, since this was the regular period of their beautifying, six months with oil of myrrh and six months with spices and ointments for women— ¹³when the young woman went in to the king in this way, she was given whatever she desired to take with her from the harem to the king's palace. ¹⁴In the evening she would go in, and in the morning she would return to the second harem in custody of Shaashgaz, the king's eunuch, who was in charge of the concubines. She would not go in to the king again, unless the king delighted in her and she was summoned by name.

15 When the turn came for Esther the daughter of Abihail the uncle of Mordecai, who had taken her as his own daughter, to go in to the king, she asked for nothing except what Hegai the king's eunuch, who had charge of the women, advised. Now Esther was winning favor in the eyes of all who saw her. 16 And when Esther was taken to King Ahasuerus, into his royal palace, in the tenth month, which is the month of Tebeth, in the seventh year of his reign, 17 the king loved Esther more than all the women, and she won grace and favor in his sight more than all the virgins, so that he set the royal crown[2] on her head and made her queen instead of Vashti. 18 Then the king gave a great feast for all his officials and servants; it was Esther's feast. He also granted a remission of taxes to the provinces and gave gifts with royal generosity.

19 Now when the virgins were gathered together the second time, Mordecai was sitting at the king's gate. 20 Esther had not made known her kindred or her people, as Mordecai had commanded her, for Esther obeyed Mordecai just as when she was brought up by him. 21 In those days, as Mordecai was sitting at the king's gate, Bigthan and Teresh, two of the king's eunuchs, who guarded the threshold, became angry and sought to lay hands on King Ahasuerus. 22 And this came to the knowledge of Mordecai, and he told it to Queen Esther, and Esther told the king in the name of Mordecai. 23 When the affair was investigated and found to be so, the men were both hanged on the gallows.[3] And it was recorded in the book of the chronicles in the presence of the king.

[1] Hebrew *who is good in the eyes of the king* [2] Or *headdress* [3] Or *wooden beam* or *stake*; Hebrew *tree* or *wood*. This Persian execution practice involved affixing or impaling a person on a stake or pole (compare Ezra 6:11)

Section Overview

We are introduced to two main characters in the story, Mordecai and Esther, and we see Esther rise from a position of total obscurity to become queen. Although God is clearly at work in Esther's life, the way the author tells this part of his story raises some questions about these two members of God's people.

Section Outline

> II. Esther Becomes Queen (2:1–23)
>> A. The Beauty Contest (2:1–4)
>> B. Introduction of Esther and Mordecai (2:5–7)
>> C. Esther's Success in the Contest (2:8–20)
>> D. Mordecai's Rescue of the King (2:21–23)

Comment

2:1 The beginning of this chapter is similar to the end of chapter 1: the king reacts to his wife (this time in sadness, not anger) and is told by others what to do. There is no remorse from the king after his anger clears: he only remembers what she did (not how he reacted) and what had been decreed about her (even though he approved the decree).

2:2–4 As always, Ahasuerus is told what to do by others: a national beauty pageant should be held to choose a new queen. Reconciling with Vashti, who has violated the king's fragile and oversensitive sense of honor, is apparently out of the question. Once again the silly ostentation of the Persian Empire is on full display.

2:5 Our two heroes are introduced. The first thing we learn about Mordecai is that he is a Jew. Although this designation will take on increasing weight as Haman's hatred focuses on him, at this point in the story it serves only to identify him as one more minority in an empire that is home to many non-Persians (1:22). His genealogy also identifies him as a son of Kish. This connection with King Saul (Kish's son) will become important later in the story.

2:6 Three times we are told Mordecai had been among those "carried away" in the exile, even though the first clause would have been sufficient to communicate that fact. This helps define Mordecai's precarious and vulnerable position in Persia. He is not there by choice and has no recourse to any of the resources Israelites enjoyed in the Promised Land. It might be significant that no desire to return to Israel or grief or worry over its fate is ever registered by Mordecai, even though Cyrus, an earlier Persian king, had already allowed for Jews to return (cf. Neh. 1:4 for a stark contrast). These concerns might have been dear to Mordecai's heart, but we are never told of them. Despite the book's support for the work of God's people in and for a pagan society, this silence is noticeable.

2:7 Esther is introduced, first by her Jewish name (Hadassah, meaning "myrtle") and then by her Babylonian name, derived from either the Mesopotamian goddess Ishtar or the Persian word for "star." She is described only in relation to her physical beauty—qualifying her for Ahasuerus's contest—and in relation to her cousin who had adopted her.

2:8 Esther is taken into the harem for the process of beautification. The passive verb is important: her wishes are not consulted and, in fact, are not even known. It could be that she had received a wonderful spiritual upbringing from her cousin and that harem life was therefore tantamount to torture for her. On the other hand, she might have thought all of her dreams were coming true. We are told nothing.

2:9 Esther wins the attention and affection of the chief eunuch, who singles her out from probably hundreds of young women for special treatment. This reminds us of Joseph (Gen. 39:2, 23) and Daniel (Dan. 1:17–20) and prompts us to interpret Esther's success as being from God, raising our expectations that God will work through Esther in redemptive ways, even if, unlike in Genesis 39 and Daniel 1, he is not explicitly mentioned.

2:10–11 Another question about the characters' motivation confronts us: Why does Mordecai tell Esther to keep her Jewish identity a secret? (Note, again, that this is phrased in terms of ethnic identity and not spiritual allegiance.) A cynical reading might suggest Mordecai is worried about ruining Esther's chances in the beauty contest and wants a high-placed insider in the royal court for the good of his own people. But Jewishness as such does not seem to have provided any obstacle to living or working in Persia; outside of Haman's scheming, it is never a particular problem when Mordecai reveals he is Jewish, nor is it an impediment in other postexilic books. Persia as a whole does not appear to have been an anti-Semitic place (cf. comment on 3:15). It is probably more likely that Mordecai understands the unstable and unfair nature of the court and is worried about possible persecution of minorities. As it turns out, this worry is well founded, but it will be Mordecai who provokes the wrong party.

2:12–14 The particular process of the beauty contest is explained. After an opulent beauty treatment extending an entire year, the contestant is allowed whatever she wants to help her chances of being chosen as queen. (We are not told what the young women would take with them to the king's palace; perhaps it was special clothing or aphrodisiacs.) A single night would be spent with the king, after which the woman would pass to the custody of another eunuch in the harem. There she would spend her life unless the king decided to pick her as queen. We learned in verses 2–3 that the main qualification for this contest was physical beauty; now we learn what "pleasing the king" (v. 4) actually involves: pleasing the king in bed. We also learn the incredibly slim odds of Esther ever seeing the king again after that first night.

2:15–16 When it is Esther's turn, she asks for no help beyond what her handler recommends. Since this is followed immediately by a statement of her finding favor not just in the eyes of Hegai (v. 9) but from everyone who sees her (again, the text focuses on physical appearance), this should be interpreted as another sign of her success—Esther is different from the other women, who were bringing whatever they thought could help them please the king sexually. As before, however, Esther's success in pleasing the Persian king in bed creates an ironic contrast with other heroes to whom God granted success in pagan settings, such as Joseph and Daniel. Although God will be at work to save many lives through Esther (cf. Gen. 45:7), and although Esther was not given a choice in the matter, there is a clear contrast with Joseph refusing Potiphar's wife (Genesis 39) and Daniel and his friends refusing normal Babylonian meals.

Esther is again identified according to her Jewish ancestry and her relation to Mordecai (Est. 2:15a), even though this information repeats what we were recently told (v. 7). Registering her Jewish ancestry as she goes to Ahasuerus might produce the effect of making her night as a sexual toy of a pagan king even more jarring and unpalatable. Notice, however, that the information given relates only to the men in control of her life: her deceased father, the cousin who had adopted her, and then the king. The repetition in verses 15–16 of the verb "take" from verse 8 creates a contrast with Mordecai's adopting her: Mordecai took her in, but now she is taken to the king. Esther is moving from the authority of Mordecai to that of the king. Esther is passive throughout, receptive and pliable to whoever stands over her, whether her cousin, the king, or his eunuchs.

2:17–18 The original terms of the contest involved pleasing the king in physical attractiveness (v. 4) or in bed (v. 14). Although Esther clearly fulfills both of these conditions, we are told not that she has fulfilled these conditions but that the king loves her. This connotes sincere attention and affection (cf. Gen. 24:67; 29:18; Song 1:7). Instead of being only a sexual plaything, Esther unexpectedly receives a genuine level of care from the king. Without delay, she is crowned queen with a great feast. The book's first feast led to Vashti's demotion; the book's second feast is Esther's promotion in place of Vashti.

The mention of tax relief could have been omitted with no loss to the narrative. There are a few hints in the book that the success and advancement of the Jews will benefit the empire as a whole (cf. comment on Est. 3:15); the end of 2:18 should probably be read as one more example of this.

2:19–20 Esther is now placed exactly where she needs to be for the story to unfold; although she is taken from the king's presence to the "second harem" (v. 19a AT; cf. Hb. and v. 14), she is the one person in the kingdom who will be able to foil Haman's plot. The repetition of her keeping her identity secret (v. 20a) is important in a number of ways. First and foremost, her rise to prominence has not given away her secret. Doubtless Haman would have thought twice about attacking the people group of the king's beloved wife; and if he had known, he would have been more suspicious of attending two banquets held by this Jewish queen. Verse 20 also emphasizes that even though Esther has been taken to the king, she has not forgotten Mordecai. Her new position has not broken her obedience to him. This, too, will be important once Mordecai needs Esther to influence the king.

Mordecai's position in the gate (v. 19) means he is a government bureaucrat. The gate was a large building with a number of offices serving as the administrative center of the palace.

2:21–23 In the briefest way, the writer recounts an assassination attempt on the king discovered by Mordecai and foiled. This interlude contributes to the story in several ways. In addition to underscoring the instability and danger within the Persian court, we see the first instance of Mordecai working through Esther to reach the king—a strategy that will save many Jewish lives later in the book. The traitors' execution by hanging foreshadows ominously the fate of the book's main villain. Mordecai's good deed is recorded but is unrewarded, contrary to normal Persian custom. This will allow the king to be reminded of his oversight later, at the most opportune moment (6:3). We also see Mordecai being honest and loyal to the king, irrespective of the king's faults or his treatment of Mordecai's adopted cousin. Revealing the plot also took courage—if the would-be assassins had known Mordecai was aware of their treason, his life would have been in danger. Finally, Mordecai says nothing about being passed over for a promotion or reward after this act of service to the king—he is not interested in self-promotion. Mordecai will continue to show these qualities throughout the story.

Response

The main purpose of this chapter is to position Esther in exactly the right place as the only one who can foil Haman's plot. In order to do this, the narrator must show Esther's rise from total obscurity to royalty. Now that Esther is queen, the main storyline about Haman and God's secret deliverance can proceed.

Along the way, however, we see God at work in subtle but unmistakable ways through deeply imperfect people. Esther was not the only beautiful woman in the harem, but her favor with the eunuch in charge of the harem (2:9) and everyone else who sees her (v. 15), and her winning not just the beauty contest but the king's love (v. 17), must be attributed to the working of God, who is already at work to provide deliverance for his people.

Although the author gives no explicit evaluation in these chapters, his silence raises a string of uncomfortable questions. Why is nothing recorded about Mordecai the exile's concern for or action on behalf of the postexilic community in Israel? How did Mordecai and Esther feel about her conscription into the king's beauty contest? How did Esther feel about sleeping with a man to see if he liked her? Although plausible answers can be given to some of these questions (such as Esther's secrecy about her Jewish identity), and although Mordecai and Esther act with admirable courage in some ways, it is difficult to admire them as heroes unambiguously or totally. Nevertheless, God is at work through these flawed people, even though they do not show any awareness of him.

Esther's passivity has also been noted throughout this chapter. The story will show her becoming someone who takes the lead with Mordecai and shows admirable courage and skill in exposing Haman. But we will also see Esther's new assertiveness express itself in chilling ways by the story's end. The foundation for these developments has been laid in this chapter.

ESTHER 3:1–15

3 After these things King Ahasuerus promoted Haman the Agagite, the son of Hammedatha, and advanced him and set his throne above all the officials who were with him. ² And all the king's servants who were at the king's gate bowed down and paid homage to Haman, for the king had so commanded concerning him. But Mordecai did not bow down or pay homage. ³ Then the king's servants who were at the king's gate said to Mordecai, "Why do you transgress the king's command?" ⁴ And when they spoke to him day after day and he would not listen to them, they told

Haman, in order to see whether Mordecai's words would stand, for he had told them that he was a Jew. [5] And when Haman saw that Mordecai did not bow down or pay homage to him, Haman was filled with fury. [6] But he disdained[1] to lay hands on Mordecai alone. So, as they had made known to him the people of Mordecai, Haman sought to destroy[2] all the Jews, the people of Mordecai, throughout the whole kingdom of Ahasuerus.

[7] In the first month, which is the month of Nisan, in the twelfth year of King Ahasuerus, they cast Pur (that is, they cast lots) before Haman day after day; and they cast it month after month till the twelfth month, which is the month of Adar. [8] Then Haman said to King Ahasuerus, "There is a certain people scattered abroad and dispersed among the peoples in all the provinces of your kingdom. Their laws are different from those of every other people, and they do not keep the king's laws, so that it is not to the king's profit to tolerate them. [9] If it please the king, let it be decreed that they be destroyed, and I will pay 10,000 talents[3] of silver into the hands of those who have charge of the king's business, that they may put it into the king's treasuries." [10] So the king took his signet ring from his hand and gave it to Haman the Agagite, the son of Hammedatha, the enemy of the Jews. [11] And the king said to Haman, "The money is given to you, the people also, to do with them as it seems good to you."

[12] Then the king's scribes were summoned on the thirteenth day of the first month, and an edict, according to all that Haman commanded, was written to the king's satraps and to the governors over all the provinces and to the officials of all the peoples, to every province in its own script and every people in its own language. It was written in the name of King Ahasuerus and sealed with the king's signet ring. [13] Letters were sent by couriers to all the king's provinces with instruction to destroy, to kill, and to annihilate all Jews, young and old, women and children, in one day, the thirteenth day of the twelfth month, which is the month of Adar, and to plunder their goods. [14] A copy of the document was to be issued as a decree in every province by proclamation to all the peoples to be ready for that day. [15] The couriers went out hurriedly by order of the king, and the decree was issued in Susa the citadel. And the king and Haman sat down to drink, but the city of Susa was thrown into confusion.

[1] Hebrew *disdained in his eyes* [2] Or *annihilate* [3] A *talent* was about 75 pounds or 34 kilograms

Section Overview

With the main characters in place, the main action of the story begins to unfold. When Mordecai slights Haman's pride, he plots the death of every Jew in Persia. Much to the consternation of the general populace, the king unthinkingly agrees to this.

Section Outline

III. Haman's Plot against the Jews (3:1–15)

    A. Mordecai's Refusal to Bow to Haman (3:1–6)

    B. The King Approves Haman's Plan to Exterminate the Jews (3:7–11)

    C. The Statute against the Jews (3:12–15)

Comment

3:1 We are not told why the king promotes Haman, but in a sense it does not matter to the story. (After reading Haman's rhetorical manipulation of the king in vv. 8–9, one perhaps wonders if he engineered his own promotion.) The first-time reader knows nothing about Haman and so will probably not think much of his promotion—but we will quickly learn what kind of person he is and again question Ahasuerus's judgment in promoting such a person to a high position. Haman's new position is also important because being set above all other officials means no one has the authority to counteract his plan against the Jews.

3:2 Why does Mordecai refuse to join the other bureaucrats in bowing before Haman? Commentators offer a number of suggestions. Some think Mordecai is avoiding idolatrous worship; but Mordecai is not being asked to worship a foreign god, only recognize someone in authority over him. (Why would the king have a subordinate treated like a god when the king himself is not?) The ESV nicely translates this verse as "bowed down and paid homage," but the verbs could be rendered more woodenly as "kneeled" and "prostrated/genuflected"; no worship is involved. (Naaman's request in 2 Kings 5:18 shows the physical action of the second verb.) Others wonder if Mordecai is acting in pride, but Mordecai has done well as a royal servant thus far; bowing to those in authority over him was probably a regular part of his job. It is implausible to imagine that the mere action of bowing before a superior grated Mordecai somehow.

It makes more sense to posit something particular about Haman that kept Mordecai from bowing. Mordecai may well have been exposed to Haman already and may well have understood what a dangerous man he was to hold the second highest position of authority in Persia. The fact that Haman was an Agagite, and thus an Amalekite, also surely rankled a man with such a strong sense of Jewish identity. This is, in fact, the reason Mordecai gives when the other officials ask why he disobeys the king in this matter (Est. 3:4). Thus, Mordecai's action is not to be attributed to some general churlishness or arrogance.

And yet, even if Mordecai's reasons are understandable—even if Haman is totally unworthy of respect and descended from an ancient enemy of Israel—he probably has had to bow in the past to many officials unworthy of such respect. Furthermore, although it would be completely inappropriate to "blame the victim," Mordecai's actions eventually put all the Persian Jews at risk. We have already learned from chapter 1 that this is a culture obsessed with giving and receiving honor. Even if the reader understands why Mordecai does not bow, it is difficult to admire him for it.

3:3–4 Haman apparently does not notice Mordecai's disrespect until told of it by other servants. Author Michael Fox notes that this adds a touch of realism to Haman's self-involved pride, as if he is too taken up with the honor being shown him to notice one dissident.[2] The sequence of events in these verses is difficult to

---

2 Fox, *Character and Ideology*, 45. Fox's treatment of this chapter and the entire book is superb and has helped me in many ways.

follow. It appears the question from the other servants in verse 3 implies a command to bow like everyone else—but when Mordecai repeatedly refuses to listen to them (v. 4a), the servants draw Haman's attention to Mordecai. They are trying to determine if "Mordecai's words would stand"—they want to see if Mordecai can get away with defying someone in authority over him on the basis of a prior ethnic hostility (between Israel and Amalek) that the other servants probably did not know about.

3:5–6 Haman's plan to compensate himself for this insult reveals a terrifying and insatiable level of evil in him. The Persian court probably saw any number of insults and petty reprisals in the normal course of events. But the only thing that will pacify Haman is not only Mordecai's death but the death of everyone related to him! After so many questions regarding the characters' inner motivations so far in the story, this exposure of Haman's character is chilling. And he holds the greatest authority in the empire beneath a fickle and unwise king.

3:7 Haman casts lots to find the most propitious time to launch his revenge. This is an interesting insight into his superstitious cast of mind, as well as another hint that God is providentially at work even in the hatred of the enemies of his people (Prov. 16:33).

3:8–9 Haman's framing of the "problem" he puts before Ahasuerus is a skillful sleight of hand, mixing half-truths with lies to deflect the king's attention from the important questions he should be asking. Haman presents himself as a friend to the king, informing him of a vague danger, "a certain people," of which the king is unaware. The anonymity will make it easier for the king to sign the decree of execution. According to Haman, this people is "scattered abroad and dispersed." This seemingly innocuous phrase is calculated to arouse suspicion and antipathy in Ahasuerus. The image is of a lurking threat, spread everywhere but never easily identifiable. Haman's next statement, that this people has a unique set of laws, is correct, but Haman spins it to portray the Jews as traitors: they have different laws, and therefore they rebel against the king's laws. This is, of course, entirely untrue; the last chapter ended with Mordecai risking his life to save the king. But the mere fact of this people being different is enough to make the suggestion of rebellion plausible and their extermination easier to swallow. Haman is trying to create prejudice where none exists.

Haman then says it is not profitable for the king to leave this certain people alone, which, at first glance, is a bit strange. Why not say it is profitable for the king to destroy them? But if Haman said that, the king may try to learn for himself what this supposed disturbance is all about. Haman must invent a problem to manipulate the king to sign this people's death warrant without making him curious enough to ask questions and expose Haman's lies. So Haman in effect says he's bringing a certain problem to light that the king did not know about, but he doesn't want to trouble the king with all the details and can take care of it himself, if only the king agrees. The passive "let it be decreed" distances the king from the killing, and the offer to pay the staggering cost of the extermination presents Haman as generously putting interests of state first when, of course, he is really advancing his own agenda. But the king will not notice this.

3:10–11 Without a moment's reflection on the morality of his decision, without a single question about Haman's claims, the king gives Haman carte blanche to do as he wishes. His support is substantiated by his refusal of Haman's "generosity" and commitment to pay for the extermination of Esther's people with state funds. In light of 4:7, however, this may be only polite convention, part of an elaborate system of offers and refusals as deals are made, meant to show the king's support.

Haman is identified again as an Amalekite, a descendant of Agag, and as the "enemy of the Jews." An ancient hatred has been revived. The lines have been drawn; this is now Haman's role in the story.

3:12–14 The massive Persian bureaucracy grinds into action to destroy the Jews, as the king's edict is published everywhere. While Haman's statement in verse 9 concerning paying for the extermination implies government servants will do the work, verse 13 suggests the populace at large is participating in the massacre. Since Haman now has free reign to do as he wishes, he may have changed the edict to allow anyone in Persian society to participate in the massacre. Verse 12 echoes tragically the edict ending chapter 1: while the earlier edict was merely ridiculous, communicating the buffoonery of the Persian royal elite, this one is terrifying. A second echo of chapter 1 is found in the way a personal insult is magnified into a national crisis; but again, where the first part of the narrative was humorous, this one is deadly serious.

3:15 As the edict is proclaimed at a national level, Ahasuerus enjoys another miniature feast with Haman, as if celebrating their accomplishment. This is the book's third feast, after the nationwide parties beginning the book and the feast at Esther's coronation. This latest feast rankles the reader as Ahasuerus relaxes and enjoys himself, oblivious to the tumult outside.

The popular response to the edict shows that, at least in general, Persia is not in favor of the edict or inherently anti-Semitic. While 9:1–5 will show some participating in an attack on the Jews, the city as a whole is in chaos as a result of this decision.

Response

As mentioned above, Persia is not an inherently anti-Semitic place. In fact, Mordecai's ethnic identity is only incidental to his slight of Haman's bottomless ego. If a member of another people group had acted as Mordecai did, Haman would have focused his murderous revenge just as easily on that group. At the same time, the book of Esther focuses repeatedly on the Jewish people as an object of persecution (3:4, 6, 10, 13; 4:7, 13–14, 16; 5:13; 6:10, 13; 8:1, 3, 5, 7, 11, 17; 9:1–3, 10). The text's highlighting Haman's Amalekite ancestry recalls the Amalekites' persecution of Israel early in their history (Ex. 17:8–16), and one cannot help but think of the long and sad history of Jewish persecution ever since, a history that found a terrifying climax in Europe in the last century and continues yet today. "Their laws are different from ours" (cf. Est. 3:8); how many times has Jewish distinctiveness been the basis for suspicion, prejudice, or violence? And sometimes the church has participated. As Christians, we must ask ourselves if we have ever engaged in anti-Semitic attitudes or behavior, or have stood by and done nothing while anti-Semitism has flourished around us. The book of Esther makes it clear that God is a dread defender of Abraham's seed.

But this passage does not apply only to Abraham's physical offspring. Jesus clearly warns that the world will hate Christians with the same hatred it showed him, because of our allegiance to him (John 15:18). Modern disciples of Jesus will inevitably find themselves in situations in which they have no choice but to incur the violent and murderous hatred of the world, because we will not bow. The book of Esther shows how God is at work to deliver his people—in this case, through a string of providential coincidences. The same promise emboldens us not to fear the wrath of any modern-day persecutor of God's people, regardless of its authority or power, as we pledge open allegiance not just to a particular ethnic heritage but to the Lord Jesus himself.

ESTHER 4:1–17

4 When Mordecai learned all that had been done, Mordecai tore his clothes and put on sackcloth and ashes, and went out into the midst of the city, and he cried out with a loud and bitter cry. [2] He went up to the entrance of the king's gate, for no one was allowed to enter the king's gate clothed in sackcloth. [3] And in every province, wherever the king's command and his decree reached, there was great mourning among the Jews, with fasting and weeping and lamenting, and many of them lay in sackcloth and ashes.

[4] When Esther's young women and her eunuchs came and told her, the queen was deeply distressed. She sent garments to clothe Mordecai, so that he might take off his sackcloth, but he would not accept them. [5] Then Esther called for Hathach, one of the king's eunuchs, who had been appointed to attend her, and ordered him to go to Mordecai to learn what this was and why it was. [6] Hathach went out to Mordecai in the open square of the city in front of the king's gate, [7] and Mordecai told him all that had happened to him, and the exact sum of money that Haman had promised to pay into the king's treasuries for the destruction of the Jews. [8] Mordecai also gave him a copy of the written decree issued in Susa for their destruction,[1] that he might show it to Esther and explain it to her and command her to go to the king to beg his favor and plead with him[2]

on behalf of her people. ⁹ And Hathach went and told Esther what Mordecai had said. ¹⁰ Then Esther spoke to Hathach and commanded him to go to Mordecai and say, ¹¹ "All the king's servants and the people of the king's provinces know that if any man or woman goes to the king inside the inner court without being called, there is but one law—to be put to death, except the one to whom the king holds out the golden scepter so that he may live. But as for me, I have not been called to come in to the king these thirty days."

¹² And they told Mordecai what Esther had said. ¹³ Then Mordecai told them to reply to Esther, "Do not think to yourself that in the king's palace you will escape any more than all the other Jews. ¹⁴ For if you keep silent at this time, relief and deliverance will rise for the Jews from another place, but you and your father's house will perish. And who knows whether you have not come to the kingdom for such a time as this?" ¹⁵ Then Esther told them to reply to Mordecai, ¹⁶ "Go, gather all the Jews to be found in Susa, and hold a fast on my behalf, and do not eat or drink for three days, night or day. I and my young women will also fast as you do. Then I will go to the king, though it is against the law, and if I perish, I perish."³ ¹⁷ Mordecai then went away and did everything as Esther had ordered him.

¹ Or *annihilation* ² Hebrew *and seek from before his face* ³ Hebrew *if I am destroyed, then I will be destroyed*

Section Overview

Since Haman is second in authority to the king, Mordecai is not able himself to do anything to stop Haman's plan. He convinces a hesitant Esther to use her position as queen to act on her people's behalf.

Section Outline

IV. Mordecai Convinces Esther to Petition the King (4:1–17)
    A. Mordecai's Tears (4:1–3)
    B. Esther Learns of the Plot from Mordecai (4:4–8)
    C. Esther Resists Helping Mordecai (4:9–12)
    D. Mordecai Convinces Esther to Help (4:13–17)

Comment

4:1–3 Haman's edict is now public knowledge, and we have already heard the general reaction to it (3:15). Now we learn of the Jewish reaction. Torn clothes, sackcloth and ashes, and public weeping are common responses in the OT to unimaginable tragedy (Job 1:20; 16:15; Ps. 35:13; Isa. 22:12; 58:5; Jer. 6:26; Joel 1:8) and are sometimes signs of repentance (1 Kings 21:27; Jonah 3:6). If Mordecai has repented of his failure to honor Haman, however, he shows no sign of it in his conversation with Esther. Mordecai is simply in unbearable pain over this turn of events; his people follow suit (Est. 4:3). Elsewhere in the OT, dressing in sackcloth and ashes is a prelude to prayer (cf. esp. Mordecai's near contemporary Daniel, in Dan. 9:3). But Mordecai says nothing to or about God. His cry is an inarticulate scream of grief and pain.

Mordecai's location at the gate (Est. 4:2) is an attempt to get as close as possible to the authorities who can do something about the Jews' looming disaster. The gravity and extreme desperation of the situation prevents Mordecai from dressing normally, even though this would have given him access to the gate.

4:4 Mordecai's ploy works, but when Esther learns of what Mordecai is doing, her reaction is strange; although Esther is deeply (and appropriately) distressed, she sends only a change of clothes, as if that would solve the problem. Mordecai's reasons for grieving do not seem to matter to her. Since Esther's existence in the harem has revolved around shallow considerations, this is not surprising, but it shows a certain superficiality on her part.

4:5–8 We learn that Esther's existence inside the harem is a virtual imprisonment; she has to be told what the entire empire knows, and she has to communicate with Mordecai through a servant. Mordecai asks Esther to beg the king on behalf of her people (v. 8). She is the only one in the entire empire high enough to overturn Haman's edict. Mordecai's public gestures of grief and distress are meant not only to relieve his pain but also to impress upon Esther the desperateness of the situation.

4:9–12 Esther's first response reveals her immaturity. Everyone knows, she says (perhaps implying she should not have to say this to Mordecai), that I will be executed if I go to the king unbidden, and he has not called me this month. She thinks the risk to her life is a valid reason for her to be excused. One wonders what sort of response Esther expected from Mordecai. Did she think he would say he understood and would try to petition some other higher official, or flee into exile? Mordecai's request is difficult but not unfair. Note further that Mordecai asked her to petition on behalf of "her people" (v. 8), but Esther is thinking only of herself, not of the Jews who will die if Haman gets his way. We will soon see, in 5:2, that her fears are unfounded.

4:13–14 In some of the book's best known and most significant verses, Mordecai manages to convince Esther to risk her life for her people. Three comments need to be made.

First, the term appropriately translated "deliverance" is often used elsewhere of God's great acts of salvation for his people (cf. Ex. 6:6; Judg. 6:9; 1 Sam. 4:8; 2 Kings 17:39; Pss. 7:1; 22:8; Isa. 43:13). This is the closest Mordecai will ever get to making a theological statement—but he does not quite get there. This salvation will come, Mordecai says, "from another place"—not necessarily from God. Mordecai has apparently picked up the language of his tradition without understanding who inspired it. It is tantamount to saying things will work out for the Jews "just because"; Mordecai believes things tend to work out in the Jews' favor but he does not give a reason for this belief. It shows no more faith than the statement of Haman's advisers and wife in Esther 6:13. Nevertheless, Mordecai's claim that relief and deliverance are coming is truer than he knows.

Second, it is not entirely clear why Mordecai says Esther will not survive if her people die (4:13). Would the king's beloved wife not be safe in the palace from the violence outside? Some have seen here a veiled threat from Mordecai, but it is hard to imagine Mordecai attempting or coordinating some kind of assassination attempt on the queen. It may be that Mordecai is thinking of what Haman will do if and when he learns Esther is Jewish. This claim may also be the correlate of his impersonal, emaciated "theology": just as there is a natural tendency for things to work out for the Jews, so there is danger for those on the other side. That the house of Esther's father will perish probably merely means that, since Esther is an orphan and apparently has no brothers or sisters, she is her father's last remaining offspring. If she dies, his name will be wiped out.

Third, Mordecai's question of whether Esther has been placed here for exactly this crisis cannot help but bring to the reader's mind the extraordinary string of coincidences guiding the story so far (and continuing past this point). Mordecai means this as a genuine question; he is not sure. But the narrator wants the reader to see that it is no impersonal, general tendency that has brought Esther to the throne.

4:15–16 Esther is convinced. She calls for a nationwide fast but makes no mention of prayer, which always accompanied fasting elsewhere in the OT. Esther seems to have picked up Mordecai's thin "theology." She apparently expects the fasting somehow to affect the outcome of events on its own, without prayer. Her final statement, too, is one more of resignation than of faith. She does not know if she will survive the encounter, but she is willing to try.

4:17 As Mordecai does everything Esther commands him, a role reversal begins to take place. This is Esther's first step away from the complete pliability she showed in chapter 2. Mordecai and Esther are beginning to act as equals. By the end of the book, Mordecai will be following Esther's lead entirely.

Response

The books of Esther and Daniel were compared in the introduction to this commentary because of their mutual concern with how God's people can survive and thrive in exile. Within this larger similarity, however, is a contrast in how the books show God at work: Daniel is full of apocalyptic visions of spectacular actions on God's part, while Esther shows God unobtrusively working through the normal course of events to save his people. Although neither Esther nor Mordecai seems fully to realize it, God has placed her on the throne exactly for this time (4:14). Esther will use the position and power she enjoys to save many Jewish lives. Similarly, it may be that the work and witness of some Christians in this world will be attended by extraordinary and unmistakable power from God. It also may be that he intends us to use our positions outside the church for the sake of the church when Christians are in danger.

But Esther is not an unambiguously positive example. Because we can see God's providential ordering of Esther's life to deliver his people, even when she is not aware of it, we can avoid her resistance and fatalistic attitude when asked to risk our jobs or livelihoods—perhaps even our lives—for the sake of persecuted believers. We cannot know ahead of time how God will work in our particular situations, but we know he works all things for our good (Rom. 8:28).

ESTHER 5:1–14

5 On the third day Esther put on her royal robes and stood in the inner court of the king's palace, in front of the king's quarters, while the king was sitting on his royal throne inside the throne room opposite the entrance to the palace. [2] And when the king saw Queen Esther standing in the court, she won favor in his sight, and he held out to Esther the golden scepter that was in his hand. Then Esther approached and touched the tip of the scepter. [3] And the king said to her, "What is it, Queen Esther? What is your request? It shall be given you, even to the half of my kingdom." [4] And Esther said, "If it please the king,[1] let the king and Haman come today to a feast that I have prepared for the king." [5] Then the king said, "Bring Haman quickly, so that we may do as Esther has asked." So the king and Haman came to the feast that Esther had prepared. [6] And as they were drinking wine after the feast, the king said to Esther, "What is your wish? It shall be granted you. And what is your request? Even to the half of my kingdom, it shall be fulfilled."[2] [7] Then Esther answered, "My wish and my request is: [8] If I have found favor in the sight of the king, and if it please the king[3] to grant my wish and fulfill my request, let the king and Haman come to the feast that I will prepare for them, and tomorrow I will do as the king has said."

[9] And Haman went out that day joyful and glad of heart. But when Haman saw Mordecai in the king's gate, that he neither rose nor trembled before him, he was filled with wrath against Mordecai. [10] Nevertheless, Haman restrained himself and went home, and he sent and brought his friends and his wife Zeresh. [11] And Haman recounted to them the splendor of his riches, the number of his sons, all the promotions with which the king had honored him, and how he had advanced him above the officials and the servants of the king. [12] Then Haman said, "Even Queen Esther let no one but me come with the king to the feast she prepared. And tomorrow also I am invited by her together with the king. [13] Yet all this is worth nothing to me, so long as I see Mordecai the Jew sitting at the king's gate." [14] Then his wife Zeresh and all his friends said to him, "Let a gallows[4] fifty cubits[5] high be made, and in the morning tell the king to have Mordecai hanged upon it. Then go joyfully with the king to the feast." This idea pleased Haman, and he had the gallows made.

[1] Hebrew *If it is good to the king* [2] Or *done* [3] Hebrew *if it is good to the king* [4] Or *wooden beam*; twice in this verse (see note on 2:23) [5] A *cubit* was about 18 inches or 45 centimeters

Section Overview

After raising our expectations in the last chapter, the story stalls somewhat as Esther delays her petitioning the king on behalf of her people while Haman furthers his plans to avenge himself on Mordecai. Although the Jews' fortunes will soon turn around, their situation looks even grimmer by the end of this chapter.

Section Outline

> V. Esther Begins Her Appeal to the King (5:1–14)
> > A. Esther Holds a Feast for the King and Requests a Second Feast (5:1–8)
> > B. Haman Plots Mordecai's Hanging (5:9–14)

Comment

5:1–2 With the three days of fasting completed, Esther literally "puts on royalty" (v. 1). She is coming before the king as "Queen Esther" (v. 2). Like Mordecai in the previous chapter, she positions herself as close as possible to the royal throne in the heart of the palace (v. 1). As soon as Ahasuerus sees her, he extends his scepter and bids her draw near (v. 2). This not only contradicts her expectation of being executed but also bodes well for her request: extending his scepter recalls Ahasuerus's giving his signet ring in response to Haman's request in 3:10, suggesting Esther will be given what she asks. And if Ahasuerus has already broken the law about executing unannounced visitors, perhaps he will contravene his agreement with Haman as well.

5:3–8 The king knows Esther is bringing some request before him. In the exaggerated style of the Persian court, he not only asks her what her request is but essentially commits himself before hearing it: "even to the half of my kingdom" means he will not refuse her wish as being too difficult. After hearing this from the king, a first-time reader probably expects Esther to launch into her petition (4:8). Instead, Esther surprises us by asking only that the king come to a feast. Very well, the reader thinks; Ahasuerus loves to eat and drink, and what better context for a wife to wheedle and coax her husband than at the dinner table? Furthermore, each feast so far has been the occasion of a significant shift in power; this raises our expectations for a similar upset at this feast.

But if a night of charming her husband is all she intends, why does Esther invite Haman as well? Surely he would disrupt anything she tried to say? Then another surprise meets us: Ahasuerus again commits himself during the meal, twice saying that whatever Esther wants will be done. But instead of taking advantage of what appears to be a perfect opportunity to beg for the lives of her people, Esther asks only that the king come to a second feast, promising to tell him then what she wants (5:8). Why these delays? Is Esther flummoxed and nervous, unable to say what she really wants?

Although the text is silent on this question, a moment's reflection will help us appreciate the difficulty of Esther's position and reveal her strategy. Ahasuerus has already shown himself to be fickle and unstable. Esther cannot appeal to his common sense about the coming atrocity, for the king has almost none. Even if she were to win a commitment not to exterminate the Jews, Haman, who has already shown his rhetorical prowess, might be able to guide the king back to his original course at some later time. Furthermore, the king's ego is highly sensitive to any slight, perceived or real, so any direct confrontation of the king about his approval of Haman's deplorable scheme will probably only provoke him. Vashti has, after all, already learned how the king deals with assertive women, even when they are right and he is wrong. Esther must somehow convince the king not to support Haman's decree without reminding him too much of his own role in it. Weak-willed as he is, it probably would have been easy for Ahasuerus to compromise by promising Esther special protection inside the palace while letting Haman murder every other Jew in Persia. Esther must somehow deal Haman a permanent defeat without offending her hypersensitive, childish husband.

This is probably why Esther holds two feasts before revealing what she wants. She is exploiting her husband's love of food and wine and raising his curiosity without satisfying it. By the time she finally reveals her request, in chapter 7, the king will have already bound himself to it three times; she can represent herself as giving in to the king's wish instead of insisting on her own way. Her requesting Haman to be present also shows an admirable shrewdness on her part—she likely wants to keep an eye on him and prevent him from manipulating the king once she has left. Furthermore, if she accuses Haman behind his back, he would probably be able to talk his way out of it. When read together with chapter 7, Esther's request for two feasts suggests a calculated plan.

5:9 Haman leaves the queen's banquet in high spirits, oblivious to the fact that the revelation Esther has promised at the second banquet directly concerns his nefarious plot. We learn why in verse 12: Haman loves honor and respect from others as much as the king, and is singularly flattered to be the only other guest at the banquet with the king and queen. His complete misinterpretation of the queen's intention is darkly humorous.

But Haman's good cheer is instantly spoiled. As he moves through the city, many are eager to genuflect before the king's second-in-command, but among all the attention, there again was Mordecai, not standing to attention nor giving the slightest indication of any fear before this great man (cf. 3:1–6). And instantly Haman is in a fury.

5:10–13 Haman reveals to his friends (and the reader) the reason for his anger. In this revelation, Haman is still terrifying but appears a little pathetic as well. From his own perspective, Haman has led a charmed life; there is no other honor or promotion or glory he can receive without becoming king (v. 11). To top it off, he alone was invited to a royal banquet—not just once, but again tomorrow (v. 12). Haman's ego is palpable in the phrase "no one but me." Haman has already won his revenge against his enemy Mordecai—and not only that, but Mordecai's entire people are about to be annihilated. But, as Haman waits for the decree to come into effect, as long as Mordecai is still alive, everything Haman has gained might as well not exist. He cannot enjoy one single part of his life if Mordecai continues to live.

We have noted the insatiable nature of Haman's evil (cf. comment on 3:5–6). This aspect of his personality seems to have infected his whole soul. What else does Haman need, in order to be happy? The self-pity of this man is half frightening, half pathetic. The person Haman hates the most has come to dominate his thoughts and happiness. Haman turns to others to tell him what to do when his limitless pride is slighted, just as Ahasuerus does; even if Ahasuerus is not as evil as his servant, Haman resembles his king in more ways than one.

5:14 Zeresh, Haman's wife, has an idea: Haman has already won permission for Mordecai's execution, but Zeresh shows Haman a way to humiliate and degrade Mordecai in his death. The exposure of a corpse without burial was regarded in the ancient world as an unmitigated tragedy (note the courage and risk of the soldiers of Jabesh-gilead to prevent this from happening to Saul's corpse; 1 Sam. 31:11–13). Ahasuerus has already (unwittingly) condemned Mordecai to death; surely it will be a small thing to specify the means of his death by being hung on the gallows and left there for all to see. Only then can Haman's terrifying neediness be satisfied and his life of luxury begin again.

The irony of Haman's interpretation of Esther's feast is heightened in Zeresh's speech in Esther 5:14, as she advises Haman to request Mordecai be hanged before attending Esther's feast in good cheer. Without their knowing it, Haman is walking directly into the trap Esther has prepared.

Response

As we will soon see, the next chapter is the turning point in the story; after the king's sleepless night, things will get steadily better for the Jews and worse for their enemies. But the narrator does not get us to that point too quickly. Esther has set her plan in motion, but so far Haman seems only to have strengthened his victory over the Jews by plotting the degrading death of one of their leaders. Haman and Zeresh's ironic misinterpretation of Esther's feast hints at a coming reversal, but these are only hints. Behind all these events, the wheels of God's providence are in motion, but they are moving slowly. So we too, as we take risks to work in the world on behalf of God's people, especially when they are in danger for their lives, may have to wait as our situations perhaps worsen. But God's providential deliverance—in whatever form it takes—is not hindered.

ESTHER 6:1–14

6 On that night the king could not sleep. And he gave orders to bring the book of memorable deeds, the chronicles, and they were read before the king. [2] And it was found written how Mordecai had told about Bigthana[1] and Teresh, two of the king's eunuchs, who guarded the threshold, and who had sought to lay hands on King Ahasuerus. [3] And the king said, "What honor or distinction has been bestowed on Mordecai for this?" The king's young men who attended him said, "Nothing has been done for him." [4] And the king said, "Who is in the court?" Now Haman had just entered the outer court of the king's palace to speak to the king about having Mordecai hanged on the gallows[2] that he had prepared for him. [5] And the king's young men told him, "Haman is there, standing in the court." And the king said, "Let him come in." [6] So Haman came in, and the king said to him, "What should be done to the man whom the king delights to honor?" And Haman said to himself, "Whom would the king delight to honor more than me?" [7] And Haman said to the king, "For the man whom the king delights to honor, [8] let royal robes be brought, which the king has worn, and the horse that the king has ridden, and on whose head a royal crown[3] is set. [9] And let the robes and the horse be handed over to one of the king's most noble officials. Let them dress the man whom the king delights to honor, and let them lead him on the horse through the square of the city, proclaiming before him: 'Thus shall it be done to the man whom the king delights to honor.'" [10] Then the king said to Haman, "Hurry; take the robes and the horse, as you have said, and do so to Mordecai the Jew, who sits at the king's gate. Leave out nothing that you have mentioned." [11] So Haman took the robes and the horse, and he dressed Mordecai and led him through the square of the city, proclaiming before him, "Thus shall it be done to the man whom the king delights to honor."

[12] Then Mordecai returned to the king's gate. But Haman hurried to his house, mourning and with his head covered. [13] And Haman told his wife Zeresh and all his friends everything that had happened to him. Then his wise men and his wife Zeresh said to him, "If Mordecai, before whom you have begun to fall, is of the Jewish people, you will not overcome him but will surely fall before him."

[14] While they were yet talking with him, the king's eunuchs arrived and hurried to bring Haman to the feast that Esther had prepared.

[1] *Bigthana* is an alternate spelling of *Bigthan* (see 2:21) [2] Or *wooden beam* (see note on 2:23) [3] Or *headdress*

Section Overview

With Mordecai and Esther offstage, the king is providentially reminded of Mordecai's unrewarded service to the king in exposing the plot against his life (Est. 2:21–23). This sets in motion a chain of events leading to the Jews' deliverance.

Section Outline

VI. The Turning Point: Ahasuerus Honors Mordecai (6:1–14)
  A. Ahasuerus Decides to Honor Mordecai (6:1–3)
  B. Ahasuerus Designates Haman to Honor Mordecai (6:4–9)
  C. Haman Honors Mordecai (6:10–14)

Comment

6:1–3 At first glance, an apparently innocuous detail is given, seemingly irrelevant to the story: the king looks for some entertainment to pass a sleepless night. But when part of the night's reading recounts Mordecai's unrewarded act of bravery and loyalty on the king's behalf, the reader sees the hand of God at work in another coincidence to save his people from their enemy. This helps show that, although Mordecai and Esther are at work in this situation, the outcome of the book is not simply a reward for their labors. They do not "cause" the victory—they are, indeed, barely involved in this chapter.

6:4 In a place as dangerous as the Persian court, the king understands it to be in his own interests to reward acts like Mordecai's. Thus, after learning that nothing had been done to honor Mordecai, the king takes action immediately, asking if there is anyone nearby in the court to help him correct this oversight. In another perfect coincidence, Haman comes just at that moment to ask permission to hang the very man Ahasuerus now wants to honor. Again the reader cannot but see God's hand at work in ordering these circumstances.

6:5–6 Ahasuerus, who never makes decisions for himself, asks the first person he sees how he should honor a particular person. The king probably thought it most opportune for his chief adviser to be present to give him the advice he sought. For his part, Haman continues his self-aggrandizing interpretation of recent events; whom else but the king's second-in-command, the sole person invited to a private feast with the king and queen, could the king be seeking to honor? Haman probably saw here a further salve to his wounded pride (5:13). His interpretation of the king's question lets his imagination run free to create whatever recompense he wants.

6:7–9 In commenting on Haman's self-pity in the last chapter, we asked what more Haman could possibly want in order to be happy. Here we learn Haman has just the scenario in mind to satisfy his boundless ego—for a time, at least. His request in verse 7 could actually be translated as a sentence fragment, as if he were savoring the thought as it came to him: "The man whom the king delights to honor—let them bring royal robes . . ." In asking to wear the king's clothes, ride in his chariot, and wear his crown, Haman is asking to be treated like royalty— and to be officially recognized as such in the most public place in the capital of the empire (the city square; v. 9). There is no other promotion left for the king's second-in-command.

6:10–12 In the first of a string of perfectly symmetrical reversals, Haman learns that instead of detailing the way he should be honored, he has described the way in which he will have to honor Mordecai—the very man for whose head he had come to ask. The phrase "Mordecai the Jew, who sits at the king's gate" is an exact echo from 5:13, used by Haman to describe the source of his unhappiness. What could have humbled Haman more perfectly or painfully than personally carrying out for his most hated enemy the extensive honors he had imagined for himself? No emotion is recorded from Mordecai or Haman—a silence that cannot help but prompt us to imagine the storm of rage and humiliation as Haman shouted Mordecai's honor in the city square. On the other hand, Mordecai simply returns to the gate of the king when it is over (6:12)—that is, he returns to his place of work. He did not seek any reward when uncovering the plot at the end of chapter 2, and seems unaffected by it now.

Haman, by contrast, rushes home with his face covered (a sign of distress and grief in 2 Sam. 15:30; Jer. 14:3–4).[3] For him, it is the beginning of the end.

6:13 Repeating his strategy from chapter 5, Haman turns to his wife and friends for advice. Mordecai's Jewish descent weighs heavily on them: If Haman's adversary were from any other people group, they imply, Haman might be able to win his way back. But somehow Haman's wife and friends, although certainly no friends of the Jews, are convinced this is only the beginning of a downward spiral out of which Haman cannot pull himself.

Why these Persian Gentiles are so certain of Jewish success is not immediately clear (have they had enough contact with Persian Jews to notice a pattern?), but surely the narrator wants us to see again God's hand at work in a way even the Jews' enemies recognize, even if they do not know to whom to attribute this success. Mordecai's Jewish identity is also now in the open. This is the first crack in Haman's plan against the Jews: how can a man so signally honored by the king be executed?

6:14 In another perfectly timed irony, Haman has no time to ponder what this means as he hurries to Esther's second feast. We can only wonder what was running through his mind as he made his way there.

Response

Esther is a book of reversals (9:2, 22), and this chapter shows their beginning. It is impossible to avoid a certain pleasure in seeing Haman caught in his own perversely grandiose designs, forced to honor the man for whose life he had come to ask. Mordecai, although failing to honor or speak of God explicitly in any way in this book, is nevertheless a man worthy of honor. Much greater reversals await the reader of the book of Esther, but they are dwarfed by those of a Jew who lived at a later time, was hailed as a king by crowds like Mordecai, but was soon

---

3 Michael Fox reports that there is some evidence of this practice among the Persians (*Character and Ideology*, 79).

crowned with thorns to die in place of sinners. The Bible's greatest reversals find echoes in Esther—one strong point of connection between the book and the rest of Scripture.

This chapter also prompts us to wonder how else God might be at work to deliver his people from enemies who would destroy them. God's deliverance of his people involved the risk and courage of Mordecai and Esther, but it did not require their involvement. The portrayal of God's slow but certain providence can embolden modern-day Christians if they find themselves in situations similar to that of Mordecai and Esther. If even the enemies of God's people can recognize the aftereffects of God's providential work, we should not shrink from risky action when his people are under attack.

ESTHER 7:1–10

7 So the king and Haman went in to feast with Queen Esther. ² And on the second day, as they were drinking wine after the feast, the king again said to Esther, "What is your wish, Queen Esther? It shall be granted you. And what is your request? Even to the half of my kingdom, it shall be fulfilled." ³ Then Queen Esther answered, "If I have found favor in your sight, O king, and if it please the king, let my life be granted me for my wish, and my people for my request. ⁴ For we have been sold, I and my people, to be destroyed, to be killed, and to be anni-hilated. If we had been sold merely as slaves, men and women, I would have been silent, for our affliction is not to be compared with the loss to the king." ⁵ Then King Ahasuerus said to Queen Esther, "Who is he, and where is he, who has dared[1] to do this?" ⁶ And Esther said, "A foe and enemy! This wicked Haman!" Then Haman was terrified before the king and the queen.

⁷ And the king arose in his wrath from the wine-drinking and went into the palace garden, but Haman stayed to beg for his life from Queen Esther, for he saw that harm was determined against him by the king. ⁸ And the king returned from the palace garden to the place where they were drinking wine, as Haman was falling on the couch where Esther was. And the king said, "Will he even assault the queen in my presence, in my own house?" As the word left the mouth of the king, they covered Haman's face. ⁹ Then Harbona, one of the eunuchs in attendance on the king, said, "Moreover, the gallows[2] that Haman has prepared for Morde-cai, whose word saved the king, is standing at Haman's house, fifty cubits[3] high." And the king said, "Hang him on that." ¹⁰ So they hanged Haman on the gallows that he had prepared for Mordecai. Then the wrath of the king abated.

[1] Hebrew *whose heart has filled him* [2] Or *wooden beam*; also verse 10 (see note on 2:23) [3] A *cubit* was about 18 inches or 45 centimeters

Section Overview

Esther springs her trap on Haman and succeeds in exposing him. In another coincidence, the king falsely interprets Haman's plea for mercy and has Haman executed.

Section Outline

VIII. Esther's Second Feast and Haman's Exposure (7:1–10)
  A. Esther Reveals Haman's Plot (7:1–6)
  B. Haman Is Hanged (7:7–10)

Comment

7:1–2 This is the third time the king has asked Esther what she wants, and Esther has already promised she will reveal her request (5:8). Esther has laid her trap the best she can; now is the time to spring it.

7:3 Esther's indirect expression of her request is made in the most humble terms. She first asks only for her own life and that of her people. Since Ahasuerus uses two words in verse 2 for her desire, Esther's dividing of her "wish" for herself and her "request" for her people shows she has bound her life with that of the Jews. To kill the Jews, Esther says, is to kill her. Esther has forsaken any safety she might have enjoyed as queen and commits herself to suffer with her people.

7:4 For Ahasuerus's queen to have to beg for her life would have been, of course, a shock to the king. Some explanation must be given, which Esther provides in the most deferential way possible: if the Jews had only been sold as slaves, Esther would not have bothered to say anything, since the suffering of the Jews in slavery would have been nothing compared to the damage the king would have incurred in canceling the sale. Only because they had been sold to be exterminated, Esther says, does she dare bother the king about it. Esther phrases the problem in reference to the king and his convenience.

All this is, of course, hyperbolic. But Persian court customs probably regularly employed such exaggerations, and Esther is dealing with an incredibly sensitive ego. She implies she would not have brought this up without the most pressing justification, appealing to Ahasuerus's self-interest. Esther still, however, has not directly named Haman as her enemy. Having aroused the king's curiosity, she is now arousing anger and a sense of injury. She will soon direct that anger toward the intended target.

7:5 When Ahasuerus asks who would threaten the life of his queen, he either does not remember giving Haman permission to enact his plan against that "certain people" (3:8) or still does not know Esther is Jewish (she does not explicitly mention the Jews by name in 7:3–4) and so does not realize the edict threatens his queen. The king does not ask for details about the plot against his wife; he seems more concerned about offense to royal honor than possible loss of life.

7:6 It is time for Esther to spring her trap. "This wicked Haman," sitting right before us, she says, is the "foe and enemy." Her speech is two brief phrases of three words each, quickened by her anger.

It is important for Ahasuerus to see Haman for what he is. Although Haman has managed to pass himself off as a friend of the king and the Persian state, Esther is trying to expose Haman as the enemy he is, a man who all along has been plotting against the king's interests. Haman's only response is mute terror before the king and queen.

7:7–8 The decisive moment in the story has been reached—Haman's plot is now exposed before the king, the one person with authority to counteract it. What will the king do? The anticlimax of Ahasuerus's storming about in a rage is probably not what the first-time reader would expect, but it is not out of character for him. At no point in the book will he take decisive action. Haman can see, as the king leaves, that he is not in the king's favor; but the king has, as yet, done nothing.

This chapter began with Esther begging for her life; now Haman begs for his to the only one in authority above him. The man who was enraged because Mordecai would neither bow (3:2) nor rise (5:9) now stands and falls before Esther to beg. The word "falling" is the same as in 6:13; what Haman's wife and friends predicted is now literally happening.

In another providential coincidence, the king returns just as this is happening and manages to draw exactly the wrong conclusion. The sight of a penitent Haman might have counted in Haman's favor, but Ahasuerus interprets Haman's falling before Esther in terms of his own honor and possessions (in this case, his wife). It is, of course, extremely unlikely the already terrified Haman would do what the king thinks he is doing. But Ahasuerus is obsessed with his own honor, especially in relation to women. It was also the practice in ancient Persia for no one to come within seven steps of a harem woman, even in the presence of others.[4] Haman's violation of social protocol probably made it easier for Ahasuerus to draw the wrong conclusion. Ironically, Haman will be executed not for the real crime—plotting the death of the Persian Jews—but for the false charge of attempted rape. The latter seems to bother Ahasuerus more than the former.

Although there appear to be other servants reasonably close by, Esther is probably the only one who can clear Haman of this charge—but she says nothing. Some commentators have faulted Esther for failing to speak up. However, if Haman were to recover from this situation and avoid execution, the man devoted to and rejoicing in Jewish destruction might get his way in the end. Haman is falling in this scene, but his defeat is not yet complete. It is important to remember that Ahasuerus is malleable and fickle and has shown no sign of regret or distress over the destruction of Esther's people.

Esther remains silent and Haman's face is covered. He earlier had covered his

---

4 Edwin M. Yamauchi, *Persia and the Bible* (Grand Rapids, MI: Baker, 1990), 262.

own face as he fled the palace (6:12); now, the king speaks and other servants perform this ritual. His fate is sealed.

7:9–10 Once again, another voice helps Ahasuerus decide what to do. Apparently the gallows are public knowledge—as well as Haman's purpose in building them. Haman's intending these gallows for the man who saved the king's life makes the decision easy for Ahasuerus. Twice in verses 9–10 it is specified that Haman built these gallows for Mordecai, emphasizing the poetic justice of Haman's fate. This is meant to give a sense of satisfaction to the reader as Haman's evil entraps him. Modern sensibilities may find this difficult, of course. But while it would be perverse to relish the suffering and death of anyone, no matter how well deserved (indeed, to do so would be to show an attitude similar to Haman himself!), a sense of somber satisfaction at the justice of God is not morally ugly. The Bible repeatedly testifies that God governs his creation in such a way that evil tends to destroy those who practice it: "Whoever digs a pit will fall into it" (Prov. 26:27; cf. Pss. 7:12–16; 9:15; 57:6; Prov. 28:10). Modern discomfort with this truth amounts to discomfort with God's judging evil and establishing justice and righteousness in the earth. If Haman wished to avoid the gallows, he should never have built them. It is worth considering, in addition, that this is a man devoted to the destruction of God's people because he is unable to be at peace otherwise (Est. 5:13–14). Is there any possible scenario imaginable in which God's people are delivered and Haman keeps his life?

Response

With the execution of Haman, the deliverance of God's people in Persia has begun. Esther is at her most admirable in this chapter, and her most cunning. She exposes Haman for what he is, and Haman's schemes entrap him. Strikingly, although Esther is the main actor of the chapter's first half, she is passive in the second half. She guides the king to see the truth about his favorite adviser, but does not call for his death. And so it may be that, when God elevates a member of his people to play a key role in the deliverance of his people from violent persecution (4:14), their time of influence passes and other forces go to work.

We see the deceptive nature of evil in this chapter. Haman's misinterpretation of Esther's banquet means he will walk right into a trap, sealing his doom. We see that one part of God's keeping his promises to his people involves judgment and destruction of evil. In fact, for God to fail to judge evil would necessitate unfaithfulness to his promises. Finally, in God's deliverance of his people in Persia—even though they seem to have forgotten him—we see a prefiguring of a much greater act of deliverance on God's part from a much greater spiritual enemy.

ESTHER 8:1–9:18

8 On that day King Ahasuerus gave to Queen Esther the house of Haman, the enemy of the Jews. And Mordecai came before the king, for Esther had told what he was to her. [2] And the king took off his signet ring, which he had taken from Haman, and gave it to Mordecai. And Esther set Mordecai over the house of Haman.

[3] Then Esther spoke again to the king. She fell at his feet and wept and pleaded with him to avert the evil plan of Haman the Agagite and the plot that he had devised against the Jews. [4] When the king held out the golden scepter to Esther, Esther rose and stood before the king. [5] And she said, "If it please the king, and if I have found favor in his sight, and if the thing seems right before the king, and I am pleasing in his eyes, let an order be written to revoke the letters devised by Haman the Agagite, the son of Hammedatha, which he wrote to destroy the Jews who are in all the provinces of the king. [6] For how can I bear to see the calamity that is coming to my people? Or how can I bear to see the destruction of my kindred?" [7] Then King Ahasuerus said to Queen Esther and to Mordecai the Jew, "Behold, I have given Esther the house of Haman, and they have hanged him on the gallows,[1] because he intended to lay hands on the Jews. [8] But you may write as you please with regard to the Jews, in the name of the king, and seal it with the king's ring, for an edict written in the name of the king and sealed with the king's ring cannot be revoked."

[9] The king's scribes were summoned at that time, in the third month, which is the month of Sivan, on the twenty-third day. And an edict was written, according to all that Mordecai commanded concerning the Jews, to the satraps and the governors and the officials of the provinces from India to Ethiopia, 127 provinces, to each province in its own script and to each people in its own language, and also to the Jews in their script and their language. [10] And he wrote in the name of King Ahasuerus and sealed it with the king's signet ring. Then he sent the letters by mounted couriers riding on swift horses that were used in the king's service, bred from the royal stud, [11] saying that the king allowed the Jews who were in every city to gather and defend their lives, to destroy, to kill, and to annihilate any armed force of any people or province that might attack them, children and women included, and to plunder their goods, [12] on one day throughout all the provinces of King Ahasuerus, on the thirteenth day of the twelfth month, which is the month of Adar. [13] A copy of what was written was to be issued as a decree in every province, being publicly displayed to all peoples, and the Jews were to be ready on that day to take vengeance on their enemies. [14] So the couriers, mounted on their swift horses that were used in the king's service, rode out hurriedly, urged by the king's command. And the decree was issued in Susa the citadel.

[15] Then Mordecai went out from the presence of the king in royal robes of blue and white, with a great golden crown[2] and a robe of fine linen and

purple, and the city of Susa shouted and rejoiced. [16] The Jews had light and gladness and joy and honor. [17] And in every province and in every city, wherever the king's command and his edict reached, there was gladness and joy among the Jews, a feast and a holiday. And many from the peoples of the country declared themselves Jews, for fear of the Jews had fallen on them.

9 Now in the twelfth month, which is the month of Adar, on the thirteenth day of the same, when the king's command and edict were about to be carried out, on the very day when the enemies of the Jews hoped to gain the mastery over them, the reverse occurred: the Jews gained mastery over those who hated them. [2] The Jews gathered in their cities throughout all the provinces of King Ahasuerus to lay hands on those who sought their harm. And no one could stand against them, for the fear of them had fallen on all peoples. [3] All the officials of the provinces and the satraps and the governors and the royal agents also helped the Jews, for the fear of Mordecai had fallen on them. [4] For Mordecai was great in the king's house, and his fame spread throughout all the provinces, for the man Mordecai grew more and more powerful. [5] The Jews struck all their enemies with the sword, killing and destroying them, and did as they pleased to those who hated them. [6] In Susa the citadel itself the Jews killed and destroyed 500 men, [7] and also killed Parshandatha and Dalphon and Aspatha [8] and Poratha and Adalia and Aridatha [9] and Parmashta and Arisai and Aridai and Vaizatha, [10] the ten sons of Haman the son of Hammedatha, the enemy of the Jews, but they laid no hand on the plunder.

[11] That very day the number of those killed in Susa the citadel was reported to the king. [12] And the king said to Queen Esther, "In Susa the citadel the Jews have killed and destroyed 500 men and also the ten sons of Haman. What then have they done in the rest of the king's provinces! Now what is your wish? It shall be granted you. And what further is your request? It shall be fulfilled." [13] And Esther said, "If it please the king, let the Jews who are in Susa be allowed tomorrow also to do according to this day's edict. And let the ten sons of Haman be hanged on the gallows."[3] [14] So the king commanded this to be done. A decree was issued in Susa, and the ten sons of Haman were hanged. [15] The Jews who were in Susa gathered also on the fourteenth day of the month of Adar and they killed 300 men in Susa, but they laid no hands on the plunder.

[16] Now the rest of the Jews who were in the king's provinces also gathered to defend their lives, and got relief from their enemies and killed 75,000 of those who hated them, but they laid no hands on the plunder. [17] This was on the thirteenth day of the month of Adar, and on the fourteenth day they rested and made that a day of feasting and gladness. [18] But the Jews who were in Susa gathered on the thirteenth day and on the fourteenth, and rested on the fifteenth day, making that a day of feasting and gladness.

[1] Or *wooden beam* (see note on 2:23) [2] Or *headdress* [3] Or *wooden beam*; also verse 25 (see note on 2:23)

Section Overview

The story could have ended with Haman's death, but because no one is allowed or willing to repeal a Persian law, Mordecai and Esther must write a second decree to counteract Haman's. A bloody conflict ensues.

Section Outline

IX. Haman's Edict Is Counteracted and the Jews Slaughter Their Enemies (8:1–9:18)
- A. Esther's Permission to Write a Decree Countering Haman's (8:1–8)
- B. The Content of the Decree (8:9–14)
- C. The Effects of the Decree (8:15–17)
- D. The Execution of the Decree (9:1–10)
- E. The Hanging of Haman's Ten Sons and a Second Wave of Killings (9:11–18)

Comment

8:1–2 Another small reversal occurs in a book full of surprising twists. In Persia, property of traitors reverted to the crown, to dispense however it pleased. Ahasuerus gives Haman's property to Esther, who appoints Mordecai as its steward. Here we see the relationship between Mordecai and Esther change from passivity to leadership on Esther's part as she charges Mordecai with the care of Haman's property.

8:3–6 Haman has been exposed, but his plot against the Jews is legally still in force. Esther did not weep and fall at the king's feet before but does so now, asking for an edict to revoke the coming destruction of the Jews. She ties the king's feelings about her ("If I have found favor in his sight") to his approval of her plan, emphasizing it was Haman's idea alone—making it easier to reverse. However, to do so is to ask the king to go against Persian custom, by which legal decrees were unchangeable (1:19). Ahasuerus may even have viewed doing so as a violation of his own integrity. Some commentators have argued that the Persian practice of unrepealable laws is impractical and, never being mentioned in extrabiblical sources, historically unlikely. But governments are not infrequently administered in impractical ways, and it fits with Ahasuerus's bloated ego for his decisions to be unalterable, no matter how foolish or harmful. Without this idiosyncrasy of Persian law, the deliverance of the Persian Jews could be fully resolved here; because of it, the story will extend a bit further.

It should be emphasized that Esther and Mordecai's original plan is to resolve the situation without bloodshed. Esther's identification with the Jews is again emphasized (8:6).

8:7–8 Although the lives of countless Jews are at stake, Ahasuerus will not change one of his own edicts, no matter how foolish. Instead, he allows Mordecai and Esther to write whatever edict they like to ensure their protection, just as he handled Haman's original request (3:10–11). He does not otherwise seem worried about the survival of the Jews.

8:9–11 The intricacies of Persian bureaucracy are on full display as Mordecai gives the Jews royal authority to defend themselves from any armed attack on the day Haman's decree takes effect (v. 11). Since Haman's decree cannot be invalidated, this edict allows the Jews to defend themselves legally. So far, their part in this conflict is wholly defensive.

The workings of divine justice in the execution of Haman were defended earlier in this commentary against modern squeamishness over Haman's fate. But it is more difficult to defend the permission for the death of women and children. On the one hand, the purpose of the edict is self-defense (v. 11), and it is unclear whether this part of the decree was carried out, for only men are mentioned in 9:12. The book's sense of perfect symmetry in reversal dictates that, just as total annihilation is decreed against the Jews, so it is to be decreed in their favor (cf. 3:13–15 with 8:11–14). The theme of holy war also shapes the decree: what Saul left unfinished against the Amalekites will finally be resolved (Ex. 17:16; 1 Sam. 15:3). Haman's twice-repeated identification as an Agagite (Est. 8:3 and 5, a term not used since 3:10) emphasizes this theme.

On the other hand, without denying the need for the Jews of Persia to defend themselves, we can find an aspect of Mordecai's counteredict chilling. A very unfortunate resemblance between the Jews and their enemies begins to emerge at this point: the Persian Jews seem capable of the same violence as their enemies. As the story proceeds, the moral justification for their actions will become even shakier.

8:12–14 As with Haman's decree, the full force of the Persian government is set in motion as the Jews are authorized to take vengeance on their enemies (v. 13). The word "vengeance" refers to the righting of a previous wrong (cf. Josh. 10:13; 1 Sam. 14:24, Ps. 99:8; Jer. 5:9). Mordecai uses his position in the Persian government to give the Jews every advantage possible in the face of unavoidable conflict.

At the previous mention of Mordecai's attire, he was sobbing in sackcloth and ashes (4:1–2). Mordecai's royal robes now show the perfect reversal of his situation. The rejoicing of the city at Mordecai's honoring reverses the city's earlier tumult over a prior royal edict (3:15). Everyone is pleased a man like Mordecai is in a position of influence.

8:16–17 The fear and anguish Haman's edict caused among the Persian Jews (4:3) is also reversed. As elsewhere in the book, a feast occurs as power shifts, but this change is entirely happy.

The apparent conversion of many Persians continues the reversal of the Persian Jews' fate (8:17). As with many other junctures in the book, however, what might look like a victory for God's cause carries some ambiguity. The text does not say that Persian Gentiles turned to Yahweh in faith and repentance—only that they took on Jewish customs and practices. As elsewhere in the book, when the narrator has a chance to talk explicitly about God, he does not. Although we are meant to see this as one aspect of the reversed fortunes of the Jews, it is difficult not to see a sharp contrast with other OT accounts of conversions, which focus on explicit allegiance to the Lord, not on merely assuming Jewish identity (Josh. 2:11; 2 Kings 5:15; Isa. 45:14).

9:1 The main teaching of the entire book is summarized in the perfect reversal of this verse: on the very day the enemies of the Jews hoped to destroy them, the Jews gained mastery over them.

9:2–4 Two parallel statements of fear are given with regard to the Persian Jews in general and Mordecai in particular. As the Jews assemble for battle, no one can stand before them (v. 2; even though battle is apparently not joined until v. 5, we are already told of its outcome). Second, because of the fear of Mordecai and his ascendency in the Persian court, its bureaucracy supports the Jews in their efforts (vv. 3–4).

The fear falling on the Jews' enemies (v. 2) recalls the same phrase in descriptions of battles earlier in Israel's history (cf. Ex. 15:16; Josh. 2:9; 1 Sam. 11:7; Ps. 105:38). Even if none of the Jewish combatants were aware of it, an incomplete strand of redemptive history will be resolved in this battle against the descendants of Amalek. Once again, however, an ambiguity meets us when we note that those earlier acts of warfare enjoyed explicit divine sanction. The only sanction for this battle comes from the Persian state. Although God is at work to deliver his people, it is difficult to argue that the actual details of this deliverance are presented in an unambiguously positive way.

9:5–10 Although the decree was to allow the Jews to defend themselves, the Jews appear to take the initiative on the appointed day to slaughter their enemies without hindrance or restraint ("[they] did as they pleased"; v. 5). That the Jews take no plunder even when allowed (v. 10) reverses the earlier failure of Saul and the people, who plundered the Amalekites (1 Sam. 15:3, 9) instead of destroying them.

9:11–12 Ahasuerus registers no relief that his wife's people are saved, nor grief over the loss of life in his kingdom. If anything, he seems impressed with the level of bloodshed. The only reason for the extension of the fighting to a second day (v. 13) is his sense that it is going well so far.

9:13 Esther asks that the Jews be given an extra day to fight and for Haman's ten sons, already killed on the first day of slaughter, to be hanged like their father. In making both requests, Esther is vindictive and even cruel. Neither is morally justifiable.

With regard to the latter, although the hanging of corpses of those who had committed serious crimes (cf. Josh. 8:29; 10:26) was common, it is hard to imagine what purpose this would serve here except as a warning to anyone who might try to harm the Persian Jews. Esther was uninvolved in Haman's suffering this fate; it is quite a change for her to request it for the sons of her enemy.

With regard to a second day of fighting, since Haman's original edict authorized only one day on which the Jews could be slaughtered, there is no need for a second day of fighting. Her intention seems to be precautionary and punitive, eliminating people possibly suspected of harboring resentments against the Jews. But should people be killed because of what the queen suspects they might do?

One notes Esther's strong reasons for exposing Haman and begging for the repeal of his decree (Est. 7:4; 8:6). Here, in contrast, she bluntly asserts her demands without providing justification. The first day's fighting had some justification; this has none. In this regard, at least, Esther is acting in a way sadly similar to her enemy.

9:14–18 The king grants Esther's two requests, which are carried out (vv. 14–15). Fighting occurs according to the various geographical locations of scattered Jews (vv. 16–18).

Response

The ambiguities of the book of Esther surrounding the subtle but clear working of God's providence to deliver his people and the moral imperfections of the people through whom he works have come to a head. On the one hand, given the rigidity of the Persian legal system and Ahasuerus's unwillingness to violate his own decree, it is difficult to imagine what other course of action Mordecai could have taken against the looming threat of violence. But the actions of Esther, Mordecai, and the Jews on a second day of fighting lack any possible justification as they take advantage of Ahasuerus's weakness as a leader and eliminate anyone they consider an enemy (9:14–15). One cannot help but wonder what this victory might have looked like if the Jews of Esther's day had shown more faith in their ancestral God to deliver them from future attacks and had been concerned more for his fame and glory among the nations than for their own safety. To the extent that the book of Esther is concerned with God's people living wisely in exile, surely the gospel gives us a better framework for dealing with hostility from Gentiles as we live among them (1 Pet. 1:1; 2:13–17). New covenant believers cannot miss their obligation to "proclaim the excellencies" of the God who has delivered them from spiritual darkness (1 Pet. 2:9). May modern-day believers prove themselves better stewards of God's acts of deliverance than the characters in the book of Esther.

ESTHER 9:19–10:3

19 Therefore the Jews of the villages, who live in the rural towns, hold the fourteenth day of the month of Adar as a day for gladness and feasting, as a holiday, and as a day on which they send gifts of food to one another. **20** And Mordecai recorded these things and sent letters to all the Jews who were in all the provinces of King Ahasuerus, both near and far, **21** obliging them to keep the fourteenth day of the month Adar and also the fifteenth day of the same, year by year, **22** as the days on which the Jews got relief from their enemies, and as the month that had been turned for them from sorrow into gladness and from mourning into a holiday; that they should make them days of feasting and gladness, days for sending gifts of food to one another and gifts to the poor. [23] So the Jews accepted what they had started to do, and what Mordecai had written to them. [24] For Haman the Agagite, the son of Hammedatha, the enemy of all the Jews, had plotted against the Jews to destroy them, and had cast Pur (that is, cast lots), to crush and to destroy them. [25] But when it came before the king, he gave orders in writing that his evil plan that he had devised against the Jews should return on his own head, and that he and his sons should be hanged on the gallows. [26] Therefore they called these days Purim, after the term Pur. Therefore, because of all that was written in this letter, and of what they had faced in this matter, and of what had happened to them, [27] the Jews firmly obligated themselves and their offspring and all who joined them, that without fail they would keep these two days according to what was written and at the time appointed every year, [28] that these days should be remembered and kept throughout every generation, in every clan, province, and city, and that these days of Purim should never fall into disuse among the Jews, nor should the commemoration of these days cease among their descendants.

[29] Then Queen Esther, the daughter of Abihail, and Mordecai the Jew gave full written authority, confirming this second letter about Purim. [30] Letters were sent to all the Jews, to the 127 provinces of the kingdom of Ahasuerus, in words of peace and truth, [31] that these days of Purim should be observed at their appointed seasons, as Mordecai the Jew and Queen Esther obligated them, and as they had obligated themselves and their offspring, with regard to their fasts and their lamenting. [32] The command of Esther confirmed these practices of Purim, and it was recorded in writing.

10 King Ahasuerus imposed tax on the land and on the coastlands of the sea. [2] And all the acts of his power and might, and the full account of the high honor of Mordecai, to which the king advanced him, are they not written in the Book of the Chronicles of the kings of Media and Persia? [3] For Mordecai the Jew was second in rank to King Ahasuerus, and he was great among the Jews and popular with the multitude of his brothers, for he sought the welfare of his people and spoke peace to all his people.

Section Overview

Purim is instituted to commemorate the change in the Jews' fortunes. The story closes with the permanently safe and happy situation of the Jews living in Persia.

Section Outline

X. Conclusion: Purim Is Instituted (9:19–10:3)
   A. The Victory Is Commemorated by the Festival of Purim (9:19–32)
   B. Epilogue: Mordecai's Greatness (10:1–3)

Comment

9:19–23 Because of some differences in the day of fighting (vv. 16–18), some Jews celebrated this victory on a different day (v. 19). Mordecai uses his authority to enshrine this celebration as a permanent holiday (vv. 20–21) commemorating the reversal of the Jews' fortunes (v. 22)—focusing more on the victory itself than on the God who provided it. The Jews accept Mordecai's decision (v. 23).

9:24–26a Many feasts and festivals in the Pentateuch bear significant names (e.g., Passover refers to the Lord's *passing over* Israelite dwellings in Egypt; Ex. 12:13). Likewise, Purim is named for the Persian word for the lot, *pur* (rather than the Hebrew word, *goral*). The very means used by Haman to plot his extermination of the Jews is appropriated by the Jews as the name of a holiday.

9:26b–28 Accepting Mordecai's decision, the Jews of Persia add Purim to their religious year as a perpetual commemoration.

9:29–32 Esther adds her authority to Mordecai concerning the holiday of Purim.

10:1 Although this verse recalls the tax relief granted at Esther's coronation (2:18), it is not clear what relevance this information has to the context. The purpose may be to show that, although the Jews' fortunes have changed (9:2, 22), normal life in the Persian Empire grinds on. The more things change, the more they stay the same.

10:2–3 The book ends by focusing not on Esther but on Mordecai (perhaps because, as queen, no further elevation was possible for her). This once ordinary royal servant is now second only to the king as a man of serious importance to both Jews and Persians (v. 2). The text shows us that the Jews' change of fortunes was permanent under Mordecai's leadership. No new threat arose after Haman, as Mordecai worked tirelessly for the good of his people.

Response

The OT frequently shows a deep connection between great actions of God and the festivals and rituals commemorating them. Although the new covenant equivalents of these are fewer and simpler (baptism and Eucharist), they are not unimportant. Even though Christians do not celebrate Purim, baptism and Eucharist are an opportunity to enter joyfully into the salvation the Lord has worked for his church.

And yet, once again, one cannot help but see a contrast between the Lord's constant presence in the rituals of the Pentateuch and his absence from Purim. All the festivals of Exodus and Deuteronomy are focused on the Lord as acts of worship for what he has done for Israel. God has been at work in the book of Esther, but Purim could be celebrated and gifts given without a single mention of his name. And yet, perhaps the Christian can find, in the joy and relief of Purim, a hint, imperfect but unmistakable, of the joy that grips all the saints (Rev. 19:6–8) after God delivers us from the spiritual Babylon that hates God and oppresses his people (Revelation 18).

The book ends by speaking to the greatness of Mordecai (Est. 10:2–3). Many other acts of deliverance by God are followed by praise (Exodus 15; Judges 5), yet here the lack of any praise to God for the series of coincidences no human could have engineered is saddening. Although the secure position of the Jews in Persia after so serious a threat is reason for genuine celebration, it is appropriate for Christians to ponder what opportunities we might have to speak of the God who fulfills his purposes and works on our behalf as we make our way in the world.

JOB

Douglas Sean O'Donnell

INTRODUCTION TO
JOB

Overview

The book of Job prefigures the purposeful sufferings of Jesus Christ. That is, the story of God's servant Job prepares us for the story of Jesus, the suffering servant who in his passion and death exhibits how innocent suffering can show forth the justice of God.

The drama of Job opens and closes with God's blessings upon the righteous man Job (1:1–5; 42:10–17). Between the prologue and the epilogue, Job suffers the arrows of inexplicable divine providence. In two days he loses his wealth, his children, and his health. In the days that follow he loses his closest and wisest friends' respect. He thinks he is losing his mind, and he wants to lose his life. While Job claims his innocence, his friends debate the nature of his offense against God (see the discourses and soliloquies of chs. 3–31). Surely such sufferings are caused by Job's sin.

It is not until God speaks—first indirectly through Elihu (chs. 32–37), then directly (chs. 38–41)—that wisdom is found. Everyone is guilty but God. Job understands, or *sees*, this (40:3–5; 42:1–6), as do his friends (42:7–9). In the end (and as the book's goal), the righteous sufferer is vindicated, sinners are atoned for through a costly blood sacrifice, and the sovereign freedom and justice of God is upheld.

Title

The book is named after its protagonist, Job. Rabbinic exegesis first noted the wordplay (without the vowel markings, added later to the original) on the name *Job* (Hb. *'yb*, later *'iyyob*) and the word *enemy* (Hb. *'yb*, later *'oyeb*). Job asks God, "Why do you hide your face and count me as your enemy?" (13:24; cf. 33:10). Perhaps the title is a double meaning, with the final twist in the title coming at the end of the drama: Job is God's blessed servant, not his cursed enemy.

Author and Date

The author of the book is anonymous and unknown. What is known is that this book was written by an Israelite about Job, a non-Israelite. While the names of the book's people[1] and places are likely from southern Edom or northern Arabia,

---

1 Of all the characters mentioned, only Elihu (which means "he is God," likely referencing "Yahweh is God") son of Barachel ("God has blessed") bears a Hebrew name.

the drama is set outside the Promised Land ("east" of the Jordan River), and none of the key events of Israel's history are mentioned, nevertheless the language (Hebrew), deity (the "God" of the dialogue in chs. 3–37 is Yahweh [cf. 1:21; 12:9], the personal Creator who speaks/reveals himself to his creation, chs. 38–41), and theology (cf. Proverbs' teaching on the blessing of the wise vs. the punishment of the fool) clearly reflect Israel's wisdom literature tradition. Thus it is reasonable to surmise that a wisdom sage from when wisdom writing flourished in Israel (from Solomon in the 10th century BC to Hezekiah in the 8th) or someone in that same tradition at a later date (C. L. Seow argues for a late 6th- to mid-5th-century composition) was the author.[2] If the latter dating is correct, the story set in the patriarchal age (with authentic language and coloring)[3] retells for exiled Israel the story of a life east of Eden *and* their own lives east of Jerusalem. Whoever the author, whatever the date of composition, and whoever its first readers, Job undoubtedly exhibits a timelessness and timeliness to its themes that transcends its original provenance.

Occasion

While we cannot be certain of the original author's occasion for writing, the text's theological themes suggest that he writes against a rigid and formulaic view of the OT retribution principle. Under God's sovereign and free rule, there is more to life than "whatever one sows, that will he also reap" (Gal. 6:7), or, as Eliphaz phrases it, "Those who plow iniquity and sow trouble reap the same" (Job 4:8). Moreover, and more broadly speaking, the author writes to address "the age-old, universal issue of human suffering in the context of the infinite wisdom, authority, and righteousness of Yahweh."[4]

Genre and Literary Features

Is the book of Job a drama, epic poem, dialogue, tragedy, lament, lawsuit, or all of the above? Whatever its precise genre or mix of genres, Job is a literary masterpiece![5] Its carefully designed structure supports its majestically high themes, while its imagery ("my belly is like wine that has no vent"; 32:19a), wit ("the bushes of the earth . . . will teach you"; 12:8–9), ironic prayers of personification ("O earth, cover not my blood"; 16:18a), dark humor (Job's digging for death "more than for hidden treasures"; 3:21), light humor (Job's couch easing his complaint; 7:13b), clever turns of phrase ("eyes to the blind"; 29:15a), biting sarcasm ("wisdom will die with you"; 12:2b), acrostic closures (14:1 begins with

---

2 Similar to Solomon, the author of Job draws from his wealth of observable wisdom, from his knowledge of the stars in the heavens (Job 9:9; 38:31) to his grasp of mining operations under the earth (28:1–11). He knows of the soaring of hawks (39:26) and the stupidity of ostriches (39:13–18). He also echoes wisdom sayings from Proverbs (e.g., Job 4:8//Prov. 22:8a; Job 5:17b//Prov. 3:11a).
3 We know this from the ancient divine names used (*El*, *Eloah*, and *Shaddai*), the nature of commerce (e.g., wealth measured in livestock, 1:3; bartering, 2:4), sacrifices' being performed not by a priest in a temple but by a patriarch in a homestead (1:5), and Job's long life span ("And after this Job lived 140 years"; 42:16). In his *Ecclesiastical History of the English People*, Venerable Bede (c. AD 673–735) labels Job "the Blessed Patriarch."
4 Daniel J. Estes, *Job*, TTT (Grand Rapids, MI: Baker, 2013), 2.
5 Alfred, Lord Tennyson called Job "the greatest poem of ancient and modern times," and Victor Hugo said it is "perhaps the greatest masterpiece of the human mind."

the first letter of the Hebrew alphabet, while the last word of 14:22 begins with the alphabet's last letter), and eloquently structured prose (e.g., 1:13–19) make each line soar. Job's story of human tragedy and divine comedy is enhanced by its realistic characters, its profound poetry, its courtroom scene, and its surprise ending.

Such rhetorical flourish leads some scholars to view the book as purely fictional, as an imaginary narrative with a moral point, much like Jesus' parables. The extremities of Job's sufferings and the book's persistent poetic dialogue seem to support this view. Who suffers like Job? Who speaks in beautiful parallelisms when arguing or in imaginative imagery when scraping their wounds? (And who was there to record more than ten thousand words of elevated extemporaneous dialogue?) However, it is also possible that the book is historical, or at least that it contains historical elements. Even if poetic license is allowed (and it is allowed in the Bible's wisdom literature!), a historical narrative is implied. The use of real names and places, as well as a seemingly real-life story (a story no more dramatically unrealistic than the Evangelists' narratives of the creatures' killing their Creator), support this view. Moreover, the references to Job in Ezekiel 14:14, 20 and James 5:11 seem to lend their God-inspired weight to understanding him as a historical figure. It makes best sense to see the book of Job as an embellished retelling of actual people and events.

Whatever the truth regarding the book's historicity (for more discussion on this, see Interpretive Challenges), Job's genre is primarily that of poetry (3:1–42:6). As such, it is important to grasp that the structure, imagery, and terseness of poetry intentionally slows the reader down so he might meditate upon and *feel* deeply the wisdom sage's "words of delight" (Eccles. 12:10). We will explore further characteristics of Hebrew poetry in Preaching from Job, as well as explain and illustrate such characteristics throughout the commentary.

Theology of Job

If we understand something of the nature of God, humanity, and our relationship with God, we can grasp the basic theological import of the book. However, before we explore that major theological theme, it would be remiss to neglect the minor theme of *major* human suffering.

THE RIGHTEOUS SUFFERER AND SUFFERING RIGHTLY

Although the book of Job was not written primarily to address the problem of evil or the issue of inexplicable suffering (as will be clarified, the book is concerned primarily with divine wisdom and our access to it), we can nevertheless learn from Job about how to suffer in a manner pleasing to God. It should come as no surprise that a practical model for suffering (Job) should be included in the Wisdom Literature of the Bible, for these books cover topics as practical as love (the Song of Solomon), the meaning of life (Ecclesiastes), and a host of other everyday topics ranging from money to marriage and from politics to parenting (Proverbs). From Job we can learn patience (chs. 1–2; cf. James 5:11),[6] as well as how to offer impatient protest to God (cf. Job's speeches) because we believe that (a) God is sovereign even over sufferings and (b) he will ultimately vindicate the righteous even if he never reveals the purpose behind the providential pains. Thus, as the earliest Christian interpreters noted (e.g., Justin Martyr, Origen, Chrysostom, Augustine), Job rightly serves the Christian church as an exemplar of faith. Indeed, the righteous shall live by such faith. Moreover, we can join the NT authors in relating the theme of suffering—notably, suffering for righteousness' sake and the gospel—to participation in the sufferings of Christ, seeing it as an impetus to turn our hearts heavenward, longing for eternal life with our ever-living Redeemer.

DIVINE WISDOM VIA THE FEAR OF GOD

In his "Some Thoughts concerning the Revival," Jonathan Edwards wrote: "There is not so much difference, before God, between children and grown persons as we are ready to imagine; we are all poor, ignorant foolish babes in his sight: our adult age don't bring us so much nearer to God as we are apt to think."[7] As it relates to the theme of human wisdom in the book of Job, Edwards's thought is instructive. Humans can gain enormous insight about God, and yet wise Job's story reminds us that we should *know* that we *know* so little. Like Job's friends, we can plumb the depths of the riches of the wisdom and knowledge of God only to learn, as they did (42:7–9), that we are still but poor, ignorant, foolish babes in his sight. We can climb the mountains of his unsearchable judgments and inscrutable ways only to find ourselves not as near to God as we thought. We can dig deep into the recesses of human understanding and mine diamonds from the caverns of human existence, experience, and observation, but on our own we cannot find wisdom "from above," from the one who "is above all" (John 3:31). We have "earthly wisdom" (2 Cor. 1:12), but the Lord alone has heavenly wisdom. He alone is wise (Job 28:23–27; 37:1–42:6).

God's wisdom wearies us if we seek to grasp it through humanly means. Saving knowledge of the Holy One cannot be found within ourselves or by climbing Jacob's ladder to peek our heads through the clouds. We cannot wrap our minds around the one who "wrapped up the waters in a garment" and "gathered the wind in his fists" (Prov. 30:4). We can see only flickers of light in the night sky, streaks of lightning that dance in the storm. And such light—momentary light—comes only through open eyes and hands and hearts, with faces to the ground.

"Where shall wisdom be found?" (Job 28:12; cf. v. 20) is not only a question central to Job's story; it is the foundational question of the Wisdom Literature. The end of Ecclesiastes (Eccles. 12:13) and the prologue to Proverbs (Prov. 1:7) echo what Job illustrates: "the fear of the Lord, that is wisdom" (Job 28:28). This wisdom from above comes only "to those who take refuge in him" (Prov. 30:5),

---

6 In *Patience* (14:2–7), Tertullian of Carthage (c. AD 160–225) uses Job as a model of patience. Like Job, Christians should wear the "breastplate and shield of patience" to fight off the Devil's temptations and patiently persevere through the loss of possessions, loved ones, or health.

7 *The Works of Jonathan Edwards*, ed. John E. Smith, vol. 4, *The Great Awakening*, ed. C. C. Goen (New Haven, CT: Yale University Press, 1972), 408.

to those who reaffirm John the Baptist's attitude about God incarnate: "He must increase, but I must decrease" (John 3:30). The wise understand what the book of Job intends to teach: wisdom of God comes from fear of God.

Relationship to the Rest of the Bible and to Christ

According to the NT, the knowledge of God's plan of salvation—the mystery of the gospel revealed (Eph. 1:7–10)—is found in Christ and his cross. Christ, in whom are hidden all of the treasures of wisdom (Col. 2:2–3), brings "wisdom from above"; he brings God's peaceable, gentle, merciful wisdom (James 3:17) down to earth. And such wisdom was demonstrated through Christ's growth in wisdom and his teaching of wisdom (Luke 2:40, 52; Matt. 13:54) and ultimately through his sacrificial death:

> The word of the cross is folly to those who are perishing, but to us who are being saved it is the power of God. For it is written, "I will destroy the *wisdom* of the wise, and the discernment of the discerning I will thwart." Where is the one who is wise? Where is the scribe? Where is the debater of this age? Has not God made foolish the *wisdom* of the world? For since, in the *wisdom* of God, the world did not know God through *wisdom*, it pleased God through the folly of what we preach to save those who believe. For Jews demand signs and Greeks seek *wisdom*, but we preach Christ crucified, a stumbling block to Jews and folly to Gentiles, but to those who are called, both Jews and Greeks, Christ the power of God and the *wisdom* of God. (1 Cor. 1:18–24)

Paul's argument is that those who trust that God through the crucifixion made Christ to be "wisdom from God, righteousness and sanctification and redemption" (1 Cor. 1:30) appear foolish to the unwise—to the overly-wise-in-its-own-eyes—world. Yet he is no fool who abandons human pride and power to find the "secret and hidden wisdom of God" (1 Cor. 2:7) now revealed in "Christ and him crucified" (1 Cor. 2:2). The seeming folly of a crucified God is God's wisdom perfected. That is where wisdom is ultimately found.

CHRISTOCENTRIC WISDOM

In his commentary on Isaiah, Jerome wrote, "To be ignorant of the Scripture is to be ignorant of Christ."[8] Jerome was right. If we know nothing of the Word of God, we will know nothing of the Son of God. Put positively, the more we know the Bible, the better we will know the person and work of Jesus Christ. Jerome's statement, however, can be reversed to make another point: "To be ignorant of Christ is to be ignorant of Scripture." In John 5:39–40 Jesus rebukes the Pharisees: "You search the Scriptures because you think that in them you have eternal life; and it is *they that bear witness about me*, yet you refuse to come to me that you may

---

8 Jerome, "Prologue," in *Commentary on Isaiah* (PL 24:17; cf. CCSL 73:1).

have life." Life does not come through Bible literacy; life comes through Jesus. And a right understanding of Scripture comes through knowledge of Jesus and trust in him. As Paul wrote, "To this day, when they [unconverted Jews] read the [Old Testament], that same veil remains unlifted, because *only through Christ* is it taken away. Yes, to this day whenever Moses is read a veil lies over their hearts. But *when one turns to the Lord*, the veil is removed" (2 Cor. 3:14–16).

Such knowledge understands that just as every book of the OT adds light to our understanding of Jesus, so the revelation of God in the person of Christ enlightens our understanding of the OT. Martin Luther put it this way: "We can only read the Bible forwards, but we have to understand it backwards."[9] Jesus demonstrates this forward-backward reading of the Word in Luke 24:44, as he teaches his disciples how every book of the OT canon—the "Law of Moses and the Prophets and the Psalms"—attests to his person and work, notably his death and resurrection. Most significant for our study is Luke's mention of "the Psalms," referencing the *ketuvim*, or "Writings," which comprises eleven Hebrew books, the first being the book of Psalms and the last being Chronicles (1–2 Chronicles in English Bibles). In some ways the book of Job is about Jesus. In what ways, this commentary seeks to show. May Christ open our minds to understand Job Christocentrically.[10]

OT SALVATION HISTORY

From Genesis to Esther, the Bible speaks of God's saving presence in the world. In Job, however, notable references to that story are missing. There is no mention of the patriarchs, the exodus, the covenants, the Torah, or the tabernacle. Why? It is not that this book does not belong in our Bibles.[11] Rather, the answer lies in a consideration of the genre of Job: it is wisdom literature (cf. Genre and Literary Features). As such, it joins Proverbs, Ecclesiastes, and the Song of Solomon in addressing a covenant audience that knows God's workings in the world but needs encouragement in walking "in a manner worthy of the Lord," being "filled with . . . all spiritual wisdom" (Col. 1:9–10). In this way, the Wisdom Literature complements the salvation story. It provides practical theology and kingdom ethics for the redeemed. It teaches us *who* God is (more than *what* he has done) and *how* (more than *why*) we should live wisely.

Preaching from Job

GRAPPLING WITH THE TEXT

While the book of Job remains one of the most popular books of the Bible for artistic expression,[12] media reference, and private devotion, it is neglected in the

---

9 Martin Luther, quoted in David Jackman, "The Hermeneutical Distinctives of Expository Preaching," in *Preach the Word: Essays on Expository Preaching: In Honor of R. Kent Hughes*, ed. Leland Ryken and Todd Wilson (Wheaton, IL: Crossway, 2007), 18.

10 For the above two sections, see the introduction in Douglas Sean O'Donnell, *The Beginning and End of Wisdom: Preaching Christ from the First and Last Chapters of Proverbs, Ecclesiastes, and Job* (Wheaton, IL: Crossway, 2011).

11 In fact, with the exception of Theodore of Mopsuestia (AD 350–428), the church throughout the ages has readily acknowledged the book of Job as canonical.

12 As C. L. Seow notes, Job "has inspired visual art throughout the ages—in catacombs and sarcophagi from the first centuries C.E., medieval manuscript illuminations, cathedral sculptures, Renaissance paintings, and modern renderings in a variety of media. There are, in fact, thousands of artistic representations of Job in various genres known from around the world. Job is amply represented in music as well, from Jewish and

pulpit. There are valid reasons for this: its story is straightforward, but its text is complex. Job requires the modern preacher to understand ancient Near Eastern customs, poetry, theology, and language.[13] And while there are a growing number of resources to help fill the knowledge gap,[14] the task remains daunting.

Perhaps three simple suggestions will help the preacher tackle this tricky text. First, if one seeks to preach a short series on Job, then 1:1–2:13; 19:23–29; 28:1–28; 38:1–11; 42:1–6; 42:7–17 are six recommended pericopes for effectively encompassing the storyline, covering key themes, and diving into some of the profound poetry. A verse-by-verse exposition of the entire book is possible, but perhaps not profitable in a congregational setting. (Even John Calvin, in his 159 sermons on Job, did not cover every chapter!) That said, with Job's linear storyline, this book can be preached in a linear fashion, beginning to end, section by section. For this reason, the material of this commentary is organized in possible preaching units along with possible sermon titles (cf. Outline), with many of the titles taken from the text itself.

Second, preachers should note the book's narrative bookends. The beginning and end of the book of Job are key for rightly interpreting the characters' words and actions. For example, because we know from chapter 1 that Satan, not Job, is to blame for Job's calamities and from chapter 42 we know that Job has spoken rightly about the Lord, we are to read Job's story and speeches sympathetically.[15] Moreover, with the prologue and epilogue as our interpretive lens, we know we are not to read every word in the three friends' discourses as inspired truth. It would be wrong to preach some of Zophar's zings as direct applications to our contemporary contexts.

Third, expositors must preach the poetry with poetic sensibilities and a basic understanding of how Hebrew poetry works. Other than the prologue and epilogue, the book of Job joins the Psalms, the Song of Solomon, Proverbs, and Lamentations in being a wholly poetic work.[16] Thus, if we are to preach the book of Job, we must understand how to do so.

We must understand common poetic structures used in biblical poetry. For example, throughout Job there are hundreds of "couplets" (two-line units) and

---

Romans chants to later motets, madrigals, oratorios, and cantatas, to contemporary music, punk rock, and hip-hop. Job has inspired poets, novelists, playwrights, and satirists." *Job 1–21: Interpretation and Commentary*, Illuminations (Grand Rapids, MI: Eerdmans, 2013), 1.

13 Due to the use of many obscure Hebrew words (the most in the Bible!), the book of Job is daunting to translate. Even the pastor with advanced Hebrew will want to compare many translations—not only to see the possible diversities of interpretation but also to find homiletical options for expression.

14 Leland Ryken, James C. Wilhoit, and Tremper Longman III, eds. *Dictionary of Biblical Imagery* (Downers Grove, IL: IVP Academic, 1998); Tremper Longman III and Peter Enns, eds., *Dictionary of the Old Testament: Wisdom, Poetry & Writings* (Downers Grove, IL: IVP Academic, 2008).

15 While it is possible that God's verdict of Job as speaking rightly (42:7–8) relates only to his two confessions (40:3–5; 42:1–6), it likely refers to his previous speeches as well (chs. 3; 6–7; 9–10; 12–14; 23–24; 26–31). There is a question as to how Job's speaking of God as an enemy archer (6:4), or as someone who mocks the innocent in their troubles (9:23) and terrifies Job with a rod in hand (9:34), fits under the rubric of right talk about God, which we shall explore further when we come to the commentary on chapter 42. For now, a clue to why language bordering on blasphemous might be acceptable to God might be that only Job addresses God. The friends speak *about* God, but Job speaks *to* God, as a member of God's household—"my servant Job" (42:7–8). Is a relationship through prayer at play? Is there such a thing as righteous rebellion that is acceptable within the human-divine relationship when tempered by brutal honesty?

16 The only OT books without a line of poetry are Leviticus, Ruth, Esther, Haggai, and Malachi.

"triplets" (three-line units), along with a variety of parallelisms in which words, phrases, syntax, and even sounds (in the original Hebrew) correspond with each other, usually opposing or contrasting each other and often building thematically upon one another. For example, note the various grammatical and lexical parallels (synonyms and antonyms) in Job 5:18–20 (e.g., the similarity of the verbs "he wounds" and "he shatters"; v. 18):

> For he wounds, but he binds up;
> > he shatters, but his hands heal.
> He will deliver you from six troubles;
> > in seven no evil shall touch you.
> In famine he will redeem you from death,
> > and in war from the power of the sword.

At times throughout the commentary, we divide the text to highlight parallel words or lines. For example 8:11, will be displayed like this:

| Can papyrus | grow | where there is no marsh? |
| Can reeds | flourish | where there is no water? |

Alongside poetic structures, we must also understand poetic imagery. The characters in Job use a variety of images to make ideas concrete, precise, memorable, lively, and engaging. Images expressed through the use of poetic devices—such as metaphor, simile, alliteration, apostrophe, assonance, personification, and hyperboles—add color and texture. If the poetic structure can be likened to the frame of a painting, then the picture painted by such poetic devices is the painting itself. And, like the frame-painting combination, no matter how artistic the frame might be, it is the painting and not the frame that is the focus. Our job in preaching the poetry in the book of Job is to recognize these images, sense them, understand them, and explain them.[17]

PREACHING CHRIST

Most experienced preachers grasp how to preach Christ from the OT, but when it comes to the book of Job, even those most experienced among us have no idea how to travel from the text to "the gospel of God" (Rom. 1:1). Part of the difficulty is the lack of apostolic hermeneutical help. Job is quoted only twice in the NT (table 4.1),[18] and these quotes offer no simple pattern of movement, as predictive prophecy does. Rather, they merely affirm OT ethics as they exalt God's greatness.

The story of Job, however, does provide us with a narrative that relates typologically to the metanarrative of Jesus. The two "passion" narratives are strikingly similar:

---

17 For further study on preaching a Hebrew poem in an English prose sermon, see O'Donnell, "Appendix A: Preaching Hebrew Poetry," in *Beginning and End of Wisdom*, 139–152.
18 "Loci Citati Vel Allegeti" in NA[28] claims there are ninety-four allusions to Job in the NT, but the majority of these are too vague to qualify as genuine echoes of the original.

TABLE 4.1: NT Quotations of Job

Job 5:13a: "He catches the wise in their own craftiness."	1 Corinthians 3:18–21a: Let no one deceive himself. If anyone among you thinks that he is wise in this age, let him become a fool that he may become wise. For the wisdom of this world is folly with God. For it is written, *"He catches the wise in their craftiness,"* and again, "The Lord knows the thoughts of the wise, that they are futile." So let no one boast in men.

Job 41:11a:
"Who has first given to me, that I should repay him?"
	Romans 11:34–36:
	"For who has known the mind of the Lord,
	    or who has been his counselor?"
	"Or *who has given a gift to him
	    that he might be repaid?"*
	
	For from him and through him and to him are all things. To him be glory forever. Amen.

- There was a righteous man.
- This man, by God's set purpose, was handed over to Satan-inflicted sufferings.
- This man, in his suffering, was mocked and mistreated.
- This man prayed for his enemies—for those who persecuted him.
- This man, after a costly and substitutionary blood sacrifice, became a priestly mediator between God and sinners.
- This man was fully and publicly vindicated by God.
- This man, in the end, was exalted, receiving honor and glory and power and wealth, even (seemingly) to a greater extent than what he first had.

The final chapter of Job reinforces this gospel-centered reading of the whole drama. Job 42:7–8 reads like a traditional gospel tract. In summary:

- Man has sinned against God. While Job's friends thought themselves to be in the right, they were very much in the wrong.
- God is angry at sin, and rightfully so, for it is an assault on his name and glory.
- In his mercy, God deals with these sinners not according to their folly. It is through a blood sacrifice and an innocent man's mediation that their sins are forgiven.

These typological connections have been recognized throughout the church's history. For example, by the fourth century AD, the prologue to Job was used in readings for Holy Week. In fifth-century Syria, Severian of Gabala preached four sermons during the evening services on Job's "passion" as foreshadowing Christ's, and in sixth-century Constantinople, Leontius the Presbyter did likewise.[19] The thirteenth- or fourteenth-century picture Bible *Speculum Humanae Salvationis* ("Mirror of Human Salvation") and William Blake's famous *Illustrations of the Book of Job* (1826) also depict Job as a type of Christ. Perhaps a modern liturgical, sermonic, and artistic recapitulation is in order.

---

19 For these examples, see Seow, *Job 1–21*, 177, 179, 196.

Moreover, we see possible linguistic/theological connections between Job 42:7–8 and Jesus (Matt. 12:17–21//Isa. 42:1–4) in regard to the Isaianic "servant." Certainly, lines in Job resemble some of Isaiah's servant texts (Job 9:8a = Isa. 44:24d; Job 12:9b = Isa. 41:20c; and perhaps Job 16:17a//Isa. 53:9c; Job 26:12a//Isa. 51:15b).[20] Based on such evidence, the question naturally arises in the Christian mind: Is what Isaiah foretold about the servant illustrated in Job and embodied in Jesus? Does Christ crucified demonstrate how an innocent man could suffer and yet God—in it and through it—could show forth his justice? Elsewhere I wrote on this possibility:

> Job's friends were not too far removed from those who cried out to our suffering Savior, "If you are the Son of God, come down from the cross" (Matt. 27:40). The last picture they could imagine was a suffering servant. How could a suffering servant demonstrate the blessing of God? How could a suffering servant bring peace between God and man? How could a suffering servant defeat Satan and his schemes? How could a suffering servant be perfectly innocent and yet God perfectly just?[21]

Beyond typological connections, we can also make thematic connections, usually from—but not limited to—the teachings of Jesus. If we are struggling to find a way to Christ through a fulfillment scheme or a typological connection, perhaps there is something Jesus taught that can (a) summarize or (b) shed further light on a text from Job. After all, Jesus is the supreme wisdom teacher, both in person and method. So, for example, if a preacher is addressing a passage from "Job's Third Test," as we have labeled the ridicule of Job's friends (Job 3–31), perhaps a good connection would be between the "steadfastness of Job" (James 5:11) in this final test and Jesus' teaching on the necessity of Christian perseverance. In Revelation 1:10–3:22, Jesus speaks to the church then and now of patiently enduring (2:2), conquering (2:11), holding fast to his name (2:13), keeping his works until the end (2:26), and so on. We might also take such a theme a step further by relating it to Christ's perseverance for our salvation (cf. Heb. 12:2).

A final way of making thematic connections is through contrast. For example, whereas Christ willingly suffered, Job did not; Christ's sufferings and vindication conquered death, Job's did not.

Interpretive Challenges

IS THE STORY OF JOB HISTORICAL?

Was there really a man named Job? Did he live in a land called Uz? Was he perfectly righteous with a perfectly blessed life? Did he in one day lose everything but his troublesome, unnamed wife? Did he have friends who sat silently for seven days? Did he then suffer the accusations of Eliphaz, the blame of Bildad, the zings of

---

20 Seow, *Job 1–21*, 42. For more on Job as a symbol of the suffering "servant of Yahweh," see Gregory the Great's *Moralia in Iob* (in Seow, *Job 1–21*, 194) and Hans Urs von Balthasar's *The Glory of the Lord* (in Seow, *Job 1–21*, 230). An illustrated manuscript of the Syriac *Rabbula Gospels* (from the 6th century AD) portrays Job and Isaiah as holding scrolls and standing side by side (Seow, *Job 1–21*, 197).
21 O'Donnell, *Beginning and End of Wisdom*, 116.

Zophar, and the admonishments of Elihu? Did God hold a heavenly chamber room conference with Satan at which he granted permission to afflict Job? Did God really speak audibly to Job? Are Leviathan and Behemoth real creatures? Put simply, did the author of Job create the whole drama out of whole cloth, much like Shakespeare did with his characters from foreign countries who speak in poetry?

The answer is not easy, and by no means should we be dogmatic. Who can know for certain? While Uz appears to be an ancient region, the names of Job's daughters provide a tinge of historic realism (42:14), and Ezekiel mentions Job alongside Noah and Daniel (Ezek. 14:14, 20; cf. James 5:11), such clues do not solve the riddle. Authors often set fictional works in real places (e.g., the Canterbury of Chaucer's *Canterbury Tales*), and Ezekiel and James could be referencing Job as a literary figure (similar to our saying, "We should not emulate the Wife of Bath's lusts").[22] Tremper Longman offers a helpful balance:

> The truth may be between the view that Job was a historical character, with the book describing events of his life in detail, and the view that Job is a purely literary figure. Job could have been known as a particularly righteous person who suffered. His story would then lend itself to further elaboration for the purposes of discussing the issue of an innocent sufferer and wisdom. Indeed, the highly literary nature of the prose and poetry . . . would suggest that this at least is true. The genre signals help us to see that the book of Job is certainly not a precise historical report. It is either the elaborated story of an actual historical figure or of a literary figure.[23]

My view is that Job was a historical person, not a fictional character, someone whose legendary sufferings were the historical ground on which the author of Job built with magnificent literary flair. Thus, while I give poetic license to how the author retells the narrative (e.g., I do not take the speeches as verbatim reports of the interchange between Job and his friends), I take all of the characters named (including Satan) and the details of the story told (including the amazing catastrophes) to be historically accurate.

HOW DO WE READ AND APPLY THE THREE FRIENDS' ADVICE?

In the end (Job 42:7–9), since God judges the friends' words about Job to be wrong, this raises the question: Is all of what they say inapplicable to kingdom life? Put differently, is it possible to hear the inspired voice of God through the uninspired voice of tradition? While Calvin is correct that "there is nothing in their speeches that we may not receive as if the Holy Spirit had spoken it" (*On Job* 1.1), we must discerningly apply how much of it was intended to make us wise unto salvation and to train us in righteousness.

---

22 Yet, to the point, John H. Walton gives a few helpful insights: "Though there may be purely literary characters in the literature of the ancient world, ancient authors were more likely to construct their literature around epic figures of the distant past than to fabricate 'fiction' as we understand it today. . . . [Moreover,] we lose nothing by accepting Job's story as historical, and we gain nothing by concluding that he is a fabricated, fictional character." *Job*, NIVAC (Grand Rapids, MI: Zondervan, 2012), 25.

23 Tremper Longman, *Job*, BCOTWP (Grand Rapids, MI: Baker Academic, 2012), 33.

Certainly, parts of their anthropology are orthodox (Eliphaz in 4:17; 15:14–16; Bildad in 25:4) and thus worth echoing today.[24] Moreover, much of their theology is God-saturated and God-centered. For example, when Job continues to bemoan his personal sufferings, Zophar seeks to turn Job's eyes heavenward—to the infinite God and his mysterious workings (11:5–7). More to the point, Paul quotes Eliphaz's words about God as truthful (Job 5:13 in 1 Cor. 3:19). So we ought to preach their lines on God's incomprehensible nature, manifold wisdom, and great works, as well as his love for the righteous, punishment of the wicked, and corrective discipline toward his people. We can display the nuggets of gold found in the rumble of the wisdom of these fools.

WHAT IS THE ROLE OF ELIHU?

The character of Elihu is of special interest. As with the three "wise" men, we wonder if none, some, much, or all of what he says is true. Is he a long-winded, arrogant buffoon pushed on stage for comic relief, a wise prophet whose words we should heed, or something in between? If we misinterpret his four uninterrupted speeches (Job 32:6–33:33; 34:2–37; 35:2–16; 36:2–37:24), then obviously our instruction will be off. When we get to his monologue in the commentary, we will explore his role in greater detail (cf. esp. Response section on 32:1–37:24). For now, it is important to grab hold of three foundational facts.

First, neither Job nor Yahweh replies to Elihu. This is the only silent response in the book. Does God like what he hears? Does Job agree? We do not know for certain. However, since God offers no rebuke and Job offers no sacrifice on Elihu's behalf, we should perhaps lean in a positive direction. Also, it is worth noting that Elihu is the only one of the four "comforters" to engage with Job's actual claims and arguments (cf. 33:9–11; 34:5–6; 35:2–3), and, moreover, some of Elihu's views are reiterated in Yahweh's speeches. Therefore, might Elihu be like young Joseph (Gen. 41:38) or Daniel (Dan. 5:12, 14), offering his wisdom only after the world's "wise" men (Job 34:2, 34; 37:24) have failed? Or does he more resemble a Jonah-like prophet—arrogant, angry, and eccentric—but one who nevertheless speaks with divine inspiration (32:8; 33:4)? Thus, does Elihu truly possess special revelation or divine wisdom (33:33)? And, despite his false accusations against Job (e.g., 34:36–37), does he rightly defend the justice of God (e.g., 37:23) and lead us forward to the fear of God (37:24)?

Second, what is certain is that Elihu shifts the focus from Job's problem to God's power. In this sense Elihu is an Elijah-like figure who prepares the way for the Lord. He prepares Job, as he also prepares the reader, to hear from God (chs. 38–41) concerning divine transcendence, an inexplicably mysterious providence, and absolute moral freedom. Such revelation is in a sense mediated (or at least introduced) in some of Elihu's lines. Perhaps it would help to picture him as a talking temple. Before Job enters the presence of God, Elihu speaks to him of

---

24 In most contexts (not Job's!), their advice is scriptural. "It is important to recall that [Job's friends] echo ideas that are fully in accord with other parts of the Bible"; Roland E. Murphy, *The Tree of Life: An Exploration of Biblical Wisdom Literature*, ABRL (New York: Doubleday, 1990), 38.

God's awesomeness. Or, to borrow another OT image, he asks Job to take off his shoes before Job hears the awesome theophany.

Third, Elihu offers a unique theological contribution to the discussion. He introduces the idea of suffering as preparatory for purity (avoiding future sin). Moreover, and more importantly, he offers a theodicy (a defense of God's justice) as he introduces the idea of Job's sufferings as a divine test. In this way, he has stuck his head into the heavens. While he is not privy to the agreement between Satan and God in the prologue, he alone introduces the possibility of divine purposes beyond retribution for sin. Similar to Joseph's sufferings under Pharaoh, it is possible that Job was not punished by God for any sin but that the sufferings were used by God ultimately to bring about a greater good. Elihu's speeches, like Yahweh's, offer no explanation for human suffering, and, like Jesus' explanation of the blind man's suffering in John 9:1–3, they point to the need to lean on God's wisdom, not human understanding, and to believe that even through severe human sufferings "the works of God" might very well "be displayed" (John 9:3).

Outline

I. Prologue (1:1–2:13)
  A. Introduction: Once Upon a Time . . . There Was a Man (1:1–5)
    1. Job's Person (1:1)
    2. Job's Possessions (1:2–3)
    3. Job's Patriarchal "Priesthood" (1:4–5)
  B. God's Servant Given into Satan's Hand (1:6–12)
    1. Into the Heavens (1:6)
    2. A Curious Conversation (1:7–8)
    3. The Challenger's Challenge (1:9–11)
    4. Into Satan's Hand (1:12)
  C. Job's First Test (1:13–22)
    1. A Disastrous Day (1:13–19)
    2. Job's Godly Response to the Loss of His Wealth (1:20–21)
    3. An Inclusio of Approval (1:22)
  D. Job's Second Test (2:1–10)
    1. Into the Heavens, Take Two (2:1)
    2. Another Curious Conversation (2:2–3)
    3. The Challenger's Challenge: Skin for Skin! (2:4–5)
    4. Into Satan's Hand (2:6–7)
    5. Job's Godly Response to the Loss of His Health (2:8–10)
  E. Introduction to Job's Third Test (2:11–13)
    1. An Appointment to Show Sympathy (2:11)
    2. Sympathy, Solidarity, and Silence (2:12–13)
II. Job's Third Test (3:1–31:40)
  A. Why Is Light Given to Him Who Suffers? (3:1–26)
    1. Let That Day Be Darkness! (3:1–10)

JOB 1:1–5

1 There was a man in the land of Uz whose name was Job, and that man was blameless and upright, one who feared God and turned away from evil. ²There were born to him seven sons and three daughters. ³He possessed 7,000 sheep, 3,000 camels, 500 yoke of oxen, and 500 female donkeys, and very many servants, so that this man was the greatest of all the people of the east. ⁴His sons used to go and hold a feast in the house of each one on his day, and they would send and invite their three sisters to eat and drink with them. ⁵And when the days of the feast had run their course, Job would send and consecrate them, and he would rise early in the morning and offer burnt offerings according to the number of them all. For Job said, "It may be that my children have sinned, and cursed[1] God in their hearts." Thus Job did continually.

[1] The Hebrew word *bless* is used euphemistically for *curse* in 1:5, 11; 2:5, 9

Section Overview

The prologue (Job 1:1–5) introduces us to an unusual world. In verse 1, we meet a man with an unprecedented name (Hb. *'iyyob*, "Job") from an uncertain place ("the land of Uz") who worships (as of yet) an undefined "God" (Hb. *'elohim*).[25] However, it is this man in that place and his relationship with that God that sets the scene for the unfolding of one of the OT's most spectacular dramas. Verses 2–5 build upon this unusual opening with an unexpected description of the "perfect" man. Job is "perfect" in a numerological sense in that he has ten children ("*seven* sons and *three* daughters"; v. 2) and ten thousand animals (v. 3).[26] Moreover, he is "perfect," or as near to perfect as is any character in the OT, in a spiritual sense. He gains the distinct designation of being "the greatest of all the people of the east" (v. 3) both because he is rich and because he is righteous. He fears God. He turns away from evil. He provides for his children physically and spiritually.

Section Outline

    I. Prologue (1:1–2:13)

        A. Introduction: Once Upon a Time . . . There Was a Man (1:1–5)

            1. Job's Person (1:1)

            2. Job's Possessions (1:2–3)

            3. Job's Patriarchal "Priesthood" (1:4–5)

Comment

1:1 This opening verse centers on Job's person. While we are told that Job resides in "the land of Uz" (a place located in the ancient Near East, likely on the border of Edom and northern Arabia), the stress of the sentence falls on his exemplary character. Four descriptions of holiness are given here: Job (1) is blameless, (2) is upright, (3) fears God, and (4) turns away from evil. The first two adjectives have to do with Job's life in relation to people and the second two with his life in relation to God. In relation to people, he is "blameless,"[27] or "upright," as the second descriptor is synonymous with the first.

Beyond being in right relationship with others, Job is also in right relationship with God, as God himself will soon confirm (see 1:8 and 2:3, which echo 1:1b). Job fears God and turns away from evil. These phrases form a parallelism, specifically a *synthetic* parallelism, in which the second half focuses or expands on (or even explains more fully) the first. Job fears God *by* turning away from evil.[28]

---

25 Job was written in Hebrew for Israelites to read. Thus, surely the "God" referenced in 1:1 is Yahweh, the covenant God of Israel. This is made plain by how God is spoken about throughout the book, especially in chapters 38–41, where God speaks for himself about himself. Also, to settle the matter, "Yahweh" is used thirty-two times in the book, including in 1:21 and 12:9, where Job addresses God as such.

26 On the round numbers representing perfection, see David J. A. Clines, "False Naivety in the Prologue of Job," *HAR* 9 (1985): 127–136.

27 Job alone receives this designation; see Job 1:1, 8; 2:3; 8:20; 9:20–22.

28 Proverbs 8:13 states that "the fear of the LORD is hatred of evil," and here the book of Job adds that such an attitude also includes action—turning from evil. Ecclesiastes 12:13 speaks of fearing God and keeping his commandments, and Job 1:1 (cf. Prov. 3:7) of fearing God and avoiding evil. To fear the Lord is to walk uprightly (Prov. 14:2), and to walk uprightly is to walk away from evil. "By the fear of the LORD one turns away from evil" (Prov. 16:6b).

In Ecclesiastes, the fear of God can be summarized as "trembling trust."[29] But here in Job 1:1 the emphasis is not on trust but on moral purity.

1:2–3 As a result of his holiness, Job embodies Proverbs 22:4: "The reward for humility and fear of the LORD is riches and honor and life." Perhaps this is why the author of Job transitions from 1:1 into 1:2 with an unusual phrase, "And there are borne to him" (AT) his ten children. It leaves the reader wondering, "Is it as a result of Job's impeccable character (not his wife's reproductive system) that the pinnacle of his blessings (his "perfect ten" children) are born?" Perhaps so. Whatever the meaning of the transitional phrase, the thought is clear: "Following the fourfold statement about Job's person, there is a fourfold build-up of evidence of Job's blessedness: his family, his livestock, his household, and his status (1:2–3)."[30] We can group those four blessings under the term "possessions," the term used in verse 3 ("he possessed").[31]

Thus, due to his possessions (vv. 2–3) and godliness (v. 1), Job earns the designation of "the greatest of all the people of the east" (v. 3).[32] Among everyone living east of the Jordan River (outside the Promised Land), he is greatest in terms of both spiritual health and material wealth. Whether he is a Hebrew or not (likely not), he is the textbook wisdom-literature man. He is the embodiment of the perfect son of Proverbs. He is the promised blessings of Deuteronomy come to life! He fears God and reaps the rewards: riches, servants, children, and honor.

1:4–5 Satan will slither on the scene soon enough (v. 6) to test the above paradigm. But for now, all is well in Job's world. The idyllic introduction moves the reader from the righteous man (v. 1), surrounded by his servants and his sons and donkeys and daughters (vv. 2–3), to the only action (perhaps a daily one; cf. v. 5) that our text focuses on, namely, Job's patriarchal "priesthood" (vv. 4–5).[33] Early in the morning ("he would rise early"; v. 5) after he cleansed his children ("consecrate them"; v. 5)—perhaps "by means of a sanctification or purification ceremony"[34]—he offered "burnt offerings" for each child (ten costly sacrifices!) on a regular basis ("continually"; v. 5).

Job provides his reason for doing so: "It may be that my children have sinned, and cursed God in their hearts" (v. 5). It is difficult to know what is meant by "cursed God in their hearts" (v. 5). Part of the difficulty is that the word for "cursed" (Hb. *barak*) can also mean "blessed," as it is translated in verse 10, "You have blessed the work of his hands," and in 42:12, "The LORD blessed the latter days of Job more than

29 See Douglas Sean O'Donnell, *Ecclesiastes*, REC (Phillipsburg, NJ: P&R, 2014). For a definition of the fear of the Lord in Proverbs, see O'Donnell, *Beginning and End of Wisdom*, 37.
30 Seow, *Job 1–21*, 253. "His wealth . . . was exceptional, for he possessed seven thousand sheep and three thousand camels, suggesting significant pastoral and mercantile interests, the large number of camels suggesting overland trade. His five hundred teams of oxen and five hundred she-asses indicate major agricultural operations" (254).
31 In the Bible, children are considered part of a father's "possessions" (e.g., Ex. 20:17; Matt. 18:23–25).
32 Job, we might say, is the OT version of the magi (Matt. 2:1–12), in that he is a wise man from "the east" who rightly worships the covenant God of Israel. Or, if we follow Martin Luther, we might even see Job as a Gentile who receives God's "irregular grace" because he is saved before the giving of the law of Moses; *Luther's Works*, vol. 6, *Lectures on Genesis, Chapters 31–37*, ed. Jaroslav Pelikan and Hilton C. Oswald (St. Louis: Concordia, 1970), 380.
33 Job is not a "priest" in the sense that he offers sacrifices in a sanctuary. However, as the family patriarch, he takes on a priestly role, offering sacrifices at open-air altars, just as Abraham and other patriarchs did.
34 John Goldingay, *Job for Everyone*, OTE (Louisville: Westminster John Knox, 2013), 9.

his beginning." As context helps determines translation, in 1:5 "cursed" is the right sense. We might express the sentiment this way: "While they praised Yahweh outwardly, they belittled him inwardly." Perhaps they turned a solemn religious festival into something resembling Herod's birthday party (cf. Matt. 14:1–12). Or perhaps they started the party with a token prayer to please their pious father but then unwisely overindulged on wine (Job 1:13, 18; cf. Prov. 20:1) until the cock crowed. Whatever the nature of their possible sin, Job's patriarchal protection and provision is the focus, and a positive one. Like Abel and Noah,[35] who offered sacrifices and were called righteous before the law of Moses came into being,[36] Job takes seriously his household's right standing before God. Verses 1 and 5 are an inclusio of admiration!

Response

In Job 1:1 we are told that Job is "blameless and upright," or, in a more spatial translation, "whole and straight." We might say, in the language of our Lord Jesus, that as Job walks the *straight* and narrow way that leads to life, he treats others the same way he wishes to be treated; his wholehearted submission, reverence, respect, and love for God show themselves in his *whole* (or "perfect"; Matt. 5:48) love for others. And because of this, his neighbors—and even his enemies—have nothing against him. He has treated them with fairness and equity and charity. He is a "man of peace [Hb. *shalom*]," namely, a "blameless" and "upright" man (Ps. 37:37). In this way, Christians should imitate Job.

We should also imitate Job in the way he cares for his children. Think afresh about Job 1:4–5. Why does Job offer sacrifices for his children? They are presented in a positive way. The sons are independent; each of the seven has his own house. They all get along. Everyone attends all of the festivals, which might be something like birthday parties ("his day," v. 4, perhaps equals "his birthday") or, more likely, seven religious feasts throughout the year.[37] Job's household is harmonious. They are all also happy—based on the fact that they eat and drink together all the time. Eating and drinking are often symbolic in the Bible for joy (e.g., Eccles. 9:7). But within all of this wholesomeness, harmony, and happiness, something is amiss. God's will in heaven is not yet done perfectly on earth. Satan is yet to appear in the book, but sin is already present.

As ideal as the introduction to the book of Job is, we are not in Eden—we are east of it. Job thinks it necessary to sanctify and sacrifice because he fears his children might have sinned. We are not sure if he thinks their cursing God would be due to the deceitfulness of riches (they are quite wealthy), the lure of pagan idols (they live in "the east"), or simply some unintentional attitude or action

---

35 Also, like Abraham and Jacob, Job sacrifices not as a priest but as the head of the family (cf. Gen. 8:20; 22:2, 13; 31:54; 46:1).

36 In the book of Job there is no mention or allusion to the line of Aaron, to a tabernacle, or to any of the specific garb or rituals associated with Israelite cultic practice.

37 That last reading fits the idea of their "blessing" God in their hearts at these events. Seow provides three common interpretations of "his day," the second being that some commentators "imagine a weeklong celebration during some annual holidays . . . , like the 'annual sacrifice' that involved the whole family (1 Sam 20:6, 29), or the Feast of Ingathering (Exod 34:22), or the Feast of Booths, which entailed seven days of offerings, followed by a day of holy convocation (Lev 23:36; Num 29:35; 2 Chr 7:9)" (*Job 1–21*, 269).

(cf. Num. 15:28). Whatever the case, the description of Job's scrupulousness is intended not to seem neurotic or in any way negative, but rather as sin-sensitive and God-honoring. He cleanses his children and sacrifices for their sins because he cares for their souls. As Christians, and in a Christian way (due to Jesus' atoning death, there is no need for animal sacrifices), we should also pray for our children and do all we can to "consecrate" them, that is, set them apart from the world.

However, with all of that noted, the apt response to Job 1:4–5 is not merely imitation. The text also foreshadows two other sacrifice scenes. The first is Job 42:8–9. Job offers blood sacrifices only at the beginning (1:5) and end (42:8–9) of the narrative. As we shall see, that final scene is the lens by which we are to read the whole narrative. But it is more than a lens that helps us look backward; it also—like the lens on a telescope—helps us look forward to the ultimate scene of sacrifice. In Job we see a righteous sufferer vindicated, sinners atoned for through a costly blood sacrifice, and the sovereign freedom and justice of God upheld. Likewise, in Jesus, we see a sacrificial death that demonstrates how innocent suffering can both show forth the justice of God and also save sinners.

JOB 1:6–12

⁶Now there was a day when the sons of God came to present themselves before the LORD, and Satan¹ also came among them. ⁷The LORD said to Satan, "From where have you come?" Satan answered the LORD and said, "From going to and fro on the earth, and from walking up and down on it." ⁸And the LORD said to Satan, "Have you considered my servant Job, that there is none like him on the earth, a blameless and upright man, who fears God and turns away from evil?" ⁹Then Satan answered the LORD and said, "Does Job fear God for no reason? ¹⁰Have you not put a hedge around him and his house and all that he has, on every side? You have blessed the work of his hands, and his possessions have increased in the land. ¹¹But stretch out your hand and touch all that he has, and he will curse you to your face." ¹²And the LORD said to Satan, "Behold, all that he has is in your hand. Only against him do not stretch out your hand." So Satan went out from the presence of the LORD.

¹ Hebrew *the Accuser* or *the Adversary*; so throughout chapters 1–2

Section Overview

Job 1:6–12 is an uncommon text in that it is one of the few places in the Bible in which the reader is allowed to peer into the heavens. Readers receive a front-row seat to the cosmic chamber room of God, where we are introduced to "the sons of God," the "Satan," and the God ("the LORD") whom Job fears (v. 6). A curious conversation follows, featuring two questions from the Lord (vv. 7a, 8) and two answers from Satan (vv. 7b, 9–11). Satan's second answer features two questions of his own, questions accusing God of providential pampering and challenging him to remove the hedge of protection around Job and his bounty of blessings. The Lord takes up the challenge. He will remove his protection from Job. However, he will not stretch out *his* hand against Job. Instead, he will allow Satan's hand to take away Job's possessions ("Behold, all that he has is in your hand"; v. 12a) but not yet his health ("Only against him do not stretch out your hand"; 1:12b; cf. 2:4–7). The scene ends with Satan leaving the "presence of the LORD" (1:12c) and presumably entering Job's world, where our protagonist has no idea of the waves of destruction soon to come his way (vv. 13–19; 2:1–9).

Section Outline

I.B. God's Servant Given into Satan's Hand (1:6–12)

    1. Into the Heavens (1:6)

    2. A Curious Conversation (1:7–8)

    3. The Challenger's Challenge (1:9–11)

    4. Into Satan's Hand (1:12)

Comment

1:6 The scene has shifted from earth (vv. 1–5) to heaven (v. 6),[38] from "continually" (v. 5) to "a day" (v. 6), from Job and his family to God and "the sons of God." Job's God, or at least the God of the book of Job, is "the LORD," the covenant God of Israel.[39] Based on their actions and access to God, "the sons of God" are supernatural beings (perhaps angels)[40] who apparently serve on what could be labeled the parliament of the universe. Within this honorable cosmic cabinet, we are introduced to someone who is, or will become, the least honorable character in the Bible—the "Satan."[41] "Satan" (Hb. *satan*) could be translated "adversary," but he seems to function here not as a direct enemy but as an opposing ally. John Goldingay sees this Satan in Job as functioning something like a prosecuting attorney or the political party in the British parliament known as the monarch's "loyal opposition." Just as the prosecuting attorney is not an opponent of the judge and the loyal opposition is not set against the government, so Satan's role in "Yahweh's cabinet" (so to speak) is to serve Yahweh by making sure that his rule and law is properly upheld.[42]

This more positive view of the Satan of Job makes sense of the honest dialogue and contractual agreement between Satan and the Lord in verses 7–12 in regard to Job, as well as the fact that only Job's three friends, not Satan, are judged in the epilogue. But it also makes sense of why the inspired authors of the NT, when

---

38 The place of "the presence of the LORD" (Job 1:12) is often described as "heaven" or "the heavens" (e.g., Job 16:19; 22:12).

39 The Hebrew name *YHWH* ("Yahweh," "LORD") is first used here in Job 1:6, and thirty-one times thereafter.

40 The NIV renders *bene ha'elohim* in Job 1:6; 2:1; 38:7 as "angels."

41 I take the particle *gam*—"And Satan *also* came among them"—as highlighting Satan's role in the story, not as indicating that he is part of "the sons of God."

42 See Goldingay, *Job*, 12.

they look for a name to describe God's great adversary, employ the title "Satan." In the NT, "the devil" (1 John 3:8) or "Beelzebul" (Matt. 12:24) or "the evil one" (Eph. 6:16), whose power and ploys are strikingly similar to Satan's activity in Job (Matt. 4:1–11; Acts 10:38; Rev. 12:10), is the ultimate enemy of God and his kingdom (Rev. 12:9; 20:2). As we will see next in Job 1:7, this "Satan" walks about the earth "like a roaring lion, seeking someone to devour" (1 Pet. 5:8).

1:7–8 These verses record one of the most curious conversations in the cosmos. What is curious is that the Lord seems limited in his knowledge ("The LORD said to Satan, 'From where have you come?'")[43] whereas Satan seems boundless in his abilities ("Satan answered the LORD and said, 'From going to and fro on the earth, and from walking up and down on it'"). What is also curious is that God is impressed not by Satan's extraordinary abilities but rather by Job's character. Echoing the narrator's fourfold commendation (v. 1), the Lord agrees that Job is "a blameless and upright man, who fears God and turns away from evil" (v. 8). Moreover, in God's estimation, Job is more than merely "the greatest of all the people of the east" (v. 3); he is unlike any other ("that there is none like him on the earth"; v. 8). Satan, who has traveled "the earth" (v. 7), is asked if he has "considered" Job, on whom Yahweh bestows the rare and cherished designation "my servant" (v. 8). Job joins Abraham (Gen. 26:24), Moses (Num. 12:7), and David (2 Sam. 7:5) in receiving this title.

1:9–11 Satan has considered God's servant and is not overly impressed. He believes God's appraisal is an overstatement because he surmises that Job's faithfulness is shallow and superficial. In fact, he suggests that it is but a refined form of selfishness,[44] for he answers Yahweh's interrogative invitation—"Have you considered my servant Job?" (v. 8)—with two interrogatives, an indictment, and an invitation of his own (table 4.2).

TABLE 4.2: Satan's Responses to God

Interrogatives	Then Satan answered the LORD and said, "Does Job fear God for no reason? Have you not put a hedge around him and his house and all that he has, on every side?" (vv. 9–10a)
Indictment	"You have blessed the work of his hands, and his possessions have increased in the land." (v. 10b)
Invitation	"But stretch out your hand and touch all that he has, and he will curse you to your face." (v. 11)

Of the many commendations God offered in verse 8, Satan focuses only on the fear of the Lord: "Does Job fear God for no reason?" (v. 9). Satan questions the depth, sincerity, and resilience of Job's relationship with God. He seeks to dive deep into the heart of Job and walk to and fro within it and expose it for what he thinks it is—hollow!

---

43 God's question here is of the same type as that which he asked Adam after the fall: "Where are you?" (Gen. 3:9). Just as God knew where Adam was hiding, he knows where Satan has been. The point of the language is to say not that the limitless God of the universe is limited but that the transcendent God of the heavens is personal. He listens to and communicates with his creatures.
44 W. H. Green, *The Argument of the Book of Job Unfolded* (1873, repr., Minneapolis: Klock, 1977), 74.

Satan not only questions Job's heart religion, he also questions Yahweh's over-protective ("you [have] put a hedge around him") and overindulgent ("you have blessed"; v. 10) providence. This so-called son of God uses the Word of God—the Deuteronomic phrase "you have blessed the work of his hands" (v. 10; cf. Deut. 28:12; 33:11)—to challenge God. Satan's solution to the problem of God's over-protection and overindulgence is simple: "Stretch out your hand and touch all that he has, and he will curse you to your face" (Job 1:11). Smite your saint! Take away the land flowing with milk and honey. Bring on some of Egypt's plagues—bestow boils, eliminate the animals, kill the firstborn son. Then we will see Job's true heart.

Satan's challenge is bold, brazen, and borderline blasphemous. The last picture we saw of Job was of his offering God sacrifices for his children's sins. He was loving God and loving others. Satan forces us to envision a very different scene. He wants us to see this blessed man eye to eye with God, cursing him to his face. To curse God is a sin worthy of the death penalty (1 Kings 21:10), and to curse God "to [his] face" (Job 1:11) connotes a direct confrontation and rejection of God, the greatest imaginable transgression.

1:12 The ESV's rendering of the Hebrew particle *hinneh* as "behold" adds theological stress in ways few words can. From Genesis ("and behold, it was very good"; Gen. 1:31) to Revelation ("Behold, I am coming soon"; Rev. 22:12) and from the incarnation announcement ("Behold, the virgin shall conceive and bear a son"; Matt. 1:23) to the empty tomb ("And behold, . . . an angel of the Lord . . . came and rolled back the stone"; Matt. 28:2), the "beholds" of the Bible are there to catch our attention. The "behold" in Job 1:12 is no different; it announces that something important is to follow—here, a surprising pronouncement.

We might expect God to follow his "behold" with a "be gone," as Jesus ordered after his final temptation: "Be gone, Satan!" (Matt. 4:10). Instead, the "behold" is followed by a bestowal of power: "Behold, all that he has is in your hand. Only against him do not stretch out your hand" (Job 1:12). It is not surprising that the brilliant author has used clever connecting metaphors:

God has blessed the work of Job's *hands* (v. 10).
Satan asks God to stretch out his *hand* against Job (v. 11).
God allows Satan to stretch out his *hand* against Job's possessions (v. 12).

What is surprising is his theology. Is God in the business of dealing with Satan? Or, worse, is God in the business of giving authority to Satan? Worse still, is God in the business of giving Satan power to do evil to good people? The answer to those questions is "yes." But the key to understanding why "yes" is the right answer is to understand and rightly apply the final phrase from our final verse, namely, "So Satan went out from the presence of the LORD" (v. 12b). This ending leaves little doubt concerning who is in control of Satan, the world, and even what is soon to befall one person living at one time in one obscure place in the world—"There was a man in the land of Uz whose name was Job" (v. 1).

Response

Carl Jung described the dialogue and decision recorded in Job 1:6–12 as a "crude representation of a divinity who cruelly permits the torture of his creation."[45] In fact, however, our text and the texts to follow present an image of a God who sovereignly rules but who also sovereignly loves through suffering. God allowed (ordained) the trials of Job, not because he wants to *know* if Job will continue to honor him (for God knows all things, including the future) but rather because God wants to *show* that Job will honor him despite his cataclysmic circumstances. God tests Job not to see if Job will succeed or fail but rather to reveal the essence of authentic faith and to demonstrate that his divine power is made perfect in human weakness. The Bible teaches that trials and testings can authenticate or refine faith and that divine love can show itself through suffering.

It is a strange sovereignty, but it is one we see played out in the Bible over and over again—and ultimately in our Lord Jesus Christ. It was "the definite plan . . . of God" (Acts 2:23) for Jesus to be "betrayed into the *hands* of sinners" (Matt. 26:45) and "delivered up" to be "crucified and killed by the *hands* of lawless men" (Acts 2:23; cf. Matt. 17:12). When Jesus calls out with a loud voice, "Father, into your *hands* I commit my spirit!" (Luke 23:46), we see the perfect picture of love triumphing through suffering and of Satan's power being crushed once and for all by the sovereign love of God. Do we believe that? If not, we must see afresh the story of Job and touch afresh our Savior's hands. "Put your finger here, and see my hands; and put out your hand, and place it in my side. Do not disbelieve, but believe" (John 20:27). The Son of Man suffered at the hands of sinful men (Luke 24:7) to bring salvation through suffering. Only the Suffering Servant could bring to the world such healing (cf. Matt. 8:3, 15 with Matt. 8:17).

Beyond the application of the truth that God can use even the schemes of Satan and the horrors of human suffering to show forth his sovereign love, we should also reflect on the importance of Satan's question. Whatever we make of Satan's attitude and accusations, we should not make little of his challenge. Why do we trust and treasure God? Do we trust and treasure him because of what he protects us from and provides us with? Is God some sort of cosmic Santa Claus to us— if he stops bestowing gifts, will we no longer believe in him? If God's hand were against us, would we still raise our hands in praise? Will tribulation prove to be our undermining? In the end, will our faith prove to be only as fruitful as a seed sown on rocky soil? Are we in a contract with God based on the blessings he bestows, or are we in a covenant with God based on his sovereign calling of us and our dutiful but delightful glorifying of him? However we understand this challenge of Satan, we ought not underestimate its richness for matters of practical theology. Why do we trust and treasure God? Good question. Do we fear God for no reason?

---

45 See R. A. F. MacKenzie and Roland E. Murphy, "Job," in *New Jerome Biblical Commentary*, ed. Raymond E. Brown, Joseph A. Fitzmyer, and Roland E. Murphy (Englewood Cliffs, NJ: Prentice Hall, 1990), 467.

JOB 1:13–22

¹³ Now there was a day when his sons and daughters were eating and drinking wine in their oldest brother's house, ¹⁴ and there came a messenger to Job and said, "The oxen were plowing and the donkeys feeding beside them, ¹⁵ and the Sabeans fell upon them and took them and struck down the servants[1] with the edge of the sword, and I alone have escaped to tell you." ¹⁶ While he was yet speaking, there came another and said, "The fire of God fell from heaven and burned up the sheep and the servants and consumed them, and I alone have escaped to tell you." ¹⁷ While he was yet speaking, there came another and said, "The Chaldeans formed three groups and made a raid on the camels and took them and struck down the servants with the edge of the sword, and I alone have escaped to tell you." ¹⁸ While he was yet speaking, there came another and said, "Your sons and daughters were eating and drinking wine in their oldest brother's house, ¹⁹ and behold, a great wind came across the wilderness and struck the four corners of the house, and it fell upon the young people, and they are dead, and I alone have escaped to tell you."

²⁰ Then Job arose and tore his robe and shaved his head and fell on the ground and worshiped. ²¹ And he said, "Naked I came from my mother's womb, and naked shall I return. The Lord gave, and the Lord has taken away; blessed be the name of the Lord."

²² In all this Job did not sin or charge God with wrong.

[1] Hebrew *the young men*; also verses 16, 17

Section Overview

Job 1:13–19 records a very structured account of a very unruly day. After the setting of a celebratory scene (v. 13), human savagery (Sabeans and Chaldeans) and natural disasters (fire and wind) crash the party (vv. 14–19). In one day Job loses all of his possessions (cf. vv. 2–3). First, some of Job's servants are massacred and his oxen and donkeys are taken. Second, a lightning storm ("the fire of God"; v. 16) consumes more servants, along with his sheep. Third, more servants are slaughtered, with his camels being taken. Fourth, "a great wind" (v. 19) blows down the walls of Job's oldest son's house, leaving all Job's children dead. Their house of celebration (vv. 4, 13) has become their burial chamber.

Job 1:20–21 records Job's extraordinary response—unspeakable grief (he "tore his robe and shaved his head"), submissive faith (he "fell on the ground and worshiped"), recognition of his own mortality ("Naked I came from my mother's womb, and naked shall I return"), and unwavering commitment to God's providential rule ("The Lord gave, and the Lord has taken away; blessed be the name of the Lord"). Verse 22 offers a brief commentary on verses 20–21. Satan was wrong (cf. vv. 9–11). Job has praised the good reputation of the Lord. Put differently, Job has not sinned or accused God of wrongdoing.

Section Outline

I.C. Job's First Test (1:13–22)
1. A Disastrous Day (1:13–19)
2. Job's Godly Response to the Loss of His Wealth (1:20–21)
3. An Inclusio of Approval (1:22)

Comment

1:13–19 Verse 13 sets the scene. Job's children are celebrating: eating and drinking. Verses 14–19 record, in four waves, the death of Job's livestock, servants, and children. The structure of this destruction is clear: (a) a messenger speaks (b) about a catastrophe that happened, (c) and, as the messenger is ending with the line "and I alone have escaped to tell you" (repeated four times), the cycle begins again (with the line "While he was yet speaking, there came another and said" repeated three times).

Job's loss is credited to two causes, the first of which is human savagery. Two Arabian tribes ruthlessly and seemingly senselessly (why not enslave the servants?) take his oxen and donkeys and destroy Job's servants through the sword—literally, by "the mouth of the sword." The nomadic "Sabeans" seem to trust in their military might when they "fall upon" (i.e., randomly come upon) Job's servants working the fields. The marauding "Chaldeans" focus on military strategy. They overtake Job's servants by dividing and conquering. Their three military units come from three different directions upon their unsuspecting targets. The record of their victory (v. 17) gives the sense of a big and bloody battle.

The second cause of Job's calamities is natural elements, with supernatural characteristics ("the fire of God," v. 16; "a great wind," v. 19). Job credits God as the one who has "taken away" (v. 21)—he is right that God is absolutely sovereign over his creation (see esp. Job 38–41). However, the supernatural elements likely come more immediately from Satan,[46] into whose hands God has placed Job ("all that he has is in your hand"; v. 12).

1:20–21 Job's immediate reflex is one of both genuine sorrow and genuine praise. He offers a fourfold response to the fourfold calamities. First, he "arose." The last time Job arose was to offer sacrifices for his children ("he would *rise* early in the morning and offer burnt offerings"; v. 5). Now he arises to mourn their deaths. Second, he "tore his robe and shaved his head," outward symbols of his inward

---

46 A case can be made that God, not Satan, is the immediate cause. The expression "fire of God" (Hb. *'esh 'elohim*) is used of God elsewhere, such as in 2 Kings 1:12; and, the equivalent but more precise expression "Yahweh's fire" is used in Numbers 11:1–3 and 1 Kings 18:38. Moreover, the destructive wilderness wind also can be attributed to God's hand by the fact that storm metaphors are used both in Job and elsewhere in the OT for God (Job 38:1; 40:6; Jer. 23:19; 30:23; Zech. 9:14).

sorrow. It is as if his heart has been torn in two and his head severed from his body. Third, Job "fell on the ground and worshiped." Fourth, Job speaks. His first short speech is perhaps his best. In wisdom, he admits his mortality ("Naked I came from my mother's womb, and naked shall I return") and God's sovereignty ("The LORD gave, and the LORD has taken away; blessed be the name of the LORD"). Other than Jesus' response in the garden of Gethsemane ("My Father, if it be possible, let this cup pass from me; nevertheless, not as I will, but as you will"; Matt. 26:39), this is the most extraordinary response in the Bible to the sovereign will of God.

1:22 Job's godliness has been praised by God (v. 8). He has also been praised by the narrator (v. 1). Now, for the third and final time in chapter 1, our author adds approval, as an inclusio (v. 22). He commends Job for his godly response to the horrific events of the day ("in all this"). Job is praised not for what he does but for what he does *not* do: he "did not sin or charge God with wrong"; or, if this is a focused parallelism, the sense is that Job does not sin in that he does not charge God with wrong. This focus on what Job does not do perhaps heightens Job's unparalleled character, as the predictable human response would be to give into the temptation to curse God and accuse him of evildoing (cf. v. 11; 2:9).

Response

The story of Job can make us wise unto salvation. It can also train us in righteousness by teaching us what it means to stay grounded in God. Why is Job able to withstand Satan's sifting? Why is his immediate response to unspeakable tragedy not to question or curse his creator but rather to prostrate himself upon the earth in sorrow, humility, and faith and to worship its sovereign sustainer? Three roots—theological foundations—help to hold up Job during this day of duress.

The first root is Job's knowledge that material and spiritual prosperity are divine gifts, and as divine gifts they can be freely given and taken away. Along with this, he might know that peace, prosperity, self-security, and happiness can become perils that may threaten to hinder or prohibit fallen human beings from undertaking and continuing the arduous journey of faith. He might even believe, in some sense, that suffering possesses the strange but beautiful power of liberating one's soul from the seduction of safety and the love of temporal, perishable goods. In these ways he anticipates the Christian life—the necessity of cross-bearing (Luke 9:23), of enduring persecution for righteousness' sake (Matt. 5:10), of learning obedience from hardship (Heb. 5:8), of sharing in the sufferings of Christ (Phil. 1:29).

The second root is Job's trust in God's providence. Job had no idea what was going on in the heavens. He was not privy to the chamber room conversation. And yet he gave God the benefit of the doubt. He knew what the Bible calls *wisdom*. He knew who was the potter and who was the clay, and as the clay he did not say to the potter, "Do you know what you are doing?" Rather, he was able to be cracked and battered about because he trusted that he was still in God's wise and just and loving hands. He trusted in the purposeful providence of God. Following Job's lead, we should trust that God rules every aspect of the universe, every event of history, and every detail of our personal lives; that God even numbers the very hairs on our heads, as Jesus taught (Luke 12:7).

The third root is to believe in the resurrection. Believe that this life is not all there is. We live. We die. And then there is the resurrection. This conviction is not apparent from Job 1. It is not apparent that Job believed in life after death and in a day in which all wrongs would be judged and made right. Yet as Job speaks with his friends, it becomes apparent that he believes in some sort of a bodily resurrection (cf. comment on 13:28–14:22 [at 14:13–17]). This is nowhere more evident than at 19:25–26, where he answers his friends' false accusations by declaring, "I know that my Redeemer lives, and at the last he will stand upon the earth. And after my skin has been thus destroyed, yet in my flesh I shall see God!" Job held the belief, or at least pondered the possibility, that there would be a resurrection and that in that day there also would be retribution—final justice. If we would look toward the afterlife and live in light of the resurrection—our future resurrection grounded in Christ's past resurrection (we know so much more than Job did!)—our troubles would be far more tolerable. The apparent tyrannies of providence would be more palatable, for we would remember that God still "has time," so to speak, to remedy any and all injustices of history (even our personal histories). By looking forward to a future vindication and the joy that will accompany it, we can affirm Paul's words in Romans 8:18: "I consider that the sufferings of this present time are not worth comparing with the glory that is to be revealed to us."

JOB 2:1–10

2 Again there was a day when the sons of God came to present themselves before the LORD, and Satan also came among them to present himself before the LORD. ² And the LORD said to Satan, "From where have you come?" Satan answered the LORD and said, "From going to and fro on the earth, and from walking up and down on it." ³ And the LORD said to Satan, "Have you considered my servant Job, that there is none like him on the earth, a blameless and upright man, who fears God and turns away from evil? He still holds fast his integrity, although you incited me against him to destroy him without reason." ⁴ Then Satan answered the LORD and said, "Skin for skin! All that a man has he will give for his life. ⁵ But stretch out your hand and touch his bone and his flesh, and he will curse you to your face." ⁶ And the LORD said to Satan, "Behold, he is in your hand; only spare his life."

⁷ So Satan went out from the presence of the LORD and struck Job with loathsome sores from the sole of his foot to the crown of his head. ⁸ And

he took a piece of broken pottery with which to scrape himself while he sat in the ashes.

⁹ Then his wife said to him, "Do you still hold fast your integrity? Curse God and die." ¹⁰ But he said to her, "You speak as one of the foolish women would speak. Shall we receive good from God, and shall we not receive evil?"¹ In all this Job did not sin with his lips.

¹ Or *disaster*; also verse 11

Section Overview

Comedians often use repetition to engender laughter. In chapter 2, the author of Job employs repetition from chapter 1 (Job 2:1 repeats 1:6; 2:2 repeats 1:7; 2:3 repeats 1:8; 2:5–6 is very similar to 1:11–12) with very different intentions in mind. The purpose of such repetition is threefold. First, it seeks to reemphasize the person and power of Job's accuser—Satan again has access to God; Satan again has walked the world. Second, it acknowledges afresh God's sovereignty over the situation—Satan has to ask and be granted permission again. Third, it helps us to notice what is new.

Two major differences should leap off the page. First, after God repeats his praise of Job's extraordinary character, he adds this commentary on Job's resilience: "He still holds fast his integrity, although you incited me against him to destroy him without reason" (2:3). We might shorten and paraphrase that sentence into "I told you so!" This is the author's way of emphasizing just how amazing it is that Job has thus far persevered. The other difference is Satan's new strategy. When we read 1:7–12 and then 2:1–6, what Satan says in verse 4 stands out like a sore thumb, or sore *everything*, as the case may be for Job: "Skin for skin!" (v. 4). Satan wants to afflict Job's "flesh" (v. 5). Like 1:12, God concedes to the challenger's challenge. Job's body is placed in Satan's "hand" (2:6). Satan spares Job's life (per God's command; cf. v. 6b) but strikes his whole body, from head to toe (v. 7). Job responds, as he did previously, with physical gestures and spiritual confessions: he scrapes his sores (v. 8) and accepts God's bitter providence (v. 10).

Section Outline

I.D. Job's Second Test (2:1–10)
1. Into the Heavens, Take Two (2:1)
2. Another Curious Conversation (2:2–3)
3. The Challenger's Challenge: Skin for Skin! (2:4–5)
4. Into Satan's Hand (2:6–7)
5. Job's Godly Response to the Loss of His Health (2:8–10)

Comment

2:1 Echoing the setting of the first heavenly chamber conversation, this verse narrows in on Satan. Whereas both this verse and 1:6 begin, "Again ["Now" in 1:6] there was a day when the sons of God came to present themselves before the

Lord," this verse ends, "and Satan also came among them to present himself before the Lord" (cf. "and Satan also came among them"; 1:6).

2:2–3 The Lord's conversation with Satan begins with identical lines from their first conversation (cf. 1:7). The Lord asks, "From where have you come?" and Satan answers, "From going to and fro on the earth, and from walking up and down on it" (2:2). Then the Lord asks, "Have you considered my servant Job, that there is none like him on the earth, a blameless and upright man, who fears God and turns away from evil?" (1:8; 2:3a). What is new is what is said next: to his question above, God adds a commendation of Job ("He still holds fast his integrity") and a critique of Satan ("although you incited me against him to destroy him without reason"; v. 3b). The word "me" opens afresh the mystery of the problem of evil. It is clear that Satan is responsible for the attacks upon Job's family and flesh. The blood is on his *hands*. However, here God acknowledges his sovereignty over all, and Job later speaks of receiving both "good" and "evil" from God (v. 10).

2:4–5 In Ephesians 5:29, Paul points out that "no one ever hated his own flesh." Our natural disposition is to protect and love our bodies. So Satan's strategy here is smart: self-preservation, aligned with self-love, is the angle of attack he takes— "Skin for skin!" (Job 2:4). The loss of wealth, children, assets, and financial legacy have not moved Job from praising God to cursing him. But, Satan surmises, "All that a man has he will give for his life" (v. 4b). That is, Satan is asking God for the green light to turn Job's body black and blue—and red. He thinks Job will then pause in his praise ("he will curse you to your face"; v. 5), or, to continue the metaphor, turn yellow. He will cower! And *then* he will curse.

2:6–7 The light turns green. God consents ("Behold, he is in your hand"), with one condition ("only spare his life"; v. 6). Then Satan attacks, striking Job "with loathsome sores from the sole of his foot to the crown of his head" (v. 7). Black. Blue. Red. But, as we will see next, not yellow!

2:8–10 Job's initial reaction is both realistic and resilient: "He took a piece of broken pottery with which to scrape himself while he sat in the ashes." Why does he sit on ashes? He sits on ashes to symbolize his mortality ("ashes to ashes, dust to dust")[47] and to show how he feels. He wants to die (to become ashes sooner than later), which is precisely what he says in chapter 3. And because he is not dying anytime soon, or at least not right now, he seeks to soothe himself from the itchiness of the awful and all-intrusive sores. "He took a piece of broken pottery with which to scrape himself." What a realistic picture. What an awful picture. We are told in 2:12 that his friends do not even recognize him when they arrive on the scene. The illness has distorted his face, his whole body.

---

47 "In sure and certain hope of the resurrection to eternal life through our Lord Jesus Christ, we commend to Almighty God our brother . . . and we commit his body to the ground; earth to earth; ashes to ashes, dust to dust." *Book of Common Prayer*, Burial Rite 1 and 2; based on Gen. 3:19; 18:27; Job 30:19; Eccles. 3:20.

But as realistic as Job's response is, it is also, and once again, amazingly resilient. His resilience first shows itself in his silence. In fact, 2:8–3:26 is structured around the themes of silence and speech. Job is *silent* (2:8), then Job's wife and Job *speak* (vv. 9–10), Job's friends are *silent* (vv. 11–13), and then Job *speaks* (ch. 3). And then, we might even add, from chapter 3 to chapter 38 there is another silence—God's. He says nothing, and the silence is deafening to Job.

Job's response is resilient. On the ash heap, he does not blame others for his troubles, and most importantly, he does not curse God. He sits in silence. But this silence is broken by his wife's voice. When we read, "Then his wife said to him" (2:9), we might hope for soothing words. Relief is at hand. His wife is alive! She is now there with him. She will hold his hand, wipe his wounds, console his soul, point her husband heavenward to their wise and good God. But instead she questions her husband's pigheaded piety ("Do you still hold fast [to] your integrity?") and offers a simple solution ("Curse God and die"; v. 9b). Her solution makes sense from a human perspective. She has lost her ten children. Her husband, "the greatest of all the people of the east" (1:3), is sitting not upon a throne but upon an ash heap (2:8). She believes in God; she does not doubt his existence and certainly not his power. So, with her advice she is saying, "Let us get this over with. Stop playing Mr. Pious. It is time to take matters into your own hands. Stop blessing God's name—curse him. Because as soon as you curse him, he will destroy you. You will be dead, and death is better than this, right?" Satan may have slithered away from the scene, but this "devil's advocate," as Augustine calls her, echoes his voice from 1:11.

Satan's test was tough, but this test might be tougher. We ought not underestimate just how tempting her suggestion is. A man often feels most helpless when his helpmate helps not. But Job does not eat from the fruit she offers. He snubs Satan's supporter: "You speak as one of the foolish women would speak" (2:10). In other words, or to put in our own context, he says, "You are thinking and speaking not like a believer would but like one of the godless who thinks that the god-thing is okay if everything is going your way. No way, wife. Stop thinking this way. Close your mouth, and listen: 'Shall *we* [notice that he includes her] receive good from God, and shall we not receive evil?' (v. 10)." Put differently, "Keep trusting God through these incomprehensible cruelties."

After this incredibly wise and pastoral response, the narrator jumps in and makes sure we applaud Job: "In all this Job did not sin with his lips" (v. 10). This comment makes the list of the top ten understatements of the Bible. Job's not sinning with his lips here was one of the hardest things to do in human history.

Response

Job stood not untouched (he was touched head to toe!) but unmoved. He would not run from God. He would not curse God. He would not sin with his lips. Instead, he would again open wide his mouth, heart, and hands to accept whatever God would give, both "good" and "evil."

But his wife was not so willing to do so. In Georges de La Tour's painting *Job and His Wife*, Job's wife is viewed positively. She brings light and sympathy to the situation. If de La Tour is depicting the moment she arrives on the scene, he is perhaps right. (Scripture gives no prelude to her visit, as it does to the three friends; cf. 2:11–13.) However, he is certainly wrong if he is depicting their conversation. She does not soothe his soul nor comfort his body. She questions his sanity. She offers devilish advice. She speaks foolishly.

Thankfully, Job speaks graciously but correctively to her, reminding her to continue to trust God through the present trials in light of past blessings. We do not know what becomes of their relationship. Does she listen? Does she sit silently with him through the storm? There is only a hint that she does. While there is only one more specific mention of his wife (a negative one [19:17], in the context of those he has loved turning against him [19:19]), Job is blessed with ten more children (42:13). It can be safely assumed that Job and his wife stay on talking ("my breath is strange to my wife"; 19:17) and *touching* terms. It can also be said that she at least sticks with him through to the end.

Whatever we make of their relationship, there is an important lesson here for us all. A lot of love from a lover and a little help from a friend (or three friends) goes a long way. It is not absolutely necessary to our perseverance in the faith that we have others to encourage and support us, but it is near impossible in the Christian journey to make it to the celestial city on our own. Job could have used some help here. We all need such help. Jesus called twelve men to follow him, eleven of whom persevered. Jesus has called us to follow him, and such discipleship involves walking with other disciples. We must pray for healthy Christian marriages, and for strong and supportive Christian communities.

JOB 2:11–13

> [11] Now when Job's three friends heard of all this evil that had come upon him, they came each from his own place, Eliphaz the Temanite, Bildad the Shuhite, and Zophar the Naamathite. They made an appointment together to come to show him sympathy and comfort him. [12] And when they saw him from a distance, they did not recognize him. And they raised their voices and wept, and they tore their robes and sprinkled dust on their heads toward heaven. [13] And they sat with him on the ground seven days and seven nights, and no one spoke a word to him, for they saw that his suffering was very great.

Section Overview

The prologue to Job (chs. 1–2) records the story of the kindness and severity of God and of the sweetness and bitterness of his providence in the life of his servant

Job. In 1:13–22 we read of Job's response to Satan's first test (the loss of his wealth) and in 2:1–10 of his response to the second test (the loss of his health). In both responses Job remains patient, resistant, and faithful. This passage (2:11–13) introduces a third test Job will undergo—the loss of his friends' trust in his word and respect of his character. While these verses offer no indication of this testing to come, they introduce to us the ironies of friends who will act like enemies and worldly-wise men who speak like fools. But before Job 4–25 highlights their condemnable words, 2:11–13 features their commendable character.

Section Outline

I.E. Introduction to Job's Third Test (2:11–13)
> 1. An Appointment to Show Sympathy (2:11)
> 2. Sympathy, Solidarity, and Silence (2:12–13)

Comment

2:11 Thus far the protagonist has persevered. But alas, there is one final test, perhaps the toughest. Satan and Job's wife bow out of the drama, while Job's closest companions cozy up to him. However, as stated above, there is no hint of testing in 2:11–13. Instead, we are introduced to Eliphaz, Bildad, and Zophar as "Job's three friends." Like Job, they are from the east (Teman, Shuah, and Naamah)[48] and apparently considered wise.

Their wisdom is shown in six ways, the first three in verse 11. First, after hearing of Job's demise (they "heard of all this evil that had come upon him"), they individually decide to act. Second, they gather together to act collectively ("they came each from his own place"). Third they decide to journey to the land of Uz to comfort him ("they made an appointment together to come").

2:12–13 Verse 12a describes what Job's friends see when they finally arrive on the scene. "They did not recognize" Job, likely because his body is emaciated and his face scarred from and scabbed with sores. While Satan struck Job's flesh apparently in an instant (v. 7), Job must have sat on that ash heap, scraping himself with pottery pieces for days, if not months (his "months of emptiness"; 7:3),[49] before his friends arrived. He is not dressed like a rich man, if he has any clothes on at all (after rending his garments and speaking of his nakedness; 1:20–21). He does not look like the righteous man described in 1:1–3 and 42:10–16.

---

48 "The three friends of Job all have southern origins known in the OT. Eliphaz is from Teman, an important city in Edom (Gen. 36:11, 15; Ezek. 25:13; Amos 1:11–12), which was apparently known for its wisdom (Jer. 49:7). Bildad is from Shuah, a name of one of the sons of Abraham from his marriage to Keturah, whose brother was Midian and whose nephews were Sheba and Dedan (Gen. 25:2; 1 Chron. 1:32), the latter being the name of a place in Edom or Arabia. Zophar is from Naamah, which is the name of a woman listed in the genealogy of Cain (Gen. 4:22), from whom the Kenites were descendants (Gen. 4:22). The Kenites are also mentioned in connection with the Midianites in the Sinai and Arabian deserts (Num. 10:29; Judg. 4:11)" (*ESV Study Bible* note on Job 2:11).
49 "For the news to reach the Friends in their several countries and for them to arrange for a meeting suggest that Job's suffering has extended over a considerable period of time." Robert Gordis, *The Book of Job: Commentary, New Translation, Special Studies* (1978, repr. New York: Jewish Theological Seminary of America, 2011), 22.

Verses 12b–13 describe what Job's friends do, the fourth and fifth ways they show wisdom. Fourth, they grieve for Job, opening their mouths not to counsel or correct but to weep ("and they raised their voices and wept"). Fifth, they not only join in his sorrow (the tears shed), they also attempt to join in his suffering via two signs of solidarity. They "tear their robes" (cf. 1:20) and grab a fistful of dirt from the ash heap and toss it "toward heaven" and upon their own "heads." Sixth, because "they saw that his suffering was very great," they show further sympathy and solidarity through sitting ("they sat with him on the ground") and silence ("no one spoke a word to him") for the *perfect* amount of time (for "seven days and seven nights"; cf. the use of "seven" in 1:2; 42:8, 13).[50] Their patience is portrayed as boundless, as Job himself will break the silence in 3:1 ("After this Job opened his mouth").

Response

There is much we will see and hear from Job's friends that we are not to emulate. They will prove to have more folly than wisdom. However, here in 2:11–13, they model loyal friendship and supportive sympathy.

When we review their actions, we find much to learn. When they hear of Job's troubles, they act upon that information. How few of us act at all? When we hear of a death in someone's family, do we make a call or write a note? When we learn that someone from church was admitted to the hospital, do we visit and sit with them? Do we pray with them, or perhaps read a comforting psalm and sing a soothing hymn to them? Moreover, like Job's friends, are we willing to put our lives on hold in order to travel to a friend who is in despair or facing death? Eliphaz, Bildad, and Zophar sacrificed weeks to show their sympathy and try to bring comfort. Imagine life on the ash heap. Months without companionship. And then, in the distance, three friends emerge. What a sight for sore eyes (and a body inflicted with sores)!

In 2 Corinthians 7:6, Paul writes that "God, who comforts the downcast, comforted us *by* the coming of Titus." The coming of Eliphaz, Bildad, and Zophar surely comforts Job. What also surely comforts Job, as it would comfort any grieving soul, is their empathy expressed in their incarnational ministry. By weeping with Job, tearing their garments like Job, accepting the ash heap alongside Job, and not speaking to Job, they model gospel grieving. They do not check into the presidential suite at the Marriott down the road but sit on the zero-stars ash heap. They do not read Romans 8:28 ("all things work together for good"), but embody Revelation 8:1 ("there was silence in heaven"). Sometimes when we enter the home of a member of our church who is dying or walk through the door at the hospital and witness the inexplicable sufferings of someone we nurtured in the faith for many years, there is no need to say anything. Our presence is felt. It is enough for us to be there, to hold their hand, to dab their tears, to join them in weeping.

There is much to commend about Job's friends in 2:11–13. However, it is difficult not to read what they later say and do back into these verses. We look at this

---

50 Seven days is also the appropriate amount of time to mourn the dead (cf. Gen. 50:10; 1 Sam. 31:13; cf. *Sir.* 22:12).

scene and just wish we had some duct tape for their mouths! The sharing in his sorrows, the silence, the tears: it is all so beautiful. They should have called it a day—or a week, to be more accurate. If they had just ridden off into the sunset after the seven days of silence, they would have gone down in history as the picture of friendship. Artists would have painted portraits, composers would have written oratorios, and Christians would have named their children after them.

But alas, such is not the case. As we will see next, a storm is about to hit. A whirlwind of words is about to blow through Job's ash heap. His "friends" (2:11), even "close" (19:14) and "intimate friends" (19:19), are about to unleash their full armory of rebukes, accusations, scorn, and mockery. It is neither sticks nor stones that breaks Job's bones but *words*. It is words that crush his inner spirit. He will soon cry out, "How long will you torment me and break me in pieces with words?" (19:2). Job 2:11–13 is not all that will be said of Job's friends. In chapter 4, Eliphaz, Bildad, and Zophar will turn on Job, misjudging his motives and attacking his claims. This is the last test, but it is no least test. How will Job fare? Will we hear again the narrator's voice, "In all this Job did not sin with his lips" (2:10)? Will Job continue to hold fast to his integrity, fear God, trust God, and believe in God's sovereign, just, and merciful providence?

JOB 3:1–26

3 After this Job opened his mouth and cursed the day of his birth. ² And Job said:

³ "Let the day perish on which I was born,
    and the night that said,
    'A man is conceived.'
⁴ Let that day be darkness!
    May God above not seek it,
    nor light shine upon it.
⁵ Let gloom and deep darkness claim it.
    Let clouds dwell upon it;
    let the blackness of the day terrify it.
⁶ That night—let thick darkness seize it!
    Let it not rejoice among the days of the year;
    let it not come into the number of the months.
⁷ Behold, let that night be barren;
    let no joyful cry enter it.
⁸ Let those curse it who curse the day,
    who are ready to rouse up Leviathan.
⁹ Let the stars of its dawn be dark;
    let it hope for light, but have none,
    nor see the eyelids of the morning,

10   because it did not shut the doors of my mother's womb,
      nor hide trouble from my eyes.

11   "Why did I not die at birth,
      come out from the womb and expire?
12   Why did the knees receive me?
      Or why the breasts, that I should nurse?
13   For then I would have lain down and been quiet;
      I would have slept; then I would have been at rest,
14   with kings and counselors of the earth
      who rebuilt ruins for themselves,
15   or with princes who had gold,
      who filled their houses with silver.
16   Or why was I not as a hidden stillborn child,
      as infants who never see the light?
17   There the wicked cease from troubling,
      and there the weary are at rest.
18   There the prisoners are at ease together;
      they hear not the voice of the taskmaster.
19   The small and the great are there,
      and the slave is free from his master.

20   "Why is light given to him who is in misery,
      and life to the bitter in soul,
21   who long for death, but it comes not,
      and dig for it more than for hidden treasures,
22   who rejoice exceedingly
      and are glad when they find the grave?
23   Why is light given to a man whose way is hidden,
      whom God has hedged in?
24   For my sighing comes instead of[1] my bread,
      and my groanings are poured out like water.
25   For the thing that I fear comes upon me,
      and what I dread befalls me.
26   I am not at ease, nor am I quiet;
      I have no rest, but trouble comes."

[1] Or *like*; Hebrew *before*

Section Overview

As we turn to chapter 3, we learn that perhaps Job should keep quiet too. That is not to say that Job sins with his lips in his nine speeches (cf. Job 42:7, 8), the first of which is recorded here. But it *is* to say that maybe he would be better off remaining silent and waiting for God to speak. What Job says in this soliloquy is both expected and unexpected. Considering Job's situation, it is expected that Job might curse the day of his birth, wondering why he was born if only to suffer such calamities. What is unexpected, following his two earlier speeches (1:21; 2:9–10), is the depths of his despair. He makes no confession of faith in God. He holds out no hope for the future. However, he will have more to say. The debate is about to begin the moment he says that "trouble comes" (3:26b). Between Job's short opening lament over life (ch. 3) and his long closing monologue on the mystery of God's ways and Job's personal integrity (chs. 26–31), an aggressive interchange of ideas—two full cycles of dialogue—will emerge (chs. 4–25).

Section Outline

II. Job's Third Test (3:1–31:40)
   A. Why Is Light Given to Him Who Suffers? (3:1–26)
      1. Let That Day Be Darkness! (3:1–10)
      2. Why Did I Not Die at Birth? (3:11–19)
      3. Why Is Light Given? (3:20–26)

Comment

3:1–10 Verse 1 summarizes the theme of Job's first speech, namely, cursing the day he was born. Verse 3 is Job's poetic summary. He curses not only the day he was born ("Let the day perish on which I was born") but the night of the birth announcement—"It is a boy!" ("and the night that said, 'A man is conceived'"). Then, using the same verb tense (note the word "let" is used thirteen times in vv. 3–9), he pounds the theme into his friends' (and the readers') heads. All of the lines and most of the metaphors focus on covering the light (let not "light shine upon it," v. 4; "let it hope for light, but have none," v. 9) and life of the day of his birth. He wishes that darkness ("darkness," v. 4; "gloom and deep darkness," v. 5; "the blackness of the day," v. 5; "thick darkness," v. 6; "let the stars . . . be dark," v. 9) and forces of darkness ("clouds," v. 5; "Leviathan," v. 8) would cover "the day" (three times) and all the joyous emotions surrounding it ("let no joyful cry enter it"; v. 7). Unlike Sarah, Hannah, and a host of other OT saints, Job wishes for barrenness (v. 7), for "the doors of [his] mother's womb" to be "shut" (v. 10).

3:11–19 As the first half of this poem (vv. 3–10) is dominated by one theme (the day of Job's birth), one key word ("let"), and one main metaphor ("darkness"), the second half takes up that same theme with a new key word ("why," six times), focusing on why Job did not die at birth (the first four occurrences of "why") if he was to live in such misery (the final two occurrences):

> Why did I not die at birth,
>   come out from the womb and expire? (v. 11)
> Why did the knees receive me?
>   Or why the breasts, that I should nurse? (v. 12)
> Why was I not as a hidden stillborn child,
>   as infants who never see the light? (v. 16)
>
> Why is light given to him who is in misery . . . ? (v. 20a)
> Why is light given to a man whose way is hidden . . . ? (v. 23a)

Job wants to "rest" in peace (v. 13; "the weary are at rest," v. 17). He wants to lie "down," be "quiet," and sleep ("I would have slept"; v. 13). He wants to be "free" from pain (v. 19) and "at ease" (v. 18). He wants to die so that he might join both the renowned upper class ("with kings and counselors of the earth who rebuilt ruins for themselves, or with princes who had gold, who filled their houses with silver"; vv. 14–15) and the despised lower class ("the wicked," v. 17; "the prisoners," v. 18; "the small . . . and the slave," v. 19). To him, death is better than life.

3:20–26 In these verses Job is both philosophical and personal. In the first half (vv. 20–23) his perspective moves beyond his own sufferings to any and all who suffer. He wonders why God allows people to be born ("light given"; v. 20) if their life is to be characterized by such extreme suffering ("who" so live "in misery" [v. 20] that they "long for death" [v. 21]). Job even uses humor, along with hyperbole and irony, to highlight the sad situation ("who . . . dig for [death] more than for hidden treasures," v. 21; "who rejoice exceedingly and are glad when they find the grave," v. 22). Job also wonders why someone is born ("light given to a man") if that person does not understand why he is suffering ("whose way is hidden, whom God has hedged in"; v. 23).

In the second half (vv. 24–26) Job becomes more personal. Notice the first-person personal pronouns: "my sighing . . . my groanings" (v. 24); "I fear . . . I dread" (v. 25); "I am not at ease, nor am I quiet; I have no rest" (v. 26). Notice also his heartbreak. He has none of the "ease," "quiet," or "rest" that he thinks death would bring. Instead of daily bread, he suffers insatiable emptiness ("sighing," and "groanings . . . poured out like water"; v. 24). Notice, finally, his final prophetic phrase: "but trouble comes" (v. 26). Trouble is to come. Job will receive only trouble and no rest from his friends' counsel. Only God's voice will soothe his soul, albeit without answering the question why.

Response

Job's six interrogatives—why, why, why, why, why, why—will be answered promptly by his friends: "Why? Let us tell you why. Because you have sinned!" But his questions will not be answered by God when he finally opens his mouth (chs. 38–41). The "why" question just lingers on throughout the OT until we find it on the lips of our Lord Jesus: "'Eli, Eli, lema sabachthani?' that is, 'My God, my God, why have you forsaken me?'" (Matt. 27:46). Our—and Job's—Redeemer has the question "why" on his lips when he dies. He does not ask God (his Father), as Job does, why, if he was to suffer this much, he was born in the first place. Instead, his "why" question takes us back to the very reason he was born. He was born to die. He was born to suffer and die. He was born to be God-forsaken.

The scene Matthew sets is quite dramatic.[51] "Darkness" comes upon the land. For three hours all is dark, and perhaps all is silent. Then, at the about the ninth

---

51 For more on the theme of the forsakenness of Jesus, see chapter 86 in Douglas Sean O'Donnell, *Matthew: All Authority in Heaven and on Earth*, PTW (Wheaton, IL: Crossway, 2013).

hour (three o'clock, the time the lamb was brought into the temple to be slaughtered), "Jesus cried out with a loud voice, saying, . . . 'My God, my God, why have you forsaken me?'" (Matt. 27:46). Why did Jesus cry out the first sentence of Psalm 22? Why not cry out its last three victorious verses ("All the prosperous of the earth eat and worship; . . ."), the first verses from Psalm 23 ("The LORD is my shepherd; I shall not want. He makes me lie down in green pastures. He leads me beside still waters. He restores my soul"), or the start of Psalm 21 ("O LORD, in your strength the king rejoices, and in your salvation how greatly he exults! You have given him his heart's desire and have not withheld the request of his lips")? Why Psalm 22:1? Also, why a question and not an affirmation on his lips? Would not something like "God loves all of you" be more soothing, or "Let there be peace on earth" be less cutting? Why a question? And why a question *to God* about where God is when Jesus needs him most?

The voice fits the setting: a dark cry for a dark hour. Furthermore, and more importantly, the verb of Jesus' question provides us with Jesus' theology of the cross: "forsaken." The world's greatest religion of the time (Judaism) has forsaken him. The world's strongest and seemingly most civilized empire (Rome) has forsaken him. His own apostles have forsaken him. (Jesus does not—like Job—have three friends, even one friend, to argue with.) And now (can it be true?), has his Father forsaken him? Is he God-forsaken? Jesus feels that he is.

But it is one thing to feel forsaken; it is another thing to actually be forsaken. Was there somehow a severing of Trinitarian fellowship? How could there be? Did the Father really forsake his Son on the cross? And, if so, what was the nature and purpose of this God-forsakenness? Matthew does not directly tell us. But he does record the darkness and the dark cry of dereliction to move us in a direction, and that direction is to what Paul later summarizes in 2 Corinthians 5:18–21, which can be stated as follows: God made sinless Jesus "to be sin" so that we might be forgiven of our sins. This fits the verses in Matthew that teach that Jesus' death was the atonement for sins: Jesus saved "his people from their sins" (Matt. 1:21) by giving "his life as a ransom" (Matt. 20:28) and by pouring out his blood "for many for the forgiveness of sins" (Matt. 26:28).

There are major Christological implications to Job's soliloquy. Job thought he was forsaken by God. But he was not. God's silence did not mean his forsakenness. Jesus, however, was forsaken. He was forsaken so that we might not suffer eternal silence and separation from God. "Why" is not the ultimate, or even the foundational, question in the book of Job, but Jesus' "Eli, Eli, lema sabachthani" is the ultimate and most foundational question in the Bible. Without Jesus' propitiation we are absolutely hopeless. Without Jesus' atoning sacrifice our hands are stained with blood. We are guilty. Without the Word's becoming flesh and dying in his flesh as the God-man, we have no hope of eternal life, eternal joy, or eternal fellowship with the wise and just and loving God. So, as we read this depressing poem in Job 3, let us thank God for Job's honesty. But let us also thank God for the gospel, for our great Redeemer who, in his death, redeemed us, saving us from sin and Satan.

JOB 4:1–5:27

4 Then Eliphaz the Temanite answered and said:

2 "If one ventures a word with you, will you be impatient?
　Yet who can keep from speaking?
3 Behold, you have instructed many,
　and you have strengthened the weak hands.
4 Your words have upheld him who was stumbling,
　and you have made firm the feeble knees.
5 But now it has come to you, and you are impatient;
　it touches you, and you are dismayed.
6 Is not your fear of God[1] your confidence,
　and the integrity of your ways your hope?

7 "Remember: who that was innocent ever perished?
　Or where were the upright cut off?
8 As I have seen, those who plow iniquity
　and sow trouble reap the same.
9 By the breath of God they perish,
　and by the blast of his anger they are consumed.
10 The roar of the lion, the voice of the fierce lion,
　the teeth of the young lions are broken.
11 The strong lion perishes for lack of prey,
　and the cubs of the lioness are scattered.

12 "Now a word was brought to me stealthily;
　my ear received the whisper of it.
13 Amid thoughts from visions of the night,
　when deep sleep falls on men,
14 dread came upon me, and trembling,
　which made all my bones shake.
15 A spirit glided past my face;
　the hair of my flesh stood up.
16 It stood still,
　but I could not discern its appearance.
　A form was before my eyes;
　there was silence, then I heard a voice:
17 'Can mortal man be in the right before[2] God?
　Can a man be pure before his Maker?
18 Even in his servants he puts no trust,
　and his angels he charges with error;
19 how much more those who dwell in houses of clay,
　whose foundation is in the dust,
　who are crushed like[3] the moth.

20   Between morning and evening they are beaten to pieces;
         they perish forever without anyone regarding it.
21   Is not their tent-cord plucked up within them,
         do they not die, and that without wisdom?'

5 "Call now; is there anyone who will answer you?
         To which of the holy ones will you turn?
2   Surely vexation kills the fool,
         and jealousy slays the simple.
3   I have seen the fool taking root,
         but suddenly I cursed his dwelling.
4   His children are far from safety;
         they are crushed in the gate,
         and there is no one to deliver them.
5   The hungry eat his harvest,
         and he takes it even out of thorns,[4]
         and the thirsty pant[5] after his[6] wealth.
6   For affliction does not come from the dust,
         nor does trouble sprout from the ground,
7   but man is born to trouble
         as the sparks fly upward.

8   "As for me, I would seek God,
         and to God would I commit my cause,
9   who does great things and unsearchable,
         marvelous things without number:
10   he gives rain on the earth
         and sends waters on the fields;
11   he sets on high those who are lowly,
         and those who mourn are lifted to safety.
12   He frustrates the devices of the crafty,
         so that their hands achieve no success.
13   He catches the wise in their own craftiness,
         and the schemes of the wily are brought to a quick end.
14   They meet with darkness in the daytime
         and grope at noonday as in the night.
15   But he saves the needy from the sword of their mouth
         and from the hand of the mighty.
16   So the poor have hope,
         and injustice shuts her mouth.

17   "Behold, blessed is the one whom God reproves;
         therefore despise not the discipline of the Almighty.
18   For he wounds, but he binds up;
         he shatters, but his hands heal.
19   He will deliver you from six troubles;
         in seven no evil[7] shall touch you.
20   In famine he will redeem you from death,
         and in war from the power of the sword.
21   You shall be hidden from the lash of the tongue,
         and shall not fear destruction when it comes.

22   At destruction and famine you shall laugh,
     and shall not fear the beasts of the earth.
23   For you shall be in league with the stones of the field,
     and the beasts of the field shall be at peace with you.
24   You shall know that your tent is at peace,
     and you shall inspect your fold and miss nothing.
25   You shall know also that your offspring shall be many,
     and your descendants as the grass of the earth.
26   You shall come to your grave in ripe old age,
     like a sheaf gathered up in its season.
27   Behold, this we have searched out; it is true.
     Hear, and know it for your good."[8]

[1] Hebrew lacks *of God* [2] Or *more than*; twice in this verse [3] Or *before* [4] The meaning of the Hebrew is uncertain [5] Aquila, Symmachus, Syriac, Vulgate; Hebrew could be read as *and the snare pants* [6] Hebrew *their* [7] Or *disaster* [8] Hebrew *for yourself*

Section Overview

Chapter 3 was a realistic picture of and poem from a devastated man. He was not cursing God but *was* cursing the day of his birth. One wonders, "What was his relationship with God at this point?" It is hard to know. He was not cursing God, but he also was not praying to God (3:4 and 3:23 were the only times Job mentioned God, and both verses are in some way negative). It appears that Job was trying to tame his tongue. He wanted to curse God, and in some instances he came quite close to crossing the line. But, no, he is still in a relationship with God. And it is a *relationship*, with its ups and downs. God is not speaking to him, and he is not (not now at least) speaking *to* God, only about God.

In chapters 4–5 a new voice is heard. Eliphaz will offer some words about God (Job 4:6, 9, 17; 5:8, 17) to Job. Essentially, his forty-seven-verse poem (4:2–5:27) is a two-point sermon to Job in response to Job's depressing monologue (3:3–26). He wants Job to understand, first, *that he is guilty before God*, and second, *that he needs to go to God* for restoration.

Section Outline

  II.B. God Is Just; Are You, Job? (4:1–5:27)
      1. Get That You Are Guilty (4:1–21)
      2. Go to God (5:1–27)

Comment

4:1–11 After the text introduces the speaker ("Eliphaz the Temanite") and what follows as a reply to Job's speech ("answered"; v. 1), Eliphaz focuses on Job's guilt before God. To him there are at least two ways in which Job is guilty. First, Eliphaz claims that Job has been impatient. In verse 2 he asks, "If one ventures a word with you, will you be impatient?" Then, in verse 5, he answers his own question in the affirmative: "But now [trouble] has come to you, and you are impatient." To the reader well acquainted with the prologue, this accusation seems out of line, for in chapters 1 and 2, Job comes across as the poster boy of patience (as James 5:11 well summarizes: "You have heard of the steadfastness of Job"). Job is only human, as he will make clear in his reply to Eliphaz:

> This would be my comfort;
> > I would even exult in pain unsparing,
> > for I have not denied the words of the Holy One.
> What is my strength, that I should wait?
> > And what is my end, that I should be patient?
> Is my strength the strength of stones, or is my flesh bronze? (Job 6:10–12)

Eliphaz himself has witnessed such steadfastness, as together they had sat in silence for seven days. Job did not complain or curse. He was patient in affliction. Thus Eliphaz must be basing his accusation of impatience solely on Job's desire to die (ch. 3) and thus not to endure patiently the pain so as to learn from it.

The second way in which Eliphaz seeks to implicate Job is to bring to bear God's perfect purity. After he has complimented Job's character—his own "integrity" (v. 6b), "fear of God" (v. 6a), and kindness to others ("you have instructed many, . . . strengthened the weak hands. . . . upheld him who was stumbling, . . . made firm the feeble knees"; vv. 3–4)—he offers his first dose of the three friends' retribution theology (vv. 7–11), followed by his reminder of God's holiness (vv. 12–21). Both ideas he introduces with rhetorical questions. In verse 7, he says,

> Remember:

> who that was　　innocent　　ever perished?
> Or where were　　the upright　　cut off?

The answer is obvious: people get what is coming to them ("those who plow iniquity and sow trouble reap the same"; v. 8). What they reap is God's judgment ("By the breath of God they perish"; v. 9). This is the way the world works; no creature is immune. Just as the mighty lioness cannot protect her cubs if she cannot eat (vv. 10–11), so even great Job cannot alter God's moral law: the upright always prosper and the wicked always perish.

4:12–21 Eliphaz's second rhetorical question—"Can mortal man be in the right before God? Can a man be pure before his Maker?" (v. 17)[52]—focuses on God's righteousness and, by implication, man's impurity. While this point is obvious and stated elsewhere throughout Scripture (e.g., Ps. 143:2; Prov. 20:9; Eccles. 7:20), Eliphaz introduces it as a supernatural revelation ("a spirit glided past my face"; Job 4:15). It was a "word . . . brought" to him (v. 12) in a nightmare (vv. 13–16) that frightened him ("the hair of my flesh stood up"; v. 15). He wants such a prophetic vision to scare

---

52 Eliphaz will come back to this later. In Job 15:14 he will say, "What is man, that he can be pure? Or he who is born of a woman, that he can be righteous?" Moreover, in 25:4 Bildad will join in the total depravity chorus, saying, "How then can man be in the right before God? How can he who is born of woman be pure?"

some sense into Job too. He seeks to remind Job that God is so holy that "even . . . his angels he charges with error" (v. 18). If such is true of immortal heavenly beings, what then of mortal men ("those who dwell in houses of clay, whose foundation is in the dust"; v. 19), who "perish" (v. 20) and "die" (v. 21) and are forgotten ("crushed like the moth," v. 19c; "perish forever without anyone regarding it," v. 20b)?

Job has to bear the second half of the sermon (ch. 5) before he can reply. But, here, at the end of chapter 4, we can imagine him muttering under his breath, "Duh. Thanks for the theology lesson, old friend." Job knew that God alone is perfectly pure. He would agree with the illustration about the angels in verse 18: if God charges even the supernatural servants in heaven with error, then clay-made man on earth must be full of folly. We know this from what Job did in 1:5 (he sought to sanctify his children because he knew the possible depths and deception of sin) and from what he will say to God in 7:21: "Why do you not pardon my transgression and take away my iniquity?"

Job will admit he is a sinner. That is not the issue, however. The issue is that Job is unaware of what sin could possibly have caused such calamities: "If I sin, what do I do to you, you watcher of mankind? Why have you made me your mark?" (7:20). Job would readily agree with Eliphaz regarding God's discipline: "Blessed is the one whom God reproves" (5:17). What he will not agree with is the assumption that he is under the discipline of God for a crime he did not commit or does not know he committed. Job would say "Amen" to 1 John 1:8 ("If we say we have no sin, we deceive ourselves, and the truth is not in us") as well as to 1 John 1:9 ("If we confess our sins, he is faithful and just to forgive us our sins and to cleanse us from all unrighteousness"). However, he needs a sin to confess first! Thus he cries out in effect, "God, Eliphaz, anybody—show me my specific curse-causing sin!"

5:1–7 In these verses Eliphaz reinforces his vision (4:12–21), reminding Job that his appeal must be to God (cf. 5:8), not "anyone" on earth or even angels ("the holy ones") in heaven (v. 1). He also reinforces his retribution theology (vv. 2–7), reminding Job that suffering does not arise from nothing ("affliction does not come from the dust"; v. 6) and warning him of the consequences ("his children . . . are crushed in the gate," v. 4; "the hungry eat his harvest," v. 5) of sin (e.g., "vexation . . . and jealousy"; v. 2).

5:8–16 After Eliphaz has pressed home his first point, *understand that you are guilty*, he moves on to the second point, *go to God*. This point is best summarized in verse 8: "As for me, I would seek God, and to God would I commit my cause." He follows this bit of personal counsel with a beautiful poem addressing God's attributes and actions (vv. 9–16), part of which (v. 13) Paul quotes in 1 Corinthians 3:19. We might call this Eliphaz's "Why Go to God Poem," which includes literary features such as eight words that start with Aleph (the first letter in the Hebrew alphabet) in Job 5:8, seven couplets, and a plethora of parallelisms. Moreover, the poem is theologically rich and soaked in scriptural language and concepts (table 4.3).[53]

---

53 The same can be said of Job 5:17 (cf. Prov. 3:11; Heb. 12:4–11); Job 5:18 (cf. Deut. 32:39; Hos. 6:1–2); Job 5:19 (cf. Ps. 34:19); and Job 5:20 (cf. Hos. 13:14).

TABLE 4.3: Scriptural Quotes and Allusions in Eliphaz's "Why Go to God Poem"

Job 5:8–16	A Sample of Possible Echoes, Allusions, and Quotes
8 As for me, I would seek God, and to God would I commit my cause,	2 Sam. 12:16; 1 Chron. 22:19
9 who does great things and unsearchable, marvelous things without number:	Ps. 71:19
10 he gives rain on the earth and sends waters on the fields;	1 Sam. 12:17–18
11 he sets on high those who are lowly, and those who mourn are lifted to safety.	1 Sam. 2:5–8

12 He frustrates the devices of the crafty,
    so that their hands achieve no success.
13 He catches the wise in their own craftiness,
    and the schemes of the wily are brought
    to a quick end.
	1 Cor. 3:19

14 They meet with darkness in the daytime and grope at noonday as in the night.	Deut. 28:29

15 But he saves the needy from the sword of
    their mouth
    and from the hand of the mighty.
	Ps. 35:10

16 So the poor have hope, and injustice shuts her mouth.	Ps. 107:42

Eliphaz has misread the situation, and thus his wise words above are applied foolishly. However, he does accurately proclaim general truths. For example, he is right that, in light of who God is and what he will do, humans should pray ("seek God"; v. 8). In chapters 1–2, Job has been faithful to God. In chapter 3, Job speaks about God. But it is not until chapter 7, at the end of Job's second speech, that he prays. And it is an interesting prayer, an honest one, a beautiful one—one that is filled with questions:

What is man, that you make so much of him,
    and that you set your heart on him,
visit him every morning
    and test him every moment? (7:17–18)

Why do you not pardon my transgression
    [maybe Eliphaz is right?]
    and take away my iniquity? (7:21)

Eliphaz is also right that God is just and that in his great and unsearchable control of his creation he eventually brings about vindication for those who fear him: "he sets on high those who are lowly, . . . frustrates the devices of the crafty, . . . [and] saves the needy" (5:11, 12, 15). In fact, the sage-prophet Eliphaz as much as promises this for Job in the next section (vv. 17–27).

5:17–27 This final poem begins and ends with the word "behold" (vv. 17, 27). The second "behold" concludes with a reminder to Job that all that has been said is simply a reiteration of what the traditional wisdom community ("we have searched out") decrees about this situation ("it is true") and about what Job should do ("Hear, and know it for your good"; v. 27), namely, admit his guilt and go to God. The first "behold" (v. 17) is a beatitude ("blessed is the one whom God reproves") introducing a poem about the blessings of God's discipline ("therefore despise not the discipline of the Almighty"). What follows are future promises for those who do not despise God's refining discipline.

These promises are a ploy to entice Job to repent. The irony is that they end up being fulfilled prophecies. When Eliphaz claims that God "will deliver you" (v. 19; cf. "he will redeem you from death," v. 20) and that "you shall be hidden from the lash of the tongue" (v. 21), shall "miss nothing" from your "fold" (v. 24), "shall know . . . that your offspring shall be many" (v. 25), and "shall come to your grave in ripe old age" (v. 26), he predicts 42:10–17. Job's life is saved; he has ten children; he is given wealth (22,000 animals, money, a ring of gold, and inheritance for his children); and he lives the perfect number of years (140)! However callous Eliphaz's theology might come across to Job, he does remind Job (and the reader) that there is "hope" (4:6): the man who fears God and walks in integrity has a promising future. Suffering will not last forever. Healing is on its way; restoration is to come.

Response

We all know that "the world is not a random place; actions have consequences, and the consequences correspond to the actions."[54] We all know that we reap what we sow (cf. Gal. 6:7). And we all know that good things often happen to good people and bad things happen to bad people. But not always—life is not that simple.

But Eliphaz did not get the message. As we examine the first response to Job's sufferings and speech, we are introduced to Eliphaz, Bildad, and Zophar's retribution theology. It is not full-blown here. In fact, chapters 4–5 sound tame compared to the later speeches (or rebukes!): "Is not your evil abundant? There is no end to your iniquities" (Job 22:5), as Eliphaz later puts it to Job. But what we have here is the first sermon to suffering Job, one that is filled with a mixture of truth and error.

So that we might not fall into the same folly as Eliphaz, it is crucial to see what he should have seen. Sight is one of the important themes in the book of Job. Job repeatedly speaks of "deep darkness" that has come upon him, a darkness that is not only that of physical suffering, but also, and more foundationally, that of not being able to see who God is and what he is up to. When God finally reveals himself to Job (chs. 38–41), Job replies to that revelation by saying, "I had heard of you by the hearing of the ear, but now my eye sees you" (42:5).

The language of sight is used also by Eliphaz in his sermon to Job in chapters 4–5. He uses it to speak of commonsense observations based on experience. In 4:8

---

54 Christopher Ash, *Job: The Wisdom of the Cross*, PTW (Wheaton, IL: Crossway, 2014), 104.

he observes, "As I have seen, those who plow iniquity and sow trouble reap the same." Then in 5:3 he reiterates this idea: "I have seen the fool taking root, but suddenly I cursed his dwelling." Put simply, Eliphaz has seen that sin has consequences. He explains to Job that just as crops perish for a reason—perhaps a bad seed or poor cultivation—so there is an obvious reason for his suffering. His suggestion is that it is Job's high anthropology (Job thinks his sin is not the cause of his calamities) and his low theology (Job should be praising God, not cursing his birth).

Yet, it is not Job but Eliphaz who is blind to himself and his God. While he claims that he has received a vision at night and heard a voice (a so-called word from the Lord; cf. 4:12–16), his vision is still obscured. He is not seeing straight. Or better, he is simply shortsighted. How so?

First, Eliphaz does not see Satan.[55] That is, the reality and forces of evil opposition are nowhere on his retribution-theology radar. He assumes that the only force fighting against Job is Job himself—the evil of his fallen condition. And while his flesh is surely waging war against him, as it does with us all, there is more to the story, as we know. We have read chapters 1–2. We know that "Satan" is to blame. We know that Job is having a devil of a fight with the Devil, or at least a supernatural being who is acting devilish. So, while Eliphaz claims that he has had supernatural spiritual vision, what he really needs is a futuristic visit from the apostle Paul. He needs a trip to the seventh heaven and a dose of Ephesians 6:11–12:

> Put on the whole armor of God, that you may be able to stand against the schemes of the devil. For we do not wrestle against flesh and blood, but against the rulers, against the authorities, against the cosmic powers over this present darkness, against the spiritual forces of evil in the heavenly places.

Eliphaz needs to know that Satan not only can hinder us ("we wanted to come to you—I, Paul, again and again—but Satan hindered us"; 1 Thess. 2:18) but is out to devour us ("Your adversary the devil prowls around like a roaring lion, seeking someone to devour"; 1 Pet. 5:8). There is a spiritual battle within us. There is a spiritual battle all around us.

Eliphaz did not see Satan, but we should. We should pray the Lord's Prayer, ending with "deliver us from evil" (or, "the evil one"; Matt. 6:13 ESV mg.). We should echo Martin Luther's Morning Prayer:

> I thank Thee, my Heavenly Father, through Jesus Christ, Thy dear Son, that Thou hast kept me this night from all harm and danger; and I pray Thee to keep me this day also from sin and all evil, that all my doings and life may please Thee. For into Thy hands I commend myself, my body and soul, and all things. Let Thy holy angel be with me, that the Wicked Foe may have no power over me. Amen.

---

55 For these three applications, see ibid., chapters 5–6.

We are to see what Eliphaz did not see, namely, that Satan is for real; although he is not the cause of all suffering, Satan loves to tempt and test and try God's people, as he did Job. As he was responsible for Job's sores and losses, so he is responsible at times (and we often do not know when) for taking from us, tempting us, squeezing us with all the powers of hell. Just because God is sovereign over Satan, this does not mean that Satan—"the ruler of this world" (John 12:31; 14:30; 16:11)—is not at work in this world, busy working against Christ's kingdom.

Second, Eliphaz does not see the possibility of a heavenly mediator. In Job 5:1 he asks, "Call now; is there anyone who will answer you? To which of the holy ones will you turn?" Eliphaz does not think that mere mortals like Job can find access to God through some supernatural being. To him, there is no angel to call nor messianic mediator to call upon. It is just sinful Job versus holy God. But that is not the full story, and Job knows it. He knows that he has, or at least hopes that he has, a "witness . . . in heaven" (16:19) and even a "Redeemer" who "lives" (19:25). And we know so much more. We know that "there is one God, and there is one mediator between God and men, the man Christ Jesus" (1 Tim. 2:5). As Christians, we know that there is someone strong enough to save. We know that in the fullness of time, God sent Jesus to save us from our sins and to crush Satan's head—to vindicate the righteous and punish the wicked. In Jesus, we have salvation. In Jesus, we have a mediator.

Third, and related to the second point, Eliphaz does not see the cross. He does not understand that an innocent mediator might one day mediate between God and man through human suffering. If he saw Jesus on the tree, he would have agreed with the mockers: "If you are the Son of God, come down from the cross" (Matt. 27:40). And if he was a disciple, he would have wanted Jesus to recover like Superman from this kryptonite moment—to push the nails out from his hands and feet, whisk away the wicked to the Hall of Justice, and rescue the weeping women. And if he was at Calvary, we can surmise that the farthest thought from his mind would have been to grasp that Jesus played the role of the true Super Man by being the Suffering Man and that through his sacrificial death and then glorious resurrection and eternal enthronement he forgave sins, destroyed the works of the Devil, and brought meaning to any and all innocent suffering.

What a blessed vantage point we have. We can answer Eliphaz's question, "Who that was innocent ever perished?" (Job 4:7) with the simplest of Sunday School answers: Jesus! "The word of the cross," as Paul writes, "is folly to those who are perishing, but to us who are being saved it is the power of God" (1 Cor. 1:18). What else is it? It is wisdom, the very wisdom of God. "Jews demand signs and Greeks seek wisdom, but we preach Christ crucified, a stumbling block to Jews and folly to Gentiles, but to those who are called, both Jews and Greeks, Christ the power of God and the wisdom of God" (1 Cor. 1:22–24). The wisdom of the cross is the word from the Lord that Eliphaz needed. It is also the wisdom we need.

JOB 6:1–7:21

6 Then Job answered and said:

2 "Oh that my vexation were weighed,
    and all my calamity laid in the balances!
3 For then it would be heavier than the sand of the sea;
    therefore my words have been rash.
4 For the arrows of the Almighty are in me;
    my spirit drinks their poison;
    the terrors of God are arrayed against me.
5 Does the wild donkey bray when he has grass,
    or the ox low over his fodder?
6 Can that which is tasteless be eaten without salt,
    or is there any taste in the juice of the mallow?[1]
7 My appetite refuses to touch them;
    they are as food that is loathsome to me.[2]

8 "Oh that I might have my request,
    and that God would fulfill my hope,
9 that it would please God to crush me,
    that he would let loose his hand and cut me off!
10 This would be my comfort;
    I would even exult[3] in pain unsparing,
    for I have not denied the words of the Holy One.
11 What is my strength, that I should wait?
    And what is my end, that I should be patient?
12 Is my strength the strength of stones, or is my flesh
        bronze?
13 Have I any help in me,
    when resource is driven from me?

14 "He who withholds[4] kindness from a friend
    forsakes the fear of the Almighty.
15 My brothers are treacherous as a torrent-bed,
    as torrential streams that pass away,
16 which are dark with ice,
    and where the snow hides itself.
17 When they melt, they disappear;
    when it is hot, they vanish from their place.
18 The caravans turn aside from their course;
    they go up into the waste and perish.
19 The caravans of Tema look,
    the travelers of Sheba hope.

20 They are ashamed because they were confident;
   they come there and are disappointed.
21 For you have now become nothing;
   you see my calamity and are afraid.
22 Have I said, 'Make me a gift'?
   Or, 'From your wealth offer a bribe for me'?
23 Or, 'Deliver me from the adversary's hand'?
   Or, 'Redeem me from the hand of the ruthless'?

24 "Teach me, and I will be silent;
   make me understand how I have gone astray.
25 How forceful are upright words!
   But what does reproof from you reprove?
26 Do you think that you can reprove words,
   when the speech of a despairing man is wind?
27 You would even cast lots over the fatherless,
   and bargain over your friend.

28 "But now, be pleased to look at me,
   for I will not lie to your face.
29 Please turn; let no injustice be done.
   Turn now; my vindication is at stake.
30 Is there any injustice on my tongue?
   Cannot my palate discern the cause of calamity?

7 "Has not man a hard service on earth,
   and are not his days like the days of a hired hand?
2 Like a slave who longs for the shadow,
   and like a hired hand who looks for his wages,
3 so I am allotted months of emptiness,
   and nights of misery are apportioned to me.
4 When I lie down I say, 'When shall I arise?'
   But the night is long,
   and I am full of tossing till the dawn.
5 My flesh is clothed with worms and dirt;
   my skin hardens, then breaks out afresh.
6 My days are swifter than a weaver's shuttle
   and come to their end without hope.

7 "Remember that my life is a breath;
   my eye will never again see good.
8 The eye of him who sees me will behold me no more;
   while your eyes are on me, I shall be gone.
9 As the cloud fades and vanishes,
   so he who goes down to Sheol does not come up;
10 he returns no more to his house,
   nor does his place know him anymore.

11 "Therefore I will not restrain my mouth;
   I will speak in the anguish of my spirit;
   I will complain in the bitterness of my soul.
12 Am I the sea, or a sea monster,
   that you set a guard over me?

13 When I say, 'My bed will comfort me,
       my couch will ease my complaint,'
14 then you scare me with dreams
       and terrify me with visions,
15 so that I would choose strangling
       and death rather than my bones.
16 I loathe my life; I would not live forever.
       Leave me alone, for my days are a breath.
17 What is man, that you make so much of him,
       and that you set your heart on him,
18 visit him every morning
       and test him every moment?
19 How long will you not look away from me,
       nor leave me alone till I swallow my spit?
20 If I sin, what do I do to you, you watcher of mankind?
       Why have you made me your mark?
       Why have I become a burden to you?
21 Why do you not pardon my transgression
       and take away my iniquity?
    For now I shall lie in the earth;
       you will seek me, but I shall not be."

¹ The meaning of the Hebrew word is uncertain ² The meaning of the Hebrew is uncertain ³ The meaning of the Hebrew word is uncertain ⁴ Syriac, Vulgate (compare Targum); the meaning of the Hebrew word is uncertain

Section Overview

In Psalm 32:3–4 the psalmist bemoans how his unconfessed sin is destroying his body ("my bones wasted away … my strength was dried up"). In Job 6–7, Job knows of no secret sin that is the cause of his extreme physical, emotional, and spiritual agony. Thus he lays the blame for his pain on the will of the Lord (6:1–13), which is only heightened by his friends' false diagnoses and disloyalty (6:14–30). Turning to God for answers, Job asks God questions that remain unanswered (ch. 7). If Job has sinned in some way, he wonders why God will not forgive such offenses.

Section Outline

II.C. Three Arrows (6:1–7:21)
      1. The Arrows of the Almighty—into Job (6:1–13)
      2. The Arrows of Job—into His Friends (6:14–30)
      3. The Arrows of Job—into Yahweh (7:1–21)

Comment

6:1–13 In Job 4–5, Eliphaz counseled Job to recognize his guilt before God and to go to him for forgiveness and restoration. In 6:1–3 Job tells ("answered"; v. 1) Eliphaz, and the other friends as well (the "you" throughout ch. 6 is plural; vv. 21, 25–27), that he has every reason to be upset and frustrated by the situation. If someone took all of Job's anger ("vexation") and agony ("calamity"; v. 2) and weighed it on a scale, it would be "heavier than the sand of the sea" (v. 3a). That is why his words have come across as "rash" (v. 3b). Job cannot keep silent any more than a beast ("the wild donkey . . . or the ox") keeps silent when it is hungry (the donkey brays "when he has grass"; the ox lows "over his fodder"; v. 5).

Job's friends fail to understand the situation properly. He will not stomach their insipid ("tasteless," v. 6; untouchable, see v. 7a; "loathsome," v. 7b) words, for he is not under the discipline of God due to some sin ("I have not denied the words of the Holy One"; v. 10). Instead, God has attacked him without cause ("the arrows of the Almighty are in me"; v. 4; cf. Lam. 3:12–13).[56] Job has already expressed his only hope—death (Job 3). He wants the arrows of God to finish him off: "Oh that I might have my request, and that God would fulfill my hope" (6:8), namely, to "crush me . . . cut me off!" (v. 9). He sees his destruction as his only possibility of future "comfort" (v. 10). He has reached his limit, perhaps the human limit, of patience ("What is my strength, that I should wait?"; v. 11). His body can only take so much ("Is my strength the strength of stones, or is my flesh bronze?"; v. 12). His self-resolve has vanished ("Have I any help in me?"; v. 13).[57]

6:14–30 As Job thinks God has attacked him (6:4), so he next expresses the arrows of his friends' attack (presumably expressed in Eliphaz's estimation and advice; chs. 4–5). Instead of showing him steadfast love ("kindness"; Hb. *hesed*), they have proved disloyal to him. His proverb about them is as sharp as any arrow: "He who withholds kindness from a friend forsakes the fear of the Almighty" (6:14). Next, Job compares his friends (whom he ironically calls "my brothers"; v. 15) to wadis (vv. 15–20). Like temporary "torrential streams" (v. 15a) that form in the Arabian Desert ("the waste"; v. 18b) after heavy rainfall but quickly dry up ("pass away," v. 15b; "vanish," v. 17b) before providing sustenance for desperate and weary travelers (those who have turned "aside from their course," v. 18; "caravans of Tema . . . travelers of Sheba," v. 19), their "wisdom" has proved an unreliable source in sustaining him through his suffering. Just as these travelers, who were "confident" there would be water in the wadi when they arrived there, are "ashamed" and "disappointed" (v. 20) once they see the streambed is dry, so Job wants his friends to know that their counsel comes from overconfident and misguided perceptions of his situation.

Next, Job takes the arrow from his friends out of his soul and sticks it in theirs. His friends are like that empty riverbed: "you now have become nothing" (v. 21a). As they look at Job ("you see my calamity"; v. 21b), they are as "afraid" as those wanderers at the waterless wadi. They shrink back in fear instead of moving toward him in friendship. Job has not asked for much; he has not asked them for money ("Have I said, 'Make me a gift'?"; v. 22a) or to take steps to rescue him ("[Have I

---

56 "The Old Testament often pictures Yahweh as a divine warrior who fights for his people (Zeph. 3:17), as he does notably in the exodus when he defeats Pharaoh and the army of Egypt (Ex. 15:1–18). Job, however, feels that instead of being his faithful protector, God has been his fierce enemy. Bending the familiar Old Testament image of God as the divine warrior fighting for his people, Job pictures him instead as an enemy attacking him with poisoned arrows that penetrate both his body and spirit" (Estes, *Job*, 39).

57 In 6:5–7, Job asks four rhetorical questions; in 6:11–13, five.

said,] 'Deliver me. . . . Redeem me. . . .'?"; v. 23). Instead he seeks wisdom. "Teach me, and I will be silent; make me understand how I have gone astray" (v. 24). He needs "upright words" (v. 25a).

But their wisdom and words have thus far proved futile: "But what does reproof from you reprove?" (v. 25b). In other words, their criticisms amount to nothing! They think they have Job's problem solved (v. 26) and treat his disagreement with their diagnosis with disdain. To them, Job is full of hot air ("the speech of a despairing man is wind"; v. 26b). Their charges are baseless and their accusations heartless. Job is a person, not an object. His *friends* are treating him like a commodity, not a companion ("you . . . bargain over your friend"), acting as cruel and careless as poker sharks gambling over a desolate child's life ("you would even cast lots over the fatherless"; v. 27).

But there is time for Job's friends to change. Verses 28–30 are his call to repentance: "Please turn. . . . Turn now" (v. 29). In essence, Job concludes, "You look me in the eye ["be pleased to look at me"; v. 28a], and I will look you in the eye. Let us treat each other like human beings. Friends. I promise I will not exaggerate the pain, hide any sins, or 'lie to your face' [v. 28b; cf. v. 30]. You promise to be fair-minded ["let no injustice be done"; v. 29a]. 'My vindication is at stake' [v. 29b]. Please believe me. You must believe me when I say that my words ["Is there any injustice on my tongue?"; v. 30a] are not the 'cause of' my 'calamity' [v. 30b]."

7:1–10 In chapter 7, Job shifts from confronting his friends ("Please turn. . . . Turn now"; 6:29) to complaining ("I will complain in the bitterness of my soul"; 7:11) to his God. His complaint is, we might say, east of Eden. The crunch of the thorns and thistles from Genesis 3:17–19 can be felt beneath Job's feet. "Man" has a "hard service on earth" (Job 7:1a). His workdays are long ("his days [are] like the days of a hired hand"; v. 1b) and his toil under the sun without respite ("like a slave who longs for the shadow"; v. 2a). And although man works like a forced laborer (cf. vv. 1–2 with 1 Kings 5:13–14) for meager pay, the weekend never seems to come around (he "looks for his wages"; Job 7:2b).

Life is hard for all humans—such is how Job begins chapter 7. Next, he turns to himself. Notice the change from "man" to "me," "my," and "I," used thirteen times in verses 3–10. Job will return to man in verse 17 ("What is man . . . ?") but will continually view the plight of man in light of his only. In chapter 7, "I" is used twenty times, "my" seventeen times, and "me" thirteen times. In verse 3, Job applies the analogy he used of man in verse 2 to himself: worse than the man who works all week and gets measly wages in return, Job suffers ("nights of misery are apportioned to me"; v. 3b) for nothing ("I am allotted months of emptiness"; v. 3a).[58] He inherits futility, along with insomnia. "The night is long" ("When I lie down I say, 'When shall I arise?'"); he tosses in his sleep ("I am full of tossing till the dawn"; v. 4).

---

58 Some manuscripts of the pseudepigraphal *Testament of Job* speculate that Job's suffering lasted forty-eight years (21:1).

His days are worse! They come and go, one sunrise after the next, quickly ending without a thread of hope ("my days are swifter than a weaver's shuttle and come to their end without hope"; v. 6). Day after day, nothing has changed: he has not been healed; he has not died. But his body is like a walking corpse ("my flesh is clothed with worms and dirt") that regenerates sores ("my skin hardens, then breaks out afresh"; v. 5).

Job's reflection on his days and nights (vv. 3b–6) and weeks and months (vv. 1–3a) leaves him realistic ("my life is a breath")[59] but not optimistic ("my eye will never again see good"; v. 7). The reason he is not optimistic is related to God's omnipresence, a theme he will return to later (v. 20), and to mankind's transiency. As God looks on him ("your eyes are on me"; v. 8b), and perhaps mankind does as well ("the eye of him who sees me"; v. 8a),[60] nothing is done to rescue Job and his fellow man. Just as he will die ("I shall be gone," v. 8b; "no more," v. 8a), man ("he"; vv. 9, 10), who has worked so hard (vv. 1–2), works for nothing. The grave ("Sheol" in Hebrew, the place of the dead) will swallow up any remembrance of him:

> As the cloud fades and vanishes,
>> so he who goes down to Sheol does not come up;
> he returns no more to his house,
>> nor does his place know him anymore. (vv. 9–10)

7:11–16 Job has had enough. What has become of his body and what becomes of every human body is one thing. It is quite another thing to consider what has become of his soul. He can close his mouth no longer ("I will not restrain my mouth; I will speak"; v. 11ab) about the "anguish of" his "spirit" and the "bitterness of" his "soul" (v. 11bc). He does not grasp what God is doing. He is not the Mediterranean Sea or the Leviathan, that God must pay special attention to him, making sure that evil on earth is held at bay ("Am I the sea, or a sea monster, that you set a guard over me?"; v. 12).[61] "Leave me alone" (v. 16b), Job cries out. Even at night, when rest should be routine, God sends nightmares, Job claims:

> When I say, "My bed will comfort me,
>> my couch will ease my complaint,"
> then you scare me with dreams
>> and terrify me with visions. (vv. 13–14)

Why will God not remove the arrows of anguish? Job knows he will "not live forever" (his "days are a breath," v. 16a; Hb. *hebel*). Death by strangulation is a far better option ("I would choose strangling and death") than what he is now enduring ("death rather than my bones"; v. 15).

---

59 This is a common theme in the Wisdom Literature (esp. Ecclesiastes; cf. Job 9:25–26; 14:1–2) and Psalms (e.g., Pss. 39:4–5; 62:9; 89:47–48; 144:3–4).
60 The parallel here ("the eye of him"/"your eyes"; 7:8) could refer to God.
61 Perhaps, as many commentators suggest, "the sea" and "sea monster" are allusions to the gods of the ancient Near East (Yam and Tannin). They certainly symbolize great forces in creation, perhaps also forces of evil or chaos.

7:17–21 Job is not done with his imprecatory poem. He next aims his arrows at the Almighty. However, he dulls their edges. He does not make accusations; rather, he asks eight questions. The first is:

> What is man, that you make so much of him,
>   and that you set your heart on him,
> visit him every morning
>   and test him every moment? (vv. 17–18)

Unlike Psalm 8, which asks, "what is man that you are mindful of him, . . . that you care for him?" (v. 4) and begins and ends in praise, "O LORD, our Lord, how majestic is your name in all the earth!" (vv. 1, 9), in Job 7:17–18 God's mindfulness of man begins and ends only in despair.[62] To Job, God's omnipresence is overbearing (Job cannot even swallow his spit; cf. v. 19). God's watchful eye ("you watcher of mankind"; v. 20a) is not that of a protective father or merciful deliverer (as it was for Israel; see Pss. 12:7; 25:20; 40:11; 61:7) or even of a tester of mankind (cf. Ps. 11:4; Eccles. 3:18). Rather, the Almighty's eye equals his arrows ("Why have you made me your mark?"; Job 7:20; cf. 6:4). Job wants to be ignored, not oppressed by God's omnipresence. And, if he cannot be ignored, he simply wants to be forgiven for whatever microscopic sin is causing his colossal catastrophe: "Why do you not pardon my transgression and take away my iniquity" before I die ("I shall lie in the earth") and our relationship is over ("you will seek me, but I shall not be"; v. 21)?"

Job's final question (v. 21) is as important and as exaggerated as the first (vv. 17–18). He is looking for some sin as eagerly as his friends are. He is hoping to find something, even the smallest sin that he could confess to release God's harsh hand. However, he cannot find anything, and the specific sins his friends name do not resonate with his own honest self-evaluation and perception. So he calls on God to rescue him by both naming the sin and forgiving it.

Response

The arrows of the Almighty are too much for Job. His body is too weak (6:11–12), his soul too depressed (6:4),[63] and his calamities too heavy to bear (6:2). Job wants to die. But "even in the midst of his death wish, Job refuses to break relationship with God."[64] He does not consider suicide, or at least never expresses such contemplation. He knows that to take his own life is not an option for one who follows God's commands ("the words of the Holy One"; 6:10). He longs for death, but he does not long for God's disfavor. He will not risk severing his relationship with

---

62 "In 7:17–18 Job parodies the words of the psalmist in Psalm 8:4 (cf. Ps. 144:3–4). Instead of humans enjoying an exalted status under God, in which they exercise rule over his creation, Job says that they are scrutinized and examined perpetually by God. Whereas the psalmists exulted in wonder and worship as they reflected on the God-given status of humans, Job at this place in the book explodes in bitter anguish and aggravation" (Estes, *Job*, 47).

63 On 6:4, note that "it is not his body that absorbs this poison but rather his spirit, an apt metaphor for Job's depression" (Longman, *Job*, 137).

64 Ibid., 139.

Yahweh (12:9; 28:28).[65] The only way he sees out of the maze of his misery is for God himself to kill him.

Whatever we might think of Job's solution, we should appreciate and apply two aspects of Job's relationship with God. First, he fears God more than he fears death. Moreover, he loves God more than he loves himself. Second, he is honest with God. We might desire Job to return to his more pious-sounding replies to his ongoing suffering ("the LORD gave, and the LORD has taken away; blessed be the name of the LORD"; 1:21; cf. 2:9–10). We might wish he were more hopeful.[66] We might even assess his prayer (ch. 7) as impudent. However, we also might find the authenticity and integrity of his lamentations to be soothing to our souls. Like the pained psalmists, the weeping prophets, and the suffering saints, God's people can cry out to him, "How long, O LORD?" (e.g., Ps. 13:1; Hab. 1:2; Rev. 6:10) and "Why" (Job 3:11, 12, 16, 20, 23; 7:20, 21). Our depressing thoughts, even our longings for death and frustrations with God, can be appropriate prayers. When we are healthy and happy, we should turn to God in praise and thanksgiving. But also, when we are sick and sad, we should cast "all" our "anxieties on" God—our physical, emotional, social, financial, and *theological* concerns—even if we cannot sense that he "cares for" us (see 1 Pet. 5:7). And we should join in the chorus of the oppressed, from "Nobody Knows the Trouble I've Seen" to "Swing Low, Sweet Chariot."

Another lesson to learn from these chapters relates to friendship, an important theme in Job (the Hebrew word *rea'* for "friend" is used fourteen times) and wisdom literature (*rea'* is used fifteen times in Proverbs, more often than in any other OT book),[67] as it is an important experience in real life. How hard it is to find a faithful friend—a Jonathan for David or a Timothy for Paul! Job's friends started well (and they will end well; Job 42:7–9), but their whirlwind of words pushes Job to the edge. To change the metaphor, Eliphaz has not soothed his wounds but salted them. This is just the beginning of Job's third test—his final, torturous endurance test. Relationships matter. The greatest commandment focuses on our relationship with God; the second greatest on our relationship with people. Job feels like he has joined Adam and Eve after being banished from the garden. He is not in relational harmony with his God, his wife, or his friends.

God will eventually speak (chs. 38–41), and the effects of that speech will bring renewed relationship between all the people involved. In no trite way, we can be thankful for "What a Friend We Have in Jesus" (cf. Luke 7:34; John 15:13–15). God has spoken to us in Jesus, the final word (Heb. 1:1–2), and that word is soothing to our souls and renewing to all our relationships. We have a mediator between God and man, someone acquainted with our sufferings (Isa. 53:3) and powerful enough to vindicate the righteous.

---

65 See Section Overview of Job 28:1–28 on the possibility of Job as the speaker.
66 "Job's friends, reflecting the wisdom instruction of Proverbs 10:28, insist that the righteous are those who have hope (4:6; 11:18), but the wicked have no hope (8:13; 11:20). Although Job readily admits his feeling of hopelessness, he strongly argues against their deduction that he then necessarily must be wicked" (Estes, *Job*, 45–46).
67 For more on this theme, see O'Donnell, *Ecclesiastes*, 99–103.

Moreover, we today have Christ's church, all those who are in relationship with God and one another through trust in Jesus. We have true "brothers" (Job 6:15) and sisters who should hold us up when we feel the arrows of painful providence in our lives. Paul puts it beautifully: the "God of all comfort, . . . comforts us in all our affliction, *so that* we may be able to comfort those who are in any affliction" (2 Cor. 1:3–4). Because we ourselves are "comforted by God," and because we ourselves "share abundantly in Christ's sufferings, so through Christ we share abundantly in comfort too" (2 Cor. 1:4–5). Out of mutual suffering comes mutual comfort! To share in afflictions and sufferings is to share in comfort (2 Cor. 1:6–7).[68]

JOB 8:1–22

8 Then Bildad the Shuhite answered and said:

2 "How long will you say these things,
    and the words of your mouth be a great wind?
3 Does God pervert justice?
    Or does the Almighty pervert the right?
4 If your children have sinned against him,
    he has delivered them into the hand of their transgression.
5 If you will seek God
    and plead with the Almighty for mercy,
6 if you are pure and upright,
    surely then he will rouse himself for you
    and restore your rightful habitation.
7 And though your beginning was small,
    your latter days will be very great.

8 "For inquire, please, of bygone ages,
    and consider what the fathers have searched out.
9 For we are but of yesterday and know nothing,
    for our days on earth are a shadow.
10 Will they not teach you and tell you
    and utter words out of their understanding?

11 "Can papyrus grow where there is no marsh?
    Can reeds flourish where there is no water?
12 While yet in flower and not cut down,
    they wither before any other plant.

---

68 I am indebted to Longman for connecting Job 6–7 to 2 Corinthians 1:3–7. Moreover, his counsel after quoting those verses is apropos: "The sad fact, though, is that the community of God, like the three friends of Job, is often like a dried-up wadi, promising succor but not delivering. The story of Job's treatment at the hands of his friends is a warning about offering facile advice to those who suffer. It is not adequate to offer pat answers to people's problems; we must approach them with compassion, thoughtfulness, and empathy" (*Job*, 152).

13   Such are the paths of all who forget God;
     the hope of the godless shall perish.
14   His confidence is severed,
     and his trust is a spider's web.[1]
15   He leans against his house, but it does not stand;
     he lays hold of it, but it does not endure.
16   He is a lush plant before the sun,
     and his shoots spread over his garden.
17   His roots entwine the stone heap;
     he looks upon a house of stones.
18   If he is destroyed from his place,
     then it will deny him, saying, 'I have never seen you.'
19   Behold, this is the joy of his way,
     and out of the soil others will spring.

20   "Behold, God will not reject a blameless man,
     nor take the hand of evildoers.
21   He will yet fill your mouth with laughter,
     and your lips with shouting.
22   Those who hate you will be clothed with shame,
     and the tent of the wicked will be no more."

[1] Hebrew *house*

Section Overview

In chapter 8, Job's friend Bildad the Shuhite adds his voice to the debate over the cause of Job's calamities. Echoing Eliphaz's retribution theology (chs. 4–5), Bildad offers the clearest expression of their system of thought. As Christopher Ash[69] summarizes:

(1) God is absolutely in control. . . .
(2) God is absolutely just and fair.
(3) *Therefore* he always punishes wickedness and blesses righteousness. . . . If he were ever to do otherwise, he would necessarily be unjust, which is inconceivable.
(4) *Therefore*, if I suffer I *must* have sinned and am being punished justly for my sin.

(And, presumably, if I am blessed I must have been good . . .).

More succinctly: "Retribution theology is based on the idea that sin leads to suffering and thus that suffering is a sign of sin."[70] Grounding his argument in tradition (8:8–10), Bildad covers all of his theological bases. Because the absolutely sovereign God ("the Almighty"; vv. 3, 5) is always absolutely just ("Does God pervert justice?"; v. 3a), Job's sin, as is true of all that of the godless (vv. 11–19; including Job's children, v. 4), has been punished. The solution is simple: stop pretending to be innocent (v. 2). Ask God for forgiveness ("seek God and plead . . . for mercy"; v. 5).

---

69 Ash, *Job*, 90, emphasis his.
70 Longman, *Job*, 159.

Then watch the blessings flow (vv. 7, 19–22)—Job's happiness ("laughter"; v. 21) and his enemies' humiliation (v. 22).

Section Outline

II.D. New Singer, Same Old Tune (8:1–22)

    1. A Concise Summary of the Retribution Principle (8:1–7)

    2. Such Theology Is Grounded in Tradition (8:8–10)

    3. Such Theology Is Supported by Observation (8:11–19)

    4. The Benefits of Submitting to the System (8:20–22)

Comment

8:1–7 Bildad shows none of the courtesy and sensitivity of Eliphaz (cf. 4:3–4). Instead of affirmation, Bildad blasts Job with a brutal appraisal (8:2).[71] He dismisses Job's passionate claims and loud lamentations ("How long will you say these things?"; v. 2a) as a lot of hot air (Job's "words" are like "a great wind," v. 2b, namely, they cannot be grasped and should not be held on to).[72] He follows such pastoral insensitivity with analytical and abstract theology. His tone is as cold and clinical as an operating table as he dissects Job's defense. With the tightness of his retribution theology (see the summary above), he finds no room for innocent suffering. Like the men on Malta who saw the snake fastened on Paul's arm as a sign that justice will punish a murderer (Acts 28:4), Bildad sees the signs of suffering as sure evidences of Job's sin.

Job's sin, however, must not be as awful as his children's. Because God is just (Job 8:3), Job's children got their just deserts ("he has delivered them into the hand of their transgression"; v. 4). But Job is still alive! And so too are his options. He can continue to act impudently, or he can go earnestly to the Almighty ("seek God"; v. 5a). God is merciful, so Bildad implores Job to "plead . . . for mercy" (v. 5b), that is, confess his sins. Or, if Job is "pure and upright" (v. 6a), as claimed, there is no need to worry:[73] God will come to Job's aid ("then he will rouse himself for you"; v. 6b) and restore health and wealth ("[He will] restore your rightful habitation. And though your beginning was small, your latter days will be very great"; vv. 6c–7). Bildad is being cynical here, but note that, ironically, he is right. God will rouse himself (chs. 38–41), vindicate Job (42:7–9), and restore Job's fortunes (42:10–17). Job will end up better than ever (8:7b).

8:8–10 Bildad is certain of his rebuke of and advice to Job because his thought is grounded in tradition. (This might be the author's way of ironically taking his

---

71 From here on out, opening insults will characterize the friends' speeches. Moreover, in the next three rebuttals, each will begin by calling Job a windbag ("Should a multitude of words go unanswered?" 11:2a]; "Should a wise man answer with windy knowledge, and fill his belly with the east wind? Should he argue in unprofitable talk, or in words with which he can do no good?" [15:2–3]; "How long will you hunt for words?" [18:2a]).

72 In 1:19 the Hebrew for the ESV translation "a great wind" is *ruakh gedolah*, and in 8:2 it is *ruakh kabbir* (lit., a *mighty* wind). If 8:2 is an intertextual allusion to 1:19, perhaps the sense is that Job's words are destroying or wreaking havoc.

73 It is also possible that 8:6 is part two of Bildad's suggested repentance ritual. First, Job should ask for forgiveness for his sins. Second, he should live a holy life. The logic would then be: "if" he seeks mercy (8:5), and "if" he starts to amend his ways (8:6a), then God will reward him (8:6b–7).

first jab at his own wisdom tradition, or the prevalent one of his culture.) Bildad counsels Job to look beyond his own experience to "inquire" into the past ("bygone ages") and to "consider" what their wise sages have found ("what the fathers have searched out"; v. 8). His reason makes sense: while there are exceptions (cf. 32:6–9), the older person is often wiser than the younger, and thus the OT wisdom literature often implores the young to listen to their parents, teachers, and elders. Likewise, the cumulative gathering of wisdom over time about God, people, and how the world works—that which is observed, studied, accepted as consensus, and handed down—is a reasonable foundation for one's thoughts and actions. Bildad asks Job to consider time-tested tradition concerning the matter at hand. Surely, compared with that, what Job thinks he knows is inconsequential ("we are but of yesterday and know nothing, for our days on earth are a shadow"; 8:9). Heed the wisdom of the ancients, for their voice is reliable:

> Will they not teach you and tell you
>   and utter words out of their understanding? (v. 10)

8:11–19 What the ancients can teach Job is what Bildad states next in verses 11–22. In one of the most beautiful poems in the Bible, elements and analogies are employed to press home the point that traditional retribution theology is right. The first synonymous parallelism contains two rhetorical questions (v. 11):

> Can papyrus   grow   where there is no marsh?
> Can reeds   flourish where there is no water?

The answer to the above questions is obvious: no. Without water, no plant can grow. Papyrus and reeds, which can grow quickly, profusely, and to great heights, will "wither before any other plant," even "while yet in flower and not cut down" (v. 12). So too is the fate of the wicked. "All who forget God" (v. 13a, not for a moment but as a lifestyle), namely, those without God in their lives ("the godless"), whatever hope they might have, "shall perish" like the two plants (v. 13b). Bildad then changes metaphors, adding another parallelism (v. 14),

> His confidence   is   severed . . .
> His trust   is   a spider's web.

The future of the godless is as fragile as the temporary masterpiece of the garden orbweaver. Worse than that (and piling on the parallelisms!) even something seemingly stable cannot hold him up (v. 15):

> He leans against   his house,   but it does not stand;
> He lays hold   of it,   but it does not endure.

At this point we must remember that this is more than a beautiful poem; it is a rebuke directed to Job. The "he" throughout is him. Job has lost his house, his possessions, everything! And it has happened as quickly as a hurricane—or even a curious kid with a stick—obliterates a spider's web. Thus we can think of verses 16–19 as especially pointed at our protagonist. Job was like a well-watered happy plant basking in the springtime rays ("before the sun"; v. 16a). His branches ("his shoots") grew so vast that they "spread over" the "garden" (v. 16b). Not only that, his roots wrapped around a seemingly permanent foundation ("his roots entwine the stone heap"; v. 17a). In fact, all that this plant sees screams, "I will be around forever!" ("he looks upon a house of stones"; v. 17b).[74] Yet, like a weed, if he is pulled out of his seemingly solid underpinning ("if he is destroyed from his place"; v. 18a), the gardener (God) will refute the relationship: "He will deny him, saying, 'I have never seen you'" (v. 18b AT), or in Jesus' words, "I never knew you" (Matt. 7:23). Indeed, as Bildad ends his poem with "behold" (Hb. *hen*, which we might paraphrase as "See this!" or "Listen up!"), we are to behold the outcome of the unrighteous.

> Behold, this is the joy of his way,
>   and out of the soil others will spring. (Job 8:19)

The irony is thick: there is no "joy" (Hb. *mesos*) for the godless. Why? They are soon to be gone. The final phrase—"and out of the soil others will spring" (which is difficult to translate and harder to understand)—could refer to how the godly will grow in the place of the wicked, or to how one wicked generation produces another (i.e., there will be no end to evil offspring). Either way, Job is on the short end of the prosperous plant analogy. Likely Bildad is saying that like the godless, if Job does not repent, another weed will take his place.

8:20–22 Bildad uses a second "behold" (Hb. *hen*; cf. v. 19) as he wants Job to make one final consideration (v. 20):

> Behold, God   will not reject   a blameless man,
>   nor take the hand   of evildoers.

This antithetical parallelism (i.e., "will reject" is the opposite of "take the hand"; "blameless" the opposite of "evildoers") restates and summarizes Bildad's theology and also initiates his final subtle appeal to Job to heed his earlier, and not so subtle, advice ("seek God and plead . . . for mercy"; v. 5). Again the imagery is awesome (e.g., God's taking someone by the hand as symbolizing a loving and protective relationship, or, in the case of the wicked, the lack thereof) but the theology too unbending. Bildad has no room in his tight theological system for a "blameless" (Hb. *tam*) sufferer such as Job (*tam* is used of Job in 1:1, 8; 2:3; and by Job of himself in 9:20, "though I am blameless"). And to the reader, as well as Job (see chs. 9–10!), Bildad's rigidity seems not only ruthless but unrealistic. Does he really think that every stillborn is a sign of God's rejection and every baby born blind a token of Yahweh's retribution?

---

74 However, while seemingly strong, rocks are deceptive foundations. The roots are superficial (cf. Matt. 13:5, 20–21).

Job 8:21–22 end on a hopeful note. *If* Job follows Bildad's advice to repent, two positive benefits are sure to follow. True joy (contra v. 19) will come:

[God] will yet fill	your mouth	with laughter,
and	your lips	with shouting. (v. 21)

This emotional triumph is based in part on Job's enemies' receiving their just due. "Those who hate you will be clothed with shame, and the tent of the wicked will be no more" (v. 22). There are multiple ironies in this final line. First, Job's friends, who have become his enemies (27:7, Hb. *'oyebi*), will soon be "clothed with shame"—the shame of having God reprimand them (42:7–8) and of having to offer a massive and expensive sacrifice through the blameless man they repeatedly shamed (42:9). Second, God in his grace will not judge these men (cf. "the wicked will be no more"; 8:22) but instead forgive them through Job. The reader is glad that God's theological system is not as rigid as Bildad's![75]

Response

When friends are hurting—depressed over the loss of a job, devastated by the loss of a loved one, distressed by the loss of health—it is difficult to know what to say and how to act around them. We might act awkward; we might say something stupid. Yet, whatever we do and say, Job 8 teaches us not to act and talk like Bildad.

First, we are not to act arrogantly or abrasively. Bildad is absolutely sure of his theology. He is confident of his claims and critiques. He even knows, through a logical deduction, that Job's children have sinned (v. 4). Worse than that, he is callous, clinical, and condescending in his criticisms. His bedside manner is more than wanting; it is biting. He opens with a rebuke (v. 2) rather than a word of "sympathy and comfort" (his original intent! see 2:11), followed by "Oh, and your children— remember those who you buried and who you prayed for every day—died due to their wicked behavior" (cf. 8:4). He is there to "solve the problem" rather than "salve the person."[76] He asks the right question, "Does God pervert justice?" (v. 3; cf. 40:8), but leaves no room for God to be God. This moralist from Shuah thinks he knows the mind of God, but, in the wisdom literature, to assume and assert such knowledge is not a safe place to be. He is sure to be humbled (cf. 42:7–9).

We too must be humbled. Bildad's folly should serve as a wake-up call to us. We must approach those who are hurting with kindness and humility. We must not think we know all the answers; we must not spout out all the answers. Sometimes silence is most soothing (2:13), weeping most comforting (2:12), and closet prayer (Matt. 6:6) most helpful.

---

75 In his excellent commentary, Estes offers this theological insight: "Bildad takes the general retribution pattern taught in traditional wisdom (e.g., Prov. 26:27), and he reduces all of life to it. By doing this, Bildad leaves no room for God to work outside the standard pattern, thus making divine actions thoroughly predictable and automatic. The book of Job, however, will go on to demonstrate that there is mystery in God's working in the world and that the retribution principle, though valid in general, must not be pressed into an inflexible formula for how God *must* act in every case" (*Job*, 53, emphasis his).

76 Ibid., 54. In this method, as Estes points us, Bildad is "in effect . . . like a doctor who confidently prescribes Job's cure without first taking care to diagnose correctly his disease." Estes offers this application: "In trying to give the right answers to others, we must be careful to give answers that are truly relevant to their situations."

Second, we are not to speak falsely about God to God's people. Both the OT and the NT repeatedly warn, with great earnestness and severity, about false teachers and false teaching (e.g., Deut. 18:18–22; Jer. 14:14–16; 23:14; Matt. 7:15; 2 Cor. 11:13; 2 Pet. 2:1–3). Bildad's version of the health and wealth or so-called prosperity gospel is damnable. Bildad is right that God is absolutely sovereign (Job 8:3, 5) and just (v. 3) and punishes the wicked (vv. 11–19), rewards the righteous (vv. 7, 20–22),[77] and forgives those who plead for mercy (v. 5). But to claim that the righteous and forgiven never suffer is satanic, because it fails to see the divine benefits of suffering. Suffering can humble us; it can refine our faith. And, most important, suffering can draw us closer to Christ, the Suffering Servant whose substitutionary suffering has atoned for all our sins.

JOB 9:1–10:22

9 Then Job answered and said:

2 "Truly I know that it is so:
     But how can a man be in the right before God?
3   If one wished to contend with him,
     one could not answer him once in a thousand times.
4   He is wise in heart and mighty in strength
     —who has hardened himself against him, and succeeded?—
5   he who removes mountains, and they know it not,
     when he overturns them in his anger,
6   who shakes the earth out of its place,
     and its pillars tremble;
7   who commands the sun, and it does not rise;
     who seals up the stars;
8   who alone stretched out the heavens
     and trampled the waves of the sea;
9   who made the Bear and Orion,
     the Pleiades and the chambers of the south;
10 who does great things beyond searching out,
     and marvelous things beyond number.
11 Behold, he passes by me, and I see him not;
     he moves on, but I do not perceive him.
12 Behold, he snatches away; who can turn him back?
     Who will say to him, 'What are you doing?'

---

77 While the book of Job was written to correct Bildad-type theology (suffering is not always connected to sin), other parts of the OT clearly advocate the general principle that God judges the wicked and rewards the righteous in this life (e.g., Prov. 15:19; 21:21). The conditions of the law, for example, must not be forgotten: "If you faithfully obey.... all these blessings shall come upon you" and "if you will not obey ... all these curses shall come upon you" (Deut. 28:1–2, 15). This is not only an OT teaching (cf. 1 Cor. 11:30).

¹³ "God will not turn back his anger;
　　beneath him bowed the helpers of Rahab.
¹⁴ How then can I answer him,
　　choosing my words with him?
¹⁵ Though I am in the right, I cannot answer him;
　　I must appeal for mercy to my accuser.[1]
¹⁶ If I summoned him and he answered me,
　　I would not believe that he was listening to my voice.
¹⁷ For he crushes me with a tempest
　　and multiplies my wounds without cause;
¹⁸ he will not let me get my breath,
　　but fills me with bitterness.
¹⁹ If it is a contest of strength, behold, he is mighty!
　　If it is a matter of justice, who can summon him?[2]
²⁰ Though I am in the right, my own mouth would condemn me;
　　though I am blameless, he would prove me perverse.
²¹ I am blameless; I regard not myself;
　　I loathe my life.
²² It is all one; therefore I say,
　　'He destroys both the blameless and the wicked.'
²³ When disaster brings sudden death,
　　he mocks at the calamity[3] of the innocent.
²⁴ The earth is given into the hand of the wicked;
　　he covers the faces of its judges—
　　　if it is not he, who then is it?

²⁵ "My days are swifter than a runner;
　　they flee away; they see no good.
²⁶ They go by like skiffs of reed,
　　like an eagle swooping on the prey.
²⁷ If I say, 'I will forget my complaint,
　　I will put off my sad face, and be of good cheer,'
²⁸ I become afraid of all my suffering,
　　for I know you will not hold me innocent.
²⁹ I shall be condemned;
　　why then do I labor in vain?
³⁰ If I wash myself with snow
　　and cleanse my hands with lye,
³¹ yet you will plunge me into a pit,
　　and my own clothes will abhor me.
³² For he is not a man, as I am, that I might answer him,
　　that we should come to trial together.
³³ There is no[4] arbiter between us,
　　who might lay his hand on us both.
³⁴ Let him take his rod away from me,
　　and let not dread of him terrify me.
³⁵ Then I would speak without fear of him,
　　for I am not so in myself.

10 "I loathe my life;
　　I will give free utterance to my complaint;
　　I will speak in the bitterness of my soul.

2   I will say to God, Do not condemn me;
     let me know why you contend against me.
3   Does it seem good to you to oppress,
     to despise the work of your hands
     and favor the designs of the wicked?
4   Have you eyes of flesh?
     Do you see as man sees?
5   Are your days as the days of man,
     or your years as a man's years,
6   that you seek out my iniquity
     and search for my sin,
7   although you know that I am not guilty,
     and there is none to deliver out of your hand?
8   Your hands fashioned and made me,
     and now you have destroyed me altogether.
9   Remember that you have made me like clay;
     and will you return me to the dust?
10   Did you not pour me out like milk
     and curdle me like cheese?
11   You clothed me with skin and flesh,
     and knit me together with bones and sinews.
12   You have granted me life and steadfast love,
     and your care has preserved my spirit.
13   Yet these things you hid in your heart;
     I know that this was your purpose.
14   If I sin, you watch me
     and do not acquit me of my iniquity.
15   If I am guilty, woe to me!
     If I am in the right, I cannot lift up my head,
     for I am filled with disgrace
     and look on my affliction.
16   And were my head lifted up,[5] you would hunt me
       like a lion
     and again work wonders against me.
17   You renew your witnesses against me
     and increase your vexation toward me;
     you bring fresh troops against me.

18   "Why did you bring me out from the womb?
     Would that I had died before any eye had seen me
19   and were as though I had not been,
     carried from the womb to the grave.
20   Are not my days few?
     Then cease, and leave me alone, that I may find a
       little cheer
21   before I go—and I shall not return—
     to the land of darkness and deep shadow,
22   the land of gloom like thick darkness,
     like deep shadow without any order,
     where light is as thick darkness."

[1] Or *to my judge* [2] Or *who can grant me a hearing?* [3] The meaning of the Hebrew word is uncertain [4] Or *Would that there were an* [5] Hebrew lacks *my head*

Section Overview

In the narrative of Job, the same Hebrew phrase *wayya'an . . . wayyo'mar* ("then . . . answered and said") is used to introduce all of the dialogues between Job and his friends (Eliphaz, 4:1; 15:1; 22:1; Bildad, 8:1; 18:1; 25:1; Zophar, 11:1; 20:1; Elihu, 32:6; 34:1; 35:1; Job, 6:1; 9:1; 12:1; 19:1; 21:1; 23:1; 26:1). While Job 9–10 is Job's response to Bildad (ch. 8) as well as Eliphaz (chs. 4–5), his subject and object is God. In the first verse of Job's response (9:2), "God" is mentioned. From that verse on, God is mentioned seventy-five times in the English translation (three times as "God," 9:2, 13; 10:2; one as the "accuser" [or "judge," 9:15; Hb. *meshophet*]; the rest as pronouns—"he" [17x], "him" [17x], "his" [3x], "you" [21x], "your" [10x]; including God and Job as "we" [1x] and "us" [2x]). In 9:2–24 Job speaks about God (only "he," "him," and "his" are used), in 9:25–35 both to and about God ("he," "him," "you," "we," and "us" are used), and in 10:1–22 only to God (only "you" and "your" are used).

Job speaks about God as the wise and mighty creator, ruler, and judge. Job speaks also of his own innocence ("I am in the right," 9:15, 20; "I am blameless," 9:20, 21; "I am not guilty," 10:7) and his pain, both physical ("my wounds"; 9:17) and psychological ("I loathe my life," 9:21; 10:1; cf. 7:16; "my suffering," 9:28; "the bitterness of my soul," 10:1). His main "complaint" (10:1) is that God's ways seem incomprehensible, and thus Job's cause appears hopeless. There is no "arbiter" between him and God (9:33) nor savior from God ("there is none to deliver out of your hand"; 10:7). And even if he could find a representative and receive a court date with God (9:32), how could he claim perfect innocence ("How then can I answer him?" 9:14; "I cannot answer him," 9:15) and win the case against a perfectly wise and strong God ("He is wise in heart and mighty in strength"; 9:4) when he cannot possibly perceive who God is and how he works (9:11)?

Job knows that God is against him ("he crushes me," 9:17; "you bring fresh troops against me," 10:17), but he cannot understand why ("he . . . multiplies my wounds without cause," 9:17; "let me know why you contend against me," 10:2). He finds such treatment of him, and others in similar situations, unfair (9:22–24; 10:3). He would love to know what is going on, but he will settle for being delivered from God's "hand" (10:7). Thus his plea is for God to have mercy and stop oppressing him ("Let him take his rod away from me," 9:34; "Do not condemn me," 10:2; "cease, and leave me alone," 10:20b) so that he might die in peace following the few days he has left on earth (10:20–22; cf. 9:25–26).

Section Outline

II.E. Can I Get a Witness? (9:1–10:22)

    1. Contending with God (9:1–35)

        a. Two Impossible Obstacles (9:1–10)

        b. The Problem with God's Power (9:11–12)

        c. How Can I Answer Him? (9:13–21)

        d. He Destroys the Blameless and the Wicked (9:22–24)

        e. Unsatisfying Alternatives (9:25–35)

2. Pleading to God (10:1–22)
   a. Five Questions (10:1–10)
   b. Order in the Court (10:11–17)
   c. Leave Me Alone (10:18–22)

Comment

9:1–10 Bildad counseled Job to "seek God and plead with the Almighty for mercy" (8:5). Job now, in his second speech in the first cycle, contemplates that suggestion and explores its complexities. While he agrees with Bildad that a hearing before God is what is needed ("Truly I know that it is so"; 9:2a), he cannot figure out how he would "contend with him" (v. 3a). Two impossible obstacles are before Job. The first obstacle is man's inability to achieve moral perfection. Echoing and agreeing with Eliphaz (cf. 4:17), Job ponders, "How can a man be in the right before God?" (9:2b). Job believes that there is no sin that he has committed that has led to his family catastrophes and personal sufferings ("I am in the right," 9:15, 20; "I am blameless," 9:20, 21; "I am not guilty," 10:7). However, Job grasps that God's holiness is greater than anything he or any holy human can achieve. The second obstacle is that subpoenaing God for questioning is a misguided idea, for if Job was to put him in the dock, God would turn the tables on him. Job would be on trial.

> If one wished to contend with him,
>> one could not answer him once in a thousand times. (9:3)

If God took the stand, it would be Job, not God, who would be unable to answer the tough questions. Job would be no match for God's wisdom.

In verses 4–10 Job moves from his legal language and a possible courtroom drama to a stunning poem addressing the power of God. This theme ties into verses 2–3 in that it is the second part of the second obstacle, namely, the idea of subpoenaing God for questioning. Such an idea is misguided not only because it will not work ("Who has hardened himself against him, and succeeded?"; v. 4b) but also because God is smart ("wise in heart") and strong ("mighty in strength"; v. 4a). The attribute of God's obvious but incalculable strength is the theme of verses 5–10, where his strength is demonstrated in doing the impossible (vv. 5–6) and ruling the heavens and seas (vv. 7–9). The concluding verse—"who does great things beyond searching out, and marvelous things beyond number" (v. 10)—simply highlights that Job is only scraping the surface of God's transcendent power, for the limits of such strength are beyond human comprehension.

First, God's strength is demonstrated in doing the impossible (vv. 5–6). Here God is viewed not merely as touching the mountains so they smoke (Ps. 144:5) but as picking up Mount Everest and Pike's Peak ("he who removes mountains") so quickly and powerfully that they have no idea how they ended up in Cleveland ("and they know it not"; Job 9:5a) or at the bottom of the sea (Mark 11:23; Rev. 8:8), as the case may be. In fact, his power is vaster than one's power over a few mountains: he can lift the earth ("who shakes the earth out of its place") from its foundations ("and its pillars tremble"; Job 9:6). This image is bigger than God sending an earthquake. Rather, it is, as stated, God moving the whole earth, just as he moved many mountains.

Second, God's strength is demonstrated in doing the impossible and ruling the heavens and seas. Between what God does in relation to the lights of the universe—in general ("commands the sun, . . . seals up the stars"; v. 7) and with specific constellations ("made the Bear and Orion, the Pleiades and the chambers of the south"; v. 9)—stands emphatic antithetical parallelism (v. 8):

> who alone   stretched out   the heavens and
>   trampled   the waves of the sea;

This imagery is that of God's awesome strength stretching throughout the universe. His power is so great that he can not only move the mountains and the earth (v. 5), as well as turn off the sun and stars, if desired (v. 7), but can also walk on water (v. 8b), an image of subduing any evil and chaotic forces that might oppose him. Just as the "thick darkness" (Ps. 18:9//2 Sam. 22:10) is under his feet, so too are the dark waves.

9:11–12 After Job's magnificent hymn lauding the power of God (vv. 5–10), we are ready for him to conclude with the doxology: "Praise God, from whom all blessings flow; Praise him, all creatures here below; Praise him above, ye heavenly host . . ." Instead, Job shares his problem with God's power (vv. 11–12). Such strength, as Job sees it, is not working toward his deliverance. He cannot sing with the psalmist of God's hearing his cry for help ("In my distress I called upon the LORD; . . . [and] he heard my voice"; Ps. 18:6) and coming to the rescue ("He bowed the heavens and came down; . . . He rescued me"; Ps. 18:9, 17) because of his godly character ("The LORD dealt with me according to my righteousness"; Ps. 18:20).

Two other aspects of God's strength, each introduced with the word "behold" (Job 9:11, 12), with which Job takes issue are that such strength makes God both incomprehensible and incontestable. In verse 11, Job starts with "behold" to attract our attention and also to highlight the irony—as he cannot behold God:

> he passes by me,   and I see him not;
> he moves on,   but I do not perceive him.

Unlike Moses, who grasped when God had crossed his path ("the LORD passed before him"; Ex. 34:6, with the Hb. verb *'abar*), Job is unaware of God's mysterious movements; God "passes" (*'abar*) by him (Job 9:11), but Job is blind to his actions.

Beyond seeing him as incomprehensible, Job also sees God as incontestable,[78] a theme Job will develop further in verses 13–21. Here, as he concludes this small section, he simply asks two basic questions. Following his "behold," he first speaks of God's taking something from someone ("he snatches away," perhaps an allusion

---

78 Later, in Job 31:35–37, Job is so at his wits' end that he thinks not only that God is contestable in "court," but also that, if summoned, Job would have the victory.

to the sudden loss of his possessions) who, because he is not strong enough, has no way to combat it ("Who can turn him back?"; v. 12a). The second question, "Who will say to him, 'What are you doing?'" (v. 12b) reinforces the notion that even humans who might seek to question God's inexplicable and seemingly unjust actions do not possess enough clout to make him stop nor to accuse him of wrongdoing.

9:13–21 The word "God" (Hb. *'eloah*) begins this next section (cf. the beginning of the first section—*'el* is used in v. 2), verses that reiterate much of what has already been stated. Again, Job sighs over God's strength. If the allies of the strong and almost supernatural sea monster ("the helpers of Rahab"; v. 13b; cf. Ps. 89:10) submit to God ("beneath him bowed"; Job 9:13b), how can a mere human like Job change God's mind if he chooses to target someone ("God will not turn back his anger"; v. 13a)? The word for anger is literally "nose" (Hb. *'ap*), which relates to the almost dragon-like picture of God's strength over any opposition:

> By the breath of God they perish,
> > and by the blast of his *anger* they are consumed. (4:9; cf. 9:5)

Beyond sighing over God's strength, Job also and again speaks of the ill-advised idea of a court date with the divine. Here the illustration starts with Job's taking the stand and playing the role of the defendant. God, playing the role of prosecuting attorney, asks Job question after question, to which Job gives no reply. He refuses to speak not because he is hiding something but because he honestly does not know the answers. Even when words come to mind, he does not know how to properly express them:

> How then can I answer him,
> > choosing my words with him? (v. 14)

This is not his only problem. The only way forward is to obstruct the judicial system—to ask the prosecuting attorney, who is his "accuser" (v. 15), to be his judge as well ("my accuser" is *meshopti* in Hebrew, often rendered "judge"):

> Though I am in the right, I cannot answer him;
> > I must appeal for mercy to my accuser. (v. 15)

Job needs "mercy" from this accuser-turned-judge. However, even if this were granted, a new problem would arise. If God agrees to play the role of judge, then Job does not think he would get a fair hearing:

> If I summoned him and he answered me,
> > I would not believe that he was listening to my voice. (v. 16)

Job does not sound like himself anymore. What is going on here? Does he no longer fear God? Why does he feel this way? The answer to this final question is simple, but hard for the reader to grasp because the reader at this point might have forgotten what Job has been through and is going through. In verses 17–18 Job reminds us:

> For he crushes me with a tempest
>> and multiplies my wounds without cause;
> he will not let me get my breath,
>> but fills me with bitterness.

To him, God's hand of suffering is too much. Job is trying to carry a cyclone over his head as his sores breed like mosquitoes after a bite of blood (v. 17). Meanwhile, with each breath he takes, God pours into his mouth a wormwood smoothie (v. 18). He gives up!

> If it is a contest of strength, behold, he is mighty!
>> If it is a matter of justice, who can summon him?
> Though I am in the right, my own mouth would condemn me;
>> though I am blameless, he would prove me perverse. (vv. 19–20)

In these verses Job summarizes the themes of verses 2–18, along with his imaginary courtroom scenario. God wins the man-versus-God weightlifting competition (v. 19a). He also wins the legal battle, in two ways. First, he cannot be subpoenaed ("who can summon him?"; v. 19b). Second, if he appears in the courtroom, he will come as the prosecuting attorney, asking Job questions that would only make him look guilty (vv. 19b–20). So what is Job to do? The reality that he cannot sue God and win leaves him hating life. He is innocent ("I am blameless") but is not concerned with what happens anymore ("I regard not myself"; v. 21a). We might say he sounds suicidal; he will say, "I loathe my life" (v. 21b).

9:22–24 Job thinks that God is unjust because he will not save Job from his sorrows and vindicate him (see 10:2–7). He is also unjust, as Job states here, because God has a pattern of treating the good badly and the bad well, or at least dealing the same hand to both the righteous ("the blameless," 9:22; "the innocent," v. 23) and the unrighteous ("the wicked"; v. 22): "It is all one; therefore I say, 'He destroys both the blameless and the wicked'" (v. 22).

Verses 23–24 develop this theme further but take it to a darker place. Job first relives his own experience (cf. 1:13–19): "When disaster" [a flood or, in Job's case, lightning and a great wind] "brings sudden death" [like to his children and servants], God "mocks at the calamity [or "despair," Hb. *massat*] of the innocent" (9:23). That God *mocks* Job's despair is a strong accusation. The image of God not only folding his arms (he does not care) but hurling insults is a statement Job will live to regret (cf. 42:1–6). So too the exaggerated claim (found elsewhere in Scripture; cf. Psalm 73) that the ungodly rule the world and God does nothing to stop it. The clause "the earth is given into the hand of the wicked" (Job 9:24a) implies that God has granted this power; the clause "he covers the faces of its judges" (v. 24b) restates the same idea at a deeper and more diabolical level—the corruption has reached even the judicial system; and the final question, "If it is not [God], who then is it?" takes the theme to its most foundational level. If injustice exists, God must be to blame.

Job's assessment of God is off, and God will confront him on this point (see 38:2–40:2, which ends, "Shall a faultfinder contend with the Almighty?"; 40:2a). But the reader is sympathetic with him at this point. Why is Job suffering? Why is a holy man writing depressing couplets on a pile of dirt? When will God rescue him? Why would anyone in Job's situation not answer Bildad's question, "Does God pervert justice?" (8:3a), with a resounding "yes," or at least a timid, "It seems to be so"?

9:25–35 Job again (cf. 7:7–10, 16) employs several similes about the brevity of his life ("my days are swifter than a runner; they flee away," 9:25; "like an eagle swooping on the prey," v. 26b). It is a miserable life (his days "see no good"; v. 25b). It is also a quick but fragile life, like a speedboat made of papyrus ("like skiffs of reed"; v. 26a).

He then in verses 27–35 returns to courtroom imagery (cf. vv. 2–3, 14–16, 19). Estes explains well the scene:

> In his soliloquy . . . Job turns over in his mind whether he should enter a legal complaint as a plaintiff against God . . . , because God appears to be almost arbitrary in his treatment of humans. As he thinks it through, Job finds himself left with three unsatisfying alternatives. Job could drop his complaint against God (9:27–28), but then he would not have the opportunity to be declared innocent by God. Job could try to purify himself (9:29–31), but he senses that this would still not satisfy God's requirements. Or Job could find an impartial arbiter to mediate the case (9:32–35), but where could he find a suitable person to fill this role?[79]

With slight alterations and additions to Estes' suggestions, we can explore each alternative.

First, Job could drop his complaint against God ("If I say, 'I will forget my complaint'"; v. 27a). In fact, he could change his disposition and demeanor completely (saying, "I will put off my sad face, and be of good cheer"; v. 27b). The problem with this is that he dreads further punishment, either for no reason or for pretending he is not in pain (cf. comment on 1:4–5):

> I become afraid of all my suffering,
>   for I know you will not hold me innocent. (9:28)

If he is to be punished ("I shall be condemned"; v. 29a) for staying on the ash heap and looking like he does or for getting off it, taking a shower, and returning to

---

79 Estes, *Job*, 56.

work, why make any changes ("why then do I labor in vain?"; v. 29b)? It is better to stay put and do nothing.

Second, Job could try to purify himself (v. 30). He could "wash" himself with a pure substance from nature ("snow") and "cleanse" his "hands" with the strongest man-made substance ("lye"; v. 30). He could do it twice, which might be part of the reason for the poetic redundancy: I wash/cleanse; myself/my hands; with snow/ with lye. "Yet" (v. 31a, and an ominous word in this context), what good would it do? God's righteous requirements will not be met. Job would soon be dirty, as soon as God decided to act against him again ("you will plunge me into a pit"; v. 31a). Then, all the scrubbing with pure frozen rain and super-soap will be in vain. For, as he speaks humorously and with hyperbole and personification, even his garments getting a whiff of him after soaking in the sewer again will be repulsed by the smell: "my own clothes will abhor me" (v. 31b).

Third, Job contemplates finding an impartial umpire to mediate his case. He reasons that if he cannot sue God ("he is not a man, as I am") or answer any of God's questions in a court of law ("that we should come to trial together"; v. 32), perhaps some supernatural arbiter will help. Again, another problem arises: this is a good idea, but where would he find such a mediator?

> There is no arbiter between us,
>> who might lay his hand on us both. (v. 33)

The image here is gentle and sweet. Oh, that there would be someone among the heavenly beings or upon the earth who would take one hand and place it on God and another and place it on Job, and then say to each party, "Can we both get along?" Job will not give up on this idea (cf. 16:19–21; 19:23–27; 33:23–28). He is surely on to something, but he wishes he knew what.

With three solutions contemplated and then dismissed, Job returns to the only realistic solution he can think of. He asks God to remove his wrath:

> Let him take his rod away from me,
>> and let not dread of him terrify me. (9:34)

Job wants to move beyond an unhealthy terror of God to a holy fear of him. He also wants to speak to God and of God without fear of further repercussions:

> Then I would speak without fear of him,
>> for I am not so in myself. (v. 35)

10:1–10 In chapter 10, the scene and speech patterns have not shifted much. Job is still speaking about abhorring his existence ("I loathe my life"; 10:1a; cf. 9:21). Although Job now turns to prayer (addressing God directly, "I will say to God"; 10:2), we wonder if he has fallen into an abysmal despair. Is he praying to God or is he accusing him in "prayer"? The start of his direct address to God is less than promising. Job follows his "I loathe my life" with

| I will give free utterance | to my complaint; |
| I will speak | in the bitterness of my soul. (v. 1) |

The pain is too deep for Job to pray properly; he has abandoned himself to bitterness. So, while he lingers briefly on familiar themes such as his hope for deliverance ("Do not condemn me"; v. 2a) and desire for understanding ("let me know why you contend against me"; v. 2b), the thrust of the petition is antagonistic and accusatory. With five questions (vv. 3–10), Job questions God's workings in the world and personal care (or lack thereof) of Job.

The first question is, "Does it seem good to you to oppress?" (v. 3a). More pointedly, why do you seem "to despise" someone you have seemingly crafted to follow your ways ("the work of your hands"; v. 3b) but to reward someone who disregards your laws ("and favor the designs of the wicked"; Job 10:3)? It is one thing to say that God "makes his sun rise on the evil and on the good, and sends rain on the just and on the unjust" (Matt. 5:45), but why, in Job's case, is the sovereign Lord sending him only thunderstorms and the wicked only rainbows after the storm?

The second question is, "Have you eyes of flesh?" (Job 10:4a). Put differently, "Do you see as man sees?" (v. 4b). Put less poetically and more pointedly, "Is your perception of reality as shortsighted as human beings?" This question is asked because it seems to Job that God is acting like a mere mortal, a human judge who does not have all of the facts in front of him.

Job knows that this cannot be the case, so he supports his second question by asking his third: "Are your days as the days of man, or your years as a man's years, that you seek out my iniquity and search for my sin, although you know that I am not guilty, and there is none to deliver out of your hand?" (vv. 5–7). The question (accusation!) here is that Job is stuck in a hard place. If God knows Job is innocent (which he does—if he is the infinite God, not a finite man), why is he actively looking for some moral flaw? What is Job to do? He cannot call on anyone but God to rescue him from God.

The fourth question follows right on the thematic tail of the third, and we might paraphrase it as, "Why, why, why? God, please tell me why?" The fuller sense of it is, "Why, if you took great care and time to create me ['Your hands fashioned and made me'; v. 8a], would you take so little time and care to abolish me ['and now you have destroyed me altogether'; v. 8b]?" In verse 9 Job puts this point differently. He asks God to "remember" (Hb. *zekar*)! This term can have very negative connotations, namely, that Job is reproving God for being forgetful, something of which God often accuses Israel (e.g., Judg. 3:7; 1 Sam. 12:9). Or the plea for remembrance can be positive, in the sense of God remembering his promises to someone or his people (cf. esp. its use in Genesis and Exodus; see Gen. 8:1; 9:15; 19:29; 30:22; Ex. 2:24; 6:5).

With Job's statement and question—"Remember that you have made me like clay; and will you return me to the dust?" (Job 10:9)—the connotation might be both positive and negative. Job is not holding out much hope at this time.

However, there might be an ounce of optimism. Even though Job is a fragile and easily breakable human ("you have made me like clay"; v. 9a) and will die like every human dies ("return . . . to the dust"; v. 9b; cf. Eccles. 12:7), Job is hopeful that God will remember why he created this unique individual, someone who has honored, loved, and served him so well, and restore him. Is he humming Psalm 139 beneath his breath?

If the fourth question has an ounce of optimism, the fifth and final question of this section has quickly drained all positivity from Job's outlook. The sense is a pause in questions, followed by a "Wait a minute."

Did you not	pour me out	like milk
and	curdle me	like cheese? (Job 10:10)

Here Job remembers that his relationship with God as of late has been quite sour. God has treated him like milk well past its expiration date.

10:11–17 Some commentators take the reference to milk and curdled cheese in verse 10 as a veiled reference to semen and the embryo produced through sexual reproduction. Whether this is the case or not, what follows takes us not to the moment of conception but to the gestation period. At this point (v. 11), we surmise that Job, or more likely the author of Job, has meditated upon Psalm 139. The verb translated "knit me together" (Hb. *tesokekeni*) is used only in Job 10:11 and Psalm 139:13:

You	clothed me	with skin and flesh
and	knit me together	with bones and sinews. (Job 10:11)

What a picture of intimacy! Job is no deist. His God took the time with him, and apparently everyone, knitting each muscle and ligament and clothing human beings with billions of freckles and millions of unique beauty marks.

In verse 12, Job continues in this theologically sentimental mood:

> You have granted me life and steadfast love,
>   and your care has preserved my spirit.

He pauses to praise. He recognizes that God (not his mother and father) has given him life and, more than that, has carefully and caringly guarded every step and breath Job has taken. The clause "your care has preserved my spirit" is special. It is an oasis in the wilderness for Job.

The "yet" that starts verse 13, however, sours any sentimentality.[80] Job wonders why God would create him if his purpose, an apparently secret and sinister purpose, is to punish him:

> Yet these things you hid in your heart;
>   I know that this was your purpose.

---

80 It is simply "and" in the Hebrew, but "yet" gets the right tenor.

The particle "if" (Hb. *'im*) begins both verses 14 and 15. The ESV also includes an implied "if" in verse 15b. This one word, used three times, introduces Job's three thoughts here. First, in verse 14 he wants to know why God does not just forgive him if some sin is the cause of Job's suffering. Job sees no sin. But he is not God. God can and should use his omniscience to help Job:

> If I sin, you watch me
>> and do not acquit me of my iniquity.

Second, in verse 15a, Job admits that if he has sinned ("If I am guilty"), he deserves what has been handed out ("woe to me!"). But, third, in verse 15bcd, if he has not sinned ("If I am in the right"), then nothing has changed. As he reflects on his present condition ("look on my affliction"), he is drowning in dishonor ("I am filled with disgrace"), so much so that he is too embarrassed to hold up his head and look his friends in the eye ("I cannot lift up my head"; v. 15). And even if he could do so ("And were my head lifted up"; v. 16a), it would only make him a bigger target. He thinks God "would hunt" him "like a lion" and once "again work" his awesome power ("wonders"; Hb. *pala'*) "against" him (v. 16). Both images are frightful, and both echo other scriptural language of judgment. In Hosea (5:14; 13:7–8) and Amos (3:4, 8; 5:19), God is pictured as "executing his judgment against his people as a lion rends its prey,"[81] and in Exodus 3:20 God speaks of stretching out his hand to "strike Egypt with . . . wonders" (Hb. *pala'*) so that Pharaoh will let his people go.

In 10:17ab Job returns to the courtroom, where God recommences his accusations:

You	renew	your witnesses	against me
and	increase	your vexation	toward me;

Worse than that, there is no order in this court. Instead of the bailiff handcuffing Job and bringing him back to his cell, God commands his army to take Job away (and perhaps do violence to him): "you bring fresh troops against me" (v. 17c).

10:18–22 Like the previous section, this one begins with Job's recollection of his gestation: "Why did you bring me out from the womb?" (v. 18a). Moreover, as in verses 3–10, Job asks God questions. The first question is about his birth: Job again (cf. 3:11–16) wonders why God brought him into the world. He wishes he were stillborn:

> Would that I had died before any eye had seen me
> and were as though I had not been,
>> carried from the womb to the grave. (10:18b–19)

The second question is about his impending death: "Are not my days few?" (v. 20a). Job's logic here is simple: he reasons with God, saying in effect, "If I am soon to

---

81 Longman, *Job*, 180.

die and go to a dark place, then stop the suffering so I can enjoy a few moments
of sunshine."

> Are not my days few?
>   Then cease, and leave me alone, that I may find a little cheer
> before I go—and I shall not return—
>   to the land of darkness and deep shadow,
> the land of gloom like thick darkness,
>   like deep shadow without any order,
>   where light is as thick darkness. (vv. 20–22)

Job's imagery ends by shedding great light on his *dark* night of the soul (note the
use of "darkness," "deep shadow," "thick darkness," "deep shadow," "thick darkness"). He has no hope in death; he has no hope in life. But he would prefer the
"land of darkness" to his apartment of ash in Uz.

Response

As a Christian it is difficult to read Job 9–10 without pitying Job. We pity his sufferings. But we also pity his lack of knowledge. We wish he had the revelation of
Job 1:6–12 and 2:1–6 to help him understand why he was suffering, and by whose
hand. We also wish he could read about the advocate we have in Jesus and the hope
we have of life after death through his mediation for us:

> We have an advocate with the Father, Jesus Christ the righteous. He is the
> propitiation for our sins, and not for ours only but also for the sins of the
> whole world. (1 John 2:1b–2)

> He is the mediator of a new covenant, so that those who are called may
> receive the promised eternal inheritance. (Heb. 9:15; cf. 12:24; 1 Tim. 2:5)

While we pity Job's lack of knowledge, we should not overlook elements of his
theological and experiential shortsightedness. Not everything he does and says is
a model for us to emulate. When we undergo adversity, like Job we should admit
and even admire God's total sovereignty. We should also pray honestly and forth-
rightly about our needs. We can even question God (Job 10:3–10; cf. esp. Ps. 77:7–9).
That said, we must be careful that we do not put God in the dock to answer every
question we might have. We certainly should not accuse God of injustice, for he
embodies perfect justice and defines it (see God's rebuke; Job 40:8). Like Job, we
are prone to oversimplify our situation in light of God's power. Like Job, it is easy
to question God's justice when our agonies make his will for us seem so unfair.
We must remember, however, as Job earlier taught us (Job 2:10), that "we must be
content to receive bad as well as good from God,"[82] even if it appears through our
agonies that all we are experiencing is bad. (Fallen humans live in a fallen world,

---

82 Goldingay, *Job*, 55.

where fallen things happen!) We must also remember that God still loves us in the silence, and he is consistently molding us into the image of his Son, "a son" who "learned obedience through what he suffered" (Heb. 5:8).

On a different note, but related to God's Son as well as to the theme of the knowledge we have through the NT, what should we make, if anything, of Job's claim that "there is no arbiter between us" (9:33)—between him and God? While many commentators caution Christians not to take the notion of an "arbiter" too far, there is no reason to be overly cautious. We are Christians who should read the Christian Scriptures with our gospel glasses on (cf. Luke 24:27, 44). Thus, with the theme of Job's hope for an arbiter, Christological connections can be made. Job speaks of a personal heavenly witness (his living "Redeemer," Job 19:25; his "witness . . . in heaven," 16:19) who will be his attorney before God ("he who testifies for me," 16:19; and "he would argue the case of a man with God," 16:21). The "mediator" will "declare to man what is right for him" (33:23); he will, through a merciful ransom ("he is merciful to him . . . 'I have found a ransom'"; 33:24ac), deliver him from hell ("Deliver him from going down into the pit"; 33:24b), and thus Job not only will be "accepted" by God but also will find joy and satisfaction in life ("he sees [God's] face with a shout of joy"; see 33:25–26). Christians can see Christ here, and thank God for him!

JOB 11:1–20

11 Then Zophar the Naamathite answered and said:

2 "Should a multitude of words go unanswered,
    and a man full of talk be judged right?
3 Should your babble silence men,
    and when you mock, shall no one shame you?
4 For you say, 'My doctrine is pure,
    and I am clean in God's[1] eyes.'
5 But oh, that God would speak
    and open his lips to you,
6 and that he would tell you the secrets of wisdom!
    For he is manifold in understanding.[2]
Know then that God exacts of you less than your guilt deserves.

7 "Can you find out the deep things of God?
    Can you find out the limit of the Almighty?
8 It is higher than heaven[3]—what can you do?
    Deeper than Sheol—what can you know?
9 Its measure is longer than the earth
    and broader than the sea.

10   If he passes through and imprisons
          and summons the court, who can turn him back?
11   For he knows worthless men;
          when he sees iniquity, will he not consider it?
12   But a stupid man will get understanding
          when a wild donkey's colt is born a man!

13   "If you prepare your heart,
          you will stretch out your hands toward him.
14   If iniquity is in your hand, put it far away,
          and let not injustice dwell in your tents.
15   Surely then you will lift up your face without blemish;
          you will be secure and will not fear.
16   You will forget your misery;
          you will remember it as waters that have passed away.
17   And your life will be brighter than the noonday;
          its darkness will be like the morning.
18   And you will feel secure, because there is hope;
          you will look around and take your rest in security.
19   You will lie down, and none will make you afraid;
          many will court your favor.
20   But the eyes of the wicked will fail;
          all way of escape will be lost to them,
          and their hope is to breathe their last."

¹ Hebrew *your* ² The meaning of the Hebrew is uncertain ³ Hebrew *The heights of heaven*

Section Overview

Zophar the Naamathite (Job 11:1) is the last of the three friends to speak. This is the first of only two speeches he gives, thus breaking the pattern of dialogues:

Job Eliphaz

Job Bildad

Job *Zophar*

Job Eliphaz

Job Bildad

Job *Zophar*

Job Eliphaz

Job Bildad

Job [____]

His speech is short, sharp, and straightforward. It is short, only 110 words (the third-shortest speech in Job). But it is not as short as one might imagine, given his rebuke to Job ("Should a multitude of words go unanswered?"; v. 2a). It is also sharp: he wastes no time cutting into Job's character, calling him a "man full of talk" (v. 2b) and in a backhanded way a "stupid man" (v. 12a) and part of "worthless men" (v. 11a). He also claims that Job has deserved what has come to him, and what will be coming to him (v. 2b) if he does not repent (vv. 14, 20). Finally, his speech is straightforward: like Eliphaz and Bildad, he holds strictly to the retribution principle. This system is almost mathematical to him:

Sin = Suffering

Job + Suffering = Job Must Have Sinned

In verses 1–6, Zophar assumes the above "equation" is true: "God exacts of you . . . [what] your guilt deserves" (v. 6c) is his bumper-sticker theology. In Job's case, God is actually being nice. The suffering Job is experiencing is "less than" his "guilt deserves" (v. 6c). In verses 7–12, Zophar holds out the wisdom of God, hoping that in light of such wisdom Job will recognize his folly. If Job will do so, Zophar next claims in verses 13–20 that all will be restored (e.g., "your life will be brighter than the noonday"; v. 17a). If Job will not repent, however, the fate awaiting him will be worse than going to the "land of darkness" (10:21).

Section Outline

II.F.　Some Zings from Zophar (11:1–20)

　　　1.　An Exacting God (11:1–6)

　　　2.　A Wise God (11:7–12)

　　　3.　A Rewarding God (11:13–20)

Comment

11:1–6 Job has just delivered a long speech (Job 9–10), and Zophar finds an angle of attack. If the traditional wisdom expressed in Proverbs 10:19, for example, is true ("When words are many, transgression is not lacking"), then Job has already sinned. With two accusing questions, Zophar seeks to silence (and answer—"answered," Job 11:1; "unanswered," v. 2; Hb. *'anah*) sinful Job:

Should a multitude of words go unanswered,
　　and a man full of talk be judged right?
Should your babble silence men,
　　and when you mock, shall no one shame you? (vv. 2–3)

Three word-related sins are mentioned. First, Job is long-winded ("a multitude of words," paralleled with "full of talk"; v. 2). Second, he has tried to "silence" good "men" (i.e., Eliphaz and Bildad) with proud claims ("babble," Hb. *bad*, v. 3a; elsewhere translated "boast," Isa. 16:6; Jer. 48:30). Third, he has ridiculed them with his empty rhetoric ("when you mock"; Job 11:3b). Zophar is intervening now to tame such a tongue, answer Job's accusations, and make sure he is aware of his sins and shamed for them.

In verses 4–6, Zophar comes across as a prophet as he introduces God (mentioned or "present" in all of the following verses) and God's point of view on the matter. Job needs to be quiet, and God needs to speak ("oh, that God would speak . . . open his lips . . . he would tell you"; vv. 5–6a).

For you say, "My doctrine is pure,
    and I am clean in God's eyes."
But oh, that God would speak
    and open his lips to you,
and that he would tell you the secrets of wisdom!
    For he is manifold in understanding.
Know then that God exacts of you less than your guilt deserves. (vv. 4–6)

Verses 5–6ab introduce the main theme of verses 7–12, namely, the wisdom of God.[83] Verses 4 and 6c seek to expose Job's folly. As stated in the overview, the claim that "God exacts of you . . . [what] your guilt deserves" (v. 6c) is the perfect summary of Zophar's systematics. In Job's case, he is suffering, in part, because his guilt is oozing out his mouth. For example, Zophar offers a quote,

For you say, "My doctrine is pure,
    and I am clean in God's eyes." (v. 4)

There are two problems with these verses. First, retribution theology is wrong. Job does not deserve what has happened to him. And to say that he deserves even more than he has gotten (that God has been lenient in his anger, see v. 6c) is not only incorrect but cruel. Second, Job did claim to be innocent ("I am in the right," 9:15, 20; "I am blameless," 9:20, 21; "I am not guilty," 10:7), and what he was saying about God, himself, and his situation was true (perhaps the sense of Zophar's paraphrase of Job's "My doctrine is pure"; 11:4a). However, Job has never claimed to be "clean" (Hb. *bar*) in the sense of morally pure or sinless; he has only claimed to be "blameless" (Hb. *tam*), something God himself has said of him ("blameless and upright man"; 1:8; 2:3; cf. 1:1).

11:7–12 While Zophar distorts the words of Job (vv. 1–6), he has the facts straight on the wisdom of God (vv. 7–12). However, what he does not have straight is how such a lesson on God's wisdom should be applied to Job. He uses it as mirror: he wants Job to see his blemishes, to reflect on God's wisdom and reflect God's wisdom. But Job does not need the belittling poem that follows:

Can you find out the deep things of God?
    Can you find out the limit of the Almighty?
It is higher than heaven—what can you do?
    Deeper than Sheol—what can you know?
Its measure is longer than the earth
    and broader than the sea. (vv. 7–9)

The opening two words—"Can you" (v. 7)—highlight that Job is getting a personal sermon, a theological talking to (talking down to!). Using a series of four rhetorical

---

83 In 9:4, Job speaks of God's wisdom and strength ("He is wise in heart and mighty in strength"), but his poem in 11:4–10 focuses on God's strength. Thus, perhaps Zophar, with his poem in 11:7–9, wants to focus on what he thinks Job has neglected.

questions, Zophar zings Job with the "profundity and sublimity of God," describing "God as someone who is too high, too deep, too long, and too wide to grasp," as "higher than the highest place imaginable (heaven), deeper than the deepest place (Sheol), longer than the longest place (the earth), and wider than the widest place (the sea)."[84] Of course, Job knows that God is inscrutable. He knows that he cannot know the mysteries of God (9:11–12). And he would readily embrace the Pauline doxology of Romans 11:33–36. What he will not embrace is reported "wisdom" on the wisdom of God from fools!

> No doubt you are the people,
>> and wisdom will die with you. (Job 12:2)

Zophar concludes this section (11:10–12) with a courtroom scenario of his own (see Job's legal language in Job 9–10), followed by an insult. In 11:10–11, he describes God's coming to earth ("he passes through"), tossing Job in jail ("and imprisons"), and holding a trial ("summons the court"; v. 10). Job has no option; he must attend, as must everyone who is summoned ("who can turn him back?"; v. 10b). Once court is in session, Zophar reminds Job, with verse 11, that God is not stupid. He knows the difference between a good man and a wicked one ("he knows worthless men"), between an evil action ("he sees iniquity"; v. 11) and a righteous one.

Zophar follows this scene with a veiled insult. Job is the target of his taunt!

> But a stupid man will get understanding
>> when a wild donkey's colt is born a man! (v. 12)

The point of this clever but cruel proverb is that it is more probable that a wild donkey would give birth to a full-grown man than that idiot Job would apply the wisdom of Zophar's brilliant sermon.

11:13–20 With verse 12, Zophar is attempting to shame and bully Job to repent. With verses 13–20 he is seeking to woo (vv. 15–19) and warn (v. 20) him to the winning side. With a few conditional clauses ("if," vv. 13–14; "then," v. 15), Zophar implores Job to repent of his sin. The call is quite beautiful, and the imagery inspiring:

> If you prepare your heart,
>> you will stretch out your hands toward him.
> If iniquity is in your hand, put it far away,
>> and let not injustice dwell in your tents. (vv. 13–14)

Here repentance involves four actions. Inwardly, Job is to set his mind on God ("prepare your heart"; v. 13a). Outwardly, he is to acknowledge God as God and reach out to him for mercy ("stretch out your hands toward him"; v. 13b; cf. 1 Kings 8:38//2 Chron. 6:29). Personally, he is to stop sinning ("if iniquity is in your hand,

---

84 Longman, *Job*, 187–188.

put it far away"; Job 11:14a). Publicly, he is to deal justly and lovingly with his household, friends, and neighbors ("let not injustice dwell in your tents"; v. 14b).

Zophar's counsel is clear and his promises certain. If Job repents, restoration will follow. Such restoration is described in terms that would be to Job's own liking. He has been asking God not for renewed wealth or health[85] but to pull him out of the darkness of despair. As he proved in 1:20–21 and 2:10, Job can live without his possessions or health! What he cannot live without is being in a right relationship with God. That relationship seems severed because God has been silent about Job's sufferings. So Zophar's words here are "tempting," if we can put it that way, because Job longs for what is offered. He wants to be unashamed ("surely . . . you will lift up your face without blemish"), safe, and without fear (11:15). He wants to "forget" his "misery," like one forgets a wave that has crashed to shore ("you will remember it as waters that have passed away"; v. 16). He wants light, not darkness:

> And your life will be brighter than the noonday;
>   its darkness will be like the morning. (v. 17; cf. 10:21–22)

He wants the security and safety that comes from hope, as well as the prestige that comes from being recognized as wise:

> And you will feel secure, because there is hope;
>   you will look around and take your rest in security.
> You will lie down, and none will make you afraid;
>   many will court your favor. (11:18–19)

Having attempted to woo Job with the promises of restoration that come with repentance, Zophar concludes by warning him of the condemnation to come following a lack of repentance. Moving from the second person directly addressing Job ("you," used twenty times above), the final verse uses the third person. This general principle is true not just for Job but for everyone:

> But the eyes of the wicked will fail;
>   all way of escape will be lost to them,
>   and their hope is to breathe their last. (v. 20)

Unlike Eliphaz (5:25–27) and Bildad (8:20–22), but like Job (10:20–22), Zophar ends on a sour note. He is holding out hope for Job, but he wants to make clear that there is no hope for the wicked.

Response

Truths about God should be used to teach, not taunt. The Bible should be used to build up, not belittle. What Zophar has said about God is good and right, but

---

85 The phrase "without blemish" (11:15) might refer to the scars and scabs on Job's face, or it might be a metaphor for being unashamed.

what he says about God *to Job* is wrong and evil. Job was his punching bag and solid theology his gloves.

That said, if we remove the situation and take in the theology, Zophar has something to teach the church today. Do we grasp that we cannot fully grasp the incomprehensible wisdom of God? When reading Job 11:7–9, do we quietly say, "Amen, preach it!"? Can we pause in prayer and shout out, as Paul did:

> Oh, the depth of the riches and wisdom and knowledge of God! How unsearchable are his judgments and how inscrutable his ways!
>
> "For who has known the mind of the Lord,
>   or who has been his counselor?"
> "Or who has given a gift to him
>   that he might be repaid?"
>
> For from him and through him and to him are all things. To him be glory forever. Amen. (Rom. 11:33–36)

Also, can we learn from Zophar's theology of repentance? Read again what he says in Job 11:13–14. We are not Job, and certainly not Jesus. Thus, as Luther put it in his *first* of ninety-five theses, "When our Lord and Master, Jesus Christ, said, 'Repent,' he called for the entire life of believers to be one of repentance." Indeed, we regularly pray the Lord's Prayer—our disciple prayer—"forgive us our debts" (Matt. 6:12). And we seek to do so with our hearts in the right place, our hands stretched out to heaven, and our lives walking in step with the Spirit and in accord with Christ's commands. Moreover, repentance does bring restoration. And holiness usually leads to happiness, and sometimes renewed health.

JOB 12:1–14:22

12 Then Job answered and said:

2 "No doubt you are the people,
    and wisdom will die with you.
3 But I have understanding as well as you;
    I am not inferior to you.
    Who does not know such things as these?
4 I am a laughingstock to my friends;
    I, who called to God and he answered me,
    a just and blameless man, am a laughingstock.
5 In the thought of one who is at ease there is
        contempt for misfortune;

it is ready for those whose feet slip.
6 The tents of robbers are at peace,
   and those who provoke God are secure,
   who bring their god in their hand.[1]

7 "But ask the beasts, and they will teach you;
   the birds of the heavens, and they will tell you;
8 or the bushes of the earth, and they will teach you;[2]
   and the fish of the sea will declare to you.
9 Who among all these does not know
   that the hand of the LORD has done this?
10 In his hand is the life of every living thing
   and the breath of all mankind.
11 Does not the ear test words
   as the palate tastes food?
12 Wisdom is with the aged,
   and understanding in length of days.

13 "With God[3] are wisdom and might;
   he has counsel and understanding.
14 If he tears down, none can rebuild;
   if he shuts a man in, none can open.
15 If he withholds the waters, they dry up;
   if he sends them out, they overwhelm the land.
16 With him are strength and sound wisdom;
   the deceived and the deceiver are his.
17 He leads counselors away stripped,
   and judges he makes fools.
18 He looses the bonds of kings
   and binds a waistcloth on their hips.
19 He leads priests away stripped
   and overthrows the mighty.
20 He deprives of speech those who are trusted
   and takes away the discernment of the elders.
21 He pours contempt on princes
   and loosens the belt of the strong.
22 He uncovers the deeps out of darkness
   and brings deep darkness to light.
23 He makes nations great, and he destroys them;
   he enlarges nations, and leads them away.
24 He takes away understanding from the chiefs of the
      people of the earth
   and makes them wander in a trackless waste.
25 They grope in the dark without light,
   and he makes them stagger like a drunken man.

13 "Behold, my eye has seen all this,
   my ear has heard and understood it.
2 What you know, I also know;
   I am not inferior to you.
3 But I would speak to the Almighty,
   and I desire to argue my case with God.

4 As for you, you whitewash with lies;
　　worthless physicians are you all.
5 Oh that you would keep silent,
　　and it would be your wisdom!
6 Hear now my argument
　　and listen to the pleadings of my lips.
7 Will you speak falsely for God
　　and speak deceitfully for him?
8 Will you show partiality toward him?
　　Will you plead the case for God?
9 Will it be well with you when he searches you out?
　　Or can you deceive him, as one deceives a man?
10 He will surely rebuke you
　　if in secret you show partiality.
11 Will not his majesty terrify you,
　　and the dread of him fall upon you?
12 Your maxims are proverbs of ashes;
　　your defenses are defenses of clay.

13 "Let me have silence, and I will speak,
　　and let come on me what may.
14 Why should I take my flesh in my teeth
　　and put my life in my hand?
15 Though he slay me, I will hope in him;[4]
　　yet I will argue my ways to his face.
16 This will be my salvation,
　　that the godless shall not come before him.
17 Keep listening to my words,
　　and let my declaration be in your ears.
18 Behold, I have prepared my case;
　　I know that I shall be in the right.
19 Who is there who will contend with me?
　　For then I would be silent and die.
20 Only grant me two things,
　　then I will not hide myself from your face:
21 withdraw your hand far from me,
　　and let not dread of you terrify me.
22 Then call, and I will answer;
　　or let me speak, and you reply to me.
23 How many are my iniquities and my sins?
　　Make me know my transgression and my sin.
24 Why do you hide your face
　　and count me as your enemy?
25 Will you frighten a driven leaf
　　and pursue dry chaff?
26 For you write bitter things against me
　　and make me inherit the iniquities of my youth.
27 You put my feet in the stocks
　　and watch all my paths;
　　you set a limit for[5] the soles of my feet.
28 Man[6] wastes away like a rotten thing,
　　like a garment that is moth-eaten.

14 "Man who is born of a woman
        is few of days and full of trouble.

2 He comes out like a flower and withers;
       he flees like a shadow and continues not.

3 And do you open your eyes on such a one
       and bring me into judgment with you?

4 Who can bring a clean thing out of an unclean?
       There is not one.

5 Since his days are determined,
       and the number of his months is with you,
       and you have appointed his limits that he cannot
           pass,

6 look away from him and leave him alone,[7]
       that he may enjoy, like a hired hand, his day.

7 "For there is hope for a tree,
       if it be cut down, that it will sprout again,
       and that its shoots will not cease.

8 Though its root grow old in the earth,
       and its stump die in the soil,

9 yet at the scent of water it will bud
       and put out branches like a young plant.

10 But a man dies and is laid low;
       man breathes his last, and where is he?

11 As waters fail from a lake
       and a river wastes away and dries up,

12 so a man lies down and rises not again;
       till the heavens are no more he will not awake
       or be roused out of his sleep.

13 Oh that you would hide me in Sheol,
       that you would conceal me until your wrath be
           past,
       that you would appoint me a set time, and
           remember me!

14 If a man dies, shall he live again?
       All the days of my service I would wait,
       till my renewal[8] should come.

15 You would call, and I would answer you;
       you would long for the work of your hands.

16 For then you would number my steps;
       you would not keep watch over my sin;

17 my transgression would be sealed up in a bag,
       and you would cover over my iniquity.

18 "But the mountain falls and crumbles away,
       and the rock is removed from its place;

19 the waters wear away the stones;
       the torrents wash away the soil of the earth;
       so you destroy the hope of man.

20 You prevail forever against him, and he passes;
       you change his countenance, and send him away.

21 His sons come to honor, and he does not know it;
        they are brought low, and he perceives it not.
22 He feels only the pain of his own body,
        and he mourns only for himself."

¹ The meaning of the Hebrew is uncertain ² Or *or speak to the earth, and it will teach you* ³ Hebrew *him*
⁴ Or *Behold, he will slay me; I have no hope* ⁵ Or *you marked* ⁶ Hebrew *He* ⁷ Probable reading; Hebrew *look
away from him, that he may cease* ⁸ Or *relief*

Section Overview

Job 12–14 records Job's third reply to his friends, concluding the end of the first
cycle (4:1–14:22). Responding to aspects of Zophar's speech (ch. 11), notably the
theme of the wisdom of God, Job unleashes a lengthy rebuttal. He begins with an
insult (12:2), followed by a lengthy defense of his knowledge (12:3–13:2), which
starts and stops with the claims,

I have understanding as well as you (12:3)	What you know, I also know (13:2)
I am not inferior to you (12:3)	I am not inferior to you (13:2)

That said, Job sees his wisdom as not only equal with theirs ("Behold, my eye has
seen all this, my ear has heard and understood it," 13:1, followed by the parallel
idea, "What you know, I also know; I am not inferior to you," 13:2) but as far superior. For he knows what they will not acknowledge, namely, that God's hand, not
Job's sin, is the cause of Job's sufferings ("Who . . . does not know that the hand
of the LORD has done this?"; 12:9). In 12:3–13:2, Job continues to dwell on God
("God" [2x]; "LORD" [1x]; "he" [18x]; "him" [2x]; "his" [2x]), offering another poem
addressing God's wisdom and strength (12:13–25).

After stating his desire to address God in 13:3, Job switches his focus in
13:4–12 from what he knows about God to what he knows about his friends ("as
for you," 13:4; with "you" and "your" repeated seventeen times). He knows that
they are wrong (e.g., "you speak falsely for God"; 13:7a). He also knows that they
will someday be judged for how they have treated Job (e.g., "He will surely rebuke
you"; 13:10a).

In 13:13–27, Job turns his attention directly to God. After expressing his hope for
salvation, he prays for it, asking God to "withdraw your hand far from me" (13:21).

In 13:28–14:22, he steps back to take a look at the bigger picture of the relationship between God and man. While Job twice speaks positively of hope in this
reply (e.g., "Though he slay me, I will hope in him"; 13:15; cf. 14:7), he ends on
another dark note, saying to God, "you destroy the hope of man" (14:19).

Section Outline

II.G. Hope for God's Vindication? (12:1–14:22)
    1. Job's Answer to His "Wise" Friends (12:1–2)
    2. The Hand of the Lord Has Done This (12:3–13:2)

Comment

12:1–2 Verse 1 continues with the formula, "Then Job answered and said." What follows this neutral opening is an insult pregnant with passion. Job mocks his wise friends: "No doubt you are the people, and wisdom will die with you" (v. 2). Peterson's paraphrase captures the biting sarcasm well: "I'm sure you speak for all the experts, and when you die there'll be no one left to tell us how to live" (MESSAGE).

12:3–13:2 In 12:3 Job builds on the theme of "wisdom" introduced in verse 2 and in answer to Zophar's speech in chapter 11. Job's musings on wisdom in 12:3–13:2—what his friends know versus what he knows—are framed by an inclusio:

I have understanding as well as you (12:3)	What you know, I also know (13:2)
I am not inferior to you (12:3)	I am not inferior to you (13:2)

Job is upset that his friends are not taking him seriously. Twice he calls himself a "laughingstock" (12:4ad). This statement—another inclusio itself—surrounds two important statements:

> I, who called to God and he answered me,
> a just and blameless man (12:4bc)

These might be quotes from his friends, mocking him. As they are laughing at him, they use his own claims to deride him, "Oh, look at Job! So devout. He prays to God and God always answers him. Some holy man he is!" Or these words might be Job's sincere claims in summary form. In other words, Job is reminding his friends—as they laugh at him—that this is no laughing matter. He is innocent. He is in relationship with God, despite God's silence and the sufferings Job is experiencing.

Next, in 12:5–9, Job returns (cf. 12:2) to mocking his friends' lack of wisdom. They are approaching Job's situation as outsiders. Unlike Job, they are not living through inexplicable sufferings. They are "at ease" as they theologize over him. Whereas they once had sympathy for Job's sufferings, now they have "contempt for [his] misfortune" (12:5a). They have arrived at such contempt because they have deduced that Job's sin is the cause of Job's sufferings. Misfortune ("it") is like a trap, one that will catch sinners the moment they slip into sin ("it is ready for those whose feet slip"; 12:5b). The friends are wrong, however. They have no category for what is happening to Job, but they should. Job illustrates the obvious using the opposite of his situation:

The tents of robbers are at peace,
>   and those who provoke God are secure,
>   who bring their god in their hand. (12:6)

Sometimes wicked men (such as "robbers") reap the rewards of the "blessed" life: prosperity ("are at peace"; the Hebrew word *yishlayu* can also be rendered "prosper") and security ("are secure"; 12:6). Even though they "provoke God" with their actions and idolatry (perhaps "their god in their hand" [12:6] means they trust in money; cf. 31:24–28), he does not punish them. If this is true (evil men are not always punished), then why would Job's story not also be true (a good man is sometimes punished)?

Job explores this idea further in Job 12:7–11, calling upon creation to testify to the truth of his claim that Yahweh is the cause of his calamities:

> But ask the beasts, and they will teach you;
>   the birds of the heavens, and they will tell you;
> or the bushes of the earth, and they will teach you;
>   and the fish of the sea will declare to you.
> Who among all these does not know
>   that the hand of the LORD has done this? (12:7–9)

God is completely sovereign. He can do whatever he deems right:

In his hand is	the life	of every living thing
and	the breath	of all mankind. (12:10)

Just as the ear is designed for hearing ("Does not the ear test words . . .") and mouths water over spicy curry (". . . as the palate tastes food?"; 12:11), God's exercising an absolute, free sovereignty is basic to how the world works. And while it is true that the older you get, the more you know from experience and observation ("Wisdom is with the aged," or, put a slightly different way, "understanding in length of days"; 12:12), God's wisdom surely surpasses even the oldest and wisest of humans. For "with God are wisdom and might; he has counsel and understanding" (12:13; cf. 12:16; 9:4).

In 12:14–25 Job expands this thought with a poem centered on God and what he does. Each line begins with the phrase "if he" or "with him," or simply "he" (only 12:25 is the exception), followed by various actions, which are a mix of synonymous, antithetic, and synthetic parallels:

> He tears down (12:14a)
> He shuts . . . in (12:14b)
> He withholds (12:15a)
> He sends . . . out (12:15b)
> He leads . . . away (12:17a)
> He makes (12:17b)

He looses (12:18a)

[He] binds (12:18b)

He leads . . . away (12:19a)

[He] overthrows (12:19b)

He deprives (12:20a)

[He] takes away (12:20b)

He pours [out] (12:21a)

[He] loosens (12:21b)

He uncovers (12:22a)

[He] brings (12:22b)

He makes (12:23a)

He destroys (12:23a)

He enlarges (12:23b)

He leads . . . away (12:23b)

He takes away (12:24a)

[He] makes (12:24b)

He makes (12:25b)

All of these actions involve something God does in his "strength and sound wisdom" (12:16) that cannot be thwarted. He cannot be thwarted by anything on earth ("the waters" or "the land"; 12:15) or under the earth ("the deeps"; 12:22a). He cannot be thwarted by "nations" (12:23). He cannot be thwarted by men, no matter how wise, holy, respected, or powerful they might be—"counselors" (12:17a), "judges" (12:17b), "kings" (12:18), "priests" (12:19a), "the mighty" (12:19b), "the elders" (12:20b), "princes" (12:21a), and "the strong" (12:21b). Even "the chiefs of the people of the earth" (12:24a) cannot resist his will. Job 12:24–25 offers the longest comparison, with 12:25 breaking the pattern of 12:14–15 and 12:17–23. The point is to emphasize that if God can make even the greatest people on earth "wander in a trackless waste" (12:24) or "grope in the dark" or "stagger like a drunken man" (12:25)—think of Pharaoh (Isa. 19:14) or Nebuchadnezzar (Dan. 4:33)—then his power is irresistible.

Job's point is plain. Job 12:16, which breaks the pattern by beginning with the phrase "with him" instead of "if he" or "he," highlights the poem's main point:

> With him are strength and sound wisdom;
>   the deceived and the deceiver are his.

Like 1 Corinthians 13, the poem of Job 12:14–25 is a rebuke. Its purpose is not just to highlight God's amazing power and wisdom but also to teach or remind Eliphaz, Bildad, and, Zophar that God in his wisdom can use his sovereign power however he deems fit. They have somehow been deceived and are imploring Job to join in such deception (12:16; cf. 13:9b). He will have none of it!

13:3–12 Verse 3 reintroduces the idea of talking directly to God about Job's situation. Job wants to "speak to the Almighty" and "argue" his "case with God" himself.

He will do so later in this chapter, in a kind of solo mock trial. First, however, he returns to confronting his friends. His accusatory "As for you," which starts verse 4, is followed by a list of what they have done wrong and the judgment that is on its way due to their behavior (vv. 4–12). Their list of offenses is shown in table 4.4.

TABLE 4.4: Offenses of Job's Friends

Crime	Specific Accusation
They have been appalling surgeons of the soul	"worthless physicians are you all" (v. 4b)
They have been false teachers	"you whitewash with lies" (v. 4a); "you speak falsely for God and speak deceitfully for him" (v. 7)
Their testimony has been slanted	"you show partiality toward [God]" (v. 8) (or "you slant your testimony in his favor," NLT)
Their wisdom is worthless	"Your maxims are proverbs of ashes; your defenses are defenses of clay" (v. 12)

Job's solution is for them to keep their "wisdom" to themselves ("Oh that you would keep silent, and it would be your wisdom!"; v. 5) and listen afresh to his version of the story ("Hear now my argument and listen to the pleadings of my lips"; v. 6).

Job not only wants to point out their sins; he also wants them to grasp the fact that judgment for such sins is looming. In verses 7–9 and 11, using a series of questions, Job informs them that their court date with God is not looking so promising. The first two questions remind them of what they have done wrong in relation to God (note the terms "for" and "toward"):

| Will you | speak falsely | for God |
| and | speak deceitfully | for him? (v. 7) |

| Will you | show partiality | toward him? |
| Will you | plead the case | for God? (v. 8) |

The second two questions speak of the coming judgment of God. Their day in court will end with a guilty verdict.

Will it be well with you when he searches you out?
    Or can you deceive him, as one deceives a man? (v. 9)

| Will not | his majesty | terrify you, |
| and | the dread of him | fall upon you? (v. 11) |

In verse 10, Job asks no rhetorical statements. He instead makes a prophetic assertion: "He will surely rebuke you if in secret you show partiality."

13:13–27 Returning to his initial goal in verse 3, Job will speak both about God (vv. 13–19) and to him (vv. 20–27), seeking to argue his case. Both at the start of verses 13–19 and in the middle, he reiterates what he said in verses 5 and 6, namely, that his friends should listen to him as he speaks: "Let me have silence, and I will speak" (v. 13a); "Keep listening to my words, and let my declaration be in your ears" (v. 17). He will live with the repercussions of his words ("and let come on me what may"; v. 13b). He is not afraid, however, to present his case to God ("argue my ways to his face"; v. 15b). While this might seem like a perilous proposal, he does not think he is putting his life in jeopardy:

> Why should I take my flesh in my teeth,
> and   put my life in my hand? (v. 14)

Put simply, he sees no risk here. He is in no mortal danger, for his case is irrefutable—he knows that he is innocent. "Behold, I have prepared my case; I know that I shall be in the right" (v. 18). He knows that God will not even grant him a hearing if this is not the case: "the godless shall not come before him" (v. 16b). He knows that his friends cannot substantiate their claims: "Who is there who will contend with me? For then I would be silent and die" (v. 19). Thus, if God indeed hears his case, Job is not certain, but quite optimistic, that the judge's verdict will be just. "Though he slay me, I will hope in him" (v. 15a). God might destroy him, but he trusts that, in the end, the Lord will vindicate the righteous: "This will be my salvation" (v. 16a).

With this groundwork laid (he has almost talked himself into actually filing the claim), Job addresses God (vv. 20–27). However, the scene is not what is expected. There is no courtroom. Instead, we find a prayerful conversation in preparation for the case. Perhaps at this point Job realizes that direct complaint to God has gotten him nowhere. So he humbly asks God for help. He petitions, "Only grant me two things, then I will not hide myself from your face" (v. 20). First, he asks God to remove his present afflictions: "Withdraw your hand far from me, and let not dread of you terrify me" (v. 21). Once Job's health is restored, he will be ready to present his case. Second, "Call, and I will answer; or let me speak, and you reply to me" (v. 22). Job knows that some present sin, or sin of the past few months, is not the cause of his sufferings. But he also knows that he is a sinner (cf. 7:21; 9:29–31) and that he has a sinful teenage past (cf. 13:23, 26b). So he asks God to reveal whatever sin might be hindering the two of them from meeting face to face to discuss and resolve the matter: "How many are my iniquities and my sins? Make me know my transgression and my sin" (v. 23).

At this point one gets the impression that Job is genuinely hopeful that all that he has laid out makes sense. God might actually agree to Job's plan. But, with the word "why" that begins verse 24 and "your enemy" that ends it, a shadow covers these glimmers of light. In verses 24–27, Job seems to return to his personal land of darkness (10:21). He has lost hope:

> Why do you hide your face
>   and count me as your enemy? (13:24)

Job cannot comprehend why (after so many days of horrific suffering) God is not communicating to him. Why not send a dream, a vision, or an angel? Why not write something upon a stone or a scroll? Why not speak truth through the three worthless physicians? Instead of treating him like a friend, God is treating him as an enemy (like the wicked of Ps. 1:4). God's opposition to him seems so senseless. Why is the great God of the universe pursuing him like a windblown "leaf" or "dry chaff," only to catch the useless and dying object in order to "frighten" and torment it (Job 13:25)? To Job, his sufferings seem like "long-delayed punishment for his sins as a young man, which God has recorded and remembered."[86]

> You write bitter things against me
> > and make me inherit the iniquities of my youth. (v. 26)

To him, "his present predicament" is that of a "prisoner closely confined and constantly watched."[87] He is incarcerated by the Almighty!

> You put my feet in the stocks
> > and watch all my paths;
> > you set a limit for the soles of my feet. (v. 27)

As Job has been "struck" physically "with loathsome sores" on "the sole of his foot" (2:7), so has he been assailed psychologically by Yahweh. He cannot even move without God's watchful eye. He has not a moment of remission from his pain. Oh, that God would speak to him!

13:28–14:22 Job was strong and confident as he rebuked his friends at the start of his third reply. And, as he has addressed God, there at times have been glimmers of hope. He hopes God will hear his case and vindicate him. However, in the final section of his speech, he is now hopeless. He despairs. This does not surprise the readers, as this has been Job's pattern thus far—every speech ends in a dark place (cf. 3:20–26; 7:19–21; 10:18–22)—but it does perhaps make this reality emphatic. When will the suffering end? When will Job get the answers he is looking for?

What has brought him to this depressing place is his meditation on humanity as a whole. Job sets aside his personal suffering (he mentions himself only in 14:3, 13–17), as the sad fate of the human condition is the subject of these verses. The ESV begins 13:28 with the word "man." The word in Hebrew is simply the pronoun "he" (*hu'*). However, "man" is a good way to start this final section because mankind is the subject of Job's musings, with the word "man" employed six times. Indeed, the state of Adam's offspring is in focus (the Hb. word for "man" in 14:1 is *'adam*).

First, Job focuses on the fragile and fleeting nature of man's existence. The statement that "man who is born of a woman is few of days and full of trouble" (14:1) is surrounded by illustrations from creation:

---

86 Estes, *Job*, 83.
87 John E. Hartley, *The Book of Job*, NICOT (Grand Rapids, MI: Eerdmans, 1988), 228.

> Man wastes away like a rotten thing,
>> like a garment that is moth-eaten. (13:28)

> He comes out like a flower and withers;
>> he flees like a shadow and continues not. (14:2)

The question then arises: if man is like a decomposing pumpkin, a pair of old moth-eaten trousers, a shriveling daisy, and a passing cloud, then why does God focus his attention on us?

> Do you open your eyes on such a one
>> and bring me into judgment with you? (14:3)

Job wonders why God would drag him into court ("bring me into judgment"; 14:3b). Job is as sinful as any human being, who can only look so presentable before a perfectly pure Judge:

> Who can bring a clean thing out of an unclean?
>> There is not one. (14:4)

And Job is as transient as any human being. He cannot live longer than God has ordained:

> Since his days are determined,
>> and the number of his months is with you,
>> and you have appointed his limits that he cannot pass. (14:5)

Thus Job offers a solution, one he has suggested before (7:16, 19; 10:20). He wants God to leave man alone ("look away from him and leave him alone"; 14:6a) so that he can find some delight in the few days he might have left ("that he may enjoy, like a hired hand, his day"; 14:6b).

The next petition from Job is in 14:13. He asks God to bury him in the grave ("Oh that you would hide me in Sheol"; 14:13a). He gives two reasons for this apparently grim prayer. First, he hopes that Sheol will protect him from his present sufferings ("conceal me until your wrath be past"; 14:13b). Second, he hopes that Sheol is not the end of the story, that God will someday retrieve Job from this pit ("that you would appoint me a set time, and remember me!"; 14:13c). What comes before 14:13 are his observations on the bleak reality of human death (14:7–12), but what follows is his hope that God might make an exception in his case (14:14–17).

In 14:7–12 Job contrasts man's death with the death of a tree. A tree dies and is chopped down. But what happens next is amazing: just a few drops of water cause new life to sprout. A sapling buds out of the dead trunk. Poetically, Job says it this way:

> There is hope for a tree,
>> if it be cut down, that it will sprout again,

and that its shoots will not cease.
Though its root grow old in the earth,
    and its stump die in the soil,
yet at the scent of water it will bud
    and put out branches like a young plant. (14:7–9)

In contrast to a tree, a man dies and that is the end of him:

But a   man   dies   and is laid low;
        man   breathes his last,   and where is he? (14:10)

Man's death is like dried-up "waters"—"a river" or "lake" that "fails" (or "disappears"), "wastes away and dries up" (14:11). Once he is dead ("so a man lies down"), there is no hope of life again ("and rises not again"; 14:12a); he is dead forevermore ("till the heavens are no more he will not awake or be roused out of his sleep"; 14:12bc).

From this bleak reality, Job asks God to act. As stated above, he petitions God to "hide" him "in Sheol" (14:13a). While the image of throwing Job into a pit or tossing him in an open grave is not a pleasant one, Job seems to take a positive angle on it. In 14:7–12 Job has bemoaned man's fate after death. In 14:14–17 he hopes that God might do something even more miraculous than sprouting a new tree from a dead one. He wants God to resurrect him! His plan has two parts to it. First, to free him from his present pain, he wants God to send him to Sheol (14:13ab). Second, when the time is right, God will (a) remember what he did with Job and (b) retrieve him from the grave (14:13c).

This plan makes good sense to Job. As it stands, there is currently no hope for such a resurrection ("If a man dies, shall he live again?"; 14:14a). But if God is willing to offer resurrection, Job is willing to wait in Sheol for it ("All the days of my service I would wait, till my renewal [or "change"] should come"; 14:14bc). It is difficult to know precisely what is being said in the second half of 14:14. What change is Job envisioning? If he is dead in Sheol, it must be a bodily resurrection. What he pictures next is his version of "Lazarus, come out" (John 11:43). God would beckon Job ("You would call"); Job would hear him ("and I would answer you"; Job 14:15a).

Why would God do this? Two reasons are given. First, as the end of 14:15 states, "you would long for the work of your hands." Put differently, the reason for this resurrection is God's love: he loves man, whom he has made from the dust with his own hands (cf. Gen. 2:7) to rule over the trees and rivers, along with the birds of the air and the fish of the sea (Gen. 1:26–27). The second reason involves the forgiving of man's iniquities. Job wants to be saved not only from Sheol, but also from his sin. He envisions God as dismissing incriminating evidence in the case against Job. Although God would still oversee every aspect of Job's life ("you would number my steps"; Job 14:16a), omniscience will not be confining but freeing, for God will not be keeping track of every transgression ("you would not keep watch over my sin"; 14:16b). Instead,

> my transgression would be sealed up in a bag,
>   and you would cover over my iniquity. (14:17)

Perhaps it is best to envision God as taking all of Job's sin, sealing it in a safe, placing the safe at the bottom of Death Valley, and then sending forth the torrents of rain.

All of this sounds good. However, Job is not done. He wakes from his delightful daydream, and 14:18–22 are a reality check. These lines are Job's pessimistic admission, "Ah, but none of this will happen." The word "but" (14:18) introduces the contrast to come. Just as a mountain erodes ("the mountain . . . crumbles away"; 14:18a) completely ("the rock is removed from its place"; v. 18b), with stormwaters eating away "the stones" (14:19a) and "the soil" (14:19b), so God levels all anticipation of life after death ("you destroy the hope of man"; 14:19c). Now, to Job, God is a destroyer, not a savior. When God overpowers a man at death, it is permanent ("you prevail forever against him, and he passes"; 14:20). When man is sent to Sheol ("you . . . send him away"), he is changed ("you change his countenance"; 14:20b), but not for the good. In the grave he is unaware of anything that happens on the earth above. If his children prosper, thrive, and enjoy life ("sons come to honor"), "he does not know it" (14:21a); if they lose it all, get sick, and die ("are brought low"), "he perceives it not" (14:21b). He sees none of their successes or failures. His eternal hell is a lonely place:

> He feels only the pain of his own body,
>   and he mourns only for himself. (14:22)

Response

Job 12–14 offers many key Bible themes to explore—wisdom, sin, salvation, prayer, hope, judgment, death, and life after death. In regard to wisdom, Job's poem on the wisdom of God is not just a beautiful ancient poem (12:14–25), something we turn into a plaque to hang on the wall, but rather is a work of art intended to work on us. In a fallen world, suffering and death, along with inexplicable injustices, are part of the curse (cf. Rom. 5:12–21). We must have the wisdom to recognize this fact. We must also let God rule his world with his wisdom, leaning on him instead of our own understanding (Prov. 3:5). And if depression sets in due to our inability to figure things out, we should still remember that God is in complete control. And, perhaps most importantly, when we find ourselves in circumstances beyond our wisdom or control, we must go to God. God may not give us answers. He may not even bring us immediate comfort. But we go to God in prayer because worship of our sovereign God is our highest calling, for "with him are strength and sound wisdom" (Job 12:16).

We can also learn something about our salvation from Job 12–14. Job's only solution to his sufferings—and sins—involves some sort of a resurrection. While there are hints of such a resurrection in the OT (e.g., Pss. 49:15; 73:24; Dan. 12:2), it is unclear what Job thinks. At times he appears confident that there is no life after death (e.g., Job 10:21; 16:22). Other times, however, he seems to imagine and hope that there might be something more (e.g., 14:13–17; 19:25–27). Of course, how blessed we are! We know that Jesus has conquered the grave. We know that in his resurrection, we are made right with God and given the unshakable hope of release from sin, suffering, and death.

It may be a coincidence, or something very deliberate, that Paul uses the phrase "this will turn out for my deliverance" (Phil. 1:19; Gk. *touto moi apobēsetai eis sōtērian*), which is precisely the phrase used in the Greek version of Job 13:16, there translated "this will be my salvation." Both Paul and Job are simply asking to be delivered from their trying circumstances. Yet, what Paul says next in Philippians is precisely what Job, and now every believer, needs to hear and heed:

> It is my eager expectation and hope that I will not be at all ashamed, but that with full courage now as always Christ will be honored in my body, whether by life or by death. For to me to live is Christ, and to die is gain. (Phil. 1:20–21)

Job was uncertain of what awaited him after the grave. For us, we are not afraid of death, for we know that death leads us into the very presence not of our destroyer but of our savior ("to depart and be with Christ"; Phil. 1:23), which is "far better" (Phil. 1:23) not only than our sufferings but also than anything else this world has to offer.

JOB 15:1–35

15 Then Eliphaz the Temanite answered and said:

2 "Should a wise man answer with windy knowledge,
  and fill his belly with the east wind?
3 Should he argue in unprofitable talk,
  or in words with which he can do no good?
4 But you are doing away with the fear of God[1]
  and hindering meditation before God.
5 For your iniquity teaches your mouth,
  and you choose the tongue of the crafty.
6 Your own mouth condemns you, and not I;
  your own lips testify against you.

7 "Are you the first man who was born?
  Or were you brought forth before the hills?
8 Have you listened in the council of God?
  And do you limit wisdom to yourself?
9 What do you know that we do not know?
  What do you understand that is not clear to us?
10 Both the gray-haired and the aged are among us,
  older than your father.
11 Are the comforts of God too small for you,
  or the word that deals gently with you?

¹² Why does your heart carry you away,
  and why do your eyes flash,
¹³ that you turn your spirit against God
  and bring such words out of your mouth?
¹⁴ What is man, that he can be pure?
  Or he who is born of a woman, that he can be righteous?
¹⁵ Behold, God[2] puts no trust in his holy ones,
  and the heavens are not pure in his sight;
¹⁶ how much less one who is abominable and corrupt,
  a man who drinks injustice like water!

¹⁷ "I will show you; hear me,
  and what I have seen I will declare
¹⁸ (what wise men have told,
  without hiding it from their fathers,
¹⁹ to whom alone the land was given,
  and no stranger passed among them).
²⁰ The wicked man writhes in pain all his days,
  through all the years that are laid up for the ruthless.
²¹ Dreadful sounds are in his ears;
  in prosperity the destroyer will come upon him.
²² He does not believe that he will return out of darkness,
  and he is marked for the sword.
²³ He wanders abroad for bread, saying, 'Where is it?'
  He knows that a day of darkness is ready at his hand;
²⁴ distress and anguish terrify him;
  they prevail against him, like a king ready for battle.
²⁵ Because he has stretched out his hand against God
  and defies the Almighty,
²⁶ running stubbornly against him
  with a thickly bossed shield;
²⁷ because he has covered his face with his fat
  and gathered fat upon his waist
²⁸ and has lived in desolate cities,
  in houses that none should inhabit,
  which were ready to become heaps of ruins;
²⁹ he will not be rich, and his wealth will not endure,
  nor will his possessions spread over the earth;[3]
³⁰ he will not depart from darkness;
  the flame will dry up his shoots,
  and by the breath of his mouth he will depart.
³¹ Let him not trust in emptiness, deceiving himself,
  for emptiness will be his payment.
³² It will be paid in full before his time,
  and his branch will not be green.
³³ He will shake off his unripe grape like the vine,
  and cast off his blossom like the olive tree.
³⁴ For the company of the godless is barren,
  and fire consumes the tents of bribery.
³⁵ They conceive trouble and give birth to evil,
  and their womb prepares deceit."

[1] Hebrew lacks *of God* [2] Hebrew *he* [3] Or *nor will his produce bend down to the earth*

Section Overview

As Eliphaz began the first cycle of dialogues (Job 4:1), so he starts the second (15:1–21:34). The structure of his speech is almost as exacting as his theology. The main accusation of 15:2–6—that Job is "doing away with the fear of God" (v. 4a)—is surrounded by words about Job's sinful words. Besides the usual introduction, which features "answered" and "said" (v. 1), Eliphaz speaks of Job's words using terms such as "answer," "argue," "talk," "words," "mouth," "tongue," "lips," and "testify." It is as if all these words are breaking apart Job's relationship with God. Or, more vividly, it is as if Job is chewing on and spitting out God!

In verses 7–14, Eliphaz moves from his accusation of Job to questions for him. Using ten rhetorical questions, Eliphaz attempts to instruct Job afresh on the basics of wisdom. He claims that Job has forgotten his foundations. Job has stopped listening to God's wisdom and traditional insight. He has forgotten how sinful human beings are (see esp. vv. 15–16). Thus, Job's claim of innocence is wrong. He is "abominable and corrupt," like "a man who drinks injustice like water!" (v. 16).

In the final section (vv. 17–35), which is a very calculated jab at Job, Eliphaz waxes eloquent on the fate of the "wicked man" (v. 20a), also called the "ruthless" (v. 20b) and the "godless" man (v. 34a). After a robust introduction ("I will show you"; v. 17), Eliphaz shows Job what happens to the man who "[stretches] out his hand against God" (v. 25a). Every line is about this man (note the plethora of pronouns: "he," "his," "him," thirty-two times), and every imaginable evil prevails against him, from present agonies (he "writhes in pain all his days"; v. 20a) to future losses ("he will not be rich"; v. 29a).

Section Outline

II.H. Empty Words (15:1–35)

    1. Eating Away the Fear of God (15:1–6)

    2. Drinking In Sin (15:7–16)

    3. The Consequences of Such a Diet (15:17–35)

Comment

15:1–6 As stated in the overview, these verses focus on Job's words ("answer," "argue," "talk," "words," "mouth," "tongue," "lips," and "testify"). Eliphaz starts with two rhetorical questions and colorful but cruel metaphors:

> Should a wise man answer with windy knowledge,
>   and fill his belly with the east wind?
> Should he argue in unprofitable talk,
>   or in words with which he can do no good? (vv. 2–3)

He pictures Job, a supposedly wise man, as digesting the wind. Then, when he opens his mouth, useless and empty claims are belched or spewed out. However, such talk, Eliphaz claims next, is not neutral. It might be like the wind, but it is a strong wind. It is breaking Job's covenant relationship with God ("But you are doing away [Hb. *parar*, "break"][88] with the fear of God"; v. 4a). Eliphaz claims that this severing of God's favor and diminishing of their relationship (the word "hindering" in v. 4b can also be translated "diminishing"; cf. Ezek. 16:27) is a sure consequence of Job's "crafty" tongue (Job 15:5). Sin has been his schoolmaster ("your iniquity teaches your mouth"; v. 5), his vocabulary that of the snake (cf. Gen. 3:1). The case is open and shut. Job's "own mouth condemns" him; his "own lips testify against" him (Job 15:6).

15:7–16 The first eight rhetorical questions to Job (vv. 7–13) are rebukes for not listening to his friends' counsel. Eliphaz attacks Job's self-autonomy and the fact that his perception is grounded in the present, not the past. Job is not older than Adam ("Are you the first man who was born?") or creation itself ("Or were you brought forth before the hills?"; v. 7). And he certainly was not there at the moment of creation, when God in his wisdom created the earth (cf. Proverbs 8). This might be the sense of the question "Have you listened in the council of God?" (Job 15:8a). Or the sense might be that "the council of God" represents others who are wise, which would then correspond with the second line, "And do you limit wisdom to yourself?" (v. 8b). Certainly, in verse 9 Eliphaz speaks of the wisdom of others, notably that of the three friends. Job is acting like he knows more than they do. Eliphaz disagrees:

> What do you   know   that we do not know?
> What do you   understand   that is not clear to us? (v. 9)

Moreover, unlike Job, their wisdom is grounded in years of experience and observation. Those "older than" Job's "father" side with them ("are among us"; v. 10). The "gray-haired and the aged" are Eliphaz, Bildad, and Zophar or perhaps represent the tradition—ancients from the past—that the three friends continue to stand upon and are counseling Job with. Job is not listening to wisdom; he is not listening to God; he is not listening to God's voice through the tradition.

> Are the comforts of God too small for you,
>   or the word that deals gently with you? (v. 11)

If "the word that deals gently with you" refers to the words of the friends, then the reader joins Job in rolling his eyes. What!? God has not spoken with Job. There is no comfort there. The friends have spoken of what is wrong about Job, and with great venom at times (e.g., vv. 2–6, 16). There is certainly no comfort there, either. Job is rightly upset about such a lack of comfort. Yet Eliphaz considers Job's "righteous," or at least "understandable" anger, and accuses him of sin. Job's passions ("your heart [carries] you away, . . . your eyes flash"; v. 12) have gotten the

---

88 Longman (*Job*, 224), citing T. F. Williams, *NIDOTTE* 3:696, records that this verb is used twenty-three times for Israel's breaking of the covenant.

better of him. And out of the heart the mouth speaks! Job's words ("words out of your mouth") testify that every part of him rages against his creator ("you turn your spirit against God"; v. 13).

The last of the ten rhetorical questions is intended to move Job to consider his case before a holy God:

> What is man,   that he can be   pure?
> Or he who is born of a woman,   that he can be   righteous?
>
> Behold, God puts no trust in his holy ones,
>   and the heavens are not pure in his sight;
> how much less one who is abominable and corrupt,
>   a man who drinks injustice like water! (vv. 14–16)

The logic is tight. The poetic parallelisms precise. The theology correct. But the application is absolutely off. It is true that man is totally depraved. It is true that even the angels are not completely holy. It is therefore true that the man Job is not perfectly pure in God's sight. But it is not correct that Job has claimed as much. Neither is it accurate that Job is "abominable and corrupt." These disreputable OT words are certainly not reserved for Job, who is "blameless and upright" (1:1, 8; 2:3). It is certainly not true that he is so unrighteous that he "drinks injustice like water" (15:16).

15:17–35 At this point, the reader is done with Eliphaz's patronizing preaching. Job is done with Eliphaz's oratorical unkindness. But, alas, there are nineteen verses left in his sermon.

If we think of Eliphaz's speech as a three-point sermon to Job, we might divide the material as follows. Point one: With your words, you are eating away the fear of God (vv. 1–6). Point two: Because you have not listened to God or tradition, you are like a man who drinks in sin like water (vv. 7–16). Point three: Such a diet will not fare well for you (vv. 17–35).

Eliphaz has not moved from his earlier stated vision:

> Remember: who that was innocent ever perished?
>   Or where were the upright cut off?
> As I have seen, those who plow iniquity
>   and sow trouble reap the same. (4:7–8)

Here he just expands upon what he meant in 4:9: "By the breath of God they perish, and by the blast of his anger they are consumed." That is, both the wisdom tradition ("what wise men have told, without hiding it from their fathers"; 15:18) and wise observation of life ("what I have seen I will declare"; v. 17b) teach the retribution principle: the good prosper, while the bad perish. The focus here is only on the downside of that principle, with the key verse being Eliphaz's opening line: "The wicked man writhes in pain all his days" (v. 20a). All the lines that follow focus on this main point. The purpose of this poem on the wicked man is for Job to hear the wisdom of Eliphaz ("hear me"; v. 17a) and see that he is that man (cf. 2 Sam. 12:7).

Job 15:21–24 illustrates various aspects of divine punishment that the wicked man suffers. Even in times of peace, suddenly he hears the sounds of marauders marching around his home. All his shalom quickly vanishes. "Dreadful sounds are in his ears; in prosperity the destroyer will come upon him" (v. 21). He fears going out at night ("he does not believe that he will return out of darkness"), because his once safe neighborhood is now filled with violence ("he is marked for the sword"; v. 22). Verses 21–22 are likely flashbacks to Job's loss of property at the hands of the Sabeans and Chaldeans (1:13–19), and 15:23–24 the aftermath. He is hungry: "He wanders abroad for bread, saying, 'Where is it?'" (v. 23a). He thinks that death is imminent: "He knows that a day of darkness is ready at his hand" (v. 23b). And like a warrior king defeating his foes, "distress and anguish terrify him" and "prevail against him" (v. 24). He is physically and psychologically a mess.

Eliphaz next tells his congregation the cause of all these calamities: sin! The only specific named sin, which makes the wicked man "wicked," is found in verses 25–26: all of this has come upon him "because he has stretched out his hand against God"; put differently, he "defies the Almighty." The phrase "he has stretched out his hand" is an image not of worshiping Yahweh but of confronting and challenging him. It is a clenched hand, a fist in the air—the ultimate posture of rebellion. This image is reinforced with another related image—that of the wicked man charging at God ("running stubbornly [or "defiantly"] against him") with a massive, "thickly bossed" shield in hand (v. 26). While the image is that of a battle scene, with Job rushing at Yahweh, the fact that a shield and not a sword is mentioned may symbolize his defensiveness. He is so stubborn in his position against God.

The ESV begins verse 27 with the word "because" (so also v. 25). This particle (Hb. *ki*) can be translated as "because," "that," "when," or "though." Since a new thought seems to be in place (the *ki* does not relate directly to vv. 25–26 but connects to what follows in vv. 27–28), "though" also fits well, the sense being:

> Though his face is covered with fat
>   and his waist bulges with flesh,
> he will inhabit ruined towns
>   and houses where no one lives,
>   houses crumbling to rubble. (vv. 27–28 NIV)

The irony is this: while this man is overweight ("he has covered his face with his fat and gathered fat upon his waist," as the ESV translates v. 27), he is not living high on the hog! His housing situation is a joke. The cities he has resided in are "desolate," his homes condemned ("houses that none should inhabit") and soon to be demolished ("ready to become heaps of ruins," v. 28; perhaps an allusion to 1:19).

Like 15:21–24 and 27–28, verses 29–35 further illustrate various aspects of divine punishment. Any "wealth" he has "will not endure" (v. 29a). He will leave no inheritance ("nor will his possessions spread over the earth"; v. 29b). He himself will join his money: he will not endure but will die ("not depart from darkness"; v. 30a). By "the breath of [God's] mouth" he will be incinerated ("the flame will dry up his shoots"; v. 30bc). With these analogies of a consuming fire (also v. 34b below) and the drastic loss of possessions, Job's own sad story is likely echoed here (cf. 1:16–17).

Then, with a mix of metaphors from botany, business, and birth, Eliphaz concludes:

> Let him not trust in emptiness, deceiving himself,
>> for emptiness will be his payment.
> It will be paid in full before his time,
>> and his branch will not be green.
> He will shake off his unripe grape like the vine,
>> and cast off his blossom like the olive tree.
> For the company of the godless is barren,
>> and fire consumes the tents of bribery.
> They conceive trouble and give birth to evil,
>> and their womb prepares deceit. (15:31–35)

All of the images are of emptiness and ineffectiveness. The wicked man, who is self-deceived because he trusts not in Yahweh (cf. v. 31), is a loser in life. He is paid "emptiness" (v. 31b). He does not flourish ("his branch will not be green"; v. 32b; cf. v. 33 for similar ideas, and the imagery of barrenness in v. 34). His shady business deals come back to bite him (cf. vv. 34–35).

Response

Eliphaz's poem is totally out of touch with reality, not only with the reality of Job's specific situation but also with plain observation of life. Does the wicked man really writhe "in pain *all* his days" (v. 20a)? Is the ruthless man always poor (vv. 21b, 29)—so poor that he begs for bread (v. 23a) and lives in a shack (v. 28b)? Do ill-gotten fortunes always vanish away (v. 29)? Is Job really shaking his fist at God and cursing him to his face (v. 25)?

Again, it is easy to make our response to this sermon a simple word to the wise: "Do not preach like Eliphaz! Do not so easily separate the godly from the ungodly. Do not scare good people into false repentance. Do not accuse every suffering saint of sin. Do not misconstrue the facts. Do not be so demeaning. Do not be so mean!" But there are two other angles on Eliphaz's otherwise worthless words, one positive and the other corrective.

The positive takeaway is that we must not shy away from teaching the topics he teaches on. Do we boldly teach the utter sinfulness of man before a holy God? Do we warn sinners about the certain wrath of this wholly righteous God? Do we caution the wealthy about the dangers of riches and the fleetingness of possessions? The corrective application would be to allow the text to shape one's framework. Or, more specifically to Eliphaz's issue, we should be willing to change our theological framework based on experience or, more importantly, Scripture. Certain theological systems are better than others. The Westminster Standards are superior to the men of the east's retribution theology. But all theological systems must accord with Scripture and be corrected, if needed, according to Scripture.

JOB 16:1–17:16

16 Then Job answered and said:

2 "I have heard many such things;
   miserable comforters are you all.
3 Shall windy words have an end?
   Or what provokes you that you answer?
4 I also could speak as you do,
   if you were in my place;
   I could join words together against you
   and shake my head at you.
5 I could strengthen you with my mouth,
   and the solace of my lips would assuage your pain.

6 "If I speak, my pain is not assuaged,
   and if I forbear, how much of it leaves me?
7 Surely now God has worn me out;
   he has[1] made desolate all my company.
8 And he has shriveled me up,
   which is a witness against me,
   and my leanness has risen up against me;
   it testifies to my face.
9 He has torn me in his wrath and hated me;
   he has gnashed his teeth at me;
   my adversary sharpens his eyes against me.
10 Men have gaped at me with their mouth;
   they have struck me insolently on the cheek;
   they mass themselves together against me.
11 God gives me up to the ungodly
   and casts me into the hands of the wicked.
12 I was at ease, and he broke me apart;
   he seized me by the neck and dashed me to pieces;
   he set me up as his target;
13   his archers surround me.
   He slashes open my kidneys and does not spare;
   he pours out my gall on the ground.

14 He breaks me with breach upon breach;
    he runs upon me like a warrior.
15 I have sewed sackcloth upon my skin
    and have laid my strength in the dust.
16 My face is red with weeping,
    and on my eyelids is deep darkness,
17 although there is no violence in my hands,
    and my prayer is pure.

18 "O earth, cover not my blood,
    and let my cry find no resting place.
19 Even now, behold, my witness is in heaven,
    and he who testifies for me is on high.
20 My friends scorn me;
    my eye pours out tears to God,
21 that he would argue the case of a man with God,
    as[2] a son of man does with his neighbor.
22 For when a few years have come
    I shall go the way from which I shall not return.

17 "My spirit is broken; my days are extinct;
    the graveyard is ready for me.
2 Surely there are mockers about me,
    and my eye dwells on their provocation.

3 "Lay down a pledge for me with you;
    who is there who will put up security for me?
4 Since you have closed their hearts to understanding,
    therefore you will not let them triumph.
5 He who informs against his friends to get a share of
        their property—
    the eyes of his children will fail.

6 "He has made me a byword of the peoples,
    and I am one before whom men spit.
7 My eye has grown dim from vexation,
    and all my members are like a shadow.
8 The upright are appalled at this,
    and the innocent stirs himself up against the godless.
9 Yet the righteous holds to his way,
    and he who has clean hands grows stronger and
        stronger.
10 But you, come on again, all of you,
    and I shall not find a wise man among you.
11 My days are past; my plans are broken off,
    the desires of my heart.
12 They make night into day:
    'The light,' they say, 'is near to the darkness.'[3]
13 If I hope for Sheol as my house,
    if I make my bed in darkness,
14 if I say to the pit, 'You are my father,'
    and to the worm, 'My mother,' or 'My sister,'

¹⁵ where then is my hope?
   Who will see my hope?
¹⁶ Will it go down to the bars of Sheol?
   Shall we descend together into the dust?"⁴

¹Hebrew *you have*; also verse 8 ²Hebrew *and* ³The meaning of the Hebrew is uncertain ⁴Or *Will they go
down to the bars of Sheol? Is rest to be found together in the dust?*

Section Overview

At this point we are used to the Hebraism "Then Job answered and said" (16:1). But
such reserved narration shakes our sensibilities. Should it not be, "And then Job
punched Eliphaz in the face!"? Job does not do so. But he comes close. He begins his
fourth reply with some verbal attacks of his own, claiming that the three friends
are "miserable comforters" and that if he were in their situation, he would say and
do the opposite: bring strength and solace to the suffering (16:1–5). The rest of his
speech focuses again on how hopeless he sees his situation. The questions "Where
then is my hope?" and "Who will see my hope?" (17:15) state the theme of these
chapters perfectly. He is without hope because God is against him (16:6–17), and
there is nothing he can do about it (16:18–17:16). He must somehow endure his
severed relationships: the scorn of his friends ("my friends scorn me"), the silence of
God ("my eye pours out tears to God"; 16:20), and the mockery of all (16:10; 17:2).

Section Outline

II.I. Where Then Is My Hope? (16:1–17:16)
    1. Job's Friends Are against Him (16:1–6)
    2. God Is against Him (16:7–17)
    3. Even Hope Will Not Lay in the Grave with Him (16:18–17:16)

Comment

16:1–6 Job has heard enough. His friends are not doing their job. They came to
"comfort him" (2:11; Hb. *nakham*). Instead, however, they are "miserable comforters" (16:2; Hb. *menakhame 'amal*). Job is not the one filled with "windy knowledge"
(15:2; cf. 8:2); they are. Their useless and oppressive counsel (their "windy words";
16:3a) seems endless. He is sick of their hot air in his face. Job wonders what their
problem is. What continues to provoke them, that they keep answering Job's
laments with their lies (cf. v. 3b)? He wants to be left alone.

In verses 4–6 Job imagines trading places with them.

I also could speak as you do,
    if you were in my place; (v. 4ab)

He could act like they are acting. He could prod them with dispassionate poetry
("I could join words together against you"; v. 4c) and shake his head in disbelief
and dismay ("and shake my head at you"; v. 4d). Or he could take the high road, the

path they should be on. He could use his words ("mouth" and "lips") to build them up, not tear them down, bringing "strength" and "solace," helping "assuage" their "pain" (v. 5). Job has tried everything. He has tried to comfort himself with such words of strength and solace, but even his own method does not work. "If I speak, my pain is not assuaged" (v. 6a). He has also tried refraining from offering himself words of comfort, and yet that too offers little relief ("and if I forbear, how much of it leaves me?"; v. 6b).

16:7–17 Job cannot find comfort from his friends (vv. 2–4). He cannot even comfort himself (v. 6). Is God, then, the solution? In verses 7–17 Job answers with an emphatic "No!" To him, God is not the solution but the problem.

Using psalm-like language of lament, Job describes with metaphor after metaphor the awfulness of his ongoing experience. The focus of his lament is God. His opening line is "surely now God has" (v. 7a). He then goes on to describe what "God has" done to him:

God has	worn me out (v. 7a)
He has	made desolate all my company (v. 7b)
He has	shriveled me up (v. 8a)
He has	torn me in his wrath (v. 9a)
He has	gnashed his teeth at me (v. 9b)

Job is exhausted (v. 7a). His friends and their words are barren and worthless (v. 7b). Yet, because he is just skin and bones, such emaciation has been seen as a sign of sin. His "shriveled" body is a "witness against" him; his "leanness" lies to his "face" (v. 8)—"See, you are guilty!" More than that, Job feels that God has turned against him. It is as if he is under God's indignation. God's "wrath" is against him. The "hatred" is so deep that Job envisions God as his "adversary," gnashing his teeth at him, fixing ("sharpening") his eyes against him (cf. v. 9), and ready to attack!

The attack comes, so Job suggests, in the form of "men"—three men who could not believe their eyes when they first spotted Job (they "gaped at me"; v. 10a; cf. 2:12) but who quickly united to turn against him ("they have struck me insolently on the cheek; they mass themselves together against me"; 16:10bc). Job admits defeat. He assumes the warrior God is their commander-in-chief.

God	gives me up	to the ungodly
and	casts me	into the hands of the wicked. (v. 11)

God throws Job to the *ungodly!*? Such is certainly how Job feels as he indeed feels the full arsenal of his friends' attack, as well as that of the mockers who stroll by to see the skinny statue of "The Wise Man of the East" deconstructed.

Job next recounts the stealthy and severe strikes:

> I was at ease, and he broke me apart;
>> he seized me by the neck and dashed me to pieces;

> he set me up as his target;
>> his archers surround me.
> He slashes open my kidneys and does not spare;
>> he pours out my gall on the ground.
> He breaks me with breach upon breach;
>> he runs upon me like a warrior. (vv. 12–14)

Job has lost wealth. His health. His children! His wife and his friends' respect. The imagery—God choking him, throwing him to the ground, then having his archers use him as target practice and afterward slashing open his innards and watching his blood flow into the soil—is not as exaggerated as we might imagine. Job once had peace and prosperity. But he did not live happily ever after. Since the end of chapter 1 (for months, perhaps years), a constant crusade of seemingly cosmic forces has been warring against him. He does not know what to do. He has done what he thinks he should do; he has repented of anything he can possibly repent of:

> I have sewed sackcloth upon my skin
>> and have laid my strength in the dust. (16:15)[89]

He has turned to God for help. He is physically exhausted, spiritually drained:

> My face is red with weeping,
>> and on my eyelids is deep darkness, (v. 16)

But the sky seems made of stone. He does not understand why God will not hear his prayer and show mercy upon him. He is, after all, innocent, and his cries for help sincere ("although there is no violence in my hands, and my prayer is pure"; v. 17).

16:18–17:16 Job 16:18 is another beautiful supplication, one that ties into what Job has said in 16:7–17. He is not sure if God can or will hear him, so he calls on the earth to vindicate him: "O earth, cover not my blood, and let my cry find no resting place" (16:18; cf. 16:13). He also calls on heaven to be his advocate:

> Even now, behold, my witness is in heaven,
>> and he who testifies for me is on high. (16:19)

He knows not if heaven and earth will come to the rescue, but he has no other hope. Both his closest companions and his faithful God have forsaken him (his "friends scorn" him, 16:20a; his "eye pours out tears to God" to no avail, 16:20b). But Job seems conflicted, as he speaks perhaps prophetically:

> that he would argue the case of a man with God,
>> as a son of man does with his neighbor. (16:21)

---

89 The ESV, with its alliteration, perfectly captures one of the greatest metaphors in the Bible. That Job has "sewed sackcloth" over his "skin" is a powerful image: he is in a constant state of humiliation before God.

Who is the "he"? Is this "son of man" the Son of Man, the one who has come to "seek and save" (Luke 19:10)? Is this intercessor the God-man or just abstract "heaven" and "earth"? We know, but Job does not. Job is neither messianic nor optimistic: "when a few years have come I shall go the way from which I shall not return" (Job 16:22). He will soon die.

Chapter 17 continues this theme of his impending death:

> My spirit is broken; my days are extinct;
> the graveyard is ready for me. (17:1)

Sheol awaits Job, where death will mock his existence. Greatest man of the east? Phooey! But for now, his friends do the job. He is surrounded by deriders ("surely there are mockers about me"; 17:2a); he is forced to stare directly into their taunts ("my eye dwells on their provocation"; 17:2b). He wants God's support—a down payment on Job's innocence ("lay down a pledge for me"; 17:3a)—because no one else is wise enough and willing enough to do it, considering the circumstances ("Who is there who will put up security for me?"; 17:3b). Since Job believes that God has barred his friends' minds from grasping the truth ("you have closed their hearts to understanding"; 17:4a), Job hopes that they will not have the last word in the debate ("therefore you will not let them triumph"; 17:4b). For, after all, their sin is obvious, and their retribution principle needs to be practiced on them! If they are going to mock and denounce Job, their children should suffer the consequences of their crimes: "He who informs against his friends to get a share of their property—the eyes of his children will fail" (17:5).

Job's words are not careless; they are crafted against those who think he is crafty (cf. 15:5). Yet they are sad words. He is lost, confused. He turns again, in 17:6, to contemplating God and his role in Job's sorrows. God, he says, "has made" him a "byword of the peoples" (the laughingstock of Uz) and the object of degrading physical scorn ("men spit" on him; 17:6). Due to Job's sufferings, he can no longer see ("my eye has grown dim from vexation"; 17:7a) or stand up straight. All of his body parts ("members") are like sticks reflecting the morning sun ("like a shadow"; 17:7b). Yet, under the shadow of the Almighty, Job still stands. He believes that his vindication is soon to come, for he knows that anyone who is truly blameless ("the upright" man) is appalled about what is happening to him, and such a man freely joins Job in his raging against the machine ("the upright are appalled at this, and the innocent stirs himself up against the godless"; 17:8). Job trusts that his "godless" friends are not wise (cf. 17:10b). Sarcastically, he encourages them to give it another try ("but you, come on again"; 17:10a). Meanwhile, he ("the righteous . . . he who has clean hands") stands firm ("holds to his way"), and in doing so only "grows stronger and stronger" (17:9).

His strength, however, has its limits. He can only hold so much weight over his head. In 17:11–16, he again sinks (as he has done thus far in all of his speeches) into despair. His good "days" are a thing of the "past," along with his heart's "desires" and "plans" for the future (17:11). All that he might have hoped for is surely not going to happen ("broken off"; 17:11). His friends have brought him to this place. They call good "evil" and evil "good" (cf. Isa. 5:20):

> They make night into day:
>> "The light," they say, "is near to the darkness." (Job 17:12)

Job again embraces this darkness:

> If I hope for Sheol as my house,
>> if I make my bed in darkness,
> if I say to the pit, "You are my father,"
>> and to the worm, "My mother," or "My sister,"
> where then is my hope?
>> Who will see my hope?
> Will it go down to the bars of Sheol?
>> Shall we descend together into the dust? (17:13–16)

Even if he embraced death as his abode ("Sheol" as his "house," "the darkness" of the grave as his "bed"; 17:13) and as the only family he now has (calling his earthen tomb "father" and the decomposition of his body "mother" and "sister"; 17:14), he will find no solace. Will hope join him in the grave ("descend together into the dust"; 17:16b)? Surely not. Hope is not going to rest in peace with him.

Response

We might wonder why this debate between Job and his friends goes on so long. But it is part of the test. It is also part of the realism of Job's story. Real suffering rarely ends after one day or a few verses. We must keep this in mind when we go through extended periods of physical or psychological pain. We also must keep this in mind when attempting to comfort others.

Job begins this fourth reply to his friends by calling them "miserable comforters" (16:2). When he needed some soul therapy, instead their theological talk terrorized him. In his commentary on Job, John Goldingay uses Boaz as the type of comforter that Job needed and that we should be:

> In the story of Ruth, Boaz provides a neat example of the way "comfort" in the Old Testament can involve both words and actions. Boaz speaks appreciatively to Ruth about the way she has cared for Naomi and prays for Yahweh to bless her as she has come to seek refuge under his wings. Boaz has also taken action to ensure that Ruth can glean successfully and safely in his fields. One might see both the actions and words as expressions of the "comfort" she thanks him for.[90]

Be like Boaz, however, is not the only application. *Marvel at Jesus* is another, one that goes to the depth of our faith. Job longed for a "witness . . . in heaven" who would

---

90 Goldingay, *Job*, 84.

testify on his behalf (16:19). We have that witness in Jesus. Yet let us not forget that his sufferings surpassed even that of Job. We have a mediator who has undergone the mockery of men ("those who passed by derided him, wagging their heads," Matt. 27:39; "the chief priests, with the scribes and elders, mocked him," Matt. 27:41; "the robbers . . . also reviled him," Matt. 27:44; cf. Ps. 22:7, 13) *and* the full weight of God's wrath. Job felt like God had thrown him to the ungodly, to attack and devour.

> God   gives me up   to the ungodly
> and   casts me   into the hands of the wicked. (Job 16:11)

However, Job was not God-forsaken. But Jesus was!

In Matthew's Gospel, following the verbal ridicule (Matt. 27:41–44), we hear Jesus' cry of dereliction, "My God, my God, why have you forsaken me?" as darkness covers the land (Matt. 27:45–46). This moment on the hill in Golgotha takes us back to Jesus' prayers in Gethsemane. What Jesus feared more than anything else was the silence of God and the separation from God his Father—drinking the cup of God's holy judgment upon sin. How could there be silence? How could there be separation? The answer is hinted at in Matthew 8:17, where the Evangelist quotes Isaiah 53:4, "He took our illnesses and bore our diseases," more directly stated by Jesus in Matthew 20:28: "the Son of Man came . . . to give his life as a ransom for many"—in other words, to "pour out" his blood "for many for the forgiveness of sins" (Matt. 26:28). How are sins forgiven? Jesus became sin for us, and in Jesus' becoming sin (cf. 2 Cor. 5:18–21) there was some inexplicable yet unavoidable silence and separation from the Father.

JOB 18:1–21

18 Then Bildad the Shuhite answered and said:

² "How long will you hunt for words?
    Consider, and then we will speak.
³ Why are we counted as cattle?
    Why are we stupid in your sight?
⁴ You who tear yourself in your anger,
    shall the earth be forsaken for you,
    or the rock be removed out of its place?

⁵ "Indeed, the light of the wicked is put out,
    and the flame of his fire does not shine.
⁶ The light is dark in his tent,
    and his lamp above him is put out.
⁷ His strong steps are shortened,
    and his own schemes throw him down.

⁸ For he is cast into a net by his own feet,
　　and he walks on its mesh.
⁹ A trap seizes him by the heel;
　　a snare lays hold of him.
¹⁰ A rope is hidden for him in the ground,
　　a trap for him in the path.
¹¹ Terrors frighten him on every side,
　　and chase him at his heels.
¹² His strength is famished,
　　and calamity is ready for his stumbling.
¹³ It consumes the parts of his skin;
　　the firstborn of death consumes his limbs.
¹⁴ He is torn from the tent in which he trusted
　　and is brought to the king of terrors.
¹⁵ In his tent dwells that which is none of his;
　　sulfur is scattered over his habitation.
¹⁶ His roots dry up beneath,
　　and his branches wither above.
¹⁷ His memory perishes from the earth,
　　and he has no name in the street.
¹⁸ He is thrust from light into darkness,
　　and driven out of the world.
¹⁹ He has no posterity or progeny among his people,
　　and no survivor where he used to live.
²⁰ They of the west are appalled at his day,
　　and horror seizes them of the east.
²¹ Surely such are the dwellings of the unrighteous,
　　such is the place of him who knows not God."

Section Overview

The traditionalist Shuhite offers his second speech to Job. Bildad believes that the world works like a computer programmed to the retribution formula. There are precise patterns and absolutes. There is moral order to the universe. Job's radical rebuttals deny that this is the way the world works, but Bildad, the theoretical ethicist, will have none of it. After he verbally abuses Job for his folly (Job 18:2) and defends his and his friends' wisdom (vv. 3–4), Bildad seeks to disabuse Job of his crazy claims (vv. 5–21). His argument is simple and straightforward. Job has heard it all before (cf. 4:7–11; 5:2–7; 8:3–4, 11–19; 11:11; 15:20–35), and Bildad obviously thinks he needs to hear it again. There are no exceptions to the rule that the wicked suffer God's punishment. Sin leads to suffering; and suffering is a sure sign that will lead the observant to a sinner—like Job!

Section Outline

II.J. Bad Things Happen to Bad People (18:1–21)
　　1. You Shut Up; We Will Speak (18:1–4)
　　2. Indeed, the Light of the Wicked Is Put Out (18:5–21)

Comment

18:1–4 In this short opening, the Shuhite tells Job to shut up. The sense of the first (of four) rhetorical questions—"How long will you hunt for words?" (v. 2a)—is that Bildad wants Job to stop with his antagonistic, adroit, and idiotic speeches (cf. 8:2).[91] Job needs to do less talking and more listening: "Consider, and then we will speak" (18:2b). Job also needs to watch what he says:

> Why are we counted as cattle?
> Why are we stupid in your sight? (v. 3)

Eliphaz, Bildad, and Zophar are not dim-witted heifers. Finally, Job needs to cool down ("you who tear yourself in your anger"; v. 4a) and stop thinking that the world revolves around him. "The earth does not need to be remodeled around your situation ["shall the earth be forsaken for you"; v. 4b]," Bildad basically says, "or the foundations of the world tossed into the sea to suit you ["or the rock be removed out of its place?"; v. 4c]." What Job needs to know is traditional wisdom. He needs to retake Retribution Principle 101.

18:5–21 Bildad next provides a summary of those class lectures. After stating his unshakable thesis that the wicked will die—"Indeed, the light of the wicked is put out, and the flame of his fire does not shine" (v. 5)—he offers a string of illustrations to support this principle.

In chapter 8, Bildad's first rebuttal of Job's claims was filled with impressive metaphors about the fate of the wicked. The unrighteous are like papyrus plants without water (8:11), a spider's web (8:14), and a falling house (8:15). Here in chapter 18, the metaphors of the judgment of the wicked abound, including a blown-out lamp (v. 6), a net (v. 8), withering branches (v. 16), and a summons before the "king of terrors" (death; v. 14). The first metaphors are about extinguished light. Job has talked so much about darkness, the "deep darkness" (3:5; 12:22; 16:16) of his sufferings. Bildad in a sense says, "You have not seen *deep* darkness yet. What you have experienced has all been surface stuff." The life ("the light," 18:5a, 6a; "the flame of his fire," v. 5b; "his lamp," v. 6b) of the ungodly man is eventually "put out" completely (vv. 5a, 6b).[92] No light whatsoever! His lamp might flicker for a moment, but soon enough darkness encompasses his whole household ("dark in his tent"; v. 6a). Perhaps his children die, his possessions are destroyed, and his health deteriorates. And then, death comes to town.

Bildad's theology is biblical ("for the evil man has no future; the lamp of the wicked will be put out"; Prov. 24:20) but in Job's case diabolical. We wish this

---

91 As the word "you" here is plural, Bildad might also include his friends in this rebuke. He wishes the whole tenor of the debate would change. Enough with the clever words! Let us have an honest theological debate over the issues.

92 While the image of "light" might include health and prosperity, it is clearly an allusion to life: "the light of life" (33:30); and,

> Why is light   given   to him who is in misery,
> and life   [given]   to the bitter in soul? (3:20)

"Darkness" is also an allusion to death (3:5; 10:21; 17:13).

sermonette were over. Job, we can safely assume, is begging for a break from the babble (cf. Job 19:2). But no such relief is given; Bildad plows through his prepared speech. Though he has had nine chapters to prepare, the message has not changed, only the metaphors.

Job 18:7–14 describes a fugitive who is caught in his own devices and eventually meets the judgment he has been running from. He runs, but soon he is out of breath ("his strong steps are shortened"; v. 7a). He falls to ground; his own sin has leveled him ("his own schemes throw him down"; v. 7b). When he regains some strength, he runs again. However, his foot is soon caught ("he is cast into a net by his own feet, and he walks on its mesh"; v. 8). We might imagine the man (Bildad has Job in mind) dragging himself along, step by slow step in this fishnet trap set for birds, and then suddenly, when it could get no worse, a metal bear trap "seizes him by the heel" (v. 9a). Imagine the pain! This "snare lays hold of him" (v. 9b). He is tired now. Bleeding. Screaming. Yet he moves on. Ah, but the way of the wicked is not safe (Ps. 1:6). Another trap is there to meet him:

> A rope is hidden for him in the ground,
> a trap   for him in the path. (Job 18:10)

He falls into a third trap. Tired. Bleeding. Screaming. And now there is no way for him to move forward.

What comes next is worse than the three traps. Terrors! "Terrors frighten him on every side" (v. 11a). He moves the mesh, snare, and rope an inch or so. And with every inch, terrors are chasing "him at his heels" (v. 11b). He has lost all might ("his strength is famished," v. 12a; or, "strength . . . consumed by hunger," NRSV).[93] Death or "calamity" is hungry as well—waiting for the white flag to be raised ("calamity is ready for his stumbling"; v. 12b). Death does not wait long to feast on the flesh. Slowly, it begins to nibble, eating away some of the outside of the entrapped man ("it consumes the parts of his skin"; v. 13a). Even death's offspring ("the firstborn of death"—perhaps the oddest image in the Bible—v. 13b), like a brood of vultures, join in the grotesque gorging ("consumes his limbs"; v. 13b). The wicked man is being *eaten* alive by death and its offspring!

Bildad is not done. His "Sinners in the Hands of an Angry *and Automated* God" has one more pointed point (vv. 14–20) and a cold conclusion (v. 21). The point made in verses 14–20 is that ruin of the wicked man's house ("tent," vv. 14, 15; "habitation," v. 15; "dwellings," "place," v. 21) and household ("memory," "name," v. 17; "posterity," "progeny," "survivor," v. 19) follows the demise of the man himself (vv. 7–14). Not only has he been torn from his seemingly secure home and given to death to devour (cf. v. 14), his secure reputation has been ousted out the window as well. It is being *eaten* with the winds of time. Instead of children—his legacy—his house is hellish.

---

93 Job 18:12a is difficult to translate. David J. A. Clines translates it as "Disaster is hungry for them" in *Job 1–20*, WBC 17 (Waco: Word, 1989), 405. It might be a synonymous parallelism, as the NIV translates it:

Calamity   is hungry   for him;
disaster   is ready   for him when he falls.

Within ("in his tent dwells") and above ("over his habitation") are not children who bear his name but scattered "sulfur" that burns all into oblivion (v. 15).

Bildad is awful here. He is directly telling Job, with the loss of his children, that his legacy has vanished. Job knows this, bemoans this. But Bildad does not care. He has another rhetorical exhibition to display:

> His roots   dry up   beneath,
> and his branches   wither   above. (v. 16)
>
> His memory perishes   from the earth,
> and he has no name   in the street. (v. 17)

Not only is "he [Job!] thrust from light into darkness" or, put another way, "driven out of the world" (v. 18) and his offspring annihilated ("he has no posterity"/"no survivor" "among his people"/"where he used to live"; v. 19); all the people "of the west"/"of the east" are disgusted by this wicked man's life as well ("are appalled at his day"/"horror seizes them"; v. 20).

All that is left are some words of consolation. But although God is finally mentioned (v. 21), this is no gospel of grace. Job receives only a poisonous sting. Like a scorpion, it is the tail of the sermon that hurts most. Bildad claims that Job, his only audience, does not know God (cf. 8:13, where he says that Job has forgotten God). The parallelism here sticks inside the reader, as it must have Job:

> Surely   such are   the dwellings   of the unrighteous,
>   such is   the place   of him who knows not God. (18:21)

The last word in both the English and the Hebrew lingers—"God" (Hb. *'el*). Will El, Elohim, or Yahweh, stand up and defend the innocent against such accusations?

Response

Speaking of the Bible's literary excellence, Jerome writes: "What is more polished than [the book of] Job?"[94] Bildad's words are indeed polished, as polished and sharpened as Ehud's dagger (Judg. 3:21). His poetry is beautiful, some of the best in the whole literary masterpiece. Whether in his simple analogies ("Can reeds flourish where there is no water?" Job 8:11; "he lays hold of [his house], but it does not endure," 8:15) or clever word pictures ("his roots entwine the stone heap," 8:17; "he is cast into a net by his own feet," 18:8), the poet philosopher impresses with his poetry but not his philosophy. Or his theology! It handcuffs God, puts him in a box, and closes the lid. It makes Yahweh not Yahweh but some deistic and robotic ruler who is as predictable as the master clock by which we set our watches.

But the God of the Bible does not think or act that way. God does not bow the knee to some fixed formula. His master is not the unchangeable law of tradition. The prologue and epilogue of Job tells us as much. The sovereign providence of

---

94 Cited in Michael Graves, *The Inspiration and Interpretation of Scripture: What the Early Church Can Teach Us* (Grand Rapids, MI: Eerdmans, 2014), 78.

God cannot be chained, or explained! The whole Bible, notably the gospel (God's becoming man and dying for our sins!), makes sure that we do not follow Bildad's philosophical and theological thought.

Bildad and his brothers in crime (against Job and God) have received their assessment from Job (they are "worthless physicians"; 13:4), and soon they will receive their verdict from God ("My anger burns against you and against your two friends, for you have not spoken of me what is right, as my servant Job has"; 42:7). We must offer our appraisal as well. We can be sympathetic with their mistake, but we should not be lenient. They are wrong! They do not speak rightly of God. They do not treat Job rightly. Like the Pharisees (Matt. 15:1–9), their tradition blinds their eyes to the truth. Like many atheists today, their system of thought is only a straightjacket against further exploration of the possibilities.

For Christians, especially Christian teachers, we must heed a warning to the wise—to become wise by not playing the fool. One qualification for being an elder in Christ's church is aptness to teach (2 Tim. 2:24). The rest of the qualifications, however, revolve around character, not skill or gifting. In fact, what surrounds that important teaching proviso in Timothy are all the qualities that Bildad does not demonstrate. Can we say that he is "not . . . quarrelsome but kind to everyone" (2 Tim. 2:24)? Can we say that he corrects his opponent "with gentleness," hoping that "God may perhaps grant [him] repentance leading to a knowledge of the truth" (2 Tim. 2:25)? And, even though we know that the friends—not Job—need to "come to their senses" and "escape from the snare of the devil" (Satan), as they are seemingly "captured by him to do his will" (2 Tim. 2:26), can we even say that they, at any point, turn to God in prayer (calling upon "the Lord from a pure heart"; 2 Tim. 2:22)—asking for his view on the matter? Sadly, the answer to all these questions is no. They breed this quarrel (contra Paul's admonition; cf. 2 Tim. 2:23)!

Moreover, these qualities, read in light of 2 Timothy and of the book of Job, remind us of James's warning: "Not many of you should become teachers . . . for you know that we who teach will be judged with greater strictness" (James 3:1). Thankfully (we breathe a sigh of relief), this warning is followed by the somewhat soothing words: "And if anyone does not stumble in what he says, he is a perfect man" (James 3:2). We are not perfect. But that does not stop James from continuing to prod our consciences. His short but provocative taming-of-the-tongue sermon follows (James 3:3–12). This sermon contains lines that both Bildad and every believer need to hear. Bildad has set ablaze a great forest with his tongue (cf. James 3:5). He has both blessed God and cursed Job in the same sentence (cf. James 3:9). The outcome is not good.

We cannot underestimate the high calling of Christian leadership. We must, by God's gracious and powerful Holy Spirit, tame our tongues. For wisdom, as James goes on to say, is shown in "meekness," not false truths (James 3:13–14). We all need the "wisdom that comes down from above," a wisdom that is not "earthly, unspiritual, demonic" but "pure, then peaceable, gentle, open to reason" (James 3:15–17). Such wisdom will produce "a harvest of righteousness" (James 3:18).

JOB 19:1–29

19 Then Job answered and said:

2 "How long will you torment me
   and break me in pieces with words?
3 These ten times you have cast reproach upon me;
   are you not ashamed to wrong me?
4 And even if it be true that I have erred,
   my error remains with myself.
5 If indeed you magnify yourselves against me
   and make my disgrace an argument against me,
6 know then that God has put me in the wrong
   and closed his net about me.
7 Behold, I cry out, 'Violence!' but I am not answered;
   I call for help, but there is no justice.
8 He has walled up my way, so that I cannot pass,
   and he has set darkness upon my paths.
9 He has stripped from me my glory
   and taken the crown from my head.
10 He breaks me down on every side, and I am gone,
   and my hope has he pulled up like a tree.
11 He has kindled his wrath against me
   and counts me as his adversary.
12 His troops come on together;
   they have cast up their siege ramp[1] against me
   and encamp around my tent.

13 "He has put my brothers far from me,
   and those who knew me are wholly estranged from me.
14 My relatives have failed me,
   my close friends have forgotten me.
15 The guests in my house and my maidservants count me as
       a stranger;
   I have become a foreigner in their eyes.
16 I call to my servant, but he gives me no answer;
   I must plead with him with my mouth for mercy.
17 My breath is strange to my wife,
   and I am a stench to the children of my own mother.
18 Even young children despise me;
   when I rise they talk against me.
19 All my intimate friends abhor me,
   and those whom I loved have turned against me.
20 My bones stick to my skin and to my flesh,
   and I have escaped by the skin of my teeth.

21 Have mercy on me, have mercy on me, O you my friends,
    for the hand of God has touched me!
22 Why do you, like God, pursue me?
    Why are you not satisfied with my flesh?

23 "Oh that my words were written!
    Oh that they were inscribed in a book!
24 Oh that with an iron pen and lead
    they were engraved in the rock forever!
25 For I know that my Redeemer lives,
    and at the last he will stand upon the earth.[2]
26 And after my skin has been thus destroyed,
    yet in[3] my flesh I shall see God,
27 whom I shall see for myself,
    and my eyes shall behold, and not another.
    My heart faints within me!
28 If you say, 'How we will pursue him!'
    and, 'The root of the matter is found in him,'[4]
29 be afraid of the sword,
    for wrath brings the punishment of the sword,
    that you may know there is a judgment."

[1] Hebrew *their way* [2] Hebrew *dust* [3] Or *without* [4] Many Hebrew manuscripts *in me*

Section Overview

Job 19 contains the most famous line from the book of Job: "I know that my Redeemer lives" (v. 25). As we shall see, in that section (vv. 23–27) Job does express hope for future vindication. However, what surrounds this fifth response to his friends are not many rays of hope but more clouds of darkness. Addressing his three friends ("my close friends," v. 14; "my intimate friends," v. 19; "my friends," v. 21), he denounces their friendship (vv. 1–6), for they have not accepted that God has brought these sufferings upon Job for no reason ("know then that God has put me in the wrong," v. 6a; "he has kindled his wrath against me," v. 11a; "the hand of God has touched me!" v. 21b). God has "stripped" him of his "glory" (v. 9a; cf. vv. 7–12), so much so that those closest to him—his wife, brothers, maidservants, etc.—distance themselves from him (vv. 13–22). Job wants Eliphaz, Bildad, and Zophar to accept these facts and to be merciful to him ("Have mercy on me, have mercy on me, O you my friends"; v. 21a). He wants them to stop their pursuit of him (v. 22). And he warns them what will happen if they do not: "be afraid of the sword" (vv. 28–29). Indeed, the final word—"judgment" (v. 29b)—is a word of warning.

Section Outline

II.K. Have Mercy on Me, Have Mercy on Me, O You My Friends
    (19:1–29)
      1. Tormented by Friends (19:1–6)
      2. Stripped of His Glory (19:7–12)

Comment

19:1–6 Bildad has used opening questions about Job's words to begin his speeches (cf. 8:2; 18:2). In 19:2 Job questions Bildad's words, along with those of Eliphaz and Zophar: "How long will you [plural] torment me and break me in pieces with words?" Job is not simply asking them to stop their useless talk; he is asking them to cease torturing him with their words. Their verbal reproaches seem endless ("these ten times"; v. 3a; cf. Gen. 31:7, 41; Num. 14:22), and these "friends" have no remorse for what they are doing to him (cf. Job 19:3b). He does not understand, for they have no case against him. There is no public, scandalous sin. And even if he has committed some small sin or inadvertent error (cf. Lev. 5:18), such a transgression and what God does with it is none of their business ("And even if it be true that I have erred, my error remains with myself"; Job 19:4). Although they have no legal leg to stand on, they exalt themselves above Job ("you magnify yourselves against me") and use his humiliation as the only proof of his sin ("and make my disgrace an argument against me"; v. 5). Job wants them to know that this is not wise. He wants them to accept his innocence and understand that his sufferings are a result of God's sovereign will ("know . . . that God has . . . closed his net about me"; v. 6).

19:7–12 Like Habakkuk (cf. Hab. 1:2–4), Job cries out, "Violence!" (Job 19:7). The difference is that Job is speaking of God's attack against him. The other difference is that God answers Habakkuk immediately, while Job still waits to hear from God: "Behold, I cry out, 'Violence!' but I am not answered; I call for help, but there is no justice" (v. 7). Job feels that God has been unjust ("God has put me in the wrong," v. 6; "there is no justice," v. 7b). Instead of treating Job like a righteous man, rewarding him with honor and lighting his way, God is treating him like the wicked:

> He has walled up my way, so that I cannot pass,
>   and he has set darkness upon my paths.
> He has stripped from me my glory
>   and taken the crown from my head.
> He breaks me down on every side, and I am gone,
>   and my hope has he pulled up like a tree. (vv. 8–10)

And instead of treating Job like a friend, providing for him and protecting him (cf. 1:10), God is treating him like an enemy:

> He has kindled his wrath against me
>   and counts me as his adversary.
> His troops come on together;

they have cast up their siege ramp against me
and encamp around my tent. (19:11–12)

With vivid images, Job describes his hopeless situation ("my hope has he pulled
up like a tree"; v. 10b). One moment he feels completely trapped (v. 8a). The next,
when he can move forward, he cannot see where he is going (v. 8b). He has lost all
the high dignity he once had (v. 9). He is the target of God's wrath (vv. 10a, 11–12).

19:13–22 From verse 6, Job has spoken about what God has done to him.

God has	put . . . in the wrong	(v. 6a)
[God has]	closed his net	(v. 6b)
He has	walled up	(v. 8a)
He has	set darkness	(v. 8b)
He has	stripped	(v. 9a)
[He has]	taken	(v. 9b)
He	breaks . . . down	(v. 10a)
He has	pulled up	(v. 10b)
He has	kindled	(v. 11a)
[He]	counts	(v. 11b)
His troops	come on together	(v. 12a)

In verse 13, he adds a final "He has":

He has put	my brothers	far from me
and	those who knew me	are wholly estranged from me.

With seven lines (vv. 13–19), Job bemoans the estrangement his sufferings have
caused between him and those closest to him: his "relatives" (v. 14a), "close friends"
(v. 14b), "wife" (v. 17a), brothers ("the children of my own mother"; v. 17b), and
"intimate friends," (v. 19; likely the "brothers" of v. 13a and "close friends" of v. 14b,
namely, Eliphaz, Bildad, and Zophar). He is even estranged from his household
servants (vv. 15, 16), former houseguests (v. 15), and children from the community
(v. 18). Collectively they have "failed" him (v. 14a), have "forgotten" him (v. 14b),
are repulsed by him (v. 17), will not help him (v. 16), "despise" (v. 18a) and "abhor"
him (v. 19a), and gossip against him (v. 18b). All those he has "loved have turned
against" him (v. 19b). His own wife and brothers will not go near him:

My breath is strange   to my wife,
and I am a stench   to the children of my own mother. (v. 17)

We can imagine the pain of such social estrangement and assaults, as well as
the physical pain. Job is literally skin and bones ("my bones stick to my skin and to
my flesh"; v. 20a). He is barely alive. He has eluded death narrowly ("I have escaped
by the skin of my teeth"; v. 20b). Job needs mercy; he begs for it: "Have mercy on
me, have mercy on me, O you my friends" (v. 21a). He needs Eliphaz, Bildad, and

Zophar to be real friends and stop their verbal attacks (v. 22; cf. v. 2). He hopes his physical condition is enough for them to show some compassion (v. 22b).

19:23–27 Following his plea for his friends to show mercy and stop attacking him (vv. 21–22), Job returns to a theme touched on in verse 7. There he said, "Behold, I cry out, 'Violence!' but I am not answered; I call for help, but there is no justice." In verses 23–27 Job's heart faints within him over the possibility of God's hearing and vindicating him. Job hopes that there might be a permanent written record of his vindication: one "inscribed in a book" (v. 23b) and another "engraved in the rock forever" (v. 24b)—two witnesses to attest to the verdict "not guilty."

Verses 25–27, perhaps the most famous verses of the book, stand out not only for their theological depth but also for their unusual tone. Job has been hopeless since chapter 3. Even in 19:10 he describes God's taking whatever deep root of hope Job still has and "pull[ing it] up like a tree." But now a new seed of hope emerges. Light flashes across the stage of this depressing drama. We can almost hear Job singing his solo from the score of Handel's *Messiah*.

> I know that my Redeemer lives,
>   and at the last he will stand upon the earth.
> And after my skin has been thus destroyed,
>   yet in my flesh I shall see God,
> whom I shall see for myself,
>   and my eyes shall behold, and not another.
> My heart faints within me! (vv. 25–27)

By capitalizing the word "Redeemer" (v. 25), the ESV is either linking the word with "God" in verse 26 or making a Christological connection (i.e., the "Redeemer" is Jesus). Some commentators think that the redeemer here is simply the advocate and witness Job has described in 9:32–35 and 16:18–22. If this is true, then Job is once again asking for an intermediator or arbitrator who can represent him before Yahweh. The hope of this representation is restoration. However, based on the immediate context, the context of the book, and other OT references, the most likely reading is that God himself is the "Redeemer" Job hopes for. In the immediate context, "Job's description of his 'Redeemer' as one who 'lives' (Job 19:25) and his following reference to 'God' (v. 26) indicate he believes that God is the one who ultimately will vindicate him."[95] In the context of the book, we learn from chapter 42 that God himself, not some human or angel, redeems (in the sense of vindicates and restores) Job. Finally, the idea of God as "Redeemer" is a familiar title (cf. Isa. 43:14; 44:6) and concept within the OT: God redeems his nation (Ex. 6:6) and individuals (Gen. 48:16).

The phrase "at the last he will stand upon the earth" (Job 19:25b) likely refers to God as Job's Redeemer, taking the stand on his behalf at the end of the ages (judgment day), or at last. Job perhaps envisions God standing next to him on the

---

95 *ESV Study Bible* note on Job 19:25–27.

ash heap ("the earth" could be translated "the dust"). Here we might say, as Hartley has, that "Job is beseeching the God in whom he has faith to help him against the God who is punishing him."[96] On that day ("at the last"; v. 25) and in that place (upon the "ashes"; 2:8), another paradox occurs. Not only is the court case *God v. God*, but Job, who has talked about death only as extinction thus far (7:9; 10:21; 14:10, 12), here speaks of dying ("after my skin has been thus destroyed"; 19:26a) and yet somehow seeing God vindicate him ("yet in my flesh I shall see God"; v. 26b), seemingly in some sort of resurrected state. "The references to skin, *flesh* and *eyes*," as Andersen points out, "make it clear that Job expects to have this experience as a man, not just as a disembodied shade, or in his mind's eye."[97] And the thought of this beatific vision ("God, whom I shall see . . . my eyes shall behold"; vv. 26–27ab) and beautiful vindication is too much for him to take in ("My heart faints within me!" v. 27c). This future theophany is the ground of his hope.

19:28–29 Job has asked his friends, in the politest manner thus far, to stop pursuing him (cf. v. 22). In these final two verses he warns them of what will happen if they do not stop:

> If you say, "How we will pursue him!"
>   and, "The root of the matter is found in him,"
> be afraid of the sword,
>   for wrath brings the punishment of the sword,
>   that you may know there is a judgment. (vv. 28–29)

Job cautions them that if they continue to harass him (v. 28a) with their false accusation that his sin is the root of his troubles (v. 28b), God's wrath that he has been experiencing (vv. 11, 29) will come upon them. Hanging above them like the sword of Damocles, Yahweh's "sword" (two times in v. 29; cf. Isa. 66:16) is soon to drop.

Response

Certainly, when Job in his historical context uttered 19:25–27 he was not thinking about Jesus' death and resurrection and the hope that Christians gain from those redemptive events. However, Christian commentators from the time of Origen on have read the text with Jesus our Redeemer in mind, and rightly so. We can and should rejoice that we have a Redeemer, a mediator who both is fully God (1 Tim. 2:5) and also has turned away the full wrath of God upon sinners (Rom. 5:9). We should celebrate that we have been redeemed by his blood (Eph. 1:7; Col. 1:20; Rev. 5:9) and have a "living hope" (1 Pet. 1:3) of a physical resurrection and final vindication because Jesus has conquered the grave. We should sing Handel's great aria in the *Messiah*, where Job 19:25–26 is juxtaposed with 1 Corinthians 15:20, "But now is Christ risen from the dead, and become the firstfruits of them that slept" (KJV). As Hartley well summarizes:

---

96 Hartley, *Job*, 295.
97 Francis I. Andersen, *Job*, TOTC (Leicester, UK: Inter-Varsity Press, 1976), 193.

Job is working with the same logic of redemption that stands as the premise of the NT doctrine of the resurrection. Both hold to the dogma that God is just even though he permits unrequited injustices and the suffering of the innocent. God, himself, identified with Job's sufferings in the sufferings of his Son, Jesus Christ, who suffered unto death even though he was innocent. Jesus overcame his ignominious death by rising from the grave. In his victory he, as God's Son and mankind's kinsman-redeemer, secured redemption for all who believe on him. While his followers may suffer in this life, he is their Redeemer, their Advocate before the Father. In this way Job's confidence in God as his Redeemer amidst excruciating suffering stands as a model for all Christians.[98]

Beyond this traditional Christian application of Job 19, we can also apply this text another way. Like Job, we must believe that vindication for the righteous will come, even if it does not come in our lifetime. Jesus' parable of the rich man and Lazarus makes this very point (Luke 16:19–31). We can trust God to do what is right in his right timing. We can "take courage" as we wait upon the Lord (Ps. 27:14).

JOB 20:1–29

20 Then Zophar the Naamathite answered and said:

2 "Therefore my thoughts answer me,
     because of my haste within me.
3 I hear censure that insults me,
     and out of my understanding a spirit answers me.
4 Do you not know this from of old,
     since man was placed on earth,
5 that the exulting of the wicked is short,
     and the joy of the godless but for a moment?
6 Though his height mount up to the heavens,
     and his head reach to the clouds,
7 he will perish forever like his own dung;
     those who have seen him will say, 'Where is he?'
8 He will fly away like a dream and not be found;
     he will be chased away like a vision of the night.
9 The eye that saw him will see him no more,
     nor will his place any more behold him.
10 His children will seek the favor of the poor,
     and his hands will give back his wealth.
11 His bones are full of his youthful vigor,
     but it will lie down with him in the dust.

---

98 Hartley, *Job*, 297.

¹² "Though evil is sweet in his mouth,
    though he hides it under his tongue,
¹³ though he is loath to let it go
    and holds it in his mouth,
¹⁴ yet his food is turned in his stomach;
    it is the venom of cobras within him.
¹⁵ He swallows down riches and vomits them up again;
    God casts them out of his belly.
¹⁶ He will suck the poison of cobras;
    the tongue of a viper will kill him.
¹⁷ He will not look upon the rivers,
    the streams flowing with honey and curds.
¹⁸ He will give back the fruit of his toil
    and will not swallow it down;
    from the profit of his trading
    he will get no enjoyment.
¹⁹ For he has crushed and abandoned the poor;
    he has seized a house that he did not build.

²⁰ "Because he knew no contentment in his belly,
    he will not let anything in which he delights escape him.
²¹ There was nothing left after he had eaten;
    therefore his prosperity will not endure.
²² In the fullness of his sufficiency he will be in distress;
    the hand of everyone in misery will come against him.
²³ To fill his belly to the full,
    God[1] will send his burning anger against him
    and rain it upon him into his body.
²⁴ He will flee from an iron weapon;
    a bronze arrow will strike him through.
²⁵ It is drawn forth and comes out of his body;
    the glittering point comes out of his gallbladder;
    terrors come upon him.
²⁶ Utter darkness is laid up for his treasures;
    a fire not fanned will devour him;
    what is left in his tent will be consumed.
²⁷ The heavens will reveal his iniquity,
    and the earth will rise up against him.
²⁸ The possessions of his house will be carried away,
    dragged off in the day of God's[2] wrath.
²⁹ This is the wicked man's portion from God,
    the heritage decreed for him by God."

[1] Hebrew *he*   [2] Hebrew *his*

Section Overview

Job 20 records Zophar's final words in the book of Job. His wisdom will not be missed. He beats the same old retribution principle drum: Sin. Leads. To. Suffering. And. Judgment. Sin. Leads. To. Suffering. And. Judgment. Verse 27 is a more poetic summary:

| The heavens | will reveal | his iniquity, |
| and the earth | will rise up | against him. |

The powers of heaven and earth will expose the evildoer eventually. Even after Job's insulting censure (cf. 19:2, 28–29), Zophar is sure that the E-B-Z brain trust is reliable in its assessment of Job's spiritual status (20:1–3). From the first moment man stepped on earth, a system of punishment and reward was put in place: do good things, get good things; do bad things, get bad things. Even if the wicked experience some joy and prosperity, the hammer of divine justice will soon be lowered. God will not let the wicked experience pleasure (vv. 4–11) or prosperity (vv. 20–29) for too long. Why? Because he is holy. He will not let the wickedness of the wicked win (vv. 12–19).

Section Outline

II.L. Heaven Reveals the Iniquity of the Wicked; the Earth Rises Up
       against Him (20:1–29)
  1. Zophar's Understanding on the Matter, Revisited (20:1–3)
  2. The Short-Lived Joys of the Wicked (20:4–11)
  3. The Wickedness of the Wicked (20:12–19)
  4. The Prosperity of the Wicked Will Not Endure (20:20–29)

Comment

20:1–3 The Naamathite speaks again. Has he listened to Job? Might Job be right? Will he ask Job clarifying questions to make sure he has the facts straight? No. No. No. He thinks. Indeed, he *thinks*. He is a theologian. Theologians think for a living. "Therefore," he starts, "my thoughts . . ." (v. 2). Do we want to hear his thoughts? Job does not. Job wants to hear from God. Zophar is troubled though. Distraught. Disturbed by Job's persistence and obvious ignorance. He must teach his troubled but confused friend. Zophar's inspired "understanding" (v. 3)[99] must take the higher ground—high above Job's "insults" (v. 3; cf. 19:2, 28–29).

20:4–11 To Job's bold attestation to the three friends—"know [*yada'*] then that God has put me in the wrong" (19:6)—Zophar replies: "Do you not know [*yada'*] this from of old, since man was placed on earth, that the exulting of the wicked is short, and the joy of the godless but for a moment?" (20:4–5).[100] Zophar's thesis here is clear: Any honor and happiness that the ungodly man might experience is like a candle burning in the wind (cf. Job's analogy in 21:18). Zophar elaborates on this thesis with further illustrations of the short-lived joys of the wicked. We might take back the high commendation we made about Bildad's poetry, for Zophar's lines soar higher!

---

99 The word "inspired" is used here because perhaps Zophar, with the use of the word "spirit" (Hb. *ruakh*), is claiming divine inspiration for his speech. This is more clearly the case with Eliphaz (4:15) and Elihu (32:8).
100 "Indeed, though he is not specifically citing Adam and Eve, Zophar could have mentioned that once Adam and Eve sinned, they suffered (Gen. 3), being cast out of Eden and then enduring pain in relationships and work" (Longman, *Job*, 268).

Though his height mount up to the heavens,
   and his head reach to the clouds,
he will perish forever like his own dung;
   those who have seen him will say, "Where is he?" (20:6–7)

These verses describe the brevity of the wicked man's honor and reputation. Even if a wicked man somehow obtains success in this life ("his height mount up to the heavens"/"his head reach to the clouds"; v. 6), he is eventually like dung sitting on a sulfur sidewalk: he will dissolve into the dirt (cf. v. 7). Verses 8–11 further embellish this theme. The question "Where is he?" (v. 7b) lingers. He is nowhere to be found. He is like "a dream"/"a vision of the night," and his achievements surreal: they "fly away"/"[are] chased away" (v. 8; cf. Prov. 23:5). All that he had and was is gone. The dream is over; reality sets in. "Where is he?" (Job 20:7b). Nowhere. Gone. He goes unnoticed even by his own household:

The eye that saw him will see him no more,
   nor will his place any more behold him. (v. 9)

The judgment is not over. Next, his iniquity is visited upon his offspring (cf. Ex. 20:5). His children become poorer than the poor. They must beg from the destitute for sustenance ("his children will seek the favor of the poor") because their father had to return all of his exploited earnings ("his hands will give back his wealth"; Job 20:10). Though he might seem healthy at the moment (his "bones are full of . . . youthful vigor"), such vigor will vanish at his sudden death ("but it will lie down with him in the dust"; v. 11).

Verses 4–11 are cruel cuts into Job. In one day, Job went from the penthouse to the poorhouse and his children from a lively party to nailed coffins. But is Zophar right? "Pride" does go "before destruction, and a haughty spirit before a fall" (Prov. 16:18), but has "the greatest of all the people of the east" (Job 1:3) fallen into such disgrace due to arrogance or some other sin? We know the answer. Job does too. But Zophar is still blind, and in his blindness he continues his barrage of true statements falsely applied.

20:12–19 While "evil" is mentioned in verse 12, the only specific stated sin comes in verse 19: "he has crushed and abandoned the poor; he has seized a house that he did not build." The picture we might envision, which is close to what Zophar sees, is that of a real estate mogul who has pushed out the poor for profit. He buys low and sells high, leaving his neighbor high and dry. Ah, but as Proverbs says, so too does Zophar: "Whoever oppresses the poor to increase his own wealth, . . . will only come to poverty" (Prov. 22:16; cf. Job 20:21, 28). More than that, this "whoever" (Job!) will eat his losses first.

Eating is the main metaphor of Job 20:12–29, with terms such as "sweet in his mouth" (v. 12a), "under his tongue" (v. 12b), "in his mouth (v. 13b), "food . . . in his stomach" (v. 14a), "swallows" (v. 15a), "vomits" (v. 15a), "belly" (v. 15b), "suck" (v. 16a), "tongue" (v. 16b), "honey and curds" (v. 17b), "fruit" (v. 18a), and "swallow" (v. 18b).

The overall image is disgusting: the wicked man is destroyed by his own appetite for evil. Put differently, his own evil eats him alive. First, the man sits down to enjoy a delicacy. While it is "sweet in his mouth"—so sweet that he savors it "under his tongue" and "holds it in his mouth"—he is actually eating "evil" (vv. 12–13). Then, what he is "loath to let ... go" will now not let go of him (v. 13a). The "food" in "his stomach" turns to wormwood (v. 14a); it is like "the venom of cobras within him" (v. 14b). What he has swallowed down are those ill-gained "riches" (v. 15a; cf. vv. 18d–19; see also 1 Tim. 6:10). He "vomits them up again" (Job 20:15a). This is one perspective on the scene; the other is God's, who also has his hand in the mess: "God casts them out of his belly" (v. 15b). The image, of course, is not of a spew of the stew on the table; rather, it is of the wicked man's wealth being taken from him (cf. v. 10).

Verses 16–18 continue with both the food metaphors and the theme of the consequences for the wicked man's wickedness. Instead of the "delicious but deadly food" of verses 12–15,[101] the cuisine of verse 16 is repulsive:

> He will suck the poison of cobras;
>   the tongue of a viper will kill him. (v. 16)

This venomous meal is his last meal. No more picnics along the riverbank ("he will not look upon the rivers"), with delicious delights to feast upon ("honey and curds"; v. 17). No more fine wines to sip. It is payback time!

> He will give back the fruit of his toil
>   and will not swallow it down;
> from the profit of his trading
>   he will get no enjoyment. (v. 18)

The joys of this wealthy wicked man were short-lived.

20:20–29 While Zophar continues with more of his digestion metaphors ("no contentment in his belly," v. 20a; "nothing left after he had eaten," v. 21a; "fill his belly to the full," v. 23a) and adds military ones ("an iron weapon," v. 24a; "a bronze arrow," v. 24b), three main points are made here. The first two have been made already: first, the joys of the wicked are temporary; second, the prosperity of the wicked will not endure. The first point appears to be made in verse 20:

> Because he knew no contentment in his belly,
>   he will not let anything in which he delights escape him.

The sense of this verse is difficult. It perhaps means that his "greed will lead to cravings that cannot be satisfied,"[102] or, in the words of Isaiah 48:22, "There is no peace ... for the wicked." The second point is made in Job 20:21, 28. After the wicked man indulged in his ill-gotten gains, "there was nothing left after he had eaten" (v. 21a). Put less metaphorically, "his prosperity will not endure" (v. 21b).

---

101 Robert Alden, *Job*, NAC 11 (Nashville: B&H, 1993), 215.
102 Estes, *Job*, 124.

The possessions of his house will be carried away,
> dragged off in the day of God's wrath. (v. 28)

The phrase "God's wrath" introduces us to the third point found in these final verses, namely, that God will strike the wicked man's body and soul before he dies. While people will attack him ("the hand of everyone in misery will come against him"; v. 22b) and all creation testify against him ("the heavens . . . and the earth will rise up against him"; v. 27), the enemy to fear most is God. When the wicked man is resting at ease with a full stomach ("in the fullness of his sufficiency," v. 22a; "fill his belly to the full," v. 23a), God's judgment will strike him. He will suffer in soul ("he will be in distress," v. 22a; "terrors come upon him," v. 25c). He will suffer in body:

> To fill his belly to the full,
> > God will send his burning anger against him
> > and rain it upon him into his body.
> He will flee from an iron weapon;
> > a bronze arrow will strike him through.
> It is drawn forth and comes out of his body;
> > the glittering point comes out of his gallbladder;
> > terrors come upon him.
> Utter darkness is laid up for his treasures;
> > a fire not fanned will devour him;
> > what is left in his tent will be consumed. (vv. 23–26)

Wicked men like Job, Zophar is saying, experience such a living hell. Utter darkness; an unquenchable fire; an impaled body. Zophar's version of the inferno of Elohim's anger is as fierce as Dante's!

Moreover, finally, and to be absolutely clear, Zophar concludes his speech, saying that such divine burning anger has been divinely decreed:

> This is the wicked man's portion from God,
> > the heritage decreed for him by God. (v. 29)

Response

Zophar is right that God has ordained such punishment for the wicked. Indeed, Jesus himself, in the parable of the rich fool (Luke 12:13–21), teaches many of the same lessons as we learn here, such as (a) watch out for wealth and (b) God often judges evildoers unexpectedly. We need to be warned about the dangers of wealth.

> [Jesus] said to them, "Take care, and be on your guard against all covetousness, for one's life does not consist in the abundance of his possessions." (Luke 12:15)

We need to be reminded of the righteous, and potentially sudden, judgment of God.

God said to him, "Fool! This night your soul is required of you, and the things you have prepared, whose will they be?" So is the one who lays up treasure for himself and is not rich toward God. (Luke 12:20–21; cf. Jer. 17:11).

But we also need to learn about God's grace. In his commentary on Job, Christopher Ash asks an excellent question: "Why do we have to go on and on listening to these dreadful speeches?" His answer is important: "These speeches stand as a warning to us to guard grace jealously."[103] What Job needed from Zophar was not a reminder of the deceitfulness of riches, the fleetingness of earthly pleasures, or the burning heat of God's anger. He needed soothing words—God's grace for sinners; God's grace for sufferers. He needed to hear a sermon not on Romans 6:23a ("for the wages of sin is death"), but on Romans 6:23b ("but the free gift of God is eternal life in Christ Jesus our Lord"). He needed to hear a sermon not on Deuteronomy 32:35 ("In due time their foot will slip"—the text for Jonathan Edwards's famous "Sinners in the Hands of an Angry God") but on 2 Corinthians 12:7–10:

> To keep me from becoming conceited . . . a thorn was given me in the flesh, a messenger of Satan to harass me. . . . Three times I pleaded with the Lord about this, that it should leave me. But he said to me, "My grace is sufficient for you, for my power is made perfect in weakness." Therefore I will boast all the more gladly of my weaknesses, so that the power of Christ may rest upon me. For the sake of Christ, then, I am content with weaknesses, insults, hardships, persecutions, and calamities. For when I am weak, then I am strong.

JOB 21:1–34

21 Then Job answered and said:

2 "Keep listening to my words,
      and let this be your comfort.
3 Bear with me, and I will speak,
      and after I have spoken, mock on.
4 As for me, is my complaint against man?
      Why should I not be impatient?
5 Look at me and be appalled,
      and lay your hand over your mouth.
6 When I remember, I am dismayed,
      and shuddering seizes my flesh.

---

103 Ash, *Job*, 219.

7 Why do the wicked live,
    reach old age, and grow mighty in power?
8 Their offspring are established in their presence,
    and their descendants before their eyes.
9 Their houses are safe from fear,
    and no rod of God is upon them.
10 Their bull breeds without fail;
    their cow calves and does not miscarry.
11 They send out their little boys like a flock,
    and their children dance.
12 They sing to the tambourine and the lyre
    and rejoice to the sound of the pipe.
13 They spend their days in prosperity,
    and in peace they go down to Sheol.
14 They say to God, 'Depart from us!
    We do not desire the knowledge of your ways.
15 What is the Almighty, that we should serve him?
    And what profit do we get if we pray to him?'
16 Behold, is not their prosperity in their hand?
    The counsel of the wicked is far from me.

17 "How often is it that the lamp of the wicked is put out?
    That their calamity comes upon them?
    That God[1] distributes pains in his anger?
18 That they are like straw before the wind,
    and like chaff that the storm carries away?
19 You say, 'God stores up their iniquity for their children.'
    Let him pay it out to them, that they may know it.
20 Let their own eyes see their destruction,
    and let them drink of the wrath of the Almighty.
21 For what do they care for their houses after them,
    when the number of their months is cut off?
22 Will any teach God knowledge,
    seeing that he judges those who are on high?
23 One dies in his full vigor,
    being wholly at ease and secure,
24 his pails[2] full of milk
    and the marrow of his bones moist.
25 Another dies in bitterness of soul,
    never having tasted of prosperity.
26 They lie down alike in the dust,
    and the worms cover them.

27 "Behold, I know your thoughts
    and your schemes to wrong me.
28 For you say, 'Where is the house of the prince?
    Where is the tent in which the wicked lived?'
29 Have you not asked those who travel the roads,
    and do you not accept their testimony
30 that the evil man is spared in the day of calamity,
    that he is rescued in the day of wrath?

31 Who declares his way to his face,
   and who repays him for what he has done?
32 When he is carried to the grave,
   watch is kept over his tomb.
33 The clods of the valley are sweet to him;
   all mankind follows after him,
   and those who go before him are innumerable.
34 How then will you comfort me with empty nothings?
   There is nothing left of your answers but falsehood."

[1] Hebrew *he* [2] The meaning of the Hebrew word is uncertain

Section Overview

Job has had it! Again. Zophar is blind to the way the world works and how God has chosen to rule. The wicked do not always die sudden deaths as they drink the venom of asps and watch their children bleed to death with God-induced iron spears sticking out their necks. No, "the wicked live" (Job 21:7)! They live in the sense that they prosper (vv. 7–16, esp. vv. 13, 16) and that God lets them flourish (vv. 17–21). "How often is it that the lamp of the wicked is put out?" (v. 17). "Not often," says shuddering, dismayed, and utterly impatient Job (cf. vv. 1–6). With a second almost theophany-like moment (cf. 19:25–27), Job seems to understand that God can do whatever he wants ("Will any teach God knowledge, seeing that he judges those who are on high?"; 21:22). Job gets that humans cannot get God completely. For, using his ash-heap observation of how the world works, Job reckons that the righteous and the wicked look the same after the dust covers them and the worms devour their flesh (v. 26). In verses 27–34, Job ends autobiographically, as he began ("I" [6x], "me" [5x], "my" [3x] in vv. 1–6, 27–34). He also ends with that great word "behold" (v. 27; used at key points throughout Job—e.g., Job 1:12; 2:6; 28:28). Job wants us to *see* something special. What is it? That his three friends are wrong. Their "comfort" is "empty nothings," false prophesies (v. 34). The wicked fare far better than pure and pious Job.

Section Outline

II.M. The Inexplicable Blessedness of the Wicked (21:1–34)
  1. Mocking the Mockers, with a Tear in His Eye (21:1–6)
  2. The Wicked Prosper, You Idiots! (21:7–21)
  3. Will You Teach God Knowledge? (21:22–26)
  4. There Is Nothing Left of Your Answers but Falsehood (21:27–34)

Comment

21:1–6 With his very autobiographical opening (note the use of "I," "me," and "my" in every verse), Job mocks his mockers with a tear in his eye. The mocking sarcasm is obvious.

> Keep listening to my words,
>> and let this be your comfort.
> Bear with me, and I will speak,
>> and after I have spoken, mock on. (vv. 2–3)

Instead of the three friends' bringing Job comfort with their words, Job is bringing them "comfort," in the sense of providing them more concepts with which to debate him. He asks them to listen just so they will have more ammunition for their next insensitive attack.

With all this, though, Job wants their sympathy for his spiritual dilemma. He is directing his complaint not against them ("Is my complaint against man?"; v. 4a) but against God. It is true that Job is "impatient" (4:2, 5), but it is a justifiable impatience, as God refuses to speak to him and settle the situation (21:4b). He also wants his friends' sympathy for his physical sufferings. He wants them to make a fresh examination of his sore and skinny body ("look at me") and be so "appalled" that they are left speechless ("lay your hand over your mouth"; v. 5). He further wants their sympathy for his psychological sufferings. When Job recalls what happened to his children and wealth on that one day and his loss of status and reputation ever since ("when I remember"), he is "dismayed" (or "terrified"; v. 6a). He is so terrified that it affects his body ("shuddering seizes my flesh"; v. 6b).

21:7–16 Job moves from a plea for their sympathy to a corrective of their theology. In response to Zophar's claim that the wicked always suffer even if they experience prosperity and pleasure for a fleeting minute, Job argues the opposite (vv. 7–21): the wicked seem to thrive in this world. And God obviously lets them.

Those two arguments are the two points of his speech. First, the wicked thrive. Using exaggerated generalizations, Job lists how "the wicked" (three times in vv. 7–17) reside in safety ("their houses are safe from fear"; v. 9a), "grow mighty in power" (v. 7b), increase in wealth ("they spend their days in prosperity," v. 13a; "prosperity [is] in their hand," v. 16a), live long lives ("live, reach old age"; v. 7), see their children and grandchildren ("their offspring are established in their presence, and their descendants before their eyes"; v. 8), and die peaceful deaths ("in peace they go down to Sheol"; v. 13b). More than that, their livestock are fruitful and multiply.

> Their bull breeds without fail;
>> their cow calves and does not miscarry. (v. 10)

And, perhaps most ironic of all, the children of the wicked are happy!

> They send out their little boys like a flock,
>> and their children dance.
> They sing to the tambourine and the lyre
>> and rejoice to the sound of the pipe. (vv. 11–12)

Second, God lets the wicked and their children sing and skip and dance through life. Job says it this way: "No rod of God is upon them" (v. 9b). God does not discipline them through disasters. He lets them live their lives, even though they do not acknowledge his gifts; the phrase "Behold, is not their prosperity in their hand?" (v. 16a) can also be rendered "But their prosperity is not their own doing" (NET). Moreover, God lets them live their lives, even though they deride him and his ways.

> They say to God, "Depart from us!
>> We do not desire the knowledge of your ways.
> What is the Almighty, that we should serve him?
>> And what profit do we get if we pray to him?" (vv. 14–15)

Praise and prayer are of no profit. Revelation of God's law—such as "Beware lest you say in your heart, 'My power and the might of my hand have gotten me this wealth'" (Deut. 8:17)—is not needed. Allegiance to the Almighty is wholly impractical. Job does not understand why this is the case. "It's beyond me how they can carry on like this!" (Job 21:16a MESSAGE) is Eugene Peterson's helpful paraphrase of "The counsel of the wicked is far from me."

21:17–21 As the last section opened with a question ("Why do the wicked live, reach old age, and grow mighty in power?"; v. 7), so too does this one ("How often is it that the lamp of the wicked is put out?"; v. 17). This second question is very similar to the first, being a different way of stating the same problem Job faces. It also connects especially with the second point of Job's speech in verses 7–16: God lets the wicked thrive. Zophar has claimed that the wicked and their offspring are destroyed, often quite suddenly ("You say, 'God stores up their iniquity for their children'"; v. 19; cf. Eliphaz in 5:4). Job disagrees. It is rare ("how often"; 21:17a) that God judges the wicked—that "calamity comes upon them" (v. 17b), that they experience pain (v. 17c) or, metaphorically, are "like straw before the wind, and like chaff that the storm carries away" (v. 18).

Job wants God to judge justly: "Let him pay it out to them, that they may know it" (v. 19b). He thinks that they should experience what he is experiencing: "Let their own eyes see their destruction, and let them drink of the wrath of the Almighty" (v. 20). But he knows this is usually not the case. He also knows that once they die and are buried for a few months ("when the number of their months is cut off"; v. 21b), the wicked are not worrying about what will happen to their children and grandchildren ("For what do they care for their houses after them . . . ?"; v. 21a).

21:22–26 Job pauses to ponder the incomprehensible way in which God governs the world, and how "God's exercise of justice transcends what humans can comprehend."[104] Starting with another rhetorical question—"Will any teach God knowledge, seeing that he judges those who are on high?" (v. 22)—Job clarifies his confusion. As he observes the world, it is not apparent—certainly not as black and white as Eliphaz, Bildad, and Zophar claim—that the retribution principle holds true in every case. Job illustrates the grayness of actual life with an illustration of

---

104 Estes, *Job*, 130.

two deaths ("one dies," v. 23a; "another dies," v. 25a). The first man dies "in his full vigor, being wholly at ease and secure" (v. 23), his body having been well nourished and his bones healthy ("his pails full of milk and the marrow of his bones moist"; v. 24) his whole life. The second man dies an awful death ("dies in bitterness of soul") after living a miserable life ("never having tasted of prosperity"; v. 25).

We might picture the first man as the wicked man described above (vv. 7–16) and righteous Job as the second man. Job, however, does not tell us who is who. What he does say is that what the two men now have in common is their decaying dead bodies:

> They lie down alike in the dust,
>   and the worms cover them. (v. 26)

Death makes their lives—whether lived for the glory of God or for the glory of self—indistinguishable. The point Job is making is the one he has been making since verse 7. The slightly new nuance is that even the death of the wicked does not necessarily correspond with how he lived. He might have a painful death or a peaceful one. God alone determines.

21:27–34 Job returns to his direct and personal confrontation of his friends, bookending this section with accusations; the first is an accusation of their evil intentions ("your thoughts and your schemes to wrong me"; v. 27) and the second of their useless and untrue counsel ("How then will you comfort me with empty nothings? There is nothing left of your answers but falsehood"; v. 34).

In between those two accusations, Job revises his argument. He first returns to the good life of bad people (cf. vv. 7–21) and how it is obvious to anyone who has observed the world that the wicked are not always judged. Using questions, Job features his friends' perspective that both the name and the place of the wicked perish with him. "You say, 'Where is the house of the prince? Where is the tent in which the wicked lived?'" (v. 28). He follows their perspective with his:

> Have you not asked those who travel the roads,
>   and do you not accept their testimony
> that the evil man is spared in the day of calamity,
>   that he is rescued in the day of wrath?
> Who declares his way to his face,
>   and who repays him for what he has done? (vv. 29–31)

Job counsels his friends, saying that simple observation, or simply asking someone who has seen the world (accepting the "testimony" of "those who travel the roads"; v. 29), will tell them that God's anger does not always show itself against the "evil man" ("he is rescued in the day of wrath"; v. 30). God neither rebukes them ("Who declares his way to his face . . . ?"; v. 31a) nor repays them for their crimes ("Who repays him for what he has done?"; v. 31b). Moreover, the funeral of the ungodly is glorious, and their name lives on—"engraved in the rock forever" (cf. 19:24).

> When he is carried to the grave,
>> watch is kept over his tomb. (21:32)

After a massive procession to the gravesite ("all mankind follows after him, and those who go before him are innumerable"; v. 33bc), he is lowered into the ground ("the clods of the valley are sweet to him"; v. 33a), where he rests in peace. Job might even picture a smile on the man's face.

Response

The same dilemma that Job expresses in Job 21 is expressed in Psalm 73, and it has been expressed by many believers throughout the centuries as well.

In her celebrated novel *Uncle Tom's Cabin*, Harriet Beecher Stowe provides a dramatic depiction of the common cruelties of slavery in America. In perhaps the most theologically charged scene of the book, George and his wife, Eliza—two runaway slaves—along with Simeon, an old, white Quaker who is assisting in their escape, learn that a party of slave traders and officers of the law are close at hand. So George in his anger, fear, and frustration thunders:

> Is God on their side? . . . Does he see all they do? Why does he let such things happen? . . . They are rich, and healthy, and happy; they are . . . expecting to go to heaven; and they get along so easy in the world, and have it all their own way; and poor, honest, faithful Christians—Christians as good or better than they—are lying in the very dust under their feet. They buy 'em and sell 'em, and make trade of their heart's blood, and groans and tears—and God *lets* them.

After George's complaint, Simeon, a courageous Christian who daily risks his life for slaves, opens his Bible and reads the first eleven verses of Psalm 73, in which the psalmist confesses his envy of the arrogant, his problem with the prosperity of the wicked. "Why do they get away with it?" is the psalmist's basic question. At this point, Simeon pauses, turns to George, and asks, "Is not that the way thee feels, George?" To that he replies, "It is so, indeed, . . . as well as I could have written it myself." Then Simeon continues, reading how the psalmist comes into the sanctuary of God, where he sees God rightly. There he has a vision of God's wrath coming upon all wrongdoers and his compassion showering his saints, loving the lowly. "It is good for me," the psalmist says, "to draw near unto God: I have put my trust in the Lord God" (cf. Ps. 73:28 KJV). These words "breathed by the friendly old man," we are told, "stole like sacred music over the harassed and chafed spirit of George." And Simeon said to him, "If this world were all, George, . . . thee might, indeed, ask, Where is the Lord? But it is often those who have least of all in this life whom He chooseth for the kingdom. Put thy trust in Him, and, no matter what befalls thee here, He will make all right hereafter."[105]

---

[105] The above quotes are all taken from Harriet Beecher Stowe, *Uncle Tom's Cabin*, EML (repr., New York: Knopf, 1995), 216–217, emphasis hers. This illustration is taken from Douglas Sean O'Donnell, *God's Lyrics: Rediscovering Worship through Old Testament Songs* (Phillipsburg, NJ: P&R, 2010), 87, 105–106.

Job needs such a vision of God. Now he can only see dimly, his vision impaired by his injuries. The wicked do not always prosper in the way he describes. And, most importantly, God will judge the wicked and vindicate the righteous. Put simply, Job needs Job 38–42! All believers need that revelation—to see God and hear from God that he is in control and working in accord with his wise plan. Eventually, God "will make all right." In the meantime, we must "put [our] trust in him . . . no matter what befalls [us] here."

JOB 22:1–30

22 Then Eliphaz the Temanite answered and said:

2 "Can a man be profitable to God?
   Surely he who is wise is profitable to himself.
3 Is it any pleasure to the Almighty if you are in the right,
   or is it gain to him if you make your ways blameless?
4 Is it for your fear of him that he reproves you
   and enters into judgment with you?
5 Is not your evil abundant?
   There is no end to your iniquities.
6 For you have exacted pledges of your brothers for nothing
   and stripped the naked of their clothing.
7 You have given no water to the weary to drink,
   and you have withheld bread from the hungry.
8 The man with power possessed the land,
   and the favored man lived in it.
9 You have sent widows away empty,
   and the arms of the fatherless were crushed.
10 Therefore snares are all around you,
   and sudden terror overwhelms you,
11 or darkness, so that you cannot see,
   and a flood of water covers you.

12 "Is not God high in the heavens?
   See the highest stars, how lofty they are!
13 But you say, 'What does God know?
   Can he judge through the deep darkness?
14 Thick clouds veil him, so that he does not see,
   and he walks on the vault of heaven.'
15 Will you keep to the old way
   that wicked men have trod?
16 They were snatched away before their time;
   their foundation was washed away.[1]
17 They said to God, 'Depart from us,'
   and 'What can the Almighty do to us?'[2]

18 Yet he filled their houses with good things—
      but the counsel of the wicked is far from me.
19 The righteous see it and are glad;
      the innocent one mocks at them,
20 saying, 'Surely our adversaries are cut off,
      and what they left the fire has consumed.'

21 "Agree with God, and be at peace;
      thereby good will come to you.
22 Receive instruction from his mouth,
      and lay up his words in your heart.
23 If you return to the Almighty you will be built up;
      if you remove injustice far from your tents,
24 if you lay gold in the dust,
      and gold of Ophir among the stones of the torrent-bed,
25 then the Almighty will be your gold
      and your precious silver.
26 For then you will delight yourself in the Almighty
      and lift up your face to God.
27 You will make your prayer to him, and he will hear you,
      and you will pay your vows.
28 You will decide on a matter, and it will be established for you,
      and light will shine on your ways.
29 For when they are humbled you say, 'It is because of pride';[3]
      but he saves the lowly.
30 He delivers even the one who is not innocent,
      who will be delivered through the cleanness of your hands."

[1] Or *their foundation was poured out as a stream* (or *river*) [2] Hebrew *them* [3] Or *you say, 'It is exaltation'*

Section Overview

As he began the first cycle of dialogues (Job 4:1), so Eliphaz begins the third and final cycle. The three friends have little left to say (Bildad only six verses in ch. 25; Zophar none). Eliphaz speaks for thirty verses in the hope that Job will see his ethical sins (22:2–11) and theological naivety (vv. 12–20), leading him to repent and be restored (vv. 21–30).

Section Outline

II.N. Accusation and Exhortation (22:1–30)
    1. Does the Almighty Concern Himself with Your Cause? (22:1–3)
    2. Job's Ethical Iniquities; God's Holy Judgments (22:4–11)
    3. Job's Theological Naivety (22:12–20)
    4. Repentance and Restoration (22:21–30)

Comment

22:1–3 As a "caring" friend (cf. 2:11), Eliphaz begins by telling Job that God could not care less about his plight. The two questions in Job 22:2–3 center on God's transcendence and self-sufficiency. God does not need man's help in running the universe ("Can a man be profitable to God?"; v. 2a). Not even a smart, sensible, and skilled man could lend God a hand ("surely he who is wise is profitable to himself"; v. 2b). Contra the depiction of God in the prologue, where he takes great notice of Job's piety, Eliphaz claims that God receives no pleasure or profit from Job's blameless and upright life.

> Is it any pleasure   to the Almighty   if you are in the right,
> or is it gain   to him   if you make your ways blameless? (v. 3)

Eliphaz calls God "the Almighty" (Hb. *shadday*) five times in this chapter, more times than in any other chapter. Perhaps this name is used because Job has recently used it (21:15, 20). Or perhaps it is employed because it is a title that well expresses the distance and detachment Eliphaz is emphasizing. Either way, the Almighty has not been impressed by Job's actions; he has not even noticed them.

22:4–11 This section also begins with a question, a sarcastic one: "Is it for your fear of him that he reproves you and enters into judgment with you?" (v. 4). Eliphaz becomes extremely aggressive here. Even though God could not care less about Job's supposed holiness, he somehow and for some reason notices his wickedness. In his punishing providence, God is rebuking Job and calling out his crimes.

> Is not your evil abundant?
> There is no end to your iniquities. (v. 5)

To call Job a sinner is one thing; to claim that his evil is abundant and his iniquities endless is quite the insensitive exaggeration. What has Job done?

The charges are next listed. Such a list is new. The friends have rarely made more than generalizations and guesses at Job's sins (e.g., impatience, pride). Now Eliphaz makes three accusations (table 4.5).[106]

TABLE 4.5: Eliphaz's Short List of Job's Sins

Charge	Verse
Exploiting the needy	You have exacted pledges of your brothers for nothing and stripped the naked of their clothing. (v. 6)
Letting the hungry starve	You have given no water to the weary to drink, and you have withheld bread from the hungry. (v. 7)
Oppressing orphans and widows	The man with power possessed the land, and the favored man lived in it.* You have sent widows away empty, and the arms of the fatherless were crushed. (vv. 8–9)

* Regarding 22:8, though it could be an additional charge, the verse could also be related to what comes either before it ("You gave no water to the weary and you withheld food from the hungry, though you were a powerful man, owning land—an honored man, living on it"; 22:7–8 NIV) or after it ("Although you were a powerful man, owning land, an honored man living on it, you sent widows away empty-handed, and the arms of the orphans you crushed"; 22:8–9 NET). We favor the second translation and interpretation.

---

106 The epistle of James perhaps echoes Eliphaz here (cf. James 1:27; 2:1–7, 14–16; 5:1–6). These crimes also relate to various OT laws (cf. Ex. 22:22, 26; Deut. 24:6, 17–18).

The reader knows that this list is outrageous, but he or she also senses that so too does Eliphaz. In the months he has been with Job, has he seen Job ripping off his own family or not sharing his food with the famished?

Whatever the specific sins, the verdict is settled in Eliphaz's mind by the fact of Job's sufferings. The self-professed innocent man is guilty as charged. His punishment is just. Job is trapped and terrified by his sins ("therefore snares are all around you, and sudden terror overwhelms you"; v. 10). God's judgment is consuming him. His feet are ensnared, the lights are turned off ("darkness, so that you cannot see"; v. 11a), and the waters of God's wrath start to fill his jail cell ("a flood of water covers you"; v. 11b).

22:12–20 Just as Eliphaz ended the last section with God's judgment depicted as "darkness" and a "flood of water" (v. 11), so he ends this section by speaking of the "fire" of God's wrath (v. 20). He begins, however, with a psalm-like statement about the exalted God. The psalmist sings, "For you, O LORD, are most high over all the earth; you are exalted far above all gods" (Ps. 97:9). Eliphaz states, with a rhetorical question, "Is not God high in the heavens? See the highest stars, how lofty they are!" (Job 22:12). The reason Eliphaz returns to the theme of God's transcendence is to correct Job's perception of reality.

In verses 13–20, three characters speak and one acts. Job speaks ("you say"; v. 13), the wicked speak ("they said to God"; v. 17), and the righteous speak ("saying"; v. 20); God acts ("he filled"; v. 18). In verses 13–14, Eliphaz misinterprets Job's early statements (e.g., perhaps 7:17), putting these words in his mouth,

> You say, "What does God know?
>   Can he judge through the deep darkness?
> Thick clouds veil him, so that he does not see,
>   and he walks on the vault of heaven." (22:13–14)

The accusation here is that Job thinks that God is so exalted ("he walks on the vault of heaven"; 14b) that he cannot see through the clouds ("through the deep darkness," v. 13b; "thick clouds," v. 14a); and, because his perception is obstructed ("What does God know?" v. 13a; "he does not see," v. 14a; cf. 21:14; Ps. 73:11), so too is his justice ("Can he judge through the deep darkness?"; Job 22:13b). In other words, God's transcendence trumps his omniscience, his otherworldliness his care for the earth and earthlings.

In verses 15–18, Eliphaz describes the way and words of the wicked and how God wipes out their way and makes them eat their words. In verses 21–30, Eliphaz encourages Job to repent so he might reap the rewards of righteousness. Here, however, he warns him to escape the path of judgment:

> Will you keep to the old way
>   that wicked men have trod?
> They were snatched away before their time;
>   their foundation was washed away. (vv. 15–16)

The image is of that of the wicked walking on the old and well-worn path of wickedness when all of a sudden the rain starts. Hours pass. Days. Soon enough, like the generation of Noah (cf. Gen. 6:5–7, 11–13; 7:4, 11–12, 17–23; Matt. 24:37–39), the wicked are wiped out. Even the foundations of their homes are swept away in the flood (cf. Matt. 7:26–27). They thought they were untouchable, but their only relationship with their Creator was to mock his power: "They said to God, 'Depart from us,' and 'What can the Almighty do to us?'" (Job 22:17). They want to be left alone. But God will not leave them alone, and he has not let them alone. In fact, he has been good to them for so much of their lives ("he filled their houses with good things"; v. 18; cf. Matt. 5:45). The way of the wicked, Eliphaz continues, makes no sense to him ("the counsel of the wicked is far from me"; Job 22:18b). Or perhaps he is saying, in a more self-righteous tone, "Is not the plan of the wicked far from me?"[107] He cannot conceive of how anyone would want to walk right into God's wrath!

Eliphaz next steps back from the judgment scene not to weep for the wicked but to rejoice over them. He sings his version of Revelation's Hallelujah chorus (cf. Rev. 19:1–4). He joins the voices of the saints:

> The righteous see it and are glad;
>   the innocent one mocks at them,
> saying, "Surely our adversaries are cut off,
>   and what they left the fire has consumed." (Job 22:19–20)

The wicked and their wealth have been consumed by the fire of God, and the godly ("the righteous"/"the innocent"; v. 19) rejoice in it as they taunt the proud and foolish ways of their "adversaries" (v. 20a).

22:21–30 Because Eliphaz believes that Job has been ethically sinful and theologically naive (vv. 2–20), he concludes his final speech with a call to repentance and a promise of restoration (vv. 21–30). Verse 21 serves as an excellent summary: "Agree with God, and be at peace; thereby good will come to you" (v. 21). To "agree with God," of course, means to agree with Eliphaz. And to "receive instruction from his mouth" (and its parallel line—"and lay up his words in your heart"; v. 22) is also to listen to God's mouthpiece: Eliphaz (cf. 4:15)!

Next, Eliphaz brings the logic of the retribution principle to bear. He gives two if-then exhortations. First, *if* Job repents of his sins ("if you return to the Almighty"), *then* God will renew Job's status and fortunes ("you will be built up"; 22:23a). Good things happen to those who go to God! Second, *if* Job ousts from his life all of his ethical iniquities ("if you remove injustice far from your tents"; v. 23b; cf. vv. 6–9) and returns his ill-gotten gain and idolatrous wealth ("if you lay gold in the dust, and gold of Ophir among the stones of the torrent-bed"; v. 24),[108]

---

107 Longman's translation; see *Job*, 288.
108 Andersen notes that "Ophir" is the "legendary source of the best gold" and that "its location is not known (cf. Gn. 10:29)" (*Job*, 205).

then his relationship with God will revive ("then the Almighty will be your gold and your precious silver" (v. 25).

In verses 26–28, Eliphaz expands on this second if-then exhortation, highlighting three aspects of that renewed relationship. First, Job will find the former happiness he has been craving:

| For then you will | delight yourself | in the Almighty |
| and | lift up your face | to God. (v. 26) |

Second, instead of silence, God will hear and answer Job's prayers ("you will make your prayer to him, and he will hear you"), even helping Job to keep his word concerning following God's ways ("and you will pay your vows"; v. 27). Third, rather than deep darkness blinding the way forward, Job will be given light to see which direction to go: "You will decide on a matter, and it will be established for you, and light will shine on your ways" (v. 28).

Eliphaz concludes his plea to Job with a reminder of the pattern of God's salvation of sinners ("he saves," v. 29b; "he delivers," v. 30a). Similar to what Peter would later write—"God opposes the proud but gives grace to the humble" (1 Pet. 5:5)—Eliphaz envisions Job as agreeing with the Almighty (Job 22:21) and in humility admitting his pride: "It is because of pride" (v. 29a). He then envisions God as saving this sinner who is now submissive (v. 29b). While Eliphaz will not speak of God's *grace*, he does count on God's *generosity* ("he delivers even the one who is not innocent"; v. 30a).

The meaning of the final phrase of this chapter is difficult to determine. If the word "your" represents God (which is unlikely, as God has been "he" throughout), then the sense is that the sinner is saved by means of God's purity. However, if the "your" symbolizes the repentant sinner but now reestablished saint, then the sense is that this sinner-saint has become an instrument of God's deliverance for others. Other sinners, in other words, will be "delivered through the cleanness of" this now restored-as-righteous man's "hands" (v. 30b). If the second interpretive option is true, it serves as an ironic allusion to Job's future deliverance of his friends (cf. 42:7–9).

Response

In the Introduction: Interpretive Challenges, we considered how to read and apply the three friends' advice. There we stated that there is value in echoing parts of their orthodox anthropology (e.g., Eliphaz in 4:17; 15:14–16; Bildad in 25:4) and components of their God-saturated and God-centered theology (e.g., Zophar in 11:5–7). Although their vision of God is skewed and will be corrected (42:7–9), we can learn from what they say about God's incomprehensible nature, manifold wisdom, and great works, as well as his love for the righteous, punishment of the wicked, and corrective discipline toward his people. There are reasons that Paul quotes Eliphaz (Job 5:13 in 1 Cor. 3:19) and that his words of counsel are alluded to in six other places in the NT! This fool has some wise things to say.

If we carefully mine the heap of rubble (their speeches in Job 4–5; 8; 11; 15; 18; 20; 22; 25), we can find gold. And what is perhaps not at all valuable to Job might be valuable to others (think about how applicable this last speech would be to Zacchaeus; see Luke 19:1–10). For example, as we consider Job 22:6–9, Eliphaz's incorrect list of Job's sins might resemble our catalog of transgressions. And even if it might not resemble our list at all, it nonetheless reminds us that we *have* a list—sexually immoral thoughts, the desire for fame, coveting our neighbor's goods, gossiping about our pastor's wife, and so on. Moreover, Eliphaz's final plea to Job (vv. 21–30) can be deconstructed and reconstructed to make a solid and scriptural sermon. The title "Agree with the Almighty" would be catchy enough. And his admonitions to repent of pride (v. 29) and of loving mammon more than God (v. 24; cf. 28:12–19; Matt. 6:33; Luke 16:13) and his admonishments to listen to God's Word (Job 22:22; John 3:31–36) and to delight in the Lord (Job 22:26; Phil. 3:1) are words we all need to hear and heed. Moreover, his reminder of the promises of answered prayer (Job 22:27; James 5:13–18), guidance (Job 22:28; John 16:13), blessings (Job 22:21; Matt. 5:3–12), and intimacy with the Almighty (Job 22:25; Rev. 21:1–4) for those who are in a right relationship with him are encouraging and uplifting. Indeed, even from Job's jaded friend—with misconceptions about God and misunderstanding of Job's situation—we can celebrate the gospel, that we are saved from God by God through the cleanness of Jesus' hands (cf. Job 22:29b–30).

JOB 23:1–24:25

23 Then Job answered and said:

2 "Today also my complaint is bitter;[1]
    my hand is heavy on account of my groaning.
3 Oh, that I knew where I might find him,
    that I might come even to his seat!
4 I would lay my case before him
    and fill my mouth with arguments.
5 I would know what he would answer me
    and understand what he would say to me.
6 Would he contend with me in the greatness of his power?
    No; he would pay attention to me.
7 There an upright man could argue with him,
    and I would be acquitted forever by my judge.

8 "Behold, I go forward, but he is not there,
    and backward, but I do not perceive him;
9 on the left hand when he is working, I do not behold him;
    he turns to the right hand, but I do not see him.

10 But he knows the way that I take;
      when he has tried me, I shall come out as gold.
11 My foot has held fast to his steps;
      I have kept his way and have not turned aside.
12 I have not departed from the commandment of his lips;
      I have treasured the words of his mouth more than my
          portion of food.
13 But he is unchangeable,² and who can turn him back?
      What he desires, that he does.
14 For he will complete what he appoints for me,
      and many such things are in his mind.
15 Therefore I am terrified at his presence;
      when I consider, I am in dread of him.
16 God has made my heart faint;
      the Almighty has terrified me;
17 yet I am not silenced because of the darkness,
      nor because thick darkness covers my face.

24

"Why are not times of judgment kept by the Almighty,
      and why do those who know him never see his days?
2 Some move landmarks;
      they seize flocks and pasture them.
3 They drive away the donkey of the fatherless;
      they take the widow's ox for a pledge.
4 They thrust the poor off the road;
      the poor of the earth all hide themselves.
5 Behold, like wild donkeys in the desert
      the poor³ go out to their toil, seeking game;
      the wasteland yields food for their children.
6 They gather their⁴ fodder in the field,
      and they glean the vineyard of the wicked man.
7 They lie all night naked, without clothing,
      and have no covering in the cold.
8 They are wet with the rain of the mountains
      and cling to the rock for lack of shelter.
9 (There are those who snatch the fatherless child from the
          breast,
      and they take a pledge against the poor.)
10 They go about naked, without clothing;
      hungry, they carry the sheaves;
11 among the olive rows of the wicked⁵ they make oil;
      they tread the winepresses, but suffer thirst.
12 From out of the city the dying⁶ groan,
      and the soul of the wounded cries for help;
      yet God charges no one with wrong.

13 "There are those who rebel against the light,
      who are not acquainted with its ways,
      and do not stay in its paths.
14 The murderer rises before it is light,
      that he may kill the poor and needy,
      and in the night he is like a thief.

15   The eye of the adulterer also waits for the twilight,
    saying, 'No eye will see me';
    and he veils his face.
16   In the dark they dig through houses;
    by day they shut themselves up;
    they do not know the light.
17   For deep darkness is morning to all of them;
    for they are friends with the terrors of deep darkness.

18   "You say, 'Swift are they on the face of the waters;
    their portion is cursed in the land;
    no treader turns toward their vineyards.
19   Drought and heat snatch away the snow waters;
    so does Sheol those who have sinned.
20   The womb forgets them;
    the worm finds them sweet;
    they are no longer remembered,
    so wickedness is broken like a tree.'

21   "They wrong the barren, childless woman,
    and do no good to the widow.
22   Yet God[7] prolongs the life of the mighty by his power;
    they rise up when they despair of life.
23   He gives them security, and they are supported,
    and his eyes are upon their ways.
24   They are exalted a little while, and then are gone;
    they are brought low and gathered up like all others;
    they are cut off like the heads of grain.
25   If it is not so, who will prove me a liar
    and show that there is nothing in what I say?"

[1] Or *defiant* [2] Or *one* [3] Hebrew *they* [4] Hebrew *his* [5] Hebrew *their olive rows* [6] Or *the men* [7] Hebrew *he*

Section Overview

Job responds to Eliphaz's thirty-verse reply with a forty-two-verse reply of his own. In fact, excluding Bildad's brief remarks in chapter 25 (only six verses), Job speaks a total of 203 verses in the next nine chapters (Job 23–31). This is not because he has silenced his accusers but because his friends see him to be so deluded by self-righteousness ("he was righteous in his own eyes"; 32:1) that they deem further counsel to be futile. In chapter 23 Job focuses on his relationship with God and in chapter 24 on God's "relationship" to the wicked. Job wonders why he, though righteous ("an upright man"), cannot find God so that he might be acquitted ("I would be acquitted forever by my judge"; 23:7). He also wonders why, meanwhile, those who should feel God's weight of judgment upon them—"the wicked" who oppress the poor (24:2–12) and "those who rebel against the light" (24:13)—are not standing in Job's shoes. This paradox is his problem. He again presents it to God, and yet there is still silence from heaven. All that Job will hear is Bildad's squawking on about God's sovereignty and man's sinfulness.

Section Outline

II.O. Why Are Not Times of Judgment Kept by the Almighty?
(23:1–24:25)

1. A New Beginning; an Old Complaint (23:1–2)
2. Looking for the Judge (23:3–7)
3. Terrified about a Possible Encounter (23:8–17)
4. What the Wicked Do; What God Does Not Do (24:1–12)
5. Two More Hideous Sins to Add to the List (24:13–17)
6. The Fortune and Fate of the Wicked (24:18–25)

Comment

23:1–2 We might label these two opening verses "A New Beginning; an Old Complaint." What is new is how Job offers no verbal jab at his friends. We do not hear his taunts, "No doubt you are the people, and wisdom will die with you" (12:2), or "miserable comforters are you all" (16:2; cf. 13:4), or "How long will you torment me . . . ?" (19:2), or "mock on" (21:3). Instead he returns to the tone he first set. His opening words—"Today also my complaint is bitter; my hand is heavy on account of my groaning" (23:2)—more resemble 6:2–3a: "Oh that my vexation were weighed, and all my calamity laid in the balances! For then it would be heavier than the sand of the sea." Is this progress a return to his earlier civility? Or has he just given up on his friends and knows that only God can speak for God?

23:3–7 Instead of turning on his three friends (cf. comment on 23:1–2), he turns to God for the rest of the chapter (vv. 3–17). Job mentions God in every verse but the last (v. 17)—God is his focus. However, Job's vision of God is out of focus. He cannot find him: "Oh, that I knew where I might find him" (v. 3a; cf. v. 8). Job wants to find God so that God might hear his case (vv. 3b–7). Job longs to come before the judgment seat ("Oh . . . that I might come even to his seat!"; v. 3). There he envisions himself as presenting his "case" before God ("my judge"; v. 7b), making his "arguments" (v. 4). He also envisions God as listening, understanding, and siding with him (vv. 5–7). Instead of contending against a mere mortal by using the "greatness of his power" (v. 6a), God would "pay attention" and, in paying attention, would surely acquit the "upright" (vv. 6b–7).[109]

23:8–17 Verse 8 echoes and expands upon verse 3. This court case sounds great. The problem is that Job still cannot find God:

> Behold, I go forward, but he is not there,
>> and backward, but I do not perceive him;
> on the left hand when he is working, I do not behold him;
>> he turns to the right hand, but I do not see him. (vv. 8–9)

---

109 This is another positive change, for "the last time Job used this kind of legal language, he was convinced that God would both ignore and condemn him (cf. 9:3, 16, 19)" (*ESV Study Bible* note on Job 23:3–7).

Job is relieved, however, to know that God knows where to find him ("but he knows the way that I take"),[110] and, when he gets around to hearing the case ("when he has tried me"), Job will be found innocent ("I shall come out as gold"; v. 10). Job knows that his life is a pure life (as pure as "gold" refined by fire), and in light of this fact he trusts that God will eventually see, vindicate, and even reward such righteousness. Like the psalmist of Psalm 119, Job has followed God's word and delighted in his words:

> My foot has held fast to his steps;
>> I have kept his way and have not turned aside.
> I have not departed from the commandment of his lips;
>> I have treasured the words of his mouth more than my portion
>>> of food. (Job 23:11–12)

However, in verse 13 Job loses focus on the positive possibilities. His hope is deferred. His trust dissipates. The problem is not *his innocence* but *God's sovereignty*. God's sovereignty should be a comfort to him, but instead it makes him tremble in fear for the future. Due to God's immutability ("he is unchangeable"), omnipotence ("and who can turn him back?"), and absolute sovereignty ("what he desires, that he does"; v. 13), Job dreads that he will have no say in *when* his case will be heard or *what* the outcome will be. He is completely in God's hands, for God "will complete what he appoints," or "decrees," for Job, doing whatever else he has planned for Job ("and many such things are in his mind"; v. 14). Job expresses his fear of the unknown and his trepidation at actually meeting God in this way:

> Therefore I am terrified at his presence;
>> when I consider, I am in dread of him.
> God has made my heart faint;
>> the Almighty has terrified me. (vv. 15–16)[111]

Job is terrified to meet God (v. 15), and God's very presence is the cause of such trepidation (v. 16). Nevertheless, Job presses on. He does the only thing he now knows to do. He returns to lament. While he is blind to God's purposes, such "darkness" will not silence him:

| yet I am not silenced | because of | the darkness, |
| nor | because | thick darkness covers my face. (v. 17) |

And speak he will! Job has another chapter to go before Bildad's brief interruption.

---

110 Another way to take Job 23:10 is summarized by Estes: "Literally, the Hebrew reads, 'God knows [his] way with me,' which means that God knows what he is doing in Job's life. This more likely reading indicates that God is sovereign in directing Job according to the path that he has ordained for his servant (cf. 23:11–12). Job here reflects his trust that God knows what he is doing, even if Job cannot discern how this all makes sense" (*Job*, 141–142). Does such a reading, however, make best sense of Job's terror of God expressed in 23:15–17?
111 The word "terrified" in 23:15, 16 captures well the sense of the Hebrew (*bahal*), as this is not the fear (*yare'*) used to describe Job's "fear" (1:1, 8, 9; 2:3) "of the Lord" (28:28).

24:1–12 In chapter 24, Job shifts from addressing God's uncommunicative relationship with him to addressing God's apathetic relationship with the wicked. This is shocking to Job, because, unlike with Eliphaz's false and short list of Job's sins (22:6–9), the wicked have a true list, and a long one (24:2–11, 13–16). Job uses the same categories as Eliphaz to detail the crimes against humanity (table 4.6).

TABLE 4.6: Eliphaz's Charges against Job; Job's Charges against the Wicked

Charge	Against Job	Against the Wicked
Exploiting the needy	"You have exacted pledges of your brothers for nothing and stripped the naked of their clothing." (22:6)	"Some move landmarks; they seize flocks and pasture them" (24:2); the poor "gather their fodder in the field, and they glean the vineyard of the wicked man" (24:6), yet they are not paid well (the poor "lie all night . . . without clothing"; 24:7a; cf. 24:10a).
Letting the hungry starve	"You have given no water to the weary to drink, and you have withheld bread from the hungry." (22:7)	The poor "go about . . . hungry," even though "they carry the sheaves" for the wicked man and make his "oil" from his "olives" (24:10–11a), and they "suffer thirst" even though "they tread the winepresses" (24:11b).
Oppressing orphans and widows	"You have sent widows away empty, and the arms of the fatherless were crushed." (22:9)	"They drive away the donkey of the fatherless; they take the widow's ox for a pledge." (24:3); they "snatch the fatherless child from the breast" (24:9a).

While Job uses the same categories as Eliphaz, he expands upon them (e.g., adding murder and adultery in 24:13–16 to the list above, and speaking more directly of stealing land and flocks in v. 2). What he also expands upon are the effects of such crimes upon the poor.

The disadvantaged are disadvantaged in the following ways: when the wicked "move landmarks" or boundary markers (v. 2a), falsely claiming that the poor man's land and animals are now theirs ("they seize flocks"; v. 2b) and stealing even the orphan's donkey and the widow's ox (v. 3), the poor have nowhere to go. Then, when the wicked turn violent, even pushing the destitute into a ditch ("thrust the poor off the road"; v. 4a),[112] "the poor" go into hiding ("hide themselves"; v. 4b). If the wicked are bold enough to steal their land and evil enough to push them off the road, the poor fear what the wicked might do to them next.

Verses 5–10 record what does happen next: stripped of their land, possessions, and dignity, the poor become scavengers, "like wild donkeys in the desert" (v. 5a). Like hardworking but unkempt animals, they go out into "the wasteland" looking for "food for their children" ("go out to their toil, seeking game"; v. 5bc). They eat whatever they can find ("game"; Hb. *tereph*, a root used only here and in Ps. 104:21: "The young lions roar for their *prey*, seeking their food from God"). The sense, as we arrive at Job 24:6, is that these wanderers in the wilderness have wandered back to town for work. But the only work they can find is with the landowning

---

112 The road or "path" likely symbolizes "their life journey" (so Longman, *Job*, 301). They have not only lost it all, they have no future to look forward to either.

wicked. Without any options, they take the job, becoming worse off than they were in the wilderness. While they provide for "the wicked man"—gathering animal feed ("fodder in the field") and picking grapes ("glean the vineyard"; v. 6)—the wicked man does not provide for them. They are deprived of "shelter" (vv. 7b, 8) and "clothing" (vv. 7a, 10a), two essentials of human life:

> They lie all night naked, without clothing,
>> and have no covering in the cold.
> They are wet with the rain of the mountains
>> and cling to the rock for lack of shelter. (vv. 7–8)

They are also deprived of food and water, the most absolute essentials. Even though they work with food ("the sheaves" of wheat, v. 10b; rows of "olives" for olive "oil," v. 11a) and drink (the wine of "the winepresses"; v. 11b) all day, "they go about . . . hungry" (v. 10) and "suffer thirst" (v. 11b).

In verse 9—a poetic parenthesis near the middle of all this misery (vv. 6–11)— Job offers a gross and graphic image of how bad times have gotten:

> (There are those who snatch the fatherless child from the breast,
>> And they take a pledge against the poor.) (v. 9)

We feel like we have entered the worst moment of Israel's exile, the aftermath of the siege of Jerusalem—or a Dickens novel, for that matter. The "those" are the wicked who have reached a new low: kidnapping a baby ("snatch the fatherless child") from the mother who is nursing him ("from the breast"; v. 9a) and selling the child to pay off a debt or using him as collateral for a debt the poor owe them ("they take a pledge against the poor"; v. 9b). Where is God in the middle of such misery? Job wonders.

As noted above, all of the sins of the wicked center around oppression of the poor (note "the poor" mentioned in vv. 4, 5, 9, and also all of the pronouns referring to them: "they" [vv. 6 (2x), 7, 8, 10 (2x), 11 (2x)]; "their" [vv. 5 (2x), 6]; "themselves" [v. 4]). And thus all of Job's difficulty centers on the problem of evil. Having described what the wicked do (vv. 2–11), he summarizes in verses 1 and 12 (which thus forms an inclusio to this section), what God does *not* do. Job first asks why, if God in his sovereignty has decided to allow evil for a season, does it seem like injustice is never dealt with ("Why are not times of judgment kept by the Almighty?"; v. 1a)? Moreover, why do the righteous ("those who know" God) look in vain for the time of God's judgment of the wicked ("never see his days"; v. 1b)? Similarly, verse 12 speaks of the unanswered cries of the poor: "From out of the city the dying groan" (v. 12a), out of the very depths of their hearts ("the soul of the wounded"; v. 12b) they cry for help, but heaven hears not nor helps not. God does not act. He "charges no one with wrong" (v. 12c). He fails to execute justice.

24:13–17 Just as every line in 23:3–16 features God, so does every line in 24:2–24 feature the wicked. Verses 13–17 continue to focus on "those who rebel against the light" (v. 13) by featuring two notorious sinners: the "murderer" (v. 14) and the "adulterer" (v. 15). The "light" likely represents God (cf. Isa. 60:19; 1 John 1:5), specifically his light of revelation. Therefore, to "rebel against the light" is to refuse to hear God's word (these rebels "are not acquainted with [God's] ways"; Job 24:13b) or to heed his directions (they "do not stay in [God's] paths"; v. 13c).

The murderer rebels in this way. He rises around 3:00 a.m. ("rises before it is light"; v. 14a). He has a premeditated plan to senselessly slaughter the already oppressed ("that he may kill the poor and needy"; v. 14b). He takes their possessions and their land, as easily as he did their lives ("in the night he is like a thief"; v. 14c). In the morning, it is as though nothing has happened; he has gotten away with this horrific crime. In a similar manner and with a similar outcome, the adulterer rebels. Right after dark ("the eye of the adulterer also waits for the twilight"; v. 15a), trusting that he will not be seen ("saying, 'No eye will see me'"; v. 15b)—both because of the time and because of his disguise ("he veils his face"; v. 15c)—he gets into the house, or many houses ("they dig through houses"; v. 16a),[113] and *into* another man's wife (they "take [their] fill of love till morning"; Prov. 7:18). The two adulterers lay together until the coast is clear—the next twilight ("by day they shut themselves up; they do not know the light"; Job 24:16bc). And, unlike what happens to the adulterers in Proverbs 6:20–7:27, where the "twilight" rendezvous (7:9) is met with a husband's rage and "revenge" (6:34), here in Job 24 the sinners escape unnoticed and "unpunished" (contra Prov. 6:29; 7:23, 26–27).

Both sinners commit their sins at night ("before it is light," Job 24:14a; "in the night," v. 14c; "waits for the twilight," v. 15a; "they do not know the light," v. 16c). In the words of Jesus, these rebels "loved the darkness rather than the light because their works were evil" (John 3:19; cf. 1 Thess. 5:4–8). In Job's rendition:

> Deep darkness is morning to all of them;
>> for they are friends with the terrors of deep darkness. (Job 24:17)

Innocent Job has experienced the "deep darkness" (16:16) of not hearing from God; to the guilty ungodly, however, the "deep darkness" (24:17) safeguards their sin. It hides them, so it seems to Job, from God's inspecting and adjudicating eye.

24:18–25 More than not being seen and judged for their sins, the wicked often experience the opposite of punishment: prosperity! As in 21:7–21, Job argues against his friends' view ("you say"; 24:18a). Job 24:18–20 is Job's summary of their bad theology. They claim that the wicked ("they," vv. 18a, 20c; "their," v. 18bc [2x]; "them," v. 20ab [2x]; "those who have sinned," v. 19b) do not get away with anything but experience a threefold fall into disgrace. First, whatever prosperity they might experience is very short-lived. They are pushed down the river and off a waterfall like driftwood ("swift are they on the face of the waters"; v. 18a),

---

113 Some commentators and a few modern Bible translations take Job 24:16 as describing a third villain, robbers, and thus supply the word "thieves" (e.g., NIV, NLT). David J. A. Clines's translation, and reordering of the verses, is "At night the thief prowls. In the dark he breaks into houses" (*Job 21–37*, WBC 18A [Nashville: Thomas Nelson, 2006], 574).

unnoticed, unimportant, unremembered. Their grapes are blighted ("their portion is cursed in the land"; v. 18b), so their business deals fall through ("no treader
turns toward their vineyards"; v. 18c) and the family winery goes bankrupt. Then,
second, comes death ("Sheol") to snatch "those who have sinned" away, like "snow
waters" are soaked up on a 100-degree day or by a seven-month "drought" (v. 19).
Third, they are forgotten. As they are buried in the ground, only the worm notices
them ("the worm finds them sweet"; v. 20b). No one else will remember them
("they are no longer remembered"; v. 20c), not even their own mothers ("the womb
forgets them"; v. 20a). In the end, they have been judged by God and rendered
useless—"so wickedness is broken like a tree" (v. 20d; cf. Ezek. 17:24). In summary,
the friends claim that the wicked (1) do not prosper, (2) suffer quick deaths, and
(3) are soon forgotten.

Job agrees with one point of his friends' analysis, that the wicked will die and
be forgotten:

> They are exalted a little while, and then are gone;
> > they are brought low and gathered up like all others;
> > they are cut off like the heads of grain. (Job 24:24)

However, he cannot concede their other points, for he still struggles with his observation of life. The absolute fact, Job is convinced ("If it is not so, who will prove
me a liar and show that there is nothing in what I say?"; v. 25), is what he has said
in 24:1–17. Even though the wicked commit the most horrendous crimes ("they
wrong the barren, childless woman, and do no good to the widow"; v. 21; cf. Ex.
22:21–27; Deut. 24:17–22), no swift justice comes. They do not suffer quick deaths;
they do not feel the hand of God's judgment. Instead, it seems that they experience
his helping hand. God "prolongs the life of the mighty by his power; they rise up
when they despair of life" (Job 24:22). He not only helps them up when they have
fallen down, he also lifts them up, giving them security and support (v. 23a). His
eye is protecting their way ("his eyes are upon their ways"; v. 23b), rather than
judging it (cf. vv. 13–17).

Response

There are many possible responses to these chapters. These chapters cause us to
reflect on the sinfulness of sin: how dark is the human heart, that out of it comes
murder and adultery and oppression of the innocent! We could dwell on that sad
fact. Or we could dwell again on the importance of honesty in prayer and how we
can talk to God, like Job did, about all of the troubles we face and complexities
we cannot understand. We could discuss the attributes of the Almighty—such
as immutability or sovereignty—and how such attributes bring both assurance
and confusion. We could cover other theological and ethical issues that Job raises,
such as the plight of the poor. How do we fight injustice in this world to make
sure those in our neighborhoods and around the globe do not suffer the same
atrocities described in 24:2–11? Do we "remember the poor," and are we "eager"

about providing for their needs (Gal. 2:10)? Do we love the "least" among us (Matt. 25:40, 45)? Indeed, do we take seriously the warnings and blessings of the parable of the sheep and the goats (Matt. 25:31–46)?

However, the one response from these chapters we need to be sure to grasp is the Bible's solution to the problem of evil, the issue that Job struggles with most (cf. Job 24:1, 12). What is the Bible's answer to Job's question, "Why are not times of judgment kept by the Almighty?" (v. 1)? The Bible's ultimate answer is the incarnation and crucifixion. There is a time for everything under the sun (Eccles. 3:1), and there was a time for *the Son* "to be born, and . . . to die" (Eccles. 3:2). Paul writes of the incarnation in this way: "When the *fullness of time* had come, God sent forth his Son, born of woman . . . to redeem" (Gal. 4:4–5). God's answer to Eliphaz's question in Job 15:14—"What is man, that he can be pure? Or he who is born of a woman, that he can be righteous?"—is the pure and holy Son of God in the flesh. Paul also writes about the crucifixion in this way:

> In him we have redemption through his blood, the forgiveness of our trespasses, according to the riches of his grace, which he lavished upon us, in all wisdom and insight making known to us the mystery of his will, according to his purpose, which he set forth in Christ as a plan for the *fullness of time*, to unite all things in him, things in heaven and things on earth. (Eph. 1:7–10)

The crucifixion of Christ was wisdom! It revealed to us the mystery of God's mysterious will. It demonstrated to us that God had a plan, a well-timed plan, whereby he conquered the wicked through the wicked men's plan of nailing his Son to a tree.

JOB 25:1–6

25 Then Bildad the Shuhite answered and said:

2 "Dominion and fear are with God;[1]
    he makes peace in his high heaven.
3 Is there any number to his armies?
    Upon whom does his light not arise?
4 How then can man be in the right before God?
    How can he who is born of woman be pure?
5 Behold, even the moon is not bright,
    and the stars are not pure in his eyes;
6 how much less man, who is a maggot,
    and the son of man, who is a worm!"

[1] Hebrew *him*

Section Overview

In what might seem like a short but straightforward systematic theology lecture—
God is good and great; man is bad and not so great—Bildad is actually ridicul-
ing Job's preposterous notion that he can stand before God, give his testimony,
and then have the Holy One find him wholly spotless. The first part of Bildad's
rebuttal (Job 25:1–3) is that God is good and great, or, in more theological terms,
majestic, mighty, and holy. The second part of the rebuttal (vv. 4–6) follows an
a fortiori argument (from the stronger to the weaker): if the bright celestial lights
(the stronger) are not perfectly pure in God's eyes, then how can mere mortals (the
weaker) be found right before his sight? Man is too bad and small to stand before
a good and great God.

Section Outline

II.P. Bildad's Brief Barb (25:1–6)
      1. God Is Too Good and Great (25:1–3)
      2. Man Is Too Bad and Small (25:4–6)

Comment

25:1–3 Is Bildad tired? Has he given up the fight? We knew that Zophar has done
so (there will be no further response from him). Bildad belts out only six verses.
The reader gets the sense at this point that this is an interruption in Job's intrigu-
ing and developing thought. We want to know more about what Job thinks about
God's incomprehensible sovereignty (chs. 23–24). "This brevity," John Walton
claims, "is defensible in light of his entrenched traditionalism, which, at this point
in the dialogue, has reduced him to platitudinous reiteration of his major salient
points." Those points?

> God is unimaginably great; humans are intrinsically flawed and, in the
> grand scheme of things, are of little consequence. He believes in an ordered
> world, and as we have seen previously, that order is founded on the RP
> [retribution principle].[114]

Fair enough. But any sermon on the greatness of God and sinfulness of man,
however flawed and short, is worth listening to. Moreover, any final word from
the friends that is not "caustic and critical"[115] is curious (cf. 8:2; 18:2), to say the
least. Elihu will foreshadow what God has to say out of the whirlwind. Might also
bumbling Bildad? As Alden notes, "It is a welcome change to hear him begin with
this lofty and worshipful theological statement. God rules."[116]

What is so worshipful and lofty about Job 25:2–3? Bildad attributes absolute
power ("dominion"), awe ("fear," or "reverence";[117] v. 2), and "peace" (Hb. *shalom*) to

---

114 Walton, *Job*, 249.
115 Alden, *Job*, 255.
116 Ibid., 255–256.
117 Marvin H. Pope, *Job*, AB (New York: Doubleday, 1965), 180.

God's rule of the highest heights of the universe ("his high heaven"; v. 2b)—the seventy-times-seventy heights. And though transcendent, there is not a corner of the world he does not see ("Upon whom does his light not arise?"; v. 3b) or where he does not rule ("Is there any number to his armies?"; v. 3a). Do not underestimate this flawed theologian's observation: our Lord Jesus will speak of the number of angelic troops who could have rushed to his rescue (Matt. 26:53), as well as how the sun rises upon both the evil and the good (Matt. 5:45).

25:4–6 Returning to a foundational question in the dialogue—"asked originally by Eliphaz (4:17), recast and used by Job in his second speech (9:2), repeated and reinforced by Eliphaz (15:14)"[118]—Bildad asks the same question in two different ways:

| How then can | man | be in the right before God? |
| How can | he who is born of woman | be pure? (25:4) |

The question, and its implied answer (no man can be innocent before God), is not a general theological statement, something we might find in a systematics textbook. Rather, it is a specific answer (26:1) to Job's claims. We can replace the words "man" and he "who is born of woman" with *Job* to get what Bildad is getting at: to Bildad there are no exceptions to the retribution principle. "Sorry Job, your hope of being acquitted before a divine judge [cf. 23:7] will never happen." The gap between the creature and the Creator is too great.

As usual, Bildad has gone too far. He has not really looked into the facts of the case. He has also pulled the rug out from under his own hope for a relationship with God. And instead of ending his short speech with a rebuttal of Job's claims that God lets wickedness go unchecked (ch. 24), he offers a contrast between God and man. To God, even the brightest and purest of the heavenly lights—"the moon" and "the stars"—are "not bright"/"not pure in his eyes" (25:5). And if this is so, then imagine what God thinks of earthlings:

| how much less | man, | who is a maggot, |
| and | the son of man, | who is a worm! (v. 6) |

Job's case is hopeless. Imagine a worthless and loathsome creature—a "maggot" or a "worm"—coming before the lofty judgment "seat" of God (23:3b). Would such a great God really "pay attention" to Job's "arguments," and acquit him (23:4–7)?

Response

Right lesson. Wrong audience. Bildad is right that God is great and humans are depraved and that we all are therefore guilty and not innocent in his eyes (Ps. 14:1–3; Rom. 3:10–12). However, what Job needs to hear is the hope of vindication for the righteous. He needs to know that God is just and that he will act justly.

---

118 *ESV Study Bible* note on Job 25:4.

We might also add that he needs to hear more about the possibility of mediation with God through an advocate. In other words, he needs to hear the gospel. As Blaise Pascal put it: "Knowing God without knowing our own wretchedness makes for pride. Knowing our own wretchedness without knowing God makes for despair. Knowing Jesus Christ strikes the balance because he shows us both God and our own wretchedness."[119]

So, again, from the friends' counsel we learn the lesson of the danger of saying the right thing to the wrong person. We need prudence and wisdom when applying biblical doctrines. *What* we say is not more important than to *whom* we are saying it. But we also need to learn another lesson: the danger of twisting a biblical truth too far. What do we make of "Bildad's maggot theology," as Longman cleverly labels it?[120] Are we really maggots and worms in God's sight and according to his design? While God's people can act wormlike (Israel is called "you worm" in Isa. 41:14), we must remember, as Longman points out, that God created human beings with unique grandeur, with "a special and dignified relationship with God."[121] Read Genesis 1–2 and Psalm 8. We are the highest achievement of creation: made in God's image, made to rule over the rest of creation, made good, and crowned with glory and honor.

JOB 26:1–27:23

26 Then Job answered and said:

2 "How you have helped him who has no power!
    How you have saved the arm that has no strength!
3 How you have counseled him who has no wisdom,
    and plentifully declared sound knowledge!
4 With whose help have you uttered words,
    and whose breath has come out from you?
5 The dead tremble
    under the waters and their inhabitants.
6 Sheol is naked before God,[1]
    and Abaddon has no covering.
7 He stretches out the north over the void
    and hangs the earth on nothing.
8 He binds up the waters in his thick clouds,
    and the cloud is not split open under them.
9 He covers the face of the full moon[2]
    and spreads over it his cloud.

119 Blaise Pascal, *Pensées*, trans. A. J. Krailsheimer, rev. ed. (London: Penguin, 1995), 57.
120 Longman, *Job*, 309.
121 Ibid., 310.

10 He has inscribed a circle on the face of the waters
      at the boundary between light and darkness.
11 The pillars of heaven tremble
      and are astounded at his rebuke.
12 By his power he stilled the sea;
      by his understanding he shattered Rahab.
13 By his wind the heavens were made fair;
      his hand pierced the fleeing serpent.
14 Behold, these are but the outskirts of his ways,
      and how small a whisper do we hear of him!
      But the thunder of his power who can understand?”

27 And Job again took up his discourse, and said:

2 “As God lives, who has taken away my right,
      and the Almighty, who has made my soul bitter,
3 as long as my breath is in me,
      and the spirit of God is in my nostrils,
4 my lips will not speak falsehood,
      and my tongue will not utter deceit.
5 Far be it from me to say that you are right;
      till I die I will not put away my integrity from me.
6 I hold fast my righteousness and will not let it go;
      my heart does not reproach me for any of my days.

7 “Let my enemy be as the wicked,
      and let him who rises up against me be as the unrighteous.
8 For what is the hope of the godless when God cuts him off,
      when God takes away his life?
9 Will God hear his cry
      when distress comes upon him?
10 Will he take delight in the Almighty?
      Will he call upon God at all times?
11 I will teach you concerning the hand of God;
      what is with the Almighty I will not conceal.
12 Behold, all of you have seen it yourselves;
      why then have you become altogether vain?

13 “This is the portion of a wicked man with God,
      and the heritage that oppressors receive from the Almighty:
14 If his children are multiplied, it is for the sword,
      and his descendants have not enough bread.
15 Those who survive him the pestilence buries,
      and his widows do not weep.
16 Though he heap up silver like dust,
      and pile up clothing like clay,
17 he may pile it up, but the righteous will wear it,
      and the innocent will divide the silver.
18 He builds his house like a moth's,
      like a booth that a watchman makes.
19 He goes to bed rich, but will do so no more;
      he opens his eyes, and his wealth is gone.

20 Terrors overtake him like a flood;
    in the night a whirlwind carries him off.
21 The east wind lifts him up and he is gone;
    it sweeps him out of his place.
22 It[3] hurls at him without pity;
    he flees from its[4] power in headlong flight.
23 It claps its hands at him
    and hisses at him from its place.

[1] Hebrew *him* [2] Or *his throne* [3] Or *He* (that is, God); also verse 23 [4] Or *his*; also verse 23

Section Overview

Should Job respond to Bildad or ignore him? He is, after all, in the middle of an interesting and important monologue about God's work in the world. But he responds. After he speaks eloquently about his awesome God (Job 26:6–14) and boldly reiterates his own innocence (27:2–6), he curses his enemies—his three friends!—lumping them in with the wicked and reminding them of the frightful fate awaiting them (27:7–23).

Section Outline

II.Q. A Last Bout with Bildad (26:1–27:23)
    1. Some Sarcasm to Start (26:1–4)
    2. The Outskirts of God's Awesome Power (26:5–14)
    3. The Stubborn Innocent (27:1–6)
    4. The Stupid Wicked (27:7–23)

Comment

26:1–4 If it is true that both Job (23:1–2) and Bildad (25:1–6) have taken a brief break from direct insults, that ceasefire ends here. Job's answer (26:1) attacks Bildad for his lack of help and sound counsel to "him" (vv. 2, 3) in his weak condition ("no power"/"no strength"; v. 2):

How you   have helped   him who has no power!
How you   have saved   the arm that has no strength! (v. 2)

Notice that these are not questions. The ESV's exclamation points rightly enhance the sarcasm. The sarcasm continues in verse 3: "How you have counseled him who has no wisdom, and plentifully declared sound knowledge!" Job, who has "no wisdom" in Bildad's eyes, has been "counseled," given plentiful "sound knowledge." The scent of sarcasm, added to what Job says in verse 4, can be smelled a mile away. "With whose help have you uttered words?" (Surely God is whispering in your ear these prophetic rebukes, for they are out of this world!) "And whose breath has come out from you?" (Surely it is the Spirit of God himself, for you speak not like a mere wormlike man but like a god.)

26:5–14 Is Job done with his opening sarcastic rebuke? It seems to be so, for he shifts from Bildad (the "you" of vv. 2–4) to the "dead" (v. 5), who seem not to be dead but to be living in some sort of hell. Though dead, they "tremble." It is as if they are being drowned over and over, trying to live with the strange, gilled creatures (the "inhabitants" of the waters) found roaming the depths of the dark sea. However, it is not the dead who will be Job's focus. Once again (see esp. 23:3–16; 24:1, 12, 22–23), it is "God,"[122] who is named in 26:6 of the ESV and mentioned in every verse thereafter (26:7–14). With one of the most remarkable parallelisms in the book of Job, Job declares:

> Sheol   is naked   before God,
> and Abaddon   has no covering. (v. 6)

"Sheol" (the place of death) and "Abaddon" (the place of destruction; "the bottomless pit," Rev. 9:11) are seen by God even though the sun ("his light"; Job 25:3) cannot possibly penetrate the depths of the lowest point of the earth.

Job is on an *inspired* theological roll. He is talking about God, and he is doing so in the right way. Everything that follows makes us say, "Amen." As we have seen earlier, God's actions are listed: "He stretches" (26:7a), he "hangs" (v. 7b), "he binds up" (v. 8a), "he covers" (v. 9a), "he spreads" (v. 9b), "he has inscribed" (v. 10a), he rebukes (v. 11b), "he stilled" (v. 12a), "he shattered" (v. 12b), and "his hand pierced" (v. 13b). God has created the universe, stretching out the northern skies over emptiness ("he stretches out the north"; v. 7a; cf. 9:8), and suspending the earth in the middle of immense blackness (he "hangs the earth on nothing"; 26:7b). How did he do it? Without any help from some other so-called deity or his own created angel, "he binds up the waters in his thick clouds, and the cloud is not split open under them" (v. 8). In other words, as he stretched out the universe, so he stretched out what is above the earth ("the heavens," Gen. 1:1; "God called the expanse Heaven," Gen. 1:8) so that the clouds would make a natural barrier between heaven and earth. And with the moon, that great light of the earth that reflects the light of the sun, he can create the remarkable eclipse, covering "the face of the full moon" with darkness, like a "cloud" might cover the earth (Job 26:9). It is awe inspiring to watch "his cloud" (what we know to be the earth doing its divinely ordained duty)!

Job is not done. He has four more wonderful verses to go. He is in awe of God. Wherever he has been in his relationship with God, he has returned here to the fear of the Lord. He is on his knees before his awesome Creator, as we should be. Verse 10 picks up the theme of the God of Genesis: "He has inscribed a circle on the face of the waters at the boundary between light and darkness." Put differently, "God separated the light from the darkness. God called the light Day, and the darkness he called Night. And there was evening and there was morning, the first day" (Gen. 1:4b–5). Job rejoices in the fact that God in his wisdom drew a horizon over the waters, setting a daily boundary between the day and the night.

---

122 It is interesting that Job does not use a specific name for God, such as El, Elohim, or Yahweh (cf. ESV mg.).

In Job 26:11–13 Job recounts the power of God not in creation but over creation. Verse 11 speaks perhaps of a thunderstorm ("the pillars of heaven tremble and are astounded at his rebuke"). Martin Luther was turned toward God in a thunderstorm. Who of us, when rightly meditating on God's power, is not taken aback by a crash in the heavens during a summer storm that makes us shake in our boots, or fear even for our lives? Even more, God demonstrates his power by taming the untamable: the sea ("he stilled the sea"/"the heavens were made fair"; vv. 12a, 13a) and its greatest monsters ("Rahab"/"the fleeing serpent"; vv. 12b, 13b).

By	his power	he stilled the sea;
by	his understanding	he shattered Rahab.
By	his wind	the heavens were made fair;
	his hand	pierced the fleeing serpent. (vv. 12–13)

We do not need to think of Jesus taming the seas (Matt. 8:23–27) or walking on the waters (Matt. 14:22–33), but we should. We do not need to think about Revelation 21:1—"the sea was no more"—but it might be a reasonable Christian way to read the text. God has absolute control over the uncontrollable!

Job concludes with perhaps the three greatest lines of the thousand or so Oscar-winning lines in the book of Job:

> Behold, these are but the outskirts of his ways,
>> and how small a whisper do we hear of him!
>> But the thunder of his power who can understand? (26:14)

His "behold" here is the best *behold* thus far (twenty-six times in the book; fifteen times from Job). What is detailed in verses 6–13 is awesome. For Job to say, "Look, what I have just recounted is just the fringes of what God has done and can do. Indeed it is but a faint whisper of his workings in the world," makes us fall on our faces—flat on the ground with poor, suffering Job—asking the only question one should ask: "The thunder of his power who can understand?" (v. 14c).

27:1–23 Why does Job pause in his praise? Is he used to interruptions? It is, after all, Zophar's turn to trounce him. We do not know. What we do know is the narrator also notices the unusual pause. We read "and Job again took up his discourse, and said" (v. 1), not, "Then Job answered and said" (Hb. *wayya'an 'iyyob wayyo'mar*; 6:1; 9:1; 12:1; 16:1; 19:1; 21:1; 23:1; 26:1). And while it is a continuation of Job's God theme ("As God lives" is his first line; 27:2; also throughout this chapter he names "God" as *'el* or *'eloah* seven times [with an eighth assumed instance in v. 8a], and four times as "the Almighty" [Hb. *shadday*]), the focus is first on Job's innocence (vv. 2–6; see the paragraph below) and second on his "enemy": the "wicked" (v. 7a; cf. v. 13a), the "unrighteous" (v. 7b), or the "godless" (v. 8a), as he calls them. Every line but one (v. 12, the second and only other "behold" of chs. 26–27) speaks of the wicked. The pronouns "he," "his," and "him" ricochet off the walls of Job's heart. He wants his friends to feel the weight of a latter wise man's beatitude: "Blessed are you when others revile you and persecute you and utter all kinds of evil against you falsely" (Matt. 5:11).

27:2–6 In Job 27:2–6 Job again speaks of his innocence. He begins with one of the most interesting parallelisms in the book:

As God lives,	who has taken away	my right,
and the Almighty,	who has made	my soul bitter (v. 2)

Is he here accusing the powerful ("Almighty") living God ("as God lives"), whom he has just worshiped (26:6–14), of foul play? He might be. He is an honest bloke. But as he returns to his friends' folly in 27:3–5 (explicit in v. 5) and speaks of God's "spirit" within (in v. 3), Job's target seems to be Eliphaz, Zophar, and Bildad. Notice the word "you" below:

As long as my breath is in me,
    and the spirit of God is in my nostrils,
my lips will not speak falsehood,
    and my tongue will not utter deceit.

Far be it from me to say that you are right;
    till I die I will not put away my integrity from me.
I hold fast my righteousness and will not let it go;
    my heart does not reproach me for any of my days. (vv. 3–6)

As long as Job lives ("as long as breath is in me, and the spirit of God is in my nostrils"; v. 3), he will maintain his purity. He will not lie ("speak falsehood"/"utter deceit"; v. 4) nor admit that his foolish friends are right ("far be it from me to say that you are right"; v. 5). Instead, he will hold to his "integrity"/"righteousness" (vv. 5b, 6a). He will be vindicated! His conscience is clear ("my heart does not reproach me"; v. 6b) for as long as he can remember ("for any of my days"; v. 6b).

27:7–23 In these verses Job turns from his awesome God and his obedient self to his enemy: his three best friends (the "you" is plural in vv. 11–12). He wants his "enemy" to "be as the wicked" (v. 7a) because they have risen up against him (v. 7b) and been his "oppressors" (v. 13b), calling him a wicked man under God's judgment for his wickedness. By the end of the drama, he will forgive his enemies. But here he curses them. He wants them dead—punished!

Unlike his last speech on the wicked (what we labeled "The Inexplicable Blessedness of the Wicked"; Job 21) but, ironically, much like Zophar's last speech (Job 20; cf. 20:29 with 27:13), Job recounts the fate of the wicked. He begins with the hopeless death of the "wicked," also called the "unrighteous" and the "godless" (vv. 7–8). When the godless man dies ("when God cuts him off"/"when God takes away his life"; v. 8), there is no hope. God will not hear him in the grave and save him from his misery ("Will God hear his cry when distress comes upon him?"; v. 9). The wicked man cannot pray to God or praise him from the grave.

> Will he   take delight   in the Almighty?
> Will he   call upon   God at all times? (v. 10)

Job pauses in verses 11–12 to inform his friends of the purpose of his imprecatory homily: he wants to teach them ("I will teach you"/"I will not conceal") about the power of God ("concerning the hand of God"/"the Almighty"; v. 11). They both believe that God judges the wicked. Their counsel to him, however, has been like smoke curling up in the air. An air bubble. "Altogether vain" (v. 12). Vaporous. Their verdict has been totally off. Job is not wicked, *they are*. They are wicked because they are saying Job is wicked. And as such, verses 13–23 serve as a reminder of what happens when God, in his time, rectifies wrongs.

What does the wicked man get ("the portion"/"the heritage") from God (v. 13)? First, after his death (vv. 8–10, 15), his family does not fare well. If he has many children ("if his children are multiplied"), it is only so that more of them might be violently killed ("it is for the sword") or so that there will be too many mouths to feed ("have not enough bread"; v. 14). Whether the sword or the plague gets them, death ("the pestilence buries"; v. 15a) will have the last laugh. No one will care that they are gone, not even their wives ("his widows do not weep"; v. 15b; cf. NASB). Second, the wealth of the wicked man will vanish with him. Though his bank account is massive ("though he heap up silver like dust") and his wardrobe extensive (he piles "up clothing like clay"; v. 16), the righteous—not his children!—will inherit it:

> But   the righteous   will wear it,
> and   the innocent   will divide the silver. (v. 17)

The wicked man might think his stone house is indestructible. But it is like a cocoon ("his house like a moth's") or a shack ("like a booth that a watchman makes"; v. 18). "He goes to bed rich" one night, but the next day he wakes up ("he opens his eyes") and everything—the house, the money, the clothing—has vanished ("his wealth is gone"; v. 19). And instead of breakfast in bed, he gets the ride of his life! Like floodwaters ("like a flood"; v. 20a) or a hurricane ("a whirlwind," v. 20b; "the east wind," v. 21a), "terrors overtake him" (v. 20a); he is lifted up, carried off, swept "out of his place" (vv. 20–21). The terrors ("it"), or perhaps God himself (as "it" can be translated "he" in vv. 22–23), mercilessly prevail upon him ("hurls at him without pity"; v. 22a). The wicked man tries in vain to escape the judgment ("he flees from its power in headlong flight"; v. 22b). The terrors of death and hell taunt him, scorning ("claps its hands at him") and deriding him ("hisses at him"; v. 23).

Response

Who doubts the theological value of Job's beautiful and inspiring poem about God (Job 26:6–14)? "Behold, these are but the outskirts of his ways" (26:14). Amen and Amen! But what do we do with the rest of what is said in these chapters? What do we make of Job's unwavering claims to innocence (27:4–6)? What do we do with his imprecatory psalm (27:7–23)?

While Job's assertions of innocence might be surprising to us (e.g., "I hold fast my righteousness," 27:6a; see esp. ch. 31), especially if we daily confess our sins ("forgive us our sins," Luke 11:4; "God, be merciful to me, a sinner!" Luke 18:13), knowing just how far we fall from the glory of God, we should not be too taken aback by them. The Bible does give us a few examples of "righteous" men; for example, the two Josephs of the first books of the OT and the NT. Job is certainly presented to us as such a man. Moreover, we know that he is innocent of all the accusations against him. There is no known sin that is the cause of his calamities. He is on death row for a crime he did not commit. Thus, for him to say that his conscience is clear ("my heart does not reproach me"; Job 27:6b) makes sense. Finally, there is something about this aspect of innocence that is important to the drama. If Job were not innocent, the book of Job would offer no corrective to the retribution principle. Also, and perhaps most importantly, this theme might be significant if Job functions as a typological figure. It appears that the author of Job is emphasizing and reemphasizing this theme for a reason. Is he, under the inspiration of the Spirit, setting up an important paradigm, one that will make sense only and ultimately in the coming of Christ?

Regarding Job's cursing of his friends, two thoughts come to mind. First, we need to know that he will eventually forgive them and even restore them to God (42:9). Second, while we might wish that he would have imitated our merciful Lord on the cross, saying, "Forgive them, for they know not what they do" (Luke 23:34)—what a perfect prayer that would be for them!—God's Word does demonstrate God's approval of such expressions. Psalm 137 or Revelation 19, for example, are not songs Christians cannot or should not sing. We long for justice. And if we long for justice, we must long for God's wrath to come.

JOB 28:1–28

28 "Surely there is a mine for silver,
   and a place for gold that they refine.
2 Iron is taken out of the earth,
   and copper is smelted from the ore.
3 Man puts an end to darkness
   and searches out to the farthest limit
   the ore in gloom and deep darkness.
4 He opens shafts in a valley away from where anyone lives;
   they are forgotten by travelers;
   they hang in the air, far away from mankind; they swing to and fro.
5 As for the earth, out of it comes bread,
   but underneath it is turned up as by fire.

6 Its stones are the place of sapphires,[1]
   and it has dust of gold.

7 "That path no bird of prey knows,
   and the falcon's eye has not seen it.
8 The proud beasts have not trodden it;
   the lion has not passed over it.

9 "Man puts his hand to the flinty rock
   and overturns mountains by the roots.
10 He cuts out channels in the rocks,
   and his eye sees every precious thing.
11 He dams up the streams so that they do not trickle,
   and the thing that is hidden he brings out to light.

12 "But where shall wisdom be found?
   And where is the place of understanding?
13 Man does not know its worth,
   and it is not found in the land of the living.
14 The deep says, 'It is not in me,'
   and the sea says, 'It is not with me.'
15 It cannot be bought for gold,
   and silver cannot be weighed as its price.
16 It cannot be valued in the gold of Ophir,
   in precious onyx or sapphire.
17 Gold and glass cannot equal it,
   nor can it be exchanged for jewels of fine gold.
18 No mention shall be made of coral or of crystal;
   the price of wisdom is above pearls.
19 The topaz of Ethiopia cannot equal it,
   nor can it be valued in pure gold.

20 "From where, then, does wisdom come?
   And where is the place of understanding?
21 It is hidden from the eyes of all living
   and concealed from the birds of the air.
22 Abaddon and Death say,
   'We have heard a rumor of it with our ears.'

23 "God understands the way to it,
   and he knows its place.
24 For he looks to the ends of the earth
   and sees everything under the heavens.
25 When he gave to the wind its weight
   and apportioned the waters by measure,
26 when he made a decree for the rain
   and a way for the lightning of the thunder,
27 then he saw it and declared it;
   he established it, and searched it out.
28 And he said to man,
   'Behold, the fear of the Lord, that is wisdom,
   and to turn away from evil is understanding.'"

[1] Or *lapis lazuli*; also verse 16

Section Overview

Is Job still speaking in Job 28? It is difficult to know. On one hand, the topic (the place where wisdom is found) and the language (there is no direct addresses to the friends or God, and no heated accusatory language to either as well) might make us surmise that this chapter contains the narrator's voice. Like the director of a play, he stops the drama, comes down from the production booth, and addresses the audience. Speaking with a voice of serenity, tranquility, and almost scientific objectivity, he reminds both the audience and the actors of the path that Job and his friends need to take in order to arrive at the answer they seek: the wisdom of God found in the fear of God (v. 28).

On the other hand, the voice might be Job's, for he has had his moments, even quite recently (cf. 26:6–14), of deep reflection on the attributes and actions of God. He has also spoken specifically of "thick darkness" (3:6; 10:22 [2x]; 23:17), valuable stones ("gold," 3:15a; 23:10; "silver," 3:15b; 27:16–17; "iron," 19:24), "Abaddon" (26:6), "death" (3:21; 7:15; 9:23), and "wisdom," including:

With God   are wisdom and might (12:13a)
With him   are strength and sound wisdom (12:16a)

Moreover, Job seems to jump intentionally from topic to topic in his final speech (Job 26–31). He speaks of the unsearchable majesty of God (26:6–14), personal integrity (27:1–6), the judgment of the wicked (27:7–23), finding wisdom (28:1–28), the good old days (29:1–25), the terrible current days (30:1–31), and his integrity again (31:1–40). In this way, chapter 28 is not out of place. In fact, if Job is the speaker, the hymn signals to the reader something of Job's (a) spiritual growth, (b) steadfastness, and (c) wisdom—his fearing God (v. 28a; cf. 26:6–14) by turning away from evil (28:8b; cf. 27:4–6; 31:1–40). Job as the speaker also fits God's commendation of Job's words in Job 42:7–8 ("spoken of me what is right"). Surely Job 28:1–28 tops the list of speaking rightly about God!

Section Outline

II.R.   Where Shall Wisdom Be Found? (28:1–28)
    1.   The Wisdom of Man (28:1–11)
    2.   The Inaccessibility of Wisdom (28:12–22)
    3.   The Wisdom of God (28:23–28)

Comment

28:1–11 The structural outline of this wisdom hymn is straightforward (cf. Section Outline above). Job begins by dwelling on man's wisdom. He does not speak of man's unique impulse and aptitude to create art (to draw, paint, sculpt, weave, etc.), which is the "signature of man" as G. K. Chesterton puts it in *The Everlasting Man*. Instead, Job illustrates human wisdom through man's unique ability to mine precious stones, metals, and jewels from the earth.

Like those brave and skillful men who carved the core of the Rocky Mountains in the late 1850s in search of treasures, this ancient poem paints a vivid scene of likeminded men who strip the mountains of their precious possessions: of the noble elements of "gold" (vv. 1b, 6b) and "silver" (v. 1a) as well as the functional ones, "iron" and "copper" (v. 2) and "ore" (v. 3). In fact, quite similar to the techniques used by nineteenth-century excavators, these ancient miners used "fire" (v. 5) and water to extract from the earth its rich treasures, including "sapphires" (or "lapis lazuli"; v. 6a ESV mg.).

The process, described in verses 3–5 and 9–11, went something like this. After setting a large fire in a hand-dug shaft, miners poured water on the hot rock, causing it to crack.

> As for the earth, out of it comes bread,
>> but underneath it is turned up as by fire. (v. 5)

Next, they "[cut] out channels in the rocks" (v. 10a; cf. "shafts," v. 4a) and controlled any nearby rivers that might have caused flooding ("he dams up the streams so that they do not trickle"; v. 11a). Then, lowered down by ropes ("they hang in the air"; v. 4c), they would enter the cavern they created in the mountain ("puts an end to darkness"; v. 3) and go as deep as they could go ("searches out to the farthest limit"; v. 3). Once they had scraped up the fallen stones ("man puts his hand to the flinty rock"; v. 9a), they would carry them to the surface ("the thing that is hidden he brings out to light"; v. 11b). Slowly but surely, through this tedious process, the earth would open itself to the hand of men, like a flower opening to the sunlight of spring. "Man . . . overturns mountains by the roots" (v. 9b)! Man's "eye" *alone* "sees every precious thing" (v. 10b): silver, gold, iron, copper, ore, sapphires.

In the poet's estimation, this amazing accomplishment highlights the greatness of man, an intelligence and an industry unsurpassed in all creation. "That path" to these precious materials even the king of the jungle and queen of the sky cannot find:

no bird of prey	knows,
and the falcon's eye	has not seen it.
The proud beasts	have not trodden it;
the lion	has not passed over it. (vv. 7–8)

As Hartley points out: "Amazingly none of the animals with all their prowess can discover the path to such beautiful gems. The falcon and the lion, two magnificent creatures that dominate the sky and the land respectively, are representative of all animals. The falcon is known for its keen eyesight. From lofty heights it surveys the land, spots its prey, and swoops down on it. But it never detects the hidden path to these minerals."[123] So, we will not find falcons wear-

---

123 Hartley, *Job*, 377.

ing silver necklaces. Then, on the ground, we have the stately lion, a creature that stalks about, taking whatever prey it desires. It is called "proud" because of "its unusual strength and its lack of fear."[124] Yet even though it is king of the jungle, it is not lord of the mines. It cannot control, it does not have power over the earth itself—the very treasures hidden in the depths of it. So, we will not find lions wearing gold earrings to match their golden manes. The falcon, celebrated for its vision, and the lion, celebrated for its courage, cannot compare to the vision and courage of human beings.[125]

28:12–22 Thus far, this poem has a very different feel than Bildad's "Requiem to Man the Maggot and Worm" (25:1–6). But before we shout, "We are man; watch us roar and soar, or at least explore . . . the recesses of the deep!" Job 28:12–22 puts us in our place. While humans above all creatures can probe the mysteries of our earthly domain, we cannot probe the mysteries of the heavenly domain. With ingenuity and determination, we can "penetrate into the foreboding darkness of the earth's interior, the underworld, the abode of the dead in search of treasures,"[126] and we can search the edge and limits of the surface of this earth, but we cannot scratch the surface of wisdom. Man can bring to light all hidden material things, but he cannot unearth wisdom, which is the true light of the world.

The key to understanding this section is noticing the beautiful symmetry used to express this point. The refrain of verses 12–14 is parallel in form and meaning to the refrain of verses 20–22. Both ask the same question: "But where shall wisdom be found? And where is the place of understanding?" (v. 12; cf. v. 20). And both give the same reply in slightly different ways, namely, that the world itself does not know where to find wisdom. All the eyes of the living, both "man" (v. 13) and the "birds of the air" (v. 21), cannot find it. The depths of the earth ("the deep"; v. 14) and even the depths of the underworld ("Abaddon and Death"; v. 22), cannot find it. The best that this world can offer to help mankind in its search for wisdom is but a "rumor of it" (v. 22b). On, in, and above the earth, wisdom cannot be found. With the living and with the dead, wisdom cannot be found. That is the message of the bookends of this middle section (vv. 12–14; 20–22). While man can extract precious metals from the earth, it is impossible for him to obtain wisdom from "the land of the living" (v. 13b).

Within these two bookends stands the unaffordable price of wisdom (vv. 15–19). Man not only fails to secure wisdom by his ingenuity, he also fails to secure it by his wealth:

> It cannot be bought for gold,
>> and silver cannot be weighed as its price.
> It cannot be valued in the gold of Ophir,
>> in precious onyx or sapphire.

---

124 Ibid.
125 See Andersen, *Job*, 226.
126 Hartley, *Job*, 376.

Gold and glass cannot equal it,
> nor can it be exchanged for jewels of fine gold.

No mention shall be made of coral or of crystal;
> the price of wisdom is above pearls.

The topaz of Ethiopia cannot equal it,
> nor can it be valued in pure gold. (vv. 15–19)

One would think that our "inquisitive nature and technological ability that enable [us] to find the riches of the earth no matter how difficult they are to obtain"[127] and the great wealth gained from such mining operations would allow us to purchase anything we wanted, including wisdom. But we do not know, as verse 13 calls it, the "worth" of wisdom. Wisdom is scarcer than a flawless, ten carat diamond. On God's scale, wisdom outweighs the earth's greatest treasures. Jewels such as "onyx," "sapphire," "coral," "crystal," "pearl," and "topaz" are "worthless in the marketplace of wisdom,"[128] and even gold and silver, the most precious metals, are "unacceptable as tender for wisdom."[129] Just as money cannot buy love, it likewise cannot buy wisdom.

28:23–28 After mining through twenty-two verses of this twenty-eight-verse poem, we are still left without an answer to the key question, "Where shall wisdom be found?" (v. 12). If wisdom cannot be found in the depths of the earth nor bought by the deepest pockets, where shall we find this rare commodity?

Thankfully, in the third stanza (vv. 23–28) wisdom gives up the secret of its location. The solution to the search for wisdom is "God" (v. 23) and the "fear of the Lord" (v. 28). While human ingenuity cannot find wisdom, and human wealth cannot buy wisdom,

God	understands	the way to it,
and he	knows	its place. (v. 23)

God alone knows where wisdom is to be found because he alone is omniscient ("he looks to the ends of the earth and sees everything under the heavens"; v. 24). He also knows where wisdom ("it") is to be found because God ("he") created wisdom and used it to establish and govern the world:

When he gave to the wind its weight
> and apportioned the waters by measure,

when he made a decree for the rain
> and a way for the lightning of the thunder,

then he saw it and declared it;
> he established it, and searched it out. (vv. 25–27)

---

127 Smick, "Job," in *The Expositor's Bible Commentary—Abridged Edition: Two-Volume Set*, ed. Kenneth L. Barker and John R. Kohlenberger III (Grand Rapids, MI: 1994), 975.
128 Hartley, *Job*, 380.
129 Alden, *Job*, 274.

This wisdom God freely shares with man:

| Behold, | the fear of the Lord, | that is wisdom, |
| and | to turn away from evil | is understanding. (v. 28) |

This verse is at the heart of the book of Job and the heart of the OT wisdom literature. Similar to the point made in Proverbs 1:7 and Ecclesiastes 12:13, here in Job 28:28, Job reminds us that it is only through a proper attitude of submission, respect, dependence, and worship of the one true God ("the fear of the Lord") and obedience to Yahweh's ways ("to turn away from evil") that we can find wisdom.

Response

In Job 28 we find a stillness that has temporarily tamed the troubled waters. In chapters 1–2 we witnessed the waves of tragedy striking righteous Job, one wave of woe after another: the wave that consumed his children; the wave that swallowed up his wealth; the wave that still crushes against his fragile body. In chapters 3–27 we observed the vain attempts of both Job and his friends to still this terrible flood of misfortune. But thankfully, before all is lost, refuge is to be found in chapter 28, where divine wisdom in a sense stands up, extends its arms, and rebukes the unsettling seas—the shallow waves of human perception and understanding. The answer to the question "But where shall wisdom be found?" (v. 12) is answered in God (v. 23) and the fear of God, which involves turning away from evil (v. 28).

We might be so familiar with the Bible that we do not find this answer odd. How would most people in our culture answer this key question? Would *God* even be in the equation? If so, there certainly will not be anything about fearing him. Most people are optimistic about finding wisdom. One can find it through natural intelligence, acquired intelligence, or just life experience. The man with the high IQ, the woman with the elite education, the kid with street smarts—they can surely find wisdom. But the Bible says no! Not the kind of wisdom that we need to really live, not the kind of wisdom that Job needs to live through inexplicable suffering.

Proverbs, Ecclesiastes, and Job are not God's version of Ben Franklin's *Poor Richard's Almanack*—"Early to bed and early to rise, makes a man healthy, wealthy, and wise"—or the ancient Chinese sayings of Confucius—"Silence is a friend who will never betray." They are certainly not just a less humorous version of "Never argue with a fool; people might not know the difference." No, what sets the content of books like Job apart from the rest of the world's wisdom literature are claims like the one we find in 28:28: the acquisition of true wisdom comes from a right relationship with Yahweh and an appropriate attitude toward him. "Behold, the fear of the Lord, that is wisdom."

As Christians who desire to read the Bible canonically and with Christ at the center, we have license to take this answer a bit further. While it is true that in creation and providence God manifests his wisdom, it is likewise true, as taught throughout the NT, that God most perfectly or more fully manifests his wisdom in the person and work of his Son, our Lord Jesus Christ. The apostle Paul speaks in Ephesians 3:8–11 of the "manifold wisdom of God" revealed or "realized" in our Lord Jesus Christ, and in Colossians 2:3 he explains how "all the treasures of wisdom and knowledge" are "hidden" in Christ; finally, in 1 Corinthians 1:23–24, he claims that the preaching of "Christ" and him "crucified" is the "wisdom of God."

So, not only does the NT teach that *all* wisdom comes to us from God through Christ; the NT likewise teaches the surprising truth that the wisdom of God is most fully displayed in the *death* of Christ. Just as it is only through the death of Christ that we have access to eternal life, so too it is only through the cross of Christ that we have access to wisdom. When we read and reread the story of Job, we have the wonderful benefit of placing (so to speak) our knowledge of Jesus Christ, and of him crucified, as a transparent grid over this OT text. And unlike the characters in the book of Job or the first several centuries of readers of Job, we can easily connect the dots between the wisdom displayed in the sufferings of innocent Job and the wisdom displayed in the sufferings of innocent Jesus. The NT sheds remarkable light on the story of Job and on this grand theme of wisdom.

JOB 29:1–31:40

29 And Job again took up his discourse, and said:

2 "Oh, that I were as in the months of old,
    as in the days when God watched over me,
3 when his lamp shone upon my head,
    and by his light I walked through darkness,
4 as I was in my prime,[1]
    when the friendship of God was upon my tent,
5 when the Almighty was yet with me,
    when my children were all around me,
6 when my steps were washed with butter,
    and the rock poured out for me streams of oil!
7 When I went out to the gate of the city,
    when I prepared my seat in the square,
8 the young men saw me and withdrew,
    and the aged rose and stood;
9 the princes refrained from talking
    and laid their hand on their mouth;
10 the voice of the nobles was hushed,
    and their tongue stuck to the roof of their mouth.
11 When the ear heard, it called me blessed,
    and when the eye saw, it approved,
12 because I delivered the poor who cried for help,
    and the fatherless who had none to help him.

13 The blessing of him who was about to perish came upon me,
and I caused the widow's heart to sing for joy.
14 I put on righteousness, and it clothed me;
my justice was like a robe and a turban.
15 I was eyes to the blind
and feet to the lame.
16 I was a father to the needy,
and I searched out the cause of him whom I did not know.
17 I broke the fangs of the unrighteous
and made him drop his prey from his teeth.
18 Then I thought, 'I shall die in my nest,
and I shall multiply my days as the sand,
19 my roots spread out to the waters,
with the dew all night on my branches,
20 my glory fresh with me,
and my bow ever new in my hand.'

21 "Men listened to me and waited
and kept silence for my counsel.
22 After I spoke they did not speak again,
and my word dropped upon them.
23 They waited for me as for the rain,
and they opened their mouths as for the spring rain.
24 I smiled on them when they had no confidence,
and the light of my face they did not cast down.
25 I chose their way and sat as chief,
and I lived like a king among his troops,
like one who comforts mourners.

30 "But now they laugh at me,
men who are younger than I,
whose fathers I would have disdained
to set with the dogs of my flock.
2 What could I gain from the strength of their hands,
men whose vigor is gone?
3 Through want and hard hunger
they gnaw the dry ground by night in waste and desolation;
4 they pick saltwort and the leaves of bushes,
and the roots of the broom tree for their food.[2]
5 They are driven out from human company;
they shout after them as after a thief.
6 In the gullies of the torrents they must dwell,
in holes of the earth and of the rocks.
7 Among the bushes they bray;
under the nettles they huddle together.
8 A senseless, a nameless brood,
they have been whipped out of the land.

9 "And now I have become their song;
I am a byword to them.
10 They abhor me; they keep aloof from me;
they do not hesitate to spit at the sight of me.

¹¹ Because God has loosed my cord and humbled me,
       they have cast off restraint[3] in my presence.
¹² On my right hand the rabble rise;
       they push away my feet;
       they cast up against me their ways of destruction.
¹³ They break up my path;
       they promote my calamity;
       they need no one to help them.
¹⁴ As through a wide breach they come;
       amid the crash they roll on.
¹⁵ Terrors are turned upon me;
       my honor is pursued as by the wind,
       and my prosperity has passed away like a cloud.

¹⁶ "And now my soul is poured out within me;
       days of affliction have taken hold of me.
¹⁷ The night racks my bones,
       and the pain that gnaws me takes no rest.
¹⁸ With great force my garment is disfigured;
       it binds me about like the collar of my tunic.
¹⁹ God[4] has cast me into the mire,
       and I have become like dust and ashes.
²⁰ I cry to you for help and you do not answer me;
       I stand, and you only look at me.
²¹ You have turned cruel to me;
       with the might of your hand you persecute me.
²² You lift me up on the wind; you make me ride on it,
       and you toss me about in the roar of the storm.
²³ For I know that you will bring me to death
       and to the house appointed for all living.

²⁴ "Yet does not one in a heap of ruins stretch out his hand,
       and in his disaster cry for help?[5]
²⁵ Did not I weep for him whose day was hard?
       Was not my soul grieved for the needy?
²⁶ But when I hoped for good, evil came,
       and when I waited for light, darkness came.
²⁷ My inward parts are in turmoil and never still;
       days of affliction come to meet me.
²⁸ I go about darkened, but not by the sun;
       I stand up in the assembly and cry for help.
²⁹ I am a brother of jackals
       and a companion of ostriches.
³⁰ My skin turns black and falls from me,
       and my bones burn with heat.
³¹ My lyre is turned to mourning,
       and my pipe to the voice of those who weep.

31 "I have made a covenant with my eyes;
       how then could I gaze at a virgin?
² What would be my portion from God above
       and my heritage from the Almighty on high?

3　Is not calamity for the unrighteous,
　　　and disaster for the workers of iniquity?
4　Does not he see my ways
　　　and number all my steps?

5　"If I have walked with falsehood
　　　and my foot has hastened to deceit;
6　(Let me be weighed in a just balance,
　　　and let God know my integrity!)
7　if my step has turned aside from the way
　　　and my heart has gone after my eyes,
　　　and if any spot has stuck to my hands,
8　then let me sow, and another eat,
　　　and let what grows for me[6] be rooted out.

9　"If my heart has been enticed toward a woman,
　　　and I have lain in wait at my neighbor's door,
10　then let my wife grind for another,
　　　and let others bow down on her.
11　For that would be a heinous crime;
　　　that would be an iniquity to be punished by the judges;
12　for that would be a fire that consumes as far as Abaddon,
　　　and it would burn to the root all my increase.

13　"If I have rejected the cause of my manservant or my maidservant,
　　　when they brought a complaint against me,
14　what then shall I do when God rises up?
　　　When he makes inquiry, what shall I answer him?
15　Did not he who made me in the womb make him?
　　　And did not one fashion us in the womb?

16　"If I have withheld anything that the poor desired,
　　　or have caused the eyes of the widow to fail,
17　or have eaten my morsel alone,
　　　and the fatherless has not eaten of it
18　(for from my youth the fatherless[7] grew up with me as with a father,
　　　and from my mother's womb I guided the widow[8]),
19　if I have seen anyone perish for lack of clothing,
　　　or the needy without covering,
20　if his body has not blessed me,[9]
　　　and if he was not warmed with the fleece of my sheep,
21　if I have raised my hand against the fatherless,
　　　because I saw my help in the gate,
22　then let my shoulder blade fall from my shoulder,
　　　and let my arm be broken from its socket.
23　For I was in terror of calamity from God,
　　　and I could not have faced his majesty.

24　"If I have made gold my trust
　　　or called fine gold my confidence,
25　if I have rejoiced because my wealth was abundant
　　　or because my hand had found much,

26 if I have looked at the sun[10] when it shone,
      or the moon moving in splendor,
27 and my heart has been secretly enticed,
      and my mouth has kissed my hand,
28 this also would be an iniquity to be punished by the judges,
      for I would have been false to God above.

29 "If I have rejoiced at the ruin of him who hated me,
      or exulted when evil overtook him
30 (I have not let my mouth sin
      by asking for his life with a curse),
31 if the men of my tent have not said,
      'Who is there that has not been filled with his meat?'
32 (the sojourner has not lodged in the street;
      I have opened my doors to the traveler),
33 if I have concealed my transgressions as others do[11]
      by hiding my iniquity in my heart,
34 because I stood in great fear of the multitude,
      and the contempt of families terrified me,
      so that I kept silence, and did not go out of doors—
35 Oh, that I had one to hear me!
      (Here is my signature! Let the Almighty answer me!)
      Oh, that I had the indictment written by my adversary!
36 Surely I would carry it on my shoulder;
      I would bind it on me as a crown;
37 I would give him an account of all my steps;
      like a prince I would approach him.

38 "If my land has cried out against me
      and its furrows have wept together,
39 if I have eaten its yield without payment
      and made its owners breathe their last,
40 let thorns grow instead of wheat,
      and foul weeds instead of barley."

The words of Job are ended.

[1] Hebrew *my autumn days* [2] Or *warmth* [3] Hebrew *the bridle* [4] Hebrew *He* [5] The meaning of the Hebrew is uncertain [6] Or *let my descendants* [7] Hebrew *he* [8] Hebrew *her* [9] Hebrew *if his loins have not blessed me* [10] Hebrew *the light* [11] Or *as Adam did*

Section Overview

Six words are of great importance in this last long speech: "days," "now," "if," "then," "oh," "let." The word "day" (Hb. *yom*, always in the plural construct "days" in these chapters) sets the scene for the contrast between two seasons in Job's life. First, Job recounts the good old days, the "days when God watched over" him (Job 29:2) and was his friend (29:4), the days when he was respected by all in the city (29:7–24), living "like a king" (29:25). Second, Job speaks of the "days of affliction" (30:16, 27; Hb. *yeme-'oni*). These "days" stretch from that dreadful day ("Now there was a day"; 1:13) when Job lost his children to the present day, in which he still suffers in every imaginable way ("My inward parts are in turmoil and never still"; 30:27; cf. 30:16a). Subsumed under the phrase "days of affliction" is the contrast between *then* and *now*, with the phrase "and now" (Hb. *weʿattah*) repeated three times: "But now they laugh at me" (30:1a); "And now I have become their song" (30:9a); "And now my soul is poured out within me" (30:16a).

The word "if" (Hb. *ʾim*, eighteen times) and the implied "then" (five times) dominate Job 31. This if-then sequence, which starts after four questions (31:1–4), ends only when Job stops speaking ("The words of Job are ended"; 31:40c). Its purpose is to catalog Job's innocence in a variety of ethical areas. Such a catalog is intended by Job not to reassure himself of his blamelessness but rather to showcase to God what he too should see and respond to. And here is where the words "oh" and "let" (both rightly conveying the sense of the Hebrew) come into play. In 31:6a Job says, "Let me be weighed in a just balance." He wants God to know that he is innocent ("Let God know my integrity!"; 31:6b) and to judge accordingly. Job longs for God both to answer him ("Oh, that I had one to hear me! . . . Let the Almighty answer me!"; 31:35) and to vindicate him ("Oh, that I were as in the months of old"; 29:2). These three chapters foreshadow precisely what will happen: God will answer him (38:1; 40:6) and vindicate him (42:7–9), returning him to his former prosperity and happiness (42:10–17). For now, however, Job has no sense that the "days of affliction" will ever pass.

Section Outline

II.S. Let God Know My Integrity and Answer Me! (29:1–31:40)
    1. Back in the Days of Friendship with God (29:1–25)
    2. But Now . . . the Days of Affliction (30:1–31)
    3. If . . . Then (31:1–40)

Comment

29:1–6 Even though God has not granted Job a hearing, chapters 29–31 can be seen as the closing argument of Job's defense. And here, in chapter 29, he begins with a very personal testimony. Job gets almost nostalgic as he recalls what life was like a few months ago ("the months of old"; v. 2a). From those days he recounts two blessings (or, we might say, what "the LORD gave"; 1:21): Yahweh's guiding presence and his generous provision. First, God was present with Job. Although God is the "Almighty," yet he was "with" Job (29:5a).[130] This close "friendship" (v. 4b) benefited his whole household (vv. 4b, 5b) and offered protection ("God watched over me"; v. 2b)[131] and guidance for Job ("his lamp shone upon my head, and by his light I walked through darkness"; v. 3). Second, God generously provided for Job. He provided Job with the blessings of children ("my children were all around me"; v. 5b) and of wealth. The odd expression that ends this introduction—"when

---

130 The "withness" of God is a subtle but important theological theme in both the OT (e.g., Gen. 39:2–3, 21, 23; Isa. 8:10; Zech. 8:23) and the NT (Matt. 1:23; Col. 2:13).
131 Compare this positive reference to God's watching Job with what Job says in 10:14 and 13:27.

my steps were washed with butter, and the rock poured out for me streams of oil!" (v. 6)—describes an unusual abundance. He was awash with wealth. He could bathe in butter, if he wanted to; he could touch stones and oil would stream out. We might say that everything that Job touched (or that *God* touched for Job) turned to gold. Back in the good old days, the luxuries of Canaan seemed small in comparison.

29:7–17 Verses 7–10 speak of the respect Job received from all ages ("young men," "the aged"; v. 8) and from every rank (even "princes," "nobles"; vv. 9–10) at the center of the city ("the gate of the city"; v. 7a)[132] when Job sat to adjudicate and educate. The scene Job paints is of his walking to the city gate to hear an important matter. When he arrives (v. 7), teenagers move to the side (v. 8a), old men stand as a sign of respect (v. 8b), and even princes and nobles stop talking because someone more important than they ("the greatest of all the people of the east"; 1:3) has arrived:

> The princes refrained from talking
>> and laid their hand on their mouth;
> the voice of the nobles was hushed,
>> and their tongue stuck to the roof of their mouth. (29:9–10)

In verses 11–17 Job recounts why (note the "because" in v. 12) he was so well respected. Perhaps seeking to defend himself specifically from Eliphaz's false testimony (cf. 22:6–9) and to reiterate what he really believes about wickedness (cf. 24:3–4, 21), Job depicts himself as a merciful and righteous judge-king. The phrase "when the ear heard, it called me blessed" and its parallel "and when the eye saw, it approved" (29:11) likely refers to legal proceedings he ruled over, with the idea being that his judgments were not only fair but also celebrated (cf. v. 14). What follows, then, in verses 12–17 are the various reasons people rejoiced in his rulings. First, he was merciful to the vulnerable—the poor, the orphan, the widow:

> Because I delivered the poor who cried for help,
>> and the fatherless who had none to help him.
> The blessing of him who was about to perish came upon me,
>> and I caused the widow's heart to sing for joy. (vv. 12–13)

He brought deliverance to the destitute, perhaps personally (out of his own pocket? serving with his own hands?) or at least in his judicial verdict:

> I put on righteousness, and it clothed me;
>> my justice was like a robe and a turban.
> I was eyes to the blind
>> and feet to the lame.

---

132 "As the center of community life, the gate combined the activities of the commercial marketplace (2 Kings 7:17–18), the legal court (Deut. 21:19; Ruth 4:1), and the intellectual interchange of ideas (cf. Ps. 127:5). . . . To have a seat in the gate is to enjoy a privilege reserved for the most prominent citizens (Gen. 19:1; Prov. 31:23)" (Estes, *Job*, 176).

I was a father to the needy,
> and I searched out the cause of him whom I did not know. (vv. 14–16)

If that was not enough, Judge Job defanged those who would take advantage of the vulnerable and destitute:

I broke the fangs of the unrighteous
> and made him drop his prey from his teeth. (v. 17)

This awesome image is a heroic one. Even though Job is talking about himself, it does not come across as self-aggrandizement. We know what the narrator has said of Job. We know what God thinks of Job. We know what will happen to Job. So, the sympathetic reader, as well as the theologically savvy one, might just feel like joining the elders in standing in awe of such a man.

29:18–20 Like Abraham, Job was a friend of God (v. 4; cf. Isa. 41:8), and he fully expected to die as the patriarch did (Gen. 25:8–9)—in his own house ("in my nest"; Job 29:18a), at an old age ("I shall multiply my days as the sand"; v. 18b), surrounded by his beloved family. In fact, reading Genesis 25:8–9 should make us weep for Job, especially the lines concerning Abraham's children burying him. It is normal for a father to grieve deeply that he will not be buried by his children. Job now has no children; he has lost all ten. This is a sad fact that we as readers should not forget. Job also thought he would remain healthy until his final breath, flourishing like a sky-high, deep-rooted tree ("my roots spread out to the waters, with the dew all night on my branches"; Job 29:19). He thought that the respect and dignity he describes in verses 8–10 and 21–25 would stay with him until the end ("my glory fresh with me"; v. 20a; cf. 19:9), still fighting on his deathbed for the causes of justice in the world ("and my bow ever new in my hand"; v. 20b). Job has lost his children; he has lost his health. He has lost his glory; he has lost his ethical reputation.

29:21–25 In these final verses, Job reminisces again about the days of old, when his words were not mocked but listened to ("men listened to me and waited"; v. 21a). There was silence when he spoke ("[men] kept silence for my counsel"; v. 21b) and afterward ("they did not speak again"; v. 22a), so convinced were they of the truth of his declarations. His words were life-giving ("my word dropped upon them"; v. 22b), like spring rain after the winter drought ("they waited for me as for the rain, and they opened their mouths as for the spring rain"; v. 23). How different than what Job has experienced from chapter 4 until now. His friends have not believed his words, listened to them, or found any sustenance in them. Instead they have repeatedly rebuked him for the folly of his lips.

Job 29:24–25 summarizes the utter honor Job then had. He did not even have to open his mouth for people to feel blessed by his presence. To the hopeless, his smile and countenance brought the confidence they needed to lift their spirits ("I smiled on them when they had no confidence, and the light of my face they did not cast down"; v. 24), and his leadership ("I . . . sat as chief"/"like a king") brought both wise guidance ("I chose their way") and compassionate consolation ("like one who comforts mourners"; v. 25).

30:1–15 The words "But now" (v. 1) beginning chapter 30 present an ominous contrast to the good old days of 29:2. As Job dreams of the past, he awakes in the present to the sounds of laughter. "But now they laugh at me" (30:1a). The word "laugh" in verse 1 is the same word for "smile" in 29:24 (Hb. *sakhaq*). This is not smiley laughter at the end of a joke but mocking laughter toward Job as the butt of their joke. The word "they" (twenty times in 30:1–15) introduces us to Job's opposition, whom Job describes as young ("men who are younger than I"; v. 1b) and of the lowest possible reputation ("whose fathers I would have disdained to set with the dogs of my flock"; v. 1cd). A gang of teenage thugs, of whom Job would not have even hired their fathers as lowly shepherds (or even as sheep dogs!), are barking after him!

In verses 2–8 Job describes in vivid color the class and character of his new enemies. They are weak (v. 2), homeless (vv. 6–7), and hungry scavengers who eat whatever they can find (vv. 3–4) and who have been ousted from honorable society (v. 5). They look, smell, and act like dogs! They are, in Job's summary estimate, "a senseless, a nameless brood" that has been expelled from any human community ("whipped out of the land"; v. 8). *That* is who "they" are! And yet "they" join Eliphaz, Bildad, and Zophar in devouring Job with their verbal cruelty:

> Now I have become their song;
>   I am a byword to them. (v. 9)

They so hate Job ("they abhor me"; v. 10a) that verbal abuse is not enough. Not only do they sing pub songs celebrating his demise and create catchy proverbs about his poverty (cf. v. 9), they also offer psychological abuse as well. They look down on him ("they keep aloof from me"), so much so that they spit in the dirt before him ("they . . . spit at the sight of me"; v. 10). This spitting might refer to spitting in his face (cf. NIV). If so, such a reading transitions from the psychological to the physical pain Job experiences. He feels helpless against their harassment. Because "God" has let go of Job ("loosed my cord"), watching him fall in the pit of poverty and ignominy ("and humbled me"), nothing can stop this street gang from pummeling him ("they have cast off restraint in my presence"; v. 11). Anything goes in their assault.

Job next, in verse 12–14, describes what they do to him with a mix of metaphors, from a street fight to a besieged city. First, he is blindsided ("on my right hand the rabble rise"; v. 12a) and knocked to the ground ("they push away my feet"; 12b). Then, as he lies powerless on the ground, they again attack his body ("they promote my calamity"; v. 13b). To him, he is a feeble victim, an easy target ("they need no one to help them"; v. 13c). To them, however, he is a mighty fortress to be conquered. They blow up any bridges over which he might escape ("they break up my path"; v. 13a) and build siege ramps against him ("they cast up against me their ways of destruction"; v. 12c). They batter down the wall, making a gaping hole ("as through a wide breach they come"; v. 14a) for wave upon wave of their forces to flood through ("amid the crash they roll on"; v. 14b).[133] Job fears for his life ("terrors are turned upon me"; v. 15) and he fears that his former glory will never return to him:

My honor   is pursued   as by the wind,
and my prosperity   has passed away   like a cloud. (v. 15bc)

30:16–23 Where are the aged, the princes, and the nobles to defend Job (cf. 29:8–10)? Worse than that, where is God to defend the innocent and lift up the honorable? How can honorable Job be so dishonored by the least honorable? How can the just judge be sentenced by unrighteous criminals? How can the father to the needy be mocked and beaten by teenage thugs from among the poorest of the poor?

In 30:16 Job introduces the key phrase "days of affliction," which he will later use in verse 27. In both places he speaks of his unimaginable sufferings of the soul. Verse 16 also begins with the phrase "and now" (Hb. *we'attah*), repeated twice earlier: "But now they laugh at me" (v. 1); "And now I have become their song" (v. 9). This final "and now" shows the greatest contrast between *then* and *now*. *Then* Job walked on thick butter (29:6), bestowing joy upon the joyless (29:13b); *but now* he sits in the mire (30:19a) with a soul that is poured on the floor like rotten milk (v. 16a). More than that, his pain is an eleven! The relentless pain is so severe that he cannot sleep ("the night racks my bones, and the pain that gnaws me takes no rest"; v. 17). His own protective garment turns into a noose ("with great force my garment is disfigured"; v. 18a), slowly tightening around his neck ("it binds me about like the collar of my tunic"; v. 18b). If a hanging is in vision in the terribly difficult to translate verse 18, Job next falls to the ground. Verse 19 is clear that Job is now in the mud. The cause, however, is not gravity but God: he "has cast me into the mire" (v. 19a).

If Job was helpless against the assaults of the street gang, how well will he fare against almighty God? He is as good as dead ("I have become like dust and ashes"; v. 19b). Job knows that the only way he will be restored is if God decides to act for him, not against him. Yet here again (cf. 23:16), with each reference to God, Job loses hope:

You do not answer me (30:20a)
You only look at me (v. 20b)
You persecute me (v. 21b)
You toss me about in the roar of the storm (v. 22b)
You will bring me to death (v. 23a)

God will not answer his prayers ("I cry to you for help and you do not answer me"; v. 20a). Even though God sees Job and knows of his plight, he stands idly by ("you only look at me"; v. 20b). And when God does lift a hand, it is only to brutalize

---

133 See Alden, *Job*, 291.

("you have turned cruel to me; with the might of your hand you persecute me"; v. 21). The persecuting pain is like God's lifting him from the ground ("you lift me up on the wind"), making him ride the fast and furious wind for a while ("you make me ride on it"), and then tossing him into the thunder ("and you toss me about in the roar of the storm"; v. 22). The ride is not yet over. This is how Job feels now. The last leg of the ride, he can only imagine, will end in death. Eventually God will drop him to the dust ("for I know that you will bring me to death"), for that is where every person eventually resides ("to the house appointed for all [the] living"; v. 23). Job is a lot closer to where he began in chapter 3 than where he was in 26:6–14. A deep darkness is slowly covering the stage.

30:24–31 God is not mentioned in these verses. Job ends with neither an accusation against heaven nor a petition to it. Instead he offers a "self-lament."[134] Job laments that no one—not even God—has extended him a helping hand: "Yet does not one in a heap of ruins stretch out his hand, and in his disaster cry for help?" (v. 24). Job has been left stranded, to struggle alone. This makes no sense to him, as he has lived a life of extending an emphatic hand to rescue. He "delivered the poor who cried for help" (29:12a) and lifted the lame (29:15b). Or, as he puts it here with two rhetorical questions:

> Did not I weep   for him whose day was hard?
> Was not my soul grieved   for the needy? (30:25)

The retribution principle is busted. Lady Justice's blindfold is pulled over her mouth. Job's world has been turned upside down. He lived by another wisdom sage's later beatitude, "Blessed are the merciful, for they shall receive mercy" (Matt. 5:7). What happened instead?

> But   when I hoped for good,   evil came,
> and   when I waited for light,   darkness came. (Job 30:26)

Job cannot cope. His philosophical struggles affect his body. His bowels boil! "My inward parts are in turmoil and never still" (v. 27a). Like Jeremiah, he writhes in pain within the walls of his heart (cf. Jer. 4:19). His skin is blackened "not by the sun" (Job 30:28a), but by his spiritual sickness and social sorrow. His deep darkness within is even changing his complexion! He suffers both outwardly ("my skin turns black and falls from me") and inwardly ("and my bones burn with heat"; v. 30). Since God is silent, his only hope is to appeal to those who once esteemed him at the city gate (cf. 29:7–11). "I stand up in the assembly," he says, "and cry for help" (30:28b). But that too is useless. His only fellowship and family is with ugly and obnoxious animals:

> I am   a brother   of jackals
> and   a companion   of ostriches. (v. 29)

---

134 Hartley, *Job*, 404.

This verse, along with the final one (below), depicts Job on the ash heap, making mournful music (cf. the use of the "flute" in Jer. 48:36; Matt. 9:23) and howling like a jackal and hissing like an ostrich (cf. Mic. 1:8):[135]

> My lyre   is turned   to mourning,
> and my pipe   to the voice of those who weep. (Job 30:31)

31:1–4 How will Job conclude? Will he make a disingenuous admission of his sins? No. A final tirade against his friends? No. Instead, he puts down his flute and the score to the Jackal's Requiem and takes up his old legal brief. He once again denies the allegations against him, calling on the Almighty to render a righteous judgment. He denies the charges his friends have libeled against him—e.g., dishonesty (22:6; 31:5–8), neglecting the needy (22:7–9; 31:16–23)—as well as other common sins such as idolatry (vv. 26–28), covetousness (vv. 7–8), sexual lust (v. 1), or adultery (vv. 9–12). Job gives what many commentators call an "oath of innocence." Daniel Estes explains how and why Job uses this "ancient legal strategy of negative confession":

> Several times, Job uses the form, "If I have done this crime, then let God punish me with this horrible consequence." Other times, Job states the condition, but he leaves the consequence undefined. By this means, Job as the defendant calls on God as judge either to condemn him to the full extent of the law or else to clear him of the erroneous charge. If Job is guilty, then he has invited God to strike him with horrific penalties. If God does not exact the punishment, then his failure to do so will tacitly acquit Job of the charges against him. By this legal procedure, even the silence of God the judge can exonerate Job.[136]

Job will deny eleven sins: lust (vv. 1–4), dishonesty (vv. 5–8), adultery (vv. 9–12), oppression (vv. 13–15), neglect of the needy (vv. 16–23), materialism (vv. 24–25), paganism (vv. 26–28), vindictiveness (vv. 29–30), inhospitality (vv. 31–32), duplicity (vv. 33–34), and exploitation (vv. 38–40).[137]

Job begins with his disavowal of *lust*: "I have made a covenant with my eyes; how then could I gaze at a virgin?" He has cut a covenant (Hb. *berit karatti*) with his eyes. In other words, he has vowed to himself, as a man who fears the Lord and turns away from evil, that he will control his eyes (or else! see v. 3). He will not "gaze" upon a teenage girl (a "virgin"), whether such looking involves looking to add another woman as a wife or, more likely, looking with lustful intent on

---

135 "The jackal's howl is a doleful, mourning sound, said to sound like the wailing of a child, while the ostrich gives out a hissing moan. Their moaning cries convey the stark loneliness of the steppe. Job feels so lonely that he senses that his only companions are these animals in their doleful crying" (ibid., 406).
136 Estes, *Job*, 188.
137 Hartley lists fourteen sins that Job denied, viewing the "use of two sevens in the list" as symbolizing Job's "faithful adherence to the entire moral law" (*Job*, 409). With some slight alterations, we have followed Derek Thomas's list in *The Storm Breaks: Job Simply Explained* (repr. Durham, UK: Evangelical Press, 2005), 237.

her. Perhaps Job starts with the sin of lust because it is a common temptation for men.[138] Also, it is something internal, a matter of the eyes and heart.

Job has been self-controlled in this vital area of sexual purity because he knows that God sees everything ("Does not he see my ways and number all my steps?"; v. 4) and judges even the secret intentions of the heart. Job asked himself the question:

What would be   my portion   from God above
and   my heritage   from the Almighty on high? (v. 2)

In other words, what would God give him if he indulged in sexual fantasies? His answer comes in verse 3: he should expect an unhappy heritage!

Is not   calamity   for the unrighteous,
and   disaster   for the workers of iniquity? (v. 3)

31:5–8 Next, Job disavows *dishonesty*. Here Job uses three walking metaphors for living dishonestly ("if I have walked with falsehood"/"my foot has hastened to deceit"/"my step has turned aside"; vv. 5, 7a). He denies that he has walked this way. He also claims that both his heart and his hands are clean: his "heart" has not chased a profit for ill-gotten gain (v. 7b), and his "hands" have no guilty blemish on them from some shady deal (v. 7c). If his honesty were weighed on an honest scale ("let me be weighed in a just balance"), it would prove to God that Job has been telling the truth ("know my integrity!"; v. 6). If this is not so, Job continues, he will reap the consequence for not keeping the covenant: someone else can eat from his fertile fields ("then let me sow, and another eat") and his land can fall forever barren after the stranger has been fed ("and let what grows for me be rooted out"; v. 8).

31:9–12 In these verses Job returns to the theme of sexual immorality (cf. v. 1). Here he denies the sin of *adultery*, which he describes briefly in two lines. First, a man is smitten by another man's wife ("if my heart has been enticed toward a woman [or "wife"]"; v. 9a). Second, he waits for an opportunity to seduce her ("and I have lain in wait at my neighbor's door"; v. 9b). Third, and implied, he succeeds; he sleeps with her.

Job has never done this! And he is repulsed by the thought of it. A lustful glance (v. 1) is a sin against God and the girl, but adultery is a more grievous sin (a "heinous crime"; v. 11) because it is premeditated and because it tears apart the very fabric of marriage and of society as a whole. The consequences for such a crime Job lays out in verses 10–12. He envisions his wife becoming the town whore ("then let my wife grind for another, and let others bow down on her"; v. 10), the elders of the city gate stoning him ("an iniquity to be punished by the judges"; v. 11b), and setting all his property ablaze (adultery is a "fire that consumes as far as Abaddon,

---

138 As Goldingay writes: "Job is a man, and it looks as if Job knows that men think about sex a lot. So sex is the concrete starting point for understanding 'wrongdoing' and 'wickedness' and for a recognition that without a commitment to sexual propriety, he is liable to God's bringing disaster on his life" (*Job*, 146).

and it would burn to the root all my increase"; v. 12). A household and a society cannot survive when this sin from the pit of hell reigns!

31:13–15 If there is a pattern to Job's denials of sin, it perhaps emerges here. He moves from *seemingly* secret sins (lust, adultery) to societal sins (dishonesty in business, oppression of household slaves). This pattern seems to play out in the rest of the chapter (table 4.7).

TABLE 4.7: Pattern of Job's Denials in Job 31

Secret Sins	Societal Sins
lust (vv. 1–4)	
dishonesty (vv. 5–8)	
adultery (vv. 9–12)	
	oppression (vv. 13–15)
	neglect of the needy (vv. 16–23)
materialism (vv. 24–25)	
paganism (vv. 26–28)	
vindictiveness (vv. 29–30)	
	inhospitality (vv. 31–32)
	exploitation (vv. 38–40)

Oppression is what Job denies in verses 13–15. He states that he would never have treated one of his household slaves ("my manservant or my maidservant") without good will or generosity if they came to him with a complaint (v. 13).[139] He knows that God judges inhumane masters (v. 14), and he knows, far before Thomas Jefferson penned "all men are created equal," that his slaves were created by his Creator: "Did not he who made me in the womb make him? And did not one fashion us in the womb?" (v. 15).

31:16–23 Job's longest denial is that he has not *neglected the needy*. Remembering the poor, in Paul's words (Gal. 2:10), is a big deal to Job. To use another NT text, Job will fare well come judgment day, according to Jesus' parable of the sheep and the goats (Matt. 25:31–46). Job claims that he has cared for the least of God's people: the "poor" (Job 31:16a), the "widow" (v. 16b), the "fatherless" (vv. 17b, 21), and anyone in need of food, clothing, or shelter (vv. 17a, 18–20).

In one of the most personal, autobiographical, and beautifully phrased lines in the book, Job recalls his childhood, when apparently orphans were a part of his family, or a consistent ministry of his family ("from my youth the fatherless

---

139 When we read about Job's slaves, we should not think of the cruelties of American antebellum slavery as depicted in *Uncle Tom's Cabin*. Rather, we should think of the relationships depicted in *Downton Abbey*. Job's servants were beloved members of his large household. And let us remember that Job lost not only all his children but most of his servants as well.

grew up with me as with a father"; v. 18a). He also recalls, in exaggerated terms, how the plight of widows has been his concern his whole life ("from my mother's womb I guided the widow"; v. 18b). Job has lived out true religion (cf. James 1:27).

Job may be exaggerating, but if he is lying, he calls on God to rip off his arms!

| then | let my shoulder blade | fall | from my shoulder, |
| and | let my arm | be broken | from its socket. (v. 22) |

31:24–28 *Materialism* is the next vice. He pairs it with *paganism*. This is an interesting, but not unexpected, combination, for as our Lord Jesus himself summarizes, the two go hand in hand:

No one can serve two masters, for either he will hate the one and love the other, or he will be devoted to the one and despise the other. You cannot serve God and money. (Matt. 6:24)

Job asserts that he has not "made gold my trust" or, put differently, "called fine gold my confidence" (Job 31:24). His joy has not come from the fortune he has made for himself (v. 25).

Money was not his god, and pagan deities were not his idols. The moon and the sun, natural candidates for worship in the ancient Near East, he did not worship. He did not look at the sun when it rose (v. 26a) or the moon "moving in splendor" at night (v. 26b) and secretly pray that such celestial lights would prosper him (v. 27a). "He never *threw a kiss* [v. 27b] to them as a sign of affection and devotion, a widespread pagan practice."[140] Why not? Because such sins are as evil as adultery ("this also would be an iniquity to be punished by the judges"; v. 28a) and idolatry is a crime against Yahweh himself ("for I would have been false to God above"; v. 28b; cf. Ex. 20:3–6).

31:29–37 In these verses, Job disavows *vindictiveness*, *inhospitality*, and *duplicity*. He states that he has not rejoiced over the ruin of his enemies, gloated over their misfortune, or prayed for their deaths (vv. 29–30). Moreover, he has been gracious to all, extending hospitality to all, from his slaves to strangers (vv. 31–32). Finally, with Job, what you see is what you get. He is not a hypocrite. He does not curse his enemies under his breath, invite only the powerful to sup at table, or hide his sins ("concealed my transgressions"/"hiding my iniquity"; v. 33) under the pretense of piety. When he has offended God or others, he has made it known. He did not keep silent, hiding in his house ("did not go out of doors"; v. 34c) because he feared what people ("the multitude"/"families"; v. 34ab) might think if they only knew his personal failings.

What is unusual here, however, is that he does not add the usual consequence of such sins (cf. vv. 2–3, 8, 10–12, 14, 22, 28). Instead, he interrupts his disavowals (he has one more to go, vv. 38–40) with a plea reminiscent of earlier ones (most

---

140 Hartley, *Job*, 419. The ESV translates this phrase "and my mouth has kissed my hand." Hartley, slightly paraphrasing, translates, "and my hand threw a kiss from my mouth" (418).

recently, v. 6b). In verses 35–37, Job again begs for a hearing ("Oh, that I had one to hear me!"; v. 35a). He has already written (or wanted to write) his testimony on stone (cf. 19:23–24). Now he signs it ("here is my signature!"; 31:35b). He demands an answer from God ("Let the Almighty answer me!" and write his own "indictment" against me; v. 35bc). Job is curious as to what the charges from his "adversary" might be.[141] Like his sins (cf. vv. 33–34), he would take seriously and make public the charges against him ("surely I would carry it on my shoulder; I would bind it on me as a crown"; v. 36). He needs an answer as soon as possible to the question of 13:23a, "How many are my iniquities and my sins?" He begs again, this time to God, "Make me know my transgression and my sin" (13:23b). Job is ready and eager to defend himself ("I would give him an account of all my steps"; 31:37a); he is confident going into this court case ("like a prince" before a king "I would approach" God; v. 37b).

31:38–40 Before we read the narrator's declaration that the "words of Job are ended" (v. 40c), Job ends with his final crime-consequence pairing ("if"/"let"). He disavows *exploitation*. Job has not exploited his land (the "land" has not "cried out against" him; parallel, "its furrows" have not "wept together"; v. 38) or his tenants who farm it (he has not "made its owners breathe their last"; v. 39b). He has not underpaid or cheated the farmers (he has not "eaten its yield without payment"; v. 39a). And if he has, the final curse should apply:

> let   thorns   grow   instead of wheat,
> and   foul weeds   instead of barley. (v. 40ab)

While this curse is anticlimactic, coming from verses 35–39, it is realistic. Like any person suffering from extreme pain, Job has often shifted from loud lament to awe-filled worship, from strong defense to utter despair, from promises to plagues.

RESPONSE

With this long section of Job's final speech, many thoughts of reflection and response might come to mind. Let us consider five possible avenues of application.

First, it is difficult to read Job's description of himself as a just judge in 29:11–17 and not long for justice in our world. As much as we long for the coming Judge and his final and perfect justice, we should pray now for godly rulers and judges. What a difference it makes when those in high office are clothed with righteousness and justice (29:14). How the world is changed for the better when godly laws are in place and enforced that protect the weak and poor. And what a difference it makes when the rich act righteously and generously with their time, treasures, and talents, being eyes to the blind, feet to the lame, and fathers to the needy (29:15–16). When those of high society look out for the lowly, look out! The kingdom of God is at hand.

---

141 For a similar statement about God, see Job 16:9.

Second, Job's memories in chapter 29 might nauseate some if they think his nostalgia is an exercise in self-love. However, the point might be, as Estes indicates, that "when adversity comes, memories of God's past faithfulness can sustain us."[142] As followers of Yahweh, we are to remember what God has done for us, a command found in both the OT (e.g., Deut. 5:15) and the NT (e.g., Luke 22:19), trusting that sometimes such memories can be therapeutic for the soul.

Third, and following closely what has been said above (and what might need to be a corrective for some Christians), we must not mistake gratitude for God's generosity—expressed in his blessings of health and wealth—for the gospel. The gospel of Jesus Christ does not promise us the happiness of a pain-free existence or extravagant lifestyle. It does not promise us respect or awed esteem when we enter the room. It does not promise us a Job-like bank account.[143] Instead, as our Lord Jesus makes clear, discipleship is a call to die to self: "If anyone would come after me, let him deny himself and take up his cross and follow me" (Mark 8:34). The apostle Paul not only followed this pattern but proclaimed it. As Longman well summarizes:

> Paul tells Christians that they are an afflicted people. Indeed, Paul speaks of the necessity of sharing in the sufferings of Christ and thereby "attaining to the resurrection from the dead" (Phil. 3:10–11 NIV). However, in their present affliction, they experience God's comfort (2 Cor. 1:3–11). Indeed, in spite of all of his troubles, Paul could still experience joy (2 Cor. 7:4). The absence of pain and the experience of unalloyed joy come not in this life but the next. Christians must endure the hardships of a fallen world today but can anticipate the joys of the future, when God will wipe away every tear (Rev. 7:17).[144]

Fourth, Job's accusations against God and his self-laments expressed in Job 30 are difficult to apply. But before we condemn Job or say, "I would never say that to God!" we must sit with him for a day. Job is totally distraught. His "days of affliction" (30:16, 27) have stricken his body and soul. He is black on the outside (30:28, 30) and blue on the inside (30:16a, 27a). He is lonely. Maligned. Mistreated. Mystified. Ashamed. His shame, however, is not due to sin. So it will not work to ask him to pray some version of Psalm 32 or Psalm 51. And, while we do not recommend using each word of this chapter in one's prayers to God or conversation with others, we do recommend that we, like Job, take whatever shame we might feel—whether it be from undeserved derision (in Job's case) or from unrepentant

---

142 Estes, *Job*, 180.
143 John Calvin's warning is also apropos here: "This must serve for our learning that we may always stand upon our guard. If God send us any prosperity, let us not be too sleepy: but let us consider this mortal life is subject to all the changes we can devise, yea truly notwithstanding all the props that we have. And although the whole world seem to favor us, and that we have a hundred thousand shoulders to bear us up: yet must we nevertheless think, that there is no settledness here below, but that all things are transitory, so as all things are changed in the turning of a hand.... For there is nothing easier with a man, than to make himself believe, that he shall always continue in a happy state, when he is once in it." *Sermons on Job* (facsimile edition of the 1574 edition; Edinburgh, UK: Banner of Truth, 1993), sermon 107, p. 502.
144 Longman, *Job*, 343.

sin (usually in our case)—and use such shame to bring us to God for answers or forgiveness.[145]

Fifth, what do we make of Job's oath of innocence (Job 31)? Perhaps we find it off-putting because Job comes across to us as self-righteous (e.g., 31:33a) and self-promoting ("I" [31x], "me" [13x], "my" [44x]). Or, if we give this chapter a more generous reading, we still might think it odd for a believer to make such a detailed inventory of sins followed by a disavowal of them. However, if we remember the historical and narrative context, it makes sense that Job is offering a final defense. In this way, he is no different than a defendant offering self-representation in a criminal case. He is dismissing, one by one, the charges against him. Beyond the original context, might this chapter speak into our contemporary context? Do such self-evaluations deny the gospel of grace? They do not have to (cf. 2 Cor. 13:5; 2 Pet. 1:10). For example, since the Protestant Reformation, Christians have used the Ten Commandments to remind us of our need for mercy *and* to show us how to live in a manner worthy of the gospel.[146]

For example, soon after we read in Answer 44 of the Westminster Shorter Catechism that "we are bound to keep all his commandments," the catechism asks, "What is required in the first commandment?" (Q. 46). The answer is, "The first commandment requireth us to know and acknowledge God to be the only true God, and our God; and to worship and glorify him accordingly." Question/Answer 47 follows:

Q. What is forbidden in the first commandment?
A. The first commandment forbiddeth the denying, or not worshiping and glorifying, the true God as God, and our God; and the giving of that worship and glory to any other, which is due to him alone.

Luther's Small Catechism similarly uses the Ten Commandments to train us in righteousness:

The Sixth Commandment.
Thou shalt not commit adultery.
What does this mean?
Answer: We should fear and love God that we may lead a chaste and decent life in words and deeds, and each love and honor his spouse.

The Seventh Commandment.
Thou shalt not steal.
What does this mean?
Answer: We should fear and love God that we may not take our neighbor's money or property, nor get them by false ware or dealing, but help him to improve and protect his property and business [that his means are preserved and his condition is improved].

---

145 See Longman on this topic (ibid., 352–353). "Shame can be redemptive when it drives a person to God" (353).
146 It is interesting to note how many of the Ten Commandments Job covers!

The Heidelberg Catechism follows the same pattern.

Question 110. What does God forbid in the eighth commandment?
Answer: God forbids not only those thefts, and robberies, which are punishable by the magistrate; but he comprehends under the name of theft all wicked tricks and devices, whereby we design to appropriate to ourselves the goods which belong to our neighbor: whether it be by force, or under the appearance of right, as by unjust weights, ells, measures, fraudulent merchandise, false coins, usury, or by any other way forbidden by God; as also all covetousness, all abuse and waste of his gifts.

Question 111. But what does God require in this commandment?
Answer: That I promote the advantage of my neighbor in every instance I can or may; and deal with him as I desire to be dealt with by others: further also that I faithfully labor, so that I may be able to relieve the needy.

JOB 32:1–37:24

32 So these three men ceased to answer Job, because he was righteous in his own eyes. ²Then Elihu the son of Barachel the Buzite, of the family of Ram, burned with anger. He burned with anger at Job because he justified himself rather than God. ³He burned with anger also at Job's three friends because they had found no answer, although they had declared Job to be in the wrong. ⁴Now Elihu had waited to speak to Job because they were older than he. ⁵And when Elihu saw that there was no answer in the mouth of these three men, he burned with anger.

⁶And Elihu the son of Barachel the Buzite answered and said:

"I am young in years,
    and you are aged;
therefore I was timid and afraid
    to declare my opinion to you.
⁷ I said, 'Let days speak,
    and many years teach wisdom.'
⁸ But it is the spirit in man,
    the breath of the Almighty, that makes him understand.
⁹ It is not the old[1] who are wise,
    nor the aged who understand what is right.
¹⁰ Therefore I say, 'Listen to me;
    let me also declare my opinion.'

¹¹ "Behold, I waited for your words,
    I listened for your wise sayings,
    while you searched out what to say.

12 I gave you my attention,
    and, behold, there was none among you who refuted Job
    or who answered his words.
13 Beware lest you say, 'We have found wisdom;
    God may vanquish him, not a man.'
14 He has not directed his words against me,
    and I will not answer him with your speeches.

15 "They are dismayed; they answer no more;
    they have not a word to say.
16 And shall I wait, because they do not speak,
    because they stand there, and answer no more?
17 I also will answer with my share;
    I also will declare my opinion.
18 For I am full of words;
    the spirit within me constrains me.
19 Behold, my belly is like wine that has no vent;
    like new wineskins ready to burst.
20 I must speak, that I may find relief;
    I must open my lips and answer.
21 I will not show partiality to any man
    or use flattery toward any person.
22 For I do not know how to flatter,
    else my Maker would soon take me away.

33 "But now, hear my speech, O Job,
    and listen to all my words.
2 Behold, I open my mouth;
    the tongue in my mouth speaks.
3 My words declare the uprightness of my heart,
    and what my lips know they speak sincerely.
4 The Spirit of God has made me,
    and the breath of the Almighty gives me life.
5 Answer me, if you can;
    set your words in order before me; take your stand.
6 Behold, I am toward God as you are;
    I too was pinched off from a piece of clay.
7 Behold, no fear of me need terrify you;
    my pressure will not be heavy upon you.

8 "Surely you have spoken in my ears,
    and I have heard the sound of your words.
9 You say, 'I am pure, without transgression;
    I am clean, and there is no iniquity in me.
10 Behold, he finds occasions against me,
    he counts me as his enemy,
11 he puts my feet in the stocks
    and watches all my paths.'

12 "Behold, in this you are not right. I will answer you,
    for God is greater than man.
13 Why do you contend against him,
    saying, 'He will answer none of man's[2] words'?[3]

¹⁴ For God speaks in one way,
 and in two, though man does not perceive it.
¹⁵ In a dream, in a vision of the night,
 when deep sleep falls on men,
 while they slumber on their beds,
¹⁶ then he opens the ears of men
 and terrifies[4] them with warnings,
¹⁷ that he may turn man aside from his deed
 and conceal pride from a man;
¹⁸ he keeps back his soul from the pit,
 his life from perishing by the sword.

¹⁹ "Man is also rebuked with pain on his bed
 and with continual strife in his bones,
²⁰ so that his life loathes bread,
 and his appetite the choicest food.
²¹ His flesh is so wasted away that it cannot be seen,
 and his bones that were not seen stick out.
²² His soul draws near the pit,
 and his life to those who bring death.
²³ If there be for him an angel,
 a mediator, one of the thousand,
 to declare to man what is right for him,
²⁴ and he is merciful to him, and says,
 'Deliver him from going down into the pit;
 I have found a ransom;
²⁵ let his flesh become fresh with youth;
 let him return to the days of his youthful vigor';
²⁶ then man[5] prays to God, and he accepts him;
 he sees his face with a shout of joy,
 and he restores to man his righteousness.
²⁷ He sings before men and says:
 'I sinned and perverted what was right,
 and it was not repaid to me.
²⁸ He has redeemed my soul from going down into the pit,
 and my life shall look upon the light.'

²⁹ "Behold, God does all these things,
 twice, three times, with a man,
³⁰ to bring back his soul from the pit,
 that he may be lighted with the light of life.
³¹ Pay attention, O Job, listen to me;
 be silent, and I will speak.
³² If you have any words, answer me;
 speak, for I desire to justify you.
³³ If not, listen to me;
 be silent, and I will teach you wisdom."

34

Then Elihu answered and said:

² "Hear my words, you wise men,
 and give ear to me, you who know;

3   for the ear tests words
     as the palate tastes food.
4   Let us choose what is right;
     let us know among ourselves what is good.
5   For Job has said, 'I am in the right,
     and God has taken away my right;
6   in spite of my right I am counted a liar;
     my wound is incurable, though I am without transgression.'
7   What man is like Job,
     who drinks up scoffing like water,
8   who travels in company with evildoers
     and walks with wicked men?
9   For he has said, 'It profits a man nothing
     that he should take delight in God.'

10   "Therefore, hear me, you men of understanding:
     far be it from God that he should do wickedness,
     and from the Almighty that he should do wrong.
11   For according to the work of a man he will repay him,
     and according to his ways he will make it befall him.
12   Of a truth, God will not do wickedly,
     and the Almighty will not pervert justice.
13   Who gave him charge over the earth,
     and who laid on him[6] the whole world?
14   If he should set his heart to it
     and gather to himself his spirit and his breath,
15   all flesh would perish together,
     and man would return to dust.

16   "If you have understanding, hear this;
     listen to what I say.
17   Shall one who hates justice govern?
     Will you condemn him who is righteous and mighty,
18   who says to a king, 'Worthless one,'
     and to nobles, 'Wicked man,'
19   who shows no partiality to princes,
     nor regards the rich more than the poor,
     for they are all the work of his hands?
20   In a moment they die;
     at midnight the people are shaken and pass away,
     and the mighty are taken away by no human hand.

21   "For his eyes are on the ways of a man,
     and he sees all his steps.
22   There is no gloom or deep darkness
     where evildoers may hide themselves.
23   For God[7] has no need to consider a man further,
     that he should go before God in judgment.
24   He shatters the mighty without investigation
     and sets others in their place.
25   Thus, knowing their works,
     he overturns them in the night, and they are crushed.

26 He strikes them for their wickedness
    in a place for all to see,
27 because they turned aside from following him
    and had no regard for any of his ways,
28 so that they caused the cry of the poor to come to him,
    and he heard the cry of the afflicted—
29 When he is quiet, who can condemn?
    When he hides his face, who can behold him,
    whether it be a nation or a man?—
30 that a godless man should not reign,
    that he should not ensnare the people.

31 "For has anyone said to God,
    'I have borne punishment; I will not offend any more;
32 teach me what I do not see;
    if I have done iniquity, I will do it no more'?
33 Will he then make repayment to suit you,
    because you reject it?
For you must choose, and not I;
    therefore declare what you know.[8]
34 Men of understanding will say to me,
    and the wise man who hears me will say:
35 'Job speaks without knowledge;
    his words are without insight.'
36 Would that Job were tried to the end,
    because he answers like wicked men.
37 For he adds rebellion to his sin;
    he claps his hands among us
    and multiplies his words against God."

35

And Elihu answered and said:

2 "Do you think this to be just?
    Do you say, 'It is my right before God,'
3 that you ask, 'What advantage have I?
    How am I better off than if I had sinned?'
4 I will answer you
    and your friends with you.
5 Look at the heavens, and see;
    and behold the clouds, which are higher than you.
6 If you have sinned, what do you accomplish against him?
    And if your transgressions are multiplied, what do you
        do to him?
7 If you are righteous, what do you give to him?
    Or what does he receive from your hand?
8 Your wickedness concerns a man like yourself,
    and your righteousness a son of man.

9 "Because of the multitude of oppressions people cry out;
    they call for help because of the arm of the mighty.[9]
10 But none says, 'Where is God my Maker,
    who gives songs in the night,

¹¹ who teaches us more than the beasts of the earth
     and makes us wiser than the birds of the heavens?'
¹² There they cry out, but he does not answer,
     because of the pride of evil men.
¹³ Surely God does not hear an empty cry,
     nor does the Almighty regard it.
¹⁴ How much less when you say that you do not see him,
     that the case is before him, and you are waiting for him!
¹⁵ And now, because his anger does not punish,
     and he does not take much note of transgression,¹⁰
¹⁶ Job opens his mouth in empty talk;
     he multiplies words without knowledge."

36 And Elihu continued, and said:

² "Bear with me a little, and I will show you,
     for I have yet something to say on God's behalf.
³ I will get my knowledge from afar
     and ascribe righteousness to my Maker.
⁴ For truly my words are not false;
     one who is perfect in knowledge is with you.

⁵ "Behold, God is mighty, and does not despise any;
     he is mighty in strength of understanding.
⁶ He does not keep the wicked alive,
     but gives the afflicted their right.
⁷ He does not withdraw his eyes from the righteous,
     but with kings on the throne
     he sets them forever, and they are exalted.
⁸ And if they are bound in chains
     and caught in the cords of affliction,
⁹ then he declares to them their work
     and their transgressions, that they are behaving arrogantly.
¹⁰ He opens their ears to instruction
     and commands that they return from iniquity.
¹¹ If they listen and serve him,
     they complete their days in prosperity,
     and their years in pleasantness.
¹² But if they do not listen, they perish by the sword
     and die without knowledge.

¹³ "The godless in heart cherish anger;
     they do not cry for help when he binds them.
¹⁴ They die in youth,
     and their life ends among the cult prostitutes.
¹⁵ He delivers the afflicted by their affliction
     and opens their ear by adversity.
¹⁶ He also allured you out of distress
     into a broad place where there was no cramping,
     and what was set on your table was full of fatness.

¹⁷ "But you are full of the judgment on the wicked;
     judgment and justice seize you.

¹⁸ Beware lest wrath entice you into scoffing,
 and let not the greatness of the ransom turn you aside.
¹⁹ Will your cry for help avail to keep you from distress,
 or all the force of your strength?
²⁰ Do not long for the night,
 when peoples vanish in their place.
²¹ Take care; do not turn to iniquity,
 for this you have chosen rather than affliction.
²² Behold, God is exalted in his power;
 who is a teacher like him?
²³ Who has prescribed for him his way,
 or who can say, 'You have done wrong'?

²⁴ "Remember to extol his work,
 of which men have sung.
²⁵ All mankind has looked on it;
 man beholds it from afar.
²⁶ Behold, God is great, and we know him not;
 the number of his years is unsearchable.
²⁷ For he draws up the drops of water;
 they distill his mist in rain,
²⁸ which the skies pour down
 and drop on mankind abundantly.
²⁹ Can anyone understand the spreading of the clouds,
 the thunderings of his pavilion?
³⁰ Behold, he scatters his lightning about him
 and covers the roots of the sea.
³¹ For by these he judges peoples;
 he gives food in abundance.
³² He covers his hands with the lightning
 and commands it to strike the mark.
³³ Its crashing declares his presence;[11]
 the cattle also declare that he rises.

37 "At this also my heart trembles
 and leaps out of its place.
² Keep listening to the thunder of his voice
 and the rumbling that comes from his mouth.
³ Under the whole heaven he lets it go,
 and his lightning to the corners of the earth.
⁴ After it his voice roars;
 he thunders with his majestic voice,
 and he does not restrain the lightnings[12] when his voice
  is heard.
⁵ God thunders wondrously with his voice;
 he does great things that we cannot comprehend.
⁶ For to the snow he says, 'Fall on the earth,'
 likewise to the downpour, his mighty downpour.
⁷ He seals up the hand of every man,
 that all men whom he made may know it.
⁸ Then the beasts go into their lairs,
 and remain in their dens.

9   From its chamber comes the whirlwind,
      and cold from the scattering winds.
10 By the breath of God ice is given,
      and the broad waters are frozen fast.
11 He loads the thick cloud with moisture;
      the clouds scatter his lightning.
12 They turn around and around by his guidance,
      to accomplish all that he commands them
      on the face of the habitable world.
13 Whether for correction or for his land
      or for love, he causes it to happen.

14 "Hear this, O Job;
      stop and consider the wondrous works of God.
15 Do you know how God lays his command upon them
      and causes the lightning of his cloud to shine?
16 Do you know the balancings[13] of the clouds,
      the wondrous works of him who is perfect in knowledge,
17 you whose garments are hot
      when the earth is still because of the south wind?
18 Can you, like him, spread out the skies,
      hard as a cast metal mirror?
19 Teach us what we shall say to him;
      we cannot draw up our case because of darkness.
20 Shall it be told him that I would speak?
      Did a man ever wish that he would be swallowed up?

21 "And now no one looks on the light
      when it is bright in the skies,
      when the wind has passed and cleared them.
22 Out of the north comes golden splendor;
      God is clothed with awesome majesty.
23 The Almighty—we cannot find him;
      he is great in power;
      justice and abundant righteousness he will not violate.
24 Therefore men fear him;
      he does not regard any who are wise in their own conceit."[14]

1 Hebrew *many* [in years] 2 Hebrew *his* 3 Or *He will not answer for any of his own words* 4 Or *seals* 5 Hebrew *he*
6 Hebrew lacks *on him* 7 Hebrew *he* 8 The meaning of the Hebrew in verses 29–33 is uncertain 9 Or *the*
many 10 Theodotion, Symmachus (compare Vulgate); the meaning of the Hebrew word is uncertain
11 Hebrew *declares concerning him* 12 Hebrew *them* 13 Or *hoverings* 14 Hebrew *in heart*

Section Overview

In chapters 32–37 we are introduced to the enigmatic Elihu. Where did he come from? How long has he been listening in? Long enough to have an opinion on the matter. He claims to speak for God ("Bear with me a little," he says in 36:2, "... for I have yet something to say *on God's behalf*"), and the reader at this point, like Job, is longing for a word from God. But does Elihu truly speak for God?

It is difficult to know what to make of Elihu. In Job 42, when everything gets sorted out, God offers no rebuke to Elihu (he is not included with the three friends), and Job offers no sacrifice on his behalf. Does this mean that God approves of his message? We are not told. Does this mean that God looks over this young man's offenses (i.e., he simply covers them like Job did his children's sins)? Again, we are not told. All this leaves us to wonder. We wonder if none, some, much, or all of what he says is wise and true. We wonder, "Is he a long-winded arrogant buffoon pushed on stage at the end of the drama for comic relief, or is he a wise prophet whose word we should heed, or is he something in between those two extremes?"

While Elihu wants us to believe that he is like a young Joseph (Gen. 41:38) or a young Daniel (Dan. 5:12, 14), offering up his inspired "wisdom" (Job 33:33) only after all the other "wise men" (34:2, 34; cf. 37:24) have offered their wisdom and failed, our take is that he is more like Jonah. That is, he is an angry young man who in his arrogance wrongly assesses the prophetic situation he has been placed into but nevertheless speaks the word of the Lord. In other words, he is not a false prophet but a flawed one. (See Response section below for a fuller evaluation.)

Here then, is the overview of his flawed, but at times truly prophetic, prophecy: after Elihu introduces himself (32:1–5) and gives a long apology for his need to speak (32:6–22), he gives the first of four speeches. The first speech is a rebuke to Job (33:1–33). Job has many words, but he does not have wisdom. Elihu is like a voice crying in the wilderness—no one is listening to him. His final three speeches, whatever their major and minor flaws, prepare the way of the Lord (Yahweh's speeches in Job 38–41). In the second speech Elihu asserts God's justice (34:1–37); in the third he extols God's greatness (35:1–16); and in his brilliant and climactic fourth speech he announces God's majesty (36:1–37:24).

Section Outline

  III. Enigmatic Elihu (32:1–37:24)
      A. A Voice Crying in the Wilderness (32:1–33:33)
          1. The Angry Young Man Who Must Speak (32:1–22)
          2. Speech One: Job Rebuked (33:1–33)
      B. Preparing the Way for the Lord (34:1–37:24)
          1. Speech Two: Asserting God's Justice (34:1–37)
          2. Speech Three: Extolling God's Greatness (35:1–16)
          3. Speech Four: Announcing God's Majesty (36:1–37:24)

Comment

32:1–5 We are told in verse 1 why Eliphaz, Bildad, and Zophar "ceased to answer Job": because they deemed him "righteous in his own eyes." This phrase perhaps means "self-righteous" but certainly includes the exasperating idea that Job will not admit guilt. Then we are introduced to Elihu. Like the three friends, we are given reference to his father (2:11; 4:1; 8:1; 11:1): he is the "son of Barachel the Buzite" (32:2). We also learn that he is "of the family of Ram" (v. 2). What is most important, however, is not his lineage but his emotional state. Because no good "answer" has been given to Job (vv. 1, 3, 5), Elihu "burned with anger" (vv. 2, 3, 5). Such anger, unlike the Lord's anger in 42:7, is a mix of righteous and unrighteous anger. Elihu is angry at the three friends because they have accused Job of wrongdoing ("they had declared Job to be in the wrong"; 32:3b) but have produced no solid evidence of sin ("they had found no answer"; v. 3a; cf. v. 5). This may well be righteous anger. He is right that they are wrong. However, is he right when he accuses Job of justifying "himself rather than God" (v. 2b)? If not, as we will suggest below, then his anger is off base.

32:6–22 Some Job scholars have become too soft on Elihu. While we are in the camp that equates him with John the Baptist (he prepares the way of the Lord, who will speak right after him), we are not in the camp that almost comes across as saying, "among those born of women there has arisen no one greater than" him (Matt. 11:11). In reaction to the historical consensus that Elihu is eccentric, angry, and arrogant, some commentators today claim that Elihu can do no wrong. Such a conclusion is wrong. And some of the wrongness of that interpretation is demonstrated in the wrongheadedness of Elihu's first words.

While Elihu might be honest in his opening statement (Job 32:6–7), his hesitancy to speak can also be read in the voice and tone of Charles Dickens's classic character Uriah Heep. As Heep consistently talks about how humble he is, the reader senses that something is amiss. Elihu might have waited to speak, as he states, because young men should not interrupt their elders or speak out of turn:

> I am young in years,
> and you are aged;
> therefore I was timid and afraid
> to declare my opinion to you.
> I said, "Let days speak,
> and many years teach wisdom." (vv. 6–7)

But we have taken the view, based on what follows, that he is not as respectful of his elders or as "timid" as he suggests. The word "but" at the start of verse 8 stands out as a massive transition from his stated humility. (In wisdom literature to stay silent rather than to speak is usually wise.) Elihu begins his long speech with a true statement about how wisdom comes from God ("it is the spirit in man, the breath of the Almighty, that makes him understand"; v. 8), not necessarily or automatically from life experience ("it is not the old who are wise, nor the aged who understand what is right"; v. 9; cf. Ps. 119:100). Poetically, we can note the carefully laid out similarities and contrasts:

It is	the spirit in man,	
	the breath of the Almighty,	that makes him understand.
It is not	the old	who are wise,
Nor	the aged	who understand what is right.

(Job 32:8–9)

In light of this possibility, Elihu feels justified in opening his mouth: "Therefore I say, 'Listen to me; let me also declare my opinion'" (v. 10). With this contrast he is implying that the "breath of the Almighty" (v. 8) is breathing words into his ear that God has not breathed into the "old"/"aged" Eliphaz, Bildad, and Zophar (v. 9).

Elihu perhaps knows that his claim (vv. 8–10) might come across as over-confident. So next, with a mixture of confidence in what he is about to say and nervousness over to whom he is about to say it, he feels the need first to justify himself further. It is not just that a young man, in principle, can know more than someone old (vv. 8–9); it is also that the three wise men have not said anything wise. "Listen ["behold"]," he says in effect, "I listened to your rebukes and arguments against Job ["I listened for your wise sayings," v. 11b; "I gave you my attention," v. 12a]—quite patiently, I might add ["I waited for your words, . . . while you searched out what to say"; v. 11ac]. The problem, however, is that all three of you did not prove that Job was wrong in what he said or did ["there was none among you who refuted Job or who answered his words"; v. 12bc] And now what do you do? Nothing! Your tongues are tied. It is no excuse to say that the wisest thing to do now ["we have found wisdom"] is to hope for God to rise up and drive Job completely away from your presence ["God may vanquish him"; v. 13]. You cannot wait for God to kill Job while you mutter, 'We did what we could. Our best shot was a good shot. Now, it is time for God to shoot the target in the heart.' I will wait no longer ["and shall I wait, because they do not speak, because they stand there, and answer no more?"; v. 16]. You might be discouraged ["dismayed"] from the war of words you have not won, so much so that you have nothing left to say ["they answer no more; they have not a word to say"; v. 15]. But I am ready to go! Job has not yet been in the ring with me ["he has not directed his words against me"; v. 14a]. And rest assured, he will not know what hit him when I use my left hook—some new and inspired logic ["I will not answer him with your speeches"; v. 14b]."

Elihu is indeed ready to go. He spends four verses telling everyone just how ready he is:

> I also will answer with my share;
>> I also will declare my opinion.
> For I am full of words;
>> the spirit within me constrains me.
> Behold, my belly is like wine that has no vent;
>> like new wineskins ready to burst.
> I must speak, that I may find relief;
>> I must open my lips and answer. (vv. 17–20)

We find plenty of first-person personal pronouns on the lips of blameless Job, but the many pronouns here ("I," "my," and "me," twelve times in four verses!) are a bit over the top, especially as there is a drama-queen attitude from this young man attached to them. Does he need to add a third "behold" (vv. 11, 12, now v. 19;

sixteen times in six chapters!)? Is he sure that God's spirit is within him, that what he is about to say will be purer than what Job and the three friends have said (v. 18; cf. v. 8)? Is he so constipated with great rebuttals to Job's stupid speeches ("I am full of words"; v. 18) that if he does not "find relief" (v. 20a) he will "burst" like unvented wine in "new wineskins" (v. 19)? Must he really speak ("I must speak"/"I must open my lips"; v. 20)?

Elihu ends his long-winded introduction to his forthcoming speech by speaking more. His introduction needs a conclusion (obviously), a conclusion in which he assures the world that what he is about to say is pure. A third justification:

I will not   show partiality   to any man
or   use flattery   toward any person. (v. 21)

Why will Elihu (presumably unlike the three friends) be impartial and abandon all obsequiousness? The answer is easy: he does not know how to do otherwise ("for I do not know how to flatter"; v. 22a), and if he did know how to do such a wicked thing (which he does not!), he knows that God would eradicate him instantaneously ("else my Maker would soon take me away"; v. 22b). What a flair for drama.

33:1–33 This chapter records Elihu's first speech. It is a twofold rebuke to Job ("But now, hear my speech, O Job," v. 1; "Pay attention, O Job, listen to me," v. 31). First, Elihu rebukes Job for claiming to be innocent (vv. 9–12). Second, he rebukes Job for not grasping that God has already spoken to Job (vv. 13–23). Both rebukes are ungrounded, but the second one adds a new and important idea to the debate.

In 32:18–20, Elihu spoke of needing to "find relief" (32:20) from all of the words fermenting inside him ("I am full of words," 32:18; "I must speak"/"I must open my lips," 32:20). In chapter 33, the wineskins crack (vv. 1–5), then burst (vv. 6–33). In verses 1–5, as well as verses 31–33, Elihu speaks a lot about speaking: "hear my speech . . . and listen to all my words" (v. 1); "my words . . . my lips . . . speak" (v. 3); "pay attention . . . listen to me . . . I will speak . . . listen to me . . . I will teach you" (vv. 31–33). And some of his statements about speaking are so redundant they almost belittle the simple beauty of the art of Hebrew parallelisms (e.g., "Behold, I open my mouth; the tongue in my mouth speaks"; v. 2).

At both the top (vv. 1–5) and the tail (vv. 31–33), Elihu calls on Job to listen to him. In these verses he gives three reasons why this would be wise. First, his words come from a pure heart and serious and sober thinking on the matter ("My words declare the uprightness of my heart, and what my lips know they speak sincerely"; v. 3). Second, his basis for speaking is grounded in God. God has created him:

The Spirit   of God   has made me,
and the breath of the Almighty   gives me life. (v. 4)

God has also, implied here (cf. 32:8, 18; 33:14), given him words to say. Elihu speaks because God has given him wisdom (cf. 32:13). Thus he can boldly declare in his final line of the first speech, "Be silent, and I will teach you wisdom" (33:33).

Third, Elihu offers a simple solution to Job's dilemma. Justification! Vindication! "I desire to justify you" (v. 32b). How? It is easy: if Job would only admit his guilt before God (say, "I sinned"; v. 27), then God would graciously "accept" (v. 26a), "deliver" (v. 24b), "ransom" (v. 24c), "redeem" (v. 28a), "bring back" (v. 30), and "restore" (v. 26c; cf. vv. 25, 28b, 30b). While Elihu claims to have something new to say, these three reasons are no different from those of the three friends. The friends did not have some deep, dark ulterior motives (2:11). They too claimed to be God-made and God-inspired (e.g., 4:12–16). They offered Job justification through confession of sin, which would lead to redemption and restoration (22:21–30).

While Elihu offers no new rationale for listening to him, he does bring fresh arguments to the debate (32:12–22). We will explore these soon. First, however, Elihu finds it necessary to rebuke Job for claiming innocence. Before this rebuke, Elihu seeks to level the playing ground (33:6–7). We might imagine him like a school principal who starts a conversation with a student who is about to be expelled with gentle and affirming words before lowering the hammer of discipline. "Behold," Elihu states, "I am toward God as you are; I too was pinched off from a piece of clay" (v. 6). Put differently, "We are both humans, created out of the earth by God." So, "Behold [his favorite word], there is no need to be afraid of me ["no fear of me need terrify you"]; I will take it easy on you ["my pressure will not be heavy upon you"; v. 7]." Yeah, right! Not a second later, the weight of an elephant of accusatory words falls on Job's head. This is all that Job needs—some "patronizing" disclaimer followed by a personal pounding.[147]

The personal pounding is no different than what Job has received thus far. Having listened carefully to the debate ("you have spoken in my ears, and I have heard the sound of your words"; v. 8), Elihu claims that Job's claim below is false. "Behold [again!], in this [vv. 9–11] you are not right" (v. 12a).

> You say, "I am pure, without transgression;
>> I am clean, and there is no iniquity in me.
> Behold, he finds occasions against me,
>> he counts me as his enemy,
> he puts my feet in the stocks
>> and watches all my paths." (vv. 9–11)

Elihu exaggerates Job's assertion of innocence (cf. 9:20). Job never claimed sinless perfection, only that there was not some sin that caused his calamities. He is even open to some unknown sin, if God would only reveal it to him (7:20), or some sin from his youth as the cause (13:26). However, Elihu does summarize well enough Job's assertion that God has acted as his adversary by seeing (16:9; cf. 19:11) and seizing him. In 13:24 Job said to God, "Why do you . . . count me as your enemy?" (cf. 16:9; 19:11) and in 13:27, "You put my feet in the stocks and watch all my paths; you set a limit for the soles of my feet."

---

147 R. N. Whybray, *Job* (repr. Sheffield, UK: Phoenix, 2008), 154.

The basic reason that Elihu believes Job is not right in claiming that he is innocent and God guilty (33:12a) is that Job has reversed the roles: "God is greater than man" (v. 12b). And because God is greater than man, a man like Job cannot "contend against him" (v. 13a). God is not obliged in any way to answer any of Job's attestations of innocence or assertions against him ("He will answer none of man's words"; v. 13b). Moreover, there is no need for God to say anything when he has already spoken. In verses 14–22, Elihu lays out two ways in which God regularly speaks ("God speaks in one way, and in two"), ways that are often missed by man ("though man does not perceive it"; v. 14).

First, God speaks through dreams, a familiar concept in the Bible that spans from the patriarchal era (Gen. 20:3, 6–7) to the birth of Christ (Matt. 1:20) and the Christian church (Acts 2:17).

> In a dream, in a vision of the night,
> > when deep sleep falls on men,
> > while they slumber on their beds,
> then he opens the ears of men
> > and terrifies them with warnings. (Job 33:15–16)

The purpose of such nightmares is to suppress sin ("that he may turn aside from his deed"), subdue pride ("conceal pride from a man"; v. 17), and warn men of the consequences of unconfessed sin: death (God, through the dreams, "keeps back his soul from the pit, his life from perishing by the sword"; v. 18). Job himself has experienced such nightmares ("you [God] scare me with dreams and terrify me with visions"; 7:14). However, he has not seen them as revelatory, and certainly not as revealing his sins or provoking him to confession or repentance.

Second, God speaks through suffering: "Man is also rebuked with pain on his bed" (33:19a). In verses 19b–22, Elihu details such pain. Man's body aches ("with continual strife in his bones"; v. 19b); his appetite is suppressed and oppressed (he "loathes" both the basics, like "bread," and delicacies, "the choicest food"; v. 20); "his flesh" is so emaciated that he is see-through ("so wasted away that it cannot be seen"), and "bones" that usually are unseen—like the rib cage and hips—now "stick out" (v. 21). God is screaming to him in the suffering, "Stop sinning before it is too late!"

> His soul   draws near   the pit,
> and his life   to those who bring death. (v. 22; cf. v. 18)

Elihu's insight—God speaks through suffering—is a crucial Christian concept. He is ahead of his time! The cross of Christ is God's ultimate revelation. It is God's bullhorn to wake up an indifferent world. But again, Elihu is assuming that Job is guilty of not listening to God in the suffering and not grasping that the pain is not punitive or purgative but preventive.[148] But is Elihu right? Is God trying to

---

148 See Hywel R. Jones, *Job*, EPSC (Darlington, UK: Evangelical, 2007), 241.

prevent Job from sinning, as he does with Paul (2 Cor. 12:7)? Is this general principle—God speaks through suffering—true for Job? Is it "the reality . . . that Job has been deaf and not that God has been dumb"?[149] We do not think so. Job 3–31 depicts Job as waiting to hear even the faintest whisper from God, and chapters 38–41 depict God as finally, and for the first time, speaking. So again, in our estimation, like the three friends Elihu offers some wise counsel but not necessarily the counsel Job needs.

And if there is one thing that Job certainly does not need to hear, it is a short sermonette on his need for repentance and the guarantee of restoration for his *definite* mortal illness. But alas, such is what follows (33:23–30). As stated above, Elihu offers a simple solution to Job's dilemma: *if* Job would only admit his guilt before God ("prays to God"; v. 26a) and others ("he sings before men and says: 'I sinned and perverted what was right'") and that the punishment he got was more lenient than he deserved ("and it was not repaid to me"; v. 27), *then* God (cf. v. 29) would graciously and joyously ("he sees his face with a shout of joy"; v. 26b) restore his health and wealth. Job's sad song will turn into a song of salvation: "He sings before men and says: . . . 'He has redeemed my soul from going down into the pit, and my life shall look upon the light'" (vv. 27a, 28).

A similar if-then solution is offered by Eliphaz in his "Agree with God" sermon (22:21–30). What is new here is that Elihu takes seriously Job's desire for a mediator (cf. 9:32–35; 16:19; 19:25). He proposes the possibility of a heavenly messenger ("an angel") who will speak on behalf of Job ("for him"; 33:23a). If such a creature exists, he is rare ("a mediator, one of the thousand"; v. 23b). And if he spoke for God to man, he would say basically what Elihu has said and will say.[150] He would "declare to man what is right for him" (v. 23c), namely, to find God's mercy through confession of sin (v. 27). This confession will serve as man's "ransom" (v. 24c), one that will "deliver him from going down into the pit" (v. 24b, parallel with v. 30a) and restore his good old (young!) life: "his flesh [will] become fresh with youth"; he will "return to the days of his youthful vigor" (v. 25); he will be "lighted with the light of life" (v. 30b).

34:1–37 Is Elihu only a pathetic prophet like Jonah? No. He may be going the wrong way, but unwittingly. Moreover, as shown above, he adds a few important new contributions to the conversation. However, he may be overly optimistic as he pauses between 33:33 and 34:1 to see what Job will say. Will Job answer him ("answer me"; 33:5, 32)? Job for the first time offers no answer. Is his silence because he agrees with Elihu or because he has had enough fighting with fools? Likely there is a mix of both. Whatever his flaws, Elihu is preparing the way for the Lord to speak, and, however bitter Job might feel after two chapters of the

---

149 As suggested and summarized by Jones (ibid, 240).

150 In his commentary *Job*, NIBCOT (Peabody, MA: Hendrickson, 2007), 377, G. H. Wilson argues that Elihu sees himself as this "angel." Though Elihu is very self-confident, it is still more likely that the angel is a heavenly creature. Longman points out the irony of Job 33:23: "Little did he [Job] (or Elihu) know that the only angel in heaven mentioned in the book of Job ('the accuser'; see 1:6 and 2:1) was working against his interests and not for them" (*Job*, 389).

angry young man telling him what is what in the world, Job will listen in silence. Perhaps he is hoping for a treasure of truth, however small, to come from the misguided messenger.

Yet, in Elihu's second speech (34:2–37), Job will only hear more overly simplistic deductions from the novice theologian. Elihu, once again "confident that he has deciphered the puzzle that has baffled Job,"[151] calls the crowd around him to learn how he has put the pieces together. He begins,

Hear my words,	you wise men,
and give ear to me,	you who know;
for the ear	tests words
as the palate	tastes food.
Let us choose	what is right;
let us know among ourselves	what is good. (vv. 2–4)

The "wise men" here (v. 2), and in verses 10, 16, and 34 ("men of understanding") do not include Job (he is counted among the wicked and "speaks without knowledge; his words are without insight"; v. 35). Elihu might also exclude Eliphaz, Bildad, and Zophar, in whom he has found no wisdom (32:11–14). His audience, then, are those who listen to him ("hear my words"/"give ear to me," 34:2; "hear me," v. 10; "hear this"/"listen to what I say," v. 16) and consider his words wise ("the wise man who hears me"; v. 34b). They are those who can discern "what is right"/"what is good" from what is wrong/bad (v. 4), just as a refined palate can taste the difference between a meal made by a master chef and one made by the cook at the local diner (cf. v. 3).

The heart of this speech is a defense of God's justice (esp. vv. 10–30), as the main issue that Elihu has with Job is that Job denies that God is fair. The structure of his argument is as follows: it begins with what Job has supposedly said ("For Job has said," v. 5; "For he has said," v. 9) and should say ("For has anyone said"; v. 31), followed by Elihu's replies (vv. 7–8, 10–30, 33–37). The first claim that Job has made, according to Elihu and rearranged by him, is that God has denied just Job justice:

For Job has said, "I am in the right,
    and God has taken away my right;
in spite of my right I am counted a liar;
    my wound is incurable, though I am without transgression." (vv. 5–6)

While it is accurate that Job has repeatedly asserted his innocence (e.g., 6:28–30; 9:15; 27:2–6), questioned God's fairness (e.g., 19:6–8), and seen God as warring against him (e.g., 6:4; 16:13), Elihu's representation is not completely fair. Elihu never gives or gets the context in which Job's words are spoken. Job is actually an innocent sufferer! Moreover, Job has more to say than these three claims. For

---

151 Estes, *Job*, 204.

example, what does Elihu make of Job's heartfelt cries to God or acknowledgements of God's greatness?

Elihu does not have time to consider the full picture. Indeed, he has no categories for Job's seemingly ridiculous claims. Thus with his damning rhetorical question he renders perhaps the harshest—and certainly the most overstated and untrue—verdict:

> What man is like Job,
>   who drinks up scoffing like water,
> who travels in company with evildoers
>   and walks with wicked men? (34:7–8)

There is simply no evidence to support a description of Job as the vilest man on earth ("what man is like Job?"). Can anyone really envision Job as sipping on sin ("drinks up scoffing like water") as he walks side by side with the wicked ("travels . . . with evildoers")?

In verse 9, Elihu advances Job's second claim: "For he has said, 'It profits a man nothing that he should take delight in God.'" Has Job ever said that it does not pay to please God? In 9:29–31, he admits struggling with living righteously if it leads only to a condemnable existence. And in 21:15 Job says that the wicked say, "What is the Almighty, that we should serve him? And what profit do we get if we pray to him?" But again, Elihu has deduced too much. His paraphrase of Job's position is a stretch and a direct contradiction of Job's answer to Satan's question (1:9). Job does not follow God for the perks.

More than that, like Elihu's rebuke above (34:7–8), his second rebuke (vv. 10–30) is over the top and unnecessary. As much as he rejects and denounces the three friends, what he says here simply echoes and affirms what they themselves have said. Because of this, some commentators suggest that no one replies to Elihu's four speeches because they have all fallen asleep during the sermon. This is easy enough to do when the preacher is preaching the same points we have heard for nearly thirty chapters!

Point one is that God is good ("far be it from God that he should do wickedness, and from the Almighty that he should do wrong"; v. 10bc) and, consequently, is just ("God will not do wickedly"; he "will not pervert justice"; v. 12). Point two is that God demonstrates such justice through enforcing the retribution principle:

> For according   to the work of a man   he will repay him,
>   and according   to his ways   he will make it befall him. (v. 11)

Point three is that God is a self-appointed sovereign ("Who gave him charge over the earth, and who laid on him the whole world?"; v. 13) who has such absolute control over creation that he can destroy people whenever he wants ("If he should set his heart to it and gather to himself his spirit and his breath, all flesh would perish together, and man would return to dust"; vv. 14–15).[152] Point four, based on points one, two, and three, is that it is inappropriate to accuse a sovereign, good, and just God of acting unjustly. Comparing God to a just king, Elihu asks two rhetorical questions:

> Shall one who hates justice govern?
>   Will you condemn him who is righteous and mighty,
> who says to a king, 'Worthless one,'
>   and to nobles, 'Wicked man,'
> who shows no partiality to princes,
>   nor regards the rich more than the poor,
>   for they are all the work of his hands? (vv. 17–19)

With the first question Elihu assumes that the answer is obvious: God, like a righteous and mighty king, loves justice and thus governs by it. With the second question, Elihu emphasizes that God, like an impartial king, does not show favoritism: he never favors the powerful over the powerless or the rich over the poor.

In verses 20–30 Elihu moves beyond the analogy of God as a good earthly king and judge to his status as the almighty God who sees all ("his eyes are on the ways of a man, and he sees all his steps," v. 21; he knows "their works," v. 25a) and judges all without any need for a drawn-out court case ("God has no need to consider a man further. . . . He shatters the mighty without investigation"; vv. 23–24). Even the seemingly invincible ("the mighty"; vv. 20, 24), who think they have gotten away with evil, are soon found out ("there is no gloom or deep darkness where evildoers may hide themselves"; v. 22), promptly punished ("in a moment they die; at midnight the people are shaken and pass away," v. 20ab; "he overturns them in the night, and they are crushed," v. 25b) directly by God ("are taken away by no human hand," v. 20c; "he strikes them for their wickedness" for turning aside "from following him" and "his ways" and for afflicting "the poor," vv. 26–28), and replaced (God "sets others in their place"; v. 24b). God acts justly! He makes sure that wicked rulers are deposed. He does not allow a "godless man" to "reign" and "ensnare the people" (v. 30). Thus only a godless man (like Job!) would ever condemn God for the way he rules the world. Job must learn the lesson of verse 29: if God chooses to be silent ("when he is quiet"/"when he hides his face"), there is no man or nation in a position to find him ("who can behold him?") and pass judgment on him ("who can condemn?"). God rules however he sees fit.

So, if Job wants to say anything further ("for Job has said," v. 5; "he has said," v. 9), Elihu suggests, he should learn from God's disciplinary hand (cf. Prov. 3:11–12) that his sins should be confessed, not his God condemned. Job should say, "I have borne punishment; I will not offend any more" (Job 34:31b) and "Teach me what I do not see; if I have done iniquity, I will do it no more" (v. 32). However,

---

152 "With these words [Job 34:14–15], Elihu comes very close to affirming the deistic dogma that whatever is, is right" (ibid., 207).

it is rare for people to do so ("has anyone said" such things "to God"; v. 31a). Job certainly has not done so yet.

Elihu ends his second speech by turning to Job (v. 33), then to what he assumes the wise will say about his brilliant assessment (vv. 34–35), and finally to all who are sitting at his feet and awaiting his climactic conclusion (vv. 36–37). First, he says to Job (the "you" is singular in v. 33) in effect, "Let me make clear to *you* that *you* have rejected God's terms. God is not going to reward *you* ["make repayment to suit you"]. *You* have a choice to make ["you must choose"]. I look forward to *your* making a wise decision. Let me know what *you* decide ["declare what you know"]." Then Elihu adds what will be the response of the wise:

Men of understanding		will say to me,
and the wise man	who hears me	will say:

"Job speaks		without knowledge;
his words	are	without insight." (vv. 34–35)

It is not enough that Elihu calls Job an idiot and does so through a pretend response to a sermon that is not finished. He must end with a curse (hoping that Job will experience even further punishment: "would that Job were tried to the end"; v. 36a) and four unfeeling and ungrounded accusations (vv. 36b–37):

(1) "He answers like wicked men."
(2) "He adds rebellion to his sin."
(3) "He claps his hands among us."
(4) "[He] multiplies his words against God."

35:1–16 This shorter third speech begins with Elihu's answering ("And Elihu answered and said"; v. 1) his own assertions. We might be surprised that he does not answer with self-congratulations, "Amen, preach it, brother!" But in light of the whole of the sermon, perhaps that would be the better option instead of once again lowering the hammer on poor Job. The word "you" (fourteen times) in the singular (namely, *you Job*) are the fourteen nails he uses to drive home his point that *God is so great that he does not care about the superficial cries of sinners like Job.*

Elihu starts with a loaded question to Job, "Do you think this to be just?" (v. 2a). The "this" follows: Elihu wants to know if Job thinks he is right in claiming, "It is my right before God" (v. 2b), the sense being, "I am right and God is wrong," or perhaps, "I am righteous before God." Elihu also wants to know if Job really believes what he has supposedly stated before, "What advantage have I? How am I better off than if I had sinned?" (v. 3). These are twisted and exaggerated representations of Job's cries to God for help and pleas to his friends to bring true wisdom to the inexplicable situation. They are loosely based on overhearing Job's press conferences: "[God,] you know that I am not guilty" (10:7a); "[God,] what profit do [I] get if [I] pray?" (21:15b); "[God,] far be it from me to say that you [in context: the friends, not God] are right; till I die I will not put away my [absolutely perfect] integrity" (27:5). These are "press conferences," by the way, given while Job is under an amazing amount of duress.

Now, while Elihu asks Job a question, "Do you think this to be just?" (35:2), it is not a serious question to Job; it is a strawman that has been set up to push down and burn. The clause "I will answer you and your friends with you" (v. 4) is perhaps the most arrogant statement in the Bible. How condescending! After putting words in Job's mouth, now Elihu makes sure his own words of "wisdom" are heard, because, after all, that is the only wisdom that can possibly shed light on this situation. Distorting Job's heartbreaking question, "What is man, that you make so much of him?" (7:17a), Elihu orates:

> Look at the heavens, and see;
>   and behold the clouds, which are higher than you.
> If you have sinned, what do you accomplish against him?
>   And if your transgressions are multiplied, what do you do to him?
> If you are righteous, what do you give to him?
>   Or what does he receive from your hand?
> Your wickedness concerns a man like yourself,
>   and your righteousness a son of man. (35:5–8)

The gist of this section of the third sermon is simple; it is merely an expansion of Eliphaz's earlier ponderings (22:2–3). God is too big and Job is too small for him to pay attention to Job's puny pleas. Both Job's righteousness and his unrighteousness might affect other human beings, but they do not affect God. But we have read the prologue, and Elihu has not, so we might be lenient here, or we might be disgusted by this deistic view of God. The latter is more appropriate. As Christians we know that God is both transcendent and immanent. We also sense that this is how Job understood God and has spoken about him. To Job, the struggle is with his theological convictions (God is not a distant and detached deity but a near and involved friend) and his experience (God seems distant and detached from his sufferings, so far removed and unfriendly).

Things get worse for Job. The sermon continues. Elihu next discounts Job's heartfelt lamentations as hypocritical defamations. When most people are in trouble because the "arm of the mighty" is oppressing them (35:9), they *finally* beg God to do something: "Save me!" Job is like these foxhole atheists. But Elihu asks, in effect, where the really righteous person is who wonders, "Where is God my Maker, who gives songs in the night, who teaches us more than the beasts of the earth and makes us wiser than the birds of the heavens?" (vv. 10–11). Elihu is a confused deist, if he is indeed the founding member of the club. Out of one side of his mouth he says, "The First Cause does not care about earthlings," but out of the other side he chides, "Why are there not more pious prayers *from the pinnacle of creation* (humans) to the glorious Creator, the One who provides and protects his people?" We know that this young man must not have gone to seminary yet, but still there is something wickedly amiss here.

This sort of nastiness continues for the rest of this sermon. It will, however, find its resting place, as Jonah does in Nineveh, when Elihu finally speaks the word of the Lord. However, first we come to verses 12–16. They are sickening: Job is being repeatedly stabbed in the soul. He has said that he cannot see what God is up to ("I do not perceive him"; 9:11), that he wishes for some sort of legal hearing before his Judge (23:4; 31:35), that he hopes that God might rescue him (13:15; 14:14) and yet that it seems as if God is not playing fair (9:24; 12:6; 21:17). But what does Elihu do with these statements? He "takes Job's words and spins them so that they sound like an arrogant rejection of God."[153]

Elihu claims that Job, and people like him, "cry out" to God but "he does not answer" or "regard" their petition because "the pride of evil men" makes God indifferent to their "empty cry" (35:12–13). He claims that the more Job complains and waits for some imaginary court case, the worse he makes matters ("How much less when you say that you do not see him, that the case is before him, and you are waiting for him!"; v. 14). What then? Well, because God is so distant and detached—"his anger does not punish" and "he does not take much note of transgression" (v. 15; Elihu is hoping to impress everyone with his high view of God)—Job's words are like dandelion petals trying to survive a hurricane. A chasing after the wind. Vanity of vanities ("empty" in v. 16a is Hb. *hebel*). "Job opens his mouth" (v. 16a), and what comes out? Mere breath; smoke in the air; dust in the wind. Job "multiplies words without knowledge" (v. 16b). Ouch. What wicked theology.

36:1–25 But wait! Finally, Jonah has arrived at Nineveh. "Please," we readers say, "give us a God-inspired message, pathetic prophet. Give us some message from God!" Every Christian reader can rejoice that, in some perverted way, Elihu has asserted God's justice and extolled his greatness. But surely, when we come to Elihu's final two chapters—in which he proclaims the good news of God's majesty—we realize that, however flawed an ass of a messenger he may be (cf. Balaam's donkey from Num. 22:21–39), there is truly something both profound and preparatory here.

After Elihu introduces his fourth speech with an arrogant admission of divine inspiration ("I have yet something to say on God's behalf. I will get my knowledge from afar"; Job 36:2–3) and God-like wisdom ("one who is perfect in knowledge is with you"; v. 4),[154] he then rightly exalts God's power. His favorite word, "behold," is used four times in chapter 36 to emphatically introduce this main point.

> Behold, God is mighty, and does not despise any;
>> he is mighty in strength of understanding. (v. 5)

> Behold, God is exalted in his power;
>> who is a teacher like him? (v. 22)

---

153 Estes, *Job*, 215. We also credit Estes for the references in the sentence above.
154 While Elihu calls God "perfect in knowledge" in 37:16, the syntax of 36:4 suggest that Elihu is saying of himself that his "words" are true and that he is "perfect in knowledge." If this is the case, he is unwittingly destroying his own argument. He claims that no one is like God. But he begins saying, "Well, except me, I suppose."

Behold, God is great, and we know him not;
> the number of his years is unsearchable. (v. 26)

Behold, he scatters his lightning about him
> and covers the roots of the sea. (v. 30)

In these verses above, God's power is linked to his wisdom and his wisdom to his justice, with the point being that God's cosmic authority assures his wise governance and judgment of the world.

While Elihu's tone has softened, his theological position has not changed. In verses 5–25 the same broken record is played, *Retribution Principle's Greatest Hits*. Job has to sit and listen to more of this off-key album. Elihu's perfect knowledge is for Job personally ("you," "your," and "yourself," fourteen times in ch. 35). What Job presumably needs to know is what he has already heard, namely, that God is using suffering to save him from his sin and that Job needs to be willing to submit to this discipline and allow God to correct him. The principle is laid out plainly in verses 5–15 and the application in verses 16–25. Verses 5–15 focuses mostly on God. He is powerful, wise, and fair (v. 5). Evil men are judged ("he does not keep the wicked alive") and the oppressed saved (he "gives the afflicted their right"; v. 6). His watchful protection ("he does not withdraw his eyes from the righteous") assures that good people prosper, promoting them as rulers ("but with kings on the throne he sets them forever, and they are exalted," v. 7; or the sense of v. 7b might be that God raises up good kings to rule over these good people). However, if these good people sin ("their transgressions, that they are behaving arrogantly," v. 9b; "iniquity," v. 10b), God sends some suffering to wake them up!

Then he declares to them their work
> and their transgressions, that they are behaving arrogantly.
He opens their ears to instruction
> and commands that they return from iniquity.
If they listen and serve him,
> they complete their days in prosperity,
> and their years in pleasantness.
But if they do not listen, they perish by the sword
> and die without knowledge. (vv. 9–12)

The godly hear God's voice in the pain and return to him: "They listen and serve him" (v. 11a). And what happens? God rewards the righteous:

They complete	their days	in prosperity,
and	their years	in pleasantness. (v. 11bc)

And what happens to those who will not listen? "If they do not listen, they perish by the sword and die without knowledge" (v. 12). "They die in youth, and their life ends among the cult prostitutes" (v. 14). An unexpected, violent, and disgraceful death awaits those who will not learn from the school of suffering ("the godless in heart" who stay angry and "do not cry for help when he binds them"; v. 13).

Elihu wants Job to understand that this general principle—that God "delivers the afflicted by their affliction and opens their ear by adversity" (v. 15)—is good news for Job personally. Through the gift of punitive pain, God is wooing Job out of the slough of despond ("he also allured you out of distress"), seeking to move him to a safe place ("into a broad place"), free from suffering ("where there was no cramping") and with a feast awaiting him (a "table . . . full of fatness"; v. 16). Basically, all that Job needs to do is to say what the psalmist says: "Before I was afflicted I went astray, but now I keep your word" (Ps. 119:67). But what has Job done instead? The opposite. And for this Elihu lays into him: *But you!* "But you are full of the judgment on the wicked; judgment and justice seize you" (Job 36:17).

In verses 18–25 Elihu offers five admonitions: "beware" (v. 18), "do not long for" (v. 20), "take care" (v. 21), "behold" (v. 22), and "remember" (v. 24). First, he warns Job that, even though his loss has been great ("let not the greatness of the ransom"),[155] he should still return to God (do not let the losses "turn you aside"; v. 18b) and should certainly not allow his anger to lead to any mocking of God ("beware lest wrath entice you into scoffing"; v. 18a). The loud angry cries need to stop, as they are not helping Job's cause: "Will your cry for help avail to keep you from distress, or all the force of your strength?" (v. 19). Second, Elihu warns Job not to "long for the night" (v. 20a; perhaps an allusion to death), because there is no safety even in sleep ("when peoples vanish in their place"; v. 20b—perhaps alluding to criminal activities that happen at night [cf. 24:14–17], including murder [24:14; cf. 36:12]).

Third, Elihu accuses Job of choosing to sin in the pain rather than listening to the pain ("for this you have chosen rather than affliction"; v. 21b), and he exhorts him to stop such wicked behavior ("take care; do not turn to iniquity"; v. 21a). Fourth, instead of touting his innocence and demanding his rights, Job needs to acknowledge God's power ("Behold, God is exalted in his power"), wisdom ("who is a teacher like him?"; v. 22), sovereign freedom ("Who has prescribed for him his way . . ."), and justice ("or who can say, 'You have done wrong'?"; v. 23). Fifth, Job also needs to "remember to extol [God's] work" (v. 24a), joining all mankind in noticing God's justice (see Deut. 32:4, "his work is perfect, for all his ways are justice"), mighty deeds (see "work"/"mighty deeds" in Ps. 77:12), and creation (see Job 37:14, 16; "All mankind has looked on it; man beholds it from afar," 36:25) and even singing about it ("of which men have sung"; v. 24b; cf. Ps. 77:6, "Let me remember my song in the night").

36:26–37:24 While the admonitions above are excellent and would apply in many situations to many people, once again they do not fit Job. Elihu's assess-

---

155 "Elihu has already alluded to the possibility of a ransom (cf. 33:24). Here [in 36:18] he makes it explicit: Job should consider the greatness of the loss of his family, his reputation, and all that belonged to his household as the means by which the Lord is arresting his attention and turning him from sin" (*ESV Study Bible* note on Job 36:18).

ment is inaccurate. However, an important shift has occurred in 36:22. As Elihu says "Behold, God is exalted in his power," he moves the discussion beyond Job alone to everyone listening and reading. He wants us all to behold God! And, as he in 36:26–37:24 "breaks into [his] hymn of praise to the God of creation,"[156] we sense that Elihu might indeed "have yet something to say on God's behalf" (36:2) about God that is true even in Job's situation. The two key admonitions here are to (1) "stop and consider the wondrous works of God" (37:14) so that we might (2) "fear him" (37:24). Both of these tie into important ideas in chapters 1–2 and 28. They also connect closely with what God himself will ask Job to do in 38:1–40:2 and 40:6–41:34, and what Job himself will do in 40:3–5 and 42:1–6.

The first admonition focuses on God's awesome power displayed throughout creation, from the sun (the "light"; 37:21) to the "roots of the sea" (36:30b). Elihu especially focuses on God's control ("he draws up," 36:27a; "he scatters," 36:30a; "he covers," 36:32a; he "commands," 36:32b; "he says, 'Fall on the earth,'" 37:6a) of storms, including clouds (36:29a), thunder (36:29b), lightning (36:32; 37:3b, 11b, 15b), rain ("drops of water," 36:27a; "skies pour down," 36:28a; "downpour," 37:6b), snow (37:6a), ice (37:10), and winds (37:9, 17). In such storms, God speaks:

> Keep listening to the thunder of his voice
>> and the rumbling that comes from his mouth.
> Under the whole heaven he lets it go,
>> and his lightning to the corners of the earth.
> After it his voice roars;
>> he thunders with his majestic voice,
>> and he does not restrain the lightnings when his voice is heard.
> God thunders wondrously with his voice;
>> he does great things that we cannot comprehend. (37:2–5)

Both man and beast acknowledge God's power (36:33; 37:7–8), but only man can hear God in the storm and "fear him" (37:24a). This is Elihu's second main admonition. In context, to fear God is not only to be in awe of his awesomeness ("God is clothed with awesome majesty"; 37:22b) or to shake before his presence ("my heart trembles and leaps out of its place"; 37:1); it is also to acknowledge that God governs the world justly (with the same storm "he judges" some people and "gives food in abundance" to others, 36:31; "for correction . . . or for love," 37:13) and that human beings cannot teach God how to run the world (37:19–20), because we do not fully comprehend how he controls everything:

> Behold, God is great, and we know him not;
>> the number of his years is unsearchable. (36:26)

> Can anyone understand the spreading of the clouds,
>> the thunderings of his pavilion? (36:29)

---

156 Thomas, *The Storm Breaks*, 281.

> God thunders wondrously with his voice;
>> he does great things that we cannot comprehend. (37:5)

> Do you know how God lays his command upon them
>> and causes the lightning of his cloud to shine?
> Do you know the balancings of the clouds,
>> the wondrous works of him who is perfect in knowledge,
> you whose garments are hot
>> when the earth is still because of the south wind? (37:15–17)

> The Almighty—we cannot find him;
>> he is great in power;
>> justice and abundant righteousness he will not violate. (37:23)

This is the meaning of the remark that God "does not regard any who are wise in their own conceit" (37:24b). Those who fear God know that they do not know what God knows, and they know that God has wise designs for the ways in which he rules his creation.

All of this is another rebuke to Job ("Hear this, O Job"; 37:14), but this time it is a right rebuke, as it aligns with what God himself will say next. God, whose voice thunders (40:9; cf. 37:2) as he speaks out of a whirlwind (38:1; 40:6; cf. 37:9), will refer to his rule of creation, including clouds (38:9, 34, 37), rain (38:25a, 28), snow (38:22), lightning (38:25b, 35), ice (38:30), and "springs of the sea" (38:16).

Response

In the Section Overview, we spoke of Elihu as a Jonah-like character: not a false prophet but a flawed one. He is an angry young man who, in his arrogance, wrongly assesses the prophetic situation he has been placed into but nevertheless speaks the word of the Lord. In this Response we will look at four negatives and two positives of Elihu's ministry.

Elihu's first flaw is that *he speaks from anger*. Righteous indignation is a biblical concept. God burns in anger in Job 42:7; Jesus burns in anger when he cleanses the temple. But that does not mean that when we read the threefold refrain in Job 32:1–5 ("He burned with anger"), Elihu's anger is righteous. It is not. Speaking out of anger, he says things like, "What man is like Job, who drinks up scoffing like water, who travels in company with evildoers and walks with wicked men?" (34:7–8). Not only are those accusations cruel, but they are false as well—Job never mocks or derides God, and he certainly does not sit with scoffers. What are also mean, and which arise from his unbridled anger, are Elihu's astringent words to Job in 35:12–16. In those verses he basically says "that there is simply no point of contact between Job and God. Job doesn't make any difference to God; God doesn't make any difference to Job."[157] How harsh. How inconsiderate. "The tongue is a fire," as James tells us; it is "a restless evil, full of deadly poison" (James 3:6, 8). Don't

---

157 Goldingay, *Job*, 173.

be like Elihu. Don't let your tongue burn your brothers. "A man of wrath stirs up strife, and one given to anger causes much transgression" (Prov. 29:22).

Elihu's second flaw is that *his pleading to be heard is annoying*. He reminds us of the kid in Sunday school who always raises his hand. "Oh, pick me. Pick me." The hand is raised for every question. That is fine. What is not fine is the continual "Oh, oh, oh." "I must speak," says Elihu, "that I may find relief; I must open my lips and answer" (Job 32:20). Must he? Later he will say, "If you have understanding, hear this; listen to what I say" (34:16). Yes, he likes saying that: "Pay attention, O Job, listen to me" (33:31). "Listen to me" (33:33; cf. 32:10). In fact, his preamble, which takes up a whole chapter (ch. 32), is a bit ridiculous. It is fine to say that one waits to speak because he is young, but he ought not take half a chapter to say just how respectful of his elders he is. He ought to get to the point, to stop saying things like, "I also will answer with my share; I also will declare my opinion" (32:17). We might think that once we get to chapter 33, we will finally get to the meat of the matter, but first we have to hear, "But now, hear my speech, O Job, and listen to all my words" (33:1), followed by "Behold, I open my mouth; the tongue in my mouth speaks" (33:2).

As Proverbs 25:11 says, "A word fitly spoken is like apples of gold in a setting of silver." But with many words comes much sinning. People treat long-windedness and excessive talking like it is a generic trait. It might be. But it also might be a sin. "When words are many, transgression is not lacking, but whoever restrains his lips is prudent" (Prov. 10:19). What D. L. Moody said of prayer, we might say of speech: "Some men's prayers need to be cut short on both ends and set on fire in the middle." Elihu has more lines in the book of Job than Eliphaz, Bildad, and Zophar combined. Oh, that some of his words were set on fire! "Whoever restrains his words has knowledge, and he who has a *cool spirit* is a man of understanding" (Prov. 17:27).

Elihu's third flaw is that when he finally opens his mouth, he not only is long-winded but also *is often arrogant*. Not only does he talk down to Job in front of others, such as when he says, "Job opens his mouth in empty talk; he multiplies words without knowledge" (Job 35:16); he further follows that with "I have yet something to say on God's behalf" (36:2). "I will get my knowledge from afar" (36:3). He claims to have heard from Yahweh—the God who has been silent to righteous Job. And what does the Lord say? He says what Elihu says. Indeed, as Elihu puts it, "Truly my words are not false; one who is perfect in knowledge is with you" (36:4).

This flaw warns us to be careful in our God talk (e.g., "God told me to say this to you"). It is so easy to hide our pride under the pretense of prophecy. For example, if someone is leaving a church because of a relational difficulty with a friend, dislike of the pastor's preaching, or a sense that the direction the church is going is unbiblical, one must not tell everyone that he is leaving because God told him to do so. We must not use the Lord's name in vain! In his book *Hope Beyond Cure*, Dave McDonald writes about Christians who tell cancer patients that God will heal them if they just believe. In one instance, one false prophet had a word from the Lord that the cancer would be gone by the end of the week. Such counsel is *devilish*. We must be careful when we "speak for God."

Finally, we come to Elihu's fourth flaw, which is that *his accusation is off*. Eliphaz, Bildad, and Zophar have claimed that Job's suffering is caused by Job's sin. Elihu claims that Job has sinned in the suffering. In other words, Job has sinned in what he has said to God from chapter 3 on. Thus Elihu has a retribution theology quite similar to the first three men's. This is why he will often sound just like them. For example, in 34:11 he says, "according to the work of a man [God] will repay him, and according to his ways he will make it [good or bad] befall him." In 34:36–37 he says, "Would that Job were tried to the end, because he answers like wicked men. For he adds rebellion to his sin; he claps his hands among us and multiplies his words against God." And in 36:11 he promises this to those who listen to God's instruction: "If they listen and serve him, they complete their days in prosperity, and their years in pleasantness." He is just the B-side to the same broken record. As John Goldingay puts it: "For all his protestations that he has something new to say, Elihu's understanding of Job's position and of how life with God works is not so different from that of the friends. Job is suffering, so he must have sinned, and he needs to repent."[158]

The B-side is better than the A-side, but it is still scratched and still playing the wrong tune. Did Job sin? Did he sin before suffering, as the first three friends claim, or during, as Elihu does? We answer these questions in two ways. First, we can read and see what God says in 42:7: "My anger burns against you [Eliphaz] and against your two friends [Bildad and Zophar], for you have not spoken of me what is right, as my servant Job has." This last line is the extended commentary we need in order to know that to God, Job has not sinned with his tongue against him. This decree teaches us how to reread Job's speeches, not only with an open mind but also with open ears and eyes to hear and see what God would teach us through Job's speeches about him. Second, we can reread chapters 3–31 and see what Job says. Here is a summary of the data:

- Job openly complains: "I will not restrain my mouth; I will speak in the anguish of my spirit; I will complain in the bitterness of my soul" (7:11).
- He curses the day he was born (3:1) and wants God to kill him: "Oh . . . that he would let loose his hand and cut me off" (6:8–9).
- He claims, in extremely strong language, that God is against him: "The arrows of the Almighty are in me" (6:4); "Why have you made me your mark?" (7:20); "You have turned cruel to me; with the might of your hand you persecute me" (30:21); "Why do you . . . count me as your enemy?" (13:24). Indeed, he directly questions God's goodness and justice *in the world* ("Why is light given to him who is in misery?"; 3:20) and especially *in his own situation* ("although you know that I am not guilty, and there is none to deliver out of your hand"; 10:7).

---

158 Ibid., 166.

- Job thinks that if he were allowed a hearing before God, the Lord would
  not challenge him: "Would he contend with me in the greatness of his
  power? No; he would pay attention to me. There an upright man could
  argue with him ["argue my ways to his face"; 13:15], and [as a result?]
  I would be acquitted forever by my judge" (23:6–7).

In all this, Job does not see right. But this is not the same as Job not speaking
right. Is it a sin to question God? Not always. "My God, my God, why have you forsaken me?" (Matt. 27:46). Remember who asked that! Is it a sin to complain against
God? Not always. "How long?" the persecuted saints call out in Revelation 6:10. Is
it a sin for Job to say that God is against him without cause (Job 9:17)? No, because
Job has not been given the cause, and because God is actually against him in one
sense. Reread the prologue: the Lord has given and the Lord has taken away. Is it
wrong to ask for personal vindication? No. Is it wrong to ask God to act justly? No.

What, then, is wrong with Job's speeches? We say "nothing." We agree with
God and say that Job does not sin with his tongue. Even though Job cannot find
God (23:8–9), this does not mean that he does not know where wisdom can be
found (28:28). Even though Job despairs of life (3:3–10), this does not mean that
he has denied the Holy One (6:10). Even though Job thinks God is acting unjustly
in his situation (9:22), this does not mean that he does not recognize his human
limitations:

> If it is a contest of strength, behold, he is mighty!
>   If it is a matter of justice, who can summon him? (9:19)

> For he is not a man, as I am, that I might answer him,
>   that we should come to trial together. (9:32)

> Will any teach God knowledge,
>   seeing that he judges those who are on high? (21:22)

And even though Job sometimes sounds so hopeless (7:6), this does not mean that
he cannot also cry out, "Though he slay me, I will hope in him" (13:15).

Having looked at the negatives of Elihu's discourse, we turn next to the positives. Having listed four flaws—he speaks from anger, his pleading to speak is
annoying, he is often arrogant, and his accusation is off—let us list two admirable
contributions of this young and aspiring theologian. Put simply, here is what is
true about Elihu's teaching.

First, what Elihu says about *God speaking through suffering* is true. In 33:14,
Elihu seeks to teach or remind Job that God speaks in many ways: "God speaks in
one way, and in two, though man does not perceive it." How does God speak? He
might speak in a prophecy or through the conscience. But he also might speak "in
a dream," especially through nightmares, because "then he opens the ears of men
and terrifies them with warnings" (33:15–16). How else might God speak? One
other way is through suffering: "Man is also rebuked with pain on his bed and

with continual strife in his bones" (33:19). This is what Elihu wants Job to *perceive*. He says in effect, "Job, God has not been silent. You keep saying, 'God is silent; God will not speak to me.' You are wrong, Job. He speaks through the suffering. You are just not listening."

What Elihu wants Job to hear from God is a rebuke. That is what God is saying. In the pain, God is disciplining Job. Now, that error in Elihu's theory aside, we still agree with what Elihu is saying here, especially as it relates to our personal histories. In *The Problem of Pain*, C. S. Lewis famously puts it, "God whispers to us in our pleasures, speaks in our conscience, but shouts in our pains: it is His megaphone to rouse a deaf world."[159] For many of us, we came to a knowledge of sin and a need for a savior through suffering. God first wounded us before he healed us. We also agree that Elihu's theory that God speaks to us through suffering as it relates to salvation history is true. Hebrews begins, "Long ago, at many times and in many ways, God spoke to our fathers by the prophets, but in these last days he has spoken to us by his Son" (Heb. 1:1–2). And how has he spoken? The ultimate revelation is through the cross. In the sufferings of the Son of God we hear God's voice: "You are forgiven," "You have been granted eternal life," and "You are my friend."

Second, *Elihu's closing argument* (Job 36:22–37:24) is both correct and convicting. Elihu does not win the case, but what he says here is beautiful and brilliant: "Behold, God is exalted in his power; who is a teacher like him?" (36:22). "Behold, he scatters his lightning about him and covers the roots of the sea" (36:30). "God thunders wondrously with his voice; he does great things that we cannot comprehend" (37:5). "Therefore men fear him" (37:24). Elihu shifts the focus from Job's problem to God's power, demonstrated in creation. Here is how John Goldingay simply summarizes the complex speech:

> Creation shows that God is too big for us to be able to tell God how to run the world, and it reminds us that we can hardly even appear before God to ask such questions and offer God such advice. If we cannot look the sun in the eye, we can hardly look God in the eye. Insightful people focus on revering and submitting to God rather than expecting to show up to see him.[160]

Exactly. So, despite Elihu's false accusations against Job, and his arrogance and verbosity, we need to appreciate here that he does rightly defend the justice of God (e.g., 37:23) as he leans us forward to the fear of God (37:24) *and the voice of God*. Yes, Elihu prepares Job, as he also prepares the reader, to hear from God in chapters 38–41. And what does God talk about? He talks so much of what Elihu has talked about: his own majestic transcendence, his inexplicably mysterious providence, and his absolute moral freedom. So in this way Elihu is an Elijah-like figure who prepares the way for the Lord. And in a way he is like a burning bush, signaling to Job that he should think about taking off his sandals because he is about to have a close encounter with the living God!

---

159 C. S. Lewis, *The Problem of Pain* (New York: Macmillan, 1962), 91.
160 Goldingay, *Job*, 183.

Many people have seen beautiful beaches, majestic mountains, colorful birds, exotic lizards, and creatures as frightening as Leviathan. And they praise Mother Nature and want to protect the environment. But how few people make the link that Elihu does, from creation to the Creator, from awe before a beautiful garden to awe before our glorious God? Nineteenth-century Romanticism and twenty-first-century planet appreciation are not what Elihu is on about. No, he calls Job, as he calls us, to "stop and consider the wondrous works of God" (37:14). Why? So we might bow before our Maker. Yes, the "awe-inspiring impressiveness of creation" should generate in us an "awe-inspiring awareness of God's greatness."[161] What is true about Elihu's speeches are his theology of the cross and his theology of creation. Indeed, he anticipates the ultimate combination of these themes, namely, the death of the Creator. How does Paul put it? The one by whom "all things were created" and in whom "all things hold together" reconciled "to himself all things, whether on earth or in heaven, making peace by the blood of his cross" (Col. 1:16–20). Oh for the day when the church will return to a robust theology of the cross and of creation! Oh for the day when the world grasps something of the greatness of God!

JOB 38:1–42:6

38 Then the LORD answered Job out of the whirlwind and said:

2   "Who is this that darkens counsel by words without knowledge?
3   Dress for action[1] like a man;
      I will question you, and you make it known to me.

4   "Where were you when I laid the foundation of the earth?
      Tell me, if you have understanding.
5   Who determined its measurements—surely you know!
      Or who stretched the line upon it?
6   On what were its bases sunk,
      or who laid its cornerstone,
7   when the morning stars sang together
      and all the sons of God shouted for joy?

8   "Or who shut in the sea with doors
      when it burst out from the womb,
9   when I made clouds its garment
      and thick darkness its swaddling band,
10   and prescribed limits for it
      and set bars and doors,

---

161 Ibid., 182.

11   and said, 'Thus far shall you come, and no farther,
         and here shall your proud waves be stayed'?

12   "Have you commanded the morning since your days began,
         and caused the dawn to know its place,
13   that it might take hold of the skirts of the earth,
         and the wicked be shaken out of it?
14   It is changed like clay under the seal,
         and its features stand out like a garment.
15   From the wicked their light is withheld,
         and their uplifted arm is broken.

16   "Have you entered into the springs of the sea,
         or walked in the recesses of the deep?
17   Have the gates of death been revealed to you,
         or have you seen the gates of deep darkness?
18   Have you comprehended the expanse of the earth?
         Declare, if you know all this.

19   "Where is the way to the dwelling of light,
         and where is the place of darkness,
20   that you may take it to its territory
         and that you may discern the paths to its home?
21   You know, for you were born then,
         and the number of your days is great!

22   "Have you entered the storehouses of the snow,
         or have you seen the storehouses of the hail,
23   which I have reserved for the time of trouble,
         for the day of battle and war?
24   What is the way to the place where the light is distributed,
         or where the east wind is scattered upon the earth?

25   "Who has cleft a channel for the torrents of rain
         and a way for the thunderbolt,
26   to bring rain on a land where no man is,
         on the desert in which there is no man,
27   to satisfy the waste and desolate land,
         and to make the ground sprout with grass?

28   "Has the rain a father,
         or who has begotten the drops of dew?
29   From whose womb did the ice come forth,
         and who has given birth to the frost of heaven?
30   The waters become hard like stone,
         and the face of the deep is frozen.

31   "Can you bind the chains of the Pleiades
         or loose the cords of Orion?
32   Can you lead forth the Mazzaroth[2] in their season,
         or can you guide the Bear with its children?
33   Do you know the ordinances of the heavens?
         Can you establish their rule on the earth?

34 "Can you lift up your voice to the clouds,
        that a flood of waters may cover you?
35 Can you send forth lightnings, that they may go
        and say to you, 'Here we are'?
36 Who has put wisdom in the inward parts[3]
        or given understanding to the mind?[4]
37 Who can number the clouds by wisdom?
        Or who can tilt the waterskins of the heavens,
38 when the dust runs into a mass
        and the clods stick fast together?

39 "Can you hunt the prey for the lion,
        or satisfy the appetite of the young lions,
40 when they crouch in their dens
        or lie in wait in their thicket?
41 Who provides for the raven its prey,
        when its young ones cry to God for help,
        and wander about for lack of food?

39 "Do you know when the mountain goats give birth?
        Do you observe the calving of the does?
2   Can you number the months that they fulfill,
        and do you know the time when they give birth,
3   when they crouch, bring forth their offspring,
        and are delivered of their young?
4   Their young ones become strong; they grow up in the open;
        they go out and do not return to them.

5   "Who has let the wild donkey go free?
        Who has loosed the bonds of the swift donkey,
6   to whom I have given the arid plain for his home
        and the salt land for his dwelling place?
7   He scorns the tumult of the city;
        he hears not the shouts of the driver.
8   He ranges the mountains as his pasture,
        and he searches after every green thing.

9   "Is the wild ox willing to serve you?
        Will he spend the night at your manger?
10 Can you bind him in the furrow with ropes,
        or will he harrow the valleys after you?
11 Will you depend on him because his strength is great,
        and will you leave to him your labor?
12 Do you have faith in him that he will return your grain
        and gather it to your threshing floor?

13 "The wings of the ostrich wave proudly,
        but are they the pinions and plumage of love?[5]
14 For she leaves her eggs to the earth
        and lets them be warmed on the ground,
15 forgetting that a foot may crush them
        and that the wild beast may trample them.

16   She deals cruelly with her young, as if they were not hers;
        though her labor be in vain, yet she has no fear,
17   because God has made her forget wisdom
        and given her no share in understanding.
18   When she rouses herself to flee,[6]
        she laughs at the horse and his rider.

19   "Do you give the horse his might?
        Do you clothe his neck with a mane?
20   Do you make him leap like the locust?
        His majestic snorting is terrifying.
21   He paws[7] in the valley and exults in his strength;
        he goes out to meet the weapons.
22   He laughs at fear and is not dismayed;
        he does not turn back from the sword.
23   Upon him rattle the quiver,
        the flashing spear, and the javelin.
24   With fierceness and rage he swallows the ground;
        he cannot stand still at the sound of the trumpet.
25   When the trumpet sounds, he says 'Aha!'
        He smells the battle from afar,
        the thunder of the captains, and the shouting.

26   "Is it by your understanding that the hawk soars
        and spreads his wings toward the south?
27   Is it at your command that the eagle mounts up
        and makes his nest on high?
28   On the rock he dwells and makes his home,
        on the rocky crag and stronghold.
29   From there he spies out the prey;
        his eyes behold it from far away.
30   His young ones suck up blood,
        and where the slain are, there is he."

40   And the LORD said to Job:

2   "Shall a faultfinder contend with the Almighty?
        He who argues with God, let him answer it."

3 Then Job answered the LORD and said:

4   "Behold, I am of small account; what shall I answer you?
        I lay my hand on my mouth.
5   I have spoken once, and I will not answer;
        twice, but I will proceed no further."

6 Then the LORD answered Job out of the whirlwind and said:

7   "Dress for action[8] like a man;
        I will question you, and you make it known to me.
8   Will you even put me in the wrong?
        Will you condemn me that you may be in the right?

9 Have you an arm like God,
     and can you thunder with a voice like his?

10 "Adorn yourself with majesty and dignity;
      clothe yourself with glory and splendor.
11 Pour out the overflowings of your anger,
      and look on everyone who is proud and abase him.
12 Look on everyone who is proud and bring him low
      and tread down the wicked where they stand.
13 Hide them all in the dust together;
      bind their faces in the world below.⁹
14 Then will I also acknowledge to you
      that your own right hand can save you.

15 "Behold, Behemoth,¹⁰
      which I made as I made you;
      he eats grass like an ox.
16 Behold, his strength in his loins,
      and his power in the muscles of his belly.
17 He makes his tail stiff like a cedar;
      the sinews of his thighs are knit together.
18 His bones are tubes of bronze,
      his limbs like bars of iron.

19 "He is the first of the works¹¹ of God;
      let him who made him bring near his sword!
20 For the mountains yield food for him
      where all the wild beasts play.
21 Under the lotus plants he lies,
      in the shelter of the reeds and in the marsh.
22 For his shade the lotus trees cover him;
      the willows of the brook surround him.
23 Behold, if the river is turbulent he is not frightened;
      he is confident though Jordan rushes against his mouth.
24 Can one take him by his eyes,¹²
      or pierce his nose with a snare?

41 ¹³ "Can you draw out Leviathan¹⁴ with a fishhook
        or press down his tongue with a cord?
2 Can you put a rope in his nose
      or pierce his jaw with a hook?
3 Will he make many pleas to you?
      Will he speak to you soft words?
4 Will he make a covenant with you
      to take him for your servant forever?
5 Will you play with him as with a bird,
      or will you put him on a leash for your girls?
6 Will traders bargain over him?
      Will they divide him up among the merchants?
7 Can you fill his skin with harpoons
      or his head with fishing spears?
8 Lay your hands on him;
      remember the battle—you will not do it again!

9 15 Behold, the hope of a man is false;
  he is laid low even at the sight of him.
10 No one is so fierce that he dares to stir him up.
  Who then is he who can stand before me?
11 Who has first given to me, that I should repay him?
  Whatever is under the whole heaven is mine.

12 "I will not keep silence concerning his limbs,
  or his mighty strength, or his goodly frame.
13 Who can strip off his outer garment?
  Who would come near him with a bridle?
14 Who can open the doors of his face?
  Around his teeth is terror.
15 His back is made of 16 rows of shields,
  shut up closely as with a seal.
16 One is so near to another
  that no air can come between them.
17 They are joined one to another;
  they clasp each other and cannot be separated.
18 His sneezings flash forth light,
  and his eyes are like the eyelids of the dawn.
19 Out of his mouth go flaming torches;
  sparks of fire leap forth.
20 Out of his nostrils comes forth smoke,
  as from a boiling pot and burning rushes.
21 His breath kindles coals,
  and a flame comes forth from his mouth.
22 In his neck abides strength,
  and terror dances before him.
23 The folds of his flesh stick together,
  firmly cast on him and immovable.
24 His heart is hard as a stone,
  hard as the lower millstone.
25 When he raises himself up, the mighty 17 are afraid;
  at the crashing they are beside themselves.
26 Though the sword reaches him, it does not avail,
  nor the spear, the dart, or the javelin.
27 He counts iron as straw,
  and bronze as rotten wood.
28 The arrow cannot make him flee;
  for him, sling stones are turned to stubble.
29 Clubs are counted as stubble;
  he laughs at the rattle of javelins.
30 His underparts are like sharp potsherds;
  he spreads himself like a threshing sledge on the mire.
31 He makes the deep boil like a pot;
  he makes the sea like a pot of ointment.
32 Behind him he leaves a shining wake;
  one would think the deep to be white-haired.
33 On earth there is not his like,
  a creature without fear.
34 He sees everything that is high;
  he is king over all the sons of pride."

42 Then Job answered the LORD and said:

2 "I know that you can do all things,
    and that no purpose of yours can be thwarted.
3 'Who is this that hides counsel without knowledge?'
    Therefore I have uttered what I did not understand,
        things too wonderful for me, which I did not know.
4 'Hear, and I will speak;
    I will question you, and you make it known to me.'
5 I had heard of you by the hearing of the ear,
    but now my eye sees you;
6 therefore I despise myself,
    and repent[18] in dust and ashes."

[1] Hebrew *Gird up your loins* [2] Probably the name of a constellation [3] Or *in the ibis* [4] Or *rooster* [5] The meaning of the Hebrew is uncertain [6] The meaning of the Hebrew is uncertain [7] Hebrew *They paw* [8] Hebrew *Gird up your loins* [9] Hebrew *in the hidden place* [10] A large animal, exact identity unknown [11] Hebrew *ways* [12] Or *in his sight* [13] Ch 40:25 in Hebrew [14] A large sea animal, exact identity unknown [15] Ch 41:1 in Hebrew [16] Or *His pride is in his* [17] Or *gods* [18] Or *and am comforted*

Section Overview

Is there a pregnant pause between Elihu's last line and the Lord's first reply? As there is no response from Job or the friends, is everyone listening stunned to silence or just bored to death? Does God interrupt Elihu? Or does Yahweh ("then the LORD answered"; Job 38:1) enter the stage on cue ("therefore men fear him"; 37:24)? The third suggestion makes most sense. Either way, the Lord now and finally speaks! The one who is "clothed with awesome majesty" (37:22) lives up to his label. This is what Job has been waiting and calling for (31:35). However, God's response does not live up to Job's expectations. Job expects God to justify and vindicate him. He will have to wait for that. First he needs to eat some humble pie. Job has not come across as a prideful man, but he has come across as an honest man who has asked one or ten too many questions. He is not God, and God will remind him of that.

As great as God is to Job, his God is too small. The creator confronts the creature; the potter asks the clay to listen and learn. Job should not have contended with the "Almighty" (40:2) or questioned God's justice (38:3; 40:8). Job learns these lessons. He understands that he is small, and so he is first silent (40:3–5), then repentant (42:1–6). The big God who controls the earth (even the unimaginably powerful Behemoth; 40:15–24) and the seas (even the unimaginably powerful Leviathan; 41:1–34) can be trusted. His incomprehensible love is sovereign but good. He has evil on a leash. And, in his time, he justifies and vindicates the righteous.

Section Outline

IV. The Unexpected Trial of Job: God Speaks! (38:1–42:6)
    A. God Calls His First Witnesses (38:1–40:2)
    B. Repentance of the Righteous, Part 1 (40:3–5)
    C. God Calls His Final Witnesses (40:6–41:34)
    D. Repentance of the Righteous, Part 2 (42:1–6)

Comment

38:1–2 Is the poetry of these chapters, or their message, the best we have heard? Yes and yes. With lofty language, the great God of the universe, speaking from a storm (v. 1; cf. Ex. 19:16), highlights the mystery of the inexplicable way in which he rules an exceedingly complex world. He begins with a question to Job, one of his seventy or so unanswerable questions.[162] The first is a tough, seemingly harsh, one: "Who is this that darkens counsel by words without knowledge?" (Job 38:2). God does not say, "Sorry, friend," or "Hang in there—only a few more chapters to go." Instead he puts his favorite human on trial. This is not "to humiliate or intimidate Job"[163] but to open his eyes to the God that makes the Milky Way look like a stream in an Arabian wadi. God is in charge. He knows what he is doing. Divine wisdom is *out of this world*! Satan will not win. Good Job will glow in the end, after some more refining fire.

38:3–11 God's forceful opening statement—"Dress for action like a man; I will question you, and you make it known to me" (v. 3)—must have startled Job, as much as it does the sympathetic reader. "Give Job a gospel tract," we might say. "God loves you and has a wonderful plan for your life!" No. Job is in the dock. He must prepare himself for the legal battle of his life.[164] He will have to answer questions that God, the prosecuting attorney, knows that even the wisest human cannot answer:

> Where were you when I laid the foundation of the earth?
>   Tell me, if you have understanding.
> Who determined its [all of creation's] measurements—surely you know!
>   Or who stretched the line upon it?
> On what were its bases sunk,
>   or who laid its cornerstone,
> when the morning stars sang together
>   and all the sons of God shouted for joy? (vv. 4–7)

Genesis 1 declares Job guilty. Job cannot possibly know how God created the earth (Job 38:4), the details of its dimensions (v. 5), the depths of its foundations (v. 6), or the first reaction of the highest constellations of heaven or the highest creation on earth.

With verses 8–11, the Bible's first chapter is not done taking the stand. God asks Job if he has any idea who was in charge of the seven seas, making sure that the oceans, which first burst forth like a quickly delivered baby (v. 8), do not flood the land. God also asks how the clouds, which could flood the world completely in forty or so days, are restrained. The answer is God alone (the awesome I!):

---

162 Cf. Estes, *Job*, 230.
163 Ibid.
164 Estes explains the command, "Dress for action like a man," in this way: "This . . . interrogation will require every effort Job can muster, as Yahweh has enrolled him in a graduate course in the divine school of wisdom. Using the familiar biblical image of girding up one's garment by inserting it in the belt (cf. Exod. 12:11; 1 Kings 18:46; Jer. 1:17; 1 Pet. 1:13 KJV), Yahweh exhorts Job to prepare himself for a formidable intellectual and theological challenge" (ibid., 243).

Or who shut in the sea with doors
  when it burst out from the womb,
when *I* made clouds its garment
  and thick darkness its swaddling band,
and prescribed limits for it
  and set bars and doors,
and said, "Thus far shall you come, and no farther,
  and here shall your proud waves be stayed"? (vv. 8–11)

38:12–21 With all of these questions, God is seeking to teach Job that his understanding is insufficient. His statements, "Tell me, if you have understanding" (v. 4b) and "Declare, if you know all this" (v. 18b)—even the sarcastic ones ("surely you know!" v. 5a; "you know, for you were born then," v. 21a)—are just as important as his questions. This son of pride (41:34b) needs to be put in his place.

The next set of questions (38:12–21) are also answered "no" in Job's head. He has not ordered the sun to rise ("commanded the morning"/"caused the dawn"; v. 12). And as the sun spreads across the earth, bringing everything to light and exposing the earth's various and diverse geological "features" (v. 14), Job cannot see what God sees. God sees all wickedness ("From the wicked their light is withheld"; v. 15a), in every imaginable hidden place on earth ("the skirts of the earth"; v. 13a), and judges it ("the wicked [are] shaken out of" the earth, v. 13b; "their uplifted arm is broken," v. 15b). Job has not swum to the bottom of the ocean ("entered into the springs of the sea"/"walked in the recesses of the deep"; v. 16) to eye all of the exotic creatures and make sure the springs are still working. Job has talked a lot about death, but he knows nothing about its place or power ("the gates of death"/"deep darkness" have not "been revealed to" him; v. 17). Job cannot fathom how huge the earth is ("Have you comprehended the expanse of the earth?"; v. 18a). He probably thinks it is flat, with Uz as the center of the universe! Job does not know the sources of light or darkness ("the dwelling of light"/"the place of darkness"; v. 19; parallel thought in v. 20), or perhaps the sense is that he does not know where heaven and Sheol are. Job was surely not there ("you were born then," v. 21, is sarcasm) when God's voice pierced the "darkness . . . over the face of the deep": "Let there be light" (Gen. 1:2, 3).

38:22–38 In these verses Job is asked to consider the sky, from the farthest stars to the closest clouds. He is to explain the weather (snow, hail, wind, thunder, lightning) and its effects on the ground (land, ice, frost, floods, dust). The main question to which Job has no answer is, "Do you know the ordinances of the heavens? Can you establish their rule on the earth?" (v. 33). As Job has no way of knowing how even his own human mind works ("Who has put wisdom in the inward parts or given understanding to the mind?"; v. 36), he certainly cannot grasp how God uses extreme weather to impact extreme situations (for example, when he releases the "storehouses" of "snow" and "hail" [v. 22] to help defeat the enemy—"I have reserved for the time of trouble, for the day of battle and war"; v. 23; cf.

Ex. 9:22–26; Josh. 10:11; Isa. 30:30; Ezek. 13:11). Job cannot fly to the heavens to eye the place where lightning originates ("the light is distributed"; Job 38:24a) or walk back to the source from which "the east wind is scattered" all over the world (v. 24b). The unpredictable power of a storm is not under Job's control. Nor is the rain. No human can perfectly predict where or when every storm ("a channel for the torrents of rain"/"a way for the thunderbolt"; v. 25) will hit. It might be in the middle of nowhere ("on a land where no man is"/"on the desert in which there is no man"; v. 26), or make grass grow in the desert, of all places ("to satisfy the waste and desolate land, and to make the ground sprout with grass"; v. 27)!

God alone is the father of rain ("Has the rain a father . . . ?"; v. 28a) and the mother ("who has begotten"/"from whose womb did . . . come forth . . . ?"; vv. 28b–29) of dew, ice, and frost. He determines the temperatures on land, even freezing a whole lake if he so desires ("the waters become hard like stone"/"the face of the deep is frozen"; v. 30). He orders and arranges the constellations ("bind the chains of the Pleiades"; "loose the cords of Orion"; "lead forth the Mazzaroth"; "guide the Bear with its children [i.e., Ursa Major and Ursa Minor]"; vv. 31–32). God also controls the countless clouds ("Who can number the clouds by wisdom?"; v. 37a). He can dictate where each bolt of lightning will strike (v. 35) and call forth rain (lift his "voice to the clouds, [so] that a flood of waters" comes, v. 34; "tilt the waterskins of the heavens," v. 37b) during a drought ("when the dust runs into a mass"/"the clods stick fast together"; v. 38).

38:39–39:30 From speaking about cosmogony (38:4–21) and meteorology (38:22–38), God turns finally to zoology (38:39–39:30).[165] This lesson centers on animals that man cannot tame, feed, see, or comprehend. The purpose of the lesson is the same as the lessons on cosmogony and meteorology: to remind Job that he is a man, not a god, and as a man his knowledge and power are quite limited. Not only are God's ways higher than Job's ways (cf. Isa. 55:9); his power is unsurpassable as well. Job cannot do all that God does. Job cannot provide food for the lion ("hunt the prey for the lion, . . . lie in wait in their thicket"; Job 38:39–40) or the raven ("provides for the raven its prey"; 38:41a) so they might provide for their young ("satisfy the appetite of the young lions," 38:39b; the raven's "young ones," 38:41b), who "cry to God for help" because of their "lack of food" (38:41bc).

Job has no idea how to spy out the birth process of the elusive ibex[166]—when they give birth ("Do you know when the mountain goats give birth?"; 39:1a), how they do so ("Do you observe the calving of the does?" v. 1b; "when they crouch, bring forth their offspring," 39:3a), how long they are pregnant ("Can you number the months that they fulfill . . . ?"; 39:2a), what season of the year that they usually give birth ("Do you know the time when they give birth?"; 39:2b), or what happens

---

165 This is Robert Alter's helpful summary and division of the text. See *The Art of Biblical Poetry* (New York: Basic, 1985), 94, quoted in Longman, *Job*, 425n36.
166 "The mountain goat here is the ibex that today can be seen in the En Gedi area of Israel. It is an elusive animal that can be observed only from a distance, and it resists domestication by humans. With telephoto lenses humans can now learn some of the habits of animals like the ibex, but until recent times little was known of its patterns of life" (Estes, *Job*, 236).

to their young soon after ("their young ones become strong; they grow up in the open; they go out and do not return to them"; 39:4).

Job cannot domesticate the wild donkey (39:5), who roams freely and swiftly throughout the wasteland (the "arid plain" is "his home," the "salt land" is "his dwelling place," 39:6; this refers to the salt flats by the Salt Sea; cf. Gen. 14:3), surviving on his own, even if he needs to roam the hills to find food ("he ranges the mountains as his pasture"/"he searches after every green thing"; Job 39:8). This wild beast will not let man be his master ("he scorns the tumult of the city; he hears not the shouts of the driver"; 39:7).

So too "the wild ox." While man could harness the "great" strength of such a creature and use it to till the fields ("harrow the valleys") and transport heavy goods to the "threshing floor" (39:10–12), this particular ox refuses to be enslaved. It is unwilling to "serve" man, even for one day ("spend the night at your manger"; 39:9). Again, the point here, as with all of the animals thus far and following, is to show Job that "Job is not in charge or control of the created order."[167]

The ostrich is another example, an odd but important one. Among the animals in Job, only the warhorse (39:19–25) will receive more verses, and only one more.[168] This is also the only section (39:13–18) with no rhetorical questions. God makes three statements about this strange creature. First, the ostrich seems useless. It has feathers ("the wings of the ostrich wave proudly"), but these aphrodisiac wings ("the pinions and plumage of love"; 39:13)[169] do not help it to fly. Second, the ostrich seems stupid ("God has made her forget wisdom and given her no share in understanding"; 39:17). This stupidity is shown in how she treats her young. Since she cannot fly, she is not like the eagle, who leaves her offspring in a safe high place. Instead, she "leaves her eggs [on] the earth" (39:14a) or slightly buried in the sand. This, of course, makes them vulnerable. Anyone or anything might step on them ("a foot may crush them"/"the wild beast may trample them"; 39:15), or a human hunter could grab them or a beastly predator devour them. This seems both cruel ("she deals cruelly with her young, as if they were not hers"; 39:16) and stupid. How will her species survive? But her ignorance is bliss ("though her labor be in vain, yet she has no fear"; 39:16b). God has made her this way (39:17). And still her species survives, and even thrives. Third, part of her survival relates to her unique (and humorous!) maneuverability and uncanny ability to flee from trouble (39:18). While the ostrich cannot dive at the speed of an eagle (100 mph/160 kmph), it can run half that speed, faster than anything on two legs. It can even outrun some incredibly fast four-legged creatures, such as the horse (39:18; see 39:19–25) and even the lion (38:39–40). It certainly would leave the mountain goat (39:1–4), wild donkey (39:5–8), and wild ox (39:9–12) in the dust.

---

167 Longman, *Job*, 436.
168 Although it should be noted that "the ostrich makes sport of the fearless warhorse [see Job 39:18]. As it flees, the ostrich reaches a height of over 8 feet (2.4 m), strides of over 15 feet in length (4.6 m), and speeds of more than 40 miles (64 km) an hour" (*ESV Study Bible* note on Job 39:18).
169 "The flapping of its stubby wings with their dull and mottled feathers is the male's courting gesture" (Alden, *Job*, 386).

These three ideas are important to Yahweh's pedagogical purposes. Why would God create such a creature? The existence of the awkward, ugly, and odd ostrich is a visual reminder that God's ways are mysterious and is a rebuttal of the retribution principle's tidy system of theology. There is nothing logical about this powerful but silly bird. Like the Leviathan (41:29), this strange creature "laughs" (39:18). Perhaps they both laugh at theology like that of Eliphaz, Zophar, Bildad, Elihu, and, even in part, Job.

From the ostrich eluding a fast horse (39:18), Yahweh turns to the horse itself. He asks Job if Job is responsible for giving such an amazing creature its "might" (39:19a), its "mane" (39:19b), its ability to jump ("leap like the locust"; 39:20a), or its imposing and fearsome sounds ("his majestic snorting is terrifying"; 39:20b). The implied answer is, "Of course not." Then God further describes this fierce beast in battle. With his hoofs digging in the ground ("he paws in the valley"; 39:21a), he rushes into battle ("he goes out to meet the weapons"; 39:21b). With each step he smiles at his strength ("and exults in his strength"; 39:21a). He is fearless ("he laughs at fear and is not dismayed") of the fight ahead ("he does not turn back from the sword"; 39:22). This warhorse is armed for war ("upon him rattle the quiver, the flashing spear, and the javelin"; 39:23). The charge has sounded; he has heard the horn. "When the trumpet sounds, he says 'Aha!'" (39:25a). He races ahead with an almost reckless courage.[170] "With fierceness and rage he swallows the ground; he cannot stand still at the sound of the trumpet" (39:24). Snorting, he kicks up the dirt. He hears the battle cry ("the thunder of the captains, and the shouting"; 39:25c), smells the bloody battle ahead ("he smells the battle from afar"; 39:25b), and races ahead. This imposing and terrifying animal may be tamed by man but is also dangerous to man, both as it attacks the enemy and as its rider gallops to the fight. It lives on the brink of being an uncontrollable force. When "plunging headlong into battle," it can steer its "own course" (Jer. 8:6). Only a powerful God could create such a powerful creature and know how to rein it in.

Next, and finally for God's first speech, we have the "hawk" (Job 39:26) and the "eagle" (39:27–30), symbolizing the "epitome of avian animals."[171] Who can harness the hawk? Who can eye the eagle? Certainly not Job. God returns Job's vision to the sky (cf. 38:9–38). Look up! Regarding both birds, Yahweh asks two rhetorical questions followed by a description that fits them both. It is only by God's "understanding that the hawk soars and spreads his wings toward the south" (39:26) and by his "command that the eagle mounts up and makes his nest on high" (39:27). Job has not taught these amazing birds to fly, soaring so far above the earth.

Up high, on the "rocky crag," they live (39:28). The eagle lives not in inaccessible light but at an inaccessible height.[172] Job cannot fly; he cannot climb to these heights to pet their young. He did not even coach them in how to build their

---

170 See Alden, *Job*, 389.
171 Ibid., 390.
172 "The 'eagle' is the most common bird in the Bible. . . . Most references to it are figurative with points made about its strength (Exod 19:4; Isa 40:31), speed (2 Sam 1:23; Jer 4:13), grandeur in flight (Prov 30:19; Jer 48:40), or ability to take pray (Job 9:26; Hab 1:8) or find carrion (Prov 30:17; Matt 24:28). Here, as in Jer 49:16 and Obad 4, the point is the 'soaring' and 'nesting' in high, craggy, inaccessible places" (ibid.).

amazing nests (their "stronghold"; 39:28b). From these heights, these birds of prey *see* their prey. An eagle can see a rabbit running 3 miles (4.8 km) away! "From there he spies out the prey; his eyes behold it from far away" (39:29). It dives. The rabbit or rodent does not have a chance. Going a 100 miles (160 km) an hour, this big and burly bird grabs its main course, uses its hard beak to kill, and returns home to feed the whole family ("his young ones suck up blood"; 39:30a). Other times, roadkill will do for dinner ("and where the slain are, there is he"; 39:30; cf. Matt. 24:28//Luke 17:37).

Again, why does God bring before Job's eyes these birds? Estes summarizes the point perfectly: "The hawk and the eagle demonstrate that there is much in Yahweh's design for the world that humans do not know or control."[173] Moreover, the eagle dovetails (no pun intended) with the first creature named, a lion. As Job cannot stakeout a meal for the king of the jungle (Job 38:39), so can he not tell the queen of the heavens where to find food. This is an inclusio of ignorance. Job is not God. Job cannot fathom even a few behaviors of some of the amazing and mysterious creatures of the earth and sky. (How will he fare with the monster of the sea? See 41:1–34.) If Job is still standing, he should not be. He should be on his knees by now.

40:1–5 Is Job on his knees? Face down? He is. If not literally, then at least metaphorically. What gets him in this humble position is everything that God has said from 38:2 to 39:30. But what also gets him there is Yahweh's final rebuke: "And the LORD said to Job: 'Shall a faultfinder contend with the Almighty? He who argues with God, let him answer it'" (40:1–2). Job now understands that he should not seek to call God to court, accuse him, or correct him. God should not be schooled in wisdom. Smallness and silence are the appropriate responses:

> Then Job answered the LORD and said:

> "Behold, I am of small account; what shall I answer you?
>   I lay my hand on my mouth.
> I have spoken once, and I will not answer;
>   twice, but I will proceed no further." (vv. 3–5)

Elihu might have taken on a John-the-Baptist role in that he prepared the way for the Lord's speech, but Job here takes on John's humble position before Jesus (cf. Matt. 3:11). Job is not worthy to be in the Lord's presence. Adding his own "behold" (see Elihu's sixteen previous "beholds"), the greatest man of the east grasps that he is not so great compared to God ("I am of small account"; Job 40:4a). Then, as Alden puts it, "With a rhetorical question of his own [v. 4b], Job replied that he could not answer any of the questions."[174] Job has given up the idea of a court case, with himself featured as the spectacular prosecuting attorney against God, masterfully defending himself. He has spoken here, even though he said he

---

173 Estes, *Job*, 239.
174 Alden, *Job*, 392.

would not speak. He is dazed, confused; he covers his mouth ("I lay my hand on my mouth"; v. 4b). He has said enough.

There is no acknowledgement of sin here. Job does not say, "Oh, the four friends were right. I have offended God." Job likely feels stuck. He knows that some secret sin has not led to his circumstances. Yet he now also knows that he spoke too much and without a better grasp of things. He regrets some of what he has said; he understands that he does not understand the mystery of God's workings in the world, and he acknowledges that he has overstepped his rank. He is hoping the ordeal will soon be over, but he is willing to sit on the ash heap a few hours more if Yahweh will condescend to speak with him and to him.

40:6–14 Again (see 38:1), "out of the whirlwind" God speaks ("the LORD answered Job . . . and said"; 40:6). Also, as in 38:3, God begins with the same command to Job ("dress for action like a man") and declaration ("I will question you, and you make it known to me"; 40:7). What is different in the short forewords to these two speeches is that God's first question in the second one comes after, not before (as in 38:2, "Who is this that darkens counsel by words without knowledge?"), that command and that declaration. In 40:8–9, God asks Job three penetrating questions:

> Will you even put me in the wrong?
>> Will you condemn me that you may be in the right?
> Have you an arm like God,
>> and can you thunder with a voice like his? (vv. 8–9)

Again, a negative answer is implied to all three questions. To the first two we can imagine Job saying, "Not anymore," and to the third, "No." Job is learning not only that he is not as powerful as God (he does not have as strong an "arm" or as thunderous a "voice"; v. 9; cf. Ps. 44:1–3) but also that he has been wrong to put God "in the wrong" (Job 40:8a), to defame God's name ("will you condemn me"; cf. 9:24; 27:2) in order to clear his own ("that you may be in the right?"; 40:8b). "He was more concerned with his own reputation for righteousness than he was with God's reputation for justice."[175]

Next, with ten imperatives God challenges Job to be God. First, Yahweh calls him to exist like God: to "adorn" himself "with majesty [*ga'on*] and dignity [*gobah*]," to "clothe" himself "with glory [*hod*] and splendor [*hadar*]" (v. 10; cf. Elihu's "God is clothed with awesome majesty," 37:22). Second, he repeatedly challenges Job to judge justly like God—to condemn the proud ("pour out . . . your anger," 40:11a; "abase him," v. 11b; "bring him low," v. 12a; "tread down the wicked," v. 12b; "hide them all in the dust," v. 13a; "bind their faces in the world below," v. 13b). If Job were able to exist and act like God, then God would be happy to let Job go on with his suggestion of a court trial in which God hears all of his defenses and answers all of his questions. God will even acknowledge that he is not needed. Job can save himself. "Then will I also acknowledge to you that your own right hand

---

175 Longman, *Job*, 440.

can save you" (v. 14). Of course, the point is that Job needs to realize afresh that God alone can save him.

40:15–24 In 38:39–39:30 God paraded the lion, raven, mountain goat, wild donkey, wild ox, ostrich, warhorse, hawk, and eagle. In 40:15–41:34 he takes Job face to face with the two fiercest creatures in the world. In 40:15 he begins, "Behold, Behemoth!" What is this creature? Who has heard of "Behemoth" (Hb. *behemot*)?[176] On one hand, it is possible that this is a hippopotamus, as the following description seems to fit (esp. vv. 20–24), and hippopotamuses were known to have existed in the ancient Near East,[177] especially in lower Egypt.[178] On the other hand, Behemoth could be a mythical beast.[179] However, the opening line, in which God speaks of creating this creature as he did man ("I made as I made you"; v. 15b) and which follows nine literal animals in chapters 38–39, favors the view that a hippopotamus is in view.[180]

At first glance, the hippopotamus merely resembles the ox. "He eats grass like an ox" (40:15c). He is extremely strong. Not only is his backside formidable ("his strength in his loins"), so too is his stomach ("his power in the muscles of his belly"; v. 16), and his massive legs look indestructible ("the sinews of his thighs are knit together"; v. 17b). Even his tail appears powerful ("he makes his tail stiff like a cedar"; v. 17a)![181] Both on the outside (vv. 16–17) and the inside he is formidable.

> His bones   are   tubes of bronze,
> his limbs   like bars of iron. (v. 18)

The animal has muscles of steel and bones of bronze—who could conquer such a beast? Humans cannot hurt him. He ranks "first" among the "works of God" (v. 19a, i.e., the greatest among the great beasts of the land); only Yahweh, who brought him to life, has the power to take his life ("let him who made him bring near his sword!"; v. 19b). Behemoth is strong, but not stronger than God! "Unafraid, Yahweh *can approach* Behemoth *with his sword*," thus symbolizing "his complete mastery of this beast."[182] Only God is his king.

But God does not slay him; rather, he provides for him. Even the mighty mountains bring him his meals ("the mountains yield food for him"; v. 20a). The sense, of course, is that this enormous beast climbs the hills (the banks of the Nile?) at night in search of a late-night gorge. His midnight playground is "where all the wild beasts play" (v. 20b). But he fears them not. What can they do to him? This nocturnal herbivore spends some of the day relaxing riverside ("under the [Zizyphus]

---

176 On the Hebrew as plural, Ash notes: "Here the plural seems to be a plural of majesty, conveying something like 'The Superbeast'" (*Job*, 410).
177 See Alden, *Job*, 396n87.
178 See Hartley, *Job*, 524.
179 See Pope, *Job*, 320–322.
180 For further support of Behemoth and Leviathan as real creatures, see David J. A. Clines, *Job 38–42*, WBC 18B (Nashville: Thomas Nelson, 2011), 1183–1201; and Gordis, *Job*, 569–572.
181 The hippopotamus's tail, while it is thick and strong at the base, is short and curly. Thus some scholars think that an elephant and its trunk are being described; others the hippopotamus's stiffened penis. The best solution might be that the poet is using hyperbole, the sense being, "Just try to find a weak spot."
182 Hartley, *Job*, 525, emphasis his.

lotus plants he lies"; v. 21a) but most of the day submerged in the swamp-like waters ("in the shelter of the reeds and in the marsh. For his shade the lotus trees cover him; the willows of the brook surround him"; vv. 21b–22).[183]

This three-ton beast does not sink.[184] He does not feed on aquatic plants or animals. Bull sharks are not his diet. The *Hippopotamus amphibius* eats only grass! Amazing. Strange. How does that work? How does he remain so strong? How does he maintain his weight? How does he assure that his body armor stays indestructible? And, strangest of all (it receives a "behold"!), how on earth does he swim?

> Behold, if the river is turbulent he is not frightened;
>   he is confident though Jordan rushes against his mouth. (v. 23)

He is not afraid of the wild beasts at night. During the day, he is not afraid of any raging river (even the "Jordan" River or the Nile River when it floods). By running underwater, he can swim! And this plump, round giant can swim faster than any svelte and successful Olympian ever dreamed (30 mph [48 kmph] bursts, compared with 6 mph [10 kmph]!). The big bird in the sky (the eagle) and the fat mammal in the marsh can do what man could never do.

This comparison with man concludes the portrait of Behemoth. Man cannot catch him (cf. 41:2, 7, 26).

> Can one take him by his eyes,
>   or pierce his nose with a snare? (40:24)

We might picture the huge and heavy hippopotamus smiling with his twenty-inch teeth as some man tries to catch him like a trout. Again (see v. 19), the point is that only God could capture him, if he wanted. But why would he want to? Such a beast boasts of his greatness!

41:1–34 Here God speaks of Leviathan, a sea creature Job was aware of (3:8; cf. "Rahab," 9:13; 26:12). The purpose of putting Behemoth and Leviathan before Job's eyes is to help Job "realize that Yahweh totally controls all threats to his order" and that "compared with the Lord, Job has paltry knowledge and feeble power."[185] Or, in Yahweh's own words, it is to teach Job that "whatever is under the whole heaven is mine" (41:11b), and that even the fierce, powerful, and seemingly uncontrollable and unconquerable Leviathan cannot "stand before" him (v. 10b). Leviathan might be the king *of* all creatures (v. 34b), but God is king *over* all creatures.

Like Behemoth, it is difficult to know if Leviathan is some real or mythical creature. However, as it is likely that Behemoth is a hippopotamus, it is also possible that Leviathan is a crocodile. While there is some evidence for this claim,

---

183 "During the day hippopotami spend much of the time submerged, except their nostrils, eyes, and ears, which remain above the water in order to sense everything around them" (Alden, *Job*, 397).

184 Unless he wants to! Hippos can float or sink by controlling their breathing and body positions.

185 Estes, *Job*, 242, 247. This reading also fits the other mentions of Leviathan in the OT. God has formed the ocean for the Leviathan to "play in" (Ps. 104:26), and God alone can destroy this beast ("crushed the heads"; Ps. 74:14), using his "strong sword" (cf. Job 40:19) to "punish . . . the twisting serpent, . . . the dragon that is in the sea" (Isa. 27:1).

it is not easy to prove. We think, however, that the point God has been making since 38:39 depends on the animals listed being real animals and not mythical creatures (e.g., Leviathan is like the Canaanite's seven-headed Lotan) or mere symbols (e.g., the "embodiment of cosmic evil itself"[186] or of "chaotic forces of evil"[187]). In what ways is an incredible sea creature more symbolic of "evil" than the lion or eagle devouring their innocent prey, or the warhorse smelling the blood of battle?

The Leviathan is, however, special. Thus Yahweh saves him for last, offers him the longest description of any creature (thirty-four verses), and concludes climactically with two statements about this creature: "On earth there is not his like" (41:33a) and "he is king over all the sons of pride" (v. 34b). Perhaps it is best to read verses 1–34 and think "this is a crocodile" but allow our imaginations to envision a hybrid of a saltwater crocodile and whatever other creature—the White Whale, the Loch Ness Monster, or the smug Smaug—we find most ferocious.

The description of Leviathan begins with the humorous idea of men trying to fish him out of the waters and raise him as a pet. Imagine baiting a "fishhook" with some wallaby (v. 1a). Then, as the mighty monster jumps out of the water and devours the bait, the hook lodges inside its mouth and its tongue is "pressed down by the rope tied to the hook"[188] ("press down his tongue with a cord"; v. 1b). Finally, via a "rope" through "his nose" and a "hook" through "his jaw" (v. 2), he is dragged to the shore. This feat in and of itself is as unlikely as a boy catching a killer whale with a toy fishing rod. And it is foolish. Who in the world is brave enough to hunt him ("no one is so fierce that he dares to stir him up"; v. 10a)? But, if we play along, we can next imagine man's relationship with this captured beast.

Will Leviathan beg for mercy ("make many pleas to you"/"speak to you soft words"; v. 3)? No! Will he admit defeat and offer himself as a bondslave for life ("make a covenant with you to take him for your servant forever"; v. 4)? No! Will he eventually be so domesticated that he would become like a dove ("will you play with him as with a bird") or a collie ("will you put him on a leash for your girls?"; v. 5)? "A girl leading on a leash a crocodile that may weigh as much as a ton is a whimsical if not absurd scene."[189]

God is leading Job from one absurd idea to another. In verse 6, another humorous picture is put in his sight. Who can imagine merchants in the afternoon fish market bargaining over Leviathan ("Will traders bargain over him?") or trying to divide ("Will they divide him up?"; v. 6) his indestructible flesh (see vv. 13, 15–17, 23, 26–30) into little pieces for sushi? Then, taking us back to the opening scene (vv. 1–2), God calls the whole scenario he has depicted in verses 1–6 absurd. Can one really fish for Leviathan: "fill his skin with harpoons or his head with fishing spears" (v. 7)? As soon as you try to get him out of the water and "lay your hands on

---

186 Robert R. Fyall, *Now My Eyes Have Seen You: Images of Creation and Evil in the Book of Job*, NSBT 12 (Downers Grove, IL: InterVarsity, 2002), 157. Fyall also argues that Behemoth symbolizes death (137).
187 Hartley, *Job*, 530.
188 Ibid.
189 Alden, *Job*, 401.

him," you might not have hands left. It will be a day you will not forget ("remember the battle") and an act of such stupidity that "you will not do it again!" (v. 8). The idea of even bringing this creature out of the waters (let alone to the market!) is an optimism of idiocy ("the hope of a man is false"; v. 9a). The mere sight of him raising his head in the waters ("when he raises himself up, the mighty are afraid"; v. 25a) or of his wake in the waters (v. 32) is enough to make even the proudest hunter shake in his boots ("he is laid low even at the sight of him"; v. 9b). Leviathan is "so fierce that" no one is foolish enough to fish for him, let alone come near him ("dares to stir him up"; v. 10a).

In verses 10b–11 God gives the reason for this imaginary fishing expedition: it is to remind Job that he should not be stirring up God and that he is not in a position to stand toe to toe with God, whether it be in some court of law or even face to face. Two reasons are given. First, God is the creator and sustainer of the world ("Who has first given to me, that I should repay him?"; v. 11a). Second, God is sovereign over all creation ("whatever is under the whole heaven"—white tigers, brown snakes, black widows, the nearly invisible box jellyfish, etc.—"is mine"; v. 11b). God cannot be challenged. God has no equal (cf. Rom. 11:33–36). Even the most deadly animals are his pets!

In Job 41:12–24, Yahweh provides an extended inventory of Leviathan's anatomy (cf. the short description of Behemoth; 40:16–18). "I will not keep silence concerning his limbs, or his mighty strength, or his goodly frame" (41:12). The inventory of his strong body begins with his skin and mouth (vv. 13–17). His skin is like a double coat of mail armor ("who can strip off his outer garment?" v. 13a; also later, "the folds of his flesh stick together, firmly cast on him and immovable," v. 23), with a thousand or so tile-like pieces of impenetrable metal interlocking together, sealed with inseparable superglue:

> His back is made of rows of shields, ["His scales are his pride," KJV; cf. NASB]
>   shut up closely as with a seal.
> One is so near to another
>   that no air can come between them.
> They are joined one to another;
>   they clasp each other and cannot be separated. (vv. 15–17)

The only opening is his mouth. But that is not the safest place to attempt an attack! No one would dare try to put a bridle around his head ("Who would come near him with a bridle?"; v. 13b). He is not a docile pony. He is not even a half-tamed warhorse. Moreover, how would one even open this beast's mighty jaws to set the mask in place ("Who can open the doors of his face?"; v. 14a)? And if some man could open them, watch out! Leviathan's greatest weapon awaits: "around his teeth is terror" (v. 14b).[190] His seventy-plus sharp and strong teeth can kill incredibly large animals, fish, and birds. That is not all. Out of his mouth comes fire!

---

190 According to the ESV, Job 41:14 contains the twelfth and final question (there are no more questions in 41:15–34) that God asks Job about Leviathan. The two questions in 41:10–11 are about God. Thus, there are

His sneezings flash forth light,
> and his eyes are like the eyelids of the dawn.

Out of his mouth go flaming torches;
> sparks of fire leap forth.

Out of his nostrils comes forth smoke,
> as from a boiling pot and burning rushes.

His breath kindles coals,
> and a flame comes forth from his mouth. (vv. 18–21)

Here is where the anatomical description fails to describe a crocodile, resembling more the long list of mythological dragons of the ancient world. However, it might be that of an extinct crocodile-like creature, one for which we have no fossil record. And even if we had some scientific record, how would we know for certain if the creature could breathe fire? It might also be that verses 18–21 are metaphors for the way in which a crocodile roams the water ("Its nostrils squirt spray that becomes translucent in the light [41:18]. . . . Spray from its mouth looks like fire in the sunshine [41:19]"[191]); "When this creature sneezes, the water spray sparkles in the sunlight like flashes of light," and "when this creature emerges from the water, it spews out its pent-up breath in a steaming spray that appears like *sparks of fire* or like *smoke from a boiling pot*."[192] Verses 20–21 might also describe the aftermath of a crocodile killing its prey. As he descends back into the waters, a captured bird or animal is totally *incinerated* (i.e., devoured, without a trace) within seconds!

A metaphorical reading also fits the context. The parallel line to "His sneezings flash forth light" (v. 18a) is a metaphor about his thin, black pupil set against reddish-green eyes resembling the morning sun peaking over the horizon ("and his eyes are like the eyelids of the dawn"; v. 18b). Moreover, there is hardly a line that is not a metaphor in verses 12–32.[193] For example, verses 18–21 are followed by verse 22, where "terror dances before him" (this is as metaphorical as it gets!) as his neck breaks the prey into pieces ("in his neck abides strength"; v. 22). Also, in verse 24 this cold-blooded and hard-hearted killer ("his heart is hard as a stone, hard as the lower millstone")[194] with his safely protected chest could not care less if he is consuming his own children or a man's wife.

In verses 25–32 Yahweh returns to the crazy notion of humans' trying to attack the super creature of the sea. In verses 1–2 we have a depiction of a man using

---

fourteen questions total. The final questions center on the terror Job would experience if face to face with this seemingly invincible crocodile and also relate back to the two questions about God in 41:10–11. As Hartley summarizes: "In contemplating taking up his case with God, Job has been concerned with being overcome by terror (cf. 9:32–35; 13:20–21). Now Yahweh is showing Job that his apprehensions were on target. If he would have to retreat in terror before Leviathan, surely he could not stand before God at court" (*Job*, 534).
191 Jones, *Job*, 278.
192 Hartley, *Job*, 532, emphasis his.
193 For example, "his face" is like "doors" (41:14a), "terror" hangs around his teeth (41:14b), "his back is made of rows of shields" (41:15a), "he counts iron as straw, and bronze as rotten wood" (41:27), "sling stones are turned to stubble" (41:28b), "clubs are counted as stubble" (41:29a), "he laughs at the rattle of javelins" (41:29b), "his underparts are like sharp potsherds" (41:30a), "he spreads himself like a threshing sledge" (41:30b), the sea is turned "white-haired" in his wake (41:32b). See also God possibly depicted metaphorically as a fire-breather (4:9).
194 These metaphors are also hyperbole. The idea is that even if a hunter could get through Leviathan's invincible body, he would be met with a surprise. This creature's heart is as hard as his hide!

fishing gear to catch this beast. Stupidity of stupidity. In verses 25–32 man employs weapons of war: the sword, spear, dart, javelin, arrow, sling stones, and clubs. Better idea; same results. Not only is Leviathan's back covered in bone (osteoderms) that look like spears, his belly is like hard and jagged stones ("his underparts are like sharp potsherds," v. 30; "sharp stones are under him," KJV). The spear can reach him under the waters, but it does not avail against his thick skin (v. 26). The sword then? No. Chop off his head when he raises it above the waters? A sword might easily cut off a man's head, but not Leviathan's. His neck is massive and strong (v. 22a). Can something be thrown from a distance? Sure. But, why lose valuable iron and bronze spears, darts, javelins, and arrows? They bounce off him like straw and rotten wood (v. 27). "He laughs at the rattle of javelins" (v. 29b).[195] How about King David's slingshot? This may work against Goliath of the Canaanites but not against Samson of the Deep. When stones strike his body, they turn to nothing— "stubble" (the short and stiff stumps of grain left after harvesting). Baseball bats too ("clubs are counted as stubble"; v. 29a).

What then? Nothing. Even the mightiest men tremble when they see him ("when he raises himself up, the mighty are afraid"); they turn green and yellow when he splashes beside the boat ("at the crashing they are beside themselves"; v. 25). Watch him laugh in the mire, crying his crocodile tears, and rubbing his belly against the mud of the earth's rivers and seas ("he spreads himself like a threshing sledge on the mire"; v. 30b). As his "fire" shows itself on the surface (vv. 19–21), so he makes the underbelly of the sea shake, rattle, roll, and boil(!) when he swims by ("he makes the deep boil" like a pot of tea, or like someone brewing the newest perfume [a "pot of ointment"; v. 31]). He leaves a boastful wake above the surface ("behind him he leaves a shining wake"; v. 32a) and turns the dark sea white as he speeds through the waters ("one would think the deep to be white-haired"; v. 32b).

Among all creatures of the "earth" (or "dust," Hb. 'apar), no creature is as inimitable ("on earth there is not his like") or intrepid ("a creature without fear"; v. 33). What Martin Luther said of the Devil, we might say of Leviathan: "on earth is not his equal" (from "A Mighty Fortress"). Indeed, this beast is like the beast of Revelation 13:4 ("Who is like the beast, and who can fight against it?"). Every arrogant creature from the blue peafowl of Sri Lanka to the Siamese cat to fallen *Homo sapiens* knows that Leviathan is the "king over all the sons of pride" (Job 41:34b).

42:1–6 The only appropriate response to this fearless creature is to fear its awesome Creator (28:28). Stop complaining; stay the avowals of innocence; submit. "Yahweh is thus calling Job to decide whether to argue his case and lose or submit to Yahweh, accepting in trust the blessing and the curse, the riches and

---

195 Hartley summarizes Habel's insight on laughter being a "thread that runs through the animal portraits." He writes: "The wild ass laughs at the noise in the city (39:7), the ostrich laughs at the horse and its rider (39:18), the horse laughs at fear (39:22), the wild animals play (laughingly) near Behemoth (40:20), and no one can play (laughingly) with Leviathan (40:29) [Eng. 41:5])" (ibid., 533, citing Norman C. Habel, *The Book of Job: A Commentary*, OTL [Philadelphia: Westminster Press, 1985], 573).

the ash heap."[196] Job's final answer ("Job answered"; 42:1, with the context of his answer in vv. 2–6) is as remarkable as his first (1:20–21). He trusts God atop the garbage dump.

As Christopher Ash summarizes: "Job's response is in three parts. He speaks of something he now knows, of things he did not know, and supremely of one he has now seen."[197] First, he states how he now knows, or knows afresh, that God "can do all things," or, put differently, that "no purpose of yours can be thwarted" (42:2). Job has acknowledged God as "the Almighty" many times (6:4, 14; 13:3; 21:15, 20; 23:16; 24:1; 27:2, 10, 11, 13; 29:5, 31:2). Now he acknowledges that Yahweh really is all-mighty. Second, Job acknowledges that there is a major knowledge gap between himself and God. To God's question, "Who is this that darkens counsel by words without knowledge?" (38:2, repeated here by Job in 42:3a, with two slight variations), Job speaks of speaking sophomorically. He has "uttered what" he "did not understand/know," concepts beyond his comprehension ("things too wonderful for me"; v. 3). Third, having heard clearly God's challenges to him ("Hear, and I will speak; I will question you, and you make it known to me"; v. 4, echoing 38:3; 40:7), Job speaks of seeing what God wants him to see, or really seeing God for more of who God is. God is bigger than Job imagined. He is greater than the traditions he has heard. Yahweh makes Leviathan look little and Behemoth brittle. This perception of reality and aural vision of the Reality causes him to tremble, tremble, tremble and to change his mind and turn away from previous thoughts and postures:

> I had heard of you by the hearing of the ear,
>   but now my eye sees you;
> therefore I despise myself,
>   and repent in dust and ashes. (42:5–6).

Here we have the repentance of the righteous. In these verses Job pours out his heart, contritely confessing that he has spoken beyond his knowledge. Job misjudged God, and for this he recants of his accusations. In self-humiliation, he retracts his case against God and despises himself for the abusive words he has foolishly hurled at God.[198] Job had never questioned God's power but had challenged God's seeming indifference. Now Job submits himself to the God who has appeared to him by acknowledging that God is lovingly involved in the operations of an exceedingly complex universe. Job admits that compared with the omniscience of God, he has drawn his conclusions from a limited examination of life. What Job now comprehends is that God and his mysterious providence are too wonderful to comprehend, and human perceptions of justice are not the scales upon which the righteousness of God is weighed. What he finally grasps is that "God has an inescapable purpose in whatever he does,"[199] even if that inescapable

---

196 Ibid., 534.
197 Ash, *Job*, 416.
198 See Clines, *Job 38–42*, 1204–1224.
199 Hartley, *Job*, 537.

purpose is never revealed to the creatures it affects. Job finally sees clearly that he cannot see clearly!

Through God's two speeches Job was given neither a bill of indictment nor a verdict of innocence; rather, he was given eyes to see the greatness of God. He sees now "with, not through, the eye" (William Blake) in such a way that the apparent madness of God becomes his only sanity. In the presence of God, all of his complaints against God now seem insignificant. His intellectual problem remains unsolved, but unimportant.[200] For, still in the midst of extreme pain, Job is spiritually healed by the revelation of God. He sings upon the ashes that his Redeemer lives!

Response

Job and his friends have been asking the question *why*. God asks the question *who*. "Who determined [the earth's] measurements . . . or who stretched the line upon it?" (38:5). "Who has put wisdom in the inward parts or given understanding to the mind?" (38:36). "Who can number the clouds by wisdom?" (38:37a). "Who provides for the raven its prey?" (38:41a). "Who has let the wild donkey go free?" (39:5). "Who can strip off [the Leviathan's] outer garment? Who would come near him with a bridle? Who can open the doors of his face?" (41:13–14). God also asks the questions *have you*, *can you*, and *do you* (e.g., "Have you comprehended the expanse of the earth?" 38:18a; cf. 38:12, 16, 17, 22; 40:9; "Can you draw out Leviathan with a fishhook?" 41:1; cf. 38:31, 32, 33b, 34, 35, 39; 39:2, 10; 40:9b; 41:2, 7; "Do you give the horse his might?" 39:19; cf. 38:33a; 39:1, 2b, 12, 20). All of these questions are designed to move Job and his friends to admit that God is God and man is not. God alone has the wisdom required to create and govern the world. Moreover, these questions are intended to teach them that God is not bound by the retribution principle. Job is an innocent sufferer; however, that does not mean that he deserves rewards from God. In his mysterious providence, God has great purposes for his people, even if those purposes are not immediately or ever revealed on earth.

We too should seek to answer the first question posed to Job, "Who is this that darkens counsel by words without knowledge" (38:2)? Who are we to question God? Our response to his revelation throughout creation should be to "acknowledge" his "invisible attributes, namely, his eternal power and divine nature," to "honor him as God or give thanks to him," and serve him as our "Creator" (Rom. 1:28, 20–21, 25). Job's first response was right: smallness and silence. We must know our smallness compared with God's greatness. We must be silent before his sovereignty. We do not and cannot know everything there is to know about even animals. What makes us think that we can tell God how to run the universe? The way God works might be as unpredictable as a thunderstorm or as seemingly illogical as an ostrich. We must trust, however, that if he can control Leviathan

---

200 See H. H. Rowley, *The Book of Job*, NCBC (Grand Rapids, MI: Eerdmans, 1980), 266.

and supervise the stars, then he also can and will deal with our problems in a wise way. Our response is worship. We worship a God we can know and who has revealed himself to us. But we also worship a God we cannot completely know[201] and who has only revealed something of himself to us. The "something" is no small revelation, as "the Word became flesh and dwelt among us" (John 1:14). However small and insignificant man is, the incarnation reminds us that we are not that small or insignificant.

A second response to God's two speeches would be to do what Job does in 42:2–6, namely, to repent. Elsewhere in Scripture, a careful observation of creation calls us to work hard (Prov. 6:6–11), give thanks (Rom. 1:21), and grasp that God cares and will provide for us (Matt. 6:26–34). Here in Job, however, such an observation calls us to worship. To be silent, take off our sandals, and bow before the awesome Lord of the heavens and the earth. Even biologists and zoologists should be prostrate, for as much as they have learned about amoebae and eagles, they must acknowledge that they have only scratched the surface of God's sovereignty. Job understands that he does not understand ostriches. Job knows that he cannot control Behemoth. So he submits to God's sovereignty and repents of his proud assumptions.

Until God spoke, nothing was worse than silence, but when God did speak (as Job so desperately wanted), the torment of silence in comparison seemed sweet. Out of the whirlwind God raised his voice, answering Job's doubts and accusations by bombarding him with questions about Job's personal knowledge of the detailed workings of God's creation. He says to Job, at the beginning of chapter 38, "Who is this that darkens counsel by words without knowledge? Dress for action like a man; I will question you, and you make it known to me" (38:2–3).

With question after question, God probes the depths of human wisdom, perception, and power. He specifically questions Job's knowledge of how the world works and why it works the way it does. To summarize, "Have you, Job, any grasp of why the stars hang in the sky, or why the sea does not spill over upon the land? Can you, Job, send forth the storehouses of snow, the torrents of rain, the bolts of lightning, the crash of thunder? Do you give the horse its might, the wild donkey its freedom, the ostrich its stupidity, and the eagle its sight?"

It may surprise us that in God's two speeches we find no superficial niceness, no artificial comfort, no tickling of ears. We might think that God has a poor bedside manner. And if we are searching for the answer to the question of why there is suffering in the world, we will find no answer here. God gives no answer to the source of Job's misery or the reason for it. In fact, he makes no mention of Job's sufferings. Instead, Yahweh gives Job the one thing he needs: a clearer vision of God. God in essence says to him, "Job, all that you need to know about your suffering is that I am God. I am still in control. I still care about you. And I am always just in everything I do." The way God demonstrates this is by asking Job to "stop

---

201 "Mystery," writes Thomas, "is the vital element of all our theologizing" (*The Storm Breaks*, 288). As Calvin said: "Our understanding is not capable of comprehending his essence" (*Institutes* 1.5.1n3, quoted in ibid., 289).

and consider the wondrous works of God" (37:14), for in the wondrous works of God's creation is the visible attestation of his "abundant righteousness" (37:23).

In Job 38–41 God offers no extravagant philosophical argument in defense of his character. Rather, he argues that the existence and maintenance and operation of the earth, stars, waters, and animals confirm his just rule and also "testify against human arrogance, ignorance, and ingratitude."[202] God calls creation to the witness stand, and creation's respectable and valid testimony renders all human beings morally inexcusable and intellectually incapable of criticizing God's character. God's control, constraint, and care, clearly portrayed every day, ought to silence all accusations against God's goodness.

Through questioning Job in this manner, God in essence says to all of us, "If you understood but a fraction of the details of my creation and of my detailed interaction with it, you would never open your mouth to accuse me of injustice. For even the mightiest of creatures I hold tight upon a leash. So, who are you, O man, to place me under the lens of your judgment, to talk back to the creator of the universe?" A mere observation of nature should be enough to acquit God of any charge of injustice. If we considered the beauty and order of creation, we would conclude that God is no cosmic bully. He is not "making sport" of us with his providential power.[203] God's "rule of human history," as Schreiner summarizes Calvin, "is inexplicable, incomprehensible, and beyond human reason. And yet nature points beyond itself and promises that the same God who brought the beauty and order of creation into being is wise and powerful enough to bring order out of what appears to be present confusion."[204] The world is the theater of God's glory. Before the vast panorama of the heavens and earth, the majestic face of God shines.

By the start of Job 42, Job finally realizes that even in the worst of life's storms the sun does not fail to warm or sustain the earth. From the whirlwind God speaks, and in the swirl of scattered dust and ashes Job confesses his ignorance and repents of his presumption. And to his credit, Job does not suffer from our obsession with the question *why*; neither does he suffer from our obsession with having felt needs met. Real needs! God does not offer Job healing, and he certainly does not offer Job a restored self-esteem. There is no therapeutic babble from the tongue of God. There is no healing here from the hand of God. And the beautiful thing is that Job is not concerned about those things anymore. Job does not want anything but God. That is what God offers. And that is what Job takes.

Job takes God for who he is, no questions asked. Job has come to the point in his struggles that he finally gets it. The light has gone on. He sees God's point. He agrees with God and finds true comfort in the character of God. Oh that we would do the same, no matter our sad or happy situation.

---

202 John H. Eaton, *Job*, OTG (Sheffield, UK: JSOT Press, 1985), 141.
203 John Calvin, *Institutes* 1.71.1, quoted in Susan E. Schreiner, *Where Shall Wisdom Be Found? Calvin's Exegesis of Job from Medieval and Modern Perspectives* (Chicago: University of Chicago Press, 1994), 93.
204 Schreiner, *Wisdom*, 152.

JOB 42:7–17

7 After the LORD had spoken these words to Job, the LORD said to Eliphaz the Temanite: "My anger burns against you and against your two friends, for you have not spoken of me what is right, as my servant Job has. **8** Now therefore take seven bulls and seven rams and go to my servant Job and offer up a burnt offering for yourselves. And my servant Job shall pray for you, for I will accept his prayer not to deal with you according to your folly. For you have not spoken of me what is right, as my servant Job has." **9** So Eliphaz the Temanite and Bildad the Shuhite and Zophar the Naamathite went and did what the LORD had told them, and the LORD accepted Job's prayer.

10 And the LORD restored the fortunes of Job, when he had prayed for his friends. And the LORD gave Job twice as much as he had before. **11** Then came to him all his brothers and sisters and all who had known him before, and ate bread with him in his house. And they showed him sympathy and comforted him for all the evil¹ that the LORD had brought upon him. And each of them gave him a piece of money² and a ring of gold.

12 And the LORD blessed the latter days of Job more than his beginning. And he had 14,000 sheep, 6,000 camels, 1,000 yoke of oxen, and 1,000 female donkeys. **13** He had also seven sons and three daughters. **14** And he called the name of the first daughter Jemimah, and the name of the second Keziah, and the name of the third Keren-happuch. **15** And in all the land there were no women so beautiful as Job's daughters. And their father gave them an inheritance among their brothers. **16** And after this Job lived 140 years, and saw his sons, and his sons' sons, four generations. **17** And Job died, an old man, and full of days.

¹ Or *disaster* ² Hebrew *a qesitah*; a unit of money of unknown value

Section Overview

Like the prologue, the epilogue to Job is prose, not poetry. It offers a happy surprise ending. We might have expected after God's barrage of questions and Job's own admittance of shortsightedness and irreverence that the Lord would "declare that Job was a blasphemous and wicked man deserving of everything that happened."²⁰⁵ This is not what happens. Instead, Job is publicly vindicated (42:7–9). His three friends are judged as speaking wrongly and he rightly. Then his former blessings are restored twofold (vv. 10–17). These blessings are not bestowed on Job out of some obligation of God to prosper the righteous. They are a gift, one that can be given or taken away. In fact, Job had no idea that his repentance would bring vindication

205 David R. Jackson, *Crying Out for Vindication: The Gospel According to Job* (Phillipsburg, NJ: P&R, 2007), 164.

and restoration. Once again, he demonstrates that he fears God not because of God's blessings (cf. 1:9–11) but because God is God and worthy to be worshiped.

With this ending we are left with questions. Why are Elihu and Satan unmentioned? Where did they go? Will they be judged too? Job's fortune and happiness are restored, but is his health? Did the boils heal that day? Ever? Did Job ever get an explanation from God as to the cause or reason for his sufferings? What is God's relationship to evil (e.g., the "evil that the LORD had brought upon him"; 42:11)? These important unanswered questions are likely part of the author's intention. We must learn, as Job did, that submission to God's wise sovereignty allows us to live with inexplicabilities and unsolved mysteries.

Section Outline

V. Epilogue: Job's Vindication and Restoration (42:7–17)
  A. The Lord's Rebuke (42:7–9)
  B. The Lord's Restoration (42:10–17)

Comment

42:7–9 Yahweh has spoken to Job (38:1–40:1; 40:6–41:34). Then, "after the LORD had spoken these words to Job," he turns to talk to "Eliphaz," the representative for Bildad and Zophar ("your two friends"; 42:7).

First, God states his emotional state. He is angry. "My anger burns against you and against your two friends" (v. 7). Second, God gives the rationale for his displeasure. He is upset because the three friends "have not spoken of me what is right, as my servant Job has" (vv. 7, 8). They have accused God of inflicting suffering on Job to punish him for his sin. This is not true. Job has spoken rightly in that even in his laments, questions, complaints, and accusations he has expressed a heart desirous to be restored with God and to grow in his relationship with him.[206] He never stopped pursuing God, even though he sensed God was in wrathful pursuit of him. He still saw God as his only salvation from God.

Third, God offers the friends restoration to him through Job. They are to "take seven bulls and seven rams and go to my servant Job and offer up a burnt offering for yourselves. And my servant Job shall pray for you, for I will accept his prayer not to deal with you according to your folly" (v. 8). In one of the most noteworthy moments in the book, we read that the two warring parties obey God ("Eliphaz the Temanite and Bildad the Shuhite and Zophar the Naamathite went and did what the LORD had told them" [v. 9a]; they presumably repent, and here Job presumably prays, as noted in v. 10) and are reconciled both to God ("the LORD accepted Job's prayer"; v. 9b)[207] and to one another. For the three friends to humble themselves in

---

206 It is possible that God is stating that Job has only spoken rightly in his two humble responses to God's speeches (40:3–5; 42:1–6), as it is difficult to categorize *everything* that Job said under the phrase "what is right." However, as the friends are judged for what they have said within the dialogue (chs. 3–31), the more natural reading is to assume that the same is true for Job.

207 "Job, the intercessor and bearer of sacrifices at the start (1:5), now intercedes for those who offer sacrifices at the end (42:8). . . . The one who longed for a mediator (9:33; 16:19; 19:25) becomes the mediator" (Ash, *Job*, 431).

this way, offering an incredibly expensive, costly, complete (7 + 7), and bloody sin sacrifice ("seven bulls and seven rams," v. 8; on this as a substitutionary sin offering, see 1 Chron. 29:21; Heb. 10:4)[208] through righteous Job's mediation (on Job's role as a patriarchal "priest," cf. Job 1:5),[209] is a great act of submission to God. And for Job to pray for his enemies is remarkable as well. Together they model what Jesus would later teach (Matt. 5:44; 6:12, 14–15) and embody (Luke 23:34).

42:10–17 In these verses we learn that more is restored to Job than his relationship with his friends. Immediately after Job offers prayer "for his friends" (v. 10a), God honors the man who has honored him by doubling his original fortunes. "And the Lord gave Job twice as much as he had before" (v. 10b). The blessings come in three ways.

First, God gives wealth. When Job's siblings arrive, they each give him "a piece of money and a ring of gold" (v. 11c). His livestock is doubled ("and he had 14,000 sheep, 6,000 camels, 1,000 yoke of oxen, and 1,000 female donkeys"; v. 12; cf. 1:3).

Second, God gives family. Job has a renewed relationship with "all his brothers and sisters" and his community ("all who had known him before"), and together they feast at table ("and ate bread with him in his house"; 42:11). Those who maligned him (cf. 19:13–22) now dine with him (cf. 1:4). He has a renewed (and repeatedly intimate) relationship with his wife, as together they have ten more children ("seven sons and three daughters," 42:13; cf. 1:2).[210] The familiarity of the family is expressed in Job naming ("Jemimah," "Keziah," and "Keren-happuch"; 42:14) his beautiful daughters ("no women so beautiful"; v. 15a)[211] and including them in his inheritance ("and their father gave them an inheritance among their brothers"; v. 15b), an unusual act in that society. It is also expressed in the second half of verse 16: "And [Job] saw his sons, and his sons' sons, four generations." They are a close-knit family. Job is involved in his children's, grandchildren's, and great-grandchildren's lives.

Third, God gives long life. "Job lived 140 years" (v. 16), a perfect or complete number of years (70 x 2) and double the norm (cf. Ps. 90:10). These 140 years are on top of what he has already lived ("after this"; Job 42:16). Does he live to 200? However old he is when he dies, he certainly does so as "an old man, and full of days" (v. 17). Like Abraham and Isaac, Job is depicted as living a full life, "full of years" (Gen. 25:8) and "full of days" (Gen. 35:29). And, like David, he is viewed (despite all his flaws) as a man after God's own heart (1 Sam. 13:14; Acts 13:22)

---

208 "The sacrifice is referred to as a 'burnt offering,' the commonest offering in the Old Testament. As part of the ritual, hands were laid on the animal's head, firstly to identify the victim with the worshipper, but also, and more importantly, to signify a representative and substitutionary significance in the act that followed. Of all the sacrifices offered, the burnt offering demonstrated most clearly God's anger poured out against sin in that the victim of the sacrifice was totally consumed. The offering, which represented and was a substitute for the offerer, quite literally went up in smoke!" (Thomas, *The Storm Breaks*, 316).

209 "The intercession of Job for his friends is the best proof of his righteousness." Dariusz Ivanski, *The Dynamics of Job's Intercession*, AnBib 161 (Rome: Pontifical Biblical Institute, 2006), 357, quoted in Longman, *Job*, 459.

210 Note that the children are not doubled. This might be to symbolize that the original ten are not forgotten, as cattle would be, for example. It might also be that ten is a perfect number, as opposed to twenty.

211 The point of mentioning their beauty is to say that these doubly endowed virgins (they have good looks and an inheritance) will not have any trouble finding a husband, an important concern for a caring father.

and as someone dying at "a good age, full of days, riches, and honor" (1 Chron. 29:28; cf. Prov. 3:16).

Response

The three words (one word in Hebrew: *wayyamat*) that do not fit with the motif of a happy ending are the words "and Job died" (v. 17a). Job does not live happily ever, or *forever*, after.

In one of the church's ancient hymns, Ephrem the Syrian (c. 306–373) sings of Job's conquering Satan, but not death, and of "Christ conquer[ing] Death where Job could not."[212] Ephrem also writes of Job's suffering being only on his own behalf, and of Christ's being on behalf of all his people.[213] These are two important insights. As Christians, thanks to Christ's suffering and conquering of the grave, we can be glad that the end of our stories will not end with merely a final "and he/she died." We can hope for heaven. We can hope for the resurrection and the return of Christ.

In James 5:11, the Lord's brother writes, "You have heard of the steadfastness of Job, and you have seen the purpose of the Lord, how the Lord is compassionate and merciful." The example of Job is set within the context of the admonition, to "be patient, therefore, brothers, until the coming of the Lord" (James 5:7). On these texts—James 5:7, 11 and Job 42:7–17—Christopher Ash writes these beautiful words and offers a moving charge to the church:

> The purpose of the Lord to show mercy and compassion will be seen finally only when the Lord Jesus returns in glory. Job 42 anticipates the return of the Lord Jesus Christ. Like all the Old Testament types of Christ, Job dies at the end of his story (v. 17); and his death proves he is not the one to come, but merely one in whose sufferings are foreshadowed that one whose sandals neither Job nor any Old Testament prophet nor even John the Baptist will be worthy to untie.
>
> The end comes at the end. The normal Christian life is warfare and waiting and being loved and humbled by God and being justified by God, all in the here and now. But it is the expectation of blessing *at the end*. Often we do get blessed now. God graciously pours out all manner of blessings here and now. But the blessings we get now are just a tiny foretaste of the blessings to be poured out at the end.
>
> And the blessings God will pour out on the believer at the end will be every bit as *real* as the blessings of Job. Job knew real prosperity, real joy and celebration, real fruitfulness and real beauty (his dazzling daughters). The blessings of the new heavens and new earth will be rock-solid real. We look forward to beauty that makes the most beautiful woman in the world seem dull. We look forward to fruitfulness that will make the most

---

212 *Nisibene Hymns* 53.14; summarized by Seow, *Job 1–21*, 179.
213 See *Hymns on Nativity* 13.34; *Hymns on Epiphany* 2.34.

abundant family in the world seem barren. We look forward to prosperity that will make the Forbes list of the world's billionaires seem poor. And we look forward to celebration that will make the best party in the world seem like a quiet glass of apple juice.[214]

Above every other passage in Job, 42:7–17 offers the most clear and valuable connections with Christ. For how this text can be viewed typologically, cf. Introduction: Preaching from Job: Preaching Christ. Moreover, as Ash points out above, this text can also serve as a great impetus for Job-like perseverance in view of the coming of Christ. As we look for vindication, the marriage supper of the Lamb, the defeat of Satan, and the new heaven and new earth wherein eternal righteousness, happiness, and prosperity dwell (Revelation 19–22), we should model patient endurance (Rev. 2:2) and holding fast to Jesus' name (Rev. 2:13).

What a book! And what a Savior! Job's journey and Jesus' life show us that God can and does triumph over evil ultimately, and thus we can trust him. We can trust him as we look at creation. We can trust him as we look at the history of salvation. We can trust him as we look at his written revelation. We can trust that he will glorify what is stronger than hate and evil and suffering and death, and that he will do so through his Son, our Lord Jesus Christ, to whom all glory and honor and praise and adoration is forever due.

---

214 Ash, *Job*, 432–433, emphasis his.

SCRIPTURE INDEX